D1518055

The Shaping of *COLONIAL VIRGINIA*

THOMAS J. WERTENBAKER

The Shaping of COLONIAL VIRGINIA

New York
RUSSELL & RUSSELL

LIBRARY OF CONGRESS CATALOG CARD NUMBER 58-5370

PRINTED IN U.S.A.

Patrician and Plebeian in Virginia

OR THE ORIGIN AND DEVELOPMENT OF THE SOCIAL CLASSES OF THE OLD DOMINION

By

THOMAS J. WERTENBAKER

Dedicated to H. R. W.

PREFACE

Forty-seven years have passed since this volume was first published; in that time a mass of source material has been made available to the historian and numerous books on early Virginia history have been published. But I believe that its main theses have not been shaken. The old belief that the Virginia aristocracy had its origin in a migration of Cavaliers after the defeat of the royalists in the British Civil War has been relegated to the sphere of myths. It is widely recognized that the leading Virginia families—the Carters, the Ludwells, the Burwells, the Custises, the Lees, the Washingtons—were shaped chiefly by conditions within the colony and by renewed contact with Great Britain.

That the Virginia aristocracy was not part of the English aristocracy transplanted in the colony is supported by contemporaneous evidence. When Nathaniel Bacon, the rebel, the son of an English squire, expressed surprise when Governor Berkeley appointed him to the Council of State, Sir William replied: "When I had the first knowledge of you I intended you and do now again all the services that are in my power to serve, for gentlemen of your quality come very rarely into the country, and therefore when they do come were used by me with all respect."

Bacon was equally frank. "Consider . . . the nature and quality of the men in power . . . as to their education, extraction, and learning, as to their reputation for honor and honesty, see and consider whether here, as in England, you can perceive men advanced for their noble qualifications . . . ."

Governor Francis Nicholson ridiculed the pretensions of

the leading planters to distinguished lineage. "This generation know too well from whence they come," he wrote in a letter to the Lords of Trade, in March 1703, "and the ordinary sort of planters that have land of their own, though not much, look upon themselves to be as good as the best of them, for he knows, at least has heard, from whence these mighty Dons derive their originals . . . and that he or his ancestors were their equals if not superiors."

On the other side of the Potomac Henry Callister was frank in refuting the similar claims of wealthy Marylanders. "Some of the proudest families here vaunt themselves of a pedigree, at the same time they know not their grandfather's name. I never knew a good honest Marylander that was not got by a merchant."

That many prominent families in Virginia also were founded by merchants is attested by the fact that they continued to be traders after they came to the colony. "In every river here are from ten to thirty men who by trade and industry have gotten very competent estates," wrote Colonel Robert Quary in 1763. "These gentlemen take care to supply the poorer sort with provisions, goods, and necessities, and are sure to keep them always in debt, and so dependent on them. Out of this number are chosen her Majesty's Council, the Assembly, the justices, and other officers of the government."

Hartwell, Blair, and Chilton, in their *The Present State of Virginia and the College,* written in 1697, divide the people into three classes—planters, tradesmen, and merchants. "The merchants live best," they said. But though profits were large, their business was carried on in the face of great difficulties. The tobacco they bought from the small planters had to be carted or rolled to the landings and put on board their sloops and shallops for transfer to the merchant ships; they had to sell imported goods on credit; often there were long delays in loading the ships.

Some of the most influential men in Virginia were importers of servants and slaves. Among them were William Claiborne,

Peter Ashton, Isaac Allerton, Giles Brent, Joseph Bridger, Thomas Milner, Henry Hartwell, and Robert Beverley.

The distinguished historian, Lyon Gardiner Tyler, in *Tyler's Magazine,* Volume I, says that Virginia owes much to the London firms, because they were continually sending over trusted young agents . . . many of whom settled down and founded Virginia families . . . The business of the merchants consisted largely in buying and selling tobacco and importing settlers and servants, for each of which if imported at their expense the merchants were entitled to fifty acres of land. Then there was the usual trade in clothing and articles of general use."

Though the Virginian who acquired a degree of wealth was no aristocrat, he longed to be one. His grandfather, or his great-grandfather might have been a younger son of an English squire. He envied the honor, wealth, and power landholding brought that ancestor, just as many Virginians today envy the life of the colonial plantation owner. So when he found himself an extensive landholder, he thought of himself as an English squire. He too would build a fine residence, decorate his walls with family portraits, have a formal garden, accumulate a library, and dress in the latest English fashion.

Virginia in the colonial period was linked to England by government, commerce, religion, reading, education. The mother country sent over governors who set the fashion in courtly living. It was the planter's agent in London or Bristol who usually selected his furniture, his silverware, his clothing, and often even his books. When on Sunday he went to church he listened to a minister who had been born and educated in England. The shelves of his library were lined with books from England, if he could afford it he sent his son to Oxford or Cambridge.

When a Virginia planter visited England in the eighteenth century, he was deeply impressed by the beauty and dignity of the great country mansions there. As he viewed Longleat, or Blenheim, or Eaton Hall, he must have resolved that he too would build a stately house on the banks of the James. If he had never been to England, he might take down an English book of architecture—Batty Langley's *Treasury of Designs,* or Abraham Swan's *The British Architect,* or James Gibb's *A Book of Architecture*—pick out a suitable design and model his house on it. He might even send to England for an architect, as did George Mason, when he engaged William Buckland to design beautiful Gunston Hall. Westover, Carter's Grove, Mount Airy, Kenmore, Brandon, all bear the stamp of the English Georgian.

If there was any doubt that the Virginia gentlemen followed the latest English fashions in dress, a glimpse at their portraits would dispel it. William Byrd II, as he appears in the painting by Sir Godfrey Kneller would have made a fine figure in any assembly in England; no English nobleman was better dressed than Robert Carter, of Nomini Hall, as shown in the Reynolds portrait.

When a Virginian went to England he not only took the opportunity to replenish his own wardrobe, but was charged by his relatives and friends to make purchases for them. In a letter to Mrs. Thomas Jones, in 1727, Mrs. Mary Stith asked: "When you come to London pray favor me in your choice of a suit of pinners suitably dressed with a crossknot roll or whatever the fashion requires, with suitable ruffles and handkerchief." In 1752 Lady Gooch, wife of Governor William Gooch, while in London bought for Mrs. Thomas Dawson a fashionable laced cap, a handkerchief, ruffles, a brocade suit, a blue satin petticoat, a pair of blue satin shoes, and a fashionable silver girdle. But it was not always necessary to send to England for clothing, for there were tailors in Virginia who advertised that they could make gentlemen's suits and dresses for the ladies "in the newest and genteelest fashions now wore in England." It was a valuable asset for a tailor if he had just arrived from London.

The Virginians also imitated the English in their outdoor sports. The fox chase, so dear to the Englishman's heart, was a favorite amusement. When the crowds gathered around the county courthouse on court days, they were often diverted from more serious business by horseraces. And like their English cousins they were fond of cockfighting, boat racing, and hunting.

The life of the wealthy planter was profoundly influenced by his reading of English books. He took his religion more from the *Sermons* of Archbishop Tillotson than from the preaching of the local clergyman; as a county magistrate he had to know Blackstone and Coke; he turned to Kip's *English Houses and Gardens*, or John James' *Theory and Practice of Gardening*, to guide him in laying out his flower beds and hedges and walks; if he or his wife or a servant became ill he consulted Lynch's *Guide to Health;* he willingly obeyed the dictates of Chippendale in furniture.

But despite all the bonds with the mother country he was slowly, but inevitably, becoming more an American, less an Englishman. It was the plantation which shaped the daily life of the Virginian and made him different from the English squire. As he looked out over his wide acres, his tobacco fields, his pastures, his woodlands, his little village of servant and slave quarters, tobacco houses, barn, and stable, he had a sense of responsibility, dignity, pride, and self-reliance. He must look after the welfare of the men and women and children under his care, seeing that they were housed, clothed, and fed, protecting their health, playing the role of benevolent despot. He had to be agriculturalist, business man, lawyer, builder, even doctor.

Visitors to the colony were quick to notice the difference between the Virginian and the Englishman. Hugh Jones, in his *The Present State of Virginia* devotes several pages to a description of the colonists. Andrew Burnaby, who visited Virginia in 1760, thought that the authority had by the planters over their slaves made them "vain and imperious.... They are haughty and jealous of their liberties, impatient of restraint..." Lord Adam Gordon, writing in 1764, gives a more favorable opinion: "I had an opportunity to see a good deal of the country and many of the first people in the province and I must say they far excel in good sense, affability, and ease any set of men I have yet fallen in with, either in the West Indies or on the Continent, this, in some degree, may be owing to their being most of them educated at home (England) but cannot be altogether the cause, since there are amongst them many gentlemen, and almost all the ladies, who have never been out of their own province, and yet are as sensible, conversible, and accomplished as one would wish to meet with."

In brief, the Virginia aristocracy was the product of three forces, inheritance, continued contact with the mother country, and local conditions. Coming largely from the middle class in England, though with some connections with the squirearchy through younger sons, they brought with them the English language, English political institutions, the Anglican Church, English love of liberty. This inheritance was buttressed by their political and cultural dependance on the mother country. But it was profoundly affected, even reshaped, by Virginia itself.

Dr. Samuel Johnson's charge that the Americans were a race of convicts, if he meant it to be taken seriously, is of course absurd. It is true that from time to time convicts were sent to the colonies. This is proved by the protests of the Assemblies and by laws passed to prohibit their importation. In Virginia there are records in some of the county courthouses of the crimes committed by these jailbirds. But they never entered in any appreciable numbers into the population of the colony, not even of the lowest class. They were never numerous, the planters considered it a risk to use them, some were forced to serve as cannon fodder in the colonial wars, others were shunted off to the frontiers.

The bulk of the immigrants to Virginia were poor men seeking to better their condition in a new country. Many came as indentured workers, who placed their signatures to contracts to work for four years in the tobacco fields in return for their passage across the Atlantic; other thousands paid their fare in advance and so entered the colony as freemen. They were not essentially different from the millions who came to the United States in the nineteenth century. Most of them, indentured workers and freemen alike, sooner or later acquired small plantations and became members of a yeoman class. A few acquired wealth. Many went into the trades to become carpenters, or bricklayers, or blacksmiths, or coopers, or saddlers, or wheelwrights.

Colonial Virginia has often been pictured as the land of the aristocratic planter, the owner of thousands of acres and hundreds of slaves. Scant attention has been paid to the far more numerous middle class. Yet this class was the backbone of the colony. It is true that most of the leaders came from the aristocracy, but it was the small farmer who owned the bulk of the land, produced the larger part of the tobacco crop, could outvote the aristocrat fifty to one, made up the rank and file of the army in the colonial wars.

Among the thousands of Englishmen who left their homes to seek their fortunes in Virginia there were no dukes, no earls, rarely a knight, or even the son of a knight. They were, most of them, ragged farm workers, deserters from the manor, ill paid day laborers, yeomen who had been forced off their land by the enclosures, youthful tradesmen tempted by the cheapness of land or by the opportunities for commerce, now and then a lad who had taken a mug of doctored grog and awakened to find himself a prisoner aboard a tobacco ship. But Virginia claimed them all, moulded them into her own pattern, made them Virginians.

Princeton, New Jersey
August, 1957

THOMAS J. WERTENBAKER

PART ONE

The Aristocracy

THE aristocratic character of Virginia society was the result of development within the colony. It proceeded from economic, political and social causes. On its economic side it was built up by the system of large plantations, by the necessity for indentured or slave labor, by the direct trade with England; politically it was engendered by the lack of a vigorous middle class in the first half of the 17th century, and was sustained by the method of appointment to office; on its social side it was fostered by the increasing wealth of the planters and by the ideal of the English gentleman.

It will be necessary, in explaining this development, to determine the origin of the men that composed this aristocracy; for it will be impossible to understand the action of the forces which prevailed in Virginia during the colonial period unless we have a knowledge of the material upon which they worked. Much error has prevailed upon this subject. It was for years the general belief, and is still the belief of many, that the wealthy families, whose culture, elegance and power added such luster to Virginia in the 18th century, were the descendants of cavalier or aristocratic settlers. It was so easy to account for the noble nature of a Randolph, a Lee or a Mason by nobleness of descent, that careful investigation was considered unnecessary, and heredity was accepted as a sufficient explanation of the existence and characteristics of the Virginia aristocracy.

We shall attempt to show that this view is erroneous. Recent investigation in Virginia history has made it possible to determine with some degree of accuracy the origin of the aristocracy. Yet the mixed character of the settlers, and the long period of time over which immigration to the colony continued make the problem difficult of accurate solution, and the chances of error innumerable. Out of the mass of evidence, however, three facts may be established beyond controversy, that but few men of high social rank in England established families in Virginia; that the larger part of the aristocracy of the colony came directly from merchant ancestors; that the leading planters of the 17th century were mercantile in instinct and unlike the English aristocrat of the same period.

Much confusion has resulted from the assumption, so common with Southern writers, that the English Cavaliers were all of distinguished lineage or of high social rank. The word "Cavalier," as used at the time of Charles I, denoted not a cast, or a distinct class of people, but a political party. It is true that the majority of the gentry supported the king in the civil war, and that the main reliance of Parliament lay in the small landowners and the merchants, but there were many men of humble origin that fought with the royalist party and many aristocrats that joined the party of the people. Amongst the enemies of the king were the Earls of Bedford, Warwick, Manchester and Essex, while many leaders of the Roundheads such as Pym, Cromwell and Hampden were of gentle blood. Thus the fact that a man was Cavalier or Roundhead proved nothing as to his social rank or his lineage.[1]

No less misleading has been the conception

---

[1] Fiske, Old Va. and Her Neighbors, Vol. II, p. 12.

that in Great Britain there existed during the 17th century distinct orders of society, similar to those of France or Spain at the same period. Many have imagined the English nobility a class sharply and definitely separated from the commonalty, and forming a distinct upper stratum of society. In point of fact no sharp line of social demarkation can be drawn between the peerage and the common people. For in England, even in the days of the Plantagenets, the younger sons of the nobles did not succeed to their fathers' rank, but sank to the gentry class, or at most became "knights." They usually married beneath the rank of their fathers and thus formed a link binding the nobility to the commons of the country. Often the sons and brothers of earls were sent to Parliament as representatives of the shires, and as such sat side by side with shopkeepers and artisans from the towns. It is this circumstance that explains why so many middle-class Englishmen of the present day can trace back their lineage to the greatest and noblest houses of the kingdom. The healthy political development which has been such a blessing to the English nation is due in no small measure to the lack of anything like caste in British society.

These facts help to explain much in the origin of the Virginia aristocracy that has only too often been misunderstood. They make evident the error of presuming that many persons of gentle blood came to Virginia because there was an immigration of so called Cavaliers, or because certain families in the colony could trace back their ancestry to noble English houses.

Immigration to Virginia during the seventeen years after the founding of Jamestown was different in character from that of any succeeding period. The London Company in its efforts to send to the colony desirable settlers induced a number of men of good family and education to venture across the ocean to seek their fortunes in the New World. Since the Company numbered among its stockholders some of the greatest noblemen of the time, it could easily arouse in the influential social classes extraordinary interest in Virginia. It is due largely to this fact that among the first settlers are to be found so many that are entitled to be called gentlemen.

Moreover, the true nature of the task that confronted the immigrants to the wilds of America was little understood in England at this time. Those unhappy gentlemen that sailed upon the Discovery, the Godspeed and the Susan Constant hoped to find in Virginia another Mexico or Peru and to gain there wealth as great as had fallen to the lot of Cortez or of Pizarro. Had they known that the riches of the land they were approaching could be obtained only by long years of toil and sweat, of danger and hardship, they would hardly have left their homes in England. That the First Supply took with them a perfumer and six tailors shows how utterly unsuited they were to the task of planting a new colony. Many, doubtless, were men of ruined fortune, who sought to find in the New World a rapid road to wealth. When it became known in England that gold mines were not to be found in Virginia and that wealth could be had only by the sweat of the brow, these spendthrift gentlemen ceased coming to the colony.

It is true, however, that the proportion of those officially termed "gentlemen" that sailed with the early expeditions to Jamestown is surprisingly large. Of the settlers of 1607, out of one hundred and five men, thirty-five were called gentlemen.[2] The First Supply, which arrived in 1608, contained thirty-three gentlemen out of one hundred and twenty persons.[3] Captain John Smith declared these men were worthless in character, more fitted "to spoyle a commonwealth than to begin or maintain one," and that those that came with them as "laborers" were really footmen in attendance upon their masters. In the Second Supply came twenty-eight gentlemen in a total company of seventy.[4] The conduct of those of the Third Supply shows them to have been similar in character to their predecessors. Smith calls them a "lewd company," among them "many unruly gallants packed thither by their friends to escape il destinies."[5] These men, however, made practically no imprint upon the character of the population of the colony; for by far the larger part of them perished miserably within a few months after their arrival. Of the five

---

[2] Nar. of Early Va., p. 125.
[3] Ibid, pp. 140-141.
[4] Ibid, pp. 159-160.
[5] Ibid, p. 192.

hundred persons alive in Virginia in October, 1609, all but sixty had died by May of the following year.[6]

As years went by, this influx of dissipated gentlemen began to wane. It could not be concealed in England that the early settlers had perished of starvation, disease and the tomahawk, and those that had been led to believe that Virginia was an Eldorado, turned with a shudder from the true picture of suffering and death told them by those that returned from the colony. Moreover, the London Company soon learned that no profit was to be expected from a colony settled by dissipated gentlemen, and began to send over persons more suited for the rough tasks of clearing woods, building huts and planting corn. Their immigrant ves-

---

[6] Fiske, Old Va. and Her Neighbors, Vol. I, p. 154. The facts here presented form a complete refutation of the assertion, so frequently repeated by Northern historians, that the Virginia aristocracy had its origin in this immigration of dissipated and worthless gentlemen. The settlers of 1607, 1608 and 1609 were almost entirely swept out of existence, and not one in fifty of these "gallants" survived to found families. Most of the leading planters of Virginia came from later immigrants, men of humbler rank, but of far more sterling qualities than the adventurers of Smith's day.

sels were now filled with laborers, artisans, tradesmen, apprentices and indentured servants. It is doubtless true that occasionally gentlemen continued to arrive in Virginia even during the last years of the Company's rule, yet their number must have been very small indeed. When, in 1624, James I took from the London Company its charter, the colony contained few others than indentured servants and freemen of humble origin and means. In 1623 several of the planters, in answering charges that had been brought against the colony by a certain Captain Nathaniel Butler, said that the inhabitants were chiefly laboring men.[7]

With the downfall of the London Company one influence which had tended to send to Virginia persons of good social standing ceased to exist. The personal interest of those noblemen that had owned stock in the enterprise was no longer exerted to obtain a desirable class of settlers, and economic forces alone now determined the character of those that established themselves in Virginia. During the remainder of the 17th century it was the profit that could be obtained from the planting of tobacco that

---

[7] Nar. of Early Va., p. 415.

brought the most desirable class of settlers to the colony. It is true, however, that dissipated and spendthrift gentlemen still came over at times, seeking in Virginia a refuge from creditors, or expecting amid the unsettled conditions of a new country to obtain license for their excesses. It was this element of the population, doubtless, that the Dutch trader De Vries referred to when he asserted that some of the planters were inveterate gamblers, even staking their servants.[8] Such a character was Captain Stone, whom DeVries met at the home of Governor Harvey. This man was related to families of good standing in England, but strutted, was lewd, swore horribly and was guilty of shameless carousals wherever he went. While in New Amsterdam he entered upon a drinking bout with Governor Von Twiller, and stole a vessel of Plymouth. In Massachusetts he called Roger Ludlow a just ass, and later, having been detected in other crimes, was forced to flee from the colony. Beyond doubt men similar to Stone were to be found in Virginia during the first half of the 17th century,

[8] Neill, Va. Carolorum.

but they became rarer and rarer as time went on.[9]

How few men of good social standing there were in the colony in this period is shown by the number of important positions filled by uneducated persons of humble origin and rank. The evidence is conclusive that on many occasions indentured servants that had served their term of bondage and had acquired property were elected by the people to represent them in the House of Burgesses. This is notably true of the first half of the 17th century, when the government was largely in the hands of a few leading planters, and when pressure from above could influence elections very decidedly. Had there been many men of ability or rank to select from, these Plebeians would never have found a place in the Assembly of the colony. The author of Virginia's Cure stated that the burgesses were "usuall such as went over as servants thither," and although this is doubtless an exaggeration, it shows that there must have been in the Assemblies many men of humble extraction. In the case of some of the burgesses, it has been

[9] Ibid.

shown definitely that they came to Virginia as servants. Thus William Popleton was formerly the servant of John Davies; Richard Townsend was in 1620 the servant of Dr. Potts; William Bentley arrived in the colony in 1624 as a hired man. All three of these men were burgesses.[10] The preacher, William Gatford, testified that persons of mean extraction had filled places of importance and trust.[11] Governor Berkeley, stated in 1651 while addressing the Assembly, that hundreds of examples testified to the fact that no man in the colony was denied the opportunity to acquire both honor and wealth. At times men of humble origin became so influential that they obtained seats in the Council, the most exclusive and powerful body in the colony. Thus William Pearce, who came over in the days of the Company as a poor settler, was a Councilor in 1632, and was before his death one of the wealthiest and most powerful men in the colony.[12] In 1635 we find in the Council John Brewer, formerly a grocer of London.[13] Mal-

---

[10] Ibid.

[11] Ibid.

[12] Ibid.

[13] Va. Mag. of Hist. and Biog., Vol. XI, p. 317.

achy Postlethwayt, a writer of several treaties on commerce, states that even criminals often became leading men in Virginia. Although this is obviously an exaggeration, Postlethwayt's testimony tends to add force to the contention that many of humble rank did at times rise to positions of honor. "Even your transported felons," he says, "sent to Virginia instead of to Tyburn, thousands of them, if we are not misinformed, have, by turning their hands to industry and improvement, and (which is best of all) to honesty, become rich, substantial planters and merchants, settled large families, and been famous in the country; nay, we have seen many of them made magistrates, officers of militia, captains of good ships, and masters of good estates."[14] In England stories of the rapid advance of people of humble origin in Virginia gave rise to the absurd belief that the most influential families in the colony were chiefly composed of former criminals. Defoe in two of his popular novels, gives voice to this opinion. In Moll Flanders we find the following: "Among the rest, she

---

[14] Fiske, Old Va. and Her Neighbors, Vol. II, p. 182.

often told me how the greatest part of the inhabitants of that colony came hither in very indifferent circumstances from England; that generally speaking, they were of two sorts: either, 1st, such as were brought over....to be sold as servants, or, 2nd, such as are transported after having been found guilty of crimes punishable with death. When they come here ....the planters buy them, and they work together in the field till their time is out.... (Then) they have....land allotted them.... and (they)....plant it with tobacco and corn for their own use; and as the merchants will trust them with tools....upon the credit of their crop before it is grown, so they plant every year a little more (etc). Hence, child, says she, many a Newgate-bird becomes a great man, and we have....several justices of the peace, officers of the trained band, and magistrates of the towns they live in, that have been burnt in the hand."[15] In Mrs. Behn's comedy The Widow Ranter, the same belief finds expression, for Friendly is made to say: "This country wants nothing but to be peopled with a well-born race to make it one of the best col-

[15] Ibid, Vol. II, p. 179.

onies in the world; but for want of a governor we are ruled by a council, some of whom have been perhaps transported criminals, who having acquired great estates are now become Your Honour and Right Worshipful, and possess all places of authority."[16] It is absolutely certain that the Virginia aristocracy was not descended from felons, but this belief that found voice in works of fiction of the 17th century must have had some slight foundation in truth. It tends to strengthen the evidence that many men of humble origin did attain places of honor and profit in the colony, and it shows that in England in this period people were far from imagining that many aristocrats had come to Virginia to settle.[17]

Although it is impossible to determine with accuracy the lineage of all the leading families of Virginia during the 17th century, it is definitely known that many of the most wealthy

---

[16] Ibid, Vol. II, p. 170.

[17] As late as the year 1775 we find Dr. Samuel Johnson, with his usual dislike of America, repeating the old error. In speaking of the rebellious colonists, he says: "Sir, they are a race of convicts, and ought to be thankful for anything we allow them short of hanging." Boswell's Life of Samuel Johnson, Temple Classics, Vol. III, p. 174.

and influential houses were founded by men that could boast of no social prominence in England. In the days immediately following the downfall of the London Company there was no more influential man in the colony than Abraham Piersey. In matters of political interest he took always a leading part, and was respected and feared by his fellow colonists. He was well-to-do when he came to Virginia, having acquired property as a successful merchant, but he was in no way a man of social distinction or rank. John Chew was another man of great distinction in the colony. He too was a plain merchant attracted to the colony by the profits to be made from the planting and sale of tobacco.[18] George Menifie, who for years took so prominent a part in the political affairs of Virginia, and who, as a member of the Council was complicated in the expulsion of Governor Harvey, speaks of himself as a "merchant," although in later years he acquired the more distinguished title of "esquire." Menifie possessed an ample fortune, most of which was acquired by his own business ability and foresight. It is stated that his "large

[18] Bruce, Econ. Hist. of Va., Vol. II, pp. 380, 366.

garden contained the fruits of Holland, and the roses of Provence, and his orchard was planted with apple, pear and cherry trees."[19] Samuel Mathews, a man of plain extraction, although well connected by marriage, was a leader in the colony. In political affairs his influence was second to none, and in the Commonwealth period he became governor. He is described as "an old planter of above 30 years standing, one of the Council and a most deserving Commonwealth man,....He hath a fine house, and all things answerable to it; he sows yearly store of hemp and flax and causes it to be spun; he keeps weavers and hath a tan house....hath 40 negro servants, brings them up to trade, in his house; he yearly sows abundance of wheat, barley, etc....kills store of beeves, and sells them to victual the ships when they come thither; hath abundance of kine, a brave dairy, swine great store and poultry."[20] Adam Thoroughgood, although he came to Virginia as a servant or apprentice, became wealthy and powerful. His estates were of great extent and at one time he owned forty-nine sheep and one-

[19] Ibid, Vol. II, p. 377.
[20] Neill, Va. Carolorum.

hundred and seventeen cattle.[21] Captain Ralph Hamor, a leading planter in the days of the Company, was the son of a merchant tailor. Thomas Burbage, was another merchant that acquired large property in Virginia and became recognized as a man of influence. Ralph Warnet, who is described as a "merchant," died in 1630, leaving a large fortune.[22] That these men, none of whom could boast of high rank or social prominence in England, should have been accepted as leaders in the colony shows that the best class of settlers were of comparatively humble extraction. Had many men of gentle blood come to Virginia during the first half of the 17th century there would have been no chance for the "merchant" class to acquire such prominence.

Nor did men of plain extraction cease to occupy prominent positions after the Restoration, when the much misunderstood "Cavalier" immigration had taken place, and the society of the colony had been fixed. Amongst the leading planters was Isaac Allerton, a man dis-

---

[21] Bruce, Econ. Hist. of Va., Vol. II, pp. 372, 377, 574.

[22] Bruce, Soc. Hist. of Va., p. 164; Econ. Hist. of Va., Vol. II, p. 531.

tinguished for his activities both in the House of Burgesses and the Council, and the founder of a prominent family, who was the son of an English merchant tailor.[23] The first of the famous family of Byrds, which for nearly a century was noted for its wealth, its influence, its social prominence, was the son of a London goldsmith.[24] Oswald Cary, who settled in Middlesex in 1659 was the son of an English merchant.[25] There was no man in the colony during the second half of the 17th century that exerted a more powerful influence in political affairs than Philip Ludwell. He was for years the mainstay of the commons and he proved to be a thorn in the flesh of more than one governor. He was admired for his ability, respected for his wealth and feared for his power, an admitted leader socially and politically in the colony, yet he was of humble extraction, his father and uncle both being mercers. The noted Bland family sprang from Adam Bland, a member of the skinners gild of London.[26] Thomas Fitzhugh, one of the wealthiest and

[23] Wm. and Mary Quar., Vol. IV, p. 39.
[24] Ibid, Vol. IV, p. 153.
[25] Va. Mag. of Hist. and Biog., Vol. XI, p. 366.
[26] Bruce, Soc. Hist. of Va., p. 91.

most prominent men of the colony, was thought to have been the grandson of a maltster.

It was during the second half of the 17th century that occurred the "Cavalier" immigration that took place as a consequence of the overthrow of Charles I. Upon this subject there has been much misapprehension. Many persons have supposed that the followers of the unhappy monarch came to Virginia by the thousand to escape the Puritans, and that it was from them that the aristocracy of the colony in large part originated. Even so eminent a historian as John Fiske has been led into the erroneous belief that this immigration was chiefly responsible for the great increase in population that occurred at this time. "The great Cavalier exodus," he says, "began with the king's execution in 1649, and probably slackened after 1660. It must have been a chief cause of the remarkable increase of the white population of Virginia from 15,000 in 1649 to 38,000 in 1670."[27] This deduction is utterly unwarranted. The increase in population noted here was due chiefly to the stream of indentured

[27] Fiske, Old Va. and Her Neighbors, Vol. II, p. 16.

servants that came to the colony at this period. At the time when the so-called Cavalier immigration was at its height between one thousand and fifteen hundred servants were sent to Virginia each year. In 1671 Governor Berkeley estimated the number that came over annually at fifteen hundred, and it is safe to say that during the Commonwealth period the influx had been as great as at this date. The constant wars in Great Britain had made it easier to obtain servants for exportation to America, for thousands of prisoners were disposed of in this way and under Cromwell Virginia received numerous batches of unfortunate wretches that paid for their hostility to Parliament with banishment and servitude. Not only soldiers from King Charles' army, but many captives taken in the Scotch and Irish wars were sent to the colony. On the other hand after the Restoration, hundreds of Cromwell's soldiers were sold as servants. If we estimate the annual importation of servants at 1200, the entire increase of population which Fiske notes is at once accounted for. Moreover, the mortality that in the earlier years had been so fatal to the newcomers, was now greatly reduced owing to the introduction of Peruvian bark and to the precautions taken by planters to prevent disease on their estates. Governor Berkeley said in 1671 that not many hands perished at that time, whereas formerly not one in five escaped the first year.

Nor can the increased number of births in the colony be neglected in accounting for the growth of population. The historian Bruce, referring to the period from 1634 to 1649, in which the population trebled, says: "The faster growth during this interval was due, not to any increase in the number of new settlers seeking homes in Virginia, but rather to the advance in the birth-rate among the inhabitants. There was by the middle of the century a large native population thoroughly seasoned to all the trying variations of the climate and inured to every side of plantation life, however harsh and severe it might be in the struggle to press the frontier further and further outward."[28] It may then be asserted positively that the growth of population between the dates 1649 and 1670 was not due to an influx of Cavaliers.

Had many men of note fled to Virginia at

---

[28] Bruce, Soc. Hist. of Va., pp. 18 and 19.

this period their arrival would scarcely have escaped being recorded. Their prominence and the circumstances of their coming to the colony would have insured for them a place in the writings of the day. A careful collection of the names of those Cavaliers that were prominent enough to find a place in the records, shows that their number was insignificant. The following list includes nearly all of any note whatsoever: Sir Thomas Lunsford, Col. Hammond, Sir Philip Honeywood, Col. Norwood, Stevens, Brodnax, Welsford, Molesworth, Col. Moryson, John Woodward, Robert Jones, Nicholas Dunn, Anthony Langston, Bishop, Culpeper, Peter Jenings, John Washington, Lawrence Washington, Sir Dudley Wiat, Major Fox, Dr. Jeremiah Harrison, Sir Gray Shipworth, Sir Henry Chiskeley and Col. Joseph Bridger. Of this number a large part returned to England and others failed to establish families in the colony. How few were their numbers is shown by the assertions of colonial writers. Sir William Berkeley reported in 1671 that Cromwell's "tyranny" had sent divers worthy men to the colony. Hugh Jones, writing in 1722, speaks of the civil wars in

England as causing several families of good birth and fortune to settle in Virginia. This language certainly gives no indication of a wholesale immigration of Cavaliers.

Some writers have pointed to the number of families in Virginia that were entitled to the use of coats-of-arms as convincing proof that the aristocracy of the colony was founded by men of high social rank. It is true that in numerous instances Virginians had the right to coats-of-arms, but this does not prove that their blood was noble, for in most cases these emblems of gentility came to them through ancestors that were mercantile in occupation and in instinct. During the 17th century the trades were in high repute in England, and to them resorted many younger sons of the gentry. These youths, excluded from a share in the paternal estate by the law of primogeniture, were forced either into the professions or the trades. It was the custom for the country gentleman to leave to his eldest son the whole of his landed estates; the second son he sent to Oxford or to Cambridge to prepare for one of the learned professions, such as divinity, medicine or law; the third was apprenticed to some local surgeon or apothecary; the fourth was sent to London to learn the art of weaving, of watchmaking or the like. It was the educating of the youngest sons in the trades that gave rise to the close connection between the commercial classes in England and the gentry. Great numbers of merchants in the trading cities were related to the country squire or even to the nobleman. These merchant families, since they did not possess landed estates, could not style themselves "gentlemen," but they clung to the use of the coat-of-arms that had descended to them from their ancestors. Thus it happened that some of the immigrants to Virginia possessed coats-of-arms. Since they still looked upon the life of the country squire as the ideal existence, as soon as they were settled upon the plantations, they imitated it as far as possible. With the possession of land they assumed the title of "gentleman." Since the squire or nobleman from whom the right to the coat-of-arms came to them might have lived many generations before the migration to Virginia, the use of this emblem could give but little ground for a claim to gentle blood.

Finally, the opinion that the leading planters

of the colony sprang from families of distinction and high social rank. in England is being discarded by the best authorities on Virginia history. The Virginia Magazine of History and Biography, which has done so much to shed light on the early history of Virginia, throws its influence without compromise against the old belief. It says: "If the talk of 'Virginia Cavaliers' indicates an idea that most of the Virginia gentry were descended from men of high rank, who had adhered to the King's side and afterwards emigrated to Virginia, it is assuredly incorrect. Some members of distinguished families, a considerable number of the minor gentry, as well as persons of the lower ranks, after the success of a party which they believe to be composed of rebels and traitors, came to Virginia, finding here a warm welcome, and leaving many descendants."[29] Again it says: "As we have before urged, and as we believe all genealogists having any competent acquaintance with the subject will agree, but few 'scions of great English houses' came to any of the colonies. Gloucester....has always been distinguished in Virginia as the resi-

[29] Va. Maga. of Hist. and Biog., Vol. I, p. 215.

dence of a large number of families of wealth, education and good birth; but in only a few instances are they descended from 'great houses' even of the English gentry. The families of Wyatt, Peyton and Throckmorton are perhaps the only ones derived from English houses of historic note; but they were never, in Virginia, as eminent for large estates and political influence as others of the same county whose English ancestry is of much less distinction. Next, as known descendants of minor gentry, were the families of Page, Burwell, Lightfoot and Clayton. Other leading names of the county, nothing certain in regard to whose English ancestry is known, were Kemp, Lewis, Warner, etc. These families were, like those of the ruling class in other countries, doubtless derived from ancestors of various ranks and professions....members of the country gentry, merchants and tradesmen and their sons and relatives, and occasionally a minister, a physician, a lawyer or a captain in the merchant service."[30] The William and Mary Quarterly makes the unequivocal statement that it was the "shipping people and mer-

---

[30] Ibid., Vol. I, p. 217.

chants who really settled Virginia." John Fiske, despite the exaggerated importance which he gives to the Cavalier immigration, agrees that the leading planters were not descended from English families of high rank. "Although," he says, "family records were until of late less carefully preserved (in Virginia) than in New England, yet the registered facts abundantly prove that the leading families had precisely the same sort of origin as the leading families of New England. For the most part they were either country squires, or prosperous yeomen, or craftsmen from the numerous urban guilds; and alike in Virginia and in New England there was a similar proportion of persons connected with English families ennobled or otherwise eminent for public service."[31]

Beyond doubt the most numerous section of the Virginia aristocracy was derived from the English merchant class.[32] It was the opportunity of amassing wealth by the cultivation of tobacco that caused great numbers of these

[31] Fiske, Old Va. and Her Neighbors, Vol. II, p. 187.

[32] Bruce, Soc. Hist. of Va., p. 83.

men to settle in the Old Dominion. Many had been dealers in the plant in England, receiving it in their warehouses and disposing of it to retailers. They kept up a constant and intimate correspondence with the planter, acting for him as purchasing agent, supplying him with clothes, with household goods, with the thousand and one articles essential to the conducting of the plantation, and thus were in a position to judge of the advantages he enjoyed. They kept him in touch with the political situation in England and in return received from him the latest tidings of what was going on in Virginia. In fact for one hundred and fifty years after the founding of Jamestown the colony was in closer touch with London, Bristol, Plymouth and other English seaports than with its nearest neighbors in America.[33]

The life of the Virginia planters offered an inviting spectacle to the English merchant. He could but look with envious eyes upon the large profits which for so many years the cultivation of tobacco afforded. He held, in common with

---

[33] Wm. & Mary Quar., Vol. IV, p. 29; Ibid., Vol. VI, p. 173; Bruce, Soc. Life of Va., p. 85; Jones' Virginia.

all Englishmen, the passion for land, and in Virginia land could be had almost for the asking. He understood fully that could he resolve to leave his native country a position of political power and social supremacy awaited him in the colony.

The civil wars in England greatly accelerated the emigration of merchants to Virginia. Business men are usually averse to war, for nothing can derange the delicate fibers of commerce more quickly than battles and sieges. And this is especially true of civil wars, for then it is the very heart of the country that suffers. Many prominent merchants of the English cities, fearing that their interests would be ruined by the ravages of the contending armies or the general business depression, withdrew to the colony, which was pursuing its usual quiet life but slightly affected by the convulsions of the mother country. William Hallam, a salter, wrote, "I fear if these times hold amongst us, we must all be faine to come to Virginia." William Mason wrote in 1648, "I will assure you that we have had several great losses that have befallen us and our charge is greater by reason of ye differences that are in our kingdom, trading is dead."[34]

The most convincing evidence that the leading settlers in Virginia were of the mercantile class is to be found by a study of the characteristics of the planters of the 17th century. Contemporaneous writers are unanimous in describing them as mercantile in their instincts. De Vries, a Dutch trader, complaining of the sharpness of the planters in a bargain, says, "You must look out when you trade with them, for if they can deceive any one they account it a Roman action."[35] Hugh Jones says, "The climate makes them bright and of excellent sense, and sharp in trade....They are generally diverted by business or inclination from profound study....being ripe for management of their affairs....They are more inclined to read men by business and conversation than to dive into books....being not easily brought to new projects and schemes; so that I question, if they would have been im-

[34] Wm. & Mary Quar., Vol. VIII, p. 243.

[35] Va. Maga. of Hist. and Biog., Vol. XI, pp. 359, 366, 453; Vol. XII, pp. 170, 173; Wm. & Mary Quar., Vol. IV, pp. 27, 39; Bruce, Soc. Life of Va.

posed upon by the Mississippi or South-Sea, or any other such monstrous Bubbles.[36]

And this evidence is corroborated fully by letters of Virginia planters to English merchants. They show that the wealthy Virginian of the 17th century was careful in his business dealings, sharp in a bargain, a painstaking manager, and in his private life often economical even to stinginess. Robert Carter, one of the wealthiest men of the colony, in a letter complains of the money spent upon the outfit of the Wormley boys who were at school in England, thinking it "entirely in excess of any need." William Fitzhugh, Philip Ludwell, William Byrd I, typical leaders of their time, by the mercantile instinct that they inherited from their fathers were enabled to build up those great estates which added such splendor to the Virginia aristocracy of the 18th century.[37]

---

[36] Jones' Virginia.

[37] Thinking Virginians of today cannot but be gratified that the old erroneous belief concerning the origin of the aristocracy is being swept away. Why it should ever have been a matter of pride with old families to point to the English nobility of the 17th century as the class from which they sprang is not easy to understand. The lords of that day were usually corrupt, unscrupulous and

Having, as we hope, sufficiently shown that the leading planters of Virginia were not in any large measure the descendants of Englishmen of high social rank, and that with them the predominant instinct was mercantile, we shall now proceed to point out those conditions to which the planters were subjected that changed them from practical business men to idealistic and chivalrous aristocrats.

Undoubtedly the most powerful influence that acted upon the character of the Virginian was the plantation system. In man's existence it is the ceaseless grind of the commonplace events of every day life that shapes the character. The most violent passions or the most stirring events leave but a fleeting impression in comparison with the effect of one's daily occupation. There is something distinctive about

---

quite unfit to found vigorous families in the "wilderness of America." How much better it is to know that the aristocracy of the colony was a product of Virginia itself! The self-respect, the power of command, the hospitality, the chivalry of the Virginians were not borrowed from England, but sprang into life on the soil of the Old Dominion. Amid the universal admiration and respect for Washington, Jefferson, Madison and Marshall, with what pride can the Virginian point to them as the products of his native state!

the doctor, the teacher, the tailor, the goldsmith. There is in each something different from the rest of mankind, and this something has been developed within him by the ceaseless recurrence of certain duties required of him by his profession. Similarly the English immigrant, isolated upon his vast plantation, surrounded by slaves and servants, his time occupied largely with the cultivation of tobacco, could not fail in the course of time to lose his mercantile instincts and to become distinctly aristocratic in his nature.

The estates of the planters were very large, comprising frequently thousands of acres. William Byrd II inherited from his father 23,231 acres, but so great was his hunger for land and so successful was he in obtaining it that at his death he owned no less than 179,440 acres of the best land in Virginia.[38] Robert Carter, of Nomini Hall, owned 60,000 acres.[39] The lands of William Fitzhugh amounted to 54,000 acres, at his death in 1701.[40] Other prominent men were possessed of estates not less extensive.

---

[38] Bassett, Writings of Wm. Byrd, lxxxiii.
[39] Fithian, Journal and Letters, p. 128.
[40] Va. Maga. of Hist. and Biog., Vol. I, p. 17.

These vast tracts of land comprised usually several plantations that were scattered in various parts of the colony and which differed widely in value and in extent. In the region to the west beyond tidewater estates of 20,000, 30,000, or 40,000 acres were not infrequent, while in the sections that had been first settled the average size was much less. Yet the plantations that stretched along the banks of the James, the York, the Rappahannock and the Potomac were so extensive that often the residences of the planters were several miles apart. From 4,000 to 6,000 acres was the average size of the farms of the wealthier men.[41]

The author of Virginia's Cure, a pamphlet printed in 1661, says: "The families....are dispersedly and scatteringly seated upon the sides of rivers, some of which running very far into the country, bear the English plantations above a hundred miles, and being very broad, cause the inhabitants of either side to be listed in several parishes. Every such parish is extended many miles in length upon the rivers' side, and usually not above a mile in breadth

---

[41] Fiske, Old Va. and Her Neighbors, Vol. II, p. 221.

backward from the river, which is the common stated breadth of every plantation, some extend themselves half a mile, some a mile, some two miles upon the sides of the rivers."[42]

The system of large plantations was in vogue in Virginia from the early years of the 17th century. Even before the days of Sir William Berkeley, many of the colonists possessed extensive tracts of land, only part of which they could put under cultivation. Doubtless the dignity which the possession of land gave in England was the principal inducement for the planter to secure as large an estate as his means would permit. The wealthier Virginians showed throughout the entire colonial period a passion for land that frequently led them into the grossest and most unjustifiable fraud.[43]

The tendency was accelerated by the law, made by the Virginia Company of London to encourage immigration, which allotted fifty acres of land to proprietors for every person they brought to the colony, "by which means

---

[42] Force, Hist. Tracts, Vol. III.

[43] The proofs of this statement are here omitted, as they are given at much length on pages 96 to 98 of this volume.

some men transporting many servants thither, and others purchasing the rights of those that did, took possession of great tracts of land at their pleasure."[44] In 1621 a number of extensive grants were made to persons thus engaging themselves to take settlers to Virginia. To Arthur Swain and Nathaniel Basse were given 5,000 acres for undertaking to transport one hundred persons. Five thousand acres was also given Rowland Truelove "and divers other patentees." Similar tracts were given to John Crowe, Edward Ryder, Captain Simon Leeke and others.[45] Sir George Yeardly received a grant of 15,000 acres for engaging to take over three hundred persons.[46]

Even more potent in building up large plantations was the wasteful system of agriculture adopted by the settlers. It soon became apparent to them that the cultivation of tobacco was very exhausting to the soil, but the abundance of land led them to neglect the most ordinary precautions to preserve the fertility of their

---

[44] Virginia's Cure.

[45] Abst. Proceedings Va. Co. of London, Vol. I, p. 154.

[46] Abst. Proceedings Va. Co. of London, Vol. I, p. 160.

fields. They planted year after year upon the same spot until the soil would produce no more, and then cleared a new field. They were less provident even than the peasants of the Middle Ages, for they failed to adopt the old system of rotation of crops that would have arrested to some extent the exhausting of their fields. Of the use of artificial fertilizers they were ignorant.

This system of cultivation made it necessary for them to secure very large plantations, for they could not be content with a tract of territory sufficiently large to keep busy their force of laborers. They must look forward to the time when their fields would become useless, and if they were wise they would secure ten times more than they could put into cultivation at once. If they failed to do this they would find at the end of a few years that their estates consisted of nothing but exhausted and useless fields. Thomas Whitlock, in his will dated 1659, says: "I give my son Thomas Whitlock the land I live on, 600 acres, when he is of the age 21, and during his minority to my wife. The land not to be further made use of or by planting or seating[47] than the first deep branch that is commonly rid over, that my son may have some fresh land when he attains to age."[48]

The plantations, thus vast in extent, soon became little communities independent in a marked degree of each other, and in many respects of the entire colony. The planter, his family, his servants and slaves lived to themselves in isolation almost as great as that of the feudal barons or of the inhabitants of the vill of the 13th century.

But this isolation was due even more to the direct trade between the planters and the foreign merchants than to the extent of the plantations. This was made possible by the nature of the waterways. The entire country was intersected with rivers, inlets and creeks that were deep enough to float the sea going vessels of the age, and salt water penetrated the woods for miles, forming of the whole country, as John Fiske has expressed it, a sylvan Venice. Thus it was possible for each planter to have his own wharf and to ship his tobacco directly

---

[47] The word seating is used here in the sense of occupying.

[48] Va. Maga. of Hist. and Biog., Vol. V, p. 285.

from his own estate. Moreover, it allowed him to receive from the foreign vessels what merchandise he desired to purchase. Hugh Jones wrote, "No country is better watered, for the conveniency of which most houses are built near some landing-place; so that anything may be delivered to a gentleman there from London, Bristol, &c., with less trouble and cost, than to one living five miles in the country in England; for you pay no freight from London and but little from Bristol; only the party to whom the goods belong, is in gratitude engaged to ship tobacco upon the ship consigned to her owners in England."[49]

This system, so remarkably convenient for the planters, was continued throughout the entire colonial period despite the many efforts made to change it. The Virginians could not be induced to bring their tobacco to towns for the purposes of shipping when the merchant vessels could so easily land at their private wharves. The merchants had less reason to like the system, for it forced them to take their

[49] An account of Virginia in 1676 written by Mrs. Thomas Slover says, "The planters' houses are built all along the sides of the rivers for the conveniency of shipping."

vessels into remote and inconvenient places; to spend much valuable time in going from plantation to plantation before their vessels were laden; to keep accounts with many men in many different places.[50] The sailors too complained of the custom, for they were frequently required to roll the tobacco in casks many yards over the ground to the landings, causing them much greater trouble than in loading in other countries. For this reason they are said to have had a great dislike of the country. Throughout the 17th century and even later the English government made repeated efforts to break up this system but without success, for the saving to the planters by local shipping was so great that threats and even attempted coercion could not make them give it up.

It is this that is chiefly responsible for the lack of towns in Virginia during the entire 17th century. Not until the settlements had spread out beyond the region of deep water did towns of any size arise. Then it became necessary to bring goods overland to the nearest deep water and from this circumstance shipping cities gradually appeared at the falls line

[50] Va. Maga. of Hist. and Biog., Vol. IV, p. 261.

on the rivers. Then it was that Richmond developed into the metropolis of Virginia.

How utterly insignificant the villages of the colony were during the 17th century is shown by a description of Jamestown given by Mrs. Ann Cotton in her account of Bacon's Proceedings. "The town," she says, "is built much about the middle of the south line close upon the river, extending east and west about three-quarters of a mile; in which is comprehended some sixteen or eighteen houses; most as is the church built of brick faire and large; and in them about a dozen famillies (for all their houses are not inhabited) getting their liveings by keeping of ordinaries at extraordinary rates." This was in 1676, sixty-nine years after the first settlement, and when the population of the colony was 45,000.

The lack of towns was a source of much uneasiness to the first promoters of the colony, for they regarded it as a sign of unhealthful and abnormal conditions and frequent directions were given to the colonial governors to put an end to the scattered mode of life and to encourage in every way possible the development of cities. Sir Francis Wyatt was instructured "to draw tradesmen and handicraftmen into towns."[51] Time and again throughout the 17th century the English kings insisted that the Assembly should pass laws intended to establish trading towns. In 1662, an act was passed at the command of Charles II providing for the building of a city at Jamestown.[52] There were to be thirty-two brick houses, forty feet long, twenty feet wide, and eighteen feet high; the roof to be fifteen feet high and to be covered with slate or tile. "And," says the Act, "because these preparations of houses and stores will be alltogether useless unless the towne be made the marte of all the adjoyning places, bee it therefore enacted that all the tobacco made in the three counties of James Citty, Charles Citty, and Surrey shall the next yeare when the stores be built be brought by the inhabitants to towne and putt in the stores there built." This absurd attempt met with utter failure. One of the complaints made to the King's Commissioners sent to investigate the causes of Bacon's Rebellion was, "That great quantities of tobacco was levied upon the

[51] Va. Maga. of Hist. and Biog., Vol. XI, p. 56.
[52] Hening's Statutes, Vol. II, p. 172.

poor people to the building of houses at Jamestown, which was not made habitable but fell down again before they were finished."[53]

In an effort to build up towns an act was passed in 1680 requiring all merchants to bring their goods to certain specified spots and there only to load their vessels with tobacco. "But several masters of ships and traders....not finding....any reception or shelter for themselves, goods or tobaccos, did absolutely refuse to comply with the said act....but traded and shipped tobaccos as they were accustomed to doe in former years, for which some of them suffered mouch trouble....the prosecution being chiefly managed by such persons....as having particular regard to their privat ends and designs, laid all the stumbling blocks they could in the way of publick traffic (though to the great dissatisfaction of the most and best part of the country)."[54]

In 1682 Lord Culpeper was instructed to do everything in his power to develop Jamestown into a city. Charles II told him to announce to the members of the Council that he would re-

---

[53] Va. Maga. of Hist. and Biog., Vol. II, p. 387.

[54] McDonald Papers, Vol. VI, p. 213.

gard with special favor those that built houses there and made it their permanent residence. Culpeper seems to have recognized the uselessness of the attempt, for he wrote, "I have given all encouragement possible for the rebuilding of James Citty,. . . .as to the proposall of building houses by those of the Counsell and the cheefe inhabitants, it hath once been attempted in vaine, nothing but profitt and advantage can doe it, and then there will be noe need of anything else."[55]

The Act of 1680 was never enforced. The planters complained that the places selected for ports were too few in number and that they were put to great expense in bringing their tobacco to them for shipment. The English government then directed the Assembly so to change the Act that it could be put into practical operation, but an attempt, in 1685, to follow these instructions proved futile. The Burgesses were willing to pass a bill providing for ports in each county, but this was not what the king wanted and so the whole matter came to nothing.[56]

---

[55] Va. Maga. of Hist. and Biog., Vol. XI, p. 398.

[56] Journal of Council, McDonald Papers, Vol. VII, pp. 457-566.

These failures were attributed by many to the obstinacy of the Virginians. Men at that time understood but dimly the supremacy of economic laws, and could not realize that so long as the planters found it profitable to do their shipping from their private wharves so long would there be no seaports in Virginia, no matter what laws were enacted. In 1701 a pamphlet was published entitled, "A Plain and Friendly Perswasive to the Inhabitants of Virginia and Maryland for promoting Towns and Cohabitation." The author tried to prove that towns would be an unmixed blessing to the colony, that they would promote trade, stimulate immigration, build up manufacture and aid education and religion.[57] A similar pamphlet, called Virginia's Cure, had been written in 1661, complaining that the scattered mode of life was the cause of the decline of religion in Virginia and advocating the building of towns.

This lack of urban life reacted strongly upon the plantations. Since there were no centers of activity in the colony where the planters could gather on occasions of universal interest, it tended to isolate them upon their estates. It

[57] Va. Maga. of Hist. and Biog., Vol. IV, p. 255.

forced them to become, except for their trade with England, self-sustaining little communities. As there were no towns to act as markets there was almost no trade between the various parts of the colony. During the 17th century a stranger in Virginia desiring to purchase any article whatever, could only obtain it by applying at some plantation. Nowhere else in the colony could it be had. The Friendly Perswasive dwelt especially on the evils of this state of affairs. "And as to a home-trade," it says, "by towns, all plantations far or near, would have some trade, less or more, to these towns, and a frequent trade, and traffic, would soon grow and arise between the several rivers and towns, by carrying and transporting passengers and goods to and fro; and supplying all places with such goods as they want most." Not until the end of the century was there even the beginning of home trade. Then it was that Williamsburg, Norfolk and Hampton, still mere villages, enjoyed a slight trade with the surrounding plantations.

This state of affairs made necessary the system of plantation manufacture. Those articles whose nature made importation from

Europe inconvenient were produced upon the plantations, and not in the towns of the colony. It had been the purpose of the Virginia Company of London to make the colony an industrial community and with this in view they had so encouraged the immigration of tradesmen and artisans, that between the years 1619 and 1624 hundreds of carpenters, smiths, coopers, bricklayers, etc., settled in Virginia. These men soon found, however, that they could not maintain themselves by their trades, and many, giving up their calling, secured tracts of land and became planters. Others took up their abode on some large plantation to serve as overseers or head workmen. In 1639 Sir Francis Wyatt was instructed to see to it "that tradesmen and handicraftsmen be compelled to follow their several trades,"[58] but this order was entirely ineffectual and soon but few artisans remained. Makensie says, "Our tradesmen are none of the best, and seldom improve from the incouragement they have. If some few stick to their trades, they demand extravigant rates, and few employ

[58] Va. Maga. of Hist. and Biog., Vol. XI, p. 56.

them but out of pure necessity."[59] Not infrequently an artisan would combine tobacco planting with his trade, since the latter alone was but a slender and insufficient source of income. On several occasions the Assembly tried to encourage the various trades by exempting free artisans from taxation, but this too proved ineffective.[60]

The planters found it necessary to secure skilled servants to fill the place of the hired workmen, and soon every estate had its smith, its carpenter, its cooper, etc. At the home plantation of "King" Carter were two house carpenters, a ship carpenter, a glazier, two tailors, a gardener, a blacksmith, two bricklayers and two sailors, all indentured servants.[61] In his will Col. Carter divided these men among his three sons.[62] The inventory of the property of Ralph Wormeley, who died in 1791, shows that at the home house there were eight English servants, among them a shoemaker, a tailor and a miller. In the 18th century, when the negro slave had to a large

---

[59] Va. Maga. of Hist. and Biog., Vol. IV, p. 267.
[60] Va. Maga. of Hist. and Biog., Vol. IX, p. 277.
[61] Va. Maga. of Hist. and Biog., Vol. VI, p. 367.
[62] Va. Maga. of Hist. and Biog., Vol. VI, p. 3.

extent taken the place of the white servant, attempts were made to teach the Africans to become artisans, but with partial success only. Hugh Jones, in speaking of the negroes, says, "Several of them are taught to be sawyers, carpenters, smiths, coopers, &c. though for the most part they be none of the aptest or nicest."[63]

An interesting picture of the life on the plantation is given in the manuscript recollections of George Mason, by his son General John Mason. "It was much the practice," he says, "with gentlemen of landed and slave estates....so to organize them as to have considerable resources within themselves; to employ and pay but few tradesmen, and to buy little or none of the course stuffs and materials used by them....Thus my father had among his slaves, carpenters, coopers, sawyers, blacksmiths, tanners, curriers, shoemakers, spinners, weavers, and knitters, and even a distiller. His woods furnished timber and plank for the carpenters and coopers, and charcoal for the blacksmiths; his cattle....supplied skins for the tanners, curriers and shoemakers; and his

[63] Jones' Virginia, p. 36.

sheep gave wool and his fields produced cotton and flax for the weavers and spinners, and his orchards fruit for the distiller. His carpenters and sawyers built and kept in repair all the dwelling houses, barns, stables, ploughs, harrows, gates, etc., on the plantations, and the outhouses at the house. His coopers made the hogsheads the tobacco was prized in, and the tight casks to hold the cider and other liquors. The tanners and curriers, with the proper vats, etc., tanned and dressed the skins as well for upper as for lower leather to the full amount of the consumption of the estate, and the shoemakers made them into shoes for the negroes. A professed shoemaker was hired for three or four months in the year to come and make up the shoes for the white part of the family. The blacksmith did all the ironwork required by the establishment, as making and repairing ploughs, harrows, teeth, chains, bolts, etc. The spinners, weavers, and knitters made all the course cloths and stockings used by the negroes, and some of finer texture worn by the white family, nearly all worn by the children of it. The distiller made every fall a good deal of apple, peach, and percimmon brandy.... Moreover, all the beeves and hogs for consumption or sale were driven up and slaughtered.... at the proper seasons and whatever was to be preserved was salted and packed away for after distribution."[64]

And the isolation that was a consequence of this industrial independence was made all the more pronounced by the condition of the roads. The task of cutting highways through the great forests was more than the first settlers could undertake. During the 17th century boats were the most common means of conveyance.[65] Each plantation possessed a number of vessels of various sizes and the settlers made use of them both in visiting their immediate neighbors and in travelling to more remote parts of the colony. Owing to the great width of the rivers, however, the use of small boats was fraught with danger.[66] For many miles from their mouths the James, the York, and the Rap-

---

[64] Rowland, Life of Geo. Mason, Vol. I, pp. 101, 102; compare Fithian, Journal and Letters, pp. 67, 104, 130, 131, 138, 217, 259; Va. Maga. of Hist. and Biog., Vol. XI, p. 62; Fiske, Old Va. and Her Neighbors, Vol. II, pp. 208, 214, 217; Bruce, Econ. Hist. of Va. Vol. II, pp. 411, 418.

[65] Force Hist. Tracts, Vol. II, Va. Maga. of Hist. and Biog., Vol. VI, p. 267.

[66] Jones' Va., p. 49.

pahannock are rather broad inlets of the Chesapeake Bay than rivers, and at many points to row across is no light undertaking.

Early in the 18th century efforts were made to construct serviceable roads. The settlements had by that time extended back from the rivers and creeks, and means of communication by land was absolutely necessary. The nature of the country, however, presented great difficulty. Hugh Jones wrote, "The worst inconveniency in travelling across the country, is the circuit that must be taken to head creeks, &c., for the main roads wind along the rising ground between the rivers, tho' now they much shorten their passage by mending the swamps and building of bridges in several places; and there are established ferries at convenient places, over the great rivers." But slight attention was given to keeping the roads in good condition and after each long rain they become almost impassable. The lack of bridges was a great hindrance to traffic and even the poor substitute of ferries was often lacking, forcing travellers to long detours or to the dangerous task of swimming the stream.[67]

[67] Fiske, Old Va. and Her Neighbors, Vol. II, p. 215.

Thus cut off from his neighbors the planter spent his life in isolation almost as great as that of the feudal barons of the Middle Ages. The plantation was to him a little world whose activities it was his business to direct and this world moulded his character far more than any outward influence.

It is a matter of no surprise that one of the first distinctive characteristics to develop among the Virginia planters was pride. This trait was natural to them even in the early years of the 17th century. The operation of economic conditions upon a society is usually very slow, and frequently the changes that it brings about may be detected only after the lapse of centuries. This fact is nowhere more apparent than in the development of the Virginia aristocracy, and we find that its distinctive character had not been fully formed until after the Revolution. Pride, however, is a failing so natural to humanity that its development may be a matter of a few years only. Conditions in the colony could not fail to produce, even in the first generations of Virginians, all the dignity and self esteem of an old established aristocracy. William Byrd I, Daniel Parke, "King"

Carter were every whit as proud as were Randolph, Madison or Jefferson.

It is interesting to note how careful were the Virginians of the 17th century not to omit in documents and legal papers any term of distinction to which a man was entitled. If he possessed two titles he was usually given both. Thus Thomas Willoughby is alluded to in the records of Lower Norfolk County as "Lieutenant Thomas Willoughby, gentleman." The term "esquire" was used only by members of the Council, and was the most honorable and respectful which could be obtained in Virginia, implying a rank which corresponded with the nobility in England. It invested those that bore it with dignity and authority such as has been enjoyed by the aristocrats of few countries. The respect shown to the leading men of the colony is evinced by an incident which befell Colonel William Byrd I, in 1685. One Humphrey Chamberlaine, a man of good birth, became angry with Byrd, and drew his sword in order to attack him. The man was immediately seized and put in jail. At his hearing before the court he declared in palliation of his act that he was a stranger in the country and ignorant of its customs, but the justices thought this a poor excuse, declaring that "no stranger, especially an English gentleman, could be insensible of ye respect and reverence due to so honorable a person" as Col. Byrd. Chamberlaine was fined heavily.[68]

The arrogance of these early aristocrats is shown even more strikingly by the conduct of Col. John Custis in 1688. As collector of duties on the Eastern Shore he had been guilty of great exactions, extorting from the merchants unjust and unreasonable fees. This had proceeded so far that it was reacting unfavorably upon commerce, and when foreign traders began to avoid entirely that part of the colony, the people of Accomack in alarm drew up a paper of grievances which they intended to present to the House of Burgesses. Custis one day seeing this paper posted in public, flew into a great rage and tore it down, at the same time shaking his cane at the crowd that had assembled around him and using many threatening words. In this Custis was not only infringing on the rights of the people, but he was offering a distinct affront to the House of Burgesses.

---

[68] Bruce, Soc. Life of Va., p. 133.

Yet so great was the awe that his authority and dignity inspired, that the people of Accomack not only allowed him to keep the paper, but "being terrified and affrighted drew up no other aggreivances att that time."[69]

Robert Carter was another planter whose "extraordinary pride and ambition" made many enemies. Governor Nicholson accuses him of "using several people haughtily, sometimes making the justices of the peace of the county wait two or three hours before they can speak to him." . . . . "In contempt of him," he adds, "he is sometimes called 'King' Carter."[70]

Beyond doubt this haughtiness was chiefly the result of the life upon the plantation. The command that the planter possessed over the lives of scores of servants and slaves could not fail to impress him with a feeling of respect for his own importance. John Bernard, the traveller, shows that he understood this matter clearly. "Woe," he says, "to the man who lives constantly with inferiors! He is doomed never to hear himself contradicted, never to be

---

[69] Jour. of Burg. 1688, pp. 81, 82; Sainsbury, Calendar of State Pap., Vol. IV, p. 252; McDonald Papers, Vol. VII, pp. 437-441.

[70] Va. Maga. of Hist. and Biog., Vol. VIII, p. 56.

told unwelcome truth, never to sharpen his wits and learn to control his temper by argument with equals. The Colonial Cavaliers were little kings, and they proved the truth of the saying of the royal sage of Rome that the most difficult of tasks is to lead life well in a palace."[71]

Political conditions also tended to the same result, for the leading men of the colony were possessed of extraordinary influence and power. Many of the prominent families of the 17th century were related to each other and they formed a compact little oligarchy that at times controlled the affairs of the colony at will.

But as time went on a decided change took place in the nature of the Virginian's pride. During the 18th century he gradually lost that arrogance that had been so characteristic of him in the age of Nicholson and Spotswood. At the time of the Revolution are found no longer

---

[71] Compare Voyages dans l'Amérique Septentrionale, Vol. II, p. 136. "On n'en pourra pas douter, si l'on considere qu'une autre cause agit encore en concurrence avec la premiere (heredity): je veux parler de l'esclavage;....parce que l'empire qu'on exerce fur eux, entretient la vanité & la paresse."

men that do not hesitate to trample under foot the rights of others as Custis, Byrd, and Carter had done. Nothing could be more foreign to the nature of Washington or Jefferson than the haughtiness of the typical Virginia planter of an earlier period. But it was arrogance only that had been lost, not self-respect or dignity. The Virginian of the later period had a most exalted conception of what a man should be, and they respected themselves as exemplifiers of their ideals, but they were always ready to accord to others the same reverence they paid themselves. The change that had taken place is shown in the lack of pretence and self-assertion in judges, councillors, in college presidents and other dignitaries. Thomas Nelson Page, in speaking of the fully developed Virginia gentleman, says, "There was the foundation of a certain pride, based on self-respect and consciousness of power. There were nearly always the firm mouth with its strong lines, the calm, placid, direct gaze, the quiet speech of one who is accustomed to command and have his commands obeyed."[72]

This change was beyond doubt the result of

[72] Page, The Old South, p. 157.

the increased political resistance which the aristocracy encountered during the 18th century. Within a few years after the founding of Jamestown the wealthy planters may be noted as a body distinct from the other settlers. Immediately after the downfall of the Virginia Company of London they became a powerful force in the colony, and when, a few years later, Governor Harvey tried to curb them, not only did they resist him successfully, but they eventually brought upon him financial and political ruin. This state of affairs was due largely to the vast superiority of the merchant settlers to the lower class of immigrants, both in intelligence and in wealth. Those English traders that made their home in the colony, became at once leaders politically and socially. Not infrequently they became burgesses, justices, or even members of the Council after a few years' residence only, taking their place quite naturally by the side of those that had come over previously. This condition of affairs continued until late in the century. Bacon the rebel was made a councillor, although he lived in Virginia less than two years altogether, while the Lees, the Washingtons and many others obtained places of influence and power as soon as they reached the colony. On the other hand, the middle class did not become a factor of very great importance in the government until the surrender of the colony to the Parliamentary Commissioners in 1652. The bulk of the immigrants during the first half of the 17th century were indentured servants, brought over to cultivate the tobacco fields. They came, most of them, from the ignorant laboring class of England, and were incapable, even after the expiration of their term of indenture, of taking an intelligent part in governmental affairs. It is true that many free families of humble means came to the colony in this period, but their numbers were not great enough to counterbalance the power of the leading planters. These families formed the neuclus of what later became an energetic middle class, but not until their ranks were recruited by thousands of servants, did they develop into a really formidable body.

It was the Commonwealth Period that gave to the middle class its first taste of power. After the surrender of the colony to Parliament, the House of Burgesses was made the ruling body in Virginia, in imitation of conditions in England. Since the Burgesses were the representatives of the common people, it might naturally be inferred that the rich planters would be excluded from any share in the government. Such, however, was not the case. By a conveniently rapid change of front the most prominent men of the colony retained much of their old influence, and the rabble, lacking leaders of ability, were forced to elect them to places of trust and responsibility. But the Commonwealth Period helped to organize the middle class, to give it a sense of unity and a desire for a share in the government. At the time of Bacon's Rebellion it had grown in numbers and strength, despite the oppression of the Restoration Period, and showed, in a way never to be forgotten, that it would no longer submit passively to tyranny or injustice.

Although England entered upon a policy of repression immediately after the submission of the insurgents, which for some years threatened to take from the common people every vestige of political liberty, it was at this very time that the House of Burgesses began that splendid struggle for its rights that was eventually to make it the supreme power in the colony. Even in the waning years of the 17th century it is evident that the middle class had become a power in political affairs that must always be taken into account. The discontented Berkeley party turned to it for support against the King's Commissioners after Bacon's Rebellion; Culpeper, at the risk of Charles' displeasure, compromised with it; Nicholson sought its support in his memorable struggle with the Virginia aristocracy. In the 18th century through the House of Burgesses its influence slowly but steadily advanced. Governor Spotswood had once to beg the pardon of the Burgesses for the insolence of the members of the Council in wearing their hats in the presence of a committee of the House.[73] Governor Dinwiddie expressed his surprise, when the mace bearer one day entered the supreme court, and demanded that one of the judges attend upon the House, whose servant he was.[74] Before the outbreak of the Revolution the House of Burgesses had become the greatest power in the colony.

It is then a matter of no surprise that the

---

[73] Compare Jour. of Coun. 1748, pp. 17, 18, and 19.

[74] Wm. & Mary Quar., Vol. VI, p. 13.

rich planters lost the arrogant spirit which had formerly characterized them. Long years of vigorous opposition from a powerful middle class had taught them to respect the privileges and feelings of others. They were no longer at such a height above their humbler neighbors. The spirit of democracy, which was fostered by the long resistance to the English government, had so pervaded Virginia society, that even before the open rupture with the mother country many of the aristocratic privileges of the old families had been swept away. And when the war broke out, the common cause of liberty in a sense placed every man upon the same footing. An anecdote related by Major Anbury, one of the British officers captured at Saratoga and brought to Virginia, illustrates well the spirit of the times. "From my observations," he says, "in my late journey, it appeared to me, that before the war, the spirit of equality or levelling principle was not so prevalent in Virginia, as in the other provinces; and that the different classes of people in the former supported a greater distinction than those of the latter; but since the war, that principle seems to have gained great ground in Virginia; an instance of it I saw at Col. Randolph's at Tuckahoe, where three country peasants, who came upon business, entered the room where the Colonel and his company were sitting, took themselves chairs, drew near the fire, began spitting, pulling off their country boots all over mud, and then opened their business, which was simply about some continental flour to be ground at the Colonel's mill: When they were gone, some one observed what great liberties they took; he replied it was unavoidable, the spirit of independence was converted into equality, and every one who bore arms, esteemed himself upon a footing with his neighbor, and concluded by saying; 'No doubt, each of these men conceives himself, in every respect, my equal.' "[75]

One of the most fertile sources of error in history is the tendency of writers to confound the origin of institutions with the conditions that brought them into life. In nothing is this more apparent than in the various theories advanced in regard to the development of chivalry during the Middle Ages. The fundamentals of chivalry can be traced to the earliest period

[75] Anbury, p. 329.

of German history. Many Teutonic writers, imbued with a pride in their ancestors, have pointed out the respect for women, the fondness for arms, the regard for the oppressed and unfortunate, of the people of the Elbe and the Rhine. Chivalry, they say, was but the expansion, the growth of characteristics natural and individual with their forefathers.[76] This is erroneous. The early Germanic customs may have contained the germ of chivalry, but that germ was given life only by conditions that came into operation centuries after the Teutons had deserted their old habits and mode of life and had taken on some of the features of civilization.

Chivalry was the product of feudalism. It was that system that gave birth to the noble sentiments, the thirst for great achievements, the spirit of humanity that arose in the 10th and 11th centuries. Feudalism, although it was the cause of much that was evil, also produced in the hearts of men sentiments that were noble and generous. If it delivered Europe into the hands of a host of ruthless and savage barons, that trod under foot the rights of the common

---

[76] Guizot, Civ. in Europe, p. 117.

people, it alone gave rise to the sentiment of honor which was so conspicuous from the 10th to the 13th centuries.

Similarly it is erroneous to look to England for the explanation of chivalry in Virginia. This spirit was almost entirely a development in the colony. The settlers of the 17th century, even of the better class were by no means characterized by gallantry and honor. The mortal enemy of chivalry is commerce, for the practical common-sense merchant looks with contempt upon the Quixotic fancies of a Bayard. His daily life, his habits of thought, his associations tend to make him hostile to all that glittering fabric of romance reared in the Middle Ages. He abhors battles and wars, for they are destructive to his trade. He may be honest, but he cares little for the idealistic honor of the days of knighthood. He ascribes to woman no place of superiority in society. We have already seen that the Virginia aristocracy had its origin largely in the emigration of English merchants to the colony, and we should naturally expect to find the planters of the 17th century lacking in the spirit of chivalry. Such indeed was the case.

The Virginians were not a race of fighters. It was their misfortune to be subjected to frequent and murderous attacks from a savage race living in close proximity to them, and on this account were compelled to keep alive the military spirit, but they never entered into war with the feeling of joy that characterized the warriors of the Middle Ages. Throughout the entire colonial period there was a numerous body of militia, which was considered the bulwark of the people both against the Indians and against attack from European armies. Its commanders were selected from the leading planters of each community and at times it numbered thousands of men. It never, however, presented a really formidable fighting force, for it was at all times lacking in discipline, owing to the fact that the people were so scattered and the country so thinly settled that it was impossible for them to meet often for military exercises. Repeated laws requiring the militia to drill at stated periods created great discontent, and were generally disobeyed. The Assembly, even in times of war, shirked the responsibility of furnishing the companies with arms, while the people were far too indifferent to purchase them for themselves. At times the English government would send guns and powder and armor from the royal arsenal, and then only would the colony be in a position to repel foreign invasion. Governor Nicholson speaks of the utter insufficiency of the militia, and spent a large part of his time in reorganizing it, but conditions were so adverse that he met with little success. Governor Spotswood, who had served under the Duke of Marlborough and was an experienced soldier, also endeavored to increase the efficiency of the militia and under his leadership better discipline was obtained than before, but even he could effect no permanent improvement. When the test of war came the militia was found to be of no practical use. The companies could not be assembled quickly enough to repel a sudden invasion, and when a considerable body was gotten together desertion was so common that the force immediately melted away. In the French and Indian War Governor Dinwiddie soon learned that no dependence whatever could be placed in the old organization and turned his attention to recruiting and arming new companies. The Virginia troops that were driven from Fort Duquesne, those that fought with Braddock, and those that held back the attacks of the Indians along the frontier of the Shenandoah Valley were in no way connected with the old militia.

This distaste of the colonists for war is shown clearly by the consistent opposition of the Assembly to all measures either of defense or of military aggression. On more than one occasion they were commanded by the English kings to render aid to other colonies in America. Thus in 1695, when there was grave danger that the French would invade New York the Virginians were directed to send men and money to aid the Northern colony, which was a bulwark to all the English possessions in America. It was only after repeated and peremptory demands and even threats that any assistance at all was sent, and then it was miserably insufficient. In 1696 the burgesses were shameless enough to assert that an attempt to impress men for service in New York would probably be the means of frightening most of the young freemen from the colony, even causing many to desert their wives and children.[77]

[77] Jour. of Bour. Apl. 1696.

Governor Spotswood met with great opposition in his attempt to aid South Carolina and North Carolina when those colonies were threatened with extermination by the savage attacks of the Indians. And in later years, when there was imminent danger of an invasion of Virginia itself by the French with their savage allies, Governor Dinwiddie was never able to persuade the Assembly to provide adequate means of defence. Not until the news of massacres of defenceless women and children upon the frontier struck terror to every family in Virginia did the legislators vote money for a body of men to drive back the enemy. And even then so niggardly were they in their appropriations that with the insufficient means granted him even the patient and frugal Washington was unable to prevent the continuance of the murderous raids of the Indians. In the Revolutionary War the same spirit prevailed. Virginia was not willing to raise and equip a standing army to defend her soil from the English invaders and as a consequence fell an easy victim to the first hostile army that entered her borders. The resistance offered to Cornwallis was shamefully weak, and the Virginians had the mortification of seeing their plantations and their towns devastated by an army that should have been driven back with ease. The militia to which the safety of Virginia was entrusted, like similar troops from the other states, proved ill disciplined, ill armed and cowardly.[78]

Although it was the House of Burgesses that offered the most strenuous opposition at all periods to the improvement of the military organization, a large measure of blame must be placed upon that wealthy clique of men represented by the Council. The commissioned officers were invariably selected from the wealthiest and most influential planters, and it was they alone that could keep alive the military spirit, that could drill the companies, that could enforce the discipline that was so essential to efficiency. It is true that the Council usually favored the measures proposed by various governors for bettering the militia and for giving aid to neighboring colonies, but this was due more to a desire to keep in harmony with the executive than to military ardour. And it is significant that when troops were en-

---

[78] Marshall, Life of George Washington.

listed for distant expeditions, the wealthy planters were conspicuous by their absence. We see not the slightest inclination on their part to rush into the conflict for the love of fighting and adventure that was so typical of the aristocrat of the Middle Ages. They were more than content to stay at home to attend to the business of the plantation and to leave to humbler hands the task of defending helpless families of the frontiers. But the economic and political conditions in the colony were destined to work a change in this as in other things in the Virginia planter. The gradual loss of the mercantile instinct, the habit of command acquired by the control of servants and slaves, and the long use of political power, the growth of patriotism, eventually instilled into him a chivalric love of warfare not unlike that of the knights of old. It is impossible to say when this instinct first began to show itself. Perhaps the earliest evidence that the warlike spirit was stirring in the breasts of the planters is given in 1756, when two hundred gentlemen, moved by the pitiful condition of the defenseless families of the Shenandoah Valley, formed a volunteer company, and marched against the Indians. It is probable that the expedition did not succeed in encountering the enemy, but it was of much value in animating the lower class of people with greater courage.[79] In the Revolutionary War the change had become quite apparent. It is to the Old Dominion that the colonies turn for the commander-in-chief of their armies. The Lees, Morgan and other Virginia aristocrats were among the most gallant leaders of the American army. But the development was even then far from its climax. Not until the Civil War do we note that dash, that gallantry, and bravery that made the Virginia gentleman famous as a warrior. Then it was that the chivalrous Stuart and the reckless Mosby rivaled the deeds of Bayard and of Rupert. Then it was that each plantation gave forth its willing sacrifice of men for the defense of the South, and thousands of the flower of Virginia aristocracy shed their blood upon the battle field. And Virginia produced for this great struggle a galaxy of chieftains seldom equalled in the world's history. Robert E. Lee, "Stonewall" Jackson, Johnston and many other great generals show that warfare had become natural to the people of the Old Dominion.

---

[79] Dinwiddie Papers, Vol. II, p. 427.

Even more striking is the development of duelling in Virginia. The history of chivalry in Europe is indissolubly connected with thousands of tournaments and duels. It was the ambition of each knight to increase his fame by triumphing over as many warriors as possible. He looked upon these fights as the greatest pleasure of his existence, and his training and education were intended largely to prepare him for them. As years passed and the feudal baron gave place to the aristocratic lord, the tournament was no longer indulged in, but as its successor the custom of duelling continued unabated. It remained, as it had been for centuries, the acknowledged way for gentlemen to settle difficulties. At the very time that the best class of settlers was coming to Virginia, duelling was in high favor with the English aristocracy. It was a common event for two gentlemen who were suitors for the hand of the same lady to settle the matter by mortal combat, and this was considered not only proper, but the highest compliment that could be paid the lady's charms. Angry joustings were frequent in places of amusement or even upon the streets.

In London the ring in Hyde Park, the back of Montague House, and the Barns Elms were the favorite places for these combats.[80]

That the custom was not continued in Virginia adds convincing testimony to the evidence that the best class of immigrants to the colony were not members of the English aristocracy. Had many country gentlemen or noblemen settled in the Old Dominion, duelling would have been as common on the banks of the James as it was in London. The most careful investigation has been able to bring to light evidence of but five or six duels in Virginia during the entire colonial period.[81] In 1619 Capt. Edward Stallings was slain in a duel with Mr. William Epes at Dancing Point. Five years later Mr. George Harrison fought a duel with Mr. Richard Stephens. "There was some words of discontent between him and Mr. Stephens, with some blows. Eight or ten days after Mr. Harrison sent a challenge to Stephens to meet him in a place, which was made mention of, they meeting together it so fell out that Mr. Harrison received a cut in the leg which did some-

[80] Pict. Hist. of Eng., Vol. IV, p. 789.

[81] Va. Maga. of Hist. and Biog., Vol. I, p. 216.

what grieve him, and fourteen days after he departed this life."[82]

After this fatal affair the custom of duelling died out almost entirely in the colony. Had there been many of these encounters frequent mention beyond doubt would have been made of them. Any deaths resulting from them could hardly have escaped mention in the records, and the general interest that always attaches itself to such affairs would have caused them to find a place in the writings of the day. Beverley, Hugh Jones, John Clayton and other authors who described the customs of colonial Virginia made no mention of duelling. Only a few scattered instances of challenges and encounters have been collected, gleaned largely from the county records, and these serve to show that duelling met with but little favor. Most of the challenges were not accepted and provoked usually summary and harsh punishment at the hands of the law. In 1643 a commissioner was disabled from holding office for having challenged a councillor.[83] Some years later Capt. Thomas Hackett sent a challenge by

---

[82] Brown, First Rep. in America, p. 582.

[83] Va. Maga. of Hist. and Biog., Vol. VIII, p. 69.

his son-in-law, Richard Denham, to Mr. Daniel Fox, while the latter was sitting in the Lancaster County court. The message was most insulting in its wording and ended by declaring that if Fox "had anything of a gentleman or manhood" in him he would render satisfaction in a personal encounter with rapiers. One of the justices, Major Carter, was horrified at these proceedings. He addressed Denham in words of harsh reproval, "saying that he knew not how his father would acquit himself of an action of that nature, which he said he would not be ye owner of for a world." Denham answered in a slighting way "that his father would answer it well enough....whereupon ye court conceivinge ye said Denham to be a partye with his father-in-law....adjudged ye said Denham to receive six stripes on his bare shoulder with a whip." The course pursued by Fox in this affair is of great interest. Had duelling been in vogue he would have been compelled to accept the challenge or run the risk of receiving popular contempt as a coward. He could not have ignored the message on grounds of social superiority, for Hackett ranked as a gentleman. Yet he requested the court to arrest Hackett, "him to detain in safe custody without baile or mainprize," in order to save himself from the risk of a personal attack.[84] A similar case occurred in 1730, when Mr. Solomon White entered complaint in the Princess Anne County court against Rodolphus Melborne for challenging him "with sword and pistoll." The court ordered the sheriff to arrest Melborne and to keep him in custody until he entered bond in the sum of 50 pounds as security for good behavior for twelve months.[85]

But though the Virginia gentleman, in the days when he still retained the prosaic nature of the merchant, frowned upon duelling, it was inevitable that in time he must become one of its greatest advocates. The same conditions that instilled into him a taste for war, could not fail in the end to make him fond of duelling. We are not surprised then to find that, at the period of the Revolutionary War, duelling began to grow in popularity in Virginia and that from that time until the Civil War appeals to

[84] Va. Maga. of Hist. and Biog., Vol. II, p. 96; Bruce, Soc. Life of Va., p. 246.

[85] Va. Maga. of Hist. and Biog., Vol. III, p. 89. Compare McDonald Papers, Vol. V, p. 35.

the code were both frequent and deadly. Writers have sought to find a reason for this change in the military customs introduced by a long war, or in the influence of the French. There can be no doubt, however, that the rapid increase of duelling at this time was due to the fact that conditions were ripe for its reception. A spirit had been fostered by the life upon the plantation which made it distasteful to gentlemen to turn to law for redress for personal insults. The sense of dignity, of self reliance there engendered, made them feel that the only proper retaliation against an equal was to be found in a personal encounter.

Perhaps the most beautiful, the most elevating feature of the chivalry of the Middle Ages was the homage paid to women. The knight always held before him the image of his lady as an ideal of what was pure and good, and this ideal served to make him less a savage and more a good and true man. Although he was rendered no less brave and warlike by this influence, it inclined him to tenderness and mercy, acting as a curb to the ferocity that in his fathers had been almost entirely unrestrained. It made him recognize the sacredness of womanhood. The true value of the wife and the mother had never before been known. In none of the ancient communities did women attain the position of importance that they occupied in the age of chivalry, for neither the Roman matron nor the Greek mother could equal the feudal lady in dignity and influence.

And this was the direct outcome of the feudal system. The ancient baron led a life of singular isolation, for he was separated in his fortress home from frequent intercourse with other men of equal rank, and around him were only his serfs and retainers, none of whom he could make his companions. The only equals with whom he came in contact day after day were his wife and children. Naturally he turned to them for comradeship, sharing with them his joys and confiding to them his sorrows. If he spent much of his time in hunting, or in fishing, or in fighting he always returned to the softening influence of his home, and it was inevitable, under these conditions, that the importance of the female sex should increase.[86]

As we have seen, the Virginia plantation bore a striking analogy to the feudal estate.

---

[86] Guizot, Hist. of Civ. in Europe, p. 106.

The planter, like the baron, lived a life of isolation, coming into daily contact not even with his nearest neighbors. His time was spent with his servants and slaves. He too could turn only to his family for companionship, and inevitably, as homage and respect for women had grown up among the feudal barons, so it developed in Virginia.

There is no proof that the colonists of the 17th century regarded womanhood in any other than a commonplace light. They assigned to their wives and daughters the same domestic lives that the women of the middle classes of England led at that time. Predominated by the instinct of commerce and trade, they had little conception of the chivalric view of the superiority of the gentle sex, for in this as in other things they were prosaic and practical.

The early Virginians did not hesitate to subject gossiping women to the harsh punishment of the ducking stool. In 1662 the Assembly passed an Act requiring wives that brought judgments on their husbands for slander to be punished by ducking.[87] In 1705 and again in

[87] Hening, Statutes, Vol. II, p. 66.

1748 the county courts were authorized to construct ducking stools if they thought fit.[88] That the practice was early in vogue is shown by the records of the county courts. We read in the Northampton records for 1634 the following, "Upon due examination it is thought fitt by the board that said Joane Butler shall be drawen over the Rings Creeke at the starn of a boat or canoux."

How inconsistent with all the ideals of chivalry was that action of Bacon in his war with Governor Berkeley which won for his men the contemptuous appellation of "White Aprons!" Bacon had made a quick march on Jamestown and had surprised his enemies there. His force, however, was so small that he set to work immediately constructing earthworks around his camp. While his men were digging, "by several small partyes of horse (2 or 3 in a party, for more he could not spare) he fetcheth into his little league, all the prime men's wives, whose husbands were with the Governour, (as Coll. Bacons lady, Madm. Bray, Madm. Page, Madm. Ballard, and others) which the next morning he presents to the view of there hus-

[88] Hening, Statutes, Vol. III, p. 268, Vol. V, p. 528.

bands and ffriends in towne, upon the top of the smalle worke hee had cast up in the night; where he caused them to tarey till he had finished his defense against his enemies shott,.... which when completed, and the Governour understanding that the gentle women were withdrawne in to a place of safety, he sends out some 6 or 700 of his soulders, to beate Bacon out of his trench."[89]

The fact that Bacon's family was one of great prominence in the colony makes this ungallant action all the more significant. His uncle, Nathaniel Bacon, was a leader in political affairs, being one of Berkeley's most trusted advisers. He himself had been a member of the Council. It is true that his harsh treatment of the ladies brought upon him some censure, yet it is highly indicative of the lack of chivalry of the times, that a gentleman should have been willing to commit such a deed. How utterly impossible this would have been to George Washington or Thomas Jefferson, typical Virginians a hundred years later!

It remained to Berkeley, however, the so-

[89] Force, Hist. Tracts, Vol. I, Our Late Troubles, p. 8.

called "Cavalier Governor" of Virginia, to strike the most brutal blow at womanhood. After the failure of Bacon's Rebellion, when the insurgents were being hunted down by the implacable anger of the Governor, Major Chiesman, one of the most prominent of the rebels, was captured. "When the Major was brought into the Governours presence, and by him demanded, what made him to ingage in Bacon's designs? Before that the Major could frame an answer to the Governours demand; his wife steps in and tould his honour that it was her provocations that made her husband joyne in the cause that Bacon contended for; ading, that if he had not bin influenced by her instigations, he had never don that which he had done. Therefore (upon her bended knees) she desired of his honour, that since what her husband had done, was by her means, and so, by consequence, she most guilty, that she might be hanged, and he pardoned." Had Berkeley had one atom of gallantry or chivalry in his nature, he would have treated this unfortunate woman with courtesy. Even though he condemned her husband to the gallows, he would have raised her from her knees and palliated her grief as best he could with kind words. That he spurned her with a vile insult shows how little this "Cavalier" understood of the sacredness of womanhood.[90]

Some years later an incident occurred which, as Bishop Meade well remarks, speaks ill for the chivalry and decorum of the times.[91] A dispute arose between Col. Daniel Parke and Commissary Blair, the rector of the church at Williamsburg. Mr. Blair's wife, having no pew of her own in the church, was invited by Mr. Ludlow, of Green Spring, to sit with his family during the services. Col. Parke was the son-in-law of Mr. Ludlow, and one Sunday, with the purpose of insulting the rector, he seized Mrs. Blair rudely by the arm, and dragged her out of the pew, saying she should no longer sit there. This ungallant act is made all the more cowardly by the fact that Mr. Blair was not present at the time. We learn with pleasure that Mr. Ludlow, who was also probably absent, was greatly offended at his son-in-law for his brutal conduct. The incident is

[90] Force, Hist. Tracts, Vol. I, Ingram's Proceedings, p. 34.

[91] Meade, Vol. II, pp. 180, 181.

the more suggestive in that both Col. Parke and Mrs. Blair were members of leading families in the colony.

In matters of courtship there was little of romance and chivalry. Women did not care for the formalities and petty courtesies of the gallant suitor. Alsop, in describing the maids of Maryland, whose social life was quite similar to that of their sisters of Virginia, says, "All complimental courtships drest up in critical rarities are meer strangers to them. Plain wit comes nearest to their genius; so that he that intends to court a Maryland girle, must have something more than the tautologies of a long-winded speech to carry on his design, or else he may fall under the contempt of her frown and his own windy discourse."

We will not attempt to trace through successive years the chivalric view of womanhood. The movement was too subtle, the evidences too few. At the period of the Revolutionary War, however, it is apparent that a great change was taking place. The Virginia gentleman, taught by the experience of many years, was beginning to understand aright the reverence due the nobleness, the purity, the gentleness of woman. He was learning to accord to his wife the unstinted and sincere homage that her character deserved.

It is unfortunate that we should be compelled to rely to so great an extent upon the testimony of travelers for our data regarding the domestic life of the Virginia aristocracy of the 18th century. These writers were frequently superficial observers and almost without exception failed to understand and sympathize with the society of the colony. Some were prejudiced against the Virginians even before they set foot upon the soil of the Old Dominion, and their dislike is reflected in their writings, while few tarried long enough to grasp fully the meaning of the institutions and customs of the people. They dwelt long on those things that they found displeasing, and passed over in silence those distinctive virtues with which they were not in harmony. It is not surprising then that they failed to grasp the dignity and importance of the place filled by the Virginia woman. When they spoke of her their criticisms were usually favorable, but only too often they ignored her entirely. The gifted John Bernard, however, was more penetrating than the others. "Of the planters' ladies," he said, "I must speak in terms of unqualified praise; they had an easy kindness of manner, as far removed from rudeness as from reserve, which being natural to them....was the more admirable....To the influence of their society I chiefly attribute their husbands' refinement."[92]

To understand fully the sentiment of respect for womanhood that finally became so pronounced a trait of the Virginia gentleman, it is necessary to turn to Southern writers. Thomas Nelson Page, in "The Old South," draws a beautiful and tender picture of the ante-bellum matron and her influence over her husband. "What she was," he says, "only her husband knew, and even he stood before her in dumb, half-amazed admiration, as he might before the inscrutable vision of a superior being. What she really was, was known only to God. Her life was one long act of devotion—devotion to God, devotion to her husband, devotion to her children,....devotion to all humanity. She was the head and front of the church;....she regulated her servants, fed the poor, nursed the sick, consoled the bereaved.

[92] Bernard, Retrospections of America, p. 150.

The training of her children was her work. She watched over them, led them, governed them....She was at the beck and call of every one, especially her husband, to whom she was guide, philosopher, and friend."

Dr. George Bagby pays to the Virginia woman a tribute not less beautiful. "My rambles before the war made me the guest of Virginians of all grades. Brightest by far of the memories of those days....is that of the Virginia mother. Her delicacy, tenderness, freshness, gentleness; the absolute purity of her life and thought, typified in the spotless neatness of her apparel and her every surrounding, it is quite impossible to convey. Withal, there was about her a naiveté mingled with sadness, that gave her a surpassing charm."[93]

Further evidence is unnecessary. Enough has been said to show clearly that in the matter of gallantry a great change took place among the wealthy Virginia planters during the colonial period; that in the 17th century they were by no means chivalrous in their treatment of women; that at the time of the Revolution and in succeeding years homage to the gentler

[93] Bagby, The Old Va. Gentleman, p. 125.

sex was an important part of the social code. It is but one more link in the long chain of evidence that shows that society in Virginia was not an imitation of society in England, but was a development in the colony; that the Virginia aristocracy was not a part of the English aristocracy transplanted to the shores of the New World, but a growth produced by local conditions.

A study of the spirit of honor in the colony leads us to the same conclusion. It is not difficult to demonstrate that during the greater part of the colonial period the Virginia aristocracy was not characterized by the chivalric conception of what was honorable. The mercantile atmosphere that they brought with them from England was not well suited to this spirit. None were quicker to seize an unfair advantage in a bargain, and the English and Dutch merchants that traded with the Virginians made repeated complaints of unfair treatment. So great were their losses by the system of credit then in vogue in the colony that it was the custom for traders to employ factors, whose business it was to recover bad debts from the planters, and prolonged lawsuits became very frequent. The use of tobacco as money caused a great amount of trouble, and the Virginians were not slow to take advantage of any fluctuation in the value of their medium of exchange. This was the occasion of great injustice and suffering. It was the standing complaint of the clergy that they were defrauded of a part of their salaries at frequent intervals by the varying price of tobacco.

Accusations of frauds in regard to weights were also made against the planters, and this species of deception at one time was so general, that it became necessary to pass a special law declaring the English statute concerning weights to be in force in Virginia. The Act is as follows, "To prevent the great abuse and deceit by false styllyards in this colony, It is enacted by this Assembly, That whoever shall use false stillyards willingly shall pay unto the party grieved three fold damages and cost of suit, and shall forfeit one thousand pounds of tobacco."[94]

It is not necessary to assume, however, that the Virginia planters were noted for dishonesty in matters of business. They were neither bet-

[94] Hening's Statutes, Vol. I, p. 391.

ter not worse than merchants in other parts of the world or in other times. It was their daily life, their associations and habits of thought that made it impossible for them to see in an ideal light the highest conceptions of honor.

In their political capacity the leading men of the colony were frequently guilty of inexcusable and open fraud. Again and again they made use of their great influence and power to appropriate public funds to their private use, to escape the payment of taxes, to obtain under false pretenses vast tracts of land.

After Bacon's Rebellion, when the King's Commissioners were receiving the complaints of the counties, from all parts of the colony came accusations of misappropriated funds. The common people asserted, with an earnestness and unanimity that carry conviction, that throughout the second period of Governor Berkeley's administration large quantities of tobacco had been collected from them which had served only to enrich certain influential individuals. Other evidence tends to corroborate these charges. In 1672, the Assembly passed a bill for the repairing of forts in the colony, and entrusted the work to associations of wealthy planters, who were empowered to levy as heavy taxes in the various counties as they thought necessary. Although large sums of money were collected under this Act, very little of it was expended in repairing the forts and there is no reason to doubt that much of it was stolen. Similar frauds were perpetrated in connection with an Act for encouraging manufacture. The Assembly decided to establish and run at public expense tanworks and other industrial plants, and these too were entrusted to wealthy and influential men. Most of these establishments were never completed and none were put in successful operation and this was due largely to open and shameless embezzlement.[95] The common people, emboldened by promises of protection by Governor Jeffries, did not hesitate to bring forward charges of fraud against some of the most influential men of the colony. Col. Edward Hill, who had been one of Berkeley's chief supporters, was the object of their bitterest attack. They even ac-

[95] Va. Maga. of Hist. and Biog., Vol. III, pp. 136, 141, 142.

cused him of stealing money that had been appropriated for the repairing of roads. Hill defended himself vigorously, but there can be little doubt that he was to some extent guilty.[96]

The Council members were the boldest of all in dishonesty, for they did not scruple to defraud even the English government. There was a tax on land in the colony called the quit rents, the proceeds of which went to the king. Since there was very little coin in Virginia, this tax was usually paid in tobacco. Except on rare occasions the quit rents were allowed to remain in the colony to be drawn upon for various governmental purposes, and for this reason it was convenient to sell the tobacco before shipping it to England. These sales were conducted by the Treasurer and through his connivance the councillors were frequently able to purchase all the quit rents tobacco at very low prices. In case the sale were by auction, intimidation was used to prevent others than Council members from bidding. In 1697, Edward Chilton testified before the Lords Commissioners of Trade and Plantations that the quit rents had brought but four or six shillings per hun-

[96] Va. Maga. of Hist. and Biog., Vol. III, p. 143.

dred pounds, although the regular price of tobacco was twenty shilling.[97]

The wealthy planters consistently avoided the payment of taxes. Their enormous power in the colonial government made this an easy matter, for the collectors and sheriffs in the various counties found it convenient not to question their statements of the extent of their property, while none would dare to prosecute them even when glaring cases of fraud came to light. Estates of fifty or sixty thousand acres often yielded less in quit rents than plantations of one-third their size.[98] Sometimes the planters refused to pay taxes at all on their land and no penalty was inflicted on them. Chilton declared that the Virginians would be forced to resign their patents to huge tracts of country if the government should demand the arrears of quit rents.[99]

Even greater frauds were perpetrated by prominent men in securing patents for land. The law required that the public territory should be patented only in small parcels, that a

[97] Sainsbury, Cal. of State Pap., Vol. V, pp. 334, 336; 360-2.

[98] Sainsbury, Cal. of State Pap., Vol. V, pp. 341-5.

[99] Sainsbury, Cal. of State Pap., Vol. V, pp. 260-2.

house should be built upon each grant, and that a part should be put under cultivation. All these provisions were continually neglected. It was no uncommon thing for councillors to obtain patents for twenty or thirty thousand acres, and sometimes they owned as much as sixty thousand acres. They neglected frequently to erect houses on these estates, or, if they wished to keep within the limits of the law, they built but slight shanties, so small and ill constructed that no human being could inhabit them. On one grant of 27,017 acres the house cost less than ten shillings. In another case a sheriff found in one county 30,000 acres upon which there was nothing which could be distrained for quit rents. At times false names were made use of in securing patents in order to avoid the restrictions of the law.[1]

Amid these acts of deception and fraud one deed is conspicuous. Col. Philip Ludwell had brought into the colony forty immigrants and according to a law which had been in force ever since the days of the London Company, this entitled him to a grant of two thousand acres of land. After securing the patent, he

[1] Sainsbury, Cal. of State Pap., Vol. V, pp. 360-2.

changed the record with his own hand by adding one cipher each to the forty and the two thousand, making them four hundred and twenty thousand respectively. In this way he obtained ten times as much land as he was entitled to and despite the fact that the fraud was notorious at the time, so great was his influence that the matter was ignored and his rights were not disputed.[2]

Alexander Spotswood was guilty of a theft even greater than that of Ludwell. In 1722, just before retiring from the governorship, he made out a patent for 40,000 acres in Spotsylvania County to Messrs. Jones, Clayton and Hickman. As soon as he quitted the executive office these men conveyed the land to him, receiving possibly some small reward for their trouble. In a similar way he obtained possession of another tract of 20,000 acres. Governor Drysdale exposed the matter before the Board of Trade and Plantations, but Spotswood's influence at court was great enough to protect him from punishment.[3]

The commonness of fraud of this kind

---

[2] Sainsbury, Cal. of State Pap., Vol. V, pp. 360-2.

[3] Sainsbury, Cal. of State Pap., Vol. IX, pp. 131-2.

among the Virginia planters of the earlier period does not necessarily stamp them as being conspicuously dishonest. They were subjected to great and unusual temptations. Their vast power and their immunity from punishment, made it easy for them to enrich themselves at the public expense, while their sense of honor, deprived of the support of expediency, was not great enough to restrain them. The very men that were the boldest in stealing public land or in avoiding the tax collector might have recoiled from an act of private dishonesty of injustice. However, it would be absurd in the face of the facts here brought forth, to claim that they were characterized by an ideal sense of honor.

But in this as in other things a change took place in the course of time. As the self-respect of the Virginian became with him a stronger instinct, his sense of honor was more pronounced, and he gradually came to feel that deceit and falsehood were beneath him. Used to the respect and admiration of all with whom he came in contact, he could not descend to actions that would lower him in their estimation. Certain it is that a high sense of honor became eventually one of the most pronounced characteristics of the Virginians.

Nothing can demonstrate this more clearly than the "honor system" that came into vogue in William and Mary College. The Old Oxford system of espionage which was at first used, gradually fell into disuse. The proud young Virginians deemed it an insult for prying professors to watch over their every action, and the faculty eventually learned that they could trust implicitly in the students' honor. In the Rules of the College, published in 1819, there is an open recognition of the honor system. The wording is as follows, "Any student may be required to declare his guilt or innocence as to any particular offence of which he may be suspected....And should the perpetrator of any mischief, in order to avoid detection, deny his guilt, then may the Society require any student to give evidence on his honor touching this foul enormity that the college may not be polluted by the presence of those that have showed themselves equally regardless of the laws of honour, the principles of morality and the precepts of religion."[4]

---

[4] Wm. & Mary Quar., Vol. IX, p. 194.

How potent an influence for good was this sense of honor among the students of the college is shown even more strikingly by an address of Prof. Nathaniel Beverley Tucker to his law class in 1834. "If," he says, "There be anything by which the University of William and Mary has been advantageously distinguished, it is the liberal and magnanimous character of its discipline. It has been the study of its professors to cultivate at the same time the intellect, the principles, and the deportment of the student, labouring with equal diligence to infuse the spirit of the scholar and the spirit of the gentleman. As such we receive and treat him and resolutely refuse to know him in any other character. He is not harrassed with petty regulations; he is not insulted and annoyed by impertinent surveillance. Spies and informers have no countenance among us. We receive no accusation but from the conscience of the accused. His honor is the only witness to which we appeal; and should he be even capable of prevarication or falsehood, we admit no proof of the fact. But I beg you to observe, that in this cautious and forbearing spirit of our legislation, you have not only proof that we have no disposition to harrass you with unreasonable requirements, but a pledge that such regulations as we have found it necessary to make will be enforced....The effect of this system in inspiring a high and scrupulous sense of honor, and a scorn of all disingenuous artifice, has been ascertained by long experience."[5]

A society in which grew up such a system as this could have no place for the petty artifices of the trader nor the frauds of leading men in public affairs. It is clear that at this period the old customs had passed away; that there was a new atmosphere in Virginia; that the planter was no longer a merchant but a Cavalier. The commercial spirit had become distinctly distasteful to him, and he criticised bitterly in his northern neighbors the habits and methods that had characterized his own forefathers in the 17th century. Governor Tyler, in 1810, said in addressing the Legislature, "Commerce is certainly beneficial to society in a secondary degree, but it produces also what is called citizens of the world—the worst citizens in the world." And in public

[5] Wm. & Mary Quar., Vol. VI, p. 184.

affairs honesty and patriotism took the place of deceit and fraud. Even in the Revolutionary period the change is apparent, and long before the advent of the Civil War the very memory of the old order of affairs had passed away. The Virginia gentleman in the 19th century was the soul of honor. Thomas Nelson Page says, "He was proud, but never haughty except to dishonor. To that he was inexorable....He was chivalrous, he was generous, he was usually incapable of fear or meanness. To be a Virginia gentleman was the first duty."[6] The spirit of these men is typified in the character of Robert E. Lee. To this hero of the Southern people dishonesty was utterly impossible. After the close of the Civil War, when he was greatly in need of money he was offered the presidency of an insurance company. Word was sent him that his lack of experience in the insurance business would not matter, as the use of his name was all the company desired of him. Lee politely, but firmly, rejected this proposal, for he saw that to accept would have been to

[6] Page, The Old South, p. 158.

capitalize the homage and reverence paid him by the people of the South.

Along with the instinct of pride and the spirit of chivalry in the Virginia planters developed the power of commanding men. Among the immigrants of the 17th century leardership was distinctly lacking, and during almost all the colonial period there was a decided want of great men. Captain John Smith, Governor William Berkeley, Nathaniel Bacon and Alexander Spotswood are the only names that stand out amid the general mediocrity of the age. If we look for other men of prominence we must turn to Robert Beverley, Philip Ludwell, William Byrd II, James Blair. These men played an important part in the development of the colony, but they are practically unknown except to students of Virginia history.

What a contrast is presented by a glance at the great names of the latter part of the 18th century. The commonplace Virginia planters had then been transformed into leaders of men. When the Revolution came it was to them that the colonies looked chiefly for guidance and command, and Washington, Jefferson,

Henry, Mason, the Lees and many other Virginians took the most active part in the great struggle that ended in the overthrow of the sway of England and the establishment of the independence of the colonies. Washington was the great warrior, Jefferson the apostle of freedom, Henry the orator of the Revolution. And when the Union had been formed it was still Virginia that furnished leaders to the country. Of the first five presidents four were Virginia planters.

This transformation was due partly to the life upon the plantation. The business of the Virginia gentleman from early youth was to command. An entire community looked to him for direction and maintenance, and scores or even hundreds of persons obeyed him implicitly. He was manager of all the vast industries of his estate, directing his servants and slaves in all the details of farming, attending to the planting, the curing, the casing of tobacco, the cultivation of wheat and corn, the growing of fruits, the raising of horses, cattle, sheep and hogs. He became a master architect, having under him a force of carpenters, masons and mechanics. Some of the wealthiest Virginians directed in every detail the construction of those stately old mansions that were the pride of the colony in the 18th century. Thus Thomas Jefferson was both the architect and builder of his home at Monticello, and gave to it many months of his time in the prime of his life.

The public life of the aristocrat also tended to develop in him the power of command. If he were appointed to the Council he found himself in possession of enormous power, and in a position to resist the ablest of governors, or even the commands of the king. In all that he did, in private and public affairs, he was leader. His constant task was to command and in nothing did he occupy a subservient position. No wonder that, in the course of time, he developed into a leader of men, equal to the stupendous undertaking of shaking off the yoke of England and laying the foundations of a new nation.

The magnificence with which the members of the aristocracy in the 18th century surrounded themselves, and the culture and polish of their social life are not so distinctly the result of local conditions. The customs, the tastes, the prejudices that were brought over from England were never entirely effaced. The earliest immigrants established on the banks of the James a civilization as similar in every respect to that of the mother country as their situation would permit. Had it not been for economic and climatic conditions there would have grown up amid the wilderness of America an exact reproduction of England in miniature. As it was, the colonists infused into their new life the habits, moral standards, ideas and customs of the old so firmly that their influence is apparent even at the present day.

And this imitation of English life was continued even after the period of immigration was passed. The constant and intimate intercourse with the mother country made necessary by commercial affairs had a most important influence upon social life. Hugh Jones, writing of society in Governor Spotswood's time, says: "The habits, life, customs, computations &c of the Virginians are much the same as about London, which they esteem their home; the planters generally talk good English without idiom and tone and can discourse handsomely upon most common subjects; and conversing with persons belonging to trade and navigation in London, for the most part they are much civilized." Again he says, "They live in the same neat manner, dress after the same modes, and behave themselves exactly as the gentry in London."

Nor had this spirit of imitation become less apparent at the period of the Revolution, or even after. Their furniture, their silver ware, their musical instruments, their coaches and even their clothes were still imported from England and were made after the latest English fashions. John Bernard noted with astonishment that their favorite topics of conversation were European. "I found," he says, "men leading secluded lives in the woods of Virginia perfectly au fait as to the literary, dramatic, and personal gossip of London and Paris." The lack of good educational facilities in Virginia led many of the wealthy planters to send their sons to England to enter the excellent schools or universities there. Even after the establishment of William and Mary College, the advantages to be derived from several years' residence in the Old World, induced parents to send their sons to Oxford or Cambridge. The culture, the ideas and habits there acquired by the young Virginia aristocrats exerted a powerful influence upon society in the Old Dominion.

But the peculiar conditions of the new country could not fail to modify profoundly the life of the colonists. Despite the intimacy with England and despite the tenacity with which the people clung to British customs, Virginia society in both the 17th and 18th centuries was different in many respects from that of the mother country. The absence of towns eliminated from colonial life much that was essentially English. There could be no counterpart of the coffee house, the political club, the literary circle. And even rural conditions were different. The lack of communication and the size of the plantations could not fail to produce a social life unlike that of the thickly settled country districts of England.

We note in Virginia a marked contrast between the 17th and 18th centuries in the mode of living of the planters. In the first hundred years of the colony's existence there was a conspicuous lack of that elegance in the houses, the furniture, the vehicles, the table ware, etc., that was so much in evidence at the time of the Revolution. This was due in part to the newness of the country. It was impossible amid the forests of America, where artisans were few and unskillful, to imitate all the luxuries of England, and the planters were as yet too busily employed in reducing the resources of the country to their needs to think of more than the ordinary comforts of life. Moreover, the wealth of the colony was by no means great. Before the end of the century some of the planters had accumulated fortunes of some size, but there were few that could afford to indulge in the costly and elegant surroundings that became so common later. And the owners of newly acquired fortunes were often fully satisfied with the plain and unpretentious life to which they were accustomed and not inclined to spend their money for large houses, fine furniture, or costly silver ware. As time went on, however, the political and social supremacy of the aristocracy, the broader education of its members, and the great increase in wealth conspired to produce in the colony a love of elegance that was second only to that of the French nobility.

During the 17th century the houses even of the wealthiest planters were made of wood. Despite the fact that bricks were manufactured in the colony and could be had at a reasonable price, the abundance of timber on all sides made the use of that material almost universal during the greater part of the colonial period. Shingles were used for the roof, although slate was not unknown. The partitions in the dwellings were first covered with a thick layer of tenacious mud and then whitewashed. Sometimes there were no partitions at all as was the case in a house mentioned by William Fitzhugh. This, however, was not usual and we find that most of the houses of the wealthiest planters contained from four to seven compartments of various sizes. The residence of Governor William Berkeley at Green Spring contained six rooms. Edmund Cobbs, a well-to-do farmer, lived in a house consisting of a hall and kitchen on the lower floor and one room above stairs. In the residence of Nathaniel Bacon, Sr., were five chambers, a hall, a kitchen, a dairy and a storeroom. The apartments in the house of Mathew Hubbard, a wealthy planter of York County, consisted of a parlor and hall, a chamber, a kitchen and buttery. Robert Beverley, who played so important a role in Bacon's Rebellion and in the political struggles following that uprising, resided in a house which contained three chambers, a dairy, a kitchen and the overseer's room. The house of William Fauntleroy, a wealthy land owner, contained three chambers, a hall, a closet and a kitchen.[7]

The surroundings of the planters' residences were entirely lacking in ornament. In the immediate vicinity of the house were usually grouped stable, hen house, kitchen, milk house, servants' house and dove-cote. Near at hand also was to be found the garden, which was devoted to both vegetables and flowers. Around it were always placed strong palings to keep out the hogs and cattle which were very numerous and were allowed to wander unrestrained.[8]

The furniture of the planters was of fairly

---

[7] Bruce, Econ. Hist. of Va. Vol. II, p. 145-158.
[8] Ibid, Vol. II, pp. 160-161.

good quality, as most of it was imported from England. The beds were similar to those used in the mother country, ranging from the little trundle-bed to the great-bed of the main chamber, which was usually surrounded by curtains upheld by a rod. Rugs were quite common, but were of very poor quality, being made frequently of worsted yarn or cotton. Various materials were used in making couches. Some were of hides, some of tanned leather, some of embroidered Russian leather. As a substitute for wardrobes or closets in every bed room were chests, in which were kept the most costly articles of clothing, the linen, trinkets of value and occasionally plate. Chairs of various kinds were used, the most costly being the Russian leather chair and the Turkey-worked chair. In the houses of the wealthiest planters the walls were sometimes hung with tapestry.[9]

When the families of the planters were large, which was frequently the case, their little houses were exceedingly crowded. Beds are found in every room except in the kitchen. In the parlor or reception room for guests are not only beds, but chests of clothing and linen,

---

[9] Ibid, Vol. II, pp. 163-166.

while in the hall which was used also as a dining room, are flock-beds, chests, guns, pistols, swords, drums, saddles, and bridles. The chamber contains every variety of article in use in the household. One of the rooms in the house of Thomas Osborn contained a bedstead with feather-bed, bolster, rug, blanket and sheets, two long table cloths, twenty-eight napkins, four towels, one chest, two warming pans, four brass candle-sticks, four guns, a carbine and belt, a silver beaker, three tumblers, twelve spoons, one sock and one dram cup.[10]

The utensils in use in the dining room and kitchen were usually made of pewter, this material being both cheap and durable. Even upon the tables of the wealthiest planters were found sugar-pots, castors, tumblers, spoons, dishes, ladles, knives and various other articles all of pewter. Silver, however, was not unknown. In the closing years of the 17th century the possession of silver plate and silver table-ware was becoming more and more frequent.[11]

As the wealth of the leading planters in-

---

[10] Ibid, Vol. II, pp. 177-179.

[11] Bruce, Econ. Hist. of Va., Vol. II, pp. 165-175.

creased they gradually surrounded themselves with elegant homes and sumptuous furnishings. At the period of the Revolution there were dozens of magnificent homes scattered throughout Virginia. Shirley, Brandon, Rosewell, Monticello, Blenheim, Mount Airy, and many more testified to the refined taste and love of elegance of the aristocracy of this time. The most common material used in the construction of these mansions was brick, manufactured by the planter himself, upon his own estate. The usual number of rooms was eight, although not infrequently there were as many as fourteen or sixteen. These apartments were very large, often being twenty-five feet square, and the pitch was invariably great. In close proximity to the mansion were always other houses, some of which contained bed rooms that could be used either by guests or by members of the family. Thus the main house was really but the center of a little group of buildings, that constituted altogether a residence of great size. How spacious they were is shown by the number of guests that were at times housed in them, for at balls and on other festive occasions it was not at all infrequent for forty or fifty persons to remain for several days in the home of their host. At a ball given by Richard Lee, of Lee Hall, Westmoreland County, there were seventy guests, most of whom remained three days.

Nomini Hall, the house of Robert Carter, is an excellent example of the residences of the wealthier planters during the middle of the 18th century. The main building was of brick, which was covered over with a mortar of such perfect whiteness that at a little distance it appeared to be marble. Although it was far larger than the houses of the preceding century it was not of great size, being but seventy-six feet long and forty-four wide. The pitch of the rooms, however, was very great, that of the lower floor being seventeen feet and that of the second floor being twelve. No less than twenty-six large windows gave abundance of light to the various apartments, while at different points in the roof projected five stacks of chimneys, two of these serving only as ornaments. On one side a beautiful jett extended for eighteen feet, supported by three tall pillars. On the first floor were the dining room, the children's dining room, Col. Carter's study, and a ball room thirty feet long, while the second story contained four bed rooms, two of which were reserved for guests. At equal distances from each corner of the mansion were four other buildings of considerable size. One of these, a two story brick house of five rooms, was called the school and here slept Col. Carter's three sons, their tutor and the overseer. Corresponding to the school house at the other corners of the mansion were the stable, the coach house and the work house. The beauty of the lawn and the graceful sweep of a long terrace which ran in front of the mansion testified to the abundant care and taste expended in planning and laying out the grounds. East of the house was an avenue of splendid poplars leading to the county road, and the view of the buildings through these trees was most attractive and beautiful. One side of the lawn was laid out in rectangular walks paved with brick and covered over with burnt oyster shells, and being perfectly level was used as a bowling green. In addition to the buildings already mentioned there were close to the mansion a wash house and a kitchen, both the same size as the school house, a bake house, a dairy, a store house and several other small buildings.[12]

Some of the mansions of the 18th century were much larger and more beautiful than Nomini Hall. Rosewell, erected by the Page family, was of immense size, containing a large number of halls and chambers, but it was singularly devoid of architectural beauty and presented somewhat the appearance of a hotel. The Westover mansion was very large and could accommodate scores of guests. It was surrounded with so many buildings and out-houses that to visitors it seemed a veritable little city.[13] Chastellux, who was a guest of the Byrds in 1782, says that Westover surpassed all other homes in Virginia in the magnificence of the buildings and the beauty of the situation.[14]

It was the interior of these mansions, however, that gave them their chief claim to elegance. The stairways, the floors, the mantles were of the finest wood and were finished in the most costly manner. In the beautiful halls

---

[12] Fithian, Journal and Letters, pp. 127-131.

[13] Voyages dans l'Amerique Septentrionale, Tome II, p. 128.

[14] Va. Maga. of Hist. and Biog., Vol. VI, p. 347.

of Rosewell richly carved mahogony wainscotings and capitals abounded.[15] At Monticello the two main halls were given an air of richness and beauty by the curiously designed mantles, the hard wood floors and the stately windows and doors. John Bernard, who thought the Virginia mansions lacking in architectural beauty, stated that internally they were palaces.

The furniture was in keeping with its surroundings. It was frequently of hard wood, beautifully decorated with hand work. All the furniture, except that of the plainest design, was imported from England, and could be bought by the planters at a price very little above that paid in London. Costly chairs, tables, book-cases, bedsteads, etc., were found in the homes of all well-to-do men.

The Virginians seem to have had at this period a passion for silver ware, and in their homes were found a great variety of articles made of this metal. There were silver candlesticks, silver snuffers, silver decanters, silver snuff-boxes, silver basins. The dining table on festive occasions groaned with the weight of silver utensils, for goblets, pitchers, plates, spoons

---

[15] Meade, Vol. II, p. 331.

of silver were then brought forth to do honor to the guests. The punch might be served in silver bowls and dished out with silver ladles into silver cups; for the fruit might be silver plates, for the tea silver pots. The silver plate at Westover was mortgaged by William Byrd III to the value of £662. Among other articles we find that ten candle-sticks brought £70, one snuffer-stand £5, two large punch bowls £30, a punch strainer £1.10, and a punch ladle £1.[16] Robert Carter, of Nomini Hall, was very fond of fine silver. In 1774 he invested about £30 in a pair of fashionable goblets, a pair of sauce-cups and a pair of decanter holders.[17]

In many homes were collections of pictures of great merit and value. In the spacious halls of the mansions were hung the portraits of ancestors that were regarded with reverential pride. The Westover collection was perhaps the most valuable in the colony, containing several dozen pictures, among them one by Titian, one by Rubens, and portraits of several lords of England.[18] Mount Airy, the beautiful home of

---

[16] Va. Maga. of Hist. and Biog., Vol. IX, p. 82.
[17] Fithian, Journal and Letters, p. 251.
[18] Va. Maga. of Hist. and Biog., Vol. VI, p. 350.

the Tayloe family, contained many paintings, which were well executed and set in elegant frames.[19] Although most of the pictures in the homes of the aristocracy were imported from England, some were painted in Virginia, for at times artists of talent came to the colony. In 1735 a man named Bridges painted William Byrd's children. It is thought also that it was he that painted the portrait of Governor Spotswood and possibly several pictures of the Page family.[20]

The use of coaches during the 17th century was not common. The universal highways of that period were the rivers. Every planter owned boats and used them in visiting, in attending church and in travelling through the colony. As the plantations for many years did not extend far back from the rivers' banks, there was no need of roads or vehicles. And even when many settlements had been made beyond tidewater, the condition of the roads was so bad that the use of vehicles was often impracticable and riding was the common method of travelling. As the colony became more

---

[19] Fithian, Journal and Letters, p. 148.

[20] Wm. & Mary Quar., Vol. I, p. 123; Vol. II, p. 121.

thickly populated and the roads were gradually improved, various kinds of carriages were introduced. During Governor Spotswood's administration most families of any note owned a coach, chariot, berlin or chaise.[21] By the middle of the 18th century their use was general throughout the entire colony.

The coaches in use at the time of the Revolution were elegant and very costly. A bill for a post chaise which has come down from the year 1784 gives the following description of that vehicle. The chaise was to be very handsome, the body to be carved and run with raised beads and scrolls, the roof and upper panels to have plated mouldings and head plates; on the door panels were to be painted Prince of Wales ruffs with arms and crests in large handsome mantlings; the body was to be highly varnished, the inside lined with superfine light colored cloth and trimmed with raised Casoy laces; the sides stuffed and quilted; the best polished plate glasses; mahogany shutters were to be used, with plated frames and plated handles to the door; there were to be double folding inside

[21] Jones' Virginia.

steps, a wainscoted trunk under the seat and a carpet.[22]

Every gentleman of means at this time owned a chariot drawn by four horses. Frequently six horses were used.[23] These animals were of the finest breed and were selected for their size and beauty from the crowded stables of the planters. The vehicles were attended by liveried negroes, powdered and dignified. Mrs. Carter, of Nomini Hall, had three waiting men for her coach; a driver, a coachman and a postillion.[24]

In the matter of dress there seems, from the earliest days, to have been a love of show and elegance. Inventories of the first half of the 17th century mention frequently wearing apparel that is surprisingly rich. Thus Thomas Warnet, who died in 1629, possessed a pair of silk stockings, a pair of red slippers, a sea-green scarf edged with gold lace, a felt hat, a black beaver, a doublet of black camlet and a gold belt and sword.[25] At times these early immigrants wore highly colored waistcoats, plush or broad

---

[22] Va. Maga. of Hist. and Biog. Vol. VIII, p. 334.

[23] Fithian, Journals and Letters, p. 58.

[24] Ibid, p. 75.

[25] Bruce, Soc. Life in Va., p. 164.

cloth trousers, camlet coats with lace ruffles. the rough surroundings of the new colony. This gaudy apparel must have seemed odd amid Not all the wealthy planters, however, indulged in the weakness of costly dress. Many of the richest men of the 17th century, obedient to the spirit of frugality which so often marks the merchant, dressed plainly.

At the time of the Revolution the use of costly apparel had become general. The usual costume of both men and women at festivals or balls was handsome and stately. Joseph Lane, while visiting at Nomini Hall, was dressed in black superfine broadcloth, laced ruffles, black silk stockings and gold laced hat.[26] Probably few even of the wealthiest aristocrats could approach in matters of dress Lord Fairfax. The inventory of this gentleman's estate shows an astonishing variety of gaudy clothes. He possessed a suit of brown colored silk, a suit of velvet, a suit of blue cloth, a suit of drab cloth, a green damask laced waistcoat, a scarlet laced waistcoat, a pink damask laced waiscoat, a gold tissue waistcoat, a brown laced coat, a green silk

[26] Fithian, Journal and Letters, p. 113.

waistcoat, a pair of black velvet breeches, and a pair of scarlet plush breeches.[27]

As might be expected, reading and study were not common among the early settlers. The rough life in the woods of the New World, the struggle to drive back the Indians and to build up civilization left no time for mental culture. During the first half of the 17th century books are mentioned very rarely in the records. As time passed, however, the planters began to build up libraries of considerable size in their homes. The lack of educational facilities and the isolation of the plantations made it necessary for each gentleman to trust to his own collection of books if he desired to broaden and cultivate his mind. Moreover, the use of overseers which became general in the 18th century left to him leisure for reading. Many of the libraries in the mansions of the aristocracy were surprisingly large and well selected. Some of Col. Richard Lee's books were, Wing's Art of Surveying, Scholastical History, Greek Grammar, Caesaris Comentarii, Praxis Medicinae, Hesoid, Tulley's Orations, Virgil, Ovid,

---

[27] Va. Maga. of Hist. and Biog. Vol. VIII.

Livius, Diogenes, Sallust, History of the World, Warrs of Italy, etc.[28] In the library of Ralph Wormeley were found Glaber's Kimistry, The State of the United Provinces, The Colledges of Oxford, Kings of England, The Laws of Virginia, The Present State of England, Ecclesastical History in Latin, Lattin Bible, Skill in Music, A Description of the Persian Monarchy, Plutoch's Lives, etc.[29] Many of these volumes were great folios bound in the most expensive way and extensively illustrated.

The planters even in the 17th century were not insensible to the refining and elevating influence of music. Inventories and wills show that many homes contained virginals, hand lyres, violins, flutes and haut boys. The cornet also was in use.[30] In the 18th century the study of music became general throughout the colony and even the classical compositions were performed often with some degree of skill. Despite the difficulty of securing teachers, music became a customary part of the education of ladies. Many of the planters themselves

---

[28] Wm. & Mary Quar. Vol. II, p. 247, 248.

[29] Wm. & Mary Quar. Vol. II, p. 172.

[30] Bruce, Econ. Hist. of Va. Vol. II, p. 175; Soc. Life of Va. p. 164.

in their leisure moments indulged in this delightful amusement. Robert Carter had in his home in Westmoreland County a harpsichord, a piano-forte, an harmonica, a guitar and a flute, and at Williamsburg an organ. He had a good ear, a very delicate touch, was indefatigable in practicing and performed well on several instruments. Especially was he fond of the harmonica, and spent much time in practicing upon it. His skill is thus described by his tutor, "The music was charming! The notes are clear and soft, they swell and are inexpressibly grand; and either it is because the sounds are new, and therefore please me, or it is the most captivating instrument I have ever heard. The sounds very much resemble the human voice, and in my opinion they far exceed even the swelling organ."[31] Thomas Jefferson, amid the cares of statesmanship and the study of philosophy, found time for music. He performed upon the violin and during the Revolutionary War, when the prisoners captured at Saratoga were encamped near his home, he took great delight in playing with a British officer, who could accompany him upon the guitar.

---

[31] Bruce, Soc. Life of Va., pp. 181-185.

Dancing was indulged in by the Virginians from the earliest period. Even when the immigrants lived in daily dread of the tomahawk of the Indians, and when their homes were but log huts in the midst of the forest, this form of amusement was not unknown. The music for dances was at times furnished by negroes, who had acquired skill upon the fiddle. There is evidence of the presence of dancing masters in the colony even during the 17th century. One of these was Charles Cheate. This man wandered through the colony for some time giving lessons, but he was forced to flee from the country after the suppression of Bacon's Rebellion, because of his attachment to the cause of the insurgents. However, the sparseness of the population, the isolation of the plantations, the lack of roads made festive gatherings infrequent during the first century of the colony's existence. The lack of towns made it necessary for dances to be held in private houses, and distances were so great that it was frequently impossible for many guests to assemble. Moreover, at this period the residences of the planter were too small either to allow room for dancing or to accommodate the visitors, who must necessarily spend the night after the close of the festivities. Not until the administration of Governor Spotswood were these difficulties somewhat overcome. Then it was, that the increasing wealth of the colony gave rise to a more brilliant social life among the aristocracy. Hugh Jones declared in 1722 that at the Governor's house at balls and assemblies were as good diversion, as splendid entertainment, as fine an appearance as he had ever seen in England.[32]

At the time of the Revolution dancing was so general that it had become a necessary part of the education of both gentlemen and ladies, and dancing schools were quite common. The masters travelled from house to house and the pupils followed them, remaining as guests wherever the school was being held. A Mr. Christian conducted such a school in Westmoreland County in 1773. Fithian thus describes one of his classes held at Nomini Hall, "There were present of young misses about eleven, and seven young fellows, including myself. After breakfast, we all retired into the dancing room, and after the scholars had their

[32] Jones' Va.

lessons singly round Mr. Christian, very politely, requested me to step a minuet....There were several minuets danced with great ease and propriety; after which the whole company joined in country dances, and it was indeed beautiful to admiration to see such a number of young persons, set off by dress to the best advantage, moving easily, to the sound of well performed music, and with perfect regularity ....The dance continued til two, we dined at half after three....soon after dinner we repaired to the dancing-room again; I observed in the course of the lessons, that Mr. Christian is punctual, and rigid in his discipline, so strict indeed that he struck two of the young misses for a fault in the course of their performance, even in the presence of the mother of one of them!"[33]

The balls of this period were surprisingly brilliant. The spacious halls of the mansions afforded ample room for a large company and frequently scores of guests would be present to take part in the stately minuet or the gay Virginia reel. The visitors were expected to remain often several days in the home of their

---

[33] Fithian, Journal and Letters, p. 63.

host resuming the dance at frequent intervals, and indulging in other forms of amusement. Fithian thus describes a ball given by Richard Lee, of Lee Hall, Westmoreland County. "We set away from Mr. Carter's at two; Mrs. Carter and the young ladies in the chariot,....myself on horseback. As soon as I had handed the ladies out, I was saluted by Parson Smith; I was introduced into a small room where a number of gentlemen were playing cards....to lay off my boots, riding-coat &c. Next I was directed into the dining-room to see young Mr. Lee; he introduced me to his father. With them I conversed til dinner, which came in at half after four....The dinner was as elegant as could be well expected when so great an assembly were to be kept for so long a time. For drink there was several sorts of wine, good lemon punch, toddy, cyder, porter &c. About seven the ladies and gentlemen begun to dance in the ball room, first minuets one round; second giggs; third reels; and last of all country dances; tho' they struck several marches occasionally. The music was a French horn and two violins. The ladies were dressed gay, and splendid, and when dancing, their skirts and brocades rustled and trailed behind them! But all did not join in the dance for there were parties in rooms made up, some at cards; some drinking for pleasure;....some singing 'Liberty Songs' as they called them, in which six, eight, ten or more would put their heads near together and roar,....At eleven Mrs. Carter call'd upon me to go." There were seventy guests at this ball, most of whom remained three days at Lee Hall.[34]

Side by side with growth in luxury, in refinement and culture may be noted a marked change in the daily occupation of the wealthy planters. In the 17th century they were chiefly interested in building up large fortunes and had little time for other things. They were masters of the art of trading, and their close bargaining and careful attention to detail made them very successful. Practically all of the fortunes that were so numerous among the aristocracy in the 18th century were accumulated in the colony, and it was the business instinct and industry of the merchant settlers that made their existence possible. The leading men in the colony in the last half of the 17th century toiled cease-

---

[34] Ibid., pp. 94-97.

lessly upon their plantations, attending to the minutest details of the countless enterprises that it was necessary for them to conduct. They were the nation builders of Virginia. It is true that they spent much of their energy upon political matters, but this was to them but another way of increasing their fortunes. Altogether neither their inclinations, nor the conditions in which they lived, inclined them to devote much of their time to acquiring culture and refinement.

But the descendants of these early planters enjoyed to the full the fruits of the energy and ability of their fathers. As time passed, there grew up in the colony the overseer system, which relieved the great property owners of the necessity of regulating in person all the affairs of their estates. Even before the end of the 17th century many men possessed plantations in various parts of the colony and it became then absolutely necessary to appoint capable men to conduct those that were remote from the home of the planter. At times the owner would retain immediate control of the home plantation, which often served as a center of industry for the remainder of the estate, but even this in the 18th century was not infrequently intrusted to the care of an overseer. These men were selected from the class of small farmers and many proved to be so capable and trustworthy that they took from their employers' shoulders all care and responsibility. They were well paid when their management justified it and cases were frequent where overseers remained for many years in the service of one man.

This system gave to the planters far greater leisure than they had possessed in the earlier part of the colony's existence, and they made use of this leisure to cultivate their minds and to diversify their interests. It is only in this way that we can fully explain why the aristocrat surrounded himself with a large library, indulged in the delicate art of music, beautified his home with handsome paintings, and revelled in the dance, in races or the fox hunt. This too explains why there grew up amid the plantations that series of political philosophers that proved so invaluable to the colonies in the hour of need. Jefferson, Henry, Madison, Marshall, Randolph, would never have been able to give birth to the thoughts that made them famous had they been tied down to the old practical life of the planters of early days. The old instinct had been distinctly lacking in the philosophical spirit. As Hugh Jones says, the planters were not given to prying into the depths of things, but were "ripe" for the management of their affairs. With the greater leisure of the 18th century this spirit changed entirely, and we find an inclination among the aristocrats to go to the bottom of every matter that came to their attention. Thus John Randolph was not only a practical statesman and a great orator, he was a profound thinker; although Thomas Jefferson was twice president of the United States, and was the author of the Declaration of Independence, it is as the originator of a political creed that he has the best claim to fame; John Marshall, amid the exacting duties of the Supreme Court, found time for the study of philosophy. In men less noted was the same spirit. Thus Robert Carter of Nomini Hall in his love for music, did not content himself with acquiring the ability to perform on various instruments, but pried into the depths of the art, studying carefully the theory of thorough bass.[35] He himself invented an appliance for tuning harpsichords.[36] This gentleman was also fond of the study of law, while he and his wife often read philosophy together.[37] Fithian speaks of him as a good scholar, even in classical learning, and a remarkable one in English grammar. Frequently the gentlemen of this period spent much time in the study of such matters as astronomy, the ancient languages, rhetoric, history, etc.

It is a matter of regret that this movement did not give birth to a great literature. Doubtless it would have done so had the Virginia planters been students only. Practical politics still held their attention, however, and it is in the direction of governmental affairs that the new tendency found its vent. The writings of this period that are of most value are the letters and papers of the great political leaders—Washington, Jefferson, Madison and others. Of poets there were none, but in their place is a series of brilliant orators. Pendleton, Henry, and Randolph gave vent to the heroic senti-

---

[35] Fithian, Journal and Letters, pp. 59 and 83.
[36] Ibid., p. 77.
[37] Ibid., pp. 83 and 90.

ments of the age in sentences that burned with eloquence.

The change that was taking place in the daily thoughts and occupations of the planters is strikingly illustrated by the lives of the three men that bore the name of William Byrd. Father, son and grandson are typical of the periods in which each lived. The first of the name was representative of the last quarter of the 17th century. He possessed to an extraordinary degree the instinct of the merchant, taking quick advantage of any opportunity for trade that the colony afforded and building up by his foresight, energy and ability a fortune of great size. Not only did he carry on the cultivation of tobacco with success, but he conducted with his neighbors a trade in a great variety of articles. In his stores were to be found duffels and cotton goods, window glass, lead and solder, pills, etc. At one time he ordered from Barbadoes 1,200 gallons of rum, 3,000 pounds of "muscovodo sugar," 200 pound of white sugar, three tons of molasses, one cask of lime-juice and two-hundredweight of ginger. A handsome profit often came to him through the importing and sale of white servants. In a letter to England he writes, "If you could send me six, eight or ten servants by the first ship, and the procurement might not be too dear, they would much assist in purchasing some of the best crops they seldom being to be bought without servants." Byrd was also interested in the Indian trade. His plantation at Henrico was well located for this business and he often sent out traders for miles into the wilderness to secure from the savages the furs and hides that were so valued in England. He was provident even to stinginess and we find him sending his wig to England to be made over and his old sword to be exchanged for a new one. Although Byrd took a prominent part in the political life of the day, it is evident that in this as in other things he was predominated by the spirit of gain, for he took pains to secure two of the most lucrative public offices in the colony. For years he was auditor and receiver-general, receiving for both a large yearly income.[38] At his death his estate was very large, the land he owned being not less than 26,000 acres.

William Byrd II was also typical of the period in which he lived. He was still the busi-

---

[38] Bassett, Writings of Wm. Byrd., Intro. XXV.

ness man, but he lacked the talent for close bargaining and the attention to details that characterized his father. His business ventures were bold and well conceived, but they did not meet with a great measure of success. His iron mines were never very productive, while his Indian trade met with frequent and disastrous interruptions from hostile tribes upon the frontier. Nor did he confine his attention to business matters. He was intensely interested in every thing pertaining to the welfare of the colony. He was one of the commissioners that ran the dividing line between Virginia and North Carolina. His writings show a brightness and wit that mark him as the best author the colony possessed during the first half of the 18th century. In his every act we see that he is more the Cavalier than his father, less the merchant.

The third William Byrd was entirely lacking in business ability. His mismanagement and his vices kept him constantly in debt, and for a while it seemed probable that he would have to sell his beautiful home at Westover. At one time he owned as much as £5,561 to two English merchants, whose importunities so embarrassed him that he was forced to mortgage one hundred and fifty-nine slaves on two of his plantations, and even his silver plate. These financial troubles were brought on him partly because of his fondness for gambling. Anbury says of him, "Being infatuated with play, his affairs, at his death, were in a deranged state. The widow whom he left with eight children, has, by prudent management, preserved out of the wreck of his princely fortune, a beautiful home, at a place called Westover, upon James River, some personal property, a few plantations, and a number of slaves."[39] Another of Byrd's favorite amusements was racing and he possessed many beautiful and swift horses. He died by his own hand in 1777. Despite his dissipation and his weakness, he was a man of many admirable qualities. In the affairs of the colony he was prominent for years, distinguishing himself both in political life and as a soldier. He was a member of the Council and was one of the judges in the parsons' case of 1763, in which he showed his love of justice by voting on the side of the clergy. In the French and Indian War, he commanded one of the two

---

[39] Anbury, Vol. II, p. 329.

regiments raised to protect the frontier from the savage inroads of the enemy, acquitting himself with much credit. He was a kind father, a cultured gentleman, and a gallant soldier; an excellent example of the Cavalier of the period preceding the Revolution, whose noble tendencies were obscured by the excess to which he carried the vices that were then so common in Virginia.

The story of the Byrd family is but the story of the Virginia aristocracy. A similar development is noted in nearly all of the distinguished families of the colony, for none could escape the influences that were moulding them. The Carters, the Carys, the Bollings, the Lees, the Bookers, the Blands at the time of the Revolution were as unlike their ancestors of Nicholson's day as was William Byrd III unlike his grandfather, the painstaking son of the English goldsmith.

Such were the effects upon the Virginia aristocracy of the economic, social and political conditions of the colony. There can be no doubt that the Virginia gentleman of the time of Washington and Jefferson, in his self-respect, his homage to womanhood, his sense of honor, his power of command, in all that made him unique was but the product of the conditions which surrounded him. And although the elegance and refinement of his social life, the culture and depths of his mind can, to some extent, be ascribed to the survival of English customs and the constant intercourse with the mother country, these too were profoundly influenced by conditions in the colony.

PART TWO

The Middle Class

LIKE the aristocracy the middle class in Virginia developed within the colony. It originated from free families of immigrants of humble means and origin, and from servants that had served their term of indenture, and its character was the result of climatic, economic, social and political conditions. There is no more interesting chapter in the history of Virginia than the development of an intelligent and vigorous middle class out of the host of lowly immigrants that came to the colony in the 17th century. Splendid natural opportunities, the law of the survival of the fittest, and a government in which a representative legislature took an important part coöperated to elevate them. For many years after the founding of Jamestown the middle class was so small and was so lacking in intelligence that it could exercise but little influence in govenrnental affairs, and the governors and the large planters ruled the colony almost at will. During the last years of the 17th century it had grown in numbers, had acquired something of culture and had been drilled so effectively in political affairs that it could no longer be disregarded by governors and aristocracy.

In the development of the middle class four distinct periods may be noted. First, the period of formation, from 1607 to 1660, when, from the free immigrants of humble means and from those who had entered the colony as servants and whose term of indenture had expired, was gradually emerging a class of small, independent farmers. Second, a period of oppression, extending from 1660 to 1676. In these years, when William Berkeley was for the second time the chief executive of the colony, the poor people were so oppressed by the excessive burdens imposed upon them by the arbitrary old governor and his favorites that their progress was seriously retarded. Heavy taxes levied by the Assembly for encouraging manufactures, for building houses at Jamestown, for repairing forts, bore with great weight upon the small farmers and in many cases brought them to the verge of ruin. During this period the evil effects of the Navigation Acts were felt most acutely in the colony, robbing the planters of the profit of their tobacco and causing suffering and discontent. This period ends with Bacon's Rebellion, when the down-trodden commons of the colony rushed to arms, striking out blindly against their oppressors, and bringing fire and sword to all parts of Virginia. The third period, from 1676 to 1700, was one of growth. The poor people still felt the effects of the unjust Navigation Acts, but they were no longer oppressed at will by their governors and the aristocracy. Led by discontented members of the wealthy planter class, they made a gallant and effective fight in the House of Burgesses for their rights, and showed that thenceforth they had to be reckoned a powerful force in the government of the colony. The representatives of the people kept a vigilant watch upon the expenditures, and blocked all efforts to impose unjust and oppressive taxes. During this last quarter of the 17th century the middle class grew rapidly in numbers and in prosperity. The fourth period, from 1700 to the Revolution, is marked by a division in the middle class.

At the beginning of the 18th century, there was no lower class corresponding with the vast peasantry of Europe. All whites, except the indentured servants and a mere handful of freemen whose indolence doomed them to poverty, lived in comparative comfort and ease. After the introduction of slaves, however, this state of affairs no longer existed and there grew up a class of poor whites, that eked out a wretched and degraded life. On the other hand planters of the middle class that had acquired some degree of prosperity benefited greatly by the introduction of slaves, for it lowered the cost of labor to such an extent that they were able to cultivate their fields more cheaply than before. At the time of the Revolutionary War the distinction had become marked, and the prosperous middle class farmers were in no way allied to the degraded poor whites.

During the first seventeen years of the colony's existence the character of immigration was different from that of succeeding periods. Virginia was at this time ruled by a private trading company. This corporation, which was composed largely of men of rank and ability, kept a strict watch upon the settlers, and excluded many whom they thought would make undesirable colonists.[40] As a consequence, the class of people that came over before 1624 were more enlightened than the mass of the settlers during the remainder of the century. The London Company looked upon the whole matter as a business affair, and they knew that they could never expect returns from their enterprise if they filled their plantations with vagabonds and criminals. Those that were intrusted with the selection of settlers were given explicit instructions to accept none but honest and industrious persons. When it was found that these precautions were not entirely effective, still stricter measures were adopted. It was ordered by the Company in 1622 that before sailing for Virginia each emigrant should give evidence of good character and should register his age, country, profession and kindred.[41] So solicitous were they in regard to this matter that when, in 1619, James I ordered them to transport to Virginia a number of malefactors whose care was burdensome to the state, they showed

[40] Abstracts of Proceedings of Va. Company of London, Vol. II, p. 164.

[41] Ibid., Vol. II, pp. 17 and 18; Bruce, Econ. Hist. of Va., Vol. I, p. 597.

such a reluctance to obey that they incurred the king's displeasure.[42]

What tended strongly to attract a desirable class of men in the earliest years of the colony was the repeated attempt to establish manufactures. Until the charter of the London Company was revoked, that body never ceased to send over numbers of skilled artisans and mechanics. In 1619, one hundred and fifty workmen from Warwickshire and Stafford were employed to set up iron works on the James.[43] Repeated attempts were made to foster the silk industry, and on more than one occasion men practiced in the culture of the silk worm came to Virginia.[44] An effort was made to start the manufacture of glass,[45] while pipe staves and clapboards were produced in considerable quantities.[46] Moreover, numerous tradesmen of all kinds were sent to the colony. Among the set-

---

[42] Abstracts of Proceedings of Va. Company of London, Vol. I, pp. 26 and 34; Bruce, Econ. Hist. of Va., Vol. I, pp. 599-600.

[43] Abstracts of Proceedings of Va. Company of London, Vol. I, pp. 162-164.

[44] Bruce, Econ. Hist. of Va. Vol. I, p. 51.

[45] Abstracts of Proceedings of Va. Company of London, Vol. I, pp. 130 and 138.

[46] Force, Vol. III.

tlers of this period were smiths, carpenters, bricklayers, turners, potters and husbandmen.[47]

With the year 1624 there came a change for the worse in the immigration, for the lack of the Company's paternal care over the infant colony was keenly felt after the king undertook personally the direction of affairs. James I and, after his death, Charles I were desirous that Virginia should undertake various forms of manufacture, and frequently gave directions to the governors to foster industrial pursuits among the settlers, for they considered it a matter of reproach that the people should devote themselves almost exclusively to the cultivation of tobacco, but neither monarch was interested enough in the matter to send over mechanics and artisans as the Company had done, and we find after 1624 few men of that type among the newcomers.[48] The immigration that occurred under the London Company is, however, not of great importance, for the mortality among the colonists was so great that but a small percentage of those that came over in the early years

[47] Abstracts of Proceedings of Va. Company of London, Vol. I, p. 12.

[48] Bruce, Econ. Hist. of Va., Vol. I, p. 286.

survived the dangers that they were compelled to face. In 1622, after the memorable massacre of that year, there were but 1258 persons in the colony and during the next few years there was no increase in the population.[49]

The immigration to Virginia of free families of humble means began in the early years of the colony's existence, and continued throughout the 17th century. The lowness of wages and the unfavorable economic conditions that existed in England induced many poor men to seek their fortunes in the New World.[50] The law which allotted to every settler fifty acres of land for each member of his family insured all that could pay for their transportation a plantation far larger than they could hope to secure at home.[51] Thus it was that many men of the laboring class or of the small tenant class, whose limited means barely sufficed to pay for their passage across the ocean, came to Virginia to secure farms of their own. The number of small grants in the first half of the 17th cen-

---

[49] Bruce, Soc. Life of Va., p. 17; Wm. & Mary Quar., Vol. IX, p. 61.

[50] Bruce, Econ. Hist. of Va., Vol. I, pp. 576-584.

[51] Force, Vol. III, Orders and Constitutions, p. 22.

tury is quite large. Frequently patents were made out for tracts of land varying from fifty to five hundred acres in extent to immigrants that had entered the colony as freemen.[52] The law allowed them to include in the head-rights of their patents their wives, children, relatives, friends or servants that came with them, and some immigrants in this way secured plantations of considerable size. Thus in 1637 three hundred acres in Henrico County were granted to Joseph Royall, "due: 50 acres for his own personal adventure, 50 acres for the transportation of his first wife Thomasin, 50 acres for the transportation of Ann, his now wife, 50 for the transportation of his brother Henry, and 100 for the transportation of two persons, Robt. Warrell and Jon. Wells."[53] These peasant immigrants sometimes prospered in their new homes and increased the size of their plantations by the purchase of the head-rights of other men, and the cheapness of land in the colony made it possible for them to secure estates of considerable size. It is probable that the average holding of the small farmers of this

---

[52] Va. Maga. of Hist. and Biog., Vol. VII, p. 191.

[53] Ibid., Vol. VIII, p. 75.

period was between three and four hundred acres.[54]

Owing to the demand for servants and the cost of transporting them to the colony, it was seldom that any other than wealthy planters could afford to secure them. The wills of the first half of the 17th century show that few of the smaller planters even when they had attained a fair degree of prosperity made use of servant labor. Thus there was in Virginia at this period a class of men who owned their own land and tilled it entirely with their own hands. This condition of affairs continued until the influx of negroes, which began about the year 1680, so diminished the cost of labor that none but the smallest proprietors were dependent entirely upon their own exertions for the cultivation of their fields.[55]

These men, like the wealthy planters, raised tobacco for exportation, but they also planted enough corn for their own consumption. Their support was largely from cattle and hogs, which were usually allowed to wander at large, seeking sustenance in the woods or upon unpatented

[54] Ibid., Vol. VI, p. 251.
[55] Ibid., Vol. VI, p. 251.

land. The owners branded them in order to make identification possible.[56] Some of the small farmers owned but one cow and a few hogs, but others acquired numbers of the animals. The testament of Edward Wilmoth, of Isle of Wight County, drawn in 1647, is typical of the wills of that period. "I give," he says, "unto my wife....four milch cows, a steer, and a heifer that is on Lawns Creek side, and a young yearling bull. Also I give unto my daughter Frances a yearling heifer. Also I give unto my son John Wilmoth a cow calf, and to my son Robert Wilmoth a cow calf."[57]

The patent rolls, some of which have been preserved to the present day, show that the percentage of free immigrants to the colony was quite appreciable during the years immediately following the downfall of the London Company. There are on record 501 patents that were issued between the dates 1628 and 1637, and in connection with them are mentioned, either as recipients of land or as persons transported to the colony, 2,675 names. Of these

---

[56] Bruce, Econ. Hist. of Va., Vol. I, pp. 378, 477 and 480.

[57] Va. Maga. of Hist. and Biog., Vol. VI, p. 251.

336 are positively known to have come over as freemen, and most of them as heads of families. There are 245 others who were probably freemen, although this has not yet been proved. The remainder are persons whose transportation charges were paid by others, including indentured servants, negroes, wives, children, etc. Thus it is quite certain that of the names on this list over one fourth were those of free persons, who came as freemen to Virginia and established themselves as citizens of the colony.[58] Although the patent rolls that have been preserved are far from complete, there is no reason to suspect that they are not fairly representative of the whole, and we may assume that the percentage of free families that came to the colony in this period was by no means small. As, however, the annual number of immigrants was as yet small and the mortality was very heavy, the total number of men living in Virginia in 1635 who had come over as freemen could not have been very large. The total population at that date was 5,000, and it is probable that at least 3,000 of these had come to the colony as servants.

---

[58] Ibid., Vol. VII, p. 441.

After 1635 the percentage of free settlers became much smaller. This was due largely to the fact that at this time the immigration of indentured servants to Virginia increased very much. Secretary Kemp, who was in office during Governor Harvey's administration, stated that of hundreds of people that were arriving nearly all were brought in as merchandise.[59] So great was the influx of these servants, that the population tripled between 1635 and 1649. It is certain, however, that at no period during the 17th century did freemen cease coming to the colony.

With the exception of the merchants and other well-to-do men that formed the basis of the aristocracy, the free immigrants were ignorant and crude. But few of them could read and write, and many even of the most prosperous, being unable to sign their names to their wills, were compelled to make their mark to give legal force to their testaments.[60] Some of them acquired considerable property and became influential in their counties, but this was due rather to rough qualities of manhood that

---

[59] Sainsbury Abstracts, year 1638, p. 8.
[60] Va. Maga. of Hist. and Biog., Vol. VI.

fitted them for the life in the forests of the New World, than to education or culture.

The use of the indentured servant by the Virginia planters was but the result of the economic conditions of the colony. Even in the days of the London Company the settlers had turned their attention to the raising of tobacco, for they found that the plant needed but little care, that it was admirably suited to the soil, and that it brought a handsome return. Naturally it soon became the staple product of the colony. The most active efforts of the Company and all the commands of King James and King Charles were not sufficient to turn men from its cultivation to less lucrative pursuits. Why should they devote themselves to manufacture when they could, with far greater profit, exchange their tobacco crop for the manufactured goods of England? It was found that but two things were essential to the growth of the plant—abundance of land and labor. The first of these could be had almost for the asking. Around the colony was a vast expanse of territory that needed only the woodman's axe to transform it into fertile fields, and the poorest man could own a plantation that in England would have been esteemed a rich estate. Labor, on the other hand, was exceedingly scarce. The colony itself could furnish but a limited supply, for few were willing to work for hire when they could easily own farms of their own. The native Americans of this region could not be made to toil in the fields for the white man, as the aborigines of Mexico and the West Indies were made to toil for the Spanish, for they were of too warlike and bold a spirit. Destruction would have been more grateful to them than slavery. Their haughtiness and pride were such that in their intercourse with the English they would not brook the idea of inferiority. No thought could be entertained of making them work in the fields. So the planters were forced to turn to the mother country. As early as 1620 they sent urgent requests for a supply of laborers, which they needed much more than artisans or tradesmen. The Company, although it did not relinquish its plan of establishing manufactures, was obliged to yield somewhat to this demand, and sent to the planters a number of indentured servants.[61] Thus early began that

[61] Abstracts of Proceedings of Va. Company of London, Vol. I, p. 92.

great stream of laborers, flowing from England to Virginia, that kept up without interruption for more than a century.

From the first the indenture system was in vogue. Circumstances made this necessary, for had no obligations been put upon the immigrants to work for a certain number of years in servitude, they would have secured tracts of ground for themselves and set themselves up as independent planters, as soon as they arrived in the country. It was found to be impossible to establish a class of free laborers. Also the system had its advantages for the immigrant. The voyage to the colony, so long and so expensive, was the chief drawback to immigration. Thousands of poor Englishmen, who could hardly earn enough money at home to keep life in their bodies, would eagerly have gone to the New World, had they been able to pay for their passage. Under the indenture system this difficulty was removed, for anyone could secure free transportation provided he were willing to sacrifice, for a few years, his personal freedom.

And, despite the English love of liberty, great numbers availed themselves of this opportunity. There came to Virginia, during the period from 1635 to 1680, annually from 1000 to 1600 servants. The immigration in the earlier years seems to have been nearly if not fully as great as later in the century. During the year ending March 1636 sixteen hundred people came over, most of whom were undoubtedly servants.[62] In 1670 Governor Berkeley estimated the annual immigration of servants at 1500.[63] But we need no better evidence that the stream at no time slackened during this period than the fact that the demand for them remained constant. So long as the planter could obtain no other labor for his tobacco fields, the great need of the colony was for more servants, and able-bodied laborers always brought a handsome price in the Virginia market. Col. William Byrd I testified that servants were the most profitable import to the colony.[64] The fact that the term of service was in most cases comparatively short made it necessary for the planter to repeople his estate at frequent intervals. The period of indenture was from four to seven years, except in the case of criminals

---

[62] Neill, Virginia Carolorum.

[63] Hening's Statutes, Vol. II.

[64] Virginia Hist. Register, Vol. I, p. 63.

who sometimes served for life, and without this constant immigration the plantations would have been deserted. Thus in 1671, when the population of the colony was 40,000, the number of servants was but 6,000.[65] Nor was there any sign of slackening in the stream until the last years of the century, when there came a great increase in the importation of negro slaves. As soon as it became practicable to secure enough Africans to do the work of the servants, the need for the latter became less pressing. For many reasons the slave was more desirable. He could withstand better the heat of the summer sun in the fields, he was more tractable, he served for life and could not desert his master after a few years of service as could the servant. We find, then, that after 1680, the importation of servants decreased more and more, until, in the middle of the 18th century, it died out entirely.

Thus it will be seen that the number of indentured servants that were brought to the colony of Virginia is very large. The most conservative estimate will place the figure at 80,000,

---

[65] Neill, Virginia Carolorum; Hening's Statutes, Vol. II, p. 510.

and there is every reason to believe that this is much too low. Now, if we consider the growth of population in conjunction with these facts, it becomes evident that the indentured servant was the most important factor in the settlement of the colony. In 1671, according to the statement of Governor Berkeley, there were but 40,000 people in the colony.[66] The immigration of servants had then been in progress for fifty years, and the number brought over must have exceeded the total population at that date. Even after making deductions for the mortality among the laborers in the tobacco fields, which in the first half of this century was enormous, we are forced to the conclusion that the percentage of those that came as freemen was small.

We have already seen that the larger part of the servants were men that came over to work in the tobacco fields. Great numbers of these were drawn from the rural districts of England, where the pitiful condition of thousands of laborers made it easy to find recruits ready to leave for Virginia. So low were the wages given the farm hands at this period that their

---

[66] Hening's Statutes, Vol. II, p. 510.

most excessive labor could hardly insure enough to support life, and, after years of hard work, they were often compelled to throw themselves upon charity in their old age. The pittance that they received seldom made it possible for them to secure food enough to sustain properly their arduous labors. Many worked for fourteen pence a day, and those that were most favored earned two shillings. The condition of the poorer class of workmen in the cities was, if possible, worse than that of the agricultural laborers, for economic conditions had combined with unwise laws to reduce them to the verge of starvation. Those that had not some recognized trade were compelled to labor incessantly for insufficient wages, and many were forced into beggary and crime. They were clothed in rags and their dwellings were both miserable and unsanitary. The number of those dependent upon charity for subsistence was enormous. In Sheffield, in 1615, a third of the entire population was compelled to rely in part on charity. No wonder these poor wretches were willing to sell their liberty to go to the New World! They had the assurance that whatever happened to them, their condition could not be altered much for the worse. In Virginia there was a chance of improvement, at home they were doomed to live lives of drudgery and misery.[67]

But not all the indentured servants came from this class. Some were persons of culture, and, on rare occasions, of means. The word "servant" did not at that time have the menial signification that it has acquired in modern times, for it was applied to all that entered upon a legal agreement to remain in the employment of another for a prescribed time.[68] There are many instances of persons of gentle blood becoming indentured servants to lawyers or physicians, in order to acquire a knowledge of those professions.[69] All apprentices were called servants. Tutors were sometimes brought over from England under terms of indenture to instruct the children of wealthy planters in courses higher than those offered by the local schools. Several instances are recorded of gentlemen of large estates who are spoken of as servants, but such cases are very rare.[70] What was of

[67] Bruce, Econ. Hist. of Va., Vol. I, pp. 576-584.
[68] Ibid., Vol. I, p. 573.
[69] Ibid., Vol. I, p. 574.
[70] Bruce, Econ. Hist. of Va., Vol. I, p. 574.

more common occurrence was the entering into indenture of persons who had become bankrupt. The severe English laws against debtors forced many to fly from the country to escape imprisonment, and there could be no surer way for them to evade their creditors than to place themselves under the protection of some planter as a servant and to sail for Virginia. How numerous was the debtor class in the colony is shown by an act of the Assembly in 1642, which exempted from prosecution persons that had fled from their creditors in England. The colonial legislators declared openly that the failure to pass such a law would have hazarded the desertion of a large part of the country.

At intervals large numbers of political prisoners were sent to Virginia. During the civil wars in England, when the royal forces were meeting defeat, many of the king's soldiers were captured, and many of these were sold to the planters as servants. A large importation took place after the defeat of Charles II at Worcester.[71] From 1653 to 1655 hundreds of unfortunate Irishmen suffered the consequence of their resistance to the government of Cromwell

---

[71] Ibid., Vol. I, p. 608.

by banishment to the plantations.[72] After 1660, when the tables had been turned, and the royalist party was once more in power, there set in a stream of Commonwealth soldiers and nonconformists.[73] These were responsible for a rising in the colony in 1663, that threatened to anticipate Bacon's Rebellion by thirteen years.[74] The Scotch rebellion of 1678 was the occasion of another importation of soldiers. Finally, in 1685, many of the wretches taken at the battle of Sedgemoor were sent to Virginia, finding relief in the tobacco fields from the harshness of their captors.[75]

These immigrations of political prisoners are of great importance. They brought into Virginia a class of men much superior to the ordinary laborer, for most of them were guilty only of having resisted the party in power, and many were patriots in the truest sense of the word, suffering for principles that they believed essential to the welfare of their country.

We have already seen that under the London Company of Virginia few criminals were sent to

---

[72] Ibid., Vol. I, p. 609.

[73] Ibid., Vol. I, p. 610.

[74] Beverley, Hist. of Va., p. 57.

[75] Bruce, Econ. Hist. of Va., Vol. I, p. 611.

the colony. After the dissolution of that body there was quite as great strictness in regard to the matter. As the Company had feared to fill the country with malefactors, knowing that it would ruin the enterprise in which they had expended so much time and money, so, in later years, the Virginia people were solicitous of the character of those that were to be their neighbors. They were firm in demanding that no "jailbirds" be sent them. On more than one occasion, when persons of ill repute arrived, they at once shipped them back to England. There existed, however, in the mother country a feeling that it was but proper to use Virginia as a dumping ground for criminals, and the magistrates from time to time insisted on shipping objectionable persons. But it is certain that the percentage of felons among the servants was not large. At one period only were they sent over in numbers great enough to make themselves felt as a menace to the peace of the colony. After the Restoration, when England was just beginning to recover from the convulsions of the preceding twenty years and when the kingdom was swarming with vicious and criminal persons, a fresh attempt was made to seek an outlet for this class in Virginia. A sudden increase in lawlessness in the colony aroused the people to the danger, and in 1670 the General Court prohibited the introduction of English malefactors into the colony.[76] Although in the 18th century criminals were sent to Virginia at times, their numbers were insignificant and their influence small.

Having examined the various types of men that entered Virginia as indentured servants, it now remains to determine to what extent these types survived and became welded into the social life of the colony. The importation of starving laborers and even of criminals was of vital importance only in proportion to the frequency with which they survived their term of service, acquired property, married and left descendants. The law of the survival of the fittest, which is so great a factor in elevating the human race, operated with telling effect in Virginia. The bulk of the servants were subjected to a series of tests so severe, that, when safely passed through, they were a guarantee of soundness of body, mind, and character.

The mortality among the laborers in the to-

[76] Hening's Statutes, Vol. II, p. 510.

bacco fields was enormous. Scattered along the banks of the rivers and creeks and frequently adjacent to swamps and bogs, the plantations were unhealthful in the extreme. Everywhere were swarms of mosquitoes,[77] and the colonists were exposed to the sting of these pests both by night and day, and many received through them the deadly malaria bacteria. Scarcely three months had elapsed from the first landing at Jamestown in 1607, when disease made its appearance in the colony. The first death occurred in August, and so deadly were the conditions to which the settlers were subjected that soon hardly a day passed without one death to record. Before the end of September more than fifty were in their graves. Part of the mortality was due, it is true, to starvation, but "fevers and fluxes" were beyond doubt responsible for many of the deaths.[78] George Percy, one of the party, describes in vivid colors the sufferings of the settlers. "There were never Englishmen," he says, "left in a forreigne countrey in such miserie as wee were in this new discovered Virginia, Wee watched every three nights, lying on

[77] Strachey's Historie of Travaile into Va., p. 63.
[78] Percy's Discourse, p. lxxii.

the bare ground, what weather soever came; ....which brought our men to be most feeble wretches,....If there were any conscience in men, it would make their harts to bleed to hears the pitifull murmurings and outcries of our sick men without reliefe, every night and day for the space of six weekes: some departing out of the World, many times three or foure in a night; in the morning, their bodies trailed out of their cabines like dogges, to be buried."[79] Of the hundred colonists that had remained at Jamestown, but thirty-eight were alive when relief came in January, 1608.

Nor were the colonists that followed in the wake of the Susan Constant, the Godspeed and the Discovery more fortunate. In the summer of 1609, the newcomers under Lord Delaware were attacked by fever and in a short while one hundred and fifty had died. It seemed for a while that no one would escape the epidemic and that disease would prove more effective than the Indians in protecting the country from the encroachment of the Englishmen.[80] How terrible was the mortality in these early years is

---

[79] Narratives of Early Va., pp. 21 and 22.

[80] Ibid., p. 200.

shown by the statement of Molina in 1613, that one hundred and fifty in every three hundred colonists died before being in Virginia twelve months.[81]

In 1623 a certain Nathaniel Butler, who had been at one time governor of the Bermuda Islands, testified to the unhealthfulness of the colony. "I found," he says, "the plantations generally seated upon meer salt marishes full of infectious boggs and muddy creeks and lakes, and thereby subjected to all those inconveniences and diseases which are soe commonly found in the most unsounde and most unhealthy parts of England whereof everie country and clymate hath some." Butler asserted that it was by no means uncommon to see newcomers from England "dying under hedges and in the woods." He ended by declaring that unless conditions were speedily redressed by some divine or supreme hand, instead of a plantation Virginia would shortly get the name of a slaughter house.[82]

The mortality was chiefly among the new-

---

[81] Ibid., p. 220.

[82] Abstracts of Proceedings of Va. Company of London, Vol. II, p. 171.

comers. If one managed to survive during his first year of residence in the colony, he might reasonably expect to escape with his life, being then "seasoned" as the settlers called it. The death rate during this first year, however, was frightful. De Vries said of the climate "that during the months of June, July and August it was very unhealthy, that then people that had lately arrived from England, die, during these months, like cats and dogs, whence they call it the sickly season."[83] So likely was it that a newcomer would be stricken down that a "seasoned" servant was far more desirable than a fresh arrival. A new hand, having seven and a half years to serve, was worth not more than others, having one year more only. Governor William Berkeley stated in 1671, "there is not oft seasoned hands (as we term them) that die now, whereas heretofore not one of five escaped the first year."[84]

Robert Evelyn, in his Description of the Province of New Albion, printed in 1648, gives a vivid picture of the unhealthful climate of Virginia. He declared that formerly five out

[83] Neill, Va. Carolorum.
[84] Hening's Statutes, Vol. II.

of every six men imported from Europe fell speedy victims to disease. "I," he said, "on my view of Virginia, disliked Virginia, most of it being seated scatteringly.... amongst salt-marshes and creeks, whence thrice worse than Essex,....and Kent for agues and diseases ....brackish water to drink and use, and a flat country, and standing waters in woods bred a double corrupt air."[85]

Much of the ill health of the immigrants was undoubtedly due to the unwholesome conditions on board the ships during their passage from Europe. The vessels were often crowded with wretched men, women and children, and were foul beyond description. Gross uncleanliness was the rule rather than the exception. William Copps, in a letter to Deputy Treasurer Ferrar, says, "Betwixt decks there can hardlie a man fetch his breath by reason there arisith such a funke in the night that it causes putrifacation of blood and breedeth disease much like the plague." Often the number of persons that died at sea was frightful. One vessel lost one hundred and thirty persons out of one

[85] Force, Historical Tracts, Vol. II, New Albion, p. 5.

hundred and eighty. The disease started in this way was often spread in Virginia after the settlers had reached their new homes, and terrible epidemics more than once resulted.

If the assertion of Berkeley that four out of five of the indentured servants died during the first year's residence in the colony, or Evelyn's statement that five out of six soon succumbed, be accepted as correct, the number of deaths must have been very large indeed. Among the hundreds of servants that were brought to the colony each year a mortality of over eighty per cent would have amounted in a few years to thousands. Statements made in regard to early Virginia history are so frequently inaccurate, and the conditions here described are so horrible that one is inclined to reject this testimony as obviously exaggerated. However, a close examination of the number of persons that came to Virginia from 1607 to 1649, and of the population between those dates forces us to the conclusion that the statements of Berkeley and Evelyn were not grossly incorrect. When, however, Evelyn adds that "old Virginians affirm, the sicknesse there the first thirty years to have killed 100,000 men," it is evident that this rumor was false.[86] Yet even this is valuable because it shows in an indefinite way that the mortality was very large.

When we consider the fact that it was the lowest class of immigrants that were chiefly exposed to these perils it becomes evident how great a purifying force was exerted. The indentured servants more than any others had to face the hot sun of the fields, and upon them alone the climate worked with deadly effect.

But disease was not the only danger that the indentured servant faced in those days. At times starvation carried off great numbers. Even after the colony had attained a certain degree of prosperity famines occurred that bore with fearful weight upon the servants. In 1636 there was great scarcity of food and in that year 1,800 persons perished. A servant, in 1623, complained in a letter to his parents that the food that was given him would barely sustain life, and that he had often eaten more at home in a day than was now allowed him for a week.[87]

But if the servant survived all these dangers,

---

[86] Ibid., p. 5.

[87] Bruce, Econ. Hist. of Va., Vol. I, p. 7.

if he escaped disease, starvation and the tomahawk, his task was not yet finished. He had then to build for himself a place in society. When the servant was discharged, upon the expiration of his term, he was always given some property with which to start life as a freeman. In the days of the Company, each was granted 100 acres of land, and, when this was seated, each was probably entitled to an additional tract of the same extent. After 1624 the servant received, at the end of his term of indenture, no allotment of land, but was given instead enough grain to sustain him for one year. Also he was to receive two sets of apparel, and in Berkeley's time a gun worth twenty shillings.[88] The cheapness of land made it easy for these men to secure little farms, and if they were sober and industrious they had an opportunity to rise. They might acquire in time large estates; they might even become leaders in the colony, but the task was a hard one, and those that were successful were worthy of the social position they obtained.

It is of importance to note that of the servants that came to the colony but a small num-

---

[88] Ibid., Vol. II, pp. 41 and 42; Jones' Va.

ber married and left descendants. Women were by no means plentiful. During the earlier years this had been a drawback to the advancement of the colony, for even the most prosperous planters found it difficult to secure wives. It was this condition of affairs that induced the Company to send to Virginia that cargo of maids that has become so famous in colonial history. As years went on, the scarcity of women became a distinct blessing, for it made it impossible for the degraded laborer, even though he ultimately secured his freedom, to leave descendants to perpetuate his lowly instincts. Of the thousands of servants whose criminal instincts or lack of industry made it impossible for them to become prosperous citizens, great numbers left the colony. Many went to North Carolina. As Virginia had served as a dumping ground for the refuse of the English population, so did this new colony furnish a vent for undesirable persons from Virginia. William Byrd II, who had an excellent opportunity to observe conditions in North Carolina while running the dividing line, bears testimony to the character of the immigrants to that colony from Virginia and Maryland. "It is certain," he says, "many slaves shelter themselves in this obscure part of the world, nor will any of their righteous neighbors discover them. Nor were the worthy borderers content to shelter runaway slaves, but debtors and criminals have often met with the like indulgence. But if the government of North Carolina has encourag'd this unneighbourly policy in order to increase their people, it is no more than what ancient Rome did before them."[89] Again he says, "The men....just like the Indians, impose all the work upon the poor women. They make their wives rise out of their beds early in the morning, at the same time that they lye and snore, til the sun has run one third of his course ....Then, after stretching and yarning for half an hour, they light their pipes, and, under the protection of a cloud of smoak, venture out into the open air; tho' if it happens to be never so little cold, they quickly return shivering into the chimney corner....Thus they loiter away their lives, like Soloman's sluggard, with their arms across, and at the winding up of the year scarcely have bread to eat. To speak the truth, tis a thorough aversion to labor that makes

[89] Bassett, Writings of Wm. Byrd, p. 47.

people file off to North Carolina, where plenty and a warm sun confirm them in their disposition to laziness for their whole lives."[90] The gangs of outlaws that infested North Carolina during the early years of the 18th century and defied the authority of the governors, were composed largely of runaway servants from Virginia. The laxness and weakness of the government made it an inviting place for criminals, while the numerous swamps and bogs, and the vast expanse of dense woods offered them a safe retreat.[91]

Many freed servants took up in Virginia unpatented land, trusting that their residence upon it might give to them in time a legal title. Others settled upon tracts that had been deserted. In some instances, where these people, or their descendants, had prospered and had built homes and barns and stables on the property, or had otherwise improved it, their claims

---

[90] Ibid., pp. 75 and 76.

[91] It is not to be supposed that these people are the ancestors of the eastern North Carolians of today. As they were cast off by society in Virginia, so were they crowded west by the influx of more industrious settlers in their new home and their descendants are at present to be found in the Blue Ridge and the Alleghanies.

to the land were confirmed by law. In other cases, when patents were made out to land already occupied by "squatters," the lowly settlers were forced to leave their farms and to seek homes elsewhere, probably on unclaimed territory in remote parts of the colony. This gave rise to that fringe of rough humanity upon the frontier, that spread continually westward as the colony grew. Many of the servants that escaped from their masters fled to the mountains, seeking refuge among the defiles and woods of the Blue Ridge or the more distant Alleghanies. The descendants of these wretched people still exist in the mountains of Virginia, North Carolina, Tennessee and Kentucky, exhibiting in their ignorance, their disregard for law, their laziness and even in their dialect the lowness of their origin.

The facts presented in the preceding paragraphs lead us inevitably to the conclusion that that portion of the vast body of indentured servants that were brought to Virginia which made its lasting imprint on the character of the population of the eastern countries was composed of men of sterling qualities, and was rather an element of strength than of weakness to the middle class into which they went. That many did rise to places of trust and influence is well established. There are numerous instances of servants, who, after serving their term of indenture, became burgesses, justices, etc. Thus John Trussell, who came over in 1622 as a servant, became a burgess in 1654.[92] The Assembly of 1629 included in its members William Warlick, William Poppleton, Richard Townsend and Anthony Pagett, all of whom had come to the colony under terms of indenture.[93] Gatford, a puritanical preacher of the Commonwealth period, wrote that at that time some of the former servants were still filling offices of trust in the colony. The author of Virginia's Cure asserted, in 1662, that the burgesses "were usuall such as went over as servants thither, and though by time, and industry, they may have obtained competent estates, yet by reason of their poor and mean condition, were unskilful in judging of a good estate, either of church or Commonwealth."[94] This,

---

[92] Neill, Va. Carolorum.

[93] Neill, Va. Carolorum; Bruce, Econ. Hist. of Va. Vol. II, p. 45.

[94] Neill, Va. Carolorum; Force, Historical Tracts, Vol. III; Bruce, Econ. Hist. of Va., Vol. II, p. 45.

however, is undoubtedly an exaggeration. Yet, in 1651, Governor Berkeley, in an address to the Assembly, stated that hundreds of examples testified to the fact that no man in the colony was denied the opportunity to acquire both honor and wealth.

The chief occupation to which the freed servant turned was agriculture. During their term of indenture it was as field laborers that most of them had spent their time, and many were ignorant of any other means of earning a living. Moreover, farming was almost the only occupation open to them in the colony. Some, who had been trained upon the plantations as artisans, doubtless made use of their skill after becoming free to increase their incomes, but even these were forced to turn their attention chiefly to farming. With the payment that was made by the former master, and the land which it was so easy to obtain, the new freeman, if he were sober and industrious, was sure to wrest from the soil an abundant supply of food and perhaps enough tobacco to make him quite prosperous. He must first plant corn, for were he to give all his land to tobacco, he would starve before he received from it any returns.

If things went well with him, he would buy hogs and cattle, and thereafter these would constitute his most valuable possession.

Some of the servants upon the expiration of their terms of indenture secured work as overseers, if they found it impossible to obtain patents to estates of their own. Throughout the greater part of the colonial period the position occupied by the overseer was preferable to that of the poorest class of independent farmers. His usual remuneration was a part of the crop. Sometimes he received only one-tenth of what was produced, but often his share was much greater, for cases are on record where he was to keep one half. Later the pay was regulated by the number of persons under his management, slaves as well as hired and indentured servants forming the basis of the calculation. Under both systems of payment he was liberally rewarded for his services.[95] The control of many laborers, the necessity for a knowledge of all the details of farming, the contact with his employer in matters of business made requisite in the overseer both intelligence and the power of command. Many were men of much ability

[95] Bruce, Econ. Hist. of Va., Vol. II, p. 47.

and were trusted by the planters with the entire management of their estates. When the overseer worked upon the "home" plantation, he usually dwelt either in the mansion itself or in one of the group of houses nearby, in which were sleeping rooms used by members of the household or guests. He was treated always with courtesy and was accorded some social recognition by his aristocratic employer. Sometimes the overseer through ability and care accumulated property and became an independent planter.

Occasionally the servants upon the close of their term of indenture earned a subsistence as hired laborers. This, however, was not very common, for the opportunities for an independent existence were so great that few would fail to grasp them. There could be no necessity for laboring for others when land could be had so cheaply. Those that did hire themselves out were tempted usually by the excessive wages that could be obtained from wealthy planters. Throughout the 17th century, the difficulty of obtaining a sufficient supply of servants to keep in cultivation the tobacco fields of the colony, created a lively demand for labor and made wages higher than in England. Even in the early years of the century this state of affairs prevailed, and we find planters complaining of the excessive cost of hired labor and making urgent requests for indentured servants.[96] Despite the high price of tobacco that prevailed before 1660, it was the general opinion that no profit could be made from it when hired laborers were used in its cultivation, and it is probable that they were never employed except when the supply of servants fell far short of the demand. In the 18th century, when the importation of many thousands of slaves had lowered the price of labor in the colony, the employment of hired hands became still less frequent.

The existence of high wages for so many years accelerated the formation of the middle class, for the hired laborer could, if he were economical, save enough to purchase land and to become an independent farmer. So crude were the agricultural methods then in use in the colony that very little capital was needed by the small planters, and tobacco and corn could be raised by them almost as economically as

[96] Ibid., p. 118.

upon the large plantations. Moreover, since men of the middle class could seldom afford to employ laborers to till their fields, they were in a sense brought into competition with the wage earner. The price of tobacco was dependent in large measure upon the cost of production, and could not, except upon exceptional occasions, fall so low that there could be no profit in bringing servants from England to cultivate it, and this fact reacted favorably upon those that tilled their fields with their own hands. On the other hand this very circumstance made it hard for the small farmer to enlarge the scope of his activities. Unless he had obtained a fair degree of prosperity, it would be impossible for him to purchase servants or hire laborers and the output of his plantation was limited to his own exertions, or those of the members of his family.

By 1660, the middle class was fully formed. From the thousands of indentured servants that had been brought to the colony numerous families had emerged which, though rough and illiterate, proved valuable citizens and played an important rôle in the development of the country. Added to the free immigrants of humble means they formed a large body that needed only organization and leaders to wield a powerful influence in governmental affairs.

In the second period, from 1660 to 1676, the prosperity of the middle class was seriously impaired by oppression by England and misgovernment and tyranny in the colony. The Navigation Acts, which were designed by the English to build up their commerce, regardless of the consequences to their colonies, injured Virginians of all classes, but bore with telling weight upon the poor independent planters. Moreover, the arbitrary rule of Governor William Berkeley, the corruption of the Assembly, the heavy and unjust taxes and the frequent embezzlement of public funds conspired to retard the advancement of the middle class and to impoverish its members.

The beginning of England's oppressive policy towards the commerce of her colonies must date from 1651, when Parliament passed a stringent Navigation Act, forbidding the importation of any commodities into England or its territories except in English vessels or vessels of the nation that produced the goods.[97]

---

[97] Bruce, Econ. Hist. of Va. Vol. I, p. 349.

This law was aimed chiefly at the Dutch carrying trade, which was so extensive that it had aroused England's jealousy, but it came as a serious blow to Virginia. A large part of her exports had for many years been transported by the Dutch, and the entire exclusion of the "Hollanders" could not fail to react unfavorably upon her prosperity. The immediate effect, since it relieved the English ship owners of much of the competition with which they had contended, was to raise the cost of transportation.

The Virginians protested strongly. In a speech to the Assembly, Governor Berkeley, fairly foaming with rage, denounced the act. "We," he said, "the Governor, Councell and Burgesses of Virginia, have seene a printed paper....wherein (with other plantations of America) we are prohibited trade and commerce with all but such as the present power shall allow of:....we think we can easily find out the cause of this the excluding us the society of nations, which bring us necessaries for what our country produces: And that is the averice of a few interested persons, who endeavour to rob us of all we sweat and labor for."[98]

But the evil was to some extent avoided during the Commonwealth period, owing to constant evasions of the law. There is abundant evidence to show that the Dutch trade, although hampered, was by no means stamped out, and Dutch vessels continued to carry the Virginia tobacco just as they had done during the reign of Charles I. In the year 1657, there was a determined effort to enforce the law, and the advance in the charges of transporting the crop of that year, indicates that this effort was partly successful. The freight rate rose from £4 a ton to £8 or £9, and in some cases to £14.[99]

A more serious blow came in 1660. A bill was passed prescribing that no goods of any description should be imported into or exported from any of the king's territories "in Asia, Africa, or America, in any other than English, Irish, or plantation built ships."[1] It was also required that at least three-fourths of the mar-

[98] Va. Maga. of Hist. and Biog., Vol. I, p. 75.
[99] Wm. & Mary Quar.
[1] Bruce, Econ. Hist. of Va., Vol. I, p. 356.

iners of these ships should be Englishmen. Moreover, another feature was added to the law which was far more oppressive than the first provision. It was enacted that "no sugar, tobacco, cotton, wool, indigo, ginger, justic, and other dying woods, of the growth or manufacture of our Asian, African, or American colonies, shall be shipped from the said colonies to any place but to England, Ireland, or to some other of his Majesty's plantations."

The results of this law were ruinous to Virginia. At one blow it cut off her trade with all countries but England and her colonies, and raised enormously the cost of transportation. Although England was the largest purchaser of tobacco, Holland and other countries had taken a large part of the crop each year. The colonists were now forced to bring all their crop to England, and an immediate glut in the market followed. The English could neither consume the enormously increased supply of tobacco, nor rid themselves of it by exportation to continental countries, and it piled up uselessly in the warehouses. An alarming decline in the price followed, which reacted on the planters to such an extent that it brought many to the verge of ruin. The profit from tobacco was almost entirely wiped out.

The effects of this law are clearly shown in a paper by a London merchant named John Bland, which was presented to the authorities in England, protesting against the injustice done to the colonies. "If," he says, "the Hollanders must not trade to Virginia how shall the planters dispose of their tobacco? the English will not buy it, for what the Hollander carried thence was a sort of tobacco, not desired by any other people, nor used by us in England but merely to transport for Holland. Will it not then perish on the planters' hands?....the tobacco will not vend in England, the Hollanders will not fetch it from England; what must become thereof? even flung to the dunghil."[2]

The people of Virginia were reduced almost to despair. They made desperate efforts to raise the price of their staple product. Communications were entered into with Maryland and North Carolina to restrict the planting of tobacco in order to relieve the overproduction, but negotiations failed, giving rise to much bit-

[2] Va. Maga. of Hist. and Biog., Vol. I, p. 141.

terness and contention.[3] Similar proposals were made by Virginia from time to time, but the effort was never successful. In 1664, the whole tobacco crop of Virginia was worth less than £8.15s for each person in the colony. In 1666 a large portion of the crop could not be sold at any price and was left on the hands of the planters.[4]

Moreover, the strict enforcement of the law placing all carrying trade in the hands of Englishmen created a monopoly for the English ship owners, and raised enormously not only the freight rates, but the cost of all imported goods. The planter, while he found his income greatly decreased by the low price of tobacco, was forced to pay more for all manufactured goods. The cost of clothing rose until the colony was almost in nakedness.

At this crisis an attempt was made to turn the energies of the people to manufacture. The Assembly offered rewards for the best pieces of linen and woolen cloth spun in the colony,[5] and put a bounty on the manufacture of silk.

---

[3] Sainsbury Abstracts, for 1662, pp. 17 and 19; Bruce, Econ. Hist. of Va., Vol. I, pp. 389-390-391-392.

[4] Bruce, Econ. Hist. of Va., Vol. I, p. 393.

[5] Hening's Statutes, Vol. II, p. 238.

A law was passed requiring each county to erect tan-houses, while encouragement was given to a salt works on the Eastern Shore. Bounties were also offered for ship-building. In 1666 a bill was passed making it compulsory for the counties to enter upon the manufacture of cloth. The reading of this act shows that the Assembly understood fully the causes of the distress of the people. It begins: "Whereas the present obstruction of trade and the nakedness of the country doe suffitiently evidence the necessity of providing supply of our wants by improving all means of raysing and promoteing manuffactures amonge ourselves.... Be it enacted by the authority of this grand assembly that within two yeares at furthest after the date of this act, the commissioners of each county court shall provide and sett up a loome and weaver in each of the respective counties."[6]

The corruption and mismanagement that attended these measures made them unsuccessful, and as time went on the planters became more and more impoverished. The Virginians chafed bitterly under the harsh enforcement of

---

[6] Ibid.

the law of 1660. Governor Berkeley when asked by the Lords Commissioners of Trade and Plantations in 1671 what obstructions there were to the improvement of trade and commerce in Virginia, answered with his accustomed vigor, "Mighty and destructive, by that severe act of Parliament which excludes us the having any commerce with any other nation in Europe but our own....If this were for his majesty's service, or the good of his subjects, we should not repine, whatever our sufferings are for it; but on my soul, it is the contrary of both."[7]

Berkeley had gone to England in 1661, and while there exerted his influence for the repeal of the act, but had been able to accomplish nothing. The desire of the English to crush the Dutch trade was so strong that they could not be induced to consider at all the welfare of the colonies. The powerful and logical appeal of Bland also was unheeded. This remarkable man, who seems to have understood fully the operation of economic laws that were only established as truths many years later, explained clearly the harmful consequences of the

[7] Ibid., Vol. II, p. 509.

act and demanded that justice be done the colonists. "Then let me," he says, "on behalf of the said colonies of Virginia and Maryland make the following proposals which I hope will appear but equitable:

"First, that the traders to Virginia and Maryland from England shall furnish and supply the planters and inhabitants of those colonies with all sorts of commodities and necessaries which they may want or desire, at as cheap rates and prices as the Hollanders used to have when the Hollander was admitted to trade thither.

"Secondly, that the said traders out of England to those colonies shall not only buy of the planter such tobacco in the colonies as is fit for England, but take off all that shall be yearly made by them, at as good rates and prices as the Hollanders used to give for the same....

"Thirdly, that if any of the inhabitants or planters of the said colonies shall desire to ship his tobacco or goods for England, that the traders from England to Virginia and Maryland shall let them have freight in their ships at as low and cheap rates, as they used to have when the Hollanders and other nations traded thither."

Bland, of course, did not expect these suggestions to be followed, but he did hope that the evils that he so clearly pointed out would be done away with by the repeal of the act. So far from heeding him, however, Parliament passed another bill, in 1673, taking away the last vestige of freedom of trade. The colonists, when the Navigation Acts began to be strictly enforced, in seeking an outlet for their commodities turned to each other, and a considerable traffic had sprung up between them. The New Englanders, tempted by the high price of manufactured goods in the south, were competing with Englishmen for the market of the tobacco raising colonies. The British merchants brought pressure to bear on Parliament, and a law was passed subjecting all goods that entered into competition with English commodities to a duty equivalent to that imposed on their consumption in England. This act crippled the new trade and deprived Virginia of even this slight amelioration of her pitiful condition.

The decline in the price of tobacco and the increased cost of manufactured goods bore with telling effect on the small farmers. It was customary for them to sow the greater part of their fields with tobacco, and the enormous decline in the price of that plant brought many to the verge of ruin. Whenever the overproduction was so great that the English traders left part of the crop in Virginia, it was the planter of the middle class that was apt to suffer most, for the merchants could not afford to affront the wealthy and influential men of the colony, by refusing to transport their crops. Had it not been for the ease with which the common people could obtain support from Indian corn and from their hogs and cattle, many might have perished during these years.

But, in addition to the causes of distress that were brought about by the unjust policy of England, there were forces at work within the colony, that were scarcely less potent for harm. Chief among these was the attempt of Governor William Berkeley to make his government independent of the people. Berkeley had, during the reign of Charles I, made a good governor, and had won the respect of the people, but as he became old there was a decided change for the worse in his nature. He is depicted in his declining years, as arbitrary, crabbed and avaricious.

He had for the populace the greatest contempt. To him they seemed a mere rabble, whose sole function in life was to toil and whose chief duty was to obey strictly the mandates of their rulers. He discouraged education because it bred a spirit of disobedience. "I thank God," he wrote, "there are no free schools and printing (in Virginia) and I hope we shall not have these hundred years; for learning has brought disobedience, and heresy, and sects into the world, and printing has divulged them, and libels against the best governments."[8] That the common people should have a share in the government seemed to him, even more than it had seemed to Charles I, a thing absurd and preposterous. After the Restoration, therefore, he resolved to free himself as far as practicable from all restraint, and to assume an arbitrary and almost absolute power.

Berkeley was far better qualified for this task than had been his royal masters the Stuarts. He possessed remarkable vigor and determination, and despite his quick temper was

---

[8] Hening's Statutes, Vol. II.

not lacking in tact and diplomacy. With a discrimination and care that marked him as a master in the art of corruption, he tried to make the Assembly dependent upon himself, by bribing the members of both houses. Selecting men that he though he could most easily manage, he gave to them places of honor and emolument in the colony, some being made collectors, some sheriffs, some justices.[9] The House of Burgesses was entirely corrupted, and so far from seeking to defend the rights of the people they represented, they proved willing instruments to the governor in his attempt to establish absolute power.[10] Nor could the colony correct this evil by returning to the Assembly new burgesses, for Berkeley would not permit an election, and having once won over the House, continued to prorogue it from year to year.[11] For nine years before Bacon's Re-

---

[9] Va. Maga. of Hist. and Biog., Vol. I, p. 59; Vol. III, p. 134.

[10] The commons of Charles City county said: "Sir William Berkeley, mindeing and aspiring to a sole and absolute power and command over us....did take upon him the sole nameing and appointing of other persons, such as himself best liked and thought fittest for his purposes."

[11] Va. Maga. of Hist. and Biog., Vol. III, p. 141.

bellion there had been no election of burgesses. "In this way," complained the commons of Charles City county, "Berkeley hath soe fortifyed his power over us, as himselfe without respect to our laws, to doe what soever he best pleased."[12]

His power over the Council became even more marked. The men composing this important body looked to the governors for appointment to lucrative offices and endeavored usually to keep their favor.[13] Berkeley, more than any other governor, made use of this power over the Council to make its members submissive to his will. When vacancies occurred he took pains to appoint none whom he thought would be at all refractory.[14] Moreover, "he very often discountenanced and placed his frowns on such as he observed in the least to thrust or cross his humor, soe that if by chance he had at any time choice of a person of honor, or conscience, that durst like a noble patriot speake his mind freely....such person by some means or other was soone made

[12] Va. Maga. of Hist. and Biog., Vol. III, p. 136.
[13] Ibid., Vol. I, p. 60.
[14] Ibid., Vol. III, p. 134.

weary of coming to councelle, and others overawed from the like boldness."[15] In making his selections for high offices, Berkeley had recourse at times to men that had recently settled in the colony, hoping, doubtless, to secure persons submissive to his will. "It has been the common practice," it was stated, "to putt persons that are mere strangers into places of great honor, profitt and trust who unduly officiating therein, do abuse and wrong the people." These men proved parasites upon the colony and many enriched themselves at the public expense. Bacon, in his proclamation, called attention to this evil. "Wee appeale," he said, "to the country itselfe what and of what nature their oppressions have bin or by what caball and mistery the designs of those whom we call great men in authority and favour to whose hands the dispensation of the countries wealth has been committed; let us observe the sudden rise of their estates compared with the quality in which they first entered this country, or the reputation they have held here amongst wise and discerning men, and lett us see wither their extraction and education have not bin vile, and

[15] Ibid., Vol. III, p. 136.

by what pretence of learning and vertue they could soe soon come into employments of so great trust and consequence. . . . let us see what spounges have suckt up the publique treasures, and wither it hath not bin privately contrived away by unworthy favorites and juggling parasites whose tottering fortunes have been repaired and supported at the publique charge."

These evils were aggravated by excessive taxation. The government at Jamestown added each year something more to the great burden that the poor were bearing. With utter recklessness they appropriated large quantities of tobacco for the repairing of forts, for stores and ammunition, for the construction of ships, the support of ministers, the establishment of new industries, the building of towns, and for other purposes, in addition to the usual expenses of maintaining the government itself. On all sides the people protested with bitterness. They declared the taxes excessive and unnecessary, and in more than one instance the approach of the collectors precipitated a riot. The fact that much of the money was appropriated, not to the purposes to which it was intended, but to the private use of individuals, was galling in the extreme to the poor people of the colony.[16] This abuse was especially notorious in the fort bill of 1672. The people of Charles City county declared after the Rebellion that large sums had been levied "for building and erecting forts which were never finished but suffered to go to ruine, the artillery buried in sand and spoyled with rust and want of care, the ammunition imbezzled. . . ." They complained also of mismanagement and fraud in connection with the bills passed for fostering manufacture in the colony. "Great quantities of tobacco have been raised on us," they said, "for building work houses and stoure houses and other houses for the propogating and encouragement of handicraft and manufactury. . . .yet for want of due care the said houses were never finished or made useful. . . .and noe good ever effected . . . .save the particular profitt of the undertakers, who (as is usually in such cases) were largely rewarded for thus defrauding us."

The expense of maintaining the Assembly itself was very heavy. This body not only added to the distress of the people by its corrupt and

[16] Va. Maga. of Hist. and Biog., Vol. III, p. 38; p. 136.

unwise legislation, but drained their resources by frequent and extended meetings, the cost of which was defrayed by taxation. The people of Surry county stated "that ye last Assembly (before the rebellion) continued many years and by their frequent meeting, being once every yeare, hath been a continuall charge and burthen to the poore inhabitants of this collony; and that the burgesses of the said Assembly had 150lb tobacco p day for each member, they usually continueing there three or 4 weeks togither, did arise to a great some."

This taxation would have been oppressive at any time, but coming as it did at a period when the colony was suffering severely from the Navigation Acts, and when the price of tobacco was so low that the smaller planters could hardly cultivate it with profit, the effect was crushing. The middle class during this period lost greatly in material prosperity. Many that had been well-to-do and happy before the Restoration, were reduced to poverty.

Politically, however, the evils of this period proved finally to be of benefit to the middle class, for when their burdens had become unbearable they rushed to arms and, striking out blindly at their oppressors, showed in no uncertain way that they would submit no longer to tyranny and injustice. It is true that Bacon's Rebellion was put down amid the blood of those that were its chief promoters, but the fury and horror of that outburst were not forgotten, and never again did governors or aristocracy drive to despair the commons of the colony by unjust taxation and arbitrary assumption of all power. Moreover, the misfortunes that preceded the Rebellion stirred in the breasts of the poor farmers a feeling of brotherhood, causing them to realize that their interests were common, and that by common action alone could they guard their interests. After 1676 we find that the middle class had become a self-conscious body, watching jealously every action of the Council or of the governors and resisting with energy and success all measures that seemed to them detrimental to their interests.

The period from 1676 to 1700 was marked by the growth of the middle class both in material prosperity and in political power. It is true that the Navigation Acts were still in force and that the price of tobacco continued for a while so low that little profit could be made from it, but the people were no longer so dependent on the plant as in former times. The poor farmers had been forced by absolute necessity to produce upon their own estates nearly all the articles necessary for their maintenance and comfort, and could no longer be put so completely at the mercy of the English merchants. Although the attempts of the Assembly to establish public industries proved futile, the end that had been held in view was in some measure attained by the petty manufacture upon the little plantations. The farmers' wives became expert spinners and weavers and supplied themselves and their husbands with coarse cloth sufficient for their humble needs. By planting less tobacco and more corn they could be sure of a plentiful supply of bread, while their cattle and hogs furnished them with milk and meat. The planting of apple or peach trees assured them not only fruit in abundance, but made it possible for them to make cider or brandy that were excellent substitutes for imported liquors. Their furniture could be fashioned with their own hands, while, except in rare cases, even household utensils might be made upon the farm. Thus the small farmer to some extent prospered.

Before the end of the 17th century it was rare indeed to find freemen in the colony living in poverty. There were none whose condition was at all comparable for misery and want to the vast body of paupers that crowded the English cities and eked out an existence as laborers upon the farms. Robert Beverley, who wrote in 1705, called Virginia the best poor man's country in the world. He declared that the real poor class was very small, and even these were not servile.[17] As early as 1664 Lord Baltimore had written that it was evident and known that such as were industrious were not destitute. Although this was certainly an exaggeration, when applied to the period succeeding the Restoration, it became strictly true after Bacon's Rebellion, when the people were no longer oppressed with burdensome taxation. Hugh Jones, writing during Governor Spotswood's administration, stated that the common planters lived in "pretty timber houses, neater than the farm houses are generally in England."[18]

---

[17] Beverley's Virginia; Wm. & Mary Quar., Vol. VI, p. 9.

[18] Jones' Virginia.

"They are such lovers of riding," he adds, "that almost every ordinary person keeps a horse." So favorable were the conditions in which the small farmers found themselves that a fair degree of prosperity was often obtained by them even though they were lacking in industry. Hugh Jones says, "The common planters leading easy lives don't much admire labour, except horse-racing, nor diversion except cock-fighting, in which some greatly delight. This easy way of living, and the heat of the summer makes some very lazy, who are said to be climate-struck."

The fourth period in the development of the middle class extends from 1700 to the Revolution. It is marked by a split in the class, some of the small planters becoming wealthy, others failing to advance in prosperity, while still others degenerated, falling into abject poverty. This was almost entirely the result of the substitution of slave labor for the labor of the indentured servant. The importation of negroes had begun early in the 17th century, but for many years their numbers were so few that the vast bulk of the work in the fields had been performed by white men. In 1625 there were about 465 white servants in Virginia and only 22 negroes.[19] In 1649, when the population of the colony was 15,000, there were but 300 slaves.[20] In 1671, Governor Berkeley stated that there were only 2,000 slaves in Virginia, although the population was at that date about 40,000.[21] Near the end of the century, the number of negroes brought to the colony increased very much. The Royal African Company, which had obtained the exclusive right to trade in slaves with the English possessions, stimulated this human traffic to such an extent that negroes were soon found in every part of Virginia. By the year 1700 the number of slaves was about 6,000.[22] The negroes proved more suited to the needs of the planters than the white servants, for they served for life, were docile and easy to manage, stood well the unhealthful conditions in the tobacco fields, and, most important of all, they cheapened vastly the cost of production. The wealthy planters who had for so many years been limited in the amount of land they could place

[19] Bruce, Econ. Hist. of Va., Vol. I, p. 572.
[20] Force, Hist. Tracts.
[21] Hening's Statutes, Vol. II, p. 515.
[22] Bruce, Econ. Hist. of Va., Vol. II, p. 108.

under cultivation by the number of servants they could procure, now found it possible to extend the scope of their operations. Before the end of the century such men as Byrd and Carter and Fitzhugh owned scores of slaves. It was this circumstance more than any thing else that accounts for the increased prosperity of the colony which is so noticeable during the first quarter of the 18th century.[23]

The more prosperous and capable members of the middle class shared to some extent the benefits resulting from negro labor. Many that had been unable to secure servants now bought slaves and thus were able to increase very much the output of their plantations. The shortness of the time that the servants served, the great cost of transporting them to the colony and the risk of losing them by death or by flight, had made it impossible for the small farmers to use them in cultivating their fields. Since negro labor was not attended with these objections, many planters of humble means bought slaves and at one step placed themselves above the class of those that trusted to their own exertions in the tilling of their fields. When once

[23] Jones' Virginia.

a start had been made, the advance of their prosperity was limited only by the extent of their ability and industry. Some became quite wealthy. Smythe, writing in 1773, stated that many of them formed fortunes superior to some of the first rank, despite the fact that their families were not ancient or so respectable.

Those members of the middle class who were unable, through poverty or incapacity, to share the prosperity of the early years of the 18th century were injured by the general use of slave labor in the colony. Since they could not purchase negroes, they were in a sense thrown into competition with them. The enormous increase in the production of tobacco brought down the price and made their single exertions less and less profitable. They were deprived of the privilege of working for wages, for no freeman could toil side by side with negroes, and retain anything of self-respect. Thus after the year 1700, the class of very poor whites became larger, and their depravity more pronounced.[24] A Frenchman, travelling in Virginia at the time of the Revolution, testified that the condition of

[24] Fiske, Old Va. and Her Neighbors, Vol. II, p. 189.

many white families was pitiful. "It is there," he said, "that I saw poor people for the first time since crossing the ocean. In truth, among these rich plantations, where the negro alone is unhappy, are often found miserable huts, inhabited by whites, whose wan faces and ragged clothes give testimony of their poverty."[25] It is certain that this class was never large, however, for those that were possessed of the least trace of energy or ambition could move to the frontier and start life again on more equal terms. Smythe says that the real poor class in Virginia was less than anywhere else in the world.

The introduction of slavery into the colony affected far more profoundly the character of the middle class farmer than it did that of the aristocrat. The indentured servants, upon whose labor the wealthy planters had relied for so many years, were practically slaves, being bound to the soil and forced to obey im-

[25] Voyages dans l'Amérique Septentrionale, Vol. II, p. 142; "C'est-là que, depuis que j'ai passé les mers, j'ai vu pour la premiere fois des pauvres. En effet, parmi ces riches plantations où le negre seul est malhereux, on trouve souvent de misérables cabanes hibitées par des blancs, dont la figure have & l'habillement déguenillé annoncent la pauvreté."

plicitly those whom they served. The influence that their possession exerted in moulding the character of the aristocracy was practically the same as that of the negro slave. Both tended to instil into the master pride and the power of command. Since, however, but few members of the small farmer class at any time made use of servant labor, their character was not thus affected by them. Moreover, the fact that so many servants, after the expiration of their term of indenture, entered this class, tended to humble the poor planters, for they realized always the existence of a bond of fellowship between themselves and the field laborers. When the negro slave had supplanted the indentured servant upon the plantations of the colony a vast change took place in the pride of the middle class. Every white man, no matter how poor he was, no matter how degraded, could now feel a pride in his race. Around him on all sides were those whom he felt to be beneath him, and this alone instilled into him a certain self-respect. Moreover, the immediate control of the negroes fell almost entirely into the hands of white men of humble means, for it was they, acting as overseers upon the large plantations, that directed their labors in the tobacco fields. This also tended to give to them an arrogance that was entirely foreign to their nature in the 17th century. All contemporaneous writers, in describing the character of the middle class in the 18th century, agree that their pride and independence were extraordinary. Smythe says, "They are generous, friendly, and hospitable in the extreme; but mixed with such an appearance of rudeness, ferocity and haughtiness, which is, in fact, only a want of polish, occasioned by their deficiencies in education and in knowledge of mankind, as well as their general intercourse with slaves." Beverley spoke of them as being haughty and jealous of their liberties, and so impatient of restraint that they could hardly bear the thought of being controlled by any superior power. Hugh Jones, John Davis and Anbury also describe at length the pride of the middle class in this century.

Thus was the middle class, throughout the entire colonial period, forming and developing. From out the host of humble settlers, the overflow of England, there emerged that body of small planters in Virginia, that formed the real strength of the colony. The poor laborer, the hunted debtor, the captive rebel, the criminal had now thrown aside their old characters and become well-to-do and respected citizens. They had been made over—had been created anew by the economic conditions in which they found themselves, as filthy rags are purified and changed into white paper in the hands of the manufacturer. The relentless law of the survival of the fittest worked upon them with telling force and thousands that could not stand the severe test imposed upon them by conditions in the New World succumbed to the fever of the tobacco fields, or quitted the colony, leaving to stronger and better hands the upbuilding of the middle class. On the other hand, the fertility of the soil, the cheapness of land, the ready sale of tobacco combined to make possible for all that survived, a degree of prosperity unknown to them in England. And if for one short period, the selfishness of the English government, the ambition of the governor of the colony and the greed of the controlling class checked the progress of the commons, the people soon asserted their rights in open rebellion, and insured for themselves a share in the government and a chance to work out their own destiny, untrammelled by injustice and oppression. At the outbreak of the Revolution, the middle class was a numerous, intelligent and prosperous body, far superior to the mass of lowly immigrants from which it sprang.

BIBLIOGRAPHY

Anbury, Major Thomas.—Travels Through the Interior Parts of America in a series of Letters. Two Volumes. Printed for William Lane, Leadenhall Street, London, 1791. Major Anbury was a British officer who was captured at Saratoga and was brought south with the Convention Prisoners. He was paroled and had an opportunity to see much of Virginia. His observations upon the social life of the state are interesting, although tinged with prejudice. Viewing life in the New World with the eyes of one accustomed to the conventional ideas of England his writings throw light upon conditions in the Old Dominion that cannot be found in the works of native authors.

Bagby, George W.—Selections from the Writings of. Whittet and Shepperson, Richmond, Va., 1884. Two volumes. The articles in this work touching on Virginia life are well worth the attention of the historian. Dr. Bagby traveled through many parts of the state and had an unsurpassed opportunity of becoming acquainted with this life. The style is pleasing and the stories entertaining.

Barton, R. T.—Virginia Colonial Decisions. The Reports by Sir John Randolph and by Edward Barradall of the Decisions of the General Court of Virginia, 1728-1741. Two volumes. The Boston Book Company, Boston. Accompanying the decisions is a prospective sketch of the contemporaneous conditions during the period covered and of the lawyers who practiced at the bar of the General

Court in that day. In addition, the first volume contains an interesting account of the settling of Virginia and its history in the seventeenth century. Chapters are devoted to a description of the land, of the people, of the government, of the church, of the lack of cities, and of education. The chief value of the work, however, lies in the light that is thrown upon the history of Virginia during the years between 1728 and 1741, by the publication of the decisions which were before in manuscript form and practically inaccessible to the investigator.

Bernard, John.—Retrospections of America, 1797-1811. Harper and Brothers, New York, 1887. One volume. Bernard was famous in his time as a comedian and one of the earliest American managers of theatrical companies. He visited Virginia in 1799 and made many excursions to the homes of the wealthy planters. He thus had an opportunity to see the inner life of the most refined class of the state. His descriptions of their manners and morals, their tastes, their hospitality and their love of out-of-door sports are interesting and usually accurate.

Beverley, Robert.—The History and Present State of Virginia, in Four Parts. Printed for R. Parker, at the Unicorn, under the Piazza's of the Royal-Exchange, 1705. One volume. The work consists of an outline of the history of the colony from 1607 to 1705; of a statement of the natural productions of Virginia; its industries and its facilities for trade; of an account of the Indians and a brief summary of the government at the time of publication. The work is of value chiefly as a description of Virginia at the beginning of the 18th century. In the account given of the history of the colony in the earlier days there are many errors.

Brown, Alexander.—The Genesis of the United States. Two volumes. Houghton, Mifflin and Company, Boston and New York. This work consists of an account of the movement which resulted in the founding of Virginia, presented in the form of a series of documents not before printed, and of rare contemporaneous tracts reissued for the first time. The author, in a later work, criticises The Genesis of the United States in the following words, "I did not fully understand the case myself. I had failed (as every one else had previously done) to give due consideration to the influence of imperial politics on the history of this popular movement. I had also failed to consider properly the absolute control over the evidences, in print and in manuscript, possessed by the crown." The chief value of the work lies in the fact that it presents to the public numerous historical evidences which were for so many years inaccessible.

The First Republic in America. One volume. Houghton, Mifflin and Company, Boston and New York. This work gives an account of the origin of the nation, written from the records long concealed in England. It not only is not based on the printed histories of the day, but expressly repudiates them as false and unjust, and as written in the interest of the Court Party. Much discredit is thrown upon the narratives of Capt. John Smith. The author says; "He never returned there (Virginia) and—if every one else had done exactly as he did, there would have remained no colonists in Virginia, but mountains of books in England, conveying incorrect ideas, and filled with a mass of vanity, 'excellent criticism' and 'good advice,' amounting really to nothing." In a later work Mr. Brown says of The First Republic in America; "I wrote from the point of the Patriot Party. It was the first effort to restore to our foundation as a nation the inspiring political features of which it was robbed by those who controlled the evidences and histories under the crown."

English Politics in Early Virginia History. One volume. Houghton, Mifflin and Company, Boston and New York. The book is divided into five parts. The First Part gives an outline of the efforts of the "Patriot Party" in England to plant popular government in America and of the Court Party to prevent. Part Two recites the effort of the Court to obliterate the true history of the origin of Virginia. In Part Three the author shows the influence of politics on the historic record while the crown retained control of the evidences. Part Four shows what has been done both towards correcting and to perpetuating the error. In the Fifth Part is given a review of some of the features of the struggle of the "Patriot Party" and the Court Party.

Bruce, Philip Alexander.—Economic History of Virginia in the Seventeenth Century. Two volumes. Printed by the Macmillan Company, New York. This work treats of aboriginal Virginia, of the agricultural development after the coming of the English, the acquisition of title to land, the system of labor, the domestic economy of the planters, the part played by manufactures in the colony, the inconvenience occasioned by the scarcity of coin. The author has expended much labor in accumulating a mass of interesting and valuable detail, and the work is a veritable store house of information which is invaluable to the historian. There is no attempt made to point out the relation of the economic history of the time with the political, religious or social developments that were taking place in the 17th century. The work is valuable chiefly as a source book.

Social Life of Virginia in the Seventeenth Century. One volume. Printed for the author by Whittet and Shepperson, Richmond, Va. In the first portion of this book the author attempts to explain in some detail the origin of the higher planters in the colony. A startling array of individual cases are cited to prove the connection of at least a portion of this class with English families of education and rank. As usual with the author little attention is paid to generalizations and he arrives at his conclusions by induction rather than by deduction. Interesting chapters are devoted to social distinctions, social spirit, popular diversions, public and private occasions and duelling.

Burke, John.—The History of Virginia from its First Settlement to the Present Day. Four volumes. Published in 1804. The chief value of this work lies in the fact that it contains a number of documents of great interest to the historian. Chief among these is a series of papers relating to the dispute over the Arlington, Culpeper grant. As a general history of Virginia the work is antiquated. At the time Burke wrote a large part of the documents and pamphlets relating to the colony were inaccessible, and as a result he is compelled to pass over very important periods with the most cursory mention.

Burnaby, Andrew.—Travels through the Middle Settlements in North America in the Years 1759 and 1760; with Observations upon the State of the Colonies. Printed for T. Payne, at the Mews-Gate, London, 1798. One volume. Burnaby's criticisms of Virginia society are less accurate than those of others who have written on the same subject because his stay in the colony was so brief. He is by no means sympathetic with the life of the colony, chiefly because he does not understand it.

Byrd, William.—The Writings of "Col. William Byrd of Westover in Virginia Esq." Edited by John Spencer Bassett. One volume. Doubleday, Page and Company, New York, 1901. Col. Byrd gives an interesting picture in this work of the life upon the frontier of the colony in the first quarter of the 18th century. The style is flowing and easy, and the author shows a literary talent unusual in colonial writers. The Introduction by the editor consists of a sketch of the Byrd family. This is ably written, and the observations made upon Virginia politics and life show keen insight into the unique conditions that were moulding the character of the colony. It is, perhaps, a more valuable contribution to Virginia history than the writings which it introduces.

Campbell, Charles.—History of the Colony and Ancient Dominion of Virginia. One volume. J. B. Lippincott and Company, Philadelphia, 1860. In his preface the author says: "Her (Virginia's) documentary history, lying, much of it, scattered and fragmentary, in part slumbering in the dusty oblivion of Trans-Atlantic archives, ought to be collected with pious care, and embalmed in the perpetuity of print." The partial accomplishment of this task, so urgently advocated by the author, has rendered his work incomplete and insufficient for the present day. Upon numerous periods of Virginia history barely touched by him, a great light has since been thrown by the unearthing of manuscripts and pamphlets.

Chastellux, E. J.—Voyages dans l'Amérique Septentrionale. Chez Prault, Imprimeur du Roi, Paris, 1786. Two volumes. Chastellux was a Frenchman who visited various parts of America at the time of the Revolution. His observations upon social life in Virginia are less prejudiced than those of many of the foreign visitors to the colony at this period. The work is valuable in that it gives the impressions made by the higher class in Virginia upon one used to the refined life of France in the second half of the 18th century.

Cooke, John Esten.—Virginia, a History of the People. Houghton, Mifflin and Company, Boston, 1884. One volume. So many valuable documents and pamphlets treating of Virginia history have been made accessible since this work was published, that it is quite antiquated. In addition, the author has failed to make the best use of the material at his hands, and there are numberless errors for which there can be no excuse. One wonders, when reading the book, whether the author has ever taken the trouble to glance at Hening's Statutes, for he repeats old mistakes that were pointed out by Hening one hundred years ago. The style is entertaining and has given to the work a popularity out of proportion to its historical worth.

Dinwiddie, Robert.—The Official Records of Robert Dinwiddie. Introduction and notes by R. A. Brock. Virginia Historical Society, Richmond, Va., 1883. Two volumes. A large number of manuscripts of various kinds relating to the administration of Dinwiddie have been printed for the first time in this work. Great light is thrown upon Braddock's disasterous expedition and other important events of the French and Indian War. Dinwiddie's account of the obstinacy and unreasonable conduct of the burgesses should be studied in conjunction with the journals of the House which have recently been published.

Fiske, John.—Old Virginia and her Neighbors. Two volumes. Houghton, Mifflin and Company, Boston and New York, 1897. This work is written in the delightful and entertaining style so characteristic of the author, and like Macaulay's History of England holds the interest of the reader from beginning to end. Only a portion of the colonial period is covered, and this in a general and hap-hazard way. The narrative is not equally sustained throughout, some periods being dwelt upon in much detail, and others, equally important, passed over with but cursory mention. Fiske did not have access to many of the sources of Virginia history, and this led him into repeating some old errors.

Fithian, Philip Vickers.—Journal and Letters, 1767-1774. Edited for the Princeton Historical Association, by John Rogers Williams. One volume. Fithian was tutor at Nomini Hall, the home of Col. Robert Carter, during the years 1773 and 1774. His observations upon the life in the midst of which he was thrown, the life of the highest class of Virginians, are intensely interesting and very instructive. The author was a young theologian, who had received his education at Princeton, and who seemed strangely out of place in the gay society of aristocratic Westmoreland. For this very reason, however, his journal and letters are interesting, for he dwells with especial emphasis upon what was new or strange to him and has thus unconsciously given an excellent account of all that was unique or distinctive in the Virginia aristocracy.

Force, Peter.—Tracts and other Papers, Relating Principally to the Origin, Settlement and Progress of the Colonies in North America. Printed in 1836. Four volumes. By the preservation of these valuable documents Mr. Force has done a great service to the history of the colony of Virginia. The papers relating to Bacon's Rebellion are of especial interest, while Virginia's Cure, A Description of New Albion and Leah and Rachel are hardly less important.

Goodwin, Maud Wilder.—The Colonial Cavalier or Southern Life before the Revolution. Lowell, Coryell and Company, New York, 1894. One volume. This little work is well written and is in the main accurate. It offers an interesting picture of the Southern planter and the unique life that he led in the second half of the 18th century.

Hening, W. W.—The Statutes at Large; Being a Collection of all the Laws of Virginia, from the First Session of the Legislature, in the Year 1619. In thirteen volumes covering the period up to October, 1792. In 1836 Samuel Shepherd published three more volumes, covering the period from

1792 to 1806. In addition to the collection of laws the work contains many historical documents of great value. The Statutes at Large are invaluable to the student of Virginia history and they throw much light upon periods otherwise obscured in gloom. It is to Hening chiefly that the historian is indebted for his knowledge of the years covered by the first administration of Sir William Berkeley, while his information of what occurred during the Commonwealth Period would be slight indeed without The Statutes at Large. Since the Journals of the House of Burgesses have been copied, and thus made available to the investigator, the work is not so indispensable for some periods, but it constitutes a valuable adjunct to these papers and no historian can afford to neglect them. The work shows throughout the greatest care even in the minutest details and will remain a monument to the indefatigable energy and patience of Mr. Hening.

Howe, Henry.—Historical Collections of Virginia; containing a collection of the most interesting facts, traditions, biographical sketches, anecdotes, etc., relating to its history and antiquaries, etc. One volume. Published by Babcock and Company, 1845. In his preface the author says: "The primary object of the following pages is to narrate the most prominent events in the history of Virginia, and to give a geographical and statistical view of her present condition." In accomplishing the latter of these tasks Mr. Howe has done a real and lasting service to the history of the state. His description of the various counties in 1843 and the life of their people was the fruit of personal observation and as a consequence is usually accurate and trustworthy.

Howison, Robert R.—A History of Virginia, from its Discovery and Settlement by Europeans to the Present Time. Two Volumes. Carey and Hart, Philadelphia, 1846. The preface of the work has the following: "In writing the Colonial History, the author has endeavored to draw from the purest fountains of light the rays which he has sought to shed upon his subject." And throughout the book there is abundant evidence to show that Mr. Howison had studied the sources of Virginia history then available and had picked out as best he could the truth whenever his authorities differed. So much has been learned of the events he treats since 1846, however, that his work is today of little value.

Johns Hopkins University Studies in Historical and Political Science. The Johns Hopkins Press, Baltimore. A number of these studies touch upon colonial Virginia history and they have done much in bringing order out of the mass of facts to be found in old books, in documents and in journals. Some of the papers are: "Justice in Colonial Virginia, O. P. Chitwood; History of Suffrage in Virginia, J. A. C. Chandler; Representation in Virginia, J. A. C. Chandler; White Servitude in the Colony of Virginia, H. R. McIlwaine, and Virginia Local Institutions, Edward Ingle.

Jones, Hugh.—The Present State of Virginia. Printed for J. Clark, at the Bible under the Royal-Exchange, 1724. Reprinted for Joseph Sabin, New York. This work gives an entertaining and valuable picture of Virginia during the administration of Governor Spotswood. Those chapters are most useful which treat of the pursuits, the religion, the manners and the government of the colonists. The descriptions given are drawn largely from the personal observations of the author. This, together with the sincere and straightforward manner in which the book is written, leaves the impression of accuracy and trustworthiness.

Journals of the Council of Virginia as Upper House. Manuscript copies made of incomplete records in the State Library at Richmond, in the Library of the Virginia Historical Society. Arranged in three volumes as follows: I, 1685-1720; II, 1722-1747; III, 1748-1767. These journals are by no means so important as those of the House of Burgesses. They are devoted quite largely to routine matters and reflect but little of the political life of the colony. The historian, if he gives careful study to their pages, will be rewarded by passages here and there which draw aside the veil, and give fleeting pictures of the strife between the Council and the Burgesses.

Journals of the House of Burgesses.—In the State Library. Session of 1619; manuscript copies of sessions from 1680 to 1718, and from 1748 to 1772. These journals, so many of which have been buried for centuries in English archives, throw a flood of light upon the political life of the colony. They constitute by far the most important source of information upon the long and tireless struggle of the middle class in Virginia for a share in the conducting of the government. Something of this, of course, may be gleaned from the official correspondence of the governors, but this evidence is partisan in spirit and does injustice to the commons of Virginia. Hening gives in the main only bare statutes, and the discussions, the quarrels and the passions of the sessions are omitted. The journals are to Hening's work what the living person is to the stone image. It is a matter of the deepest regret that the journals from 1619 to 1680 are missing, for they leave a gap in Virginia history that it is impossible to fill.

Keith, Sir William.—The History of the British Plantations in America. Part One contains the History of Virginia. Printed by S. Richardson, London, 1738. The work is devoted almost entirely to the colony under the London Company. It contains little of value, following John Smith's account throughout and presenting nothing new either of documentary evidence or of criticism.

Long, Charles M.—Virginia County Names, Two Hundred and Seventy Years of Virginia History. The Neale Publishing Co., New York. This little volume throws much light upon the history of Virginia through the record left in the names of the counties. The work contains several valuable tables. One of these gives the governors of Virginia from 1607 to 1908.

McDonald Papers.—Copies of Papers in Brit. Rec. Office. Virginia State Library, Richmond. There were seven volumes of these documents, but two of them have been missing for many years. Vol. I covers the years from 1619 to 1626; Vol. II from 1627 to 1640; Vols. III and IV are missing; Vol. V from 1675 to 1681; Vol. VI from 1681 to 1685; Vol. VII from 1683 to 1695. This collection contains many papers that are to be found in Sainsbury, but they are usually more full, being often exact copies of the originals. In addition there are many papers in the McDonald collection not to be found elsewhere.

Maury, Richard L.—The Huguenots in Virginia. Col. Maury in this work has rendered an important service to Virginia history. On every page are evidences of the utmost care for truth and the greatest diligence in reaching it. Col. Maury made, before writing this book, a thorough study of the sources of Virginia history and the accuracy of his work reflects this labor.

Maxwell, William.—The Virginia Historical Register. Printed by Macfarlane and Ferguson, Richmond. In six volumes. This work is one of the fruits of the revival of interest in Virginia history which took place in the two decades preceding the Civil War. It contains many papers and documents printed for the first time, and no student of colonial history can afford to neglect it.

Meade, William.—Old Churches, Ministers and Families of Virginia. J. B. Lippincott and Co., Philadelphia. Two volumes. The title does not indicate all, nor the most valuable part, of the contents of this work. In addition to giving numerous facts in regard to the old churches and their ministers and congregations, the author has presented an ecclesiastical history of Virginia. The contest of the vestries with the governors to obtain and to keep control of the church, is carefully and ably set forth. Also, the relation of this struggle to the political life of the colony is kept constantly in sight. The appendix contains several papers relating to church affairs that are invaluable to the historian.

Miller, Elmer I.—The Legislature of the Province of Virginia. One volume. The Columbia University Press. The Macmillan Co., Agents. This work is but the assembling and arranging of numerous facts in regard to the General Assembly. It presents no new thoughts, it teaches no lessons in Virginia history, it settles none of the old problems, it presents no new ones. Unfortunately, also, the author did not have access to a large number of the journals of the House of Burgesses, which, it need hardly be added, are indispensable for an exhaustive study of the Assembly.

Neill, Edward D.—Virginia Vetusta, during the Reign of James I. Joel Munsell's Sons, Albany, 1885. The value of this work lies in the printing of numerous documents throwing light on the affairs of the colony under the London Company. Mr. Neill takes the ground that John Smith's narratives are not to be trusted, and he has made a long step towards correcting the errors contained in the works of that writer.

Virginia Carolorum: The Colony under the Rule of Charles the First and Second A. D. 1625-A. D. 1685, based upon manuscripts and documents of the period. Joel Munsel's Sons, Albany, 1886. Mr. Neill has been, with some justice, called the scavenger of Virginia history. In Virginia Carolorum he has gathered many papers and documents which are bitterly hostile to the colony, and represent it in a light far from attractive. As, however, it is the duty of the historian to present truth, no matter whether pleasant or disagreeable, this volume is of undoubted value. Its chief fault lies in the author's failure to point out the prejudices of some of those writers that are quoted, thus leaving the reader to give to their statements more weight than they can justly claim.

Page, Thomas Nelson.—The Old Dominion her Making and her Manners. Charles Scribner's Sons, New York, 1908. This work consists of a series of essays, in part addresses delivered before various societies at different times. It is written in the delightful style for which Dr. Page is so well known and is as entertaining as Fiske's The Old Dominion and her Neighbors. Perhaps the most valuable chapter is that devoted to Colonial Life.

The Old South, Essays Social and Political. Charles Scribner's Sons, New York, 1892. This work consists of a series of well written articles upon anti-bellum Virginia. Among these are Glimpses of Life in Colonial Virginia, The Old Virginia Lawyer, and the Negro Question. Dr. Page's intimate knowledge of the life upon the plantation makes him peculiarly well qualified to write a book of this nature.

Perry, William Stevens.—Papers Relating to the History of the Church in Virginia, 1650-1776. Printed in 1870. One volume. This collection of manuscripts is invaluable to the historian. Some of the papers have been preserved in other works, but many are to be had here only. The documents relating to the controversy between the vestries and the governors for control of the appointing of ministers are of great importance. Not only do these papers give much information upon the ecclesiastical history of the colony, but they throw light that cannot be gotten elsewhere upon political conditions.

Sainsbury, Noel W.—Papers. Twenty manuscript volumes in the Virginia State Library. These papers are chiefly copies in abstract of the official correspondence of the home government, and the governors and secretaries of Virginia. They cover the long period from the founding of the colony until the year 1730. The letters of the governors to the Lords of Trade and Plantations are often quite frank and give the student an insight into their purposes and their methods that can be gained from no other source. They should be studied in connection with the Journals of the House of Burgesses, for they will make clear many points that are purposely left obscure in the transactions of the Assembly. It is a matter for regret that the papers are but abstracts and the State of Virginia should have exact copies made of the originals.

Sale, Edith Tunis.—Manors of Virginia in Colonial Times. One volume. J. B. Lippincott Co., 1909. This work contains accounts of no less than twenty-four manors, including in the list Shirley, Westover, Brandon, Rosewell, Monticello, Gunston Hall, etc. The descriptions of the houses are made more vivid and entertaining by sketches of the families that occupied them. The volume is rich in illustrations.

Smith, Capt. John.—Works of, edited by Edward Arber. On Montague Road, Birmingham, England, 1884. Capt. Smith's account of the settling of Jamestown and the struggle of the colonists there was for many years accepted without cavil by historians. His story of his own heroism and of the wickedness of his colleagues has been embodied in almost every American school history. Mr. Charles Dean, in 1860, was the first to question Smith's veracity, and since that date many historians have taken the ground that his works are quite unreliable. Alexander Brown has contended that his account of Virginia was purposely falsified to further the designs of the Court Party during the reign of James I. The discovery of numerous documents relating to the years covered by Smith's histories, and the application of historical criticism to his work, cannot but incline the student to distrust much that he has written.

Spotswood, Alexander.—The Official Letters of. Edited by R. A. Brock. Virginia Historical Society. Two volumes. These letters are of great value, for they touch upon the most important events of Spotwood's administration. They present, of course, the governor's views upon public matters, and must be studied in conjunction with other evidence for a just understanding of the times. This, fortunately, is to be had in various manuscripts, in the Journals of the House of Burgesses, the Journals of the Council and in scattered papers, some of which have been printed.

Stanard, Mary Newton.—The Story of Bacon's Rebellion. The Neale Publishing Co., 1907. One volume. The authoress has had before her in this work the general interest that attaches to the picturesque subject and has written in a light and pleasing style. No deep analysis of the causes and results of the Rebellion are given, but the reader has the feeling throughout that the facts presented have been gathered with great care and that the narrative is as accurate as labor and research can make it.

Stanard, William G. and Mary Newton.—The Colonial Virginia Register. Joel Munsell's Sons, Albany, 1902. This work contains the names of the Governors of Virginia in the Colonial Period, the Secretaries of State, the Auditors General, the Receivers General, the Treasurers, the Attorneys General, the Surveyors General, the Council members, the members of the House of Burgesses and the members of the Conventions of 1775 and 1776.

Stith, William.—The History of the First Discovery and Settlement of Virginia. William Parks, Williamsburg, 1747. Stith had in the preparation of this work access to some manuscripts which are not now in existence. For this reason the work will retain a certain value as a source book of Virginia history. In the main, however, he follows Smith's story with servility, for it did not occur to him that much of the latter was not trustworthy. Stith takes his history no further than the year 1624.

The Lower Norfolk County Virginia Antiquary. Press of the Friedenwald Co., Baltimore. Five volumes. This magazine has rendered a true service to Virginia history by publishing many valuable documents hitherto hidden or inaccessible. These papers touch Virginia life in the Colonial Period in many phases and throw light on points hitherto obscure or misunderstood.

The Southern Literary Messenger.—In 1845 and in the years immediately following, this magazine, stimulated by the great interest that was being shown in Virginia history at that time, published a number of documents and articles relating to colonial times. Among these is a reproduction of John Smith's True Relation; papers relating to Sir William Berkeley, contributed by Peter Force; and an account of the General Assembly of 1715.

The Virginia Magazine of History and Biography. —Published by the Virginia Historical Society. Seventeen volumes. The wealth of material contained in these volumes can hardly be estimated. Countless papers, formerly scattered abroad, or hidden in the musty archives of libraries, have been published and rendered accessible to the historian. So vastly important are they that no account of colonial Virginia, no matter of what period, can afford to neglect them. They touch every phase of the life of the colony, political, social, economic and religious. Much space has been given to biography. From the standpoint of the constructive historian it is to be regretted that the magazine has devoted so little of its space to short articles culling and arranging and rendering more serviceable the facts published in documentary form. But the magazine has done and is still doing a work of vast importance in collecting and preserving historical material.

Tyler, Lyon G.—Narratives of Early Virginia, 1606-1625. Charles Scribner's Sons. One volume. This work includes many important and interesting papers of the period of the London Company. Selections are made from Capt. John Smith's works. Among the papers given are Observations by Master Geo. Percy; The Relation of the Lord De-La-Ware; Letter of Don Diego de Molina; Letter of Father Pierre Biard; Letter of John Rolfe; and The Virginia Planters' Answer to Capt. Butler.

Williamsburg, the Old Colonial Capital. Whittet and Shepperson, Richmond. An account is given of the settlement and history of the town. This is followed by a brief description of Bruton church and its ministers and by a long chapter on the college. Other chapters are devoted to the capitol, the governors' house, the State prison, the powder magazine, the theatre, the Raleigh Tavern, the printing office, the jail, the court-houses, the hospital for the insane, etc.

The Cradle of the Republic: Jamestown and James River. Whittet and Shepperson, Richmond. The author has described carefully and minutely the village, locating, when possible, public buildings and the homes of the inhabitants. The last chapter is devoted to the places along the river and interesting accounts are given of their origin and their history.

Virginia Historical Society.—Abstract of the Proceedings of the Virginia Company of London, 1619-1624, prepared from the records in the Library of Congress by Conway Robinson and edited by R. A. Brock. Two volumes. Since the infant colony at Jamestown was so intimately connected with the great company which gave it life that the one cannot be understood without a knowledge of the other, this publication of the proceedings of the company is of great importance to a correct understanding of early Virginia history.

Miscellaneous Papers. Edited by R. A. Brock, 1887. On volume. This collection contains the Charter of the Royal African Company; A Report on the Huguenot Settlement, 1700; Papers of Geo. Gilmer, of Pen Park; and other valuable papers.

Proceedings of the Society at the Annual Meeting Held in 1891, with Historical Papers Read on the Occasion, and Others. Edited by R. A. Brock. One Volume.

William and Mary Quarterly.—Edited by Dr. Lyon G. Tyler. Williamsburg, Va. Seventeen volumes. This magazine is devoted to the history of Virginia and has published numerous papers relating to that subject. Great space has been devoted to biography and much light has been thrown upon the ancestry of scores of families. Of great value are a number of articles giving in condensed and clear form the results of study of the new material brought forth. Thus there is a paper upon Education in Colonial Virginia, another on Colonial Libraries, etc. The magazine, like the Virginia Magazine of History and Biography, has rendered an invaluable service to Virginia history.

Thomas J. Wertenbaker was born at Charlottesville, Va., Feb. 6, 1879. After receiving his primary education at private schools he entered Jones' University School. Later he attended the Charlottesville Public High School. In the fall of 1896 he entered the Academic Department of the University of Virginia, where he remained as a student until 1900. During the session of 1900-1901, he taught at St. Matthew's School, of Dobbs Ferry, N. Y. In September, 1901, he re-entered the University of Virginia and in 1902 received the degrees of Bachelor of Arts and Master of Arts. For some years after this he was engaged in newspaper work, being editor of the Charlottesville Morning News and editor on the Baltimore News. In the fall of 1906 he re-entered the University of Virginia as a graduate student. In 1907 he was elected Associate Professor of History and Economics at the Texas Agricultural and Mechanical College and filled that position for two sessions. In 1909 he was made Instructor of History at the University of Virginia and once more matriculated in the Graduate Department of that institution. He is a member of the American Historical Association and the Virginia Historical Society and is the author of several historical articles and essays.

The Planters of Colonial Virginia

The PLANTERS OF COLONIAL VIRGINIA

By THOMAS J. WERTENBAKER

THE PLANTERS OF COLONIAL VIRGINIA

PREFACE

America since the days of Captain John Smith has been the land of hope for multitudes in Europe. In many an humble home, perhaps in some English village, or an Ulster farm, or in the Rhine valley, one might find a family assembled for the reading of a letter from son, or brother, or friend, who had made the great venture of going to the New World. "Land is abundant here and cheap," the letter would state. "Wages are high, food is plentiful, farmers live better than lords. If one will work only five days a week one can live grandly."

In pamphlets intended to encourage immigration the opportunities for advancement were set forth in glowing colors. In Virginia alone, it was stated, in 1649, there were "of kine, oxen, bulls, calves, twenty thousand, large and good." When the traveller Welby came to America he was surprised to "see no misery, no disgusting army of paupers, not even beggars; while Henry B. Fearson noted that laborers were "more erect in their posture, less careworn in their countenances" than those of Europe.

In Virginia, as in other colonies, it was the cheapness of land and the dearness of labor which gave the newcomer his chance to rise. The rich man might possess many thousands of acres, but they would profit him nothing unless he could find the labor to put them under cultivation. Indentured workers met his needs in part, but they were expensive, hard to acquire, and served for only four years. If he hired freemen he would have to pay wages which in England would have seemed fantastic.

Thus the so-called servants who had completed their terms and men who had come over as freemen found it easy to earn enough to buy small plantations of their own. That thousands did so is shown by the Rent Roll which is published as an appendix to this book. One has only to glance at it to see that the large plantations are vastly outnumbered by the small farms of the yeomen. It proves that Virginia at the beginning of the eighteenth century was not the land of huge estates, worked by servants and slaves, but of a numerous, prosperous middle class.

Owning plantations of from fifty to five hundred acres, cultivating their fields of tobacco, their patches of Indian corn and wheat, their vegetable gardens and orchards with their own labor or the labor of their sons, the yeomen enjoyed a sense of independence and dignity. It was their votes which determined the character of the Assembly, it was they who resisted most strongly all assaults upon the liberties of the people.

As the small farmer, after the day's work was over, sat before his cottage smoking his long clay pipe, he could reflect that for him the country had fulfilled its promise. The land around him was his own; his tobacco brought in enough for him to purchase clothes, farm implements, and household goods.

But he frowned as he thought of the slave ship which had come into the nearby river, and landed a group of Negroes who were all bought by his wealthy neighbors. If Virginia were flooded with slaves, would it not cheapen production and lower the price of tobacco? Could he and his sons, when they hoed their fields with their own hands, compete with slave labor?

The event fully justified these fears. The yeoman class in Virginia was doomed. In the face of the oncoming tide they had three alternatives—to save enough money to buy a slave or two, to leave the country, or to sink into poverty.

It was the acquiring of a few slaves by the small planter which saved the middle class. Before the end of the colonial period a full fifty per cent. of the slaveholders had from one to five only. Seventy-five per cent. had less than ten. The small farmer, as he led his newly acquired slaves from the auction block to his plantation may have regretted that self-preservation had forced him to depend on their labor rather than his own. But he could see all around him the fate of those who had no slaves, as they became "poor white trash." And he must have looked on with pity as a neighbor gathered up his meager belongings and, deserting his little plantation, set out for the remote frontier.

It was one of the great crimes of history, this undermining of the yeoman class by the importation of slaves. The wrong done to the Negro himself has been universally condemned; the wrong done the white man has attracted less attention. It effectively deprived him of his American birthright—the high return for his labor. It transformed Virginia and the South from a land of hard working, self-respecting, independent yeomen, to a land of slaves and slaveholders.

Princeton, New Jersey
August, 1957

THOMAS J. WERTENBAKER

CONTENTS

CHAPTER I

England in the New World

At the beginning of the Seventeenth century colonial expansion had become for England an economic necessity. Because of the depletion of her forests, which constituted perhaps the most important of her natural resources, she could no longer look for prosperity from the old industries that for centuries had been her mainstay. In the days when the Norman conquerors first set foot upon English soil the virgin woods, broken occasionally by fields and villages, had stretched in dense formation from the Scottish border to Sussex and Devonshire. But with the passage of five centuries a great change had been wrought. The growing population, the expansion of agriculture, the increasing use of wood for fuel, for shipbuilding, and for the construction of houses, had by the end of the Tudor period so denuded the forests that they no longer sufficed for the most pressing needs of the country.

Even at the present day it is universally recognized that a certain proportion of wooded land is essential to the prosperity and productivity of any country. And whenever this is lacking, not only do the building, furniture, paper and other industries suffer, but the rainfall proves insufficient, spring floods are frequent and the fertility of the soil is impaired by washing. These misfortunes are slight, however, compared with the disastrous results of the gradual thinning out of the forests of Elizabethan England. The woods were necessary for three all-important industries, the industries upon which the prosperity and wealth of the nation were largely dependent —shipbuilding, for which were needed timber, masts, pitch, tar, resin; the manufacture of woolens, calling for a large supply of potash; smelting of all kinds, since three hundred years ago wood and not coal was the fuel used in the furnaces. It was with the deepest apprehension, then, that thoughtful Englishmen watched the gradual reduction of the forest areas, for it seemed to betoken for their country a period of declining prosperity and economic decay. "When therefore our mils of Iron and excesse of building have already turned our greatest woods into pasture and champion within these few years," says a writer of this period, "neither the scattered forests of England, nor the diminished groves of Ireland will supply the defect of our navy."[1]

From this intolerable situation England sought relief through foreign commerce. If she could no longer smelt her own iron, if she could not produce ship-stores or burn her own wood ashes, these things might be procured from countries where the forests were still extensive, countries such as those bordering the Baltic—Germany, Poland, Russia, Sweden. And so the vessels of the Muscovy Company in the second half of the Sixteenth century passed through the Cattegat in large numbers to make their appearance at Reval and Libau and Danzig, seeking there the raw materials so vitally necessary to England. "Muscovia and Polina doe yeerly receive many thousands for Pitch, Tarre, Sope Ashes, Rosen, Flax, Cordage, Sturgeon, Masts, Yards, Wainscot, Firres, Glasse, and such like," wrote Captain John Smith, "also Swethland for Iron and Copper."[2]

But this solution of her problem was obviously unsatisfactory to England. The northern voyage was long, dangerous and costly; the King of Denmark, who controlled the entrance to the Baltic, had it within his power at any moment to exclude the English traders; the Muscovy company no longer enjoyed exemption from customs in Prussia, Denmark and Russia. In case war should break out among the northern nations this trade might for a time be cut off entirely, resulting in strangulation for England's basic industries. "The merchant knoweth," said the author of *A True Declaration,* "that through the troubles in Poland & Muscovy, (whose eternall warres are like the Antipathy of the Dragon & Elephant) all their traffique for Masts, Deales, Pitch, Tarre, Flax, Hempe, and Cordage, are every day more and more indangered."[3] Moreover, the trade was much impeded by the ice which for several months each year choked some of the northern ports.

The most alarming aspect of this unfortunate situation was the effect of the shortage of shipbuilding material upon the merchant marine. Situated as it was upon an island, England enjoyed communication with the nations of the world only by means of the ocean pathways. Whatever goods came to her doors, whatever goods of her own manufacture she sent to foreign markets, could be transported only by sea. It was a matter of vital import to her, then, to build up and maintain a fleet of merchant vessels second to none. But this was obviously difficult if not impossible when "the furniture of shipping" such as "Masts, Cordage, Pitch, Tar, Rossen" were not produced in quantity by England itself, and could be had "only by the favor of forraigne potency."[4] Already, it was stated, the decay of shipping was manifest, while large numbers of able mariners were forced to seek employment in other countries. "You know how many men for want of imploiment, betake themselves to Tunis, Spaine and Florence," declared one observer, "and to serve in courses not warrantable, which would better beseeme our own walles and borders to bee spread with such branches, that their native countrey and not forreine Princes might reape their fruit, as being both exquisite Navigators, and resolute men for service, as any the world affords."[5]

It must be remembered that the merchant vessel three hundred years ago constituted an important part of the nation's sea defence. The fleet which met the mighty Spanish Armada in the Channel and inflicted upon it so decisive a defeat, was made up in large part of volunteer ships from every English port. And the Britisher knew full well that the merchant marine constituted the "wooden walls" of his country, knew that its decay would leave England almost defenseless. At the moment when one able writer was pointing out that "the Realme of England is an Island impossible to be otherwise fortified than by stronge shippes," another was complaining that there were scarce two vessels of 100 tons belonging to the whole city of Bristol, and few or none along the Severn from Gloucester to Land's End on one side, and to Milford Haven on the other.[6]

For this intolerable situation there could be but one remedy —England must secure colonial possessions to supply her with the products for which her forests were no longer sufficient. Her bold navigators had already crossed the Atlantic, returning with alluring stories of the limitless resources of the New World, of mighty forests spreading in unbroken array for hundreds of miles along the coast and back into the interior as far as the eye could see.[7] Why, it was asked, should Englishmen be forced to make the hazardous journey to the Baltic in order to procure from other nations what they might easily have for themselves by taking possession of some of the limitless unoccupied areas of America? It was folly to remain in economic bondage while the road to independence stretched so invitingly before them.

Long before the Goodspeed, the Discovery and the Sarah

Constant turned their prows into the waters of the James, able English writers were urging upon the nation the absolute necessity for colonial expansion. In 1584 the farseeing Hakluyt pointed out that the recent voyage of Sir Humphrey Gilbert had proved that "pitche, tarr, rosen, sope ashes" could be produced in America in great plenty, "yea, as it is thought, ynoughe to serve the whole realme."[8] Captain Christopher Carleill had the previous year made an effort to persuade the Muscovy Company to divert its energies toward America. Why remain under the power of the King of Denmark, he asked, or other princes who "command our shippes at their pleasure," when all the products of the Baltic regions were to be had from unoccupied territories which so easily could be placed under the English flag?

It has often been taken for granted that the statesmen and merchants of three centuries ago pursued always a mistaken and shortsighted economic policy. John Fiske assures us that even at the close of the Eighteenth century the barbarous superstitions of the Middle Ages concerning trade between nations still flourished with scarcely diminished vitality. Yet it requires but a cursory study of the theories and arguments of the Elizabethan economists to realize that they were men of ability and vision, that they knew what was needed and how to procure it, that they were nearer right than many have supposed. In fact, they acted upon sound economic principles a century and a half before Adam Smith formulated and expounded them.

These men realized keenly that England's safety demanded a larger measure of economic independence and they pointed out what seemed to be the only available means of securing it. Since her forests upon which her prosperity in the past had been so largely based, were nearing the point of exhaustion, she must expand to embrace new lands where the virgin growth of trees stood untouched. If this is barbarous, then the recent efforts of Italy to gain an independent coal supply, of Great Britain to get control of various oil fields, of the United States to build up a dye industry, are all likewise barbarous. In fact the world today in matters of economic policy has by no means gotten away from the conceptions of the men whose able writings cleared the way for the beginning of the British colonial empire.

But it must not be supposed that England in this matter was concerned only for her supply of naval stores, potash and pig iron. There were other products, not so vital it is true, but still important, which she was forced to seek abroad. From the south of Europe came salt, sugar, wine, silk, fruits; from the Far East saltpetre and dyes, together with spices for making palatable the winter's stock of food; from Holland came fish, from France wine and silk. And as in the Baltic, so elsewhere the merchants of London and Bristol and Plymouth found their activities resented and their efforts blocked and thwarted.

All commerce with the dominions of the King of Spain was carried on with the greatest difficulty. "Our necessitie of oiles and colours for our clothinge trade being so greate," pointed out Hakluyt, "he may arreste almoste the one halfe of our navye, our traficque and recourse beinge so greate in his dominions." The rich trade with the Far East was seriously hampered by the Turks, through whose territories it had to pass, and often a heavy tribute was laid upon it by the Sultan and his minions. Even after the merchants had succeeded in lading their vessels in the eastern Mediterranean with goods from the Orient, they still had to run the gauntlet of the hostile Powers who infested that sea. If they escaped the Knights of Malta, they might be captured by the corsairs of Algeria or Tripoli.

The trade with France had also declined greatly during the closing years of the Sixteenth century. Not only had the religious wars proved a tremendous obstacle, but the government at Paris discriminated against the woolens from England by means of custom duties, while the French workmen were themselves manufacturing cloth of excellent quality in larger amounts than had hitherto been thought possible. In the Low Countries the long and bitter struggle of the people against the bloody bands of Alva had wrought such destruction and had so ruined industry that all foreign commerce had greatly declined.[9]

There can be no surprise, then, that many English economists felt that a crisis had been reached, that nothing save the immediate establishment of colonies would prevent disaster. With the woolen industry declining, with the shipbuilding centres almost idle, with able mariners deserting the service, with the foreign market gradually closing to English wares, with the country overrun with idle and starving laborers, with some of her chief natural resources nearly exhausted and the trade by which her needs were replenished in constant danger, England turned to America as her hope for salvation. Upon securing a foothold in the New World, hitherto monopolized by Spain and Portugal, depended Albion's future greatness and prosperity.

It is this which gave to the London Company its national character, and made its efforts to establish a colony across the Atlantic a crusade, a movement in which every Englishman was vitally concerned. The great lords and wealthy merchants who comprised the Company knew well enough that there was little hope of immediate returns upon the money they subscribed so liberally. They expected to receive their reward in another way, in the revival of English industrial life and the restoration of English economic independence. It is a singular perversion of history, an inaccurate interpretation of men and events, which for so many years beclouded our conception of the beginning of the British colonial empire. The settlement at Jamestown was not the product of a selfish, private venture, but the fruition of long years of thought and endeavor, long years of pleading with the English public, of the conscious and deliberate efforts of the nation to expand to the New World, to break the bonds of economic dependence and to restore to England the place in the world which rightfully was hers.

In addition to, but closely associated with, the economic causes of Anglo-Saxon expansion was the realization in England of the need for prompt action in putting a limit to the growing domains of the King of Spain. In the century which had elapsed since Columbus opened a new world to the peoples of Europe, this monarch had seized the richest part of the great prize, and was still reaching forward to the north and to the south. Unless England took advantage of the present opportunity, the vast American continents might be closed to her forever. Anglo-Saxon civilization in that case might well remain permanently cooped up in the little island that had seen its inception, while the Spanish language and Spanish institutions expanded to embrace the garden spots of the world.[10]

There were still other motives for this great movement. The English felt the prime necessity of discovering and controlling a new route to the East, they wished to expand the influence of the Anglican church and convert the Indians, they hoped to seize and fortify strategic points in America which would aid them in their struggles with the Spaniards. But these things, important as they were, paled beside the pressing necessity of national expansion, of rehabilitating English industrial life, restoring the merchant marine and securing economic independence.

Thus, when Captain Newport returned in 1607 to report that the colony of Virginia had been safely launched, many Englishmen were aroused to a high pitch of hope and expectation. Now at last a province had been secured which could supply the raw materials which England so greatly needed. The active supporters of the undertaking were lavish in their promises. Virginia would yield better and cheaper timber for shipping than Prussia or Poland, she would furnish potash in abundance, and since wood could there be had for the cutting, her copper and iron ore could be smelted on the spot. Wine could be made there, as excellent as that of the Canaries, they boasted, while it was hoped soon to manufacture silk rivalling in fineness that of Persia or of Turkey. The waters of the colony were full of "Sturgion, Caviare and new land fish of the best," her fields could produce hemp for cordage and flax for linen. As for pitch, tar, turpentine and boards, there was a certainty of a rich return.[11] In February 1608, the Council of Virginia wrote to the corporation of Plymouth: "The staple and certain Comodities we have are Soap-ashes, pitch, tar, dyes of sundry sorts and rich values, timber for all uses, fishing for sturgeon and divers other sorts . . . making of Glass and Iron, and no improbable hope of richer mines."[12]

And no sooner had the infant colony been established than the Company turned with enthusiasm to the production of these highly desired commodities. A number of foreigners, Dutchmen and Poles skilled in the manufacture of ship-stores, were sent over to make a start with pitch, tar, turpentine and potash. They were to act as instructors, also, and it was expected that within a few years the Virginia forests would be filled with workers in these trades. Unfortunately their efforts met with ill success, and save for a few small samples of pitch and tar which were sent to England, nothing of value was produced.

For this failure the reason is apparent. All the able economists and statesmen who had predicted that the colony would become an industrial center had overlooked one vitally important factor—the lack of cheap labor. No matter how rich in natural resources, Virginia could not hope to compete with the long-established industries of Europe and Asia, because she lacked the abundant population requisite to success. It had been imagined by Hakluyt and others that the colony could avail herself of the surplus population of England, could drain off the upper stratum of the idle and unemployed. What more feasible than to set these men to work in the forests of the New World to produce the raw materials the want of which was responsible for unemployment in England itself!

But the voyage across the Atlantic was so long and costly, that it proved impossible to transport in any reasonable length of time enough workers to Virginia to supply her needs. And the few thousand that came over in the early years of the Seventeenth century were in such great demand that they could secure wages several times higher than those in vogue throughout Europe. Thus the London Company, from the very outset, found itself face to face with a difficulty which it could never surmount. Virginia could not compete with the ship-stores of the Baltic nations because her labor, when indeed it was found possible to secure labor at all, was far more expensive than that of Poland or Sweden or Russia. It mattered not that the Company sent over indentured servants, bound by their contracts to work for a certain number of years; the effect was the same. The cost of transportation swallowed up the profits from the servant's labor, when that labor was expended upon industries which had to face the competition of the cheap workers of the Old World.

It speaks well for the acumen of Captain John Smith that

he seems to have been the first to grasp clearly this truth. He wrote that the workingmen had made a beginning of "Pitch and Tarre, Glass, Sope-ashes and Clapboard," but that little had been accomplished. "If you rightly consider what an infinite toyle it is in Russia and Swetland, where the woods are proper for naught else, and though there be the helpe both of man and beast in those ancient Common-wealths, which many a hundred years have used it, yet thousands of those poor people can scarce get necessaries to live . . . you must not expect from us any such matter."[13]

The attempt to produce iron in Virginia was pursued even more vigorously, but with equally poor success. The early settlers, eager to assure the Company that the venture they had entered upon would soon yield a rich return, spoke enthusiastically of the numerous indications of the presence of iron ore. In 1609 Captain Newport brought with him to England a supply of ore from which sixteen or seventeen tons of metal were extracted of a quality equal or superior to that obtained from any European country. The iron was sold to the East India Company at the rate of £4 a ton.[14] Immediately plans were launched for taking advantage of what seemed to be a splendid opportunity. In the course of the first three years machinery for smelting and manufacturing iron was sent over and men were set to work to operate it. But the difficulties proved too great and ere long the attempt had to be abandoned.

The Company had no idea of relinquishing permanently its quest for staple commodities, however, and soon a new and far more ambitious project was set on foot for extracting the ore. The spot selected was at Falling Creek, in the present county of Chesterfield, a few miles below the rapids of the James river. George Sandys had noted with satisfaction some years before that the place was in every respect suited for iron smelting, for in close proximity to the ore was wood in abundance, stones for the construction of the furnace and deep water for transportation. To him it seemed that nature itself had selected the site and endowed it with every facility which the enterprise could require.[15] Here the London Company spent from £4,000 to £5,000 in a supreme effort to make their colony answer in some degree the expectations which had been placed in it. A Captain Blewit, with no less than 80 men, was sent over to construct the works, upon which, they declared, were fixed the eyes of "God, Angels and men." But Blewit soon succumbed to one of the deadly epidemics which yearly swept over the little colony, and a Mr. John Berkeley, accompanied by 20 experienced workers, came over to take his place.

At first things seem to have gone well with this ambitious venture. Soon the Virginia forests were resounding to the whir of the axe and the crash of falling trees, to the exclamations of scores of busy men as they extracted the ore, built their furnace and began the work of smelting. Operations had progressed so far that it was confidently predicted that soon large quantities of pig iron would be leaving the James for England, when an unexpected disaster put an abrupt end to the enterprise. In the terrible massacre of 1622, when the implacable Opechancanough attempted at one stroke to rid the country of its white invaders, the little industrial settlement at Falling Creek was completely destroyed. The furnace was ruined, the machinery thrown into the river, the workmen butchered. This project, which had absorbed so much of the attention and resources of the Company, is said to have yielded only a shovel, a pair of tongs and one bar of iron.[16]

The history of the attempts to establish glass works in Virginia is also a story of wasted energy and money, of final failure. The Dutch and Polish workers who came in 1608 set up a furnace at Jamestown,[17] but nothing more is heard of them, and it is clear that they met with no success. Nor did Captain William Norton, who arrived in 1621 with a number of skilled Italian glass workers fare any better.[18] In 1623 George Sandys wrote: "Capt. Norton dyed with all save one of his servants, the Italians fell extremely sick yet recovered; but I conceave they would gladly make the work to appear unfeasable, that they might by that means be dismissed for England. The fier hath now been for six weeks in ye furnace and yet nothing effected. They claim that the sand will not run." Shortly after this the workmen brought matters to an end by cracking the furnace with a crowbar.[18]

Thus ended in complete failure the efforts of England to reap what she considered the legitimate fruits of this great enterprise. The day of which her farseeing publicists had dreamed had arrived; she had at last challenged the right of Spain to all North America, her sons were actually settled on the banks of the James, a beginning had been made in the work of building a colonial empire. But the hope which had so fired the mind of Hakluyt, the hope of attaining through Virginia British economic independence, was destined never to be fulfilled. However lavishly nature had endowed the colony with natural resources, however dense her forests, however rich her mines, however wide and deep her waterways, she could not become an industrial community. Fate had decreed for her another destiny. But England was reluctant to accept the inevitable in this matter. Long years after Sir Edwin Sandys and his fellow workers of the London Company had passed to their rest, we find the royal ministers urging upon the colony the necessity of producing pig iron and silk and potash, and promising every possible encouragement in the work. But the causes which operated to bring failure in 1610 or 1620 prevented success in 1660 and 1680. Virginia had not the abundant supply of labor essential to the development of an industrial community and for many decades, perhaps for centuries, could not hope to attain it. Her future lay in the discovery and exploitation of one staple commodity for which she was so preëminently adapted that she could, even with her costly labor, meet the competition of other lands. The future history of Virginia was to be built up around the Indian plant tobacco.

CHAPTER II

THE INDIAN WEED

HISTORY is baffling in its complexity. The human mind instinctively strives for simplicity, endeavors to reproduce all things to set rules, to discover the basic principles upon which all action is based. And in various lines of research much success has attended these efforts. We know the laws underlying the movements of the planets, of various chemical reactions, of plant and animal life. It is inevitable, then, that attempts should be made to accomplish similar results in history, to master the vast multitude of facts which crowd its pages, many of them seemingly unrelated, and show that after all they obey certain fundamental laws. Despite the vaunted freedom of the human will, it is maintained, mankind like the planets or the chemical agents, cannot escape the operation of definite forces to which it is subjected. And if these forces are studied and understood, to some extent at least, the course of future events may be predicted.

Thus it may be accepted as practically established that in any country and with any people a condition of continued disorder and anarchy must be succeeded by one of despotism. History records, we believe, no exception to this rule, while there are many instances which tend to confirm it. The absolute rule of the Caesars followed the anarchy of the later Roman republic, the Oliverian Protectorate succeeded the British civil wars, the first French Empire the Reign of Terror, the Bolshevik despotism the collapse of the old regime in Russia. Such will always be the case, we are told, because mankind turns instinctively to any form of government in quest of protection from anarchy, and the easiest form of government to establish and operate is despotism.

Not content with generalizations of this kind, however, certain historians have undertaken to reduce all human action to some one great fundamental principle. The Freudian view emphasizes the influence of sex; Buckle maintains that the effect of climate is all-powerful. In recent years many students, while not agreeing that the solution of the problem is quite so simple, yet believe that underlying all social development will be found economic forces of one kind or another, that in commerce and industry and agriculture lies the key to every event of moment in the history of mankind. Often these forces have been obscured and misunderstood, but close study will always reveal them. It is folly to waste time, they say, as writers have so long done, in setting forth the adventures of this great man or that, in dwelling upon the details of political struggles or recounting the horrors of war. All these are but surface indications of the deeper movements underneath, movements in every case brought about by economic developments.

But this interpretation of history is by no means universally accepted. While admitting readily that the conditions surrounding the production and exchange of useful commodities have affected profoundly the course of events, many historians deny that they give the key to every important movement. We must study also the progress of human thought, of religion, of politics, or our conception of history will be warped and imperfect. How is it possible to explain the French religious wars of the Sixteenth century by the theory of economic causes? In what way does it account for the rebellion of Virginia and North Carolina and Maryland against the British government in 1775? How can one deny that the assassination of Abraham Lincoln affected profoundly the course of American history?

These efforts to simplify the meaning of human events have often led to error, have stressed certain events too strongly, have minimized others. The complexity of history is self-evident; we must for the present at least content ourselves with complex interpretations of it. If there be any great underlying principles which explain all, they have yet to be discovered.

Thus it would be folly in the study of colonial Virginia to blind ourselves to the importance of various non-economic factors, the love of freedom which the settlers brought with them from England, their affection for the mother country, the influence of the Anglican church. Yet it is obvious that we cannot understand the colony, its social structure, its history, its development unless we have a clear insight into the economic forces which operated upon it. These Englishmen, finding themselves in a new country, surrounded by conditions fundamentally different from those to which they had been accustomed, worked out a new and unique society, were themselves moulded into something different.

And in colonial Virginia history there is a key, which though it may not explain all, opens the door to much that is fundamental. This key is tobacco. The old saying that the story of Virginia is but the story of tobacco is by no means a gross exaggeration. It was this Indian plant, so despised by many of the best and ablest men of the time, which determined the character of the life of the colony and shaped its destinies for two and a half centuries. Tobacco was the chief factor in bringing final and complete failure to the attempts to produce useful raw materials, it was largely instrumental in moulding the social classes and the political structure of the colony, it was almost entirely responsible for the system of labor, it even exerted a powerful influence upon religion and morals. In a word, one can understand almost nothing of Virginia, its infancy, its development, its days of misfortune, its era of prosperity, its peculiar civilization, the nature of its relations to England, unless one knows the history of tobacco.

As though they had a prophetic vision of its future importance, the Virginia Indians revered the plant. To them it was an especial gift direct from the Great Spirit, and as such was endowed with unusual properties for doing good. When the fields of maize were dried and parched for lack of rain they powdered the tobacco and cast it to the winds that the evil genii might be propitiated; their priests on great occasions fed it to the sacrificial fires; when the usual catch of fish failed it was scattered over the water.[1] Smoking was considered a token of friendship and peace. When the white men first visited the native villages they soon found that to reject the proffered pipe was to offend their savage hosts and incur their hostility.

It was John Rolfe, celebrated as the husband of Pocahontas, who first experimented with the native leaf. This gentleman was himself fond of smoking, but he found the Virginia tobacco as it came from the hands of the savages, decidedly inferior to that of the West Indies. The leaf itself was small, and although the flavor was weak it was biting to the tongue.[2] Rolfe's efforts proved entirely successful. In 1614, two years after his first attempt, he had obtained a product which Ralph Hamor declared to be as "strong, sweet and pleasant as any under the sun."[3]

Thus, early in its history, Virginia had found a commodity for which she was preëminently suited, in the production of which she could compete successfully with any country in the world. And for her tobacco she had a ready market. During the reign of Queen Elizabeth the habit of smoking had spread rapidly among the upper classes of English, until at the end of the sixteenth century, it was almost universal. When

James I ascended the throne, although feeling a strong aversion to tobacco, he was forced to take up its use in order not to appear conspicuous among his courtiers, for the dictates of custom seem to have been as strong three hundred years ago as at present.[4] At the time that Rolfe was making his experiments England was spending yearly for the Spanish product many thousands of pounds.

It is not surprising, then, that the colonists turned eagerly to tobacco culture. The news that Rolfe's little crop had been pronounced in England to be of excellent quality spread rapidly from settlement to settlement, bringing with it new hope and determination. Immediately tobacco absorbed the thoughts of all, became the one topic of conversation, and every available patch of land was seized upon for its cultivation. The fortified areas within the palisades were crowded with tobacco plants, while even the streets of Jamestown were utilized by the eager planters.[5] In 1617 the George set sail for England laden with 20,000 pounds of Virginia leaf, the first of the vast fleet of tobacco ships which for centuries were to pass through the capes of the Chesapeake bound for Europe.[6] By 1627, the tobacco exports amounted to no less than half a million pounds.[7]

The London Company, together with the host of patriotic Englishmen who had placed such great hopes in the colony, were much disappointed at this unexpected turn of events. They had sought in the New World those "solid commodities" which they realized were fundamental to the prosperity of their country, commodities upon which English industrial life was founded. And they had found only the Indian weed—tobacco. This plant not only contributed nothing to the wealth of the kingdom, it was felt, but was positively injurious to those who indulged in its use. Surely, declared one writer, men "grow mad and crazed in the brain in that they would adventure to suck the smoke of a weed." James I thought there could be no baser and more harmful corruption, while Charles I expressed himself with equal emphasis. So late as 1631 the latter protested against the growing use of tobacco, which he termed "an evil habit of late tymes."[8]

Yet England soon learned to welcome the colonial tobacco as far better than no product at all. Hitherto the leaf in use had been raised in the Spanish colonies, and England's annual tobacco bill was becoming larger and larger. It seemed calamitous that British industry should be drained of good and useful commodities in exchange for a plant the consumption of which was harmful rather than beneficial. It was at least some satisfaction to know, then, that England could substitute for the Spanish leaf the growth of their own colonies. Apparently it was only later, however, that there came a full realization of the opportunity afforded for enriching England and building up her merchant marine by exporting tobacco to foreign countries. For the present they accepted this one product of their experiment in colonial expansion, reluctantly and with keen disappointment, as the best that could be obtained.

Yet it was obvious to the London Company that tobacco held out the only prospect, not only of securing a profit from their venture, but of bringing to Virginia some measure of prosperity. The first consignment of leaf which came from the colony sold for no less than 5s. 3d. a pound, a price which promised a rich return to the planters on the James and their backers in England.[9] And they much preferred to have a prosperous colony, even when prosperity was founded on tobacco, than a weak, impoverished settlement, which would be a drain upon their personal resources and of no value to the nation. Thus they accepted the inevitable, gave what encouragement they could to the new product, and sought to use it as a means for building up the British empire in America. When once England had established herself firmly in the New World, it would be time enough to return to the attempt to secure from the colony ship-stores, potash, iron and silk.

With the overthrow of the Company, however, the Crown made repeated efforts to direct the energies of Virginia away from the all-absorbing cultivation of tobacco. In 1636 Charles I wrote to the Governor and Council bidding them moderate the excessive quantities of the plant laid out each year and to endeavor to produce some other staple commodities.[10] "The King cannot but take notice," he reiterated the next year, "how little that colony hath advanced in Staple commodities fit for their own subsistence and clothing," and he warned the planters to emulate the Barbados and Caribee Islands, where a beginning had been made in cotton, wool and other useful things.[11] But the colonists paid no heed to these repeated warnings. The King's commands were no more effective in establishing new industries than had been the first attempts of the Company. Virginia was not prepared to compete with the workers of Europe in their own chosen fields, and persisted, had to persist, in the production of the one commodity for which she possessed unsurpassed natural advantages.

It is remarkable how universally the plant was cultivated by all classes of Virginians throughout the colonial period. It was difficult to find skilled artisans in any line of work, since those who had pursued in England the various trades usually deserted them, when they landed in the colony, in order to turn to the raising of tobacco. And the few who continued to pursue their old vocations usually rented or purchased a small tract of land and devoted a part of their time to its cultivation. Blacksmiths, carpenters, shipwrights, coopers all raised their little tobacco crop and sold it to the British merchants,[12] while even the poor minister sought to make ends meet by planting his glebe with Orinoco or Sweet-scented. The Governor himself was not free from the all-prevailing custom, and frequently was the possessor of a farm where his servants and slaves, like those of other gentlemen in the colony, were kept busy tending the tobacco crop.

It is doubtful whether the members of the London Company, even Sir Edwin Sandys himself, ever attempted to visualize the social structure which would develop in the Virginia they were planning. If so, they unquestionably pictured a state of affairs very different from that which the future held in store. They took it for granted that Virginia would to a large extent be a duplicate of England. In the forests of the New World would grow up towns and villages, centers of industry and centers of trade. The population would be divided into various classes—well-to-do proprietors boasting of the title of gentleman; professional men, lawyers, physicians, ministers; skilled artisans of all kinds; day laborers.

We catch a glimpse of the Virginia of their minds from a Broadside issued in 1610, appealing for volunteers for service in the colony.[13] We can see the shipwrights at work in the busy yards of thriving ports; the smelters caring for their iron and copper furnaces; the "minerall-men" digging out the ore; saltmakers evaporating the brackish waters for their useful product; vine-dressers tending their abundant crops of grapes and coopers turning out the hogsheads in which to store the wine which came from the presses; bricklayers and carpenters fashioning substantial houses; fishermen bringing in the plentiful yield of the day and dressers preparing the fish for foreign shipment; joiners, smiths, gardeners, bakers, gun-founders, ploughwrights, brewers, sawyers, fowlers, each plying his trade in the New Brittania.

But how different was the reality. Virginia became, not an industrial, but a distinctly agricultural community. For more than a century it could boast not a single town worthy of the name.[14] It was but a series of plantations, not large in extent, but stretching out for miles along the banks of the rivers and creeks, all devoted to the raising of tobacco. The population of the colony was but the aggregate of the population of the plantation—the owner, the wage earners, the indentured servant, a few slaves. Virginia in the Seventeenth century, despite the design of its founders, developed a life of its own, a life not only unlike that of England, but unique and distinct.

Immigration, like everything else in the colony, was shaped by the needs of tobacco. For its successful production the plant does not require skilled labor or intensive cultivation. The barbarous natives of Africa, who later in the century were imported in such large numbers, eventually proved quite adequate to the task. But it does require the service of many hands. For decades after Rolfe's discovery had opened a new vista of prosperity for Virginia, fertile land was so cheap that a person even of moderate means might readily purchase an extensive plantation,[15] but it would be of little service to him unless he could find hands for clearing away the forests, breaking the soil, tending and curing the plants.

Of the three requirements of production—natural resources, capital and labor—the fertile soil furnished the first in abundance, the second could readily be secured, but the last remained for a full century the one great problem of the planters. From the days of Sir George Yeardley to those of Nicholson and Andros there was a persistent and eager demand for workers. Of this there can be no better evidence than the remarkably high wages which prevailed in the colony, especially in the years prior to the Restoration. In fact, it is probable that the laborer received for his services four or five times the amount he could earn in England. Even during the time of the London Company we find George Sandys writing to a friend in London to procure indentured servants for the colony as the wages demanded were intolerable. A day's work brought, in addition to food, a pound of tobacco valued at one shilling, while in England the unskilled worker considered himself fortunate if he could earn so much in a week.[16]

In his efforts to solve this acute problem the planter found little hope in the aborigines. The Spaniards, it is true, had made use of the Indians to till their fields or work in the gold and silver mines, but the Pamunkey and the Powhatan were cast in a different mold from the Aztec and the Peruvian. To hunt them out of their native lairs and bind them to arduous and ignominious servitude was hardly to be thought of. Their spirit was too proud to be thus broken, the safe refuge of the woods too near at hand. One might as well have attempted to hitch lions and tigers to the plough shaft, as to place these wild children of the forest at the handles. At times it proved practicable to make use of Indian children for servants, and there are numerous instances on record in which they are found in the homes of the planters.[17] But this, of course, could be of little service in solving the pressing labor problem, in clearing new ground or tilling the idle fields. The Virginia landowner was forced to turn elsewhere for his helpers.

In 1619 a Dutch privateer put into the James river and disembarked twenty Africans who were sold to the settlers as slaves. This event, so full of evil portent for the future of Virginia, might well have afforded a natural and satisfactory solution of the labor problem. Slaves had long been used in the Spanish colonies, proving quite competent to do the work of tending the tobacco plants, and bringing handsome returns to their masters. But it was impossible at this time for England to supply her plantations with this type of labor. The slave trade was in the hands of the Dutch, who had fortified themselves on the African coast and jealously excluded other nations. Thus while the demand for negro slaves remained active in the colony, they increased in numbers very slowly. The muster of 1624-25 shows only 22.[18] During the following half century there was a small influx of negroes, but their numbers were still too small to affect seriously the economic life of the colony.[19]

The settlers were thus forced to look to England itself to supply them with hands for their tobacco fields. They knew that in the mother country were many thousands of indigent persons who would welcome an opportunity to better their lot by migrating to the New World. And the English statesmen, feeling that there was need for blood letting, welcomed an opportunity to divert the surplus population to the new colony in America.[20] The decline in English foreign trade and the stagnation of home industry had brought unemployment and suffering to every class of workers. Wages were so low that the most industrious could not maintain themselves in comfort, while to provide against want in case of sickness or old age was hardly to be thought of. Every parish, every town swarmed with persons stricken with abject poverty. In some parts of the country no less than 30 per cent of the population were dependent in part upon charity for their daily bread, while many were driven into vagabondage and crime, becoming an element of danger rather than of strength to the nation.[21] It seemed to the planters that the mother country constituted an abundant reservoir of labor, a reservoir already overflowing and capable of supplying indefinitely their every need.

The only drawback was the long and expensive voyage across the Atlantic. The fare, even for the poorest and most crowded accommodations, was no less than six pounds sterling, a sum far beyond the means of the thriftiest laborer.[22] Obviously some scheme had to be evolved to overcome this difficulty before Virginia could make use of English labor. And so the planters turned to the simple expedient of advancing the passage money to the immigrant and of placing him under strict legal bonds to work it out after reaching the colony.

This system, around which the economic life of Virginia centered for a full century, proved satisfactory to all concerned. The credit advanced to the immigrant made it possible for him to earn his ocean fare, not in England where labor was cheap, but in America where it was dear. In other words, he was enabled without delay to enjoy the full benefits of selling his services in the best market. The necessity for placing him under a stringent contract or indenture is evident. Had this not been done the immigrant, upon finding himself in Virginia, might have refused to carry out his part of the bargain. But the indenture was in no sense a mark of servitude or slavery. It simply made it obligatory for the newcomer, under pain of severe penalties, to work out his passage money, and until that was accomplished to surrender a part of the personal liberty so dear to every Englishman.

It is erroneous to suppose that most of the servants were degenerates or criminals. It is true that the English Government from time to time sought to lessen the expense of providing for convicted felons by sending some of them to the colonies, among them on rare occasions a few decidedly objectionable characters. More than once the Virginians protested vigorously against this policy as dangerous to the peace and prosperity of the colony.[23] By far the larger part of these penal immigrants, however, were but harmless paupers, driven perhaps to theft or some other petty offense by cold and hunger. Often they were sentenced to deportation by merciful judges in order that they might not feel the full weight of the harsh laws of that day.[24]

And of the small number of real criminals who came in, few indeed made any lasting imprint upon the social fabric of the colony. Many served for life and so had no opportunity of marrying and rearing families to perpetuate their degenerate traits. Those who escaped fled from the confines of settled Virginia to the mountains or to the backwoods of North Carolina. Many others succumbed to the epidemics which proved so deadly to the newcomers from England. In fact the criminal servant was but a passing incident in the life and development of England's greatest and most promising colony.[25]

An appreciable proportion of the so-called criminal laborers were no more than political prisoners taken in the rebellions of the Seventeenth century. These men frequently represented the sturdiest and most patriotic elements in the kingdom and were a source of strength rather than of weakness to the colony. When Drogheda was captured by Cromwell's stern Puritan troops in 1649, some of the unfortunate rebels escaped the firing squad only to be sent to America to serve in the sugar or tobacco fields. Just how many of these Irishmen fell to the share of Virginia it is impossible to say, but the number rises well into the hundreds, and the patent books of the period are full of headrights of undoubted Irish origin.[26]

When Charles II was restored to the throne in 1660 it became the turn of the Puritans to suffer, and many non-conformists and former Oliverian soldiers were sent to Virginia. In fact so many old Commonwealth men were serving in the tobacco fields in 1663 that they felt strong enough to plot, not only for their own freedom, but for the overthrow of the colonial government.[27] In 1678, after the suppression of the Scottish Covenanters by the Highland Host, a new batch of prisoners were sent to the plantations.[28] Seven years later many of Monmouth's followers taken at Sedgemour, who were fortunate enough to escape the fury of Jeffreys and Kirk, were forced to work in the plantations.

But the bulk of the servants were neither criminals nor political prisoners, but poor persons seeking to better their condition in the land of promise across the Atlantic. They constituted the vanguard of that vast stream of immigrants which for three centuries Europe has poured upon our shores. The indentured servant differed in no essential from the poor Ulsterite or German who followed him in the Eighteenth century, or the Irishman, the Italian or the Slav in the Nineteenth. Like them he found too severe the struggle for existence at home, like them he sought to reach a land where labor, the only commodity he had to sell, would bring the highest return. The fact that his passage was paid for him and that he was bound by contract to work it out after reaching America, in no wise differentiates him from the newcomers of later days. In 1671 Sir William Berkeley reported to the Board of Trade that the colony contained "6,000 Christian servants for a short tyme," who had come with the "hope of bettering their condition in a Growing Country."[29]

Virginia is fortunate in having preserved a record of this, the first great migration to the English colonies, which in some respects is remarkably complete. In fact, the names of fully three-fourths of all the persons who came to the colony, whether as freemen or servants during the first century of its existence, are on record at the Land Office at Richmond, and at all times available to the student of history. In the early days of the settlement a law was passed designed to stimulate immigration, by which the Government pledged itself to grant fifty acres of land to any person who would pay the passage from Europe to Virginia of a new settler. Thus if one brought over ten indentured servants he would be entitled to

500 acres of land, if he brought 100, he could demand 5,000 acres. But the headright, as it was called, was not restricted to servants; if one came over as a freeman, paying his own passage, he was entitled to the fifty acres. Should he bring also his family, he could demand an additional fifty acres for his wife and fifty for each child or other member of the household.[30]

When the Government issued a grant for land under this law, the planter was required to record with the clerk of the county court the names of all persons for whose transportation the claim was made. Some of these lists have been lost, especially for the period from 1655 to 1666, but most of them remain, constituting an inexhaustible storehouse of information concerning the colony and the people who came to its shores.[31] How the papers escaped destruction during the fire which did so much damage in the Secretary's office at the time of Andros, it is impossible to say. The explanation is to be found perhaps in the fact that copies of the records were kept, not only at Williamsburg, but in the several counties, so that in case of loss by fire new entries could be made.

Immigration to Virginia continued in unabated volume throughout the Seventeenth century. The needs of the tobacco plantations were unceasing, and year after year the surplus population of England poured across the Atlantic in response. An examination of the list of headrights shows that the annual influx was between 1500 and 2000. Even during the Civil War and Commonwealth periods this average seems to have been maintained with surprising consistency. Apparently the only limit which could be set upon it was the available space on board the merchant fleet which each year left England for the Chesapeake bay. Thus in the year ending May 1635 we find that 2000 landed in the colony,[32] while in 1674 and again in 1682 the same average was maintained.[33]

At times the numbers dropped to 1200 or 1300, but this was the exception rather than the rule. All in all, considerably more than 100,000 persons migrated to the colony in the years that elapsed between the first settlement at Jamestown and the end of the century.[34]

This great movement, which far surpassed in magnitude any other English migration of the century, fixed for all time the character of the white population of tidewater Virginia. The vast bulk of the settlers were English. An examination of the headright lists shows here and there an Irish or a Scotch name, and on very rare occasions one of French or Italian origin, but in normal periods fully 95 per cent were unmistakably Anglo-Saxon. In fact, such names as Dixon, Bennett, Anderson, Adams, Greene, Brooke, Brown, Cooper, Gibson, Hall, Harris, King, Jackson, Long, Martin, Miller, Newton, Philips, Richards, Turner, White, appear with monotonous repetition. Except in the years 1655 and 1656, after the Drogheda tragedy when one sees such names as O'Lanny, O'Leaby, O'Mally, and Machoone, or in 1679 when there was a sprinkling of Scottish names, the entire list is distinctly English.

It must not be supposed that immigration to Virginia in the Seventeenth century was restricted to indentured servants. Some of the settlers were freemen, paying their own passage and establishing themselves as proprietors immediately after arriving in the colony. But the conditions which attracted them were the same as those which brought over the servants. In both cases it was tobacco, the rich returns which it promised and the urgent need it had of labor, which impelled them to leave their homes in England to seek their fortunes in the strange land beyond the seas.

Having seen the character of the immigration to Virginia, it remains to determine what was the fate of the settler after he reached the colony, what rôle lay before him in its social and economic life. Would he remain permanently in the status of a servant, entering into a new agreement with his master after the expiration of the old? Would he eventually become a day laborer, working for wages upon the estates of the wealthy? Would he become a tenant? Could he hope to become a freeholder, making of Virginia, like Rome in the early days of the republic, the land of the small proprietor?

CHAPTER III

THE VIRGINIA YEOMANRY

THE system of indentured labor differed vitally from negro slavery. The servant usually was bound to his master for a limited period only, and at the expiration of four or five years was a free man, to go where he would and pursue what employment seemed most lucrative. And of tremendous importance to the future of Virginia was the fact that he was of the same race and blood as the rest of the population. There was no inherent reason why he might not take up land, marry and become a part of the social structure of the colony.

When races of marked physical differences are placed side by side in the same territory, assimilation of one or the other becomes difficult, and an age long repugnance and conflict is apt to result. Perhaps the greatest crime against the southern colonies was not the introduction of slavery, but the introduction of negroes. It was inevitable that eventually slavery would be abolished. But the negro race in America cannot be abolished, it cannot be shipped back to Africa, it cannot well be absorbed into the white population. Today California is struggling to avoid a like problem by excluding the Japanese, while Canada, Australia and New Zealand are closing their doors to Orientals of all kinds.

Thus Virginia, during its century of white immigration, was storing up no perplexing difficulties for the future, was developing slowly but surely into an industrious, democratic, Anglo-Saxon community. Not until the black flood of slaves was turned loose upon her, strangling her peasantry and revolutionizing her industrial and social life, was her future put in pawn. The white servants, so far as they remained in the colony, became bone of her bone, flesh of her flesh, promised her a homogeneous race, a sound economic and political development.

When the alien newcomer to the United States sees from the deck of his steamer the Statue of Liberty and the ragged sky line of lower Manhattan, he feels that the goal of his ambition has been reached, that the land of opportunity lies before him. But to the indentured settler of the Seventeenth century, his arrival in the James or the York was but the beginning of his struggles. Before he could grasp the riches of the New World, he must pay the price of his passage, must work out through arduous years the indenture to which he had affixed his signature.

And these years were filled not only with toil, perhaps with hardship, but with the greatest peril. He might account himself fortunate indeed if during the first twelve months he escaped the so-called Virginia sickness. Tidewater Virginia for the English settlers was a pest-ridden place. The low and marshy ground, the swarming mosquitoes, the hot sun, the unwholesome drinking water combined to produce an unending epidemic of dysentery and malaria. And at frequent intervals, especially in the early years, yellow fever, scurvy and plague swept over the infant colony, leaving behind a ghastly train of suffering and death.[1] At one time the mortality among the settlers upon the James ran as high as 75 per cent and for a while it seemed that this attempt of the British nation to secure a foothold upon the American continent must end in failure.[2]

But as the years wore on better conditions prevailed. Governor Berkeley testified in 1671, "there is not oft seasoned hands (as we term them) that die now, whereas heretofore not one of five escaped the first year."[3] This improvement was brought about by the use of Peruvian bark, a clearer understanding of sanitary matters and the selection of more healthful sites for plantations. At the time when Sir William wrote it is probable that 80 per cent or more of the indentured servants survived the dangers of the tobacco fields, completed their terms of service and, if they remained in the colony, became freedmen with the full rights of Englishmen and Virginians.

In the period from 1660 to 1725 there was, as we shall see, an exodus of poor whites from Virginia. This, however, was chiefly the result of the influx of slaves which marked the end of the century, and it is safe to assume that prior to the Restoration there was no extensive movement from Virginia to other colonies. The servant, upon attaining his freedom, usually remained in the colony and sought to establish himself there.

Although it is impossible to determine accurately the average length of service required by the indentures, there is reason to believe that it did not exceed five years. In cases of controversy between masters and servants who had come in without written contracts as to when their terms should expire, it was at first required by law that the period be fixed at five years if the age was in excess of twenty-one.[4] In 1654, however, a new act was passed by the Assembly, making it necessary for those who had no indentures, if over sixteen to serve six years, if less than sixteen until the twenty-fourth year had been reached.[5] This was found to work to the disadvantage of the colony by discouraging immigration, and in 1662 the law was changed so that in all doubtful cases the legal term should be five years for persons over sixteen.[6] Since the Assembly, which was so largely made up of persons who themselves held servants, would certainly not fix the legal term for a period shorter than that normally provided for in the indentures, we may assume that usually the servant secured his freedom within four or five years after his arrival in the colony.

Thus it is evident that the bulk of the population could not have been, as is so often supposed, made up of large landed proprietors with their servants and slaves. Such a conception takes no account of the annual translation of hundreds of men and women from bondsmen into freedmen. The short duration of the average term of service, together with the fact that the servants were usually still young when freed, made it inevitable that in time the freedmen would outnumber those in service. The size of the annual immigration could in no wise alter this situation, for the greater the influx of servants, the greater would be the resulting graduation into the class of freedmen.

The average number of headrights, as we have seen, was probably not less than 1750 a year. If it is assumed that 1500 of these were servants, five per cent of whom served for life and 20 per cent died before the expiration of their terms, no less than 1125 would remain to become freedmen. While the number of those under indenture remained practically stationary, the size of the freedman class grew larger with the passing of the years.

Placing the average term at five years, then, and the average mortality at twenty per cent, there would be in service at any given time some 6,000 men and women. In fact, Sir William Berkeley, in his famous report of 1671, estimated the number of servants in the colony at this figure.[7] On the other hand an annual accession of 1125 to the class of freedmen would in five years amount to 5,625, in ten years to 11,250, in fifteen to 16,875, in twenty to 22,500. At the end of half a century no less than 56,250 persons would have emerged from servitude to become free citizens. Although there is every reason to believe that these figures are substantially correct,[8] their accuracy or lack of accuracy in no way affect the principle involved. From its very nature it was impossible that the system of indentured servants should long remain the chief factor in the industrial life of the colony or supply most of the labor.

It is true, of course, that the number of those completing their terms of indenture is not an absolute gauge, at any given date, of the size of the freedman class. To determine this it would be necessary to know the average span of life of the freedman, a thing certainly not worked out at the time and impossible of accomplishment now. We may assume, however, that it was relatively long. The newcomer who had lived through the first terrible year in the tobacco fields had been thoroughly tested, "seasoned" as the planters called it, and was reasonably certain of reaching a mature age. Moreover, the servants were almost universally of very tender years. Seldom indeed would a dealer accept one over twenty-eight, and the average seems to have been between seventeen and twenty-three. The reasons for this are obvious. Not only were young men and women more adaptable to changed conditions, more capable of resisting the Virginia climate, stronger and more vigorous, but they proved more tractable and entered upon the adventure more eagerly.[9] These conclusions are fully borne out by an examination of the lists of servants given in Hotten's *Emigrants to America*. Of the first 159 servants here entered whose ages are attached, the average is twenty-three years.[10] And as many of these persons were brought over as skilled artisans to take part in the industrial life which the Company had planned for the colony, it is probable that they were much older than the average servant of later days who came as an agricultural laborer. There is every reason to believe, then, that the average servant was still in his prime when he completed his term, perhaps not more than twenty-six or twenty-seven, with many years of usefulness and vigor before him.

It must also be remembered that the freedman, by a display of energy and capability, might acquire property, marry and rear a family. While the number of indentured servants was strictly limited to those who were brought in from the outside, the class of poor freemen might and did enjoy a natural increase within itself. Thus it was inevitable that with the passing of the years the servants were more and more outnumbered by the growing group of freemen. In 1649, when the population was but 15,000,[11] 6,000 servants might well have performed most of the manual labor of the tobacco fields, but in 1670, when the inhabitants numbered 40,000,[12] or in 1697 when they were 70,000,[13] they would form a comparatively small proportion of the people, so small in fact that most of the work of necessity had to be done by freemen. In other words the picture so often presented, even by historians of established reputation, of a Seventeenth century Virginia in which the land was divided into large plantations owned by rich proprietors and tilled chiefly by indentured servants is entirely erroneous. Such a state of affairs was made impossible by the very nature of the system of indentures itself.

It becomes a matter of prime interest, then, to determine what became of the mass of freedmen, what rôle they played in the social and economic life of the colony. Because the servant who had completed his term was free to follow his own bent, we have no right to assume that he sought at once to establish himself as an independent proprietor. He might seek service with the large planters as a hired laborer, he might become a tenant. In either case the population would have been divided into two classes—the wealthy landowner and those who served him.

We know that at all periods of Virginia history there were a certain number of persons employed as wage earners. The colonial laws and the county records contain many references to them. Payment of wages was not unusual even under the Company, and we are told by George Sandys that hired laborers received one pound of tobacco a day in addition to their food.[14] In later years we have from time to time references to wage rates, and in some cases copies of contracts entered into between employer and wage earner. But such cases are comparatively rare, and it is evident that the use of hired labor throughout the colonial period was the exception rather than the rule. In fact it would seem that few save servants newly freed and lacking in the funds necessary for purchasing and equipping little farms of their own ever sought employment upon the large plantations. And even in such cases the contracts were for comparatively short periods, since it often required but a year or two of labor for the freedman to save enough from his wages to make a beginning as an independent proprietor.

When once established, there was no reason, in the days prior to the introduction of slavery, why he should not hold his own in competition with his wealthy neighbor. In the production of tobacco the large plantation, so long as it was cultivated only by expensive white labor, offered no marked advantage over the small. With the cost of land very low, with the means of earning the purchase price so readily in hand, with the conditions for an independent career all so favorable, it was not to be expected that the freedman should content himself permanently with the status of a hired laborer.

Nor was there any reason why he should become a tenant. Had all the fertile land been preëmpted, as was the case on the banks of the Hudson, the poor man might have been compelled to lease the soil upon which he expended his efforts or do without entirely. But such was not the case. It is true that at the end of the Seventeenth century certain wealthy men got possession of large tracts of unsettled land, but their monopoly was so far from complete that they gladly sold off their holdings in little parcels to the first purchasers who presented themselves. Apparently they made no attempts to establish themselves in a position similar to that of the great landlords of England.

The records afford ample evidence that the leasing of property was by no means unknown in colonial Virginia, but the custom was comparatively rare. Hugh Jones, writing in 1721, declared that the tenant farmers constituted but a small fraction of the population, a fact which he explained by the unusual facilities for acquiring property in fee simple.[15] It would have been folly for the tobacco planter to expend his labor upon another man's property, perhaps erecting barns and fences and otherwise improving it, when he could for so small an outlay secure land of his own.

Thus we are led to the conclusion that the average Virginia plantation must have been comparatively small in extent. The development of large estates was narrowly limited by the various factors which made it impossible to secure an adequate labor supply—the restrictions upon the slave trade, the insufficient number of indentured servants and the shortness of their terms, the unwillingness of freedmen and others to work for wages. On the other hand, it would be expected that the servants upon securing their freedom would purchase land of their own, and cover all tidewater Virginia with little farms.

Turning to the various records of the time that deal with the distribution of land—deeds, wills, transfers, tax lists, inventories—we find that these conclusions are fully borne out. All reveal the fact that the average plantation, especially in the Seventeenth century, so far from vieing with the vast estates in existence in certain parts of America, was but a few hundred acres in extent.

The land transfers of Surry county afford an interesting illustration. In thirty-four instances mentioned during the years from 1684 to 1686, for which the exact number of acres is given, the largest is 500 acres, the smallest twenty. The aggregate of all land which changed hands is 6,355 acres, or an average of 187 for each sale. There are eleven transfers of 100 acres or less, twenty-three transfers of 200 or less and only four of more than 300 acres.[16] One can find in this no evidence of the fabled barons of colonial Virginia, but only of a well established class of small proprietors.

The York county books for the years from 1696 to 1701 tell the same story. Here we find recorded forty-one transfers and leases. Twenty-two are for 100 acres or less, 33 for 200 acres or less, and four, one for 1,400, one for 1,210, one for 600 and one for 550, are more than 300 acres in extent. The aggregate is 8,153 acres and the average 199.[17]

In the Rappahannock county records from 1680 to 1688 of fifteen land transfers taken at random from the books, the largest is 400 while the average is 168 acres.[18] Of the forty-eight transfers mentioned in the Essex county books for the years from 1692 to 1695, the largest is 600 acres and the smallest 50. Twenty are for 100 acres or less, 31 for 200 or less and only four for over 300.[19]

That conditions not fundamentally different prevailed in the early days of the colony is shown by the census taken of the landowners in 1626. Of the holdings listed no less than 25 were for 50 acres or less, 73 for 100 and most of the others for less than 300 acres. The total number of proprietors listed is 224 and the total acreage 34,472, giving an average for each plantation of 154 acres.[20]

It has been assumed by certain writers that the land grants

preserved in the Registrar's Office in Richmond tend to contradict this evidence. Although the average patent is by no means large, it is much more extensive than the typical land transfer. In 1638 this average was 423 acres, in 1640 it was 405, in 1642 it was 559, in 1645 it was 333, in 1648 it was 412, in 1650 it was 675. During the entire period from 1634 to 1650 inclusive the size of the average land grant was 446 acres. From 1650 to 1655 the average was 591 acres, from 1655 to 1666 six hundred and seventy-one, from 1666 to 1679 eight hundred and ninety acres, from 1679 to 1689 six hundred and seven acres, from 1689 to 1695 six hundred and one acres, from 1695 to 1700 six hundred and eighty-eight acres.[21] In the course of the entire second half of the Seventeenth century the average size of the patent was 674 acres.

Yet these facts have little direct bearing upon the extent of the plantations themselves. The system of granting land, as we have seen, was not based upon the individual needs of the planters, but upon the number of headrights presented to the Government. Obviously it was the question of the most economical method of transporting immigrants which would determine the average size of the grant. If it proved best to bring in servants in small groups, distributed among vessels devoted chiefly to merchandise, the patents would be small; if they came in on immigrant vessels, in numbers ranging from 50 to 200, the patents would be large.

Apparently both methods were in vogue. There are grants recorded varying in size from 50 acres to 10,000 acres.[22] Beyond doubt many merchants, finding that their vessels on the western voyage were not fully laden, from time to time took on a few indentured servants. If they furnished accommodation for from ten to twenty immigrants, they could demand, in addition to the sale of the indentures, 500 to 1,000 acres of land. It was a frequent practice, also, for planters in Virginia to send orders to their agents in England to procure and ship one or more servants as need for them arose.[23] "Your brother George hath moved you in his letters to send him over some servants the next year," wrote Richard Kemp to Robert Read in 1639.[24] Undoubtedly in cases of this kind the servants usually sailed in small parties upon the regular merchant vessels.

On the other hand it would appear that large numbers of persons arrived on strictly immigrant vessels, in which they made the chief if not the only cargo. Some of the best known men in the colony were dealers in servants and reaped from the business very large profits. Of these perhaps the best known in the earlier period was William Claiborne, celebrated for his dispute with the Maryland proprietors over the possession of Kent Island. Peter Ashton was another extensive dealer in servants, at one time receiving 2,550 acres for his headrights, at another 2,000. Isaac Allerton, Lewis Burwell, Giles Brent, Joseph Bridger and many others of like prominence are upon the patent rolls for large grants. The most inveterate dealer in servants, however, was Robert Beverley. This well known planter, so famous for his part in Bacon's Rebellion and in the political contests which grew out of it, is credited with patents aggregating 25,000 or 30,000 acres.[25]

Often partnerships were formed for the importation of servants, in which cases the patents were made out jointly. Among the more interesting are patents to Robert Beverley and Henry Hartwell, to Thomas Butt and Thomas Milner, to William Bassett and James Austin, to Thomas Blunt and Richard Washington. When associations of three or more persons were formed for the importation of servants, a not infrequent occurrence, the number of headrights is unusually large and the grants patented in consequence extensive. Thus

Edmund Bibbie and others are credited with 3,350 acres, Robert Ambrose and others with 6,000, George Archer and others with 4,000.[26]

It is clear, then, that the size of the average patent in the Seventeenth century is not an indication of the extent of the average plantation. If economic conditions were such as to encourage large holdings, extensive farms would appear regardless of the original patents, for the small proprietors would be driven to the wall by their more wealthy rivals and forced to sell out to them. On the other hand, if the large planters found it difficult to secure adequate labor they would of necessity have to break up their estates and dispose of them to the small freeholders. That the latter development and not the former actually took place in Virginia during the Seventeenth century a careful examination of the country records makes most apparent.

Over and over again in the records of various land transfers it is stated that the property in question had belonged originally to a more extensive tract, the patent for which was granted under the headright law. A typical case is that of John Dicks who purchased for 8,500 pounds of tobacco, "all the remaining part of 900 acres gotten by the transporting of 19 persons."[27] Similarly we find John Johnson in 1653 selling to Robert Roberts half of 900 acres which he had received by patent.[28] In 1693 John Brushood sold to James Grey 200 acres, a part of 5,100 acres originally granted to Mr. Henry Awbrey.[29] Such cases could be multiplied indefinitely.

Perhaps the most instructive instance left us of this development is the break up of a tract of land known as Button's Ridge, in Essex country. This property, comprising 3,650 acres, was granted to Thomas Button in the year 1666.[30] The original patentee transferred the entire tract to his brother Robert Button, who in turn sold it to John Baker. The latter, finding no doubt that he could not put under cultivation so much land, cut it up into small parcels and sold it off to various planters. Of these transactions we have, most fortunately, a fairly complete record. To Captain William Moseley he sold 200 acres, to John Garnet 600, to Robert Foster 200, to William Smither 200, to William Howlett 200, to Anthony Samuell 300, to William Williams 200. It is probable that he sold also a small holding to Henry Creighton, for we find the latter, in 1695, transferring to William Moseley 100 acres, formerly a part of Button's Ridge.[31]

Important as are these gleanings from the county records, we have at our disposal even better and more conclusive evidence that colonial Virginia was divided, not into baronial estates of vast proportions, but into a large number of comparatively small farms. Governor Nicholson's rent roll, which is published as an appendix to this volume, for the early years of the Eighteenth century at least, places the matter beyond doubt. Here we have before us an official inventory of all Virginia save the Northern Neck, giving the name of every proprietor and the number of acres in his possession.

It will be remembered that in the Crown colonies there was a perpetual obligation imposed upon all land when first granted known as the quit-rent. In Virginia this duty amounted to one shilling for every fifty acres, payable in tobacco at the rate of a penny per pound.[32] Despite the fact that some 27 per cent of the returns was consumed by the cost of collection, and that there were frequent frauds in disposing of the tobacco, the revenue derived from this source was of considerable importance.[33] The amount collected in 1705 was £1,841. 1. 6¾. When James Blair, the Virginia Commissary of the Bishop of London, petitioned William and Mary for a fund from the accumulated quit-rents for his proposed college at Williamsburg, some of the British governmental officials objected strenuously. "This sum is perhaps the only ready cash in all the plantations," it was declared, "which happens to be by good husbandry and is a stock for answering any emergency that may happen in Virginia."[34]

Throughout the entire Seventeenth century, however, the Governors had experienced great difficulty in collecting this tax. Over and over again they reported in their letters to the Board of Trade that there were large arrears of quit-rents which it was impossible to make the landowners pay.[35] The reason for this was obvious enough. In each county the tax collector was the sheriff. Although this officer was appointed by the Governor, he usually had a wholesome respect for the larger proprietors and in consequence was wary of giving offense by holding them to too strict an account of their estates.[36] At times the sheriffs themselves were the sufferers by this state of affairs, for they were held responsible for the rents upon all land patented in their counties, for which returns had not been made.

Although the Governors from time to time made rather feeble attempts to remedy the prevailing laxness in this matter, nothing of importance was accomplished before the first administration of Francis Nicholson. The chief executive himself had much need of the good will of the richer inhabitants, and he was not over forward in forcing them to bring in accurate returns. Nicholson, however, who prided himself on his executive ability and who was bent on breaking the power of the clique which centered around the Council of State, exerted himself to the utmost to secure full payment for every acre.

So early as 1690 we find him issuing orders to the sheriffs for the drawing up of an accurate rent roll, through an examination of the patent lists and the records of land transfers.[37] May 15, 1691, he took up the matter again, warning the sheriffs that he expected more accurate returns than they had yet made.[38] With the appointment of Sir Edmund Andros as Governor, however, interest in the quit-rents lapsed, and not until his removal and the reappointment of Nicholson was the attempt resumed.

In July, 1699, Nicholson wrote the Commissioners of Trade and Plantations that he was doing his best to improve the quit-rents and that the auditor had been ordered to draw up a scheme for securing a more exact list of land holdings.[39] But for a while the matter still hung fire. The leading men in the Government were ready enough in making suggestions, but they were extensive landholders themselves and apparently rendered no real assistance. "I have considered those papers given me by your Excellency relating to a perfect rent roll," the auditor, William Byrd I wrote Nicholson, Oct. 21, 1703, "notwithstanding I have, according to your repeated directions used my utmost diligence in giving charge to sheriffs and taking their oaths to rolls, I am sensible there is still very great abuse therein."[40]

Despite these discouragements Nicholson persisted and in 1704 succeeded in obtaining the first really accurate rent roll of the colony. These lists have long been missing, and perhaps were destroyed in one of the several fires which have wrought so much havoc with the records of colonial Virginia, but a true copy was made by the clerk, William Robertson, and sent to the Board of Trade. Fortunately the British Government has been more careful of its priceless historical manuscripts than has Virginia, and this copy today reposes in the Public Record Office in London, a veritable treasure trove of information concerning economic and social conditions in the colony.[41]

Even a cursory examination of the rent roll is sufficient to dispel the old belief that Virginia at this time was the land of the large proprietor. As one glances down the list of plantations he is struck by the number of little holdings, the complete absence of huge estates, the comparative scarcity even of those that for a newly settled country might be termed extensive. Here and there, especially in the frontier counties is listed a tract of four or five or even ten thousand acres, but such cases are very rare. In Middlesex county there is but one plantation of more than 2,500 acres, in Charles City county the largest holding is 3,130, in Nansemond 2,300, in Norfolk county 3,200, in Princess Anne 3,100, in Elizabeth City county 2,140, in York 2,750, in Essex 3,200.

On the other hand the rolls reveal the existence of thousands of little proprietors, whose holdings of from 50 to 500 acres embraced the larger part of the cultivated soil of the colony. Thus we find that in Nansemond, of 376 farms 26 were of 50 acres or less, 66 were between 50 and 100 acres, 110 between 100 and 200 acres, 88 between 200 and 400 acres, 78 between 400 and 1,000 acres, and only eight over 1,000 acres. In Middlesex county out of 122 holdings eleven were of 50 acres or less, 33 between 50 and 100 acres, 32 between 100 and 200 acres, 25 between 200 and 500 acres, 19 between 500 and 2,500 acres, one of 4,000 acres and one of 5,200 acres. Of the 94 plantations in Charles City county 26 were of 100 acres or less, 21 between 100 and 200 acres, 25 between 200 and 500 acres, 19 between 500 and 2,500 acres and three more than 2,500 acres.[42]

Although the average size of the plantations varied considerably in different counties it was everywhere comparatively small, far smaller than the average land grant of the time, far smaller than has been imagined by some of the closest students of the period. For Nansemond the rolls reveal the average holding as 212 acres, for James City county 400, for York 298, for Warwick 308, for Elizabeth City county 255, for Princess Anne 459, for Gloucester 395, for Middlesex 406, for Charles City county 553.[43]

In the past few decades much has been written of the social life and customs of the people of colonial Virginia. But except in the able works of Dr. Philip Alexander Bruce little has been said concerning the small planter class, the men who made up the vast bulk of the population, the true Seventeenth century Virginians. We have long and detailed descriptions of the residences of the small group of the well-to-do, their libraries, their furniture, their table ware, their portraits, their clothing, their amusements. The genealogy of the leading families has been worked out with minute care, their histories recorded, some of their leading members idealized by the writers of fiction. The mention of colonial Virginia brings instantly to mind a picture of gay cavaliers, of stately ladies, of baronial estates, of noble manors. And the sturdy, independent class of small farmers who made up a full 90 per cent of the freeholders at the time the rent roll was taken, have been relegated into undeserved obscurity.

It is to be noted that the roll does not include the names of proprietors residing in the Northern Neck, as the peninsula between the Potomac and the Rappahannock is called. This territory, although acknowledging the jurisdiction of the Government at Williamsburg in most matters and sending representatives to the House of Burgesses, paid its quit-rents, not to the Crown but to a proprietor. Nicholson, therefore, was not concerned in their collection and took no steps to list its landholders in his new roll. There is no reason to believe, however, that conditions in that part of the colony were fundamentally different.

Nor can the accuracy of the rent roll be challenged. There existed always the incentive to make false returns, of course, in order to escape the payment of taxes, and not many sheriffs were so diligent as the one in Henrico who unearthed 1,669 acres that had been "concealed."[44] Yet it must be remembered that the Governor brought to bear all the pressure at his disposal to make this particular roll accurate, that the sheriffs were his appointees, that they could not lightly defy him in so important a matter. And even though in isolated cases they may have winked at false returns from men of wealth and rank, from the mass of small proprietors they must have insisted upon reports as accurate as the records or actual surveying could make them. No doubt certain uncultivated tracts in the frontier counties were omitted, but with these we are not immediately concerned. For conditions in the older parts of the colony, where the slow evolution of economic factors had been at work for a century, the roll presents unimpeachable evidence that the bulk of the cultivated land was divided into small plantations.

But it still remains to prove that their owners were men of meagre fortunes, men who tilled the soil with their own hands. After all a farm of two or three hundred acres might give scope for large activities, the employment of many servants and slaves, the acquisition of some degree of wealth. Might it not be possible that though the acres of the planter were limited, his estate after all corresponded somewhat with the popular conception?

This leads us to a study of the distribution of servants and slaves among the planters. At the outset we are faced with convincing evidence that at the end of the Seventeenth century the average number for each farm was very small. This is shown by a comparison of the number of plantations listed in the rent roll of 1704 with the estimated number of workers. In the counties for which the sheriffs made returns for Governor Nicholson there were some 5,500 landholders. When to these is added the proprietors of the Northern Neck the number must have approximated 6,500. If at this time the servants numbered 4,000, as seems probable,[45] and the slaves 6,000, together they would have averaged but 1.5 workers for each plantation. A decade earlier, when the use of slaves was still comparatively infrequent, the figure must have been still lower.

Fortunately we have even more direct and detailed evidence. Throughout almost all of Virginia colonial history one of the chief methods of raising revenue for the Government was the direct poll tax. This levy was laid, however, not only on every freeman over sixteen years of age, but upon male servants over 14, female servants who worked in the fields, and slaves above 16 of either sex, all of whom were officially termed tithables.[46] The tax rolls in which these persons were listed, some of which have been preserved among the county records, throw much light upon social and economic conditions in the colony.

In one district of Surry county we find in the year 1675 that there were 75 taxpayers and only 126 tithables. In other words only 51 persons in this district had this duty paid for them by others, whether parents, guardians or masters. And of the taxpayers, forty-two were liable for themselves alone, having no servants, slaves or dependent sons over 16; fifteen were liable for one other person, eight for two others, and only one, Lieutenant-Colonel Jordan, for so many as seven.[47]

In other districts the story is the same. In one there were forty taxpayers, 75 tithables and 25 persons who paid for themselves alone; in another 28 taxpayers, 62 tithables, fifteen who had no servants or slaves; in a third 48 taxpayers, 83 tithables, 28 who paid only for themselves, eleven who paid for two, five who paid for three; in a fourth district 29 taxpayers, 63 tithables, fourteen who had no servants or slaves; in a fifth 25 taxpayers, 45 tithables, 12 who paid only for themselves.[48] Thus in Surry county in the year 1675 there were in all 245 taxpayers and 434 tithables. In other words the men who paid their own tax outnumbered all those whose tax was paid for them, whether servants, slaves or relatives, at the ratio of about 4 to 3.

A study of the records of the same county ten years later leads to almost identical results. At that time Surry seems to have been divided into four districts. In the first there were 78 taxpayers, 132 tithables, 30 persons who paid only for themselves; in the second, 63 taxpayers, 133 tithables, 33 persons who paid for themselves alone; in the third there were 38 taxpayers, 74 tithables and 22 persons paying only for themselves; in the fourth 125 taxpayers, 201 tithables and 81 persons having no dependents to pay for. Thus there were 540 tithables in all and 304 taxpayers. In the entire county there were about 122 persons who paid the poll tax for others. The largest holders of servants or slaves were Mr. Robert Randall with seven, Lieutenant-Colonel William Browne with nine, Mr. Robert Canfield with seven, Mr. Arthur Allen with six, Mr. William Edwards with six, Mr. Francis Mason with seven and Mr. Thomas Binns with eight.[49]

Here again is proof that the popular conception of the Virginia plantation life of the Seventeenth century is erroneous. Instead of the wealthy planter who surrounded himself with scores of servants and slaves, investigation reveals hundreds of little farmers, many of them trusting entirely to their own exertions for the cultivation of the soil, others having but one or two servants, and a bare handful of well-to-do men each having from five to ten, or in rare cases twenty or thirty, servants and slaves.

A further confirmation of these conclusions is to be had by comparing the number of plantations listed in the rent roll of 1704 with the official returns of tithables for 1702.[50] Thus in

Nansemond there were 375 plantations and 1,030 tithables, Henrico with 162 plantations had 863 tithables, Middlesex with 122 plantations had 814 tithables, Gloucester with 381 plantations had 2,626, James City with 287 plantations had 1,193, York with 205 plantations had 1,180, Warwick with 122 plantations had 505, Elizabeth City with 116 plantations had 478, Princess Anne with 215 plantations had 727, Surry with 273 plantations had 739, Isle of Wight with 262 plantations had 896, Norfolk with 303 plantations had 693, New Kent with 497 plantations had 1,245, King William with 217 plantations had 803, King and Queen with 403 plantations had 1,848, Essex with 376 plantations had 1,034, Accomac with 392 plantations had 1,041, Northampton with 258 plantations had 693, Charles City and Prince George together with 420 plantations had 1,327.[51]

In Nansemond the average number of tithables as compared with the number of plantations was 2.7, in Henrico 5.1, in Middlesex 6.7, in Gloucester 6.9, in James City 4.2, in York 5.7, in Warwick 4.1, in Elizabeth City 4, in Princess Anne 3.4, in Surry 2.7, in Isle of Wight 3.3, in Norfolk 2.3, in New Kent 2.5, in King William 3.7, in King and Queen 4.6, in Essex 2.8, in Accomac 2.6, in Northampton 2.3, in Charles City and Prince George combined 3.1. In all Virginia, with the exclusion of the Northern Neck, there were 19,715 tithables and some 5,500 plantations, an average of 3.6 tithables for each plantation. If we deduct from the tithables all the male freeholders included in the rent roll, there remains only some 14,700 persons south of the Rappahannock to make up the list, not only of servants and slaves, but of professional men, wage earners, artisans and dependent sons of landholders over 16 years of age.

Another invaluable source of information concerning the distribution of servants and slaves is provided by the numerous inventories, deeds, and wills which have been preserved in the records. Thus in Surry during the years from 1671 to 1686 we find listed the estates of fifty-nine persons. Of these no less than fifty-two were apparently without servants or slaves; two, William Rooking and Captain Robert Spencer, had five each; one, Mr. William Chambers, had three; and four, Captain William Corker, John Hoge, Mr. John Goring and Samuel Cornell, had one each.[52]

In Elizabeth City of twenty-seven estates recorded during the years from 1684 to 1699 sixteen were without servants or slaves; of twenty-six recorded in York during the period from 1694 to 1697 thirteen had no servants or slaves; of twenty-three recorded in Henrico from 1677 to 1692 fourteen were without servants or slaves.[53] It is true that these inventories and wills, since they would usually pertain to persons of advanced age, perhaps do not furnish an absolutely accurate gauge of the average number of servants held by each planter. On the other hand, it is equally probable that a larger proportion of big estates than of the small found their way into the records. At all events it is evident that a goodly proportion of the landholders, perhaps sixty or sixty-five per cent possessed no slaves or indentured servants, and trusted solely to their own exertions for the cultivation of their plantations.

Thus vanishes the fabled picture of Seventeenth century Virginia. In its place we see a colony filled with little farms a few hundred acres in extent, owned and worked by a sturdy class of English farmers. Prior to the slave invasion which marked the close of the Seventeenth century and the opening of the Eighteenth, the most important factor in the life of the Old Dominion was the white yeomanry.

CHAPTER IV

FREEMEN AND FREEDMEN

IT is obvious that the small planter class had its origin partly in the immigration of persons who paid their own passage, partly in the graduation into freedmen of large numbers of indentured servants. But to determine accurately the proportion of each is a matter of great difficulty. Had all the records of Seventeenth century Virginia been preserved, it would have been possible, by means of long and laborious investigation, to arrive at strictly accurate conclusions. But with the material in hand one has to be satisfied with an approximation of the truth.

It must again be emphasized that the indentured servants were not slaves, and that at the expiration of their terms there was no barrier, legal, racial or social to their advancement. The Lords of Trade and Plantations, in 1676, expressed their dissatisfaction at the word "servitude" as applied to them, which they felt was a mark of bondage and slavery, and thought it better "rather to use the word service, since those servants are only apprentices for years."[1] "Malitious tongues have impaired it (Virginia) much," Bullock declared in 1649, "for it hath been a constant report among the ordinary sort of people that all those servants who are sent to Virginia are sold into slavery, whereas the truth is that the merchants who send servants and have no plantations of their own doe not only transferre their time over to others, but the servants serve no longer than the time they themselves agreed for in England, and this is the ordinary course in England, and no prejudice or hurt to the servant."[2]

The terms of indenture not only took for granted that the servant, upon completing his contract, would establish himself as a proprietor, but usually made it obligatory for the master to furnish him with the equipment necessary for his new life. With rare exceptions he received a quantity of grain sufficient to maintain him for one year; two suits, one of Kersey, the other of cotton; a pair of canvas drawers; two shirts; and one felt hat.[3] The historian Beverley states that to this outfit was added a gun worth twenty shillings.[4] Another writer tells us that the freedman received "a year's provision of corne, double apparel" and a supply of tools.[5]

There existed in England a widespread impression that the servant, upon securing his freedom, was entitled by law to fifty acres of land. This appears to have been a mistake arising from a misapprehension of the nature of the headright, which belonged not to the servant himself, but to the person who paid for his transportation. In many cases the indentures do not state the exact rewards to be received by the new freedman, but only that they are to accord with "the custom of the country," a very elastic term which could be construed by the master to suit his own interest.[6] John Hammond, in his *Leah and Rachel,* strongly advised the immigrant before affixing his signature to the indenture to insist upon the inclusion of a clause specifically providing for the payment of the fifty acres.[7] But the importance which attaches to this matter lies as much in the servant's expectation as in its fulfilment. Whether or not he received his little plantation, he believed that he was to get a tract of land, a very extensive tract it must have seemed to him, which would assure him a good living and make it possible for him to rise out of the class to which he belonged.[8]

In 1627 the Virginia General Court issued an order which is significant of the attitude of the colony itself to the freedmen. "The Court, taking into consideration that the next ensueing year there will be many tenants and servants freed unto whom after their freedom there will be no land due, whereby they may without some order taken to the contrary settle and seat themselves . . . have ordered that the Governor and Council may give unto the said servants and tenants leases for terms of years such quantities of land as shall be needful."[9] Thus, at this period at least, not only was it expected in the colony that servants would become land holders, but it was felt that for them not to do so was a matter of such grave concern as to require the special attention of the Government.

After all, however, the key to the situation must be sought in the history of tobacco culture and the tobacco trade. Tobacco was the universal crop of the colony and upon it every man depended for his advancement and prosperity. If the market was good and the price high, the planters flourished; if sales fell off and the price was low, they suffered accordingly. It is evident, then, that the ability of the freedman to secure a position of economic independence hinged upon the profit to be derived from his little tobacco crop. It does not matter whether he worked as a wage earner, tenant or freeholder, in the end the result would be the same. If the returns from his labor greatly exceeded his expenses, his savings would make it possible for him to establish himself firmly in the class of the colonial yeomanry. On the other hand, if he could wring from the soil no more than a bare subsistence, he would remain always a poor laborer, or perhaps be forced to seek his fortune in some other colony. Thus if we are to understand the status of the freed servant and the hope which he could entertain of advancement, it is necessary to turn our attention once more to economic conditions in the colony. First, we must determine the amount of tobacco the freedman could produce by his unassisted labor; second, the price he received for it; third, how much he had to give the merchants in exchange for their wares; and finally, the margin of profit left after all expenses had been paid.

Despite a marked divergence of testimony regarding the amount of tobacco one man could cultivate, we are able to determine this matter with some degree of exactness. In 1627 the King, in outlining a plan to take into his own hands the entire tobacco trade, proposed to limit the imports to 200 pounds for each master of a family and 125 for each servant.[10] To this, however, the planters entered a vigorous protest, claiming that the quantity was "not sufficient for their maintenance." They in turn suggested that the King take a total of 500,000 pounds a year, which for a population of 3,000 meant 167 pounds for each inhabitant, or perhaps about 500 pounds for each actual laborer.[11] Again in 1634 it was proposed that the Crown purchase yearly 600,000 pounds of Virginia tobacco.[12] As the population of the colony at that date was about 5,000, this would have allowed only 120 pounds for each person, and once more the planters protested vigorously.[13] It would seem that both of these offers were based not so much upon the amount that one man could raise as upon the quantity which could be sold in England at a certain price. In fact it is probable that even so early as 1628 the average output of one freedman was not less than 1,000 pounds. It is interesting to note that in 1640, soon after Governor Francis Wyatt's arrival from England, it was found that the excessive crop of the previous year had so clogged the market that upon the advice of the merchants the Government was "forced to a strict way of destroying the bad and halfe the goode."[14]

The author of *A New Description of Virginia,* published in 1649, claims that one man could plant from 1,600 to 2,000 pounds a year.[15] As the pamphlet presents a somewhat optimistic picture of affairs in general in the colony, this estimate must be taken with some reserve. More trustworthy is the statement of Secretary Thomas Ludwell in 1667 that 1,200 pounds was "the medium of men's yearly crops."[16]

At all events, it is evident that the planter, even when entirely dependent upon his own exertions, could produce a goodly crop. It is now necessary to ascertain what he got for it. In the second and third decades of the Seventeenth century the price of tobacco was very high. The first cargo, consisting of 20,000 pounds consigned in the George, sold for no less than £5,250, or 5s. 3d. a pound.[17] No wonder the leaders of the London Company were pleased, believing that in the Indian weed they had discovered a veritable gold mine! No wonder the settlers deserted their pallisades and their villages to seek out the richest soil and the spots best suited for tobacco culture! The man who could produce 200 pounds of the plant, after all freight charges had been met, could clear some £30 or £35, a very tidy sum indeed for those days. It was the discovery that Virginia could produce tobacco of excellent quality that accounts for the heavy migration in the years from 1618 to 1623. In fact, so rich were the returns that certain persons came to the colony, not with the intention of making it their permanent residence, but of enriching themselves "by a cropp of Tobacco," and then returning to England to enjoy the proceeds.[18]

But this state of affairs was of necessity temporary. Very soon the increasing size of the annual crop began to tell upon the price, and in 1623 Sir Nathaniel Rich declared that he had bought large quantities of tobacco at two shillings a pound.[19] This gentleman felt that it would be just to the planters were they to receive two shillings and four pence for the best varieties, and sixteen pence for the "second sort." In the same year Governor Wyatt and his Council, in a letter to the Virginia Company, placed the valuation of tobacco at eighteen pence a pound.[20] Three years later, however, the Governor wrote the Privy Council advising the establishment in Virginia of a "magazine" or entrepot, where the merchants should be compelled to take the tobacco at three shillings a pound.[21] This proposal did not seem reasonable to the King, and when Sir George Yeardley came over as Governor for the second time he was instructed to see to it that "the merchant be not constrained to take tobacco at 3. P. Pound in exchange for his wares," and to permit him to "make his own bargain."[22]

Apparently not discouraged by this rebuff, in 1628 the Governor, Council and Burgesses petitioned the King, who once more was planning to take the trade into his own hands, to grant them "for their tobacco delivered in the colony three shillings and six pence per pound, and in England four shillings."[23] This valuation undoubtedly was far in advance of the current prices, and King Charles, considering it unreasonable would not come to terms with the planters. In fact, it appears that for some years the price of tobacco had been declining rapidly. In May, 1630, Sir John Harvey wrote the Privy Council that the merchants had bought the last crop with their commodities at less than a penny per pound,[24] and two years later, in a statement sent the Virginia Commissioners, he claimed that the price still remained at that figure.[25]

It may be taken for granted, however, that this estimate was far below the actual price. The planters showed a decided tendency to blow hot or cold according to the purpose in view, and in these two particular statements Sir John was pleading for better treatment from the merchants. Yet it is reasonably certain that tobacco was at a low ebb in the years from 1629 to 1633, and sold at a small fraction of the figures of the preceding decade.[26] The Governor repeatedly wrote asking for relief, while in the Assembly attempts were made to restore the market by restricting the size of the annual crop.[27]

Yet things must have taken a favorable turn soon after, for in 1634 the planters informed the King's Commissioners that they would not sell him their tobacco at less than six pence in Virginia and fourteen pence delivered in England.[28] Later the King wrote to the Governor and Council that the rate had recently "doubly or trebly advanced."[29] This is substantiated by the fact that the Commissioners, in 1638, allowed the planters "4d. a pound clear of all charges," despite which they complained that in an open market they could do better.[30]

In 1638 several prominent Virginians estimated that on an average during the preceding eleven years they had received not more than two pence for their tobacco, but here again it is probable that there was some exaggeration.[31] In 1649 the author of *A New Description of Virginia* stated that tobacco sold in Virginia for three pence a pound.[32] All in all it seems that prices in the early years of the settlement varied from five shillings to a few pence, that a disastrous slump occurred at the end of the third decade, followed by a rapid recovery which brought the rate to about three pence, at which figure it remained fairly constant for twenty-five years or more throughout the Civil War and most of the Commonwealth periods.

The return which the Virginia farmer received from his one staple crop was determined by a number of factors over which he himself had but little control. Had he been permitted to seek his own market and drive his own bargain free from the restraining hand of the British Government, no doubt he would have secured a much better price. But from the moment it became apparent that the Virginia tobacco rivalled in flavor that of the Spanish colonies and could command as ready a sale throughout Europe, the trade was subjected to various regulations and restrictions which proved most vexatious to the colony and elicited frequent and vigorous protests. Neither James nor Charles had any idea of permitting free trade. In their prolonged struggle with the liberal party both saw in tobacco a ready means of aiding the Exchequer, and so of advancing toward the goal of financial independence. These monarchs were by no means hostile to Virginia. In fact, both took great interest in the tiny settlement upon the James, which they looked upon as the beginning of the future British colonial empire. Yet they lent too willing an ear to those who argued that tobacco might be made to yield a goodly revenue to the Crown without injury to the planters.

The policy adopted by the early Stuart kings and adhered to with but minor changes throughout the colonial period consisted of four essential features. First, the tobacco raised in the plantations should be sent only to England; second, upon entering the mother country it must pay a duty to the Crown; third, Spanish tobacco should be excluded or its importation strictly limited; lastly, the cultivation of the plant in England itself was forbidden.

In the years when the colony was still weak and dependent upon the mother country this program was not unfair. The prohibition of tobacco growing in England, however unnecessary it would have been under conditions of free trade, was felt by the planters to be a real concession, while the restrictions upon foreign importations saved them from dangerous competition at the very time when they were least able to combat it. Nor were they seriously injured by the imposition of the customs duties. The planters themselves imagined that the incidence of this tax fell upon their own shoulders and that they were impoverished to the full extent of the revenues derived from it. But in this they were mistaken. The duty, in the last resort, was paid not by the planters but by the British consumers. The colonists were affected adversely only in so far as the enhanced price of tobacco in England restricted the market.

On the other hand, the prohibition of foreign trade was a very real grievance and elicited frequent protests from the planters. Dutch merchants paid high prices for the Virginia tobacco and offered their manufactured goods in return at figures far below those of the British traders. The Virginians could not understand why they should not take advantage of this opportunity. "I humbly desire to be informed from your honors," wrote Governor Harvey to the Virginia Commissioners in 1632, "whether there be any obstacle why we may not have the same freedome of his Majesties other subjects to seek our best market."[33]

But Harvey was attacking what already had become a fixed policy of the Crown, a policy which was to remain the cornerstone of the British colonial system for centuries. The Government had, therefore, not the slightest intention of yielding, and from time to time issued strict orders that all colonial tobacco, whether of Virginia or the West Indies, be brought only to England or to English colonies. When Sir William Berkeley was appointed Governor in 1642 he was instructed to "bee verry careful that no ships or other vessels whatsoever depart from thence, freighted with tobacco or other commodities which that country shall afford, before bond with sufficient securities be taken to his Majesty's use, to bring the same directly into his Majesty's Dominions and not elsewhere."[34]

Despite the insistence of the British Government in this matter, there is abundant evidence to show that the Virginians continued to indulge in direct trade with the continent for many years after the overthrow of the Company. In 1632 Governor Harvey wrote that "our intrudinge neighbours, the

Dutch, doe allow us eighteen peance p. pound" for tobacco, while a few months later we find him reporting the attempt of John Constable and others "to defraud his Majesty of his duties by unloading in the Netherlands."[35]

With the advent of the English Civil War and throughout the Commonwealth period Virginia enjoyed a large degree of independence and found it possible to trade with the Dutch almost with impunity. Even the strict Berkeley seems to have felt it no disloyalty for the planters to seek foreign markets for their staple while the mother country was torn by the contending armies of King and Parliament. And so the merchantmen of Flushing and Amsterdam pushed their prows into every river and creek in Virginia and Maryland, taking off large quantities of tobacco and giving in return the celebrated manufactured goods of their own country. At Christmas 1648, if we may believe the testimony of the author of *A New Description of Virginia,* there were trading in the colony ten ships from London, two from Bristol, seven from New England and twelve from Holland. In 1655 the statement was made that "there was usually found intruding upon the plantation divers ships, surruptitiously carrying away the growth thereof to foreign ports to the prejudice of this Commonwealth."[36]

Thus in the years prior to the Restoration Virginia was never fully subjected to the operation of the British colonial system. When the price of tobacco in the London market fell lower and lower, the planters might and often did find relief by defying the King's commands and trading directly with the Dutch.[37] And this benefitted them doubly, for not only did they strike a better bargain with the foreign traders, but every cargo of tobacco diverted from England tended to relieve the market there and restore prices. In fact there can be little doubt that the frequent violations of the trade restrictions of this period alone saved the colony from the poverty and distress of later days and made possible the prosperity enjoyed by the planters.

It must be noted also that of the tobacco sent to England itself, a part was reshipped to foreign countries. In 1610 a law was enacted for the refunding of all import duties upon articles that were re-exported. This drawback applied also to colonial products, but under Charles I an exception was made in their case and the privilege withdrawn. In consequence the importers made a vigorous protest in Parliament, and the King, in 1631, modified his policy by ordering that of the nine pence duty then in operation, six pence should be refunded when the tobacco was shipped abroad. In 1632 the drawback was increased to seven pence leaving the total duty paid by the merchants who traded through England to foreign countries two pence a pound only.[38] Although this constituted a most serious obstacle to trade and at times aroused the merchants to bitter protest, it by no means completely blocked re-exportation. So great were the natural qualifications of Virginia for producing tobacco, that it was possible to purchase a cargo from the planters on the James, proceed with it to London, pay there the two pence a pound duty, reship it to the continent and sell it there at a profit.[39] Although this trade was not extensive, it must have had an important influence in maintaining prices and in bringing prosperity to all classes in the colony.

Thus Virginia, contrary to the wishes of the mother country and in defiance of her regulations, enjoyed for its staple product in the years prior to 1660, a world market. Whether by direct trade or by re-exportation from England a goodly share of the annual crop was consumed in foreign countries, a share which had it been left in England to clog the market, would have reacted disastrously upon all concerned.

It is apparent, then, that in the first half century of its existence Virginia was the land of opportunity. The poor man who came to her shores, whether under terms of indenture or as a freeman, found it quite possible to establish himself as a person of some property and consideration. We may imagine the case of the servant who had completed his term and secured his freedom at any time during the third decade of the Seventeenth century. As we have seen, it was an easy matter for him to secure a small patch of land and the tools with which to cultivate it. By his unassisted efforts, if he applied himself steadily to the task, he could produce a good crop of tobacco, consisting perhaps of some 400 pounds. This he could sell to the merchants for from two shillings to six pence a pound, or a total of from £10 to £40.[40]

In the years from 1630 to 1640, when the price of tobacco seems to have stabilized itself at from two to three pence, cases of such extraordinary returns must have been of less frequent occurrence, but to some extent lower prices were offset by larger crops. If our freedman in 1635 could raise 800 pounds of leaf and dispose of it for four pence, his income would be £13.6.8; in 1649, by producing 1,000 pounds, he could sell it at three pence for £12.10.0. In fact, it is not too much to say that the average annual income from the labor of one able worker at any time prior to 1660 was not less than £12. When we take into consideration the fact that the planter produced his own food, and that out of the proceeds of his tobacco crop he paid only his taxes and his bills to the English importers, it is evident that he had a goodly margin of profit to lay aside as working capital.

It must not be forgotten, however, that this margin was greatly reduced by the high cost of clothing, farm implements and all other articles brought from across the ocean. The long and dangerous voyage from London to the Chesapeake made the freight rates excessive, while the merchants did not scruple to drive a hard bargain whenever possible. The letters of the Governors are filled with complaints against the exactions of these men. "This year the Merchants have bought our tobacco with their commodities at less than a penny the pounde," Harvey wrote in 1630, "and have not shamed to make the planters pay twelve pounds Sterlinge the tunn freight home."[41] Two years later he complained that a certain Captain Tucker had just sailed leaving his stores well stocked with goods, but with "instructions to his factors not to sell but at most excessive rates."[42] In 1628, the Governor, Council and Burgesses, in a petition to the King, declared that for years they had "groaned under the oppression of unconscionable and cruel merchants by the excessive rates of their commodities."[43] Six years later Governor Harvey stated that all things which "come hither" are sold at "thrice the value they cost in England."[44]

It is obvious, however, that after all expenses had been paid, a goodly margin of profit was left, a margin perhaps averaging some three or four pounds sterling. The provident and industrious immigrant, a few years after the conclusion of his term, might well lay aside enough to make it possible for him in turn to secure a servant from England. This accomplished, he at once rose into the class of employers and his future advance was limited only by his capabilities and his ambition.

We would naturally expect to find, then, that during these years a large percentage of those who came to the colony under terms of indenture, sooner or later acquired land, perhaps bought servants, and became persons of some standing in the colony. Certainly the opportunity was theirs. It will be interesting therefore to study the early records in order to glean what evidence we may concerning this matter. If the servants graduated in any appreciable numbers into the planter class, the patents, wills, inventories, land transfers and muster rolls could hardly fail to yield some evidence of the fact.

Turning first to the earliest period, we find that of the laborers who were imported by the London Company to cultivate the public lands, a fair proportion became proprietors and were regarded by later comers with especial esteem as "ancient planters." At the termination of their service they were granted 100 acres and when this was fully cultivated received another tract of the same extent. To the apprentices bound out to tenants even more liberal treatment was accorded, for they were provided with a year's store of corn, a house, a cow, clothing, armor, household utensils, farm tools and as much land as they could till.[45]

The guiding hand of the Company was missed by the freedmen after the revoking of the charter, for the Governors seem to have left them to shift for themselves. Yet this fact did not prevent many from forging ahead, acquiring land, and in some cases positions of trust in the Government itself. In Hotten's *Immigrants* is published a muster roll for the year 1624 of all the settlers in Virginia, in which servants are carefully distinguished from freemen.[46] By following, as well as the imperfect records of the period permit, the after careers of the former, it is possible to determine with a fair degree of accuracy to what extent the small farmer class at this period was recruited from persons coming to the colony under terms of indenture.

Of the forty-four Burgesses who sat in the Assembly of 1629, no less than seven—John Harris, William Allen, William Popleton, Anthony Pagett, Richard Townsend, Adam Thoroughgood and Lionell Rowlston—were listed as servants in the muster of 1624.[47] Thus some sixteen per cent of this important body, the Virginia House of Commons, at this time was made up of men who five years previously had been working out their passage money. Among the thirty-nine members of the House of 1632, six appear as servants in the muster—Thomas Barnett, Adam Thoroughgood, Lionell Rowlston, Thomas Crump, Roger Webster and Robert Scotchmon. Whether there were other members who came over under terms of indenture but secured their freedom before 1624, we have no means of determining.

The author of *Virginia's Cure,* published in 1662, asserted that the Burgesses "were usual such as went over as servants thither; and though by time, and industry, they may have obtained competent estates, yet by reason of their poor and mean condition, were unskilful in judging of a good estate, either of church or Commonwealth."[48] This statement is a gross exaggeration both as to the composition of the Burgesses and their abilities. Instances of the election of freedmen to the House, fairly frequent in the early years of the colony, became rarer as the century advanced and the field of selection widened. Yet in the Assembly of 1652, of the thirty-five members, eight or nine appear on the patent rolls as headrights brought over by others.[49] It is evident that even so late as the middle of the century the door of opportunity was still open to the freedmen.

In the absence of a complete census for the decades after 1624, it is very difficult to determine what proportion of the servants listed in the muster roll of that year subsequently became landowners. Some light is thrown on the matter by a search through the patent books. Here are found a surprisingly large number of persons who in 1624 were servants. Among these are Anthony Jones, John Sparkes, John Cooke, Roger Delk, John Trussell, William Woolritch, Pettyplace Cloyse, Edward Sparshott, William Dawson, Richard Bell, Robert Browne, Nicholas Browne, John Chandler, Lionell Rowlston, Thomas Savadge, Samuel Bennett, Daniel Shurley,

James Hatfield, Adam Thoroughgood, John Robinson, John Hill, John Seaward, William Ramshaw, Samuel Weaver, John Upton, John Watson, Thomas Crompe and John Russell.[50]

Of these persons several acquired a fair degree of wealth and became of importance in the early life of the colony. It is interesting to note also, that some were men of good condition in England, the case of Adam Thoroughgood, whose brother Sir John Thoroughgood was at one time secretary to the Earl of Pembroke, is notable in this respect. John Hill, before coming to Virginia, had been a book binder in Oxford university, and his father had been a fletcher.[51] The patents of Thomas Crompe and John Russell state that fifty acres was due in each case for the "personal adventure" of the patentee, but since they are distinctly listed as servants in 1624 it seems probable that subsequently each made a visit to England and put in claims for the headright for the return voyage.[52]

Thus it is evident that a large proportion of the landholders during and prior to 1635 had come to the colony under terms of indenture, either under the Company or with private individuals. Perhaps it would not be unfair to estimate this proportion at from thirty to forty per cent, but it must be distinctly understood that the matter cannot be determined with any degree of accuracy or finality. Some years later Governor Berkeley in an address before the Assembly, stated that hundreds of examples testified to the fact that no man in Virginia was denied the opportunity to rise and to acquire both property and honor.[53] Careful research tends to corroborate this assertion but it does not and cannot show whether the bulk of the early planters came to the colony as freemen or as indentured servants.

During the years from 1635 to 1660 the process of building up a class of small farmers in large part from freedmen continued unabated. But the difficulties of the investigator in studying this period are also very great. Yet it is possible, by examining the names that appear in the land patents and wills, and comparing them with the list of headrights, to arrive at fairly satisfactory results. We find that of the 131 persons listed in the York county wills from 1646 to 1659 no less than twenty-five appear as headrights for others. Of these the major part became landowners, some of them men of influence in Virginia.[54] The Rappahannock wills for the years from 1656 to 1664 show a like result. Thirty-nine persons appear in the records, of whom seven came in as headrights.[55]

There is always the possibility of error in identifying these persons for the recurrence of such names as Smith, Jones, Turner, Davis, Hall, the monotonous repetition of a few common given names, and the universal omission of middle names add greatly to our difficulties. Moreover, mistakes are apt to occur because of the transfer of headrights by sale. The free immigrant to whom was due fifty acres for his "personal adventure" might not care to settle on the frontier where alone unpatented land could usually be found. At times he sold his right and purchased a plantation in some one of the older and more advanced counties. It is not conclusively proved, then, that a certain person came as a servant merely because he is listed as a headright. On the other hand, the fact that it was the custom to set forth such transfers clearly in the patent itself, justifies the conclusion that in the cases where no statement of the kind is made, the headright for which the land was granted usually came in under terms of indenture.

In Volume III of the land patents are listed in the years from 1635 to 1653 patents to fifty-seven persons in James City county.[56] Of these no less than thirty-one are found also as headrights belonging to others, although a duplication of names in several cases makes identification uncertain. One person only claimed the fifty acres for having paid his own passage to Virginia. When all possible allowance is made for transfers of rights it is obvious that at this time freedmen were still entering freely into the class of landowners.

An examination of the James City county patents in Volume IV, covering the years from 1653 to 1663, leads to similar results, for of the eighty-five names which appear there, forty-five are listed as headrights belonging to others. And although the tracts granted these men were usually small in size, in certain cases they were far in excess of the average plantation. Thus Edward Cole, who appears as a headright in 1642, patented 900 acres in 1655;[57] Thomas Warburton patented 1,664 acres;[58] George Gilbert 1,000 acres; Francis Burwell 1,000 and John Underwood 2,000 acres.[59] The number of years which elapsed between the listing of the headrights and the granting of the patents varied from two to twenty-eight. The average for the thirty-five cases in which the dates are given is twelve years. As the claims for headrights were often made long after the actual arrival of the servant, it may be assumed that the average was even greater than this. Once more, however, it must be remembered that these lists do not record personal transfers of land, while it is quite certain that many freedmen, instead of patenting unoccupied tracts, secured their little farms by purchase. Some probably became proprietors in the very first year of their freedom and set to work with hoe and plow to wrest their living from the soil.

In the patent rolls the bulk of the headrights are alluded to simply as "persons," leaving it undecided whether those included in the various lists are freemen or servants. But occasionally the newcomers are specifically described as "servants," in which case, of course, there can be no doubt whatever as to their status. By selecting at random a number of names from those so termed, avoiding for convenience sake all Smiths, Joneses and others the frequent recurrence of whose names would make identification difficult, it is possible to arrive at definite conclusions by following, as best we can, their careers in after life. With this in view we have made up the following list of servants: Henry Arnetrading, George Archer, Silvester Atkins, Nicholas Atwell, Edward Ames, John Aram, Robert Arnall, Peter Asheley, William Baldwin, Edward Burt, Francis Baile, John Bauchees, John Bishop, John Blackstone, Anthony Box, Michael Brichley, Peter Buck, William Burcher, John Causey, Robert Chesheire, Thomas Chilcott, Thomas Clayton, Annanias Coplestone, James Courtney, Thomas Cropp, Thomas Connagrave, John Day, John Dodman, Jonathan Ellison, Edward Eastwood, James Fletcher, Thomas Foanes, John Fouke, Francis Francklin, Armstrong Foster, Robert Fossett, John Farr, Robert Garsell, George Gilbert, Henry Giles, Hector Godbear, Francis Gray, Reginald Griffin, Thomas Halcock, Thomas Hand, Henry Hartwell, Hugh Hayes, John Hedler, Richard Huett, John Hodgbins, John Holdin, William Hankinson, John Hether, Lazarus Manning, Thomas Pattison, John Pullapin, Sampson Robins, George Walton, Francis Withers, Robert Webstie and Thomas Warden. A search through the patent rolls, wills, tithable lists and other data found in the records of the period, has led to the more or less positive identification of fifteen of these persons.

John Bishop, who was transported by Thomas Gray, became a man of influence and means. He represented Charles City county in the House of Burgesses in the sessions of 1644, 1652 and 1653, and was variously known as Captain Bishop or Mr. Bishop.[60] Although he became a landowner so early as 1638,[61] his family arrived from England only in 1651. Francis Gray, brought to Virginia at the age of fifteen by Joseph Johnson, also became prominent, securing a seat in the Assembly and acquiring a fair estate. In 1653 he took up 750 acres in Charles City county, while ten years later he is credited with 374 acres more in Westmoreland.[62] His will was recorded in 1667.[63]

George Archer became an extensive landowner, patenting 250 acres in 1663, 550 acres in 1665, 784 acres in 1671 and 1,395 acres in 1673.[64] In 1691 he received, in conjunction with others, title to a tract of 2,827 acres in Henrico.[65] John Holding patented in York county 850 acres in 1649 and 389 acres in 1653.[66] William Baldwin, who came in the Plaine Joan when he was twenty-four years of age, received three grants of land, one for 600 acres in York county, one for 67 acres in Isle of Wight, and one, in conjunction with Richard Lawrence, for 300 in Rappahannock.[67]

Thomas Pattison, transported by Francis Epes in 1635, took up in Lancaster two tracts, one for 200 acres and one for 400.[68] He also became part owner of two more tracts, one for 220 acres and the other for 504.[69] John Dodman secured a patent for 350 acres in Westmoreland in the year 1662.[70] Thomas Warden is mentioned as a landowner in James City county in 1643.[71] George Gilbert, transported in 1635 by Joseph Johnson, took up fifty acres in James City county in 1643.[72] In 1663, in partnership with Richard Scruely, he patented 1,000 acres in the same county north of the Chickahominy river.[73] John Blackstone acquired two tracts, one for 100 acres and the other for 151 acres,[74] while William Burcher received a grant for 300 acres.[75]

Several of these men who came as servants to the Eastern Shore are found in succeeding years among the yeomanry of Accomac and Northampton. Henry Arnetrading, Armstrong Foster, William Burcher and Sampson Robins were signers of the Northampton submission to the Commonwealth in 1652.[76] Henry Arnetrading was the owner of 300 acres of land.[77]

Armstrong Foster was the official tobacco viewer for Hungers, a position entailing no little responsibility.[78] Sampson Robins received a patent for a tract of land in Northampton in 1655.[79] Thomas Clayton is listed among the Northampton tithables of 1666.[80]

In the case of John Day some uncertainty arises. Apparently there were two men of this name in the colony, one transported by John Slaughter, and the other not only paying for his own passage, but for that of a servant as well.[81] A John Day later secured 400 acres in Gloucester county,[82] but whether it was the one who had come as a servant or the one who had entered the colony as a freeman, apparently there is no way of ascertaining.

All in all the story of these men tends to confirm the conclusions hitherto arrived at. It must be remembered that the mortality among the servants in the tobacco fields in the early days of the colony was extremely heavy. It is not improbable that of our sixty-one servants, twenty or more succumbed before the completion of their first year. That of the remaining forty-one, fourteen or fifteen established themselves as solid farmers, while several became men of influence in the colony, is a striking proof that at this period many freedmen had the opportunity to advance. Taking it for granted that the records of some of the sixty-one have been lost, or that our research has failed to reveal them, we once more come to the conclusion that a full thirty or forty per cent of the landowners of the period from 1635 to 1666 came to the colony under terms of indenture.

On the other hand, it is equally positive that the class of poor planters was recruited in part from free immigrants, men who paid their own passage across the ocean and at once established themselves as freeholders. Of this too, the records furnish ample testimony. Thus in 1636 we find that

Richard Young was granted 100 acres in Warwick "due him for his personal adventure and for the transportation of his wife Dorothy Young."[83] A year later Roger Symonds received 100 acres in Charles City "due him for the transportation of his wife, Alice, and one servant, Richard Key."[84] Similarly in May 1636, Thomas Wray was allowed 50 acres for his "personal adventure." Such cases could be multiplied indefinitely.[85]

A careful analysis of the patent rolls from 1623 to July 14, 1637, published in the *Virginia Magazine of History and Biography* for April, 1901, shows conclusively that the lists contain the names of many persons who at no time were under terms of indenture. Of the 2,675 names appearing in the records, the editor states that 336 are positively known to have come over as freemen, many of them being heads of families. "There are 245 persons whose names do not occur as headrights and yet of whom it is not positively shown that they were freemen, though the probability seems to be that by far the greater number were. And there were 2,094 persons whose transportation charges were paid by others. This last number includes some negroes, all those specifically termed 'servants' and all others. . . . It would probably be a fair estimate to say that of the names represented in the patents cited, there were about 675 free men, women and children who came to Virginia and about 2000 servants and slaves."[86] Similarly in the issue of the magazine for January, 1902, the editor says that "for some years, about this period, it is probable (from the best calculations which can be made) that seventy-five per cent of the emigrants to Virginia were indentured servants."[87]

There seems to be no reason to doubt the accuracy of these conclusions. Certainly any study of immigration to Virginia in the Seventeenth century is woefully incomplete if it fails to take into consideration the very considerable proportion of free settlers. On the other hand, it is probable that a similar study of the lists for a later date would show a smaller percentage of freemen. However this may be, it is evident that by far the larger part of the newcomers at all periods must have been indentured servants intended for service in the tobacco fields. In 1638 Richard Kemp wrote Secretary Windebanke that "of hundreds which are yearly transported, scarce any but are brought in as merchandise to make sale of."[88]

Yet it must not be forgotten that any immigration of poor freemen, however small, would have a very marked influence upon the formation of the small farmer class. Of the host of servants a certain proportion only, a proportion probably less than fifty per cent, could hope even in the most favorable times to become freeholders. If they survived the hardships and dangers of the service with their masters, it still remained for them to acquire property and win for themselves a place in the life of the colony. And to accomplish this they must display determination, intelligence, industry and thrift, qualities by no means universal among the classes in England from which the servants were chiefly drawn. But for the free immigrant there need be no period of probation. He might at once purchase his farm, erect his home, secure all necessary tools and put out his crop of tobacco. And whereas the servant usually found it possible to maintain a family only after many years of hard work, perhaps not at all, the free settler often married before leaving England and brought his wife and children with him.

In conclusion it may be said that in the first fifty years of the colony's existence conditions were very favorable for the graduation of the servant into the class of small freeholders, that the records amply prove that many succeeded in doing so, but that at this period a fair proportion of free immigrants also came to the colony. Before the expiration of the Commonwealth period was formed from these two sources, perhaps in not unequal proportions, a vigorous, intelligent, independent yeomanry, comprising fully 90 percent of all the landowners.

CHAPTER V

The Restoration Period

The people of Virginia hailed the Restoration with unaffected joy. Not only did they anticipate that the termination of the long period of civil war and unrest in England would react favorably upon their own prosperity, but they felt that Sir William Berkeley's well known loyalty and his action in proclaiming Charles II immediately after the execution of his father, might assure them the King's especial favor now that he at last had come into undisputed possession of his throne. They were doomed to bitter disappointment, however, for the Restoration brought them only hardship and suffering, discontent and rebellion.

No sooner had the royal Government been safely installed than it set to work to perfect and to enforce the colonial policy which in principle had been accepted from the first. The ties which united the colonies with the mother country were strengthened, those which gave them a common interest with foreign nations in so far as possible were snapped. The British empire was to become a unit, closely knit by economic bonds and presenting to all other nations a hostile front. With this in view Parliament passed a series of Navigation Acts, under which the trade of the colonies was regulated for many years to come.

It is necessary for us to enquire, therefore, into the effects of these laws upon the tobacco trade, for tobacco, as we have seen, was the key to the prosperity of the colony, and favorable economic conditions alone could make it possible for the newcomer to establish himself as a member of the Virginia yeomanry. If the strict enforcement of the Navigation Acts should bring low prices for tobacco and wipe out the margin of profit for the man who tilled the soil with his own hands, not only would the small planter class not expand, but might actually decline in numbers.

There were three main features of the colonial legislation of Parliament during this period, all of them interrelated and all tending toward the one great object of keeping the English plantations for the English. It was provided that the chief colonial products such as tobacco and sugar should be sent only to England or to English colonies, that the colonies should with few exceptions import goods only from British territory, that all products taken to or from any colony should be conveyed only in English vessels manned by crews composed mainly of Englishmen.

In committing itself to this policy the royal Government felt that the plantations would play a useful and necessary part in the great system which was planned, and in so doing would find prosperity. It had been the hope of the English people that their colonies would produce the articles which were so badly needed by the mother country to revive her waning industry and permit a greater measure of economic independence. Although more than half a century had passed since the first foothold had been gained upon the American continent, this expectation was as far from realization as ever. The colonies, from Massachusetts to Barbados were producing, not the articles which England especially needed, but those for which they had the greatest natural aptitude, especially tobacco and sugar. And these staples they sent, not to England alone, but to various foreign countries as well.

In short the vision of a closely knit, self-sustaining empire, the vision which had been in men's minds for many decades before the founding of Jamestown, seemed to have proved delusive. The colonies were developing interests and commercial connections hostile to those of the mother country, were nourishing the manufactures and shipping of foreign nations almost as much as those of England. And this the Government at London would not tolerate. The colonial trade with strangers must come to an end. If Virginia and Maryland produced more tobacco than the English market could absorb, they could find ready relief by turning their energies into other channels. Let them furnish the old country with pig iron or potash or silk or ship-stores and they would find ready and eager purchasers. So reasoned the English, and as their views were backed by the mandates of Crown and Parliament, the colonists were forced to submit. If they could fit themselves into the system prescribed for them, all would be well and good; if they found this impossible, they would have to suffer without hope of redress.

And suffer Virginia did for a full quarter of a century. The tobacco of the Chesapeake bay colonies had long since reached the point where it required a world market. If confined to England alone, only a fraction of the output could be consumed and disaster was certain. It was well enough for the Government to restrict the importation of Spanish leaf and to prohibit the planting of tobacco in England, these regulations could do no more than give the colonists undisputed possession of the home market, and the home market was not enough. This point seems to have been ignored by those writers who have contended that the strict enforcement of the British colonial system in itself entailed no hardship upon the tobacco colonies.

"It is obvious that any criticism of England's regulation of the colonial tobacco trade, which is based on a laissez-faire social philosophy," says George Lewis Beer, in *The Old Colonial System,* "is equally applicable to the arrangement by means of which the tobacco planter secured exlusive privileges in the home market."[1] Yet it is certain that the tobacco growers of England could never have competed with Maryland and Virginia had there been free trade. The prohibition of planting in the old country was necessary only because of the tariff, varying from 200 per cent in 1660 to 600 per cent in 1705, upon the colonial product. And though the exclusion of Spanish tobacco was a more real benefit, for the Spaniard produced varieties unknown in Virginia, there is exaggeration here also. This is clearly shown by the fact that at the end of the Seventeenth century England was sending millions of pounds of her colonial tobacco to Spain itself.[2] The leaf was brought from Virginia and Maryland, forced to pay a duty of about fifty per cent, and re-exported to the Spanish ports, where it found a ready sale. Had there been free exchange of commodities, the English colonies would have sold to Spain more tobacco than the Spanish colonies to England.

In truth the loss of the foreign market was a terrible disaster. In framing the Navigation Acts it was not the intention of the Government to stop entirely the flow of tobacco to the continent of Europe, but to divert it from the old channels and make it pass through England. It was therefore provided that in case the leaf was shipped out again to foreign ports, all the duties, except one half of the Old Subsidy, should be withdrawn.[7] The remaining half penny, however, amounted to forty or fifty per cent of the original cost of the goods, and proved at first an almost insuperable barrier to the European trade. Moreover, the shortage of ships which resulted from the exclusion of the Dutch merchants, the expense of putting in at the English ports, the long and troublesome procedure of reshipping, all tended to discourage the merchants and hamper re-exportation.

We may take for granted also that the resentment of Holland at the Navigation Acts, which struck a telling blow at her maritime prestige, played an important part in blocking foreign trade. The Dutch had been the chief European distributors of the Virginia and Maryland tobacco, and if they refused to take it, now that it could be secured only in England, it would pile up uselessly in the London warehouses. They understood well enough that the half penny a pound duty was a tribute levied upon them by their most dangerous rival. It is not surprising that instead of bowing to the new restrictions, they sought to free their trade entirely from dependence on British tobacco, by fostering the cultivation of the plant in their own country.

The colonists found an able defender in the merchant John Bland. In a Remonstrance addressed to the King this man set forth with remarkable clearness the evils which would result from the Navigation Acts, and pleaded for their repeal. The Hollander was already beginning to plant tobacco, he said, and would soon be able to supply all his needs at home. "Will he, after accustomed to the tobacco of his own growth," he asked, "ever regard that which is in Virginia? Will he ever afterwards be induced to fetch it thence, when he finds his profit nigher at home? Will he ever buy that of us, when by passing so many hands, and so much charge contracted thereon, is made so dear, that he can have it cheaper in his own territories? (Surely no.) Therefore it clearly appears, that being so, of necessity we must lose that Trade and Commerce."

"If the Hollanders must not trade to Virginia, how shall the Planters dispose of their Tobacco? The English will not buy it, for what the Hollander carried thence was a sort of tobacco not desired by any other people, nor used by us in England but merely to transport for Holland. Will it not then perish on the Planters hands? . . . Can it be believed that from England more ships will be sent than are able to bring thence what tobacco England will spent? If they do bring more, must they not lose thereby both stock and Block, principle and charges? The tobacco will not vend in England, the Hollanders will not fetch it from England; what must become thereof? . . . Is not this a destruction to the commerce? For if men lose their Estates, certainly trade cannot be encreased."[8]

The enforcement of the trade laws was indirectly the cause of still another misfortune to the colonies, for the two wars with Holland which grew out of it reacted disastrously upon their trade. In fact, on each occasion the small stream of tobacco which had trickled over the dam of restrictions into foreign countries was for a time almost entirely cut off. Not only did the tobacco exports to Holland itself come to an end, but the Dutch war vessels played havoc with the trade between England and other countries and even between England and her colonies.

The loss of their foreign exports was calamitous to the planters. Had the demand for tobacco been more elastic, the consequences might not have been so fatal, for declining prices would have stimulated consumption and made it possible for England to absorb most of the output. But the duty kept up the price and the result was a ruinous glut in the English market. Tobacco sufficient for a continent poured into the kingdom, where since the normal outlet was blocked by the half penny a pound on re-exported leaf, it piled up uselessly.

The effect upon prices was immediate. The planters were forced to take for their crops half of what they had formerly received and had reason for rejoicing if they could dispose of it at all. In 1662 Governor Berkeley and other leading citizens stated that the price of tobacco had fallen so low that it would not "bear the charge of freight and customs, answer the adventure, give encouragement to the traders and subsistence to the inhabitants."[9] In 1666 Secretary Thomas Ludwell told Lord Arlington that tobacco was "worth nothing."[10] Later in the same year the planters complained that the price was so low that they were not able to live by it.[11] "For the merchants, knowing both our necessities and the unconsumable quantities of tobacco we had by us," they said, "gave us not the twentieth part of what they sold it for in England."[12] Tobacco had so glutted the markets, it was declared, and brought the planter so small a return, that he could "live but poorly upon it." In fact, the merchants in 1666 had left the greater part of the two preceding crops upon their hands.[13]

"Twelve hundred pounds of tobacco is the medium of men's crops," wrote Secretary Ludwell to Lord John Berkeley in 1667, "and half a penny per pound is certainly the full medium of the price given for it, which is fifty shillings out of which when the taxes . . . shall be deducted, is very little to a poor man who hath perhaps a wife and children to cloath and other necessities to buy. Truly so much too little that I can attribute it to nothing but the great mercy of God . . . that keeps them from mutiny and confusion."[14] The following year he wrote in similar vein. The market was glutted; a third of the planters' tobacco was left on their hands; the rest sold for nothing.[15]

The Governor and Council declared that the merchant "allows not much above a farthing a pound for that which the planter brings to his door. And if there shall be any amongst us who shall be able to ship his tobacco on his own account, it will be at such a rate as the tobacco will never repay him, since they are inforced to pay from £12 to £17 per ton freight, which usually was but at seven pounds."[16] "A large part of the people are so desperately poor," wrote Berkeley in 1673, "that they may reasonably be expected upon any small advantage of the enemy to revolt to them in hopes of bettering their condition by sharing the plunder of the colony with them."[17] That matters had not changed in 1681 is attested by the statement of the Council that the impossibility of disposing of their tobacco without a heavy loss overwhelmed both Virginia and Maryland, and brought upon them a "vast poverty and infinite necessity."[18] "The low price of tobacco staggers the imagination," Lord Culpeper wrote to Secretary Coventry, "and the continuance of it will be the speedy and fatal ruin of this noble Colony."[19]

These distressing conditions bore with telling weight upon the small planters. The margin of profit which formerly had made it possible for the freedman to advance rapidly was now wiped out entirely and the poor man found it impossible to keep out of debt. In 1668 Secretary Ludwell declared that no one could longer hope to better himself by planting tobacco.[20] Eight years later Nathaniel Bacon, in justifying his rebellion declared that the small farmers were deeply in debt and that it was "not in the power of labor or industry" to extricate them.[21] "The poverty of Virginia is such," said a certain John Good in 1676, "that the major part of the inhabitants can scarce supply their wants from hand to mouth, and many there are besides can hardly shift without supply one year."[22] In 1673 the Governor and Council reported that of the planters, "at least one third are single persons (whose labor will hardly maintain them) or men much in debt," who might reasonably be expected to revolt to the Dutch upon any small advantage gained by them.[23] In 1680 they again reported that "the indigency of the Inhabitants is such that they are in noe manner capacitated to support themselves."[24] Three years later they wrote that "the people of Virginia are generally, some few excepted, extremely poor, not being able to provide against the pressing necessities of their families."[25]

Despite this repeated and explicit testimony of the misery and poverty of the colony during this period, which resulted from the stagnation of the tobacco market after the passage of the Navigation Acts, the surprising statement is made by Mr. George Lewis Beer, in *The Old Colonial System,* that England's trade restrictions had nothing to do with Bacon's Rebellion. "It has been at various times contended," he says, "that the uprising was, in part at least, one against the laws of trade and navigation. If there had existed in Virginia any widespread and well defined feeling of antagonism to these laws, it would unquestionably have found expression in the county grievances. Most of these reports were drawn up in a number of articles, and in all there were nearly two hundred of such separate subdivisions, yet only three of this number refer in any way to these statutes. There is no valid reason for assuming that the commercial system played any part whatsoever, or was in any degree, an issue, in the upheaval of 1676."[26]

If by this statement it is meant that Bacon and his men did not rebel in order to force the repeal of the Navigation Acts, or even that they did not have the acts in mind at the time, there are many students of Virginia history who will agree with it. But if Mr. Beer means that these laws, with their baleful effect upon the prosperity of Virginia, did not produce the conditions fundamental to the rising, he is certainly wrong. The evidence is overwhelming.

Surely no one will deny that misery, poverty and nakedness are breeders of sedition. Had it not been for the Navigation Acts there would not have been so many desperate persons in Virginia ready at any excuse to fly in the face of the Government. Bacon's men were just the type of miserably poor freemen that Berkeley several years before had feared would rebel. He himself, in his proclamation of Feb. 10, 1677, spoke of them as "men of mean and desperate fortunes."[27] William Sherwood called the rebels rude and indigent persons, alluding to them as "tag, rag and bobtayle."[28] Over and over again they are described as the multitude, the rabble, the skum.

Exception must be taken also to the statement that had there existed in Virginia any well-defined feeling of antagonism to the Navigation Acts it would have found expression in the county grievances. It should be remembered that these reports had been called for by the commissioners sent over by Charles II to investigate the troubles. The men who drew them up occupied the position of defeated rebels, and the grievances were primarily a list of excuses for their treason. They all stood trembling for their property, if they had any, and for their miserable lives. The memory of the fate of Drummond and Bland and Arnold and many others of their fellow rebels was fresh in their minds. It is not reasonable to suppose that they would tell the King that they had risen in arms against his authority in order to secure the overthrow of laws which his Majesty considered of such vital importance, laws which concerned intimately the royal revenue. Such a declaration would not have seconded successfully their plea for mercy. This is made amply clear by the reception accorded one of the few complaints which did actually touch the Navigation Acts. The commissioners report it to the King as "an extravagant request for liberty to transport their tobacco to any of his Majesty's plantations without paying the imposts, payable by act of Parliament, etc. This head is wholly mutinous—to desire a thing contrary to his Majesty's royal pleasure and benefit and also against an act of Parliament."[29]

Despite the obviously ruinous effects of the Navigation Acts upon Virginia, Mr. Beer makes the assertion that there was no very serious and general opposition to them in Virginia. "Apart from the criticisms of Bland and Berkeley," he says, "there was virtually no complaint against the system of trade enjoined by the Navigation Acts. While the Barbados Assembly and that colony's governors were vociferous in their protests, the Virginia legislature remained strangely mute."[30]

This silence on the part of the Virginia Assembly can by no means be interpreted as an indication that the people of the colony felt the Navigation Acts to be equitable and not injurious to their interests. It meant only that no Assembly under Sir William Berkeley would dare protest against an act which had received the royal sanction. That would have seemed the veriest treason to the fiery old loyalist. And the Assembly was entirely under Sir William's control. The members of both Houses were his creatures and his henchmen. Over and over again it is testified that the Assembly did nothing more than register his will.[31] If then it did not protest, it was because Sir William did not wish it to protest.

But this does not prove that the planters were not angered and alarmed at the stringent acts. That they considered them baleful is amply proved by their continuous complaints of the economic ruin which had overtaken the colony. The method they chose of combatting the trade laws, a method apt to be far more effective than the angry protests of the Barbados Assembly, was to send the Governor to England to use his influence at Court to have the acts modified or repealed. And Berkeley did what he could. While in England he wrote a paper called *A Discourse and View of Virginia,* which he hoped would induce the Government to change its policy in regard to the colonies. "Wee cannot but resent," he said, "that 40,000 people should be impoverished to enrich little more than 40 merchants, who being the whole buyers of our tobacco, give us what they please for it. And after it is here sell as they please, and indeed have 40,000 servants in us at cheaper rates, than other men have slaves, for they find them meat and drink and clothes. We furnish ourselves and their seamen with meat and drink, and all our sweat and labor as they order us, will hardly procure us coarse clothes to keep us from the extremities of heat and cold."[32] That Sir William was but the mouthpiece of the colony in this protest there can be no doubt.

But his pleadings were in vain. England would not change the laws which were the expression of her settled colonial policy. The planters must adjust themselves to changed conditions no matter how bitter was the experience. Sir William was told to go home to report to the Virginians that they need not kick against the pricks, but that England would be most pleased could they turn from the all-absorbing culture of tobacco to the production of the raw materials she so greatly desired. And Berkeley did return determined to exert every effort to lead the colonists into new prosperity by inducing them to devote a part of their energies to basic commodities. In fact he promised that in seven years he would flood the British market with new Virginia goods.[33]

Although he set to work with his accustomed vigor to make good this boast, he met with but scant success. Lack of efficient and skilled labor, high wages, and not very favorable natural conditions, made it impossible for him to compete with the long-established industries of Europe. After a few years all attempts to make silk and potash and naval stores were abandoned, and the planters continued to put their trust in tobacco.

That Berkeley was never persuaded that the Navigation Acts were just or beneficial is shown by his answer to the query of the Lords of Trade in 1671, when they asked him what impediments there were to the colony's trade. "Mighty and destructive," he replied, "by that severe act of Parliament which excludes us from having any commerce with any nation in Europe but our own, so that we cannot add to our plantation any commodity that grows out of it . . . for it is not lawful for us to carry a pipe-staff or a bushel of corn to any place in Europe out of the King's dominions. If this were for his Majesty's service or the good of his subjects we should not repine, whatever our sufferings are for it. But on my soul it is the contrary of both."[35]

Nor is this the only direct testimony that the colonists were filled with bitterness against the Navigation Acts. In 1673, during the war with Holland, Sir John Knight declared that "the planters there do generally desire a trade with the Dutch and all other nations, and speak openly there that they are in the nature of slaves, so that the hearts of the greatest part of them are taken away from his Majesty and consequently his Majesty's best, greatest and richest plantation is in danger, with the planters' consent, to fall into the enemy's hands, if not timely prevented."[36] This is corroborated by the Council itself, in an official letter to the King. "For in this very conjuncture had the people had a distasteful Governor," they wrote, "they would have hazarded the loss of this Country, and the rather because they doe believe their Condicon would not be soe bad under the Dutch in Point of Traffique as it is under the Merchants who now use them hardly, even to extremity."[37]

It is evident, then, that throughout the entire reign of Charles II the unhappy effects of the trade restrictions made of Virginia, which formerly had been the land of opportunity for the poor man, a place of suffering, poverty and discontent. The indentured servant who came over after 1660 found conditions in the colony hardly more favorable for his advancement than in England. The price of tobacco was now so low that it was not possible for a man, by his unassisted efforts, to make a profit by its cultivation. If Thomas Ludewell is correct in estimating the return from the average crop at fifty shillings, the lot of the poor man must have been hard indeed. Hungry he need not be, for food continued to be abundant and easy to obtain, but of all that the merchants gave him in return for his tobacco—clothing, farm implements, household furnishings—he had to content himself with the scantiest supply. And only too often his pressing needs brought him into hopeless debt. As for imitating his predecessors of the earlier period in saving money, purchasing land and servants and becoming a substantial citizen, the task was well nigh impossible of accomplishment.

It would be expected, then, that even the most exhaustive investigation could reveal but a few indentured servants, coming over after 1660, who succeeded in establishing themselves in the Virginia yeomanry. And such, indeed, is the case. Fortunately we have at hand for the period in question the means of determining this matter with an exactness impossible for the first half of the century. Nicholson's rent roll of 1704 supplies a complete list, with the exception of those in the Northern Neck, of every landowner in Virginia. At the same time we have in the Land Office at Richmond, the names of many thousands of persons listed as headrights, constituting almost all the immigrants who came in during the years from 1666 to the end of the century. Thus by comparing the two lists and trying to identify on the rent roll the names found in the patents, it is possible to fix the proportion of servants who won for themselves at this time places among the landowning class.

Selecting the year 1672 as typical of the Restoration period, we find that an examination of 672 of the names which are listed as headrights, eleven only can be identified with any degree of certainty upon the rent roll. Of 1116 names examined in the years from 1671 to 1674 inclusive, only 26 are positively those of persons listed as landowners in 1704. After making due allowance for the fact that uncertainty exists in a number of other cases, and that some who prospered must have died in the intervening years, it is safe to say that not more than five or six per cent of the indentured servants of this period succeeded in establishing themselves as independent planters.

These conclusions are borne out by the slowness with which the population increased during the years following the passage of the Navigation Acts. In the Commonwealth period the colony had advanced by leaps and bounds, and the inhabitants, estimated at 15,000 in 1649,[38] were placed by Berkeley thirteen years later at 40,000.[39] Under the system which existed during these years, when the colonists enjoyed a comparatively free trade, the population had tripled. But after 1660, while the Virginia tobacco was dumped upon the restricted English market and prices fell lower and lower, no such rapid growth is noted. In 1671, nine years after his first estimate, Governor Berkeley still placed the population at 40,000.[40] And even if we accept the statement of the Virginia agents sent to England to secure a charter for the colony that in 1675 the number of inhabitants was 50,000, it is evident that some pernicious influence was at work to retard the development of England's most important American province.[41] A drop in the rate of increase from 200 per cent during the thirteen years prior to 1662, to 25 per cent in the thirteen years following, is a clear index to the startling change brought about in the colony by the British trade regulations.

These figures are the more significant in that there was no appreciable slackening of the stream of servants. It is probable that in the period from 1662 to 1675, which marked this estimated increase of 10,000 persons, fully 20,000 immigrants had come to the colony.[42] The patent rolls for 1674 alone give the names of 1931 headrights, and this year is by no means exceptional. No wonder Edward Randolph was surprised at the smallness of the population and wrote to the Board of Trade that it should be investigated why Virginia had not grown more, "considering what vast numbers of servants and others had been transported thither."[43]

But Randolph failed to realize that it is not the volume of immigration but the number of people a country will support which in the end determines the size of the population. It was not enough to pour into the colony tens of thousands of poor settlers; opportunity had also to be afforded them for earning an adequate living. And this opportunity, because of the enforcement of the Navigation Acts and the consequent ruin of trade, they did not have in Virginia. Throughout the Restoration period not more than forty or fifty thousand people could exist upon the returns from the tobacco crop, and beyond that the population could hardly rise. If more poured in, they must of necessity live in misery and rags, or migrate to other colonies where more favorable conditions existed.

We are not at present concerned with what become of this surplus population, but only with the fact that the Navigation Acts brought to a dead halt the process of moulding freedmen and other poor settlers into a prosperous yeomanry. By the year 1660 this class seems to have reached its highest development, and had a rent roll of land owners been drawn up at that date it would doubtless have shown almost as many names as that of 1704. In fact it is fortunate that in the bitter years from 1660 to 1685 it did not succumb entirely. With the price of tobacco so low that no profit was to be derived from it, with his family in rags, the small planter might well have sold his land to his more wealthy neighbor and joined the newly freed servants in moving on to western Carolina or to the northern colonies.

In fact it is an indication of the solid character of the Virginia yeomanry that it survived to enter the Eighteenth century, that under Andros and Nicholson as well as under Sir William Berkeley it was the soundest element in the life of the colony. Had it not been for the crowning misfortune of the introduction of great swarms of negro slaves, sooner or later it would have come once more into its own, would have carved out for itself a new prosperity, would have filled Virginia from the Atlantic to the Alleghanies.

CHAPTER VI

The Yeoman in Virginia History

Perhaps it would have been impossible for the Virginia yeoman to survive the dark days of the Restoration period had it not been for the fact that in the matter of his food supply he was independent of England and her vexatious trade restrictions. He might be in rags, but there was no reason why he should ever feel the pangs of hunger. Seldom in any climate, in any age has food existed in such extraordinary variety and in such lavish abundance.

Almost every planter, even the poorest, was possessed of cattle. The *Perfect Discription* states that in 1649 there were in the colony "of Kine, Oxen, Bulls, Calves, twenty thousand, large and good."[1] Fifteen years later the number had increased to 100,000.[2] Many a little farmer, too poor to afford the help of a servant or a slave, had cattle more than sufficient for his every need. John Splitimber, a planter of meagre means, died in 1677 owning eight cows and one bull.[3] John Gray, whose entire personal estate was valued only at 9,340 pounds of tobacco, possessed at his death six cows, six calves, two steers and one heifer.[4] The inventory of the goods of Richard Avery, another poor planter, shows three steers, one heifer, three small cattle and one calf.[5] The yeoman not only secured from these animals a goodly supply of beef, but milk in abundance from which he made butter and cheese. The steers he used as beasts of burden.

The meat which most frequently appeared upon the table of the poor man was that of swine. The planter marked his hogs and turned them loose in the woods to feed upon roots and acorns. On the other hand, sheep did not multiply in the colony, for the woods were not suited for their maintenance, and those areas which had been cleared of trees could more profitably be utilized for agriculture than for pasture lands. Mutton was a rare delicacy even with the well-to-do.[6]

Poultry were exceedingly numerous. At the time of the Company it was stated that the planter who failed to breed one hundred a year was considered a poor manager. The *Perfect Discription* says that the poultry—"Hens, Turkies, Ducks, Geece"—were without number.[7] Moreover, the wild fowls of the inland waterways were so numerous that even the least skilful of huntsmen could readily bring down enough for the needs of his family, and the mallard, the goose, the canvas-back appeared regularly in season upon every table.[8]

The planter always devoted a part of his land to the production of the grain which was needed for his personal requirements. "They yearly plow and sow many hundred acres of Wheat," it was said, "as good and faire as any in the world."[9] At the same time maize grew so readily and its cultivation proved so cheap, that cornbread formed a part of the diet not only of the planters themselves, but of their servants and slaves.

From his garden, an inevitable accompaniment of every plantation, the farmer secured a large variety of vegetables—potatoes, asparagus, carrots, turnips, onions, parsnips, besides such fruits as strawberries, gooseberries, raspberries; from his orchard he had apples, pears, quinces, apricots, peaches.[10] Honey was abundant, and there were few householders who did not have hives under the eaves of their outbuildings. One planter, a Mr. George Pelton, is said to have made a profit of £30 from his bees.[11] There were also many wild swarms in the woods, which yielded a delicious return to the colonial bee-hunters.[12]

It is easy to understand, then, why there were no complaints of hunger even in the days when poverty was almost universal. The Virginia yeoman spread always an abundant table. "He that is lazy and will not work," said the author of *New Albion,* "needs not fear starving, but may live as an Indian, sometimes Oysters, Cockles, Wilkes, Clams, Scollons two moneths together; sometimes wilde Pease and Vetches, and Long Oates, sometimes Tuckaho, Cuttenoman ground, Nuts, Marhonions, sometimes small nuts, Filbirds, Wallnuts, Pokeberries, ten sorts of Berries, Egs of Foul, small Fish in Coves at low water will teach him to live idly." "It must needs follow then that diet cannot be scarce, since both rivers and woods afford it, and that such plenty of Cattle and Hogs are every where, which yield beef, veal, milk, butter, cheese and other made dishes, porke, bacon and pigs, and that as sweet and savoury meat as the world affords, these with the help of Orchards and Gardens, Oysters, Fish, Fowle and Venison, certainly cannot but be sufficient for a good diet and wholsom accommodation, considering how plentifully they are, and how easie with industry to be had."[13]

But the little planter, with the advent of the Navigation Acts, often suffered keenly from a lack of adequate clothing. Again and again the letters of the period state that the poor man was reduced to rags, that he could not protect his family from the winter's cold. There was some manufacture of cloth in the home, but the planter usually trusted to the foreign trader to bring him every article of clothing. He had neither the implements nor the skill to supply his own needs. During the Restoration period, and again at the time of the war of the Spanish Succession, when the price of tobacco fell so very low, many families succeeded in producing enough homespun to supply their most pressing needs.[14] But with the return of better conditions they laid aside the loom and the wheel, and resumed their purchase of English cloth.

In normal times the poor planter was comfortably clad. Edward Williams, in *Virginia Richly Valued,* advised every new immigrant to bring a monmouth cap, a waistcoat, a suit of canvas, with bands, shirts, stockings and shoes.[15] The author of *New Albion* thought that each adventurer should provide himself with canvas or linen clothes, with shoes and a hat.[16]

The houses of the small planters were small but comfortable. "Pleasant in their building," says John Hammond, "which although for most part they are but one story besides the loft, and built of wood, yet contrived so delightfully that your ordinary houses in England are not so handsome, for usually the rooms are large, daubed and whitelimed, glazed and flowered, and if not glazed windows, shutters which are made very pritty and convenient."[17] *The New Description of Virginia,* published in 1649, says: "They have Lime in abundance for their houses, store of bricks made, and House and Chimnies built of Brick, and some of Wood high and fair, covered with Shingell for Tyle."[18]

In the days of the Company most of the houses seem to have been made of logs, and Butler, in his *Virginia Unmasked*. declared that they were the "worst in the world," and that the most wretched cottages in England were superior to them.[19] But the period of which Butler wrote was exceptional, and before long the growing prosperity of the colony made possible a great improvement in the dwellings of the people. The rough log cabin gave way to the little framed cottage with chimneys at each end.

A residence erected in one of the parishes of the Eastern Shore in 1635 to serve as a parsonage may be accepted as typical of the better class of houses in Virginia at this time. It was made of wood, was forty feet wide, eighteen deep and had a chimney at each end. On either side was an additional apartment, one used as a study, the other as a buttery.[20] For the poor man this was far too pretentious, and he had to content himself with a home perhaps thirty by twenty feet, containing at times two or three apartments, at times only one.

But such as it was it gave him ample protection against the heat of summer and the cold of winter. Fuel he never lacked. When the frosts of December and January came upon him, he had only to repair to the nearest forest, axe in hand, to supply himself with wood in abundance. In this way, not only would he keep a roaring blaze in his open fireplace, but would widen the space available for the next summer's tobacco crop.

The surroundings of the planter's residence were severely plain. In the yard, which usually was uninclosed, towered a cluster of trees, a survival of the primeval forest. Nearby was the garden, with its flowers and vegetables, the dove-cote, the barn, the hen house, perhaps a milk house or even a detached kitchen. In some cases wells were sunk, but the use of natural springs was more common.[21]

Of the plantation itself, only a fraction was under cultivation at one time. Tobacco was exceedingly exhausting to the soil, but the cheapness of land led the planters to neglect the most ordinary precautions to preserve its fertility. They sowed year after year upon the same spot, until the diminishing yield warned them of approaching sterility, and then would desert it to clear a new field. This system made it necessary for them to provide for the future by securing farms far larger in extent than was dictated by their immediate requirements. They had to look forward to the day when their land would become useless, and if they were provident, would purchase ten times more than they could cultivate at any one time. Thomas Whitlock, in his will dated 1659, says: "I give to my son Thomas Whitlock the land I live on, 600 acres, when he is of the age 21, and during his minority to my wife. The land not to be further made use of or by planting or seating than the first deep branch that is commonly rid over, that my son may have some fresh land when he attains to age."[22]

One may gain an idea of the condition of the very poorest class of freemen by an examination of the inventory of the estate of Walter Dorch, drawn up in 1684. This man possessed two pairs of woollen cards, and one spinning wheel, valued at 100 pounds of tobacco, one chest at eighty pounds, four old trays at twenty pounds, two runletts at forty pounds, one pail and one skillet at sixty pounds, one bowl at two pounds, one feather bed, two pillows and three old blankets at 120 pounds of tobacco, three glass bottles at twenty pounds, one couch frame at forty pounds, one pair of pot-hooks at forty, 800 tenpenny nails at forty-five, and one old table and one sifter at twenty pounds. In all the estate was valued at 587 pounds of tobacco.[23]

John Gray, who died in 1685, left personal property worth 9,340 pounds of tobacco, consisting in part of six cows and six calves, four yearlings, two steers, one heifer, one barrel of corn, one bull, ten hogs and one horse. He had no servants and no slaves.[24] In better circumstances was Richard Avery, who seems to have been a tanner by profession. The inventory of his estate, recorded in 1686, includes one horse with bridle and saddle, a cart and a yoke of steers, eight head of cattle, 25 hogs, 118 hides, various kinds of tools, lumber to the value of 400 pounds of tobacco, four pieces of earthenware, four beds with mattresses and covers, poultry to the value of 180 pounds of tobacco, some wheat in the ground and a batch of wearing linen. The entire personal estate was valued at 14,050 pounds of tobacco. It included no servants or slaves.[25]

John Splitimber, who is entered as a headright to Thomas Harwood in 1635, is typical of the planter who rose from small beginnings to a state of comparative prosperity. This man, at his death in 1677, possessed eight cows, one bull, four yearlings, four mares, 35 hogs, two horses, two bolsters, a pillow, two blankets, a mattress, two bedsteads, two guns, fifty-six pounds of pewter, two rugs, a table, three chests, one old couch, two iron pots, two kettles, two stilyards, shovel and tongs, two smothering irons, two axes, a few carpenter's tools, a saddle and bridle, four casks, clothing to the value of 1,100 pounds of tobacco, a frying pan, a butter pat, a jar, a looking glass, two milk pans, one table cloth, nine spoons, a churn, a bible. The appraisers placed the total value at 18,277 pounds of tobacco.[26] The inventory records no servants or slaves, but it is probable that Splitimber at times made use of indentured labor, as in November 1648 and again in 1652, we find him taking up land due for the transportation of certain persons to the colony.[27]

Of similar estate was Christopher Pearson, of York county. His personal property included bedding valued at £7, linen at 18 shillings, pewter at £1.18.0, brass at six shillings, wooden ware at £4.13.6 comprising three chairs and one table, a couch, four old chests, a cask, two ten gallon rundletts, a cheese press, a box of drawers, an old table, three pails, a spinning wheel with cards, two sifting trays, a corn barrel, three bedsteads, four sives, a funnel; iron ware valued at £2.12.0, including three pots, two pot-rocks, a pestal, a frying pan, a looking glass; three cows appraised at £6.5.0, a yearling at ten shillings, a colt at two pounds sterling. The entire estate was valued at £25.19.6.[28]

It must not be imagined, however, that Virginia, even in the early years of its settlement, contained no men of wealth or rank. Industry and intelligence bore their inevitable fruit in the little colony, with the result that here and there certain planters acquired an enviable pre-eminence among their fellows. The *New Description* mentions several such cases.

Captain Matthews "hath a fine house," it says, "and all things answerable to it; he sowes yeerly store of Hempe and Flax, and causes it to be spun; he keeps Weavers, and hath a Tanhouse, causes Leather to be dressed, hath eight Shoemakers employed in their trade, hath forty Negro servants, brings them up to Trades in his house. He yeerly sowes abundance of Wheat, Barley, &c. The Wheat he selleth at four shillings the bushell; kills store of Beeves, and sells them to victuall the Ships when they come thither: hath abundance of Kine, a brave Dairy, Swine great store, and Poltery; he married a Daughter of Sir Thomas Hinton, and in a word, keeps a good house, lives bravely, and a true lover of Virginia; he is worthy of much honor."[29]

This description is interesting because it shows not only the extent of the holdings of certain planters at this early date, but that their prosperity had the same foundation as that of the more numerous class of wealthy men of the Eighteenth century. In both cases slavery and plantation manufacture would seem to have been the open sesame to success. It is notable that of the very limited number of men in Virginia prior to 1700 who stand out above their fellows in the readiness with which they acquired property, almost all gathered around them a goodly number of negroes.

Among the prominent planters of the first half of the Seventeenth century was George Menefie, famous for his orchard which abounded in apple, pear and cherry trees, and for his garden which yielded all kinds of fruits, vegetables, and flowers; Richard Bennett, a man of large property who had in one year "out of his Orchard as many Apples as he made 20 Butts of Excellent Cider"; Richard Kinsman, who for three or four years in succession secured "forty or fifty Butts of Perry made out of his Orchard, pure and good."[30]

In the second half of the century the class of the well-to-do, although somewhat more numerous, was still restricted to a small group of prominent families, many of them connected by marriage. Among the best known men are Nathaniel Bacon, Sr., Thomas Ballard, Robert Beverely, Giles Brent, Joseph Bridger, William Byrd I, John Carter, John Custis I, Dudley Digges, William Fitzhugh, Lewis Burwell, Philip Ludwell I, William Moseley, Daniel Parke, Ralph Wormeley, Benjamin Harrison, Edward Hill, Edmund Jennings and Matthew Page. But so few were their numbers that the Governors more than once complained that they could not find men for the Council of State qualified for that post by their wealth and influence.

The depository of power for the Virginia yeomanry was the House of Burgesses. This important body was elected by the votes of the freeholders, and faithfully represented their interests. Here they would bring their grievances, here express their wishes, here defend themselves against injustice, here demand the enactment of legislation favorable to their class. The hope of the people lay always in the Burgesses, Bacon the rebel tells us, "as their Trusts, and Sanctuary to fly to."[31] And though the commons usually elected to this body the leading men of each county, men of education and wealth if such were to be found, they held them to a strict accountability for their every action.[32] Many of the best known members of the Council of State served their apprenticeship in the Burgesses. But whatever the social status of the Burgess, he felt always that he was the representative of the poor planter, the defender of his interests, and seldom indeed did he betray his trust.[33] This no doubt was with him in part a matter of honor, but it also was the result of a consciousness that unless he obeyed the behests of his constituency he would be defeated if he came up for re-election.

The House of Burgesses, even in the days when the colony

was but an infant settlement stretching along the banks of the James, did not hesitate to oppose the wishes of the King himself. In 1627 Charles I sent instructions for an election of Burgesses that he might gain the assent of the planters through their representatives to an offer which he made to buy their tobacco.[34] Although the Assembly must have realized that its very existence might depend upon its compliance with the King's wishes, it refused to accept his proposal.[35] In 1634 Charles again made an offer for the tobacco, but again he encountered stubborn opposition. The Secretary of the colony forwarded a report in which he frankly told the British Government that in his opinion the matter would never go through if it depended upon the yielding of the Assembly.[36]

In 1635 the people again showed their independent spirit by ejecting Sir John Harvey from the Government and sending him back to England. It is true that the Council members took the lead in this bold step, but they would hardly have gone to such lengths had they not been supported by the mass of small planters.[37] In fact, one of the chief grievances against the Governor was his refusal to send to the King a petition of the Burgesses, which he considered offensive because they had made it "a popular business, by subscribing a multitude of hands thereto." And some days before the actual expulsion Dr. John Pott, Harvey's chief enemy, was going from plantation to plantation, inciting the people to resistance and securing their signatures to a paper demanding a redress of grievances.[38]

The attitude of the small planters during the English civil war and Commonwealth period is equally instructive. Certain writers have maintained that the people of Virginia were a unit for the King, that upon the execution of Charles I his son was proclaimed with the unanimous consent of the planters, that the colony became a refuge for English cavaliers, that it surrendered to Parliament only when conquered by an armed expedition and that it restored Charles II as King of Virginia even before he had regained his power in England.

All of this is either misleading or entirely false. It is true that the Assembly proclaimed Charles II King in 1649 and passed laws making it high treason for any person to uphold the legality of the dethronement and execution of his father.[39] But this was largely the work of Sir William Berkeley and the small group of well-to-do men who were dependent upon him for their welfare. The very fact that it was felt necessary to threaten with dire punishment all who spread abroad reports "tending to a change of government," shows that there existed a fear that such a change might be effected.[40] How many of the small planters were at heart friendly to Parliament it is impossible to say, but the number was large enough to cause Sir William Berkeley such serious misgivings as to his own personal safety that he obtained from the Assembly a guard of ten men to protect him from assassination.[41]

Nor can it be said that Virginia was forced into an unwilling submission to Parliament. It is true that an expedition was sent to conquer the colony, which entered the capes, sailed up to the forts at Jamestown and there received the formal surrender of the colony.[42] But this surrender was forced upon the Governor as much by the wishes of the people as by the guns of the British fleet. In fact, the expedition had been sent at the request of certain representatives of the Parliamentary faction in Virginia, who made it clear to the Commonwealth leaders that the colony was by no means unanimous for the King, and that it was held to its allegiance only by the authority and firm will of the Governor.[43] That the British Council of State expected to receive active assistance from their friends in Virginia is evident, for they gave directions for raising troops there and for appointing officers.[44] And there can be no doubt that the imposing military force which had been gathered to defend Jamestown was not called into action chiefly because Berkeley became convinced that it could not be relied upon to fight against the Commonwealth soldiers.

The new regime which was introduced with the articles of surrender made of Virginia virtually a little republic. In England the long cherished hope of the patriots for self-government was disappointed by the usurpation of Oliver Cromwell. But the commons of Virginia reaped the reward which was denied their brothers of the old country. For a period of eight years all power resided in the House of Burgesses. This body, so truly representative of the small planter class, elected the Governor and specified his duties. If his administration proved unsatisfactory they could remove him from office. The Burgesses also chose the members of the Council. Even the appointing of officials was largely theirs, although this function they usually felt it wise to delegate to the Governor.[45] In fact, Virginia was governed during this period, the happiest and most prosperous of its early history, by the small proprietor class which constituted the bulk of the population.

Nor is it true that the people voluntarily surrendered this power by acknowledging the authority of Charles II before the actual restoration in England. After the death of Cromwell, when the affairs of the mother country were in chaos and no man knew which faction would secure possession of the government, the Virginia Assembly asked Sir William Berkeley to act again as their chief executive. But it was specifically stipulated that he was to hold his authority, not from Charles, but from themselves alone.[46] In this step the people were doubtless actuated by an apprehension that the monarchy might be restored, in which case it would be much to their advantage to have as the chief executive of the colony the former royal Governor; but they expressly stated that they held themselves in readiness to acknowledge the authority of any Government, whatever it might be, which succeeded in establishing itself in England. So far was Sir William from considering himself a royal Governor, that when the King actually regained his throne, he wrote with no little apprehension, begging forgiveness for having accepted a commission from any other source than himself.[47]

It was the small farmer class which suffered most from the despotic methods of Berkeley during the Restoration period—the corrupting of the House of Burgesses, the heavy taxes, the usurpation of power in local government, the distribution of lucrative offices—and it was this class which rose in insurrection in 1676. It is notable that in the course of Bacon's Rebellion the great mass of the people turned against the Governor, either approving passively of his expulsion, or actually aiding his enemies. When Sir William appealed for volunteers in Gloucester county while Bacon was upon the Pamunkey expedition, he could hardly muster a man.[48] And the forces which eventually he gathered around him seem to have included only a handful of leading citizens, such men as Philip Ludwell, Nathaniel Bacon, Sr., Giles Brent and Robert Beverley, together with a mass of indentured servants and others who had been forced into service. It is this which explains the apparent cowardice of the loyal forces, who almost invariably took to their heels at the first approach of the rebels, for men will not risk their lives for a cause in which their hearts are not enlisted.

And though the small farmers lost their desperate fight, though their leaders died upon the scaffold, though the oppressive Navigation Acts remained in force, though taxes were heavier than ever, though the governors continued to encroach upon their liberties, they were by no means crushed and they continued in their legislative halls the conflict that had gone against them upon the field of battle. But the political struggle too was severe. It was in the decade from 1678 to 1688 that the Stuart monarchs made their second attempt to crush Anglo-Saxon liberty, an attempt fully as dangerous for the colonies as for England. The dissolving of the three Whig Parliaments, and the acceptance of a pension from Louis XIV were followed not only by the execution of liberal leaders and the withdrawal of town charters in the mother country, but by a deliberate attempt to suppress popular government in America. It was not a mere coincidence that the attack upon the Massachusetts charter, the misrule of Nicholson in New York, the oppressions of the proprietor in Maryland and the tyranny of Culpeper and Effingham in Virginia occurred simultaneously. They were all part and parcel of the policy of Charles II and James II.

These attempts met with failure in Virginia because of the stubborn resistance they encountered from the small farmer class and their representatives in the House of Burgesses. The annulling of statutes by proclamation they denounced as illegal; they protested bitterly against the appointment of their clerk by the Governor; they fought long to retain their ancient judicial privileges; they defeated all attempts of the King and his representatives in Virginia to deprive them of the right to initiate legislation and to control taxation. And with the Glorious Revolution of 1688-89, which put an end forever to Stuart aggressions, they could feel that their efforts alone had preserved liberty in Virginia, that they might now look forward to long years of happiness and prosperity. The Virginia yeoman reckoned not with slavery, however, and slavery was to prove, in part at least, his undoing.

CHAPTER VII

World Trade

In 1682 the depression which for nearly a quarter of a century had gripped the tobacco trade, somewhat abruptly came to an end. "Our only commodity, tobacco, having the last winter a pretty quick market, hath encouraged ye planters," wrote Secretary Spencer to the Board of Trade in May, 1683.[1] Apparently the tide had turned. From this time until the beginning of the War of the Spanish Succession more than two decades later we hear little complaint from Virginia, while there are excellent reasons to suppose that the colony was experiencing a period of growth and prosperity.

In truth the tobacco trade, upon which the planters staked their all, now expanded with startling rapidity, and each year the merchants were forced to add more bottoms to the fleet which sailed for England from the Chesapeake. During the early years of the Restoration period tobacco exports from Virginia and Maryland had made but little advance. In 1663 they amounted to 7,367,140 pounds, six years later they were 9,026,046 pounds.[2] In 1698, however, the output of Virginia and Maryland was estimated by the merchant John Linton to be from 70,000 to 80,000 hogsheads.[4] Since the hogshead usually contained from 500 to 600 pounds, these figures mean that the planters were then raising from 35,000,000 to 48,000,000 pounds of tobacco. And this conclusion is supported by the fact that the crop of 1699 is valued at £198,115, which at a penny a pound would indicate about 47,000,000 pounds.[5] In fact, the production of tobacco in the ten years from 1689 to 1699 seems to have tripled, in the years from 1669 to 1699 to have quadrupled. In 1669 the planters considered themselves fortunate if their industry yielded them a return of £30,000; at the end of the century they could count with a fair degree of certainty upon six times that amount.

For Virginia this startling development was all-important. During the darkest days of the Restoration period her share of the total returns from the tobacco crop could hardly have exceeded £10,000; in 1699 it was estimated at £100,000. Even if we accept the conservative statement that the average number of hogsheads exported from Virginia in the last decade of the century varied from 35,000 to 40,000,[6] the planters still would have received £75,000 or £80,000. From dire poverty and distress the colony, almost in the twinkling of an eye, found itself in comparative ease and plenty.

Nor is the reason difficult to discover. It had never been the intention of the British Government to destroy the foreign trade of the colonies, the Navigation Acts having been designed only to force that trade through English channels. The planters were still at liberty to send their tobacco where they would, provided it went by way of England and paid the duty of a half penny a pound. That these restrictions so nearly put an end to shipments to the continent of Europe was an unfortunate consequence which to some extent had been foreseen, but which for the time being it was impossible to avoid.

It was undoubtedly the hope of the Government that the foreign market would eventually be regained and that the colonial tobacco would flow from the colonies into England and from England to all the countries of Europe. Prior to 1660 Holland had been the distributing centre for the tobacco of Virginia and Maryland; now England insisted upon taking this rôle upon herself. But the authorities at London were hardly less concerned than the planters themselves at the difficulties encountered in effecting this change and the unfortunate glut in the home markets which followed.

None the less they persisted in the policy they had adopted, even clinging stubbornly to the half penny a pound re-export duty, and trusting that in time they could succeed in conquering for their tobacco the lost continental markets. In this they were bitterly opposed by the Dutch with whom it became necessary to fight two wars within the short space of seven years. Yet steadily, although at first slowly, they made headway. In 1681 the commissioners of the customs refused the request for a cessation of tobacco planting in the colonies, on the ground that to lessen the crop would but stimulate production in foreign countries and so restrict the sale abroad of the Virginia and Maryland leaf.[7] This argument has been denounced by some as both specious and selfish, yet it was fully justified by the situation then existing. After all, the only hope for the planters lay in conquering the European market and the way to do this was to flood England with tobacco until it overflowed all artificial barriers and poured across the Channel. And eventually this is just what happened. Since tobacco was piling up uselessly in the warehouses and much of it could not be disposed of at any price, it was inevitable that it should be dumped upon the other nations of Europe. There is in this development a close parallel with the commercial policy of Germany in the years prior to the world war, when no effort was spared to produce a margin of all kinds of wares over the home needs, which was to be exported at excessively low prices. This margin was a weapon of conquest, a means of ousting the merchants of other nations from this market or that. And when once this conquest had been effected, the price could be raised again in order to assure a profit to the German manufacturers.

It is improbable that the English economists of the Seventeenth century, like those of modern Germany, had foreseen exactly what would happen, but the results were none the less similar. When once the English leaf had secured a strong hold upon the Baltic and upon France and Spain, it was a matter of the greatest difficulty to oust it, especially as the ever increasing influx of slaves made it possible for the planters to meet the lower prices of foreign competitors and still clear a profit. Thus it was that during the years from 1680 to 1708 the Chesapeake tobacco succeeded in surmounting all the difficulties placed in its way by the Navigation Acts, the necessity of the double voyage, the re-export duty of a half penny a pound, and so gradually flooded the continental market.

It is unfortunate that figures for re-exported tobacco during the earlier years of the Restoration period are lacking. In 1688, however, it is stated that the duty of a half penny a pound was yielding the Crown an annual revenue of £15,000, which would indicate that about 7,200,000 pounds were leaving for foreign ports.[8] Ten years later, if we may believe the testimony of John Linton, exports of tobacco totalled 50,000 or 60,000 hogsheads, or from 25,000,000 to 30,000,000 pounds. Not more than a fourth of the colonial leaf, he tells us, was consumed in England itself.[9] Once more Virginia and Maryland were producing tobacco for all Europe, once more they enjoyed a world market.

This trade was extended from one end of the continent to the other. Vessels laden with American tobacco found their way not only to the ports of France and Holland and Spain, but even to the distant cities of Sweden and Russia.[10] The Baltic trade alone amounted to from 5,000 to 10,000 hogsheads, and added from £10,000 to £24,000 to the income of the planters. The chief Russian port of entry was Narva, which took annually some 500 hogsheads, but large quantities were shipped also to Riga and Raval.[11] The northern nations bought the cheaper varieties, for no tobacco could be too strong for the hardy men of Sweden and Russia.

The trade was of great importance to England, as the leaf, after it had gone through the process of manufacture, sold for about six pence a pound, yielding to the nation in all from £60,000 to £130,000.[12] As the English were still largely dependent upon the Baltic for potash and ship stores, this constituted a most welcome addition to the balance of trade. To the colonies also it was vital, carrying off a large part of the annual crop, and so tending to sustain prices.

France, too, proved a good customer for English tobacco, and in the years prior to the War of the Spanish Succession took annually from 8,000 to 10,000 hogsheads, or from 4,000,000 to 6,000,000 pounds.[13] Micajah Perry reported to the Lords of Trade that from 6,000 to 10,000 hogsheads went to France from London alone, while a very considerable amount was sent also from other ports.[14]

Far more surprising is the fact that even Spain consumed millions of pounds of English leaf. With her own colonies producing the best tobacco in the world and in the face of its practical exclusion from the English market, it is strange that the Government at Madrid should have permitted this commerce to continue. The obvious course for the Spaniards under the economic theories of the day would have been to exclude English tobacco, both in order to protect their own planters and to retaliate for the restrictions upon their product. Yet it is estimated that from 6,000 to 10,000 hogsheads entered Spain each year.[15] A pamphlet published in 1708 entitled *The Present State of Tobacco Plantations in America* stated that before the outbreak of the war then raging, France and Spain together had taken annually about 20,000 hogsheads.[16]

The Dutch, too, despite their bitter rivalry with the British, found it impossible to do without Virginia tobacco. Purchasing the finest bright Orinoco, they mixed it with leaf of their own growth in the proportion of one to four, and sold it to other European nations. In this way they sought to retain their position as a distributing center for the trade and to give employment to hundreds of poor workers. In all the Dutch seem to have purchased from England about 5,000 hogsheads a year.[17]

The enhanced importance of the tobacco trade is reflected in a steady increase of British exports to Virginia and Maryland. The planters, now that they found it possible to market their leaf, laid out the proceeds in the manufactured products of England. At the end of the Seventeenth century the two colonies were importing goods to the value of £200,000 annually. In 1698, which was an exceptionally good year, their purchases were no less than £310,133.[18]

In short the tobacco colonies had at last found their proper place in the British colonial system. Both they and the mother country, after long years of experimentation, years of misfortune and recrimination, had reached a common ground upon which to stand. Although Maryland and Virginia still fell short of the ideal set for the British colonies, although they failed to furnish the raw stuffs so urgently needed by the home industries, at least they yielded a product which added materially to shipping, weighed heavily in the balance of trade and brought a welcome revenue to the royal Exchequer.

The Crown reaped a rich return from tobacco, a return which grew not only with the expansion of the trade, but by the imposition from time to time of heavier duties. In the period from 1660 to 1685, when the tariff remained at two pence a pound, the yield must have varied from £75,000 to £100,000. If we assume that the average consumption in England was 9,000,000 pounds and the average exports 3,000,000 the total revenue would have been £81,250. In 1685, however, an additional duty of three pence a pound was placed upon tobacco upon its arrival in England, all of which was refunded when the product was re-exported. In 1688, when the tobacco consumed in England was 8,328,800 pounds, the old and new duties, amounting in all to five pence, must have yielded £173,515. When to this is added £15,000 from the half penny a pound on the 7,200,000 pounds of leaf sent abroad, the total reaches £188,515.

In 1698 still another penny a pound was added to the tax, making a grand total of six pence on colonial tobacco disposed of in England. This new duty, together with the rapid increase in the foreign trade, enriched the Exchequer by another £100,000. In 1699, if we assume that 12,000,000 pounds were consumed in England, the return would have been £300,000; while half a penny a pound on 36,000,000 pounds of re-exported leaf, would have brought the total to £375,000. That this figure was approximately correct we have evidence in the statement of the author of *The Present State of the Tobacco Plantations,* written in 1705, that the revenue yielded by the tobacco of Virginia and Maryland amounted annually to £400,000.[19] This sum constituted a very appreciable proportion of the royal income, so appreciable in fact as to make the tobacco trade a matter of vital importance in the eyes of the King's ministers. They were charged at all times to avoid any contingency which might lessen the imports and reduce the customs.

The increase in the tobacco trade stimulated industry, not only by increasing exports to Virginia and Maryland, but also by creating a new English industry. For most of the tobacco, before it was sent abroad, was subjected to a process of manufacture, by which the leaf was cut and rolled and otherwise prepared for the consumer. This industry gave employment to hundreds of poor persons in England and required a considerable outlay of capital.[20]

To British navigation the trade was vital. Each year scores of merchantmen crossed to the Chesapeake and swarmed in every river and creek, delivering their English goods to the planters and taking in return the hogsheads of tobacco. In 1690 the tobacco fleet numbered about 100 ships, aggregating 13,715 tons; in 1706 it counted no less than 300 sails.[21] Nor must it be forgotten that re-exported tobacco also added many a goodly merchantman to the navy and gave employment to many a seaman. Altogether Virginia and Maryland constituted an invaluable asset, an asset which ranked in importance secondly only to the sugar plantations.

It would naturally be supposed that the fortunate turn of events which restored to the tobacco colonies their European market would have reacted favorably upon the small planters of Virginia, not only insuring plenty to those already established, but adding new recruits from the ranks of the indentured servants; that the process of making prosperous freemen from the poor immigrants who flocked to the colony, the process interrupted by the passage of the Navigation Acts, would have been resumed now that these laws no longer prevented the flow of tobacco into the continental countries.

Such was not the case, however. A comparison of the lists of immigrants with the rent roll of 1704 shows that but an insignificant proportion of the newcomers succeeded in establishing themselves as landowners. In four lists examined for the year 1689, comprising 332 names, but seven persons can be positively identified upon the rent roll. In 1690, eight lists of 933 names, reveal but twenty-eight persons who were landowners in 1704. Of 274 immigrants listed in 1691, six only appear on the Roll. In 1695, seven lists comprising 711 names, show but ten who possessed farms nine years later. Of 74 headrights appearing in 1696, but two are listed on the roll; of 119 in 1697 only nine; of 169 in 1698 one only; of 454 in 1699, only seven; of 223 in 1700 but six.[22] All in all not more than five per cent. of the newcomers during this period prospered and became independent planters. Apparently, then, the restored prosperity of the colony was not shared by the poorer classes, the increased market for tobacco did not better materially the chances of the incoming flood of indentured servants.

The explanation of this state of affairs is found in the fact that tobacco, despite its widened market, experienced no very pronounced rise in price. The average return to the planters during the good years seems to have been one penny a pound.[23] This, it is true, constituted an advance over the worst days of the Restoration period, but it was far from approaching the prices of the Civil war and Commonwealth periods. For the poor freedman, it was not sufficient to provide for his support and at the same time make it possible to accumulate a working capital. He could not, as he had done a half century earlier, lay aside enough to purchase a farm, stock it with cattle, hogs and poultry, perhaps even secure a servant or two. Now, although no longer reduced to misery and rags as in the years from 1660 to 1682, he could consider himself fortunate if his labor sufficed to provide wholesome food and warm clothing. How, it may be asked, could Virginia and Maryland produce the vast crops now required by the foreign trade, if the price was still so low? Prior to and just after Bacon's Rebellion the planters repeatedly asserted that their labors only served to bring them into debt, that to produce an extensive crop was the surest way for one to ruin himself. Why was it that twenty years later, although prices were still far below the old level, they could flood the markets of the world?

The answer can be summed up in one word—slavery. The first cargo of negroes arrived in the colony in 1619 upon a Dutch privateer. Presumably they were landed at Jamestown, and sold there to the planters.[24] The vessel which won fame for itself by this ill-starred action, was sailing under letters of marque from the Prince of Orange and had been scouring the seas in search of Spanish prizes. Although the Dutch master could have had no information that slaves were wanted in the colony, he seems to have taken it for granted that he would not be forbidden to dispose of his human freight.

The introduction of this handful of negroes—there were butt wenty in all—was not the real beginning of the slave system in the colonies. For many years the institution which was to play so sinister a part in American history did not flourish, and the slaves grew in numbers but slowly. In the Muster Roll of Settlers in Virginia, taken in 1624, there were listed only 22 negroes.[25] Sixteen years later the black population probably did not exceed 150.[26] In 1649, when Virginia was growing rapidly and the whites numbered 15,000, there were but 300 negroes in the colony.[27] A sporadic importation of slaves continued during the Commonwealth period, but still the number was insignificant, still the bulk of the labor in the tobacco fields was done by indentured servants and poor freeholders.

In 1670 Governor Berkeley reported to the Board of Trade that out of a total population of 40,000, but five per cent were slaves.[28] Eleven years later the number of blacks was estimated at 3,000.[29] In 1635 twenty-six negroes were brought in, the largest purchaser being Charles Harmar.[30] In 1636 the importations were but seven, in 1637 they were 28, in 1638 thirty, in 1639 forty-six, in 1642 seven only, in 1643 eighteen, in 1649 seventeen.[31] But with the passage of the years somewhat larger cargoes began to arrive. In 1662 Richard Lee claimed among his headrights no less than 80 negroes, in 1665 the Scarboroughs imported thirty-nine. In 1670, however, Berkeley declared that "not above two or three ships of Negroes" had arrived in the province in the previous seven years.[32]

It is evident, then, that during the larger part of the Seventeenth century slavery played but an unimportant rôle in the economic and social life of the colony. The planters were exceedingly anxious to make use of slave labor, which they considered the foundation of the prosperity of their rivals of the Spanish tobacco colonies, but slave labor was most difficult to obtain. The trade had for many years been chiefly in the hands of the Dutch, and these enterprising navigators sold most of their negroes to the Spanish plantations. Ever since the days of Henry VIII the English had made efforts to secure a share of this profitable traffic, but with very meagre success.[33]

The Dutch had established trading stations along the African coast, guarded by forts and war vessels. Any attempts of outsiders to intrude upon the commerce was regarded by them as an act of open aggression to be resisted by force of arms. To enter the trade with any hope of success it became necessary for the English to organize a company rich enough to furnish armed protection to their merchantmen. But no such organization could be established during the Civil War and Commonwealth periods, and it was not until 1660 that the African Company, under the leadership of the Duke of York entered the field.[34]

This was but the beginning of the struggle, however. The Dutch resisted strenuously, stirring up the native chieftians against the English, seizing their vessels and breaking up their stations. Not until two wars had been fought was England able to wring from the stubborn Netherlanders an acknowledgment of her right to a share in the trade. Even then the Virginians were not adequately supplied, for the sugar islands were clamoring for slaves, and as they occupied so important a place in the colonial system they were the first to be served. Throughout the last quarter of the Seventeenth century negroes in fairly large numbers began to arrive in the Chesapeake, but it was only in the years from 1700 to 1720 that they actually accomplished the overthrow of the old system of labor and laid the foundations of a new social structure. Throughout the Seventeenth century the economic system of the tobacco colonies depended upon the labor of the poor white man, whether free or under terms of indenture; in the Eighteenth century it rested chiefly upon the black shoulders of the African slave.

There could be no manner of doubt as to the desirability of the slaves from an economic standpoint, apparently the only standpoint that received serious consideration. The indentured servant could be held usually for but a few years. Hardly had he reached his greatest usefulness for his master than he demanded his freedom. Thus for the man of large means to keep his fields always in cultivation it was necessary constantly to renew his supply of laborers. If he required twenty hands, he must import each year some five or six servants, or run the risk of finding himself running behind. But the slave served for life. The planter who had purchased a full supply of negroes could feel that his labor problems were settled once and for all. Not only could he hold the slaves themselves for life, but their children also became his property and took their places in the tobacco fields as soon as they approached maturity.

Thus in the end the slave was far cheaper. The price of a servant depended largely upon the cost of his passage across the ocean. We find that William Matthews, having three years and nine months to serve, was rated in the inventory of his master, John Thomas, at £12.[35] A servant of Robert Leightenhouse, having two years to serve, was put at £9;[36] while on the other hand we find another listed in the estate of Colonel Francis Epes, also having two years to serve, at only £5.[37] A white lad under indenture for seven years to Mr. Ralph Graves was valued at £10.[38] On the whole it would seem that the price of a sturdy man servant varied from £2 to £4 for each year of his service. On the other hand a vigorous slave could be had at from £18 to £30. Assuming that he gave his master twenty-five years of service, the cost for each year would be but one pound sterling. There could be no doubt, then, that in the mere matter of cost he was much cheaper than the indentured white man.

It is true that the negro was none too efficient as a laborer. Born in savagery, unacquainted with the English tongue, knowing little of agriculture, it was a matter of some difficulty for him to accustom himself to his task in the tobacco fields. Yet when his lesson had been learned, when a few years of experience had taught him what his master expected him to do, the slave showed himself quite adequate to the requirements of the one staple crop. The culture of tobacco is not essentially difficult, especially when pursued in the unscientific manner of the colonial period. It required many, but not skilled hands. The slave, untutored and unintelligent, proved inadequate to the industrial needs of the northern colonies. The niceties of shipbuilding were beyond his capacities, he was not needed as a fisherman, he was not a good sailor, he was useless in the system of intensive agriculture in vogue north of Maryland. But in the tobacco field he would do. He could not at first tend so many plants as his white rival, he could not produce tobacco of such fine quality, but what he lacked in efficiency he more than made up for in cheapness.

The African seems to have withstood remarkably well the diseases indigenous to eastern Virginia. There are occasional reports of epidemics among the slaves, but usually they were fairly immune both to malaria and dysentery. A census taken in 1714, when there were perhaps 15,000 negroes in the colony, records burials for sixty-two slaves only.[39] The births of slaves for the same year totalled 253.[40] These figures indicate not only the excellent physical condition in which these black workers were kept by their masters, but the rapidity with which they were multiplying. The low death rate is in part explained by the fact that only strong men and women were transported to the colonies, but it is none the less clearly indicative of the ease with which the African accustomed himself to the climate of tidewater Virginia.

As a rule the negro was more docile than the white servant, especially if the latter happened to be from the ruder elements of English society. He was not so apt to resist his master or to run away to the mountains. Yet plots among the blacks were not unknown. In 1710 a conspiracy was discovered among the slaves of Surry and James City counties which was to have been put into execution on Easter day. The negroes planned to rise simultaneously, destroy any who stood in their way, and make good their escape out of the colony. Among the chief conspirators were Jamy, belonging to Mr. John Broadnax, Mr. Samuel Thompson's Peter, Tom and Cato of Mr. William Edwards, Great Jack and Little Jack of Mr. John Edwards, and Will belonging to Mr. Henry Hart. "Two or three of these were tried this general court," wrote Colonel Jennings, "found guilty and will be executed. And I hope their fate will strike such a terror in the other Negroes as will keep them from forming such designs for the future."[41] The lesson did not prove lasting, however, for in 1730 a number of slaves from Norfolk and Princess Anne counties assembled while the whites were at church, and chose officers to command them in a bold stroke for freedom. As in the previous attempt they were discovered, many arrested and several of the ringleaders executed.[42]

Neither the merchants nor the planters seem to have been conscious of any wrong in the seizure and sale of negroes. They regarded the native Africans as hardly human, mere savages that were no more deserving of consideration than oxen or horses. And as it was right and proper to hitch the ox or the horse to the plow, so it was equally legitimate to put the negro to work in the fields of sugar cane or tobacco. Whatever hardships he had to endure upon the voyage to America or by reason of his enforced labor, they considered amply compensated by his conversion to Christianity.

It is true that the colony of Virginia early in the Eighteenth century imposed a heavy duty upon the importation of slaves, but it did so neither from any consciousness of wrong in slavery itself or a perception of the social problems which were to grow out of it. At the time the price of tobacco was declining rapidly and many planters were losing money. Feeling that their misfortunes arose from overproduction, which in turn was the result of the recent purchases of negroes, the colonial legislators decided to check the trade. "The great number of negroes imported here and solely employed in making tobacco," wrote Governor Spotswood in 1711, "hath produced for some years past an increase in tobacco far disproportionate to the consumption of it . . . and consequently lowered the price of it."[43] "The people of Virginia will not now be so fond of purchasing negroes as of late," declared President Jennings of the Virginia Council in 1708, "being sensibly convinced of their error, which has in a manner ruined the credit of the country."[44]

During the years from 1680 to 1700 slaves arrived in the colony in increasing numbers. In 1681 William Fitzhugh, in a letter to Ralph Wormeley, refers to the fact that several slave ships were expected that year in the York river.[45] At this period, for the first time in Virginia history, we find negroes in large numbers entered as headrights upon the patent rolls. In 1693 Captain John Storey received a grant of land for the importation of 79 negroes, in 1694 Robert Beverley brought in seventy, in 1695 William Randolph twenty-five.[46] Before the end of the century it is probable that the slaves in Virginia numbered nearly 6,000, and had already become more important to the economic life of the colony than the indentured servants.[47]

The chief purchasers at this time were men of large estates. The advantages of slave labor were manifest to planters of the type of William Byrd or William Fitzhugh, men who had built up fortunes by their business ability. It is but natural that they should have turned early from the indentured servant to stock their plantations with the cheaper and more remunerative African workers.

As the English secured a stronger hold upon the African trade slaves arrived in ever increasing numbers. During the years from 1699 to 1708 no less than 6,843 came in, a number perhaps exceeding the entire importations of the Seventeenth century.[48] In the summer of 1705 alone 1,800 negroes arrived.[49] With what rapidity the black man was taking the place of the indentured servant and the poor freeman as the chief laborer of the colony is shown by the fact that in 1708, in a total tithable list of 30,000, no less than 12,000 were slaves. President Jennings at the same time reported that the number of servants was inconsiderable.[50] "Before the year 1680 what negroes came to Virginia were usually from Barbadoes," Jennings told the Board of Trade in 1708. "Between 1680 and 1698 the negro trade become more frequent, tho not in any proportion to what it hath been of late, during which the African Company have sent several ships and others by their licence having bought their slaves of the Company brought them here for sale, among which lately Alderman Jeffreys and Sir Jeffry Jeffreys were principally concerned."[51]

The wars of Charles XII, however, which proved disastrous to the Baltic trade, and the War of the Spanish Succession which cut off exports of tobacco to France and Spain, caused a serious decline in prices and made it impossible for the planters to continue the large purchases of slaves. This fact, together with the duty which had been imposed with the express purpose of keeping them out, reduced the importations to a minimum during the years from 1710 to 1718.[52] But with the reopening of the tobacco market and the return of prosperity to Virginia, the black stream set in again with redoubled force. In 1730, out of a total population of 114,000, no less than 30,000 were negroes.[53] In other words the slaves, who in 1670 had constituted but five per cent of the people, now comprised twenty-six per cent. Slavery, from being an insignificant factor in the economic life of the colony, had become the very foundation upon which it was established.

As we have seen it was not slavery but the protracted accumulation of surplus stocks of tobacco in England which had broken the long continued deadlock of the tobacco trade during the Restoration period and caused the overflow into continental markets. That the labor of blacks at first played no essential part in the movement is evident from the fact that in 1682 when it first became pronounced, the slave population of Virginia and Maryland was still insignificant. But that the trade not only continued after the glut in England had been cleared up, but increased with startling rapidity, was unquestionably the result of more universal use of negroes in the years immediately preceding the War of the Spanish Succession. Slavery so cheapened the cost of production that it was now quite possible for those who used them to pay the half penny a pound duty on reëxported tobacco in England, and still undersell all rivals in the European market. Before many years had passed the tobacco trade, with all that it meant both to England and to the colonies, rested almost entirely upon the labor of the savage black man so recently brought from the African wilds.

That this fact was fully understood at the time is attested by various persons interested in the colony and the trade. In 1728 Francis Fane, in protesting against the imposition of a new tax in Virginia on the importation of slaves declared "that Laying a Duty on Negroes can only tend to make them scarcer and dearer, the two things that for the good of our Trade and for the Benefit of Virginia ought chiefly to be guarded against, since it is well known that the cheepness of Virginia tobacco in European Marketts is the true Cause of the great Consumption thereof in Europe, and one would have therefore Expected rather to have seen an Act allowing a premium on the Importation of Negroes to have Encouraged the bringing them in, than an Act laying so large a Duty to discourage their Importation."[54] Similarly Colonel Spencer wrote to the Board of Trade. "The low price of tobacco requires it should be made as cheap as possible. The Blacks can make it cheaper than Whites, so I conceive it is for his Majesty's interest full as much as the Country's or rather much more, to have Blacks as cheap as possible in Virginia."[55]

It is evident, then, that the opening of the European market and the vast expansion of the tobacco trade, while bringing prosperity to the larger planters, was no great boon to the man who tilled his fields with his own hands. It assured him a ready sale for his crop, it is true, but at prices so low as to leave him a very narrow margin of profit. The new era which was opening, the so-called golden era of Virginia history, was not for him. Virginia in the Eighteenth century was to be the land of the slave holder, not of the little planter.

CHAPTER VIII

Beneath the Black Tide

THE importation of slaves in large numbers reacted almost immediately upon the migration of whites to Virginia. As we have seen, the stream of indentured servants that poured across the Atlantic remained remarkably constant throughout almost all of the Seventeenth century. The larger planters were always in need of laborers, and they looked to the surplus population of England to supply them. But with the coming of the blacks all was changed. The Virginians saw in the slave ships which now so frequently entered their rivers the solution of all their problems. And so the influx of white men and women from the mother country dwindled and almost died out, while in its place came a still greater stream from the coast of Africa.

At the time of Bacon's Rebellion the annual importation of servants was between 1,500 and 2,000. The headrights for 1674 show 1931 names.[1] Seven years later the whites were still arriving in large numbers, the rolls for 1682 having 1,565 names. As the century drew to a close, however, the effect of the slave trade upon white immigration is reflected in the dwindling number of headrights. The change that was taking place is illustrated by a patent of 13,500 acres to Ralph Wormleley for the transportation of 249 persons, 149 of whom were white and 100 black.[2] Yet so late as 1704 the servants were still coming in appreciable numbers. In 1708 however, the number of servants at work in the colony had dwindled away almost entirely.[3] In 1715 the names of white persons listed as headrights was but ninety-one; in 1718 but 101.[4] In other words, the first great migration of Englishmen to continental America, a migration extending over a century and comprising from 100,000 to 150,000 men, women and children, had practically come to an end.

English statesmen at the time looked upon this event as an unalloyed blessing. The day had passed when they felt that there existed a surplus of labor at home and that the country was in need of blood letting. The proper policy was to keep Englishmen in England, to devote their energies to local industries and so strengthen the economic and military sinews of the nation. And if unemployment existed, it was the correct policy to bring work to the idle rather than send the idle out of the country in quest of work.[5] And the colonies were to be utilized, no longer as outlets for the population, but as a means to the upbuilding of local industry. They were to supply a market for English goods, keep employed English mariners and furnish the tobacco and sugar which when re-exported weighed so heavily in the balance of trade. And since these great staple crops could be produced by the work of slaves, it was thought highly advantageous for all concerned that the negro should replace the white servant in both the tobacco and the sugar fields. The planters would profit by the lowered cost of production, English industry would gain by the increased volume of traffic, the Crown revenues would be enhanced and English laborers would be kept at home.[6]

Apparently the deeper significance of this great movement was entirely lost upon the British economists and ministers. They had no conception of the advantage of having their colonies inhabited by one race alone and that race their own. From the first their vision was too restricted to embrace the idea of a new and greater Britain in its fullest sense. They could not bring themselves to look upon the soil of Virginia and Maryland as a part of the soil of an extended

England, upon the Virginians and Marylanders as Englishmen, enjoying privileges equal to their own. They could not realize the strength that would come from such an empire as this, the mighty future it would insure to the Anglo-Saxon race.

Their conception was different. The British empire must consist of two distinct parts—mother country and colonies. And in any clash of interest between the two, the former must prevail. It was not their intent that the colonies should be purposely sacrificed, that they should be made to pay tribute to a tyrannical parent. In fact, they earnestly desired that the plantations should prosper, for when they languished English industry suffered. But in their eyes the colonies existed primarily for the benefit of England. England had given them birth, had defended them, had nurtured them; she was amply justified, therefore, in subordinating them to her own industrial needs.

Thus they viewed the substitution of the importation of slaves to the tobacco colonies for the importation of white men purely from an English, not an Anglo-Saxon, point of view. Had it been a question of bringing thousands of negroes to England itself to drive the white laborers from the fields, they would have interposed an emphatic veto. But with the structure of colonial life they were not greatly concerned. In 1693, when James Blair secured from the King and Queen a gift for his new college at Williamsburg, Attorney-General Seymour objected vigorously, stating that there was not the least occasion for such an institution in Virginia. Blair reminded him that the chief purpose of the college was to educate young men for the ministry and begged him to consider that the people of the colony had souls to be saved as well as the people of England. "Souls! Damn your souls," snapped the Attorney-General, "make tobacco."[7] It would be unfair to say that the British Government took just the same view of the colonists as did Seymour, but there can be no doubt that their chief concern in the plantations was centered upon the size of their exports to England and of their purchases of English goods. And as the slaves could make more tobacco than the indentured servants, it became the settled policy of the Crown to encourage the African trade in every possible way.

The influx of slaves not only put almost a complete end to the importation of white servants, but it reacted disastrously upon the Virginia yeomanry. In this respect we find a close parallel with the experience of ancient Rome with slave labor. In the third and second centuries before Christ the glory of the republic lay in its peasantry. The self-reliant, sturdy, liberty-loving yeoman formed the backbone of the conquering legion and added to the life of the republic that rugged strength that made it so irresistible. "To say that a citizen is a good farmer is to reach the extreme limit of praise," said Cato. Some of the ablest of the early Roman generals were recruited from the small farmer class. Fabius Maximus, the Dictator, in need of money, sent his son to Rome to sell his sole possession, a little farm of seven jugera. Regulus, while in Africa, asked that he be recalled from his command because the hired man he had left to cultivate his fields had fled with all his farm implements, and he feared his wife and children would starve.[8]

This vigorous peasantry was destroyed by the importation of hordes of slaves and the purchase of cheap foreign grain. So long as the wars of Rome were limited to Italy the number of slaves was comparatively small, but as her armies swept over the Mediterranean countries one after another and even subdued the wild Gauls and Britains, an unending stream of captives poured into the city and filled to overflowing the slave markets. Cicero, during his short campaign against the

Parthians wrote to Atticus that the sale of his prisoners had netted no less than 12,000,000 sestercias. In Epirus 100,000 men were captured; 60,000 Cimbries and 100,000 Germans graced the triumph of Marius; Caesar is said to have taken in Gaul another 100,000 prisoners. Soon the slave became the cheapest of commodities, and he who possessed even the most extensive lands could readily supply himself with the labor requisite for their cultivation.

Thus thrown into competition with slave labor the peasant proprietor found it impossible to sustain himself. The grain which he produced with his own hands had to compete in the same market with that made by slaves. It must, therefore, sell for the same price, a price so low that it did not suffice to feed and clothe him and his family. So he was forced to give up his little estate, an estate perhaps handed down to him by generations of farmers, and migrate to the city of Rome, to swell the idle and plebeian population. And once there he demanded bread, a demand which the authorities dared not refuse. So the public treasury laid out the funds for the purchase of wheat from all parts of the world, from Spain, from Africa, from Sicily, wheat which was given away or sold for a song. This in turn reacted unfavorably upon the peasants who still clung to the soil in a desperate effort to wring from it a bare subsistence, and accelerated the movement to the city.

Thus Italy was transformed from the land of the little farmer into the land of big estates cultivated by slaves. A sad development surely, a development which had much to do with the decay and final overthrow of the mighty structure of the Roman Empire. In former times, Titus Livius tells us, "there was a multitude of free men in this country where today we can hardly find a handful of soldiers, and which would be a wilderness were it not for our slaves." "The plough is everywhere bereft of honor," wrote Virgil, while Lucian bewailed the departed peasants whose places were taken by fettered slaves.[9]

The importation of slaves to Virginia had somewhat similar results. While not destroying entirely the little farmer class, it exerted a baleful influence upon it, driving many families out of the colony, making the rich man richer, reducing the poor man to dire poverty. Against this unfortunate development the Virginia yeoman was helpless. Instinctively he must have felt that the slave was his enemy, and the hatred and rivalry which even today exists between the negro and the lowest class of whites, the so-called "poor white trash," dates back to the Seventeenth century.

The emigration of poor persons, usually servants just freed, from Virginia to neighboring colonies was well under way even at the time of Bacon's Rebellion. In 1677 complaint was made of "the inconvenience which arose from the neighborhood of Maryland and North Carolina," in that Virginia was daily deprived of its inhabitants by the removal of poor men hither. Runaway servants were welcomed in both places, it was asserted, while the debtor was accorded protection against prosecution.[10] This early emigration was caused, of course, not by the importation of slaves, for that movement had not yet assumed important proportions, but by the evil consequences of the Navigation Acts. The Virginia yeoman moved on to other colonies because he found it impossible to maintain himself at the current price of tobacco.

The continuance of the movement, for it persisted for a full half century, must be ascribed to the competition of negro labor. Like the Roman peasant, the Virginia yeoman, to an extent at least, found it impossible to maintain himself in the face of slave competition. The servant, upon the expiration of his term, no longer staked off his little farm and settled down to a life of usefulness and industry. The poor planter who had not yet fully established himself, sold or deserted his fields and moved away in search of better opportunities and higher returns.

This migration was not the first of its kind in the English colonies, for the movement of Massachusetts congregations into the valley of the Connecticut antedated it by several decades. Yet it furnishes an interesting illustration of the lack of permanency in American life, of the facility with which populations urged on by economic pressure of one kind or another change localities. The great movement westward over the Appalachian range which followed the War of 1812, the pilgrimages of homesteaders to the northwest and the Pacific coast, find their precedent in the exodus of these poor families from the tobacco fields of Virginia.

In the last decade of the Seventeenth century the migration assumed such large proportions that the Board of Trade became alarmed and directed Francis Nicholson to enquire into its cause in order that steps might be taken to stop it. The emigrant stream that directed itself northward did not halt in eastern Maryland, for conditions there differed little from those in Virginia itself. The settlers went on to the unoccupied lands in the western part of the colony, or made their way into Delaware or Pennsylvania. "The reason why inhabitants leave this province," wrote Nicholson, while Governor of Maryland, "is, I think, the encouragement which they receive from the Carolinas, the Jerseys, and above all from Pennsylvania, which is so nigh that it is easy to remove thither. There handicraft tradesmen have encouragement when they endeavor to set up woolen manufactures."[11]

Although this explanation does not go to the root of the matter, it was in part correct. The northern colonies held out far greater opportunities for the poor man than the slave choked fields of tidewater Maryland and Virginia. The industries of Pennsylvania and Delaware and the Jerseys demanded a certain degree of skill and yielded in return a very fair living. In other words, the poor settlers in Virginia, finding that tobacco culture was now based upon the cheap labor of African slaves, moved away to other localities where intelligence still brought an adequate reward.

The Maryland House of Delegates, when asked to give their opinion in this matter, thought that it was a desire to escape the payment of debts which made some of the "meaner inhabitants" seek shelter in Delaware Bay and the Carolinas. They came nearer the real cause when they added that the low price paid by the merchants for tobacco obliged many to leave.[12] Nicholson was not satisfied with this answer. "They will not directly own," he wrote, "that setting up manufactures and handicraft-trades in Pennsylvania, the large tracts of land held by some persons here and the encouragement given to illegal traders are the causes that make people leave this province. They would have it that they wish to avoid the persecution of their creditors, which causes them to shelter themselves among the inhabitants of the Lower Counties of Delaware Bay and of Carolina. The low price of tobacco has obliged many of the planters to try their fortune elsewhere, and the currency of money in Pennsylvania, which here is not, draws them to that province from this."[13]

In Virginia the difficulty of securing desirable land because of the large tracts patented by rich planters was usually assigned as the reason for the migration of poor families. This view of the matter was taken by Edward Randolph, the man who had won the undying hatred of the people of Massachusetts by his attempts to enforce the Navigation Acts there and by his attacks upon their charter. In 1696 Randolph did Virginia the honor of a visit, and although encountering there none of the opposition which had so angered him in New England, he sent to the Board of Trade a memorial concerning the colony, criticising the government severely. It should be inquired into, he said, how it comes to pass that the colony (the first English settlement on the continent of America, begun above 80 years ago) is not better inhabited, considering what vast numbers of servants and others have yearly been transported thither. . . . The chief and only reason is the Inhabitants and Planters have been and at this time are discouraged and hindered from planting tobacco in that colony, and servants are not so willing to go there as formerly, because the members of the Council and others, who make an interest in the Government, have from time to time procured grants of very large Tracts of land, so that there has not for many years been any waste land to be taken up by those who bring with them servants, or by such Servants, who have served their time faithfully with their Masters, but it is taken up and ingrossed beforehand, whereby they are forced to hyer and pay a yearly rent for some of those Lands, or go to the utmost bounds of the Colony for Land, exposed to danger and often times proves the Occasion of Warr with the Indians."[14]

For their large holdings the wealthy men paid not one penny of quit rents, Randolph said, and failed to comply with the regulations for seating new lands. The law demanded that upon receipt of a patent one must build a house upon the ground, improve and plant the soil and keep a good stock of cattle or hogs. But in their frontier holdings the wealthy men merely erected a little bark hut and turned two or three hogs into the woods by it. Or else they would clear one acre of land and plant a little Indian corn for one year, trusting that this evasion would square them with the letter of the law. By such means, Randolph adds, vast tracts were held, all of which had been procured on easy terms and much by means of false certificates of rights. "Which drives away the inhabitants and servants, brought up only to planting, to seek their fortunes in Carolina or other places."[15]

Randolph suggested that the evil might be remedied by requiring a strict survey of lands in every county, by demanding all arrears of quit rents, by giving strict orders that in the future no grant should exceed 500 acres. These measures, he believed, would cause 100,000 acres to revert to the Crown, and "invite home those who for want of Land left Virginia." It would encourage other persons to come from neighboring colonies to take up holdings and "mightily increase the number of Planters." This would augment the production of tobacco by many thousands of hogsheads, stimulate trade and industry in England, and aid his Majesty's revenue.

The Board of Trade was deeply impressed. They wrote to Governor Andros explaining to him the substance of Randolph's report and asking what steps should be taken to remedy the evils he had pointed out. "But this seeming to us a matter of very great consequence," they added, "we have not been willing to meddle in it without your advice, which we now desire you to give fully and plainly." But Andros knew full well that it was no easy matter to make the large landowners disgorge. The thing had been attempted by Nicholson several years earlier, when suit was instituted against Colonel Lawrence Smith for arrears of quit rents upon tracts of land which had never been under cultivation.[16] But before the case came to trial Nicholson had been recalled and it was afterward compounded for a nominal sum. The proceedings had caused great resentment among the powerful clique which centered around the Council of State, and Andros was reluctant to reopen the matter. He knew of no frauds in granting patents of land, he wrote the Board, and could suggest no remedy for what was past, "being a matter of Property." He agreed, however, that to limit the size of future patents would tend to "the more regular planting and thicker seating of the frontier lands."[17]

Consequently when Francis Nicholson was commissioned as Governor in 1698, he received strict instructions to advise with the Council and the Assembly upon this matter and to report back to the Board.[18] That nothing was accomplished, however, may clearly be inferred from a letter of a certain George Larkin written December 22, 1701. "There is no encouragement for anyone to come to the Plantation," he declared, "most of the land lying at all convenient being taken up. Some have 20,000, 30,000 or 40,000 acres, the greater part of which is unimployed."[19] Two years later Nicholson himself wrote that certain recent grants were for ten or twenty thousand acres each, so that privileged persons had engrossed all the good land in those parts, by which means they kept others from settling it or else made them pay for it.[20]

Despite all the concern which this matter created, it is doubtful whether it was to any appreciable extent responsible for the continued emigration of poor families. The mere granting of patents for large tracts of land could not of itself fix the economic structure of the colony, could not, if all other conditions were favorable, prevent the establishment of small freeholds. Rather than have their fields lie idle while the poor men who should have been cultivating them trooped out of the colony, the rich would gladly have sold them in small parcels at nominal prices. In the first half century after the settlement at Jamestown, as we have seen, such a breakup of extensive holdings into little farms actually occurred. Had similar conditions prevailed in the later period a like development would have followed. But in 1630 or 1650, when slaves were seldom employed and when tobacco was high, the poor man's toil yielded a return so large that he could well afford to purchase a little farm and make himself independent. In 1680 or 1700, in the face of the competition of slave labor, he was almost helpless. Even had he found a bit of unoccupied ground to which he could secure a title, he could not make it yield enough to sustain him and his family.[21]

In 1728 Governor Gooch wrote the Board of Trade that the former belief that large holdings of frontier land had been an impediment to settlement was entirely erroneous. It was his opinion, in fact, that extensive grants made it to the interest of the owners to bring in settlers and so populate the country. In confirmation of this he pointed to the fact that Spotsylvania country, where many large patents had been issued, had filled up more rapidly than Brunswick, where they had been restricted in size.[22]

In the first decade of the new century the emigration out of the tobacco colonies continued without abatement. With another disastrous decline in the price of tobacco following the outbreak of the wars of Charles XII and Louis XIV, so many families moved over the border that the Board of Trade, once more becoming seriously alarmed, questioned the Council as to the causes of the evil and what steps should be taken to remedy it. In their reply the Councillors repeated the old arguments, declaring that the lack of land in Virginia and the immunity of debtors from prosecution in the proprietory colonies were responsible for the movement. But they touched the heart of the matter in their further statement that the great stream of negroes that was pouring into the colony had so increased the size of the tobacco crop that prices had declined and the poor found it difficult to subsist. Not only "servants just free go to North Carolina," they wrote, "but old planters whose farms are worn out."[23]

A year later President Jennings stated that the migration

was continuing and that during the summer of 1709 "many entire families" had moved out of the colony.[24] In fact, although but few indentured servants arrived from England after the first decade of the century, poor whites were still departing for the north or for western Carolina so late as 1730. William Byrd II tells us that in 1728, when he was running the dividing line between Virginia and North Carolina, he was entertained by a man who "was lately removed, Bag and Baggage from Maryland, thro a strong Antipathy he had to work and paying his Debts." Indeed he thought it a "thorough Aversion to Labor" which made "People file off to North Carolina."[25]

It is impossible to estimate the numbers involved in this movement, but they must have run into the thousands. For a full half century a large proportion of the white immigrants to Virginia seem to have remained there for a comparatively short time only, then to pass on to other settlements. And the migration to Virginia during these years we know to have comprised not less than thirty or thirty-five thousand persons. In fact, it would seem that this movement out of the older colony must have been a very important factor in the peopling of its neighbors, not only western Carolina and western Maryland, but Delaware and Pennsylvania.

Though many thus fled before the stream of negroes which poured in from Africa, others remained behind to fight for their little plantations. Yet they waged a losing battle. Those who found it possible to purchase slaves, even one or two, could ride upon the black tide, but the others slowly sank beneath it.

During the first half of the Eighteenth century the poor whites sought to offset the cheapness of slave made tobacco by producing themselves only the highest grades. The traders who dealt in the finest Orinoco, which brought the best prices, found it not upon the plantations of the wealthy, but of those who tended their plants with their own hands. "I must beg you to remember that the common people make the best," wrote Governor Gooch to the Lords of Trade in 1731.[26]

In fact, the wealthy planter, with his newly acquired gangs of slaves, found it difficult at this time to produce any save the lower grades of tobacco. The African was yet too savage, too untutored in the ways of civilization to be utilized for anything like intensive cultivation. "Though they may plant more in quantity," wrote Gooch, "yet it frequently proves very mean stuff, different from the Tobacco produced from well improved and well tended Grounds." "Yet the rich Man's trash will always damp the Market," he adds, "and spoil the poor Man's good Tobacco which has been carefully managed."[27] Thus the small farmer made one last desperate effort to save himself by pitting his superior intelligence against the cheapness of slave labor.

But his case was hopeless. As slavery became more and more fixed upon the colony, the negro gradually increased in efficiency. He learned to speak his master's language, brokenly of course, but well enough for all practical purposes. He was placed under the tutelage of overseers, who taught him the details of his work and saw that he did it. He became a civilized being, thoroughly drilled in the one task required of him, the task of producing tobacco. Thus the rich planter soon found it possible to cultivate successfully the higher grades, and so to drive from his last rampart the white freeholder whose crop was tended by himself alone.

Placed at so great a disadvantage, the poor man, at all times in very difficult circumstances, found it almost impossible to exist whenever conditions in Europe sent the price of tobacco down. In the years from 1706 to 1714, when the tobacco trade was interrupted by the wars of Charles XII in the Baltic region and the protracted struggle known as the War of the Spanish Succession, he was reduced to the utmost extremities.

Virginia and Maryland were learning that a prosperity founded upon one crop which commanded a world market was in unsettled times subject to serious setbacks. It was a long cry from the James and the Potomac to the Baltic ports, yet the welfare of the Virginia and Maryland planters was in no small degree dependent upon the maintenance of peaceful conditions in Poland and Sweden and Russia. A war which seriously curtailed the exportation of English leaf to the northern countries would inevitably react on the price and so bring misfortune to the colonial planters. When called before the Board of Trade to testify as to the decay of the tobacco trade, the manufacturer John Linton declared that the Baltic countries, which formerly had purchased thousands of hogsheads a year, now took comparatively few. "The Russian trade is ruined," he said.[28]

The war against France and Spain, coming at this unfortunate juncture, still further restricted the market, sent prices down to new depths and filled to overflowing the planters' cup of misfortune. "The war has stopped the trade with Spain, France, Flanders and part of the Baltic," Colonel Quary reported in a memorial to the Board of Trade, "which took off yearly 20,000 hogsheads of tobacco. Now our best foreign market is Holland."[29] The pamphlet entitled *The Present State of the Tobacco Plantations in America* stated, in 1708, that France and Spain alone had imported 20,000 hogsheads, but that both were now otherwise supplied. "The troubles in Sweden, Poland, Russia, etc., have prevented the usual exportation of great quantities to those ports. Virginia and Maryland have severely felt the loss of such exportation, having so far reduced the planters that for several years past the whole product of their tobacco would hardly clothe the servants that made it."[30]

Their misfortunes were accentuated by the fact that the Dutch took advantage of the European upheavals to gain control of a part of the tobacco trade. Upon the outbreak of the war with Louis XIV, England prohibited the exportation of tobacco either to France or to Spain, but Holland, despite her participation in the struggle, apparently took no such action. On the contrary she strained every nerve to entrench herself in the markets of her ally before peace should once more open the flood gates to Virginia and Maryland tobacco. With this in view the acreage in Holland devoted to the cultivation of the leaf was rapidly extended. "The Dutch are improving and increasing their tobacco plantations," wrote John Linton in 1706. "In 1701 they produced only 18,000 hogsheads. Last year it was 33,500 hogsheads." Plantations at Nimwegen, Rhenen, Amersfoort and Nijkerk turned out 13,400,000 pounds, while great quantities were raised on the Main, in Higher Germany and in Prussia.[31]

The Dutch mixed their own leaf with that of Virginia and Maryland in the proportion of four to one, subjected it to a process of manufacture and sent it out to all the European markets.[32] In 1707 a letter to John Linton stated that they had from thirty to forty houses for "making up tobacco in rolls," employing 4,000 men, besides great numbers of women and girls. Their Baltic exports were estimated at 12,350,000 pounds; 2,500,000 pounds to Norway, 1,500,000 to Jutland and Denmark, 4,000,000 to Sweden, 2,350,000 to Lapland, 2,000,000 to Danzig and Königsberg.[33]

With the continuation of the war on the continent Dutch competition became stronger and stronger. In 1714, when peace was at last in prospect, they seemed thoroughly entrenched in many of the markets formerly supplied by the English. "The planting of tobacco in Holland, Germany, Etc.," it was reported to the Board of Trade, "is increased to above four times what it was 20 years ago, and amounts now to as much as is made in both Virginia and Maryland." The tobacco trade, which had formerly produced some £250,000 in the balance of trade, had declined to about half that figure, exports of manufactured goods to the Chesapeake were rapidly dwindling, the number of ships engaged in carrying tobacco was greatly reduced, the merchants were impoverished, the planters were ruined.[34]

"It is hardly possible to imagine a more miserable spectacle than the poorer sort of inhabitants in this colony," the Council wrote in 1713, "whose labour in tobacco has not for several years afforded them clothing to shelter them from the violent colds as well as heats to both which this climate is subject in the several seasons. The importation of British and other European commodities by the merchants, whereby the planters were formerly well supplied with clothing, is now in a manner wholly left off and the small supplies still ventured sold at such prodigeous rates as they please. Many families formerly well clothed and their houses well furnished are now reduced to rags and all the visible marks of poverty."[35]

This unfortunate period was but temporary. With the conclusion of peace English tobacco was dumped upon the European market at a figure so low as to defy competition. And when once the hogsheads began to move, the reaction on Virginia and Maryland was rapid and pronounced. Soon prices rose again to the old levels, and the colony entered upon a period, for the larger planters at least, of unprecedented prosperity.[36] But the eight years of hardship and poverty made a lasting imprint upon the poorest class of whites. Coming as they did upon the heels of the first great wave of negro immigration, they accelerated the movement of the disrupting forces already at work. It was not by accident that the largest migration of whites to other settlements occurred just at this time and that the inquiries as to its cause are most frequent. The little planter class never fully recovered from the blow dealt it by the temporary loss of the larger part of the European tobacco trade.

The small freeholders who possessed neither servants nor slaves did not disappear entirely, but they gradually declined in numbers and sank into abject poverty. During the period of Spotswood's administration they still constituted a large part of the population. The tax list for 1716 in Lancaster, one of the older counties, shows that of 314 persons listed as tithables, 202 paid for themselves only[37] Making ample deductions for persons not owning land it would appear that more than half the planters at this date still tilled their fields only with their own labor. At the time of the American Revolution, however, the situation had changed materially, and a decided dwindling of the poor farmer class is noticeable. In Gloucester county the tax lists for 1782-83 show 490 white families, of which 320 were in possession of slaves. Of the 170 heads of families who possessed no negroes, since no doubt some were overseers, some artisans, some professional men, it is probable that not more than eighty or ninety were proprietors.[38] In Spotsylvania county similar conditions are noted. Of 704 tithable whites listed in 1783 all save 199 possessed slaves.[39] In Dinwiddie county, in the year 1782, of 843 tithable whites, 210 only were not slave holders.[40] Apparently the Virginia yeoman, the sturdy, independent farmer of the Seventeenth century, who tilled his little holding with his own hands, had become an insignificant factor in the life of the colony. The glorious promises which the country had held out to him in the first fifty years of its existence had been belied. The Virginia which had formerly been so largely the land of the little farmer, had become the land of masters and slaves. For aught else there was no room.

Before the end of the Eighteenth century the condition of the poorest class had become pitiable. The French philosopher Chastellux who spent much time in Virginia during the American Revolution testifies to their extreme misery. "It is there that I saw poor persons for the first time since crossing the ocean," he says. "In truth, near these rich plantations, in which the negro alone is unhappy, are often found miserable huts inhabited by whites whose wan faces and ragged garments give testimony to their poverty."[41]

Philip Fithian, in his *Journal,* describes the habits of this class and is vigorous in his condemnation of the brutal fights which were so common among them. "In my opinion animals which seek after and relish such odius and filthy amusements are not of the human species," he says, "they are destitute of the remotest pretension of humanity."[42] Even the negroes of the wealthy regarded these persons with contempt, a contempt which they were at no pains to conceal.

The traveller Smyth thought them "kind, hospitable and generous," but illiberal, noisy and rude," and much "addicted to inebriety and averse to labor." This class, he says, "who ever compose the bulk of mankind, are in Virginia more few in numbers, in proportion to the rest of the inhabitants, than perhaps in any other country in the universe."[43]

But it must not be imagined that slavery drove out or ruined the entire class of small farmers, leaving Virginia alone to the wealthy. In fact, most of those who were firmly established remained, finding their salvation in themselves purchasing slaves. Few indeed had been able to avail themselves of the labor of indentured servants; the cost of transportation was too heavy, the term too short, the chances of sickness or desertion too great. But with the influx of thousands of negroes, the more enterprising and industrious of the poor planters quite frequently made purchases. Although the initial outlay was greater, they could secure credit by pledging their farms and their crops, and in the end the investment usually paid handsome dividends and many who could not raise the money to buy a full grown negro, often found it possible to secure a child, which in time would become a valuable asset.

This movement may readily be traced by an examination of the tax lists and county records of the Eighteenth century. In Lancaster even so early as 1716 we find that the bulk of the slaves were in the hands, not of wealthy proprietors, but of comparatively poor persons. Of the 314 taxpayers listed, 113 paid for themselves alone, 94 for two only, 37 for three, 22 for four, thirteen for five, while thirty-five paid for more than five. As there were but few servants in the colony at this time it may be taken for granted that the larger part of the tithables paid for by others were negro slaves. It would seem, then, that of some 200 slave owners in this country, about 165 possessed from one to four negroes only. There were but four persons listed as having more than twenty slaves, William Ball with 22, Madam Fox with 23, William Fox with 25 and Robert Carter with 126.[44]

Nor did the class of little slave holders melt away as time passed. In fact they continued to constitute the bulk of the white population of Virginia for a century and a half, from the beginning of the Eighteenth century until the conquest of the State by Federal troops in 1865. Thus we find that of 633 slave owners in Dinwiddie county in 1782, 95 had one only, 66 had two, 71 three, 45 four, 50 five, making an aggregate of 327, or more than half of all the slave holders, who possessed from one to five negroes.[45] In Spotsylvania there were, in 1783, 505 slave owners, of whom 78 possessed one each, 54 two, 44 three, 41 four, and 30 five each. Thus 247, or nearly 49 per cent of the slave holders, had from one to five slaves only. One hundred and sixteen, or 23 per cent, had from six to ten inclusive.[46] The Gloucester lists for 1783 show similar conditions. There were in this country 320 slave holders, having 3,314 negroes, an average of about 10⅓ for each owner. Fifty had one each, 41 had two each, 9 had three, 30 had four and twenty-six had five. Thus 156, or about half of all the owners, had from one to five slaves.[47] In Princess Anne county, of a total of 388 slave owners, 100 had one each, 56 had two each and forty-five had three each.[48]

Records of transfers of land tend to substantiate this testimony, by showing that the average holdings at all times in the Eighteenth century were comparatively small. In the years from 1722 to 1729 Spotsylvania was a new county, just opened to settlers, and a large part of its area had been granted in large tracts to wealthy patentees. Yet the deed book for these years shows that it was actually settled, not by these men themselves, but by a large number of poor planters. Of the 197 transfers of land recorded, 44 were for 100 acres or less and 110 for 300 acres or less. The average deed was for 487 acres. As some of the transfers were obviously made for speculative purposes and not with the intent of putting the land under cultivation, even this figure is misleading. The average farm during the period was probably not in excess of 400 acres. One of the most extensive dealers in land in Spotsylvania was Larkin Chew who secured a patent for a large tract and later broke it up into many small holdings which were sold to new settlers.[49]

This substitution of the small slave holder for the man who used only his own labor in the cultivation of his land unquestionably saved the class of small proprietors from destruction. Without it all would have been compelled to give up their holdings in order to seek their fortunes elsewhere, or sink to the condition of "poor white trash." Yet the movement was in many ways unfortunate. It made the poor man less industrious and thrifty. Formerly he had known that he could win nothing except by the sweat of his brow, but now he was inclined to let the negro do the work. Slavery cast a stigma upon labor which proved almost as harmful to the poor white man as did negro competition. Work in the tobacco fields was recognized as distinctly the task of an inferior race, a task not in keeping with the dignity of freemen.

Jefferson states that few indeed of the slave owners were ever seen to work. "For in a warm climate," he adds, "no man will labour for himself who can make another labour for him."[50] Chastellux noted the same tendency, declaring "that the indolence and dissipation of the middling and lower classes of white inhabitants of Virginia is such as to give pain to every reflecting mind."[51]

Slavery developed in the small farmers a spirit of pride and haughtiness that was unknown to them in the Seventeenth century. Every man, no matter how poor, was surrounded by those to whom he felt himself superior, and this gave him a certain self-esteem. Smyth spoke of the middle class as generous, friendly and hospitable in the extreme, but possessing a rudeness and haughtiness which was the result of their "general intercourse with slaves."[52] Beverley described them as haughty and jealous of their liberties, and so impatient of restraint that they could hardly bear the thought of being controlled by any superior power. Hugh Jones, Anbury, Fithian and other Eighteenth century writers all confirm this testimony.

Despite the persistence of the small slave holder it is obvious that there were certain forces at work tending to increase the number of well-to-do and wealthy planters. Now that the labor problem, which in the Seventeenth century had proved so perplexing, had finally been solved, there was no limit to the riches that might be acquired by business acumen, industry and good management. And as in the modern industrial world the large corporation has many advantages over the smaller firms, so in colonial Virginia the most economical way of producing tobacco was upon the large plantations.

The wealthy man had the advantage of buying and selling in bulk, he enjoyed excellent credit and could thus often afford to withhold his crop from the market when prices were momentarily unfavorable, he could secure the best agricultural instruments. Most important of all, however, was the fact that he could utilize the resources of his plantation for the production of crude manufactured supplies, thus to a certain extent freeing himself from dependence upon Birtish imports and keeping his slaves at work during all seasons of the year. Before the Eighteenth century had reached its fifth decade every large plantation had become to a remarkable degree self-sustaining. Each numbered among its working force various kinds of mechanics—coopers, blacksmiths, tanners, carpenters, shoemakers, distillers. These men could be set to work whenever the claims of the tobacco crop upon their time were not imperative producing many of the coarser articles required upon the plantation, articles which the poor farmer had to import from England. For this work white men were at first almost universally made use of, but in time their places were taken by slaves. "Several of them are taught to be sawyers, carpenters, smiths, coopers, &c.," says the historian Hugh Jones, "though for the most part they be none of the aptest or nicest."[53]

The carpenter was kept busy constructing barns and servants' quarters, or repairing stables, fences, gates and wagons. The blacksmith was called upon to shoe horses, to keep in order ploughs, hinges, sickles, saws, perhaps even to forge outright such rough iron ware as nails, chains and hoes. The cooper made casks in which to ship the tobacco crop, barrels for flour and vats for brandy and cider. The tanner prepared leather for the plantation and the cobbler fashioned it into shoes for the slaves. Sometimes there were spinners, weavers and knitters who made coarse cloth both for clothing and for bedding. The distiller every season made an abundant supply of cider, as well as apple, peach and persimmon brandy.

And the plantation itself provided the materials for this varied manufacture. The woods of pine, chestnut and oak yielded timber for houses and fuel for the smithy. The herd of cattle supplied hides for the tanner. The cloth makers got cotton, flax and hemp from the planter's own fields, and wool from his sheep. His orchard furnished apples, grapes, peaches in quantities ample for all the needs of the distiller. In other words, the large planter could utilize advantageously the resources at hand in a manner impossible for his neighbor who could boast of but a small farm and half a score of slaves.[54]

It was inevitable, then, that the widespread use of slave labor would result in the gradual multiplication of well-to-do and wealthy men. In the Seventeenth century not one planter in fifty could be classed as a man of wealth, and even so late as 1704 the number of the well-to-do was very narrowly limited. In a report to the Lords of Trade written in that year Colonel Quary stated that upon each of the four great rivers of Virginia there resided from "ten to thirty men who by trade and industry had gotten very competent estates."[55] Fifty years later the number had multiplied several times over.

Thus in Gloucester county in 1783, of 320 slave holders no less than 57 had sixteen or more. Of these one possessed 162, one 138, one 93, one 86, one 63, one 58, two 57, one 56, one 43 and one 40.[56] In Spotsylvania, of 505 owners, 76 had sixteen or more. Of these Mann Page, Esq., had 157, Mrs. Mary Daingerfield had 71, William Daingerfield 61, Alexander

Spotswood 60, William Jackson 49, George Stubblefield 42, Frances Marewither 40, William Jones 39.[57]

The Dinwiddie tax lists for 1783 show that of 633 slave holders, no less than 60 had twenty-one or more negroes. Among the more important of these were Robert Turnbull with 81, Colonel John Banister with 88, Colonel William Diggs with 72, John Jones with 69, Mrs. Mary Bolling with 51, Robert Walker with 52, Winfield Mason with 40, John Burwell with 42, Gray Briggs with 43, William Yates with 55, Richard Taliaferro with 43, Major Thomas Scott with 57, Francis Muir with 47.[58] The wealth of the larger planters is also shown by the large number of coaches recorded in these lists, which including phaetons, chariots and chairs, aggregated 180 wheels.

Thus it was that the doors of opportunity opened wide to the enterprising and industrious of the middle class, and many availed themselves of it to acquire both wealth and influence. Smyth tells us that at the close of the colonial period there were many planters whose fortunes were "superior to some of the first rank," but whose families were "not so ancient nor respectable."[59] It was the observation of Anbury that gentlemen of good estates were more numerous in Virginia than in any other province of America.[60]

In fact the Eighteenth century was the golden age of the Virginia slave holders. It was then that they built the handsome homes once so numerous in the older counties, many of which still remain as interesting monuments of former days; it was then that they surrounded themselves with graceful furniture and costly silverware, in large part imported from Great Britain; it was then that they collected paintings and filled their libraries with the works of standard writers; it was then that they purchased coaches and berlins; it was then that men and women alike wore rich and expensive clothing.

This movement tended to widen the influence of the aristocracy and at the same time to eliminate any sharp line of demarkation between it and the small slave holders. There was now only a gradual descent from the wealthiest to the poor man who had but one slave. The Spotsylvania tax lists for 1783 show 247 slaveholders owning from one to five negroes, 116 owning from six to ten inclusive, 66 owning from eleven to fifteen inclusive, and seventy-six owning more than fifteen.[61] In Gloucester 156 had from one to five slaves, 66 from five to ten inclusive, 41 from eleven to fifteen inclusive, and fifty-seven over fifteen. Thus in a very true sense the old servant holding aristocracy had given way to a vastly larger slave holding aristocracy.

It is this fact which explains the decline in power and influence of the Council in Virginia, which was so notable in the Eighteenth century. This body had formerly been representative of a small clique of families so distinct from the other planters and possessed of such power in the government as to rival the nobility of England itself. Now, however, as this distinction disappeared, the Council sank in prestige because it represented nothing, while the House of Burgesses became the mouthpiece of the entire slave holding class, and thus the real power in the colonial Government.

Historians have often expressed surprise at the small number of Tories in Virginia during the American Revolution. The aristocratic type of society would naturally lead one to suppose that a large proportion of the leading families would have remained loyal to the Crown. Yet with very few exceptions all supported the cause of freedom and independence, even though conscious of the fact that by so doing they were jeopardizing not only the tobacco trade which was the basis of their wealth, but the remnants of their social and political privileges in the colony. When the British Ministry tried to wring from the hands of the Assembly the all-important control over taxation which all knew to be the very foundation of colonial self-government, every planter, the largest as well as the smallest, felt himself aggrieved, for this body was the depository of his power and the guardian of his interests. A hundred years before, when the commons rose against the oppression and tyranny of the Government, the wealthy men rallied to the support of Sir William Berkeley and remained loyal to him throughout all his troubles. In 1775 there was no such division of the people; the planters were almost a unit in the defense of rights which all held in common.

It is obvious, then, that slavery worked a profound revolution in the social, economic and political life of the colony. It practically destroyed the Virginia yeomanry, the class of small planters who used neither negroes nor servants in the cultivation of their fields, the class which produced the bulk of the tobacco during the Seventeenth century and constituted the chief strength of the colony. Some it drove into exile, either to the remote frontiers or to other colonies; some it reduced to extreme poverty; some it caused to purchase slaves and so at one step to enter the exclusive class of those who had others to labor for them. Thus it transformed Virginia from a land of hardworking, independent peasants, to a land of slaves and slave holders. The small freeholder was not destroyed, as was his prototype of ancient Rome, but he was subjected to a change which was by no means fortunate or wholesome. The wealthy class, which had formerly consisted of a narrow clique closely knit together by family ties. was transformed into a numerous body, while all sharp line of demarkation between it and the poorer slave holders was wiped out. In short, the Virginia of the Eighteenth century, the

Virginia of Gooch and Dinwiddie and Washington and Jefferson, was fundamentally different from the Virginia of the Seventeenth century, the Virginia of Sir William Berkeley and Nathaniel Bacon. Slavery had wrought within the borders of the Old Dominion a profound and far reaching revolution.

NOTES TO CHAPTER I

[1] Peter Force, Tracts and Other Papers, Vol. III, A True Declaration, p. 25.

[2] Purchas, Vol. XVIII, pp. 437-438.

[3] Peter Force, Tracts and Other Papers, Vol. III, A True Declaration, p. 23.

[4] Alexander Brown, The Genesis of the United States, Vol. I, p. 37.

[5] Peter Force, Tracts and Other Papers, Vol. I, Nova Brittania, pp. 21-22.

[6] Hakluyt, Discourse, pp. 89-90.

[7] Hakluyt, Discourse, p. 105.

[8] Hakluyt, Discourse, p. 31.

[9] Hakluyt, Discourse, pp. 14-15.

[10] Alexander Brown, The First Republic in America, p. 49.

[11] Alexander Brown, The Genesis of the United States, Vol. I, p. 349; Peter Force, Tracts and Other Papers, Vol. I, Nova Brittania, pp. 16-17.

[12] Alexander Brown, The Genesis of the United States, Vol. I, p. 239.

[13] Alexander Brown, The Genesis of the United States, Vol. I, p. 202.

[14] P. A. Bruce, Economic History of Virginia, Vol. II, p. 445.

[15] Neill, The Virginia Company of London, p. 338.

[16] Randolph Manuscript, p. 212.

[17] P. A. Bruce, Economic History of Virginia, Vol. II, p. 440; Alexander Brown, The Genesis of the United States, Vol. I, p. 239.

[18] P. A. Bruce, Economic History of Virginia, Vol. II, p. 441.

[19] P. A. Bruce, Economic History of Virginia, Vol. II, p. 443.

NOTES TO CHAPTER II

[1] P. A. Bruce, Economic History of Virginia, Vol. I, p. 161; Alexander Brown, The First Republic in America, p. 232.

[2] William Strachey, Historie of Travaile into Virginia Britannia, p. 121; P. A. Bruce, Economic History of Virginia, Vol. I, p. 162.

[3] Ralph Hamor, True Discourse, pp. 24, 34.

[4] G. L. Beer, The Origins of the British Colonial System, p. 79.

[5] Edward Arber, The Works of Captain John Smith, p. 535.

[6] Alexander Brown, The First Republic in America, p. 268.

[7] G. L. Beer, The Origins of the British Colonial System, p. 87.

[8] G. L. Beer, The Origins of the British Colonial System, p. 81.

[9] Alexander Brown, The First Republic in America, p. 268.

[10] Virginia Magazine of History and Biography, Vol. IX, pp. 40-41.

[11] Virginia Magazine of History and Biography, Vol. IX, pp. 176-177.

[12] P. A. Bruce, Economic History of Virginia, Vol. II, p. 416.

[13] Alexander Brown, The Genesis of the United States, Vol. I, pp. 355-356.

[14] The lack of towns in Virginia was a source of great regret to the English Government, and more than once attempts were made to create them by artificial means.

[15] Even at the end of the Seventeenth century the average price for land in the older counties was about thirty pounds of tobacco an acre.

[16] P. A. Bruce, Economic History of Virginia, Vol. I, p. 578; Vol. II, p. 48.

[17] It was Chanco, an Indian boy living with a Mr. Pace, who revealed the plot to massacre the whites in 1622, and so saved the colony from destruction. Edward Arber, The Works of Captain John Smith, p. 578.

[18] P. A. Bruce, The Economic History of Virginia, Vol. II, p. 70.

[19] For a full discussion of this matter see p. —.

[20] Hakluyt, Vol. VII, p. 286.

[21] P. A. Bruce, Economic History of Virginia, Vol. I, p. 582.

[22] Abstracts of Proceedings of Virginia Company of London, Vol. I, pp. 28, 172; Edward Arber, The Works of Captain John Smith, p. 609.

[23] Hening, Statutes at Large, Vol. II, p. 510.

[24] P. A. Bruce, Economic History of Virginia, Vol. I, p. 603.

[25] P. A. Bruce, Economic History of Virginia, Vol. I, p. 605.

[26] Virginia Land Patents, Vol. V, Register of Land Office, Virginia State Capitol.

[27] Hening, Statutes at Large, Vol. II, p. 510.

[28] P. A. Bruce, Economic History of Virginia, Vol. I, p. 611.

[29] British Public Record Office, CO1-26-77, Berkeley to the Board of Trade.

[30] Peter Force, Tracts and Other Papers, Vol. III, Orders and Constitutions, 1619, 1620, p. 22.

[31] Virginia Land Patents, Register of Land Office, Virginia State Capitol.

[32] Calendar of State Papers, Colonial Series, 1574-1660, p. 208.

[33] Princeton Transcripts, Virginia Land Patents, Princeton University Library.

[34] Virginia Land Patents, Register of Land Office, Virginia State Capitol.

NOTES TO CHAPTER III

[1] L. G. Tyler, Narratives of Early Virginia, pp. 21-22.

[2] Abstracts of Proceedings of Virginia Company of London, Vol. II, p. 171.

[3] British Public Record Office, CO1-26-77, Berkeley to Board of Trade.

[4] Hening, Statutes at Large, Vol. I, p. 257.

[5] Hening, Statutes at Large, Vol. I, p. 411.

[6] Hening, Statutes at Large, Vol. I, p. 539.

[7] British Public Record Office, CO1-26-77, Berkeley to Board of Trade.

[8] Virginia Land Patents, Register of Land Office, Virginia State Capitol.

[9] P. A. Bruce, Economic History of Virginia, Vol. I, p. 595.

[10] J. C. Hotten, Original Lists of Emigrants to America (1600-1700).

[11] Peter Force, Tracts and Other Papers, Vol. II, New Description of Virginia, p. 3.

[12] British Public Record Office, CO1-26-77, Berkeley to Board of Trade.

[13] British Public Record Office, CO5-1359, p. 119, Colonial Entry Book, Governor Andros to the Lords of Trade.

[14] E. D. Neill, Virginia Vetusta, p. 123.

[15] Hugh Jones, Present State of Virginia, p. 61.

[16] Surry County Records, 1684-1686, Virginia State Library.

[17] York County Records, 1696-1701, Virginia State Library.

[18] Rappahannock County Deeds, 1680-1688, Virginia State Library.

[19] Essex County, Orders, Deeds, Etc., 1692-1695, Virginia State Library.

[20] J. C. Hotten, Original Lists of Emigrants to America, pp. 266-275.

[21] P. A. Bruce, Economic History of Virginia, Vol. I, pp. 529-532.

[22] Virginia Land Patents, Register of Land Office, Virginia State Capitol.

[23] Virginia Magazine of History and Biography, Vol. I, p. 30.

[24] Virginia Magazine of History and Biography, Vol. XII, p. 387.

[25] Virginia Land Patents, Register of Land Office, Virginia State Capitol.

[26] Virginia Land Patents, Register of Land Office, Virginia State Capitol.

[27] Essex County, Orders, Deeds, Etc., 1692-1695, Virginia State Library.

[28] Surry County Records, 1645-1672, p. 17.

[29] Essex County, Orders, Deeds, Etc., 1692-1695, p. 348, Virginia State Library.

[30] Virginia Land Patents, Register of Land Office, Virginia State Capitol, Vol. V.

[31] Essex County, Orders, Deeds, Etc., 1692-1695, pp. 199, 202, 205, 209, 216, 348, 394, 407, 413, Virginia State Library.

[32] H. R. McIlwaine, Journals of the House of Burgesses, 1686, p. 37.

[33] British Public Record Office, CO5-1359, pp. 91-92, Colonial Entry Book.

[34] British Public Record Office, CO5-1306, Document 116, Correspondence of the Board of Trade.

[35] British Public Record Office, CO5-1355, p. 361, Colonial Entry Book.

[36] British Public Record Office, CO5-1359, pp. 91-92, Colonial Entry Book.

[37] British Public Record Office, CO5-1405, p. 460, Council Minutes, 1680-1695.

[38] British Public Record Office, CO5-1405, pp. 544-545, Council Minutes, 1680-1695.

[39] British Public Record Office, CO5-1359, p. 345, Colonial Entry Book, 1696-1700.

[40] British Public Record Office, CO5-1339, Document 33V. Correspondence of the Board of Trade.

[41] British Public Record Office, CO5-1314, Document 63VIII, Correspondence of the Board of Trade. A copy of this interest-

ing document is published as an appendix to this volume.

[42] See appendix.

[43] See appendix.

[44] Of this land 15 acres belonged to Thomas Jefferson, probably the grandfather of President Jefferson.

[45] In the opening years of the Eighteenth century the increased importation of slaves brought about an immediate decline in the migration of whites to Virginia from England.

[46] Hening, Statutes at Large, Vol. II, p. 480. The laws governing the tithables were altered slightly from time to time.

[47] Surry County, Wills, Deeds, Etc., 1671-1684, pp. 134-138, Virginia State Library.

[48] Surry County, Wills, Deeds, Etc., 1671-1684, pp. 134-138, Virginia State Library.

[49] Surry County, Deeds, Wills, Etc., 1684-1686, pp. 59-63, Virginia State Library.

[50] Virginia Magazine of History and Biography, Vol. I, pp. 364-373.

[51] Prince George county was formed out of Charles City in 1703.

[52] Surry County, Wills, Deeds, Etc., 1671-1684; Surry County, Deeds, Wills, Etc., 1684-1686, Virginia State Library.

[53] Elizabeth City County Records, 1684-1699, Virginia State Library.

NOTES TO CHAPTER IV

[1] William and Mary Quarterly, Vol. VIII, p. 273.

[2] William and Mary Quarterly, Vol. VIII, p. 273.

[3] P. A. Bruce, Economic History of Virginia, Vol. II, p. 42.

[4] Robert Beverley, History of Virginia, p. 221.

[5] Peter Force, Tracts and Other Papers, Vol. III, Leah and Rachel, p. 11.

[6] William and Mary Quarterly, Vol. XXVI, p. 31.

[7] Peter Force, Tracts and Other Papers, Vol. III, Leah and Rachel, p. 11.

[8] In fact, it was stated by John Hammond in 1656 that many servants acquired considerable property even before the expiration of their indentures. "Those servants that will be industrious may in their time of service gain a competent estate before their Freedomes," he says, "which is usually done by many, and they gaine esteeme and assistance that appear so industrious:

There is no master almost but will allow his Servant a parcell of clear ground to plant some tobacco in for himselfe, which he may husband at those many idle times he hath allowed him and not prejudice, but rejoyce his Master to see it, which in time of Shipping he may lay out for commodities, and in Summer sell them again with advantage, and get a Sow-Pig or two, which any body almost will give him, and his Master suffer him to keep them with his own, which will be no charge to his Master, and with one year's increase of them may purchase a Cow calf or two, and by that time he is for himself; he may have Cattle, Hogs and Tobacco of his own, and come to live gallantly; but this must be gained (as I said) by Industry and affability, not by sloth nor churlish behaviour." Peter Force, Tracts and Other Papers, Vol. III, Leah and Rachel, p. 14.

[9] Virginia Magazine of History and Biography, Vol. IV, p. 157.

[10] Virginia Magazine of History and Biography, Vol. VII, p. 262.

[11] Virginia Magazine of History and Biography, Vol. VII, p. 261.

[12] R. L. Beer, Origins of the British Colonial System, p. 154.

[13] Virginia Magazine of History and Biography, Vol. VIII, p. 160.

[14] Virginia Magazine of History and Biography, Vol. XIII, p. 381.

[15] Peter Force, Tracts and Other Papers, Vol. II, New Description of Virginia, pp. 4-6.

[16] British Public Record Office, CO1-21, Secretary Ludwell to Lord John Berkeley.

[17] Alexander Brown, The First Republic in America, p. 268.

[18] Virginia Magazine of History and Biography, Vol. VII, p. 267, King Charles I to the Governor and Council of Virginia.

[19] Virginia Magazine of History and Biography, Vol. I, p. 293.

[20] Virginia Magazine of History and Biography, Vol. VI, p. 376.

[21] Virginia Magazine of History and Biography, Vol. II, p. 53.

[22] Virginia Magazine of History and Biography, Vol. II, p. 394.

[23] Virginia Magazine of History and Biography, Vol. VI, p. 260.

[24] Virginia Magazine of History and Biography, Vol. VII, p. 382.

[25] Virginia Magazine of History and Biography, Vol. VIII, p. 149.

[26] Governor Yeardley's Instructions of 1626 contain the statement that "tobacco falleth every day more and more to a baser price."

[27] Virginia Magazine of History and Biography, Vol. VII, p. 376.

[28] Virginia Magazine of History and Biography, Vol. VIII, p. 159.

[29] Virginia Magazine of History and Biography, Vol. IX, p. 177.

[30] Virginia Magazine of History and Biography, Vol. X, p. 425.

[31] G. L. Beer, Origins of the British Colonial System, p. 159.

[32] Peter Force, Tracts and Other Papers, Vol. II, New Description of Virginia, p. 4.

[33] Virginia Magazine of History and Biography, Vol. VIII, p. 150.

[34] Virginia Magazine of History and Biography, Vol. II, p. 288. In Feb. 1627, orders were issued once more that all colonial tobacco, whether of Virginia or of the West Indies, should be shipped only to London. Calendar of State Papers, 1574-1660, p. 84.

[35] Virginia Magazine of History and Biography, Vol. VIII, pp. 149, 155.

[36] British Public Record Office, CO1-12, Petition of Jan. 2, 1655.

[37] P. A. Bruce, Economic History of Virginia, Vol. I, pp. 349-356.

[38] G. L. Beer, Origins of the British Colonial System, pp. 203-204.

[39] G. L. Beer, Origins of the British Colonial System, p. 216.

[40] The author of A New Description of Virginia, published in 1649, states that "in Tobacco they can make L20 sterling a man, at 3d a pound per annum." Peter Force, Tracts and Other Papers, Vol. II, New Description of Virginia, p. 6.

[41] Virginia Magazine of History and Biography, Vol. VII, p. 382.

[42] Virginia Magazine of History and Biography, Vol. VIII, p. 149, Vol. II, p. 53, Vol. VII, p. 259.

[43] Virginia Magazine of History and Biography, Vol. VII, p. 260.

[44] Virginia Magazine of History and Biography, Vol. VIII, p. 158.

[45] Abstracts of Proceedings of Virginia Company of London, Vol. I, pp. 41-42.

[46] J. C. Hotten, Original Lists of Emigrants to America, pp. 201-265.

[47] Colonial Virginia Register, pp. 54-55.

[48] Peter Force, Tracts and Other Papers, Vol. III, p. 16.

[49] Colonial Virginia Register, pp. 68-69.

[50] Virginia Land Patents, Register of Land Office, Virginia State Capitol.

[51] Virginia Magazine of History and Biography, Vol. II, p. 420.

[52] Virginia Magazine of History and Biography, Vol. II, p. 421; Vol. IV, p. 75.

[53] Virginia Magazine of History and Biography, Vol. I, p. 77.

[54] W. A. Crozier, Virginia County Records, Vol. VI, pp. 15-18.

[55] W. A. Crozier, Virginia County Records, Vol. VI, p. 56.

[56] Virginia Land Patents, Register of Land Office, Virginia State Capitol.

[57] William and Mary Quarterly, Vol. XI, p. 271.

[58] William and Mary Quarterly, Vol. XI, p. 276.

[59] William and Mary Quarterly, Vol. XI, pp. 271-276.

[60] Virginia Colonial Register, pp. 64, 68, 70.

[61] William and Mary Quarterly, Vol. IX, p. 72.

[62] Virginia Land Patents, Vol. V, p. 224, Register of Land Office, Virginia State Capitol.

[63] W. A. Crozier, Virginia County Records, New Series Vol. I, p. 4.

[64] W. A. Crozier, Virginia County Records, Vol. VI, pp. 83, 84, 125, 126.

[65] W. A. Crozier, Virginia County Records, Vol. VII, p. 5.

[66] W. A. Crozier, Virginia County Records, Vol. VI, p. 78.

[67] W. A. Crozier, Virginia County Records, Vol. VI, pp. 77, 191, 281.

[68] W. A. Crozier, Virginia County Records, Vol. VI, p. 122.

[69] W. A. Crozier, Virginia County Records, Vol. VI, p. 192.

[70] W. A. Crozier, Virginia County Records, Vol. VI, p. 76.

[71] William and Mary Quarterly, Vol. IX, p. 144.

[72] William and Mary Quarterly, Vol. IX, p. 144.

[73] William and Mary Quarterly, Vol. XI, p. 276.

[74] Virginia Land Patents, Vol. III, Register of Land Office, Virginia State Capitol. The name is here spelled John Blackborne.

[75] Virginia Land Patents, Vol. III, Register of Land Office,

Virginia State Capitol. On the lists the name is spelled William Butcher.

[76] J. C. Wise, The Early History of the Eastern Shore of Virginia, pp. 135-137.

[77] Virginia Land Patents, Vol. IV, Register of Land Office, Virginia State Capitol.

[78] J. C. Wise, The Early History of the Eastern Shore of Virginia, p. 95.

[79] G. C. Greer, Early Virginia Immigrants, p. 68.

[80] J. C. Wise, The Early History of the Eastern Shore of Virginia, p. 376.

[81] Virginia Magazine of History and Biography, Vol. V, p. 101.

[82] W. A. Crozier, Virginia County Records, Vol. VII, p. 177.

[83] Virginia Magazine of History and Biography, Vol. VI, p. 92.

[84] Virginia Magazine of History and Biography, Vol. VI, p. 298.

[85] In 1656 John Hammond declared that though it cost six pounds sterling to go to Virginia, those who decided to make the venture could be sure that their money was well spent. He advised "any that goes over free, but in a mean condition, to hire himself for reasonable wages of Tobacco and Provision, the first year," for by that means he could live free of disbursement, and "have something to help him the next year." Peter Force, Tracts and Other Papers, Vol. III, Leah and Rachel, p. 14.

[86] Virginia Magazine of History and Biography, Vol. VIII, p. 441.

[87] Virginia Magazine of History and Biography, Vol. IX, p. 27.

[88] Virginia Magazine of History and Biography, Vol. X, p. 271.

NOTES TO CHAPTER V

[1] G. L. Beer, The Old Colonial System, Vol. II, p. 109.

[2] British Public Record Office, CO5-1315, Document 26, Correspondence of the Board of Trade.

[3] P. A. Bruce, Economic History of Virginia, Vol. I, p. 401.

[4] R. L. Beer, The Old Colonial System, Vol. I, p. 160.

[5] British Public Record Office, CO5-1316, Perry and Hyde to the Lords of Trade, Correspondence of the Board of Trade.

[6] British Public Record Office, CO5-1316, The Present State of the Tobacco Plantations in America, Correspondence of the Board of Trade.

[7] British Public Record Office, CO5-1316, Correspondence of the Board of Trade; Statutes of the Realm, Vol. IX, p. 917.

[8] Virginia Magazine of History and Biography, Vol. I, pp. 141-155.

[9] British Public Record Office, CO1-16, Petition of Berkeley and Others, Aug. 26, 1662.

[10] British Public Record Office, CO1-20, Thomas Ludwell to Secretary Arlington, May 1, 1666.

[11] British Public Record Office, CO1-20, Sir William Berkeley and others to Secretary Arlington, July 13, 1666.

[12] British Public Record Office, CO1-20, Sir William Berkeley and others to Secretary Arlington, July 13, 1666.

[13] British Public Record Office, CO1-21, Thomas Ludwell to Lord Arlington, Feb. 12, 1667.

[14] British Public Record Office, CO1-21, Thomas Ludwell to Lord John Berkeley.

[15] British Public Record Office, CO1-23, p. 19, Ludwell to Lord Arlington.

[16] British Public Record Office, CO1-21, Governor and Council to the King.

[17] British Public Record Office, CO1-30, p. 51, Petition of the Governor and Council.

[18] British Public Record Office, CO5-1356, p. 408, Report of the Council to the King.

[19] British Public Record Office, CO5-1355, p. 385, Colonial Entry Book.

[20] British Public Record Office, CO1-23, p. 19, Ludwell to Lord Arlington, July 20, 1665.

[21] British Public Record Office, CO5-1371, p. 246, Colonial Entry Book.

[22] British Public Record Office, CO5-1371, pp. 232-240, Dialogue Between John Good and Nathaniel Bacon, Colonial Entry Book, 1677.

[23] British Public Record Office, CO1-30, p. 51, Petition of the Governor and Council to the King, July 1673.

[24] British Public Record Office, CO5-1355, p. 410, Colonial Entry Book.

[25] British Public Record Office, CO5-1356, p. 179, Colonial Entry Book.

[26] G. L. Beer, The Old Colonial System, Vol. II, p. 147.

[27] British Public Record Office, CO5-1371, p. 276, Colonial Entry Book.

[28] British Public Record Office, CO5-1371, p. 276, Colonial Entry Book.

[29] This view of the matter has the support of the dean of Virginia historians, Dr. Philip Alexander Bruce. Dr. Bruce writes: "No less an authority than Robert Beverley, the historian, states that the Navigation Acts had a sensible influence in precipitating Bacon's Rebellion. In the early life of this writer he must have been closely associated with hundreds of people who had been through the uprising, and knew much, by direct observation, of the currents that governed it. The elder Beverley was thoroughly informed and thus, in his own home, the son had the best of opportunities of learning the truth. Beverley himself declared that the Acts were causing discontent among the people, long before the Rebellion actually occurred, and so did John Bland in his memorable petition. There is no doubt that the Acts, by keeping alive a sense of friction, left the people in just the state of mind to seize with eagerness on the more palpable wrongs which were specifically brought forward as the justification for resistance. It was really the groundwork of the movement, though if it had been the only cause, might not have precipitated open resistance to the Government.

[30] G. L. Beer, The Old Colonial System, Vol. II, p. 115.

[31] Secretary Thomas Ludwell in a long report to the British Government spoke of the Virginia Government as Berkeley's own, "Which I so term," he explains, "because he is the sole author of the most substantial parts of it, either for Lawes or other inferior institutions." British Public Record Office, CO1-20.

[32] British Museum, Egerton Manuscript, 2395, f. 356b.

[33] British Public Record Office, CO1-19, Berkeley to Lord Arlington, Aug. 1, 1665.

[34] P. A. Bruce, Economic History of Virginia, Vol. I, pp. 399-400.

[35] British Public Record Office, CO1-26-77, Berkeley to the Board of Trade.

[36] British Public Record Office, CO1-30-78, Memorial of John Knight, Oct. 29, 1673.

[37] British Public Record Office, CO1-30-71, Council of Virginia to the King, 1673.

[38] Peter Force, Tracts and Other Papers, Vol. II, New Description of Virginia, pp. 1-16.

[39] British Museum, Egerton Manuscript, 2395, f. 356b, A Discourse and View of Virginia.

[40] British Public Record Office, CO1-26-77, Berkeley to the Board of Trade.

[41] British Public Record Office, CO1-34-95, Petition of Francis Moryson, Thomas Ludwell and Robert Smith.

[42] Virginia Land Patents, Register of Land Office, Virginia State Capitol.

[43] British Public Record Office, CO5-1359, pp. 20, 21, 22, Colonial Entry Book.

NOTES TO CHAPTER VI

[1] Peter Force, Tracts and Other Papers, Vol. II, New Description of Virginia, p. 3.

[2] British Public Record Office, CO1-30, pp. 17, 51.

[3] Surry County Wills, Deeds, Etc. 1671-1624, Virginia State Library.

[4] Surry County Wills, Deeds, Etc. 1684-1686, pp. 34-35, Virginia State Library.

[5] Surry County Wills, Deeds, Etc. 1684-1686, pp. 86-87, Virginia State Library.

[6] P. A. Bruce, Economic History of Virginia, Vol. II, p. 199.

[7] Peter Force, Tracts and Other Papers, Vol. II, New Description of Virginia, p. 3.

[8] P. A. Bruce, Economic History of Virginia, Vol. II, p. 200.

[9] Peter Force, Tracts and Other Papers, Vol. II, New Description of Virginia, p. 3.

[10] Peter Force, Tracts and Other Papers, Vol. II, New Description of Virginia, p. 18.

[11] Peter Force, Tracts and Other Papers, Vol. II, New Description of Virginia, p. 15.

[12] P. A. Bruce, Economic History of Virginia, Vol. II, p. 201.

[13] Peter Force, Tracts and Other Papers, Vol. III, Leah and Rachel, p. 13.

[14] British Public Record Office, CO5-1316, Statement of Mr. Perry and Captain Hyde, Correspondence of the Board of Trade.

[15] Peter Force, Tracts and Other Papers, Vol. III, Virginia Richly Valued, p. 10.

[16] Peter Force, Tracts and Other Papers, Vol. II, New Albion, p. 32.

[17] Peter Force, Tracts and Other Papers, Vol. III, Leah and Rachel, p. 18.

[18] Peter Force, Tracts and Other Papers, Vol. II, New Description of Virginia, p. 7.

[19] Abstracts of Proceedings of the Virginia Company of London, Vol. II, p. 171.

[20] P. A. Bruce, Economic History of Virginia, Vol. II, p. 153.

[21] P. A. Bruce, Economic History of Virginia, Vol. II, pp. 160-161.

[22] Virginia Magazine of History and Biography, Vol. V, p. 285.

[23] Surry County Wills, Deeds, Etc. 1684-1686, p. 7, Virginia State Library.

[24] Surry County Wills, Deeds, Etc. 1684-1686, pp. 34-35, Virginia State Library.

[25] Surry County Wills, Deeds, Etc. 1684-1686, pp. 86-87, Virginia State Library.

[26] Surry County Wills, Deeds, Etc. 1671-1684, Virginia State Library.

[27] John Splitimber paid for himself alone in the tithable lists of 1675.

[28] York County Records, 1694-1702, Virginia State Library.

[29] Peter Force, Tracts and Other Papers, Vol. II, New Description of Virginia, p. 15.

[30] Peter Force, Tracts and Other Papers, Vol. II, New Description of Virginia, p. 14.

[31] British Public Record Office, CO5-1371, p. 241.

[32] "I would have all men consider how meanly we are provided of men of learning, ability and courage, nay indeed of honesty, to stand up in the people's behalf and oppose the oppressing party," said Nathaniel Bacon in 1676. British Public Record Office, CO5-1371, p. 246.

[33] The most notable case of betrayal is that of Isaac Allerton, who sold himself to the Governor for the promise of a seat in the Council of State. British Public Record Office, CO5-1356, pp. 125-126, Colonial Entry Book.

[34] British Public Record Office, CO1-4.

[35] P. A. Bruce, Economic History of Virginia, Vol. I, pp. 287-288.

[36] Virginia Magazine of History and Biography, Vol. X, p. 271.

[37] British Public Record Office, CO1-8, p. 48.

[38] British Public Record Office, CO1-8.

[39] Hening, Statutes at Large, Vol. I, pp. 360-361.

[40] Hening, Statutes at Large, Vol. I, p. 361.

[41] Hening, Statutes at Large, Vol. I, p. 355.

[42] Hening, Statutes at Large, Vol. I, p. 363.

[43] Sixth Report of Royal Commission on Historical Manuscripts, Part I, Instructions to Sir George Ayscue, Sept. 26, 1651.

[44] The commissioners were Capt. Robert Dennis, Richard Ben-

nett, Thomas Stegge and Captain William Claiborne, all of whom with the exception of Dennis were Virginians.

[45] Hening, Statutes at Large, Vol. I, pp. 371, 373.

[46] Southern Literary Messanger, Jan. 1845; Charles Campbell, History of Virginia, p. 74.

[47] Southern Literary Messanger, Jan. 1845.

[48] British Public Record Office, CO5-1371, p. 387, Colonial Entry Book.

NOTES TO CHAPTER VII

[1] British Public Record Office, CO5-1356, p. 104, Colonial Entry Book.

[2] G. L. Beer, The Old Colonial System, Vol. I, p. 40.

[3] British Public Record Office, CO5-1305, Document 23, Correspondence of the Board of Trade.

[4] British Public Record Office, CO5-1345, Document 16, Correspondence of the Secretary of State.

[5] G. L. Beer, The Old Colonial System, Vol. I, p. 42.

[6] Calendar of State Papers, Colonial Series, 1702.

[7] British Public Record Office, CO5-1355, pp. 381-385, Colonial Entry Book.

[8] G. L. Beer, The Old Colonial System, Vol. I, p. 168.

[9] British Public Record Office, CO5-1315, Document 16, Correspondence of the Board of Trade.

[10] British Public Record Office, CO5-1315, Document 91.

[11] British Public Record Office, CO5-1345, Document 16, John Linton to the Board of Trade, Correspondence of the Secretary of State.

[12] British Public Record Office, CO5-1315, Report of John Linton on the Tobacco Trade, Correspondence of the Board of Trade.

[13] British Public Record Office, CO5-1345, Document 16, Correspondence of the Secretary of State.

[14] British Public Record Office, CO5-1315, Document 26, Correspondence of the Board of Trade.

[15] British Public Record Office, CO5-1315, Document 26, Correspondence of the Board of Trade.

[16] British Public Record Office, CO5-1316, Correspondence of the Board of Trade.

[17] British Public Record Office, CO5-1340, Document 91, Col. Quary's Memorial.

[18] R. L. Beer, The Old Colonial System, Vol. I, p. 42.

[19] British Public Record Office, CO5-1316, Correspondence of the Board of Trade; CO5-1360, p. 233, Governor Nicholson to the Lords of Trade.

[20] British Public Record Office, CO5-1315, Document 91, Col. Quary's Memorial.

[21] British Public Record Office, CO5-1315, Correspondence of the Board of Trade, Letter of Col. Quary Sept. I, 1706.

[22] Princeton Transcripts, Virginia Land Patents, Princeton University Library.

[23] Britain Public Record Office, CO5-1359, pp. 107-108, Colonial Entry Book. In 1699 Gov. Nicholson stated that Orinoco was bringing 20 shillings the hundredweight and Sweetscented 25 shillings and up, which he considered an unusually good return. British Public Record Office, CO5-1359, p. 322.

[24] P. A. Bruce, Economic History of Virginia, Vol. II, p. 66.

[25] J. C. Hotten, Original Lists of Emigrants to America, pp. 202-265.

[26] P. A. Bruce, Economic History of Virginia, Vol. II, p. 89.

[27] Peter Force, Tracts and Other Papers, Vol. II, New Description of Virginia, p. 3.

[28] British Public Record Office, CO1-26-77, Berkeley to the Board of Trade.

[29] British Public Record Office, CO5-1355, p. 345, Lord Culpeper's account of his compliance with the King's instructions, Dec. 1681.

[30] P. A. Bruce, Economic History of Virginia, Vol. II, p. 75.

[31] P. A. Bruce, Economic History of Virginia, Vol. II, p. 75.

[32] British Public Record Office, CO1-26-77, Berkeley to the Board of Trade.

[33] G. L. Beer, The Old Colonial System, Vol. I, p. 323.

[34] G. L. Beer, The Old Colonial System, Vol. I, pp. 324-325.

[35] York County Records, 1664-1672, Virginia State Library.

[36] York County Records, 1694-1702, Virginia State Library.

[37] Henrico Records, 1677-1692, Virginia State Library.

[38] York County Records, 1694-1697, Virginia State Library.

[39] British Public Record Office, CO5-1317, Correspondence of the Board of Trade.

[40] British Public Record Office, CO5-1317, Correspondence of the Board of Trade.

[41] British Public Record Office, CO5-1406, Minutes of the

Council March 21, 1710, CO5-1363, pp. 189-191, Colonial Entry Book.

[42] British Public Record Office, CO5-1322, Governor Gooch to the Lords of Trade, Sept. 14, 1730; Feb. 12, 1731.

[43] British Public Record Office, CO5-1363, pp. 317-324, Colonial Entry Book.

[44] British Public Record Office, CO5-1362, pp. 369-373, Colonial Entry Book.

[45] P. A. Bruce, Economic History of Virginia, Vol. II, p. 83.

[46] Princeton Transcripts, Virginia Land Patents, Princeton University Library.

[47] P. A. Bruce, Economic History of Virginia, Vol. II, p. 108.

[48] British Public Record Office, CO5-1316, Correspondence of the Board of Trade.

[49] British Public Record Office, CO5-1314, Document 66, Governor Nott to the Board of Trade.

[50] British Public Record Office, CO5-1362, pp. 365-367, Colonial Entry Book.

[51] British Public Record Office, CO5-1362, pp. 365-367, Colonial Entry Book.

[52] During these years the planters were too impoverished to purchase slaves. The decline in the tobacco trade produced a feeling among the people that the colony had been overstocked with blacks.

[53] British Public Record Office, CO5-1322, Correspondence of the Board of Trade, Report of Governor Gooch.

[54] British Public Record Office, CO5-1322, Francis Fane to the Lords of Trade, Dec. 10, 1728.

[55] British Public Record Office, CO5-1356, p. 139, Colonial Entry Book.

NOTES TO CHAPTER VIII

[1] Princeton Transcripts, Virginia Land Patents, Princeton University Library.

[2] Princeton Transcripts, Virginia Land Patents, Princeton University Library.

[3] British Public Record Office, CO5-1362, pp. 365-367, Colonial Entry Book.

[4] Virginia Land Patents, Register of Land Office, Virginia State Capitol.

[5] G. L. Beer, The Old Colonial System, Vol. I, p. 28.

[6] G. L. Beer, The Old Colonial System, Vol. I, pp. 320-321.

[7] Jared Sparks, The Works of Benjamin Franklin, Vol. X, iii.

[8] Maurice Vanlaer, La Fin d'un Peuple, pp. 38-39.

[9] Maurice Vanlaer, La Fin d'un Peuple, pp. 112-117.

[10] British Public Record Office, CO1-39-38.

[11] Calendar of State Papers, Colonial Series, 1696-1697, p. 420.

[12] Calendar of State Papers, Colonial Series, 1696-1697, p. 500.

[13] Calendar of State Papers, Colonial Series, 1696-1697, p. 546.

[14] British Public Record Office, CO5-1359, pp. 20, 21, 22.

[15] British Public Record Office, CO5-1359, pp. 20, 21, 22.

[16] British Public Record Office, CO5-1359, p. 23, Colonial Entry Book.

[17] British Public Record Office, CO5-1359, p. 113, Andros to the Lords of Trade, July 1, 1697.

[18] British Public Record Office, CO5-1359, pp. 266-303, Colonial Entry Book.

[19] British Public Record Office, CO5-1312, p. 409A, Correspondence of the Board of Trade.

[20] British Public Record Office, CO5-1360, p. 441, Colonial Entry Book.

[21] Rent Roll of 1704, p. 46.

[22] British Public Record Office, CO5-1321, Correspondence of the Board of Trade, Gooch to the Lords of Trade, Nov. 6, 1728.

[23] British Public Record Office, CO5-1362, pp. 374-382, Colonial Entry Book.

[24] British Public Record Office, CO5-1364, p. 27, Colonial Entry Book.

[25] J. S. Bassett, Writings of William Byrd, p. 31.

[26] British Public Record Office, CO5-1322, Gooch to the Lords of Trade, Feb. 27, 1731.

[27] British Public Record Office, CO5-1321, Gooch to the Lords of Trade, Aug. 9, 1728.

[28] British Public Record Office, CO5-1315, Document 16, Correspondence of the Board of Trade.

[29] British Public Record Office, CO5-1315, Document 91, Correspondence of the Board of Trade.

[30] British Public Record Office, CO5-1316, Correspondence of the Board of Trade.

[31] British Public Record Office, CO5-1315, Document 16.

[32] British Public Record Office, CO5-1315, Document 91, Correspondence of the Board of Trade.

[33] British Public Record Office, CO5-1315, Correspondence of the Board of Trade.

[34] British Public Record Office, CO5-1316, Account of the tobacco trade by Perry and Hyde, June 2, 1714.

[35] British Public Record Office, CO5-1316, Petition of the Council, Correspondence of the Board of Trade.

[36] British Public Record Office, CO5-1318, Address of King and Queen county inhabitants to Spotswood; address of Westmoreland inhabitants; letter of Spotswood to Lords of Trade, Dec. 22, 1718.

[37] William and Mary Quarterly, Vol. XXI, pp. 106-122.

[38] Virginia Magazine of History and Biography, Vol. XII, pp. 414-416.

[39] Virginia Magazine of History and Biography, Vol. IV, pp. 297-299.

[40] William and Mary Quarterly, Vol. XXVI, pp. 97-106, 196-201, 250-258.

[41] Chastellux, Travels in North America, p. 291.

[42] Philip Fithian, Journal and Letters, p. 243.

[43] Smyth, A Tour of the United States, Vol. I, p. 58.

[44] William and Mary Quarterly, Vol. XXI, pp. 106-122.

[45] William and Mary Quarterly, Vol. XXVI, pp. 97-106, 196-201, 250-258.

[46] Virginia Magazine of History and Biography, Vol. IV, pp. 297-299.

[47] Virginia Magazine of History and Biography, Vol. XII, p. 415.

[48] Lower Norfolk County Antiquary, Vol. IV, p. 144.

[49] W. A. Crozier, Virginia County Records, Vol. I, pp. 88-110.

[50] Thomas Jefferson, Notes on Virginia, Edition of 1801, p. 321.

[51] Chastellux, Travels in North America, p. 292 note.

[52] Smyth, A Tour of the United States, Vol. I, p. 66.

[53] Hugh Jones, History of Virginia, p. 36.

[54] Rowland, Life of George Mason, Vol. I, pp. 101, 102; Philip Fithian, Journal and Letters, pp. 67, 104, 130, 130, 138, 217, 259; P. A. Bruce, Economic History of Virginia, Vol. II, pp. 411, 418.

[55] British Public Record Office, CO5-1314, Document 63IV.

[56] Virginia Magazine of History and Biography, Vol. XII, p. 415.

[57] Virginia Magazine of History and Biography, Vol. IV, pp. 292-299.

[58] William and Mary Quarterly, Vol. XXVI, pp. 97-106, 196-201, 250-258.

[59] Smyth, A Tour of the United States, p. 67.

[60] Anbury, Travels Through America, Vol. II, p. 330.

[61] Virginia Magazine of History and Biography, Vol. XII, p. 415.

APPENDIX

RENT ROLL OF VIRGINIA

1704-1705

A True and Perfect Rent Roll of all the Lands held of her Maj^{tie} in Henrico County, Aprill 1705

A

Andrews Thomas	396
Ascoutch Mary	633
Archer Jno	335
Adkins Jno	125
Archer Geo	1738
Aldy John	162
Akins James Senr	200
Asbrook Peter Senr	200
Akins James Junr	218
Allin Widd^{o}	99
	4106

B

Byrd Esqr	19500
Bolling Robt	500
Bolling John	831
Bevill John	495
Branch X^{to}	646
Blackman Wm	175
Bridgwater Sam	280
Bowman John Junr	300
Bowman Edwd	300
Branch Benj	550
Brown Martha	893
Bullington Benj	100
Bowman Lew	65
Bullington	144
Bevell Essex	200
Baugh John	448
Baugh James	458
Burton Isaac	100
Bottom John	100
Bayley Abr	542
Brooks Jane belonging to Wm Walker New Kent	550
Braseal Henry	200
Brazeal Henry Junr	300
Burton Robt	1350
Burgony John	100
Branch James	555
Burrows Wm. Wm. Blackwell New Kent	63
Branch Thomas	540
Bailey Thomas	251
Branch Matthew	947
Burton Wm	294
Bullington Robt	100
Broadnax Jno Jr	725
Beverley Robt	988
	33590

C

Cheatham Tho	300
Cox Batt	100
Cox John	150
Cox George	200
Chamberlaine Maj. Tho	1000
Childers Abr. Senr	368
Cannon John	108
Cox Wm	300
Childers Ab^{r} Junr	100
Clark Wm	333
Clark John	300
Cox Rich^{d}	300
Cardwell Tho	350
Crozdall Roger	200
Cock Wm	1535
Cock Richd Senr	2180
Childers Philip Senr	50
Childers Philip	300
Childers Tho	300
Carter Theod	75
Cock Capt Thomas	2976½
Couzins Charles	362
Clerk Alonson	604

Cock James	1506
Curd Edw[d]	600
Cock Rich[d]	476
Cock Jno	98
	15171½

D

Dixon Nicholas	150
Dodson Wm	100
Douglas Charles	63
	313

E

Edw[d] Tho	676
Entroughty Derby	200
Ealam Rob[t]	400
Ellis John	217
East Tho Sen	475
East Tho	554
East Edw[d]	150
Epes Capt Fra[s]	2145
Evans Charles	225
Ealam Martin	130
Epes Isham, Epes Fra. Jun[t] each 444½ acres	889
	6061

F

Field Peter Major	2185
Farrar Capt Wm	700
Farrar Tho	1444
Farrar Jno	600
Fowler Godfrey	250
Ferguson Robert	230
Ferris Wm	50
Franklin James Sen	250
Franklin James Jun	786
Ferris Rich[d] Sen	550
Farmer Henry	100
Forrest James	138
Forrest John	150
Fetherstone Henry	700
Farloe John Sen	100
Farloe John Jun	551
Faile John	240
	9024

G

Gilley Grewin Arrian	2528
Gee Henry	435
Good John Sen	600
Garthwaite Sam[l]	50
Garthwaite Ephriam	163
Granger John	472
Gill John	235
Good Sam[l]	588
Gower James Grigs Land	500
	5571

H

Hill James	795
Holmes Rich	100
Harris Thomas	357
Harris Tim[o]	250
Hill Rosam[d]	1633
Hobby Lawrence	500
Hatcher John	215
Haskins Edward	225
Hatcher Edward Sen	150
Hunt Geo	200
Hughs Edward	100
Hancock Samuel	100
Holmes Thomas	50
Hambleton James	100
Hutchins Nich[o]	240
Hatcher Benj Sen	250
Hatcher Wm Jun	50
Hobson Wm	150
Hatcher Wm Sen	298
Hatcher Henry	650
Hancock Robert	860
Harris Mary	94
Hall Edward	184
Herbert Mrs	1360
Hudson Robert	281
	9242

J

Jones Hugh	934
Jefferson Thomas	492
Jones Philip	1153
Jorden Henry	100
Jamson John	225
Jackson Ralph	250
	3154

K

Kennon Elizabeth	1900
Knibb Samuel	209
Knibb Solomon	833
Kendall Richard	400
	3342

L

Liptroll Edward	150
Lewis Wm	350
Lester Darens	100
Ladd Wm	70
Ligon Elizabeth Widdow / Ligon Mary Widdow	1341
Laforce Reu	100
Lochett James	50
Lownd Henry	516
Lockitt Benj	104
Ligon Richard	1028
Ligon Hugh	150
	3959

M

Mann Robert	100
Matthews Edward	330
Moseby Edward	150
Moseby Arthur	450
	1030

N

Nunnally Richard	70

O

Osbourn Thomas	288
Owen Thomas	68
	356

P

Perkinson John	622
Perrin Ann	500
Pleasants John	9669
Parker Wm	100
Parker Nich Sen	500
Pledge Jno	100
Powell Robert	150
Peice John	130
Pleasants Jos	1709
Porter Wm	305
Peirce Wm	175
Peirce Francis	312
Paine Thomas	300
Portlock Elizabeth	1000
Pero Henry	350
Pattram Ira	778
Pride Wm Sen	1280
Pollard Thomas Sen	130
Perkinson Seth	50
Pinkitt Wm	192
Pinkitt Thomas	300
Pattison Joseph	500
Porter John	100
Pollard Thomas Jun	235
Pollard Henry	235
Pinkitt John	215
	19937

R

Robertson Geo	1445
Ragsdaile Godfrey	450
Rawlett Peter	164
Russell Charles	200
Rowlett Wm	200
Rowen Francis	148
Robertson John	415
Rouch Rachell	300
Robertson Thomas	200
Russell John	93
Royall Joseph	783
Redford John	775
Randolph Col Wm including 1185 acres swamp	9465
	14648

S

Steward Jno Jun	902
Scott Walter	550
Soane Capt Wm	3841
Stanley Edward	300
Snuggs Charles	400
Sewell Wm	59
Smith Humphrey	40
Sharp Robert	500
Stovoll Barth°	100
Skerin Widdow	75
Steward Daniell	270
Smith Obadiah	200
Stowers Widdow	200
Sarrazin Stephen	120
	7557

T

Tancocks Orphans	1230
Trent Henry	224
Turpin Thomas	491
Turpin Philip	444
Turpin Thomas	100

Turner Henry	200
Taylor Thomas	475
Tanner Edward	217
Traylor Edward	100
Totty Thomas	260
Traylor Wm	730
	4471

V

Veden Henry	100

W

Woodson John	4060
Williams Robert	300
Woodson Robert Jun	1157
Ward Richard	300
Watson John Sen	1603
Walthall Wm	500
Walthall Henry	832
Whitby Wm	215
Watkins Henry Sen	100
Webb John	100
Watkins Thomas	200
Woodson Rich	180
Woodson Widdow	650
Williamson Thomas	1077
Webb Giles	7260
Wood Thomas	50
Watkins Wm	120
Watkins Jos	120
Watkins Edward	120
Ward Seth	700
Wood Moses	100
Wilkinson Jos	75½
Wilkinson John	130
Worsham John	1104
Womack Abr	560
Willson Jno Sen	1686
Willson Jno Jun	100
Walthall Richard	500
Wortham Geo	400
Wortham Charles	90
Womack Wm	100
	24489½

W	24489½
V	100
T	4471
S	7557
R	14648
P	19937
O	396
N	70
M	1030
L	3959
K	3342
J	3154
H	9242
G	5571
F	9024
E	6061
D	313
C	15171½
B	33590
A	4106
	165814

Out of which must be deducted these several quantities of land following Viz:

Tancocks Orphans Land	1230
Allens Orphans Land	99
	1329

An account of Land that hath been concealed

John Steward Jun	2
Thomas Jefferson	15
Thomas Turpin	10
Henry Gee	10
Stephen Sarrzen	10
Mr. Lownd	1
James Atkin Sen	32
Matthew Branch	10
James Franklin	360
James Hill	50
Rosemond Hill	33
John Bullington	44
Benjamin Lockett	4
John Russell	23
Charles Douglas	13
Col Randolph Carless Land	1049
	1669

The Quit Rent being 162719 acres.

A Rent Roll of all the Lands held in the County of Prince George for the Year 1704

A

Thomas Anderson	450
Wm Aldridge	160
Mr. Charles Anderson	505
Richard Adkinson	200
Thomas Adams	250
Matthem Anderson	349
Henry Ally	390
Wm Anderson	235
Jno Anderson	228
Henry Anderson	250
Robert Abernathy	100
Jno Avery	100
	3217

B

Richard Bland	1000
Robert Birchett	375
Arthur Biggins	200
James Benford	461
Jno Barloe	50
Charles Bartholomew	600
Philip Burlowe	350
Nicholas Brewer	100
Jno Bishop Sen	100
Jno Bishop Jun	100
Isaac Baites	360
Thomas Busby Capt	300
Thomas Busby	200
Wm Batt	750
Coll Byrd Esq	100
Edward Birchett	886
Coll Bolling	3402
Edmund Browder	100
Matus Brittler	510
Jno Butler	1385
Andrew Beck	300
Henry Batt	790
Wm Butler	283
Thomas Blitchodin	284
	12986

C

Thomas Curiton	150
Henry Chammins	300
Capt Clements	1920
Wm. Claunton	100
Robert Catte	100
Bartho Crowder	75
Thomas Clay	70
Jno Coleman	200
George Crook	489
Francis Coleman	150
Jno Clay	350
Wm Coleman Jun	100
George Croohet	30
James Cocke	750
Robert Carlill	100
Jno Clerk	83
Richarl Claunton	100
Stephen Cock for Jones Orphans	2405
	7622

D

Thomas Daniell	150
Roger Drayton	270
Joseph Daniell	50
Jno Doby	500
George Dowing	100
Wm Davis	100
Jno Duglas	300
Richard Darding	500
Christopher Davis	50
Thomas Dunkin	136
	2156

E

Robert Ellis	50
Jno Epes Sen	530
Wm Epes Sen	750
Jno Epes	300
Wm Epes	633½
Edward Epes	500
Littlebury Epes	833½
Benj Evans	700
Thomas Edwards	250
Dan Epes	200
Jno Evans	800
Jno. Ellis Jun	400
John Ellis Sen	400
Mary Evans	400
Peter Evans	270
Capt Francis Epes	226
	7243

F

Jno Freeman	300
Wm Frost	50
Jno Fountaine	350
Robert Fellows	418
Elizabeth Flood	100
Benj Foster	923
Jno Field	100
	2241

G

Jno Green	125
Richard Gord	100
David Goodgamd	479
James Greithian	363
Major Goodrich	900
Thomas Goodwin	150
Hubert Gibson	250
Richard Griffith	335
James Griffin	100
Charles Gee	484
Charles Gillam	200
Hugh Goelightly	500
Lewis Green	149
Wm Grigg	200
John Gillam	1000
John Goelightly	100
	5435

H

Coll Hill	1000
Daniell Hickdon	280
Robert Harthorn	243
Jno Hamlin	1484½
Coll Harrison Esq	150
Ralph Hill	175
Wm Harrison	1930
Wm Heath	320
Edward Holloway	100
Robert Hobbs	100
Jno Hobbs Sen	250
Edward Holloway Sen	620
Jno Hobbs	100
James Harrison	200
Gilbert Haye	200
Richard Hudson	75
Gabriell Harrison	150
Robert Hix	1000
Joseph Holycross	84
Charles Howell	125
Sam Harwell	125
Isaac Hall	450
Jno Howell	183
Thomas Howell	25
Mrs. Herbert	3925
Jno Hixs	216
Richard Hamlin	240
Thomas Harnison	1077
Elizabeth Hamlin	250
Wm Hulme	100
Jeffrey Hawkes	125
Adam Heath	300
Jno Hill	160
Jno Hardiman	872
Justance Hall	614
	17366

J

Wm Jones Jun	230
Wm Jones Sen	600
Henry Jones	200
Robert Jones	241
Edmund Irby	800
Nich. Jarrett	700
James Jackson	80
Adam Ivie	200
Thomas Jackson	60
James Jones Sen	1100
Henry Ivye	450
Peter Jones	621
Ricard Jones	600
Ralph Jacskon	110
Joshua Irby	200
John Jones	350
	6542

K

Richard Kirkland	300
John King	50
Henry King	650
Arthur Kavanah	60
Ensobius King	100
	1160

L

John Livesley	300
Samuel Lewey	100
Jno Lumbady	400
Jno Leeneir	100
Mrs Low	70
Sam Lewey for Netherland Orphans	498

Thomas Lewis Sen	200
Hugh Liegh	762
Francis Leadbeatter	100
Jno Leadbeatter	400
Wm Low	1584
	3114

M

Wm Madox	190
Robert Munford	339
James Mingo Sen	500
Matt Marks	1500
Samuell Moody	328
Francis Mallory	100
Daniell Mallone	100
Jno Mayes	365
Richard More	472
Henry Mitchell Sen	100
Jno Mitchell	170
Wm Mayes	763
Edward Murrell	100
Thomas Mitchell Jun	100
Peter Mitchell	305
Henry Mitchell Jun	200
Francis Maberry	347
James Matthews	100
Jno Martin	200
	6839

N

Richard Newman	120
Walter Nannaley	299
	419

O

Nicholas Overburry	809
Jno Owen	25
	834

P

George Pasmore	330
Francis Poythwes Sen	1283
Joseph Pattison	200
George Pail	246
Nathaniel Phillips	150
Jno Price	50
Wm Peoples	150
Elizabeth Peoples	235
Joseph Perry	275
Richard Pigeon	524
Thomas Potts	200
Joseph Pritchett	50
Jno Petterson	373
George Pace	1000
Ephram Parkam	300
Thomas Poythres	616
Dand Peoples	60
Grace Perry	100
Jno Poythres Jun	916
Jno Petterson	420
Mr Micajah Perry	600
	9203

R

Jno Roberts	316
Nath. Robinson	100
Roger Reace Jun	100
Henry Read	75
Roger Reace Sen	100
Wm Reanes	250
Frances Raye	300
Jno Reeks	50
Wm Rachell	100
Timothy Reading Sen	460
Jno Riners	200
Edward Richardson	300
Coll Randolph	226
	2677

S

Matthew Smart	100
Wm Standback	150
Thomas Symmons	566
James Salmen	477
Wm Savage	150
Wm Sandborne	40
Jno Scott	300
Martin Shieffield	150
James Smith	67
John Stroud	60
Richard Seeking	100
Wm Sexton	50
James Leveaker	710
Chichester Sturdivant	214
Daniell Sturdivant	850
Richard Smith	550
Jno Spaine	118
Matthew Sturdivant	150
Capt Stith	470½
	8272½

T

Major Henry Tooker for the Merchants in London ...	4600
George Tilliman	446
Jno Tilliman	530
Wm Tomlinson	400
Adam Tapley	977
Capt Jno Taylor	1700
Mich. Taburd	150
Maj[r] Tooker	181
Robert Tooker	400
Robert Tester	170
Joseph Tooker	200
Wm Tempel	100
Jno Thornhill	350
Jno Taylor	100
Nath. Tatham Jun	200
Samuel Tatham Sen	100
Samuel Tatham Jun	195
Henry Talley	639
Richard Turberfield	140
Francis Tucker	100
Nath. Tatham Sen	501
Jno Thrower	250
Thomas Thrower	150
James Taylor	306
Sanders Tapley	300
Thomas Tapley	300
James Thweat Sen	715
James Thweat Jun	100
Elizabeth Tucker	212
Thomas Taylor	400
Edward Thrower	150
	14462

V

Jno Vaughan	169
Samuel Vaugham	169
Nath. Vrooin	150
Daniell Vaughan	169
James Vaughan	169
Richard Vaughan	309
Wm Vaughan	309
Thomas Vinson	550
Nicholas Vaughan	169
	2163

W

John Woodlife Sen	644
Wm Wallis	200
Jno Wickett	250
Capt. James Wynn	860
Jno Woodlife Jun	750
Jno Winningham Jun	200
Richard Wallpoole	625
Jno Womack	550
Capt Thomas Wynn	400
Jno Wall	233
Thomas Winningham	100
Elizabeth Woodlife	844
Richard Worthern	1600
Richard Winkles	450
Capt Nicholas Wyatt	700
Antho Wyatt	250
Valentine Wiliamson	250
Hurldy Wick	600
Wm Wilkins	900
Francis Wilkins	150
Robert Winkfield	107
Jarvis Winkfield	100
Henry Wall	275
Jno Wilkins	150
James Williams	1436
George Williams	216
Jno White	150
Edward Winningham	100
Samuel Woodward	600
	13684

Y

Dannell Young	283
John Young	200
	583

A	3217
B	12986
C	7622
D	2156
E	7243
F	2241
G	5435
H	17366½
J	6542
K	1160
L	5114
M	6839
N	419
O	834
P	9203
R	2677
S	8272

T 14462
V 2163
W 13684
Y 583

127218½

Deduct the new discovered Land 10000

Accounted for 117218½

Orphans Land which is refulld paying Quit Rents for viz:

Mr. John Bannister Orphans per Stephen Cock 1970

Capt Henry Batesorph and their Mother Mrs Mary Bates 1200

Capt Henry Randolph Orphans per Capt Giles Webb 129

Morris Halliham Orphans ped Robert Rivers 200

Crockson Land formerly & who it belongs to now I cannot find 750

4245

117218½ acres at 24 lb tob° per 100 is ....28132 lb tobacco

at 5s per lb is......	70	6	6
Sallary 10 per cent....	7	0	10½
	63	5	7½

per William Epes Sheriff

Rent Roll of all the Lands held of her Maj^tie In Surry County Anno Domini 1704

A

Allin Arthur Major 6780
Andrews Bartho 375
Avery Jno 150
Atkins Thomas 80
Averett Jno 120
Atkinson Richard 100
Andrews Thomas 190
Andrews Robert 130
Andrews David 225

8150

B

Baker Henry Coll 850
Bruton James 500
Bennett James 200
Bland Sarah 1455
Browne Jno 600
Benbridge George 200
Bighton Richard 590
John Bell 180
Berham Robert 650
Blake Wm 200
Browne Edward 200
Bincham Jno 100
Bennett Richard 200
Baker Sarah 50
Briggs Sarah 300
Baxter Joell 100
Briggs Samuel 300
Blico Christopher 50
Brigs Charles 331
Brigs Henry 100
Bentley 180
Blackbun Wm 150
Blunt Thomas 1355
Bookey, Edward 180
Browne Wm Coll 2510
Browne Wm Capt 398
Bineham James 157
Bullock Mary 100
Barker Jno 1160
Bagley Peter 100
Barker Jery 420
Bunell Hezichiah 150
Bougher Phill 100
Baile Jno 250
Bagley Edward 350

14716

C

Chapman Benjamin 500
Cockin Wm 100
Cocker Jno 900
Crafort Robert 1000
Crafort Carter 100
Chambers Wm 50
Clark Jno 100

Cook Elizabeth	200
Carriell Thomas	100
Clements Jno	387
Clarke Jno	100
Cook Elizabeth	200
Carriell Thomas	100
Clements Jno	387
Clark Robert	400
Checett James	50
Cotten Walter	257
Cotten Thomas	257
Collier Jno	350
Collier Joseph	40
Cock Wm	630
Cock Walter	875
Cooper James	100
Cleaments Francis	600
Collier Thomas	550
Candenscaine Obedience	200
	7746

D

Dicks James	400
Davis Arthur	460
Drew Thomas	800
Drew Edward	600
Delk Roger	790
David Arthur	50
Dean Richard	100
Davis Nath.	157
	3357

E

Edward Wm Mr.	2755
Evans Antho	100
Edward John	470
Ellitt Wm	250
Edmund Howell	300
Ellis James	180
Edmund Wm	100
Ellis Edward	30
Ellis James	170
Ezell Geirge	150
Ellis Jere	50
Evans Abrah.	150
	4705

F

Flake Robert	200
Foster Anne	200
Ford George	100
Flood Walter	820
Flood Thomas	150
Ford Elias	200
Flemin Lawrence	360
Foster Christo	500
Foster Wm	100
Ferieby Benj	170
	2800

G

Gray Wm Capt	1750
Gray Wm Jun	1050
Grines Austis	100
Gwalney Wm	400
Gray Jno	200
Gwalney Wm	225
Goodman Wm	200
Gillham Hinche	658
Griffin John	200
Gully Richard	50
Gray Wm	100
Green Edward	200
Green Richard	260
	5393

H

Harrison Benj Coll	2750
Harrison Nath. Capt	2177
Hunt Wm	4042
Holt Elizabeth	1450
Holt John	150
Holt Thomas Capt	538
Holt Wm	630
Harris Wm	150
Hart Henry	725
Humfort Hugh	150
Hancock John	60
Hart Robert	600
Humphrey Evan	70
Hollyman Mary	290
Harde Thomas	900
Hill Robert	200
Holloman Richard	480
Hargrove Bryan	100
Humfort Wm	50
Hill Lyon	300
Holloman Thomas	450
Heath Adam	200
Harrison Daniell	70
Ham Richard	75
Heart Thomas	750

Name	Acres
Hyerd Thomas	50
Hunt Wm	696
Horne Richard	100
Hollingsworth Henry	60
Howell Wm	50
	18413

J

Name	Acres
Jackman Jos John Mr.	2980
Jones James	1000
Jarrell Thomas	115
Jarrett Charles	615
Judkins Samuell	100
Judkins Wm	100
Jurdan George	620
Jarrett Fardo	630
Johnson Wm	360
Johnson John	350
Jurdan Richard	350
	7220

K

Name	Acres
Kigan Mary	200
Killingworth Wm	60
Knott Wm	300
	560

L

Name	Acres
Ludwell Philip Coll	1100
Lancaster Robert	100
Lacey Mary	100
Lang Mary	77
Lane Thomas	200
Lane Thomas Jun	200
Laughter Jno	300
Laneere George	300
Lasley Patrick	520
Lucas Wm	315
	3212

M

Name	Acres
Matthew Edmund	50
Merriell George	250
Moorland Edward	225
Mason Elizabeth	300
Mallory Francis	147
Merrett Matt.	60
Middleton Thomas	100
Moss Wm	100
Moreing John	695
Mierick Owen	250
	2177

N

Name	Acres
Newton Wm	225
Newton Robert	250
Newitt Wm	330
Norwood Richard	80
Nicholl George	150
Nichols Robert	230
Noeway Barefoot	150
Norwood George	330
	1745

P

Name	Acres
Park Mary	100
Pittman Thomas Jun	100
Phillips, John	270
Price John	340
Pettoway Elizabeth	650
Pulystone Jno	1400
Parker Richard	269
Phelps Humphrey	100
Pully Wm	300
Procter Joshua	660
Persons John	830
Phillips Wm	300
Pettfort Jno	200
Pettfort Wm	50
	5569

R

Name	Acres
Randolph Wm Coll	1655
Ruffice Elizabeth	3001
Reynolds Robert	150
Richardson Joseph	300
Reynolds Elizabeth	150
Reagon Frances	200
Roads Wm	150
Rolling George	106
Road Wm	450
Rose Richard	100
Raehell George	70
Rowling Jno	476
Rohings Wm	596
Roger Wm	450
	7854

S

Scat Joseph	295
Sims George	200
Secoms Nicholas	800
Savage Charles	358
Stringfellow Richard	75
Suger Jno	250
Sewurds Anne	300
Sharp Thomas	70
Sewins Thomas	400
Steward John	200
Smith Richard	200
Savage Mary	263
Smith Thomas	750
Swann Wm	1800
Shrowsbury Joseph	260
Shrowsbury Francis	820
Savage Henry	200
Short Wm	400
Scarbro Edw	150
Scagin Jno	100
Simmons Jno	1300
Shrowsbury Thomas	566
Stockly Richard	100
Smith Thomas	380
	10237

T

Thompson Samuell	3104
Tooker Henry Major	700
Taylor Ethelred	538
Thorp Joseph	250
Tyous Thomas	400
Taylor Richard	77
	5069

V

Vincent Mary	187

W

Wright Thomas	100
Williams Charles	100
Wall Joseph	150
Williams Wm	300
Ward Thomas	100
Wall Joseph Jun	150
Warren Allen	300
Warren Thomas	1040
Watkins Richard	1345
Williams Roger	150
Webb Robert	340
Wattkins John	1160
Warren Robert	150
Welch Henry	100
Warrick John	80
Wilkinson Matthew	200
Wiggins Thomas	300
Waple Jno	300
Witherington Nicholas	100
Will Roger	78
White Charles	136
	6679

Y

Young John	300

A	8150
B	14716
C	7746
D	3357
E	4705
F	2800
G	5393
H	18413
J	7220
K	560
L	3212
M	2177
N	1745
P	5569
R	7854
S	10237
T	5069
V	187
W	6679
Y	300
	116089
New Land allowed per order	3841
	112248

Aprill 19th 1705

Errors excepted per
Jos Jno. Jackman Sheriff.

Persons denying payment for Lands held in this County (viz) Capt Tho Holt as belonging to Mr. Tho

Benules Orphans	950
Mrs. Mary White	200
	1150

Lands held by persons living out of the Country

Capt Jno Taylor	850
Mrs. Sarah Low	500
Mr. Jno Hamlin	100
Capt Thomas Harrison	530
	1150
	3130

Bartho Clement one tract of Land he living in England the quantity unknowne

Jno Davis one Tract Living in Isle of Wight

Geo & River Jorden one Tract & denys to pay Qt Rents for it & no persons living thereon, there is one Bray Living in Warwick has a small tract Land

A List of her Maj[tys] Q[t] Rents For the Isle Wighte County in the Year 1704

Jno Atkins	200
James Atkinson	400
Wm Exam	1440
Wm Brown	150
Francis Exam	200
Richard Bennett	70
James Briggs	100
Ph. Bratley	200
Abr. Drawler	200
Jno Branch	45
Francis Branch	50
Edward Brantley	175
John Brantley	364
Edward Boykin	1100
George Barloe	80
Jno Geoge	200
Thomas Carter	700
Reubin Cooke	250
Jno Clarke	850
Thomas Cook	300
Wm Clark	600
Edward Champion	600
Jno Dowles	150
Peter Deberry	100
Thomas Davis	100
Jno Davis	250
Peter Hayes	600
Christo. Hollyman	400
Richard Hardy	700
Thomas Holyman	150
Jno Harris	365
Silvester Hill	925
Roger Hodge	300
Arthur Jones	900
Edward Jones	250
Richard Jones	250
Jno Johnson	890
Roger Ingram	300
Matt. Jorden	1950
Thomas Newman	360
George Readich	790
Francis Lee	100
Ph. Pardoe	100
Jno Parsons	155
George Moore	400
Jno Mangann	100
Robert Mongo	400
Henry Martin	200
Jno Murray	650
Francis Rayner	80
Jno Richardson	150
James Sampson	1200
Jno Stevenson	150
Thomas Sherrer	200
Jno Sherrer	200
Wm Thomas	250
Thomas Tooke	1228
Thomas Throp	350
Baleaby Terrell	100
Peter Vasser	230
Jno Williams	600
George Williamson	2735
Fra. Williamson	2035
Thomas Wood	50
James Lupe	45
Elizabeth Reynolds	100
Jno Sojourner	240
Robert Hoge	60
Andrew Woodley	770
Arthur Allen	1800
Henry Baker	750
Rubin Prochter	250
Thomas Howell	100
Nath Whitby	170
Jane Atkins	600
Jno Mongo	100

Natt Ridley	200
Jno Bell	200
Wm West	250
Charles Goodrich	80
Jno Britt	350
Jno Barnes	200
Henry Goldham	1000
Jno Waltham	450
Charles Edwards	400
Wm Exam	150
Major Lewis Burwell	7000
Henry Applewaite	1500
Thomas Pitt	300
Jno Pitt	3400
Mary Benn	675
Robert Clark	450
Antho Holliday	860
Wm Westrah	450
Elizabeth Gardner	100
Jno Gardner	246
Jno Turner	950
Antho Foulgham	100
Anne Williams	150
Edward Harris	240
Jno Cotton	200
Thomas Joyner	1400
Jno Lawrence	400
Thomas Mandue	200
Wm Mayo	300
Jno Garcand	100
James Bryan	1200
Wm Keate	200
Jno Browne	100
Francis Sanders	100
John Rogers	200
Hodges Councie	420
Hardy Councie	900
Jno Councie	760
Thomas Reeves	600
Wm Crumpler	580
Bridgeman Joyner	1100
Elizabeth Swan	600
Thomas Jones	700
Arthur Whitehead	250
Thomas Allen	150
Jerimiah Exam	300
Nicholas Casey	550
Jno Giles	1150
Alexander Camoll	200
Jno Rutter	300
Godfrey Hunt	600
Wm Trygell	100
Benj Jorden	150
Thomas Jorden	207
Jno King	300
Wm Wilkinson	200
Thomas Grace	160
Wm West	50
Jno Penny	300
Robert Richards	100
Thomas Northworthy	600
Fra Parker	210
Widdo Long	104
Trustram Northworthy	1000
George Green	250
Jno Druer	100
Philip Peerce	500
Wm Best	100
Humphrey Marshall	600
Thomas Brewer	200
Wm Smith	2100
Samuel & Wm Bridger	12900
Wm Williams	100
Richard Ratcliffe	380
Joshua Jordan	150
Daniall Sandbourne	180
Nicholas Houghan	780
Mary Marshall	200
Joseph Godwin	250
Joseph Bridger	580
Henry Pitt	700
James Baron	300
Arthur Smith	3607
Robert Broch	400
Wm Godwin	400
Hugh Bracey	1000
Henry Turner	350
Thomas Wootten	963
Richard Reynolds Esq	853
Richard Reynolds	746
Jno Parnell	400
Benj Deall	467
Thdo. Joyner	595
Jno Jordan	100
Henry Wiggs	506
Wm Body	1375
Arthur Purcell	750
Jno Porteus	100
Wm West	690
Simon Everett	1100
Walter Waters	150
John Jordan	150
John Nevill	433
Robert Colman	1500
Wm Green	150
Mary Cobb	150

Robert Edwards	150
Anne Jones	100
Abraham Jones	600
John Jones	200
Richard Lewis	100
Henry Dullard	100
Thomas Williams	100
James Mercer	100
Poole Hall	350
Jno Howell	100
Thomas Lovett	100
George Anderson	150
Daniell Nottiboy	100
Henry Wilkinson	350
Jno Watkins	200
Thomas English	100
Thomas Page	203
Francis Davis	100
Richard Braswell	100
Robert Johnson	2450
Jno Minshea	300
Wm Pryan	200
Wm Dawes	400
Nicholas Tyner	300
Isaac Ricks	700
Robert Scott	300
Jno Roberts	950
Wm Duck	180
Robert Lawrence	400
Jno Denson	200
Robert Smelly	600
Francis Bridle	250
Roger Fearlton	237
Thomas Bullock	100
Wm. Marfry	600
Thomas Powell	100
Widdo Glyn	390
Jno Pope	250
Thomas Gayle	200
Wm Powell	200
Richard Hutchins	300
Henry Boseman	100
Henry Pope	557
John Williams	971
Henry Sanders	700
Jno Selloway	900
Jno Bardin	100
Phill Rayford	650
Phill Pearse	500
Jno Terseley	150
Geo Northworthy	1176
Robert Richards	450
Thomas Bevan	100
Wm Hunter	150
Madison Street	150
Thomas Wheatley	400
Richard Wilkinson	150
James Bragg	500
Jno Portous	300
Thomas Harris	350
Edward Harris	100
Nicholas Askew	80
Ambrose Hadley	100
Widdo Powell	480
Thomas Jones	100
Thomas Underwood	100
Robert King	300
Thomas Giles	880
Lewis Smelly	550
Wm Smelly	280
Godfrey Hunt	600
Edmund Godwin	400
Wm Williams	1000
John Wilson	1200
John Bryan	200
John Askew	100
Samuell Bridger	200
Roger Nevill	200
Coll Godwin	600
Jacob Durden	500
	138533

Wm Bridger.

A Compleat List of the Rent Roll of the Land in Nansemond County In Anno 1704

John Murdaugh	300
Jno Duke	113
Thomas Duke Jun	930
Edward Roberts	250
Paul Pender	240
Thomas Duke	400
James Fowler	440
Robert Baker	50
Isaac Sketto	100
Edward Sketto	200
Antho Gumms	50
Francis Sketto	100
Wm Parker	100
Francis Parker	170

Name	Acres
Thomas Parker	300
Jno Small	100
Moses Hall	95
Edward Beamond	550
Richard Parker	514
Capt James Jessey	550
Wm Sanders	200
Jno Sanders	165
Thomas Mansfield	60
Wm Woodley	350
Andrew Bourne	200
Gilbert Owen	120
Wm Sanders Jun	165
Capt John Speir	500
Capt James Reddick	943
James Griffin	500
Nicholas Stallings	965
John Stallings	250
Richard Stallings	165
Elias Stallings Jun	250
Joseph Baker	740
Wm Jones	500
Robert Roundtree	245
John Roundtree	475
George Spivey	200
James Spivey	600
James Knight	300
Jno Gorden	330
Edward Arnold	80
James Mulleny	500
Thomas Docton	200
Wm Britt	400
Nath Newby	850
Elias Stalling	470
Robert Lassiter	850
Patrick Wood	200
Wm Thompson	133
Jonathan Kitterell	300
Adam Rabey	586
Jno Powell	758
John Reddick	300
Henry Copeland	150
Thomas Davis	250
Jno Smith	100
Thomas Harrald	652
Richard Baker	40
Samuell Smith	230
Wm Hood	200
Thomas Roundtree	350
Henry Hill	175
Jno Larkhum	500
Wm Vann	100
Joseph Cooper	267
John Harris	600
Francis Copeland	513
Elizabeth Price	150
Wm Hill	150
Thomas Spivey	200
Jno Campbell	400
Jno Morley	100
Jos Rogers	15
Jno Cole	814
Thomas Harrald	100
Christopher Gawin Jun	20
Daniell Horton	200
Wm Bruin	300
Peter Eason	400
Anne Pugh	2300
Benj Blanchard	130
Thomas Norfleet	500
John Odum	50
Thomas Gough	150
Hugh Gough	150
Epapap Boyne	100
Henry Baker	375
Christopher Gwin	1010
James Speirs	200
Epaphra Benton	250
Wm Eason	180
Andrew Brown	25
Wm Horne	100
Robert Reddick	200
Henry Hackley	210
Thomas Roberts	30
Abr. Reddick	400
Jno Parker	240
Richard Barefield	900
John Benton	660
Jno Pipkin	100
Jos Brady	250
Christopher Dudley	200
Thomas Norris	100
Thomas Wiggins	100
Patrick Lawley	50
Robert Warren	100
Richard Odium	50
Thomas Davis	340
Thomas Barefield	100
John Eason	150
Jerimiah Arlin	250
Jno Perry	870
Jno Drury	87
Joseph Booth	987
Cresham Cofield	350
Richard Sumner	600
Edward Norfleet	200

Name	Acres
Jno Norfleet	600
Edward Moore	250
Thomas Moore	200
James Lawry	40
James Daughtie	400
John Wallis	150
Richard Sanders Jun	100
Wm Byrd	300
James Howard	700
John Brinkley	430
Robert Horning	80
Wm Speirs	200
Sarah Exum	150
Jno Larrence	175
Nicholas Perry	200
Sampson Merridith	400
Coll Thomas Milner	1484
Joseph Merridith	250
Thomas Kinder	160
Henry King	300
Joseph Hine	150
Wm King	140
Julian King	700
Mich. King	80
Capt Tho Godwin Jun	697
Henry Lawrence	200
Jno King	1000
Richard Hyne	200
Capt Francis Milner	479
Benj Nevill	475
Elizabeth Marler	80
Wm Keene	200
Jno Symmons	678
Hen: Johnson	150
Jno Darden	500
Wm Everett	150
Wm Pope	890
Joseph Worrell	270
Thomas Jemegan Jun	135
Richard Lawerence	200
Jonathan Robinson	400
Robert Yates	150
Thomas Odium	20
John Barefield	300
John Raules	600
Thomas Boyt	400
Thomas Vaughan	200
Jno Parker	300
Richard Green	200
Elizabeth Ballard	300
Samuell Watson	200
Francis Spight	400
Joseph Ballard	200
John Oxley	100
Benj. Rogers	600
Robert Rogers	300
Henry Jerregan	200
Jno Hansell	500
Henry Jenkins	400
Capt William Hunter	800
Jno Moore	200
Richard Moore	250
Edward Homes	300
Fra. Cambridge	100
Wm Ward	200
Jno Rice	140
Wm Battaile	800
Wm Spite	500
Abr. Oadham	20
Jacob Oadam	20
Jno Lee	100
Wm Macklenny	200
Robert Coleman	1400
Jno Bryan	200
Wm Daughtree	100
Jno Copeland	600
Jno Butler	200
James Butler	75
Thomas Roads	75
Wm Collins	1220
Jno Hedgpath	700
Jno Holland	700
Robert Carr	200
Wm Waters	600
Robert Lawrence	400
Wm Bryon	350
Lewis Bryon	400
James Lawrence	100
Wm Gatlin	100
Joseph Gutchins	250
George Lawrence	400
Lewis Daughtree	100
Thomas Rogers	50
Jno Rogers	200
Henry Core	50
Edward Cobb	100
Richard Taylor	300
Robert Brewer	200
Wm Osburne	200
Thomas Biswell	400
Jno Gatlin	200
Richard Folk	100
Thomas Parker	100
Peter Parker	140
Wm Parker	140
Richard Hine Jun	200

Stephen Archer	200
Charles Roades	800
Henry Roades	100
James Collings	300
Henry Holland	400
Wm Kerle	325
Joseph Holland	100
Jno Thomas Jun	100
Jno Thomas	275
Thomas Mason	350
Edward Mason	150
Jno Sanders	150
Mich Brinkley	200
James Moore	400
Henry Blumpton	1500
Jno Symmons	100
Jeremiah Edmunds	70
John Gay	200
Philip Aylsberry	100
James Copeland	390
Jno Brothers	460
Richard Creech	200
Richard Bond	90
Thomas Handcock	30
James Knott	1050
Wm Edwards	150
Robert Elkes	175
Edward Price	140
Jane Belson	100
Wm Staples	210
Robert Mountgomery	150
John Moore	100
Capt Edmund Godwin	800
Thomas Wakefield	150
Godfrey Hunt	360
Henery Wilkinson	250
Nicholas Dixon	200
George Keeley	650
Richard Taylor	300
Anne Coefield	300
Joseph Hollyday	1000
Mr. Jno Braisseur	400
Thomas Best	160
Alexander Campbell	500
Capt Charles Drury	570
Thomas Drury	75
Luke Shea	650
John Babb	500
Abraham Edwards	400
Richard Sanders	500
Antho Wallis	80
Daniell Sullivan	100
Joseph Ellis	290
Nicholas Hunter	190
Richard Webb	200
John Hare	190
Christopher Norfleet	400
Jno Heslop	148
Francis Benton	200
Capt Wm Sumner	275
Elizabeth Syrte	100
Anne Hare	600
Jno Porter	450
Edward Welsh	100
Jno Winbourne	400
Paul Pender	200
Mich Cowling	100
John Cowling	100
Rowland Gwyn	75
Andrew Ross	150
Jno Ballard	400
Benjamin Montgomery	910
Thomas Corbell	200
Jno Yates	400
Jno White	150
George White	50
Jno Bond	150
Wm Hay	100
Henry Bowes	600
Wm Sevill	85
Jno Hambleton	200
Robert Jordan	850
James Howard	25
Ruth Coefield	110
Jno Chilcott	100
Jno Rutter	80
Thomas Rutter	75
Wm. Rutter	75
Capt Barnaby Kerney	460
Thomas Cutchins	150
Robert Lawrence	130
Samuell Cahoone	240
Jno Iles	220
Thomas Sawyer	180
Wm Outland	400
Coll George Northworthy	650
Coll Thomas Godwin	810
Caleb Taylor	200
Thomas Carnell	320
Richard Bradley	250
Jno Corbin	300
Wm Sykes	150
Major Thomas Jorden	700
Richard Lovegrove	150
Thomas Davis	144
Samuell Farmer	160

Henry Bradley	500
Jno Clarke	25
Margarett Jorden	200
Wm Elkes	100
Humphrey Mires	150
James Ward	100
Widdow Hudnell	45
Wm Grandberry	300
Israell Shepherd	200
Benj. Small	100
Anne Crandberry	75
Charles Roberts	50
Richard Sclator	300
Robert Murrow	320
Elizabeth Peters	334
Thomas Jones	200
Elizabeth Butler	200
Coll Samuell Bridger	500
Jno Lawrence	100
Thomas Jarregan	165
Thomas Jarregan Jun	600
Wm Drury	80
Wm Butler	120
Henry Jenkins	860
Edward Bathurst	250
Thomas Houffler	200
Edward Streater	200
Wm Duffield	50
Charles Thomas Jun	50
Jnọ Blessington	150
Ursula Goodwin	100
Thomas Acwell	440
Wm Peale	180
John Lambkin	50
James Murphice	160
Robert Peale	275
John Peters	368
James Peters	340
John Wakefield	50
Richard Wynn	890
James Lockhart	800
John Keeton	2000
	117024
Jno Murrow	200
	117224
Added to make up equll the last year list which may be supposed to be held by persons that have not made both	13850
	131074

Persons living out of the County and other that will not pay or give account. Viz:

Capt Thomas Lovett
Capt Jno Wright
Fra Parker Jun
Tho Martin
Jno Wright
Wm Lapiter
Jno Lapiter
Capt Luke Haffield
Mrs Elizabeth Swann

Errors excepted per me
Henry Jenkins

An Alphabetical List of the Quit Rents of Norfolk County 1704

Ashley Dennis	150
Avis Widdow	50
Adam Wm	100
Alexander John	300
Barington Wm	100
Bartee Robert	150
Bull Robert Sen	1050
Blanch Wm	100
Bond Wm	200
Brown Widdow	270
Bruce Abraham	1010
Brown Wm	100
Bowers Jno	166
Bolton Wm	212
Byron Roger	200
Bayley Walter	290
Bruce Jno	300
Bishop Wm	100
Bull Henry	1500
Bucken Wm	410
Babington Thomas	150
Babington Jno	150
Babington Rich	50
Burges George	200
Burges Robert	535
Butt Richard	1840
Brown Edward	300
Bigg Thomas	100
Balingtine Alexander	300
Balengtine George	510

Bull Thomas	2200
Bramble Henry	100
Blake Arthur	200
Bolton Richard	700
Branton John	330
Bacheldon Joseph	300
Bush Samuell Major	1628
Balingtine Wm	60
Bowles Henry	330
Cartwright Peter	1050
Cooper Wm	150
Cooper Jno	150
Cramore George	100
Carling Walton	50
Carling Joseph	200
Curch Richard	1050
Churey Widdow	600
Cuthrell Going	470
Crekmore Edward	800
Cartwright Widdow	800
Corprew Jno	650
Corprew Thomas	650
Crekmore Jno	750
Caswell Widdow	350
Colley Jno	100
Cottell Thomas	200
Conden Thomas	390
Conner Lewis	2200
Carney Jno	100
Carney Richard	100
Collins Wm	100
Crekmore Edmund	690
Charleton Jno	50
Cutrell Thomas	150
Chapman Richard	50
Churey Thomas	100
Churey Jno	150
Dixon Jno	300
Davis Wm Sen	250
Davis Wm	158
Dresdall Robert	318
Davis Thomas	332
Desnall Wm	100
Davis Edward	300
Dalley Henry	1524
Dalley Wm	156
Davis Thomas	340
Denby Edward	100
Daniell Hugh	100
Etherdge Thomas Cooper	75
Etherdge Thomas B R	50
Etherdge Thomas Sen	34
Etherdge Thomas Jun	33
Etherdge Edward	66
Etherdge Wm	250
Etherdge Wm Jun	80
Etherdge Marmaduke	525
Edmonds John	50
Ellis Wm	200
Etherdge Edward Cooper	200
Estwood Thomas	170
Estwood John	75
Etherdge Edward Sen	33
Edwards John	250
Etherdge Charles	75
Evans Abrigall	100
Furgison Thomas	100
Freeman Jno	190
Foreman Alexander	750
Foster Henry	1000
Ferbey Jno	500
Fulsher Jno	1396
Godfry Waren	350
Godfry John	1470
Godfry Matthew	450
Grefen Jno	200
Garen Daniell	50
Guy John	110
Gwin Wm	350
Gilhgun Ferdinando	182
Gilhgan John	200
Gresnes James	150
Gaines John	50
Guy James	100
Herbert Thomas	150
Hayes Wm	200
Harris John	110
Holyday Jno	440
Hodges Joseph	50
Hoges Thomas	407
Hoges John	520
Hollowell Jno Sen	524
Hollygood Thomas	100
Hollowell Jno	200
Holsted Henry	633
Hollowell Joseph	1280
Holsted John	350
Hues Edward	1304
Hullett Jno	300
Hodges Roger	109
Hodges Thomas	50
Hodges Richard	375
Harvey Richard	265
Handberry	300
Hollowell Elener	1550
Herbert Jno	400

Hargrave Benjamin	250
Hartwell Richard	150
Henland Jno	800
Ivey George	496
Jackson Symon	720
Ives Timothy	400
Ives Timothy Jun	100
Ives John	434
Johnston John	275
Johnston Mercey	275
Joles Thomas	200
Joyce Jno	200
Jolef Jno Jun	300
Jenings Henry	100
Jolef Jno Sen	840
Kaine Richard	50
Langley Wm	1487
Langley Thomas	878
Loveney James	100
Luelling Edward	315
Luelling Richard	200
Lovell Widdow	740
Low Henry	191
Lane Robert	460
Ludgall Matthew	250
Levima John	510
Lenton Wm	150
Mercer Thomas	600
Maning Thomas	97
Maning Nicholas	260
Mones Joseph	73
Matthias Matthew	100
Miller Wm	1090
Miller Jno	200
Miller Widdow	100
Murden Widdow	2000
Miller Thomas	1050
Maund Wm	200
Maning Jno Sen	300
Miller Joseph	882
Mocey Dennis Sen & Jun	160
Mohan James	100
Murfrey Alexander	800
Maning Jno Jun	100
Moseley Widdow	300
Miller Widdow Sen	200
Mason Thomas	125
Masom Lemuell	400
Mason Thomas	653
Mason George	300
Mockey Adam	400
Newton George	1119
Nicholson Jno	160
Nash Thomas	50
Nicholson Henry	320
Nash Richard	100
Nicholson Wm	300
Norcote Thomas	273
Outlaw Edward	208
Owens Wm	650
Odyam Wm	200
Pearce Wm	100
Peters Widdow	698
Portlock	360
Porter Samuell	100
Prescot Moses	1200
Philpot Richard	200
Powell Richard	100
Powell Lemuell	246
Powell Wm	624
Perkins Wm	50
Patison Robert	350
Roberts Jos	100
Robert Samuell	800
Rose Robert	385
Rose Jno	60
Randall Giles	150
Richardson Thomas	379
Spring Robert	98
Spivey Matt	600
Smith John	127
Scoll Thomas	400
Smith Richard	600
Smith John	200
Silvester Richard	1280
John Smith Sen	1200
Sickes Walter Sen	550
Sickes John	200
Sugg George	408
Sugg Wm	200
Sayer Francis	600
Smith Humphrey	100
Standbro Jno	40
Standley Richard	200
Sharples Henry	100
Sugg Joseph	300
Symons Thomas	166
Symon James	200
Sparrow Wm	350
Tuker Wm	100
Thornton Francis	200
Thurston Matthew	100
Theobald James	140
Thellaball Widdow	600
Tuker Richard	100
Tuker Thomas	280

Taylor Jno 100
Taylor Richard 75
Tully Jno 165
Tarte Elezar Sen 300
Taylor Andrew 222
Tuker Jno 400
Tart Alice 300
Tarte Elezar Jun 595
Taylor Wm 265
Trigoney Henry 200
Velle Moriss 335
Walice Thomas 150
Weston Edward 100
Willoughby Thomas Coll .. 3200
Weshart John 150
Woodly Robert 350
Williams John 125
Wilder Mich 200
Watkins Thomas 190
Williamson Jno 750
Whedon Jno Jun 100
Willoughby Thomas Capt .. 660
Whedon Wm 200
West John 500
Watson Robert 80
Wallis Richard 250
Wallis Jno 135
Wallis Wm 450
Whithurst Richard 150
Whithurst Wm 150
Wilkins Wm 200
Williams John 200
Whedbey George 200
Worden James 400
Wilson James Jun 200
Wilson Lemuell 300
Wilson James Coll 2800
Woodward Henry 280
Whedon Jno Jun 320
White Patrick 500
Willis John 470
Weldey Dorothy 25
Ward Jno 320
Wakfield Thomas 40
Wilden Nath 100
Wooding Thomas 170
Wood Edward 100
Watford Joseph 97
Wate John 400
Wright Wm 574
Wright James 216
Wadborn Mich 500
Williams Jane 400
Webb Mary 100
Worminton John 200
Wilden Francis 100
Widdick Henry 343

113684

New discovered Land 1615

112069

An Account of the Land belonging to such persons out of the County and also others out of the County.

Coll Cary ....
Tully Robinson ....
James Daves ....
Robert Berrey 95
Jno Bennett 33
Coll Nasareth 400
Cornelius Tullery 150

James Wilson
Sherriff

Princess Anne County Rent Roll 1704

John Carraway 180
Thomas More 100
Henry Chapman 250
George Poole 1085
James Whithurst 600
Thomas Morris 63
Thomas Joy 600
Thomas Scott 100
George Smith 250
Thomas Hife 200
Richard Smith 200
Thomas Hattersley 90
Thomas Jolley 150
Mich Ventres 450
Capt Blomer Bray 270
James Mecoy 200
Francis Bond 264
Edward Wood 50
Jno Morrah 200
Alexander Morrah 200
Ruth Woodhouse 450
Horatia Woodhouse 525
Joseph White 330
Jon Basnett 250

Owen Wilbe	100	Wm. Moore	414
Mr. Wm. Corneck	1974	Mr. Henry Woodhouse	3000
Jno Oakham	390	Tully Emperor	300
David Scott	600	Jno. Godfrey	170
Jno Keeling	2000	Wm Dyer	700
Adam Keeling	500	Edward Cooper	200
Humphrey Smith	50	Wm Ship	300
Jno Halise	130	Jno Buck	250
Capt Wm Crawford	2650	Peter Mallbourn	280
Richard Williamson	450	Benjamin Roberts	100
Edward Tranter	180	Capt Jno Gibbs	3100
Jno. Sherland	800	Sarah Sanford	1200
Robert Rany	70	Henry Harrison	300
Edward Old	450	James Lemon	1500
Coll Lemuell Mason	650	Wm Wallsworth	100
Mr. Francis Emperor	400	Wm Capps	1050
James Kemp	681	Jacob Taylor	80
Bartho: Williamson	400	Stephen Pace	50
Symon Hancock Jun	200	Adam Hayes	1360
George Batten	150	Wm Chichester	400
Matth: Brinson	250	Robert Dearemore	514
Mr. Edward Mosseley Sen.	1000	Capt. Francis Morse	1300
Wm Martin	200	Patrick Anguish	150
James Joslin	100	Thomas Brock	400
Alexander Lilburn	500	Wm Brock	100
James William	100	Jno Sullivant	200
Mr. Henry Spratt	1736	Francis Sheene	300
Symon Hancock Sen	300	Jno Acksted	400
Thomas Walk	298	Charles Hendley	100
Jno Kemp	340	Duke Hill	70
Randolph Lovett	100	Job Brooks	150
Edward Davis	200	Jno Brooks	100
Jno Sammons	150	Thomas Turton	110
Elizabeth Edwards	50	Peter Crosby	250
Mr. Benj. Burroughs	800	Jno Pisburn	314
Jno Muncreef	140	James Sherwood	200
Matt: Pallett	600	Edward Cannon	550
Mrs. Thurston	290	Richard Capps	100
Lancaster Lovett	1850	John Doley	640
Robert Cartwright	260	Matthew Mathias	80
Jno. Cartwright	100	Mr. James Peters	889
Nath: Macklakan	100	Jno Owens	190
Adam Thorowgood	700	Josvas Morris	900
Henry Walstone	800	Thomas Mason	140
Edward Land	400	Wm. Wishart	200
Thomas Hall	400	Jno Russell	300
Wm. Catherill	150	Stephen Sall	250
Doctor Browne	600	Timothy Dennis	100
John Richardson	1000	George Walker	425
Robert Richmond	1000	Wm. Ashby	100
Thomas Benson	225	Charles Griffin	216
Lewis Pervine	800	Symon Franklin	100
Edward Attwood	400	Alice Thrower	125

James Wishart	225
Richard Draught	500
Doctor Wm. Hunter	80
Mr. Jon Sanders	203
Wm Grinto	650
Henry Fithgerreld	200
Coll. H. Lawson	3100
Capt. John Thorowgood	1000
Robert Thorowgood	940
Henry Southern	640
John Wharton	850
Joseph Doller	150
Jno Briggs	600
Francis Jones	100
Thomas Lurrey	100
Thomas Walker	820
Steph Swaine	450
Edward Mulsin	100
George Bullock	300
Jno Leggett	400
Mark Tully	300
Wm. Walstone	400
Mark Powell	550
Elizabeth Nicholls	500
Hugh Hoskins	50
Wm. Burrough	50
Wm. Warren	100
Capt. Hugh Campble	800
George Worrinton	400
James Tully	400
Wm. Lovett	1300
Wm. Grant	150
Thomas More	100
Richard Whithurst	350
Capt. Thomas Cocke	800
John Comins	175
Thomas Griffin	200
Thomas Spratt	600
Jno Russell	150
James Heath	550
David Duncon	100
Daniell Lane	350
George Fowler	600
Jno Booth	350
Giles Collier	500
Jacob Johnson	1700
Alexander Willis	150
Richard Bonny	2000
Mr. James Doage	784
Antho: Barnes	200
Jno. Macklalin	120
Thomas Etherington	108
Jno James	328
Wm. Woodhouse	300
John Mayho	160
Joseph Perry	35
Thomas Perry	650
Mr. Argoll Thorowgood	1000
Capt. Wm. Moseley	600
Jno Moseley	325
Wm. Smith	180
Wm. Symmons	400
Adam Forguson	120
Banj. Commins	200
Jno Elkes	500
Patrick White	1250
Richard Jones	200
Evan Jones	600
Mich. Jones	200
Richard Wicker	300
Henry Snaile	250
Mr. Samiel Bush	550
Mr. Tully Robinson	500
Jno Briberry	50
Wm. Moseley	50
Capt. Christ. Merchant	400
Richard Cox	50
Matt. Godfrey	150
Thomas Tully	600
Hector Denby	600
Thomas Keeling	700
Wm. More	100
Thomas Cason	550
Sarah Jackson	600
Jacob More	200
	98728

Henry Spratt

A True and Perfect Rent Roll of the Lands In Elizabeth City County for the Year 1704

Coll. Wm. Wilson	1024
Mr. Wm. Smelt	150
Mr. Pasquo Curle	300
Mr. Nicho. Curle	950
Coll. Dudley Diggs	216
Samuell Pearce	100
Mary Jenings	250
Mark Powell	184

Name	Acres
Wm. Davis	42
Jno Skinner	50
Thomas Baines	50
Wm. Latham	90
Thomas Tucker	60
Matthew Smell	100
Charles Cooley	200
Jno Chandler	150
Wm. Umpleet	25
Charles Tucker	240
Thomas Allin	227
Wm. Williams per the School	600
Wm Williams per himself	260
Mrs. Bridgett Jenkins	100
Christopher Davis	25
Wm. Spicer	60
Thomas Hawkins	270
Jno Bowles	260
Jno Theodam	100
Bartho. Wetherby	300
Jos: White	200
Capt. Henry Royall	750
Robert Bright Sen.	100
Thomas Naylor	100
George Cooper Sen	100
Thomas Needham	100
Cha: Cooper	100
Wm. Dunn	100
Charles Jenings	225
Samuell Davill	100
Paltey Davill	100
Francis Rogers	200
Thomas Babb per Selden	300
Richard Horsley	90
Sarah Nagleer	230
Henry Dunn	50
Peter Pearce	50
Moses Davis	150
Mich: Breltuen	100
Henry Robinson	200
Christo. Copeland	340
Thomas Faulkner	50
Mr. James Wallace	1300
Mr. Berthram Servant	418
Robert Taylor	50
Joseph Harris	50
Wm. Robinson	50
Wm. Boswell	220
Wm. Winter	70
John Lowry per Selden	110
Edward Roe	100
Henry James	100
Richard Roatton	50
Thomas Poole	1200
John Wheat Land	66
George Bell	80
Widdow Ballis	350
George Walker	325
Mr. Robert Beverley	777
Jno House	157
Jno Bushell Jun	150
Roger Masinbred	50
John Shepherd	210
Wm. Minsor	150
Edward Lattimore	190
James Baker	225
Thomas Tucker	60
Jno. Cotton	50
Mark Johnson	400
Major Wm. Armistead	460
Coll. Antho. Armistead	2140
Daniell Preeday	50
Matthew Watts	454
Bryan Penny	50
Giles Dupra	150
Jno Bayley	415
Mary Simmons	200
Jno Parish	50
Antho. Griggs	50
Abr: Parish	100
Mark Parish	200
Benj. Smith	650
Thomas Nobling per Archer	212
Wm. Mallory	200
Widdow Croashell	100
Charles Powers	400
Robert Charwill per Jno Young	440
Samuell Fingall	333
Francis Savoy	50
Mr. Edward Mihills	600
Jane Nichols	50
John Francis	25
James Priest	50
Simon Hollier	200
Mr. Thomas Gebb	630
Mr. Richard Booker	526
Mr. Wm. Lowry	526
Mr. Merry or Mrs Dunn	500
Wm. Haslyitt	100
Capt. Augustine More	285
John More	250
John Passones	780
Rebeckha Morgan	50
Thomas Roberts	250

Mr. John Turner	50	Mr. Francis Ballard per Selden	460
Henry Lais	50		
Capt. Henry Jenkins	300		
			29560

Henry Royall Sgeriff

A True & Perfect Rent Roll of all the Lands that is held in Warwick County 1704

Major Wm. Cary	300	Francis Jones	150
Mr. Nedler Plantacon	80	Matthew Jones	750
Rober Hubbert	101	Jno. Read	875
Wm. Harwood	625	Mr. Brewer Land	1350
Richard Glanvills Orphans	165	Mr. Henry Cary	670
Wm. Hubbert	200	Langhorne Orphans	602
Henry Gibbs	315	Coll. Coles Orphans	1350
Wm. Hewitt	150	Peter Jones	150
James Hill	135	Samuell Crew Orphans	150
John Golden	50	Samuell Symons	173
Thomas Harwood	575	Mrs. Elizabeth Whitaker	600
Jno. Harwood	704	Capt. Miles Cary	600
Capt. Thomas Charles	100	John Cannon	75
Hump: Harwood	400	John Linton	75
Matthew Wood	300	Richard Gough	60
Edward Joyner	60	Coll. Miles Cary	1960
Coll. Dudley Diggs	4626	Mr. Jno. Mallnote	61
Elizabeth Lucas	800	Rowlands Williams	170
John Hillard	74	Robert Chapell	150
Edward Loftes	60	James Chapell	100
Wm. Rowles Orphans	150	Edward Powers	200
Samuell Hatton	225	James White	40
Isaac Goodwin	225	Peter Sawers Orphans	95
George Robinson	70	Wm. Cotton	143
Seymon Powell	250	James Cotton	70
John Dawson	300	John Croley	100
Wades Orphans	100	Stephen Burgess	128
Henry Dawson	200	Widdow Yorgen	60
John Bowger	100	George Jackson	193
Joseph Cooper	200	Sarah Ranshaw	125
Robert Roberts	60	Richard Wootton	243
George Burton	330	Samuell Hoggard	120
Capt. Mills Wells	425	James Floyd	100
Roger Daniell Orphans	196	Fr: Rice Orphans	200
Jno Hansell	100	Mr. Math Hoggard	270
Emanuell Wells	325	Widdow Chapell	321
Elizabeth Wells Widdow	155	Thomas Ascow	50
Widdow Lewelling	100	Garrett Ridley	300
Wm. Wells	615	Samuell Ranshaw	238
Elias Wells	50	Charle Stuckey	86
Widdow Pierce	155	Jos Naylor	100
Thomas Haynes	850	Jos Russell	150
John Scarsbrook	850	Charles Allen	295

Wm. Newberrey	100
John Turmer	100
Wm. Smith	150
Elizabeth Holt	150
James Browne	150
Henry Royall	246
Edward Rice	375
Thomas Blackistone	75
Mark Noble	215
James Reynolds	75
John Holmes	200
Samuell Duberry	200
Edward Powers	200
Jno Hatton Orphans	93
Wm. Lowland	25
Thomas Morey	363
Wm. Bracey	150
Cope Doyley	500
Nath Edwards	100
Samuel Groves	490
Croncher Orphans	50
Henry Whitaker	60
Woodman Land	200
Wm Cook	29
Jno Tignall	392
Thomas Mountfort	890
Joseph Mountfort	558
James Priest	50
Abr· Cawley	80
Wm. Jones	70
Edward Davis	200
The County Land	150
Denbigh per Gleab	130
Mulberry Island Gleab	50
Thomas Hansford	75
Mr. Rascows Orphans	1195
	37685
Thomas Hansford never before paid	75
	37610

Persons out of the County

Jno Trevillian	248	
Holman Orphans	200	448

Robert Hubberd Sherriff

A Rent Roll of all the Land In York County 1704

Wm. Jackson	200
Matt: Pierce	100
Jno. Latin	150
Robert Cobbs	100
Francis Sharp	100
Geo: Baskewyle	350
Richard Gilford	100
Jos: Frith	50
Wm. Jones	70
Nath: Crawley	384
Thomas Crips	750
Wm. Davis	200
Lewis Barnoe	80
Arthur Lun	50
Jno. Bates	669
Jno Serginton	150
Wm. Taylor	100
Richard Page	150
Wm. Jorden	580
Jno. Lynes	150
Alex: Banyman	50
Wm. Cobbs	50
Mary Whaley	550
Henry Tyler	180
Richard Kendall	150
Wm. Hansford	300
Nicholas Sebrell	150
David Stoner	50
Ralph Hubberd	50
Wm. Harrison	50
Jno. Wyth	100
Thomas Hill	930
Thomas Vines	200
Morgan Baptist	100
Phil. Deadman	75
Bazill Wagstaff	127
Wm. Allen	117
Robert Read	750
Jos: Mountford	307
Roger Boult	100
Edward Fuller	70
Thomas Jefferson	100
Henry Duke	25
Jno. Hansford	100
Robert Peters	160
Jno. Morland	100
Wm. Lee	350
Richard Burt	200
John Eaton	170
Rob: Starke	250
Robt. Harrison	200
Jno. Morris	125
James Bates	117
Elizabeth Jones	94

Name	Acres
Edward Young	100
Robert Green	200
Tho: Fear	100
Edward Thomas	223
John Loyall	100
Stephen Pond	200
Wm. Wise	850
Cornelius Shoohorn	100
Joseph White	750
Daniell Park Esq.	2750
Thomas Fear Jun	130
Orlando Jones	450
Ambrose Cobbs	163
Henry Dyer	50
Wm. Davis	100
Wm. Buckner	302½
Tho. Barber	600
Elizb. Tindall	60
Dudley Diggs	1350
Wm. Hewitt	150
Mary Collier	433
Charles Collier	684
Tho. Hansford	75
Geo. Browne	150
Wm. Gibbs	50
Wm. Pekithman	650
Jno. Smith	150
Baldwin Matthews	1300
Jno Daniell	200
Seamor Powell	130
Jno. Lewis Esq.	300
Wm. Timson	1000
Jno. Page	490
Jos. Benjafield	80
Tho. Stear	60
Stephen Fouace	565
Edmund Jenings Esq.	850
Elizb. Archer	370
Wm. Coman	50
Elizb. Hansford	100
Samll: Hill	25
Jno. Anderson	50
Tho Buck	250
Lewis Burwell	2100
Robt. Crawley	400
Robt. Hyde	200
Robt. Harrison	250
Jeffry Overstreet	50
Tho. Overstreet	50
John Myhill	52
Mary Roberts	25
Benja. Stogsdall	50
Tho Wade	375

Name	Acres
Jos: Walker	615
Jno. Sanders	100
Mongo Inglis	400
Tho Holyday	100
Jno. Williams	100
Antho: Sebrell	50
Robt. Jones	100
James Cansebee	200
Richd. Booker	200
James Morris	100
Henry Adkinson	82
Robt. Jackson	150
Anthoney Robinson	183
Hannah Lamb	50
James Calthorp	900
Tho Boulmer	265
Peter Pasque	12
Jno. Chapman	70
Jno. Pond	112
Sarah Tomkins	250
Robt. Kirby	200
Tho. Kirby	270
Edward Curtis	200
Jno. Forgison	200
Wm. Row	902
Jno. Hunt	550
Wm. Taverner	100
Armiger Wade	424
Richard Dixon	450
Edmund Jennings Esq.	1650
Jno. Persons	300
Tho. Nutting	375
Peter Manson	150
Richard Slaughter	275
James Persons	350
Tho. Roberts	450
Jno. Toomer	335
Daniell Taylor	225
Robert Hayes	220
Henry Andros	274
Jno. Wells	750
Robert Curtis	250
Tho. Cheesman Sen.	1800
Jos Potter	25
Hen: Heywood	1300
David Holyday	600
John Northern	130
Jno. Doswell	367
Isaac Powell	100
Symon Staice	200
Jno. Drewet	200
Robert Topladie	100
Jno. Potter	93

Lewis Vernum 150
James Slaughter 250
Tho: Burnham 50
Jno: Doswell Jun 100
Robert Shields 400
Wm. Wilson 50
Owen Davis 247
Tho. Walker 100
Richard Nixon 150
Henry Clerk 100
Elias Love 25
Wm. Howard 100
Jno. Sanderver 100
Jno. Cox 50
Tho. Gibbins 100
Tho. Hind 100
Tho Cheesman Jun 600
Wm. Browne 200
Jno. Rogers 650
Jno. Moss 150
Jno. Lawson 100
Nicho. Philips 150
Wm. Sheldon 750
Jno. Wayman 100
Tho Edmonds 150
Lawrence Smith 1700
James Paulmer 150
Wm. Gurrow 150
Peter Goodwin 400
Robt. Snead 50
Edward Cawley 150
Wm. Gorden 150
Jno. Hilsman 75
Jno. Wright 100
Jno. Gibons 50
Elizb. Goodwin 1200
Samuell Cooper 150
Jno. Fips 150
Tho Wooton 150
Edward Moss 759
Rebecka Watkins 100
Wm. Whitaker 1800
Hampton Parish 200
Bruton parish Gleabe 300
Robt. Ivy he living in James City County & no Tennt. on ye Land.... 100

61132½

Added to make up the old Roll 168

61300½

Wm. Barbar S Y C

The Rent Roll of the Land in James City County 1704

A

Adkinson Tho 50
Adkinson Henry 250
Armestone Joshua 50
Adams Anne 150
Argo James 200
Abbitt Francis 100
Apercon Wm. 80
Allen Richard 540

1420

B

Baker Jno. 100
Bentley Jno 125
Bess Edmund 75
Burwell Lewis 1350
Beckitt Tho 60
Bray James 3500
Bryon Jno. 100
Bingley James 100
Benham Jno. 50
Brown James 250
Bowers Wm. 50
Broadnax Wm. 1683
Bayley Wm 100
Black Geo 200
Bush Jno 800
Ballard Tho 100
Bray David 5758
Burton Ralph 200
Blankitt Henry 100
Brand Richard 125
Breeding Jno. 100
Bruer Thackfield 350
Blackley Wm 142
Barratt Wm. 305
Barron Tho 100
Blankes Henry 650
Bagby Tho 180
Barnes Francis 200
Brackitt Tho 150
Browne Wm. 1070
Buxton Samuell 300
Bimms Christo. 300
Ballard Wm. 300

Boman	90
Benge Robert	60
	19123

C

Center Jno	100
Clerk Wm.	1100
Charles Phill	200
Capell Tho.	200
Cearley Wm.	450
Clerk Robert	300
Clerk Sarah	200
Cole Richard	80
Cooper Tho	60
Cook Richard	75
Cosby Charles	250
Crawley Robert	460
Cryer George	100
Cobbs Ambrose	350
Cock Jonathan	250
Cowles Thomas	675
	4850

D

Dormar Jno.	100
Drummond Wm	150
Deane Jno	150
Duckitt Abraham	290
Danzee Jno Jacob Coignan	4111
Deane Tho	80
Deane Wm	100
Drummond Jno	700
Deane Tho	150
Duke Tho	750
Davey Francis	778
Doby Jno.	300
Duke Henry Jun	50
Duke Henry Esq.	2986
	11695

E

Elerby Elizabeth	600
Edmunds Elizabeth	175
Eggleston Joseph	550
Eglestone Benj.	1375
	2700

F

Fearecloth Tho	277
Farthing Wm.	50
Frayser Jno	250
Fox Wm.	50
Fouace Stephen	150
Fish Jno.	100
Freeman George	197
Furrbush Wm.	400
Flanders Francis	350
	1824

G

Goodrich Benj.	1650
Gwin Jno.	100
Garey Tho.	60
Guilsby Tho.	300
Graves Joseph	250
Goss Charles	171
Goodall Jno.	400
Geddes	476
Gill Jno.	100
Green Tho.	50
Gregory Nicho.	50
Green Wm.	100
Ginnings Phill.	400
Gibson Gibey	150
Goodman John	275
Goodwin Robert	150
Grice Aristotle	700
Greene Tho	500
	5882

H

Hudson Wm	50
Herd Leph.	100
Hadley Dyonitia	100
Hall Jno.	50
Harvey George	1425
Howard Jno.	25
Hughes Geo.	250
Harfield Mich	50
Hudson George	100
Hudson Leonard	170
Hood Jno.	250
Harris Wm.	140
Hamner Nicho.	500
Henley Leonard	360
Hooker Edward	1067
Higgins Jno.	75
Henley Jno.	100
Holiday Tho.	250
Hitchcock John	100
Holeman James	150

Hubert Matt	1834
Handcock Robt.	300
Haley James	310
Hook Mick	260
Hill Tho.	310
Hatfield Richard	100
Hilliard Jerimiah	225
Hilliard John	200
Hopkins John	120
Hunt Wm.	1300
Hix John	115
Harrison Wm.	150
Hawkins John	200
Hix Joseph	100
Harrison Benj. Jun	100
	10936

J

Inch Jno.	30
Jone Fred	300
Inglis Mingo	1300
Jenings Edmund Esq.	200
Jaquelin Edward	400
Jeffrys Tho	60
Jackson Elizabeth	200
Jackson Richard	150
Jeffrys Matt.	100
Johnson Antho	100
Jones Wm.	50
Johnson Jno	260
Jones Wm.	150
Jordan John	1000
	4265

K

Knowstarp	150

L

Lawrence Richard	250
Ludwell Phil Esq	6626
Lattoon John	75
Lund Thomas	100
Lillingtone Benj.	100
Lidie Robt.	500
Loftin Comeles	200
Lightfoot Phil	1650
Lightfoot Jno. Esq	250
Love Jno.	100
Loftin Comeles Jun	200
Liney Wm.	55
	10106

M

Mookins Roger	160
Macklin Wm	300
Marston Wm	150
Morris Edward Jun	100
Manningaren	150
Marston Tho	1000
Martin Richard	150
Maples Tho	300
Muttlow Jno	170
Morris James	800
Moris David	170
Myers Wm Jun	100
Mountfort Tho	600
Morris John	195
Marble Geo	135
Mallard Poynes	100
Merryman James	300
Morecock Tho	700
Meekings Tho	175
Marraw Dennis	30
Major John	100
	5885

N

Norrell Hugh	328
Nicholson Jno	144
Nicholls Henry	100
Nailer Wm	300
O'Mooney Mary	126
	998

P

Prince George	50
Page John	1700
Page Mary	900
Pigot Benj.	90
Pall Wm	450
Parker Tho	1650
Peper Stephen	100
Phillips Jno	300
Pattison Alex	100
Perkins Charles	320
Philips Edward	100
Philips Wm	300
Pearman Wm	270
Pearman Jno	200
Pendexter Tho	550
Parish Tho	100
Pattisson Tho	200

Name	Acres
Parke Daniell Esq	1800
Pattison Catherine	150
	9330

R

Name	Acres
Rhodes Randall	50
Ryder Mary	350
Rhodes Francis	100
Rovell Jno	50
Revis Wm.	150
Russell Samuell	350
	1050

S

Name	Acres
Stafford Mary	210
Sanders Jno.	50
Sewell Jno.	75
Sprattley Jno.	350
Smith Christo.	450
Short Jno.	90
Smallpage Robt.	190
Santo Robt.	100
Smith Jno.	114
Slade Wm.	80
Soane Henry	750
Sykes Barnard	1012
Selvey Jacob	50
Sharp Jno.	800
Shaley Jno	150
Simes Wm.	650
Sorrell Mary	500
Sherman Elizb.	500
	6121

T

Name	Acres
Tinsley Edward	100
Tinsley Richard	100
Tomson James	100
Thackson John	289
Tyery Wm.	1590
Thurston John	500
Thomas Wm.	150
Tyler Henry	730
Tullett John	625
Thomas Hanah	100
Thomson Henry	150
Twine Tho.	100
Thomas Jno.	250
	4784

V

Name	Acres
Vaughn Henry	1900
Udall Matthew	50
Verney Wm.	50
Vaiding Isaac	300
	2300

W

Name	Acres
Weathers Tho.	130
Wood Richard	130
Whitaker Wm.	320
Ward Tho.	100
Weldon Sarah	100
Whaley Mary	200
Winter Timo.	250
Wilkins Samll.	170
Wright Samll.	100
Winter Wm.	100
Williams Matt.	75
Walker Alex.	500
Williamson John	120
Walker David	150
Walker Alex. Jun.	2025
Warberton Tho.	190
Weldey Geo.	317
Wragg Tho.	500
Wooton Jno.	150
Willson Jno.	140
Wilkins Tho.	600
Wood Edward	300
Wood Tho.	200
Walker David	100
Ward Robt.	800
Wright Mary	175
Woodward Lanslett	650
Woodward John	650
Woodward Geo.	350
Woodward Samll.	350
Ward Henry	150
Ward Edward	150
	10662

Y

Name	Acres
Young Robt.	350
Young Thomas	350
	700

114780

Benj. Shottwater of York County 300
Tho. Sorrell 300
Mary Nosham at the Blackwater 168

768

Henry Soane Junr. Sher.

The Totall of the Acres in James City County 114780

Discovered of this for which the Shreiff is to be allowed the Qt. Rts. according to his Ex.cy odrs in Council 6000

108780

108780 acres at 24 tob per 100 is .... 26107 tob

Whereof pd in Aronoco at 6 per Ct 4000 12.0.0

In Sweet Scented at 3s " 4d per Ct. 22107 92.2.3

104.2.3

New Kent County Rent Roll

A Rent Roll of the Lands held of her Maj[tie] in the Parish of St. Peters and St. Paulls. Anno 1704.

Alford John	240
Allen Richard	550
Alex Abraham	100
Allen Robt.	100
Austin	245
Austin James	700
Amos Fran	100
Ashcroft Tho	180
Aldridge Jno	250
Atkinson Jno	300
Anthony Mark	190
Anderson Jno	100
Anderson Robt	900
Arise Margt	200
Austin Rich	50
Anderson Robt.	700
Anderson David	300
Anderson Rich	200
Allen Reynold	205
Allvis George	325
Aron Josiah	200
Amos Nocho	50
Allen Daniell	250
Allen Samll	150
Anderson John	100
Ashley Charles	100
	6785

B

Bourn Wm	140
Bray Sarah	790
Bradbury Geo	100
Brothers Jno	200
Bayley Jno	80
Beck Wm Mr.	200
Butts Alice	150
Burnell Mary Mrs.	2750
Bassett Wm.	550
Ball David	200
Baughan Jno Junr	300
Bassett Tho	350
Blackburn Rowland	700
Baker Christo	100
Beer Peter	100
Brooks Richd	85
Burnell Edwd	200
Brown Jno	100
Bullock Richd	450
Blackwell James Junr	200
Brooks Robt	45
Bulkley Benj	200
Blackwell	950
Baughan Jno	100
Baughan Joseph	100
Bostock Jno	100
Bostock Wm	80
Bumpus Robt.	100
Burwell Lewis	200
Bryan Charles	100
Bullock Edwd	450
Blalock Jno	492
Baker Jno	130
Bearne Henry	50

Buhly Jno	225
Bow Henry	200
Bradley Tho	255
Barker Cha	100
Bugg Samll	60
Baskett Wm. Esq.	1250
Beck Wm.	433
Beare Joseph	150
Barrett Christo	60
Baughtwright Jno	250
Bad Samll	150
Banks Andrew	50
Baker Richd	80
Bowles John	500
Bunch John	100
Burnett Jno	150
Barnhowes Richd	1600
Barbar Tho	500
Burkett Tho	41
Bates Edwd	50
Breeding John	300
Brewer Mary	100
Bassett Wm. Esq.	4100
Bradingham Robt.	150
Baxter James	90
	21786

C

Cotrell Richd	200
Clarkson David	200
Crump Stephen	60
Crump Wm.	330
Clopton Wm.	454
Chandler Robt.	160
Crump Richd.	60
Cambo Richd.	80
Crawford David Junr	400
Crawford David Mr.	300
Chambers Edwd	235
Clerk Edwd	282
Collett Tho	100
Clerk Christo	300
Cocker Wm.	1000
Case Hugh	100
Carley Richd	80
Chiles Henry	700
Cook Abraham	200
Crump Elizb	80
Colum Richd	130
Crump James	150
Crump Robt	150
Clough Capt.	80
Chandler Wm.	300
Chandler Francis	150
Cordey Tho.	150
Currell Andrew	30
Croome Joell	600
Crutchfield Peter	400
Chesley Wm.	500
Crutchfield Junr	400
Carlton Wm.	140
Chambers George	100
Cox Wm.	350
	9251

D

Dolerd Wm	50
Dennett John	350
Durham James	100
Dumas Jerimiah	250
Deprest Robt	350
Dodd John	300
Dabony James	320
Davis Elizar	375
Duke Henry Esq.	325
Dibdall Jno	800
Darnell Rachell	100
Duke Henry Esq.	170
Davis John	80
Davenport Mest	125
Daniell John	150
	3845

E

Eperson John	120
Elmore Tho	300
Elmore Tho Junr	100
Ellicon Garratt Robt	520
England Wm.	490
Elderkin John	300
Elmore Peter	100
English Mungo	500
Ellis Wm.	100
	2530

F

Finch Edwd	300
Foster Joseph	800
Forgeson Wm	507
Fleming Charles	920
Francis Tho	150
Freeman Wm.	200

Fenton Widdo	270
Feare Edmd	200
Fisher Wm.	100
	3447

G

Goodger Jno	200
Green Edwd	200
Gibson Tho	370
Garrat James	375
Gonton Jno	250
Glass Tho	150
Graham Tho	250
Gleam Jno	300
Giles Jno	120
Gentry Nicho	250
Garland Edwd	2600
Glass Anne	150
Granchaw Tho	480
Greenfield Fran.	80
Gillmett Jno	160
Gawsen Phillip	50
Gillmett Richd	150
Glassbrook Robt	400
Gadberry Tho	200
Gill Nicho	222
Gosling Wm	460
Goodring Alexander	100
Gills John	100
Grindge Richd	225
	7442

H

Herlock John	320
Hilton Jno	300
Hughs Jno	180
Huberd Jno	827
Howle Jno	150
Howle Jno Junr	100
Hughs Robt	966
Harris Edmd	100
Harris Tho	100
Hawes Haugton	850
Harris John	146
Hill Jno	250
Hester Fra	300
Horsley Rowland	250
Horman Robt	300
Hughes Rees	400
Hill Samll	300
Holled Samll	100
Harrelston Paul	360
Hatfield Wm	318
Harris Wm	125
Harris Benj	100
Horkeey John	800
Hairy John	280
Haiselwood Jno	200
Haiselwood Tho	150
Hockiday Wm	300
Holdcroft Henry	95
Hogg Mary	140
Harmon Wm	350
Hogg Jno. Junr	260
Harris Wm	100
Hopkins Wm	200
Howes Job	300
Hight John	100
Hankins Charles	340
Harris Wm	150
Harris Robt	75
Handey Wm	150
Hogg Wm	200
Haselwood Richd	100
Harlow Tho	230
Hutton Geo	150
	11312

J

Jackson Tho	500
Izard Fran	1233
Jarratt Robt	1600
Johnson Mich	40
Jones John	100
Johnson Wm	265
Jones Jane	200
Johnson John	100
Johnson Edwd	150
Jennings Robt	100
Jones Fredirick	500
Johes John	100
Jeeves Tho	100
Jones Francis	200
Jones John	100
Jones Evan	500
	5838

K

King Elizb	300
Kembro Jno	540
Kembro Jno Junr	150
Keeling Geo	1500
	2490

L

Lightfoot John Esq.	3600
Littlepage Richd	2160
Losplah Peter	100
Lestrange Tho	200
Liddall Geo	100
Lawson Nicho	200
Levermore Phill	1000
Lewis John Esq	2600
Lawson John	50
Lewis John	375
Lovell Geo	920
Lovell Charles	250
Leak Wm	280
Logwod Tho	100
Lacey Wm	500
Lacey Tho	100
Lacey Emanuell	180
Luke Jno	150
Lochester Robt	80
Lewis Tho	115
Lee Edwd	120
Lochester Edwd	80
Law James	100
Laton Reubin	100
Linsey Joseph	1150
Linsey Wm	50
Lane Tho	100
	14760

M

Millington Wm Junr	450
Mitchell Stephen Junr	75
Millington Wm	200
Moss Samll	200
Mitchell Tho	300
Meanley Wm	100
Minis Tho	200
Mitchell Stephen	200
Moor Pelham	125
Martin Tho	100
Martin Martin	150
Morris Robt	245
Moss Tho	430
Morgan Edwd	50
Moon Stephen	70
Major Wm	456
Murroho Jno	100
Moor Jno	250
Masey Tho	300
Martin John	400
Masey Peter	100
Madox John	300
Martin Wm	230
Martin James	100
Moss James	720
Moon Tho	65
McKing Alexander	170
McKoy Jno	300
Merridith Geo	400
Melton Richd	290
Morreigh John	110
Merfield John	210
Mills Nicho	300
Mask Jno	411
Medlock John	350
Moor Edwd	65
McKgene Wm	13½
Merriweather Nicho	3327
Mage Peter	450
Mitchell Wm	512
Marr Geo	100
Moor Anne	75
Mutray Tho	382
Mirideth James	270
Mohan Warwick	850
Muttlow James	150
Morgan Matthew	210
Morris John	450
Markham Tho	100
Moxon Wm	100
Mackony Elizb	250
Meacon Gideon	270
	16149½

N

Nucholl James	300
Neaves James	150
Nonia Richd	100
Norris Wm	100
	650

O

Osling John	150
Otey John	290
Oudton Matt	190
	630

P

Page John Junr	400
Pendexter Geo	1490
Pattison David	300

Park Jno Junr	300
Park John	200
Pease John	100
Philip Geo	100
Penix Edwd	200
Plantine Peter	240
Pendexter Tho	1000
Pyraul James	150
Pullam Wm	575
Purdy Nicho	200
Page Mary Madm	3450
Perkins John	120
Paite Jerim	220
Pasley Robt	300
Perkins Wm	305
Pait John	1500
Petever Tho	100
Pittlader Wm	147
Pickley Tho	281
Pittlader Tho	295
Petty Stephen	200
Porter John	100
Petty John	2190
Park Coll	7000
Purly John	100
	21573

R

Raglin Evan	300
Raglin Evan Junr	100
Raglin Tho	100
Ross Wm	150
Richardson Henry	300
Raymond James	80
Reynold Tho	255
Reyley Jno	100
Reynolds Jonah	50
Rhoads Charles	175
Reynolds Samll	820
Rice Tho	300
Redwood John	1078
Rule Widdo	50
Richardson Richard	890
Russell John	550
Richardson John	1450
Richard Eman	1250
Round Free Wm	100
Randolph Widdo	100
	8928

S

Styles John	200
Smith Nathll	82
Sanders Wm	40
Spear Robt	450
Sanders James	60
Scott John	300
Scrugg Richd	100
Strange Alexander	450
Smith Wm	110
Scrugg Jno	50
Snead Tho	200
Sunter Stephen	478
Symons Josiah	100
Sanders John	130
Stephens Wm	100
Stanley Tho	150
Sandidge Jno	100
Sprattlin Andrew	654
Snead John	75
Smith James	80
Sexton Wm	80
Sims Jno	1000
Smith Roger	300
Sherritt Henry	100
Salmon Thomas	50
Sanders Tho	25
Symons George	125
Stamp Ralph	625
Stanop Capt	1024
Stanup Richd	325
Shears Paul	200
Stepping Tho	350
Slater James	700
	9813

T

Tony Alexandr	170
Tovis Edmd	100
Turner Henry	250
Turner Wm	250
Turner Geo	400
Thorp Tho	200
Thurmond Richd	131½
Tucker Tho	700
Turner James	50
Thompson James	100
Tully Wm	200
Turner Geo Junr	200
Tate James	160
Town Elizb	100
Thomasses Orphans	500
Tinsley Cournelius	220
Tyler	100

Tinsley Tho	150
Tirrell Wm	400
Taylor Tho	25
Tinsley Jno	130
Tapp Jno	110
Tyrrey James	150
Tyrrey Alexandr	210
Thompson Capt.	2600
Tyrey Thom	190
Taylor Joseph	150
Taylor Lemuell	212
Taylor Thomas	350
Twitty Thomas	200
	8708½

V

Upsherd Jon	60
Vaughan Wm	300
Via Amer..	50
Venables Abr.	100
Venables John	200
Vaughan John	250
Vaughan Vincent	410
	1370

W

Wintby Jacob	250
Winfry Charles	100
Waddill Jno	40
Walker Wm	650
Walton Edwd	150
Wilson Jno	200
Waddill Wm	375
Warring Peter	88
Wingfield Tho	150
Weaver Sam	100
Wyatt Alice	1300
West Nath	6370
Webb Mary	200
Wilmore Jno	100
Webster Joseph	80
West Giles	200
Wharton Tho	270
Willis Fran	134
Waddy Samll	150
Willford Charles	100
Waid James	150
White Jno	320
Wood Henry	100
Woody Symon	50
Woody Jno	100
Winstone Antho	310
Winstone Isaac	850
Woody James	130
Winstone Sarah	275
Watson Theophilus	325
Woodson Jno	600
Walton Edwd	450
Wood Walter	100
Watkins Wm	50
Wilkes Joseph	250
Williams Clerk	300
Willis Stephen	500
Williams Tho	100
Worrin Robt	300
Woodull James	200
Walker Capt	400
Wilson James	60
Wheeler John	75
Williams Wm.	100
White John	190
	17292

Y

Yeoman John	50
Yeoell Judith	150
	200

Quit Rents that hath not been paid this 7 year viz.

Richarson Matt	200
Wm Wheeler	150
Coll Parkes	300
	650

Lands that the Persons lives out of the County viz.

Coll Lemuell Batthurst	800
Robt Valkes	500
The Heirs of Bray	500
	1800

A	6785
B	21786
C	9251
D	3845
E	2530
F	3447
G	7442
H	11312

J	5838	S	9813
K	2490	T	8708½
L	14760	V	1370
M	16149½	W	17292
N	650	Y	200
O	630		
P	21573		173870
R	8298	James Mosse Sherriff	

A full & Perfect Rent Roll of all the Land held of her Majtie in Charles City County this Present Year 1704 by Patents &c.

A

Aliat John	100

B

Bradley Joseph	200
Baxter John	250
Bishop Robt	200
Bedingfield Theo	110
Botman Harman	100
Burton Henry	100
Burwell Lewis	8000
Brooks Robt	150
Blanks Richard Senr	250
Blanks Richd Junr	125
Blanks Tho	125
Bradford Richd	1397
Brown Marmaduke	100
Bray David	230
	11337

C

Cole Robt	80
Codell Richd	100
Clark Edwd	962¼
Clark Daniell	250
Clark Joseph	230
Christian Tho	1273
Cock Edwd	350
Cock Richd	975
	3258

D

Davis Thomas	200
Davis Richd	118
	318

E

Edwards John	287½
Epes Littlebury	400
Epes John	500
Ele Samll	682
Evans John	800
	2669½

F

Floyd Geo	243
Fowler Richd	150
Flowers Samll	200
	593

G

Gunn James	250
Grosse Edwd	100
	350

H

Hamlin Jno	143½
Hill Edwd	2100
Haynes Nicho	125
Harwood John	100
Howood James	200
Hattle Shard	112
Harwood Joseph	659
Harwood Samll	350
Harwood Robt	312½
Hunt Wm	3130
Hunt John	1500
Harmon Elizb	479
Hyde Wm	120
Hamlin Stephen	80
Hamlin Tho	264
	16015

J

Irby Wm	103
Javox James	100

Name	Acres
Jordin Edwd	100
Justis Justinian	200
	503

L

Name	Acres
Lowlin Danll	600
Lawrence James	100
	700

M

Name	Acres
Manders James	100
Minge James	1086
Mountford Jeffry	100
Marvell Tho	1238
Moodie Samll	82
Muschamp John	80
	2686

N

Name	Acres
New Edwd	100
New Robt	300
	400

O

Name	Acres
Owen Wm	100
Owen David	100
	200

P

Name	Acres
Parker Tho	1667
Parish Wm	100
Parish Charles	100
Parker James	160
Parish Edwd	100
Parish John	100
	2227

R

Name	Acres
Roach Jno Senr	630
Renthall Joseph	270
Russell Samll	253
Roper John	220
Royall Joseph	262
	1635

S

Name	Acres
Smith Obidiah	100
Sampson Widdo	211
Stith Drewry	1240
Stith John	1395
Stockes John	476
Stockes Silvanus Senr	250
Stokes Silvanus Junr	550
Speares Geo	225
	4447

T

Name	Acres
Tanner Tho	2000
Tarendine John	150
Turner Edwd	195
Trotman Anne	120
	2465

V

Name	Acres
Vernon Walter	240

W

Name	Acres
Wyatt Widdo	800
Woodam Tho	100
Waren John	54
	954

Letter	Acres
A	100
B	11337
C	3258
D	318
E	2669½
F	593
G	350
H	16015
J	503
L	700
M	2686
N	400
O	200
P	2227
R	1635
S	4447
T	2465
V	240
W	954
	52059½

An account of what Land that I cannot get the Quit Rents the Persons living out of the County

Josep Parish at Kiquotan...	100
Richd Smith James City Cty	350
Danll Hayley	200
Wm Lagg Henrico Cty	100
	750

Tho Parker Sherif

The Quit Rent Roll of King William County

Armsby John	200
Alvey Robt	400
Andrew Wm	100
Abbott Robt	100
Arnold Anthony	100
Arnold Benj	1000
Alcock John	190
Adam James	400
Anderson Wm Capt	150
Burwell Majr	4700
Bunch Paul	150
Baker John	250
Burges Edwd	150
Buttris Robt	400
Bibb Benj	100
Browne Joseph	270
Bell Edwds	580
Burch Henry	200
Burrel Suprian	350
Baker Tho	100
Bobo Elizb	200
Bird Wm Maj Qr	1200
Burrus John	60
Butler Thomas	150
Burrus Thomas	60
Bassett Coll Qr	1550
Bray James Qr	1400
Browne Abraham	250
Brightwell Elizb	300
Bickley Joseph	150
Claibourne Wm Coll	3000
Claibourne Tho Capt	1000
Claibourne John	50
Coakes Robert	100
Cradock Samll	600
Cockram Wm	200
Cockram Joseph	600
Celar John	100
Chadwick Wm	150
Cathern John	180
Carr Thomas	500
Chiles Henry Qr	700
Craushaw Thomas	150
Clark Margarett	100
Coates Wm	50
Douglas Wm	200
Davis Lewis	200
Davis Wm	200
Downer John	300
Downes Elias	300
Davenport Davis	200
Dorrell Sampson Qr	5000
Davenport Martin	100
Davis Robert	200
Dickason Wm	100
Dickason Thomas	100
Dillon Henry	150
Dabney James	200
Dabney George	290
Dabney Benj	200
Davis John	200
Elly Richd	100
Egny Elizb	100
Elliot Thomas	480
Edward James	350
Elliott James	1700
Fox John Capt.	600
Fox Henry	2000
Finton Francis	100
Fuller Anthony	150
Foord John Junr	300
Foord Wm	800
Fullalove Thomas	100
Fleming Charles Qr	1700
Graves John Qr	100
Garratt Thomas	200
Geeres Thomas	100
Green John	100
Gravatt Henry	150
Goodin Majr Qr	200
Glover Wm	100
Herriott George	200
Hollins John	200
Higgason John	350
Holderbee Wm	100
Holliday Wm	100
Hayfield Wm	100
Hampton John	50

Huckstep Edwd	150
Hurt Wm Junr	90
Hurt Wm Senr	250
Hurt John	500
Hendrick Hans	700
Handcock Thomas	200
Hayden John	150
Hobday Edwd	150
Hill Thomas	150
Hutchinson Wm	600
Hill Francis	300
Hill Gabriell	250
Hill Edwd Coll Qr	3000
Hayle Joseph	200
Johns Jane	240
Johnson Wm	300
Johnson Coll Qr	600
Johns Wm	100
Isabell Wm	150
James Jonathan	300
Inge Vincent	100
Jones Frederick Qr	2850
Jenings Coll Qr	4000
King Robert Qr	300
Kettlerise Symon	200
Lee John	20
Lypscomb Ambrose	600
Lasy Wm	100
Lypscomb Wm	300
Littlepage Richd Capt Qr	2600
Lypscomb John	200
Mallory Thomas	150
Mallory Roger	100
Miles Daniell	350
Mr Gehee Thomas	250
Marr John	200
Morris Wm	440
Maybank Wm	100
Mr Donnell John	150
Maddison Henry	650
Merriweather Nicho Qr	600
Mullene Matthew	150
Madison John Qr	300
Norment Joseph	800
Norment Samll	100
Noyce Wm	650
Napier Robert	100
Owens Hugh	300
Oustin John	350
Oakes John	350
Oliver John	140
Palmer Martin	1200
Peek John	100
Pynes Nathaniell	1400
Pee Thomas	400
Purlevant Arthur	100
Powers David	200
Pollard Wm Qr	500
Pemberton Geo	180
Page John Qr	1000
Pickrell Gabriell	100
Parks Coll Qr	4500
Quarles John	100
Reynolds Wm	100
Robert Maurice	200
Randall John	100
Ray James	100
Rhodes Nicholas	150
Sandlan Nicholas	700
Strutton Thomas	150
Streett Wm	350
Shilling George	300
Satterwhite Charles	150
Slaughter Geo	100
Slaughter Martin	130
Stark John	500
Sanders Jushua	100
See Mathew	200
Sellers Jacob	350
Spruse Jeremy	150
Smith Edmd	150
Spencer Thomas	600
Slaughter John	90
Smith Christo Qr	800
Slaughter Henry	100
Toms Wm	150
Towler Matthew	150
Terry Thomas	300
Terry Stephen	330
Tomason Thomas	150
Terry James	400
Traneer John	100
Vickrey Henry	450
West John Coll	1800
Winfree Henry	300
West Tho Capt	1000
Whitworth John	200
Whitlock John	200
Willeroy Abraham	550
Williams Phillip	100
Williams Griffith	240
Wood Thomas	300
Whitehead John	100
Woolsey Jacob	130
Williams John	150
Williams Samll	600

Wright Thomas	150
Whitbee Robert	800
West Nathanll Capt	2000
Waller John Majr	800
Willis Wm	250
Wheelis Joseph	130
Wormley Madam Qr	3000
Winston William	170
Whitehead Phillip	3000
Yancey Charles	100
Yarborough John	150
Yarborough Richard	300
	100950
Wm Stanard M.S.	1000
James Wood K.Q.	500
Zachary Lewis K.Q.	450
Peter Kemp G.C.	600
Wm Beck N.K.	1600
Tho. Hickman K.Q.	550
Benj Clement G.C.	600
David Bray J.C.C.	1000
Job House N.K.	2000
Harry Beverley M.S.	600
Chillian White G.C.	300

A True Account of the Lands in King & Queen County as it was taken by Robt. Bird Sherriff in the year 1704.

A

Alford John	200
Austin Danll	80
Asque John	320
Adams Johns	200
Arnold Edwd	150
Allin Thomas	100
Adkinson John	250
Austin Thomas	100
Adamson David	100
Anderson Richd	650
Allcock Dorothy	150
	2300

B

Baker Wm	350
Beverley Robt. Qr.	3000
Bennett Alexander	200
Breeding Geo	200
Bennett Wm	150
Bowles Robt	100
Bennett Sawyer	150
Baylor John	3000
Bell Roger	150
Burford Wm	150
Bray John	230
Blake Wm	290
Boisseau James Quart	900
Blake Wm Junr	210
Brown Lancelet	385
Burch Jno	100
Burch Wm	100
Brown Tho. Blakes Land	300
Bridgeforth James	355
Bagby Robt	550
Banks Wm	1079
Bullock John	200
Bird Wm	572
Broach Jno	1200
Braxton Geo	2825
Blanchet John	125
Bowker Ralph	330
Bine Edmd	111
Barber James	750
Burgess Wm	100
Bond Jno	100
Breemer John	1100
Bland Henry	150
Breemer John Junr	200
Bowden Tho.	150
Barton Andrew	150
Barlow Henry	200
Baskett John	150
Batterton Tho.	100
Baker James	322
Bill Robt.	150
Bocus Reynold	150
Bourne George	200
Bird Robt.	1324
	22535

C

Cane Jno	300
Chessum Alexandr	150
Cook Benjamin	200
Cook Thomas Junr	50
Cook Thomas Senr	100
Cook Jno	50
Cleyton John	400

Chapman Mary	200
Cleyton Jeremy	325
Crane Wm	120
Camp Thomas	250
Carleton Christo	200
Carleton Jno.	300
Carter Timo.	350
Coleman Tho.	300
Coleman Daniell	470
Cleyton Susannah Widdo	700
Collier Robt.	100
Crane Wm.	300
Crane Tho.	320
Chapman John	200
Caughlane James	100
Cotton Catherine	50
Collier Charles	450
Collier John	400
Collins Wm.	350
Cammell Alexandr.	200
Chin Hugh	100
Conner Timo.	1410
Collins James Yard Qr	300
Corbin Gowin	2000
Crisp Tobias	100
Carters Qr	300
Carlton Tho.	200
Carlton Anne	300
Clough George Qr	390
	12235
Clerk and Cordell both in Glocester	1000

D

Widdo Durrat	200
Day Alexander Maj. Beverley Qr	300
Doe Wm.	300
Dilliard Nicho.	150
Dilliard Edwd.	150
Dimmock Tho.	150
Dismukes Wm.	200
Duett Charles	900
Didlake James	200
Durham John	100
Dunkley John	380
Duson Tho.	448
Davis Nathll.	300
Deshazo Peter	450
Davis Jno	90
Davis Edwd	100
Dillard Thomas	170
Davis Richd	250
Dillard Geo	325
Duglas James	275
Dayley Owen	180
	5618

E

Eachols John	220
Ellis John	400
Eastham George	300
Ewbank Wm	350
Eastham Edwd Junr	800
Edwds John	100
Eastham Edwd	100
Eastes Abraham	200
Eyes Cornelius	100
Emory Ralph	100
Ellis Timothy	350
	3020

F

Forsigh Thomas	150
Farquson James	300
Flipp John	80
Farish Robt	1400
Fielding Henry	1000
Farmer John	50
Fothergill Richd	675
Fortcon Charles	400
Forgett Charles	150
Robt Fothergill	150
	4355
Farmer John not paid for	200
Fox Margarett not pd for	100

G

Gadberry Edwd	100
Griffin Edwd	100
George Richd	100
Griffin David	100
Graves Robt	150
Graves Jno	150
Gardner Ringing	200
Gray Joseph	200
Gilby John	300
Gray Samll	40
Gresham Jno	200
Gresham Edwd	175
Good John	200
Gresham George	150

Garrett Danll	200
Gamble Tho. Majors Land	450
Gresham Tho	225
Graves Jno	150
Guttery Jno	230
Greogory Frances Widdo	700
Gough Alice Widdo	800
Griggs Francis	250
Garrett John	330
Garrett Humphrey	200
Gibson Widdo	200
Garrett Robt	200
	6100

H

Hand Thomas	150
Hayle John Qr	685
Honey James	200
Holloway Wm	100
Herndon James	100
Hoomos George	725
Hodges Thomas	250
Hayle Joseph	250
Hayes John	100
Haynes Wm	494
Holcomb Wm Bradfords Land	700
Henderson John Thackers , Land	200
Hodgson Widdo	200
Henderson Widdo	300
Henderson Wm	162
Housburrough Morris, Harts Land	200
Hesterley John	200
Hill John	200
Hordon Wm	70
Harris Wm	250
Hart Tho	200
Hockley Robt	100
Howard Peter	300
Hardgrove Wm	100
Herring Arthur	50
Hickman Thomas	700
Hunt Wm	312
Hobs Wm	250
Hicks Richd	250
Howden Wm	100
Howerton Thomas	300
	8098

Holt Joseph lives in Maryland	321
Mayward Tho in Glocester	600

J

Jones Tho	150
Jones Robt	200
Jeffrys Richd	337
Jones Robt Junr	130
Johnson James	200
Jones Wm	900
	1917

K

King John	150
Kallander Timo	100
Kink Anne	275
King Edwd	200
Knowles Dorothy Qr	150
King Robt	100
Kenniff Danby	100
King Daniell	200
	1335

L

Loveing John	100
Lyon Peter	250
Leigh John	6200
Lumpkin Robt	400
Lee Wm	230
Loob Wm	100
Loft Richd	320
Lewis Tachary	350
Lumpkin Jacob	950
Lewis David	120
Lewis John Esq	10100
Lewis Edwd	1400
Lemon Elizb	100
Lynes Rebecea	405
Levingstone John	600
Levingstone Samll	100
Lawrence Matthew	210
Letts Arthur	475
Langford John	150
Levingstone Jno Sowels Land	750
	23310

Leftwich Thomas in Essex	75

M

May John 300
Musick George 100
Major Jno 250
Martin John 300
More Austines Qr 200
May Tho 300
Moore Samll 100
Maddison Jno 500
Morris Wm 130
Martin Elizb 400
Mackay Sarah 177
May John Piggs Land 200
Major Francis 700
Mansfield Thomas 60
Morris Henry 100
Major John 400
Melo Nicho 200
Marcartee Daniell 200
Morris Wm 300
Mead Wm 100
Matthews Edwd 160
Martin Cordelia Wido 200

5377

N

Nelson Henry 440
Neal John 50
Nason Joshua 200
Norman Wm 300
Norris James 100

1090

O

Owen Ralph 120
Ogilvie Wm 300
Orrill Lawrence 290
Orrill Wm 500
Orsbourn Michaell 90
Overstreet James Qr 180
ditto at home 50

1530

P

Powell Robt 500
Prewitt Wm 200
Paine Bernard 130
Pomea Francis 100
Philip Charles 250
Pettitt Thomas 548
Pollard Robt 500
Pollard Wm 100
Phinkett Elizb 500
Pemberton Tho. 115
Pickles Tho 93
Potters Francis Wido Neals Land 100
Parks James 200
Purchase Geo Qr 580
Page Jno 100
Pritchett David 225
Pigg Henry 61
Page John Junr 300
Pigg Edwd 250
Phelps Tho 400
Pendleton Philip 300
Pendleto Henry 700
Pann John 200
Paytons quarts 500
Pigg John 100
Pamplin Robt 150
Pryor Christo 175
Paulin Elizb 175

7552

Pate John in Glocester 1000

Q

Quarles James 300
Quarles Dyley Zacha: Lewis Land 300

600

R

Richard Robt 300
Rings Quarter 1000
Robinson Daniel 100
Roger Giles 475
Rice Michaell 200
Richeson Tho 460
Richeson Elias 180
Read Elizb 550
Russell Alexandr Wyatts Land 400
Robinson Robt 980
Rowe John 100
Richards John 914
Richards Wm 400
Richards Oliver 250
Riddle Tho Reads Land 700
Roy Richd 1000
Ryley Elias 200

Rollings Peter	150
	8359
John the son of Robt Robinson hold, which nobody pays for	750

S

Sebrill John	130
Stone Mary	100
Smiths in Bristoll Qr	2800
Stone Jno	295
Stubbelfield Geo Qr	400
Scandland Denis	1470
Swinson Richd	170
Smith Christo	200
Smith Jno Cooper	273
Smith Alexander	275
Seamour Wm	268
Sones Tho	150
Shepard Jane	100
Southerland Danll	200
Shoot Tho	100
Shepheard Joseph	100
Shea Patrick	200
Southerland Danll	200
Smith Nicho	700
Sanders Nathll	200
Smith John Sawyer	80
Shuckelford Roger	250
Skelton John	100
Snell John	150
Simpio Charles	100
Sawrey John	113
Stringer Margt	175
Spencer Tho	300
Sykes Stephen	50
Smith Francis	100
Smith Richd	150
Sparks John	200
Surly Tho	100
Stapleton Tho	200
Story John	3000
Spencer Katherine	600
	14599
Shippath Sr Wm Which is not paid for	700
Stark Tho of London which is not paid for	920
Stubblefield Geo in Glocester	400
Smith Austin in Glocester	4000

T

Turner Richard	200
Todd Thomas Quarts	2300
Taylor James	4000
Toy Thomas	175
Taylor Danll	70
Thomas Rowland	610
Tunstall Tho	550
Todd Richd	1050
Towley John	200
Trice James	350
Tureman Ignatius	100
Turner Thomas	267
Thacker C. C.	1000
	10872

U

Vaughan Cornelius	500
Vize Nathll	100
Uttley John	200
	800

W

Wood James	800
Wilkinson John	100
Wright Tho	300
Watkins Wm	137
Wiltshier Joseph	60
Watkins Edwd	98
Watkins Philip	203
White Thomas	200
Walker John	6000
Wilson Benj Wyats Land	420
Wyat Richd	1843
Walton Thomas	200
Wyat John	530
Withy Thomas	50
Williams Thomas	200
Watts Tho	235
Ward Samll	160
Watkins Benj	60
Watkins Tho Junr	125
Williams Elizb	900
Waldin Samll	275
Ware Edwd	735
William John	125
Ware Vallentine	487
Willbourn Tho	250
Wildbore Wm	100
Ware Nicho	718
White Jerimiah	200

Whorein John	200
Wise Richd quarts	209
Walker John, Johnsons Land	1000
	16920
Wadlington Paul not paid for being	150

Y

York Matthew	100

A	2300
B	22535
C	12235
D	5618
E	3020
F	4355
G	6100
H	8098
J	1917
K	1335
L	23310
M	5377
N	1090
O	1530
P	7552
Q	600
R	8359
S	14599
T	10872
U	800
W	16920
Y	100
	158522

Lands returned not paid for

C	1000
F	300
H	920
L	75
P	1000
R	750
S	6020
W	150
	10215

Glocester Rent Roll

A Rent Roll in Petso Parish

Capt David Alexander	1050
James Amis	250
John Acre	100
Wm Armistead	430
Ralph Baker	150
Martha Brooken	600
Thomas Buckner	850
Samll Bernard	550
Wm Barnard	810
Richd Bailey	600
Mary Booker	100
Thomas Cook	350
Wm Crymes	400
Jno Cobson	100
Robt. Carter	1102
Wm Collone	400
Hannah Camell	100
Benj Clements	400
Jno Cleake	100
Wm Cook	135
Jno Coleman	200
Jno Day	400
Jerim Darnell	150
Jno Darnell	60
James Dudley	780
Richd Dudley	400
Thomas Dudley	200
Thomas Dixon	300
Jno Drument	80
Samll Fowler	150
Wm Fleming	600
Wido Forginson	150
Wm Fockner	180
Jno Grymes	1400
Susannah Grinley	200
Darcas Green	400
Jno Grout	300
Jno Harper	100
Wm Howard	300
Richd Hubard	100
Wm Hasford	500
Jno Hanes	150
Alextnder How	120
Richd Hill	70
Robt Hall	100
Richd Hull	250
Sanll Hawes	200
Stephen Johnson	150

Wm Jones for Northington	530
Glebe Land	127
Jno Kingson	400
Capt Edwd Lewis	1000
Richd Lee Esq	1140
Nicho Lewis orphen	350
Wm Milner	900
Richd Minor	250
Edwd Musgrove	100
Hayes an orphan	60
Elizb Mastin	360
Jno Mackwilliams	50
Robt Nettles	300
Wm Norman	150
Isaac Oliver	100
Dorothy Oliver	130
Jno Pritchett	850
Jno Pate	1100
Richd Price	600
Madm Porteus	500
Madm Page	550
Pobt Porteus	892
Guy Parish	100
Wm Roane	500
James Reynolls	200
George Robinson	300
John Royston	570
Thomas Read	2000
Wm Richards in Pamunkey	150
Jno Shackelford	280
Edward Symons	500
Nicho Smith	280
John Stubs	300
Thomas Sivepson	280
John Smith	1300
Augustin Smith	200
Augustin Smith Junr	500
Wm Starbridge	159
Wm Thornton Senr	525
Wm Thornton Junr	800
Wm Thurston	200
Wm Upshaw	490
Francis Wisdom	150
Thomas West	112
Thomas Whiting	450
George Williams	100
Conquest Wyatt	2200
Seth Wickins	50
Walter Waters	200
Jane Wothem	60
Robt Yard	450
Robt Hall	250
Wm Whittmore Desarted	150
Wm Parsons Orphen	100
Edwd Stephens	70
John Kelley Orphen	150
	41132

Tho Neale

Glocester Rent Roll

A Rent Roll of Kingston Parish

Rose Curtis	400
Robt Peyton	680
Richd Perrott	35
Henry Preston	1500
Sarah Green	200
Robt Cully	200
Thomas Hayes	140
Andrew Bell	128
Humphry Toy	1100
Anne Aldred	350
Dunkin Bahannah	113½
Richd Hunley	50
Capt Gayle	164
Math. Gayle Junr	250
James Hundley	100
John Hundley	130
Philip Hundley	660
Tho Cray	200
Hen. Knight	240
John Williams	50
Richd Beard	380
Timothy Hundley	300
Thomas Bedford	50
Jno Floyd	250
John Bohannah	113½
Capt Armistead	3675
Christopher Dixon	300
Robt Bristow Esqr	900
Edwd Gowing	100
Tho Ryland	272
John Nevill	100
Lawrence Parrott	340
Wm Brooks	720
Joseph Bohannah	148

Wm Hampton	348	Benj. Read	550
Widdo Green	150	Walter Keble	550
Capt Dudley	650	Joseph Brooks	500
Capt. Knowles	575	Capt. Gwin	1100
Capt. Tho. Todd	775	Lindseys Land	390
Wm Beard	100	Thomas Garwood	77
Wm. Tomkins	100	John Callie	1000
Henry Bolton	50	Tho. Miggs	100
Wm Eliott	1060	Richd Glascock	500
Humphrey Tompkins	100	Jno Lylley	584
Daniel Hunter	200	Geo. Billups	1200
Thomas Peyton	684	Robt. Singleton	650
Richd Dudley	350	James Foster	225
James Ransom Junr	310	John Andrews	50
Tho. Peters	30	Thomas Rice	34
Robt. Elliott	1247	John Martin	200
Mich. Parriett	100	Capt. Smith	550
Jno. Meachen Junr	600	Capt. Sterling	1100
Caleb Linsey	140	John Diggs	1200
Alexandr Ofield	23	Wm. Howlett	300
Mark Thomas	300	Jno. Miller	100
Jno. Garnet	250	Andrew Ripley	40
Wm. Plumer	510	Francis Jarvis	460
Wm. Brumley	750	Wm. Armistead	300
Wm. Credle	50	John Banister	650
Charles Jones	225	Tho. Plumer	400
Robt. Sadler	50	Isaac Plumer	200
Edwd Sadler	20	James Taylor	50
Geo Roberts	170	Edwd Borum	360
Richd Longest	600	Widdo Davis	300
Tho. Fliping	300	Sam. Singleton	300
Charles Watters	100	Wm. Morgan Senr	50
Wm. Grundy	200	Wm. Morgan Junr	200
Thomas Kemp	200	John Bacon	825
Tho. Allaman	842	Henry Singleton	600
Coll Kemp	200	John Edwards	534
Ralph Shipley	430	Patrick Berry	250
George Turner	50	Anne Forest	500
Coll. James Ransom	1400		
Thomas Putman	300		46537
Richd Marchant	180	Ambrose Dudley	
Widdo Sinoh	300	1705	
Christopher Rispue	200		

Glocester Rent Roll

A Rent Roll in Ware Parish

Thomas Poole	600	Simon Stubelfield	200
Anne Croxson	300	Jno. Price	600
Thomas Purnell	163	Saml. Vadrey	400
Nocholas Pamplin	210	Samll Dawson	350

Nathan: Burwell	600
John Dawson	780
Tho. Bacop	200
Robt. Francis	400
Walter Greswell	50
Tho. Read	400
James Shackelfield	35
Robt. Freeman	135
Jno. Marinex	100
Isaac Valine	100
Tho. Haywood	70
Hugh Marinex	50
Leonard Ambrose	200
Philip Grady	200
Capt. Wm. Debnam	1250
James Burton	100
Jno. Spinks	300
Wm. Hurst	200
Sarah More	67
John Ray	100
Robt. Pryor	300
Christo. Greenaway	270
Capt. Throgmorton	500
James Clark	250
Philip Cooper	200
Jno. Kindrick	100
Samll. Simons	120
Wm. Radford	200
John Robins	900
Alice Bates	200
Jno. Easter	350
James Davison	100
Robt. Morrin	200
Anne Bray	100
Grace Easter	200
Sampson Dorrell	300
Capt. Francis Willis	3000
Thomas Powell	460
Wm. Holland	300
Capt. Cook	1500
Giles Cook	140
Wm. Jones	120
Tho. Collis	100
Philip Smith	700
Tho. Cheesman	650
Geo. More	40
James Morris	250
Abraham Iveson Senr.	1000
Robert Bristow Esqr.	2050
Anthony Gregory	700
Richd. Bailey	800
Wm. Foulcher	100
Widdo. Jeffes	216
Richd. Dudley Junr.	300
John Buckner	900
Thomas Todd	884
John and Peter Waterfield	143
Henry Whiting	800
Madm. Whiting	950
Jno. Goodson	150
Wm. Morris	350
Mary Lassells	200
Peter Ransone	220
Charles Waters	200
Dorothy Kertch	220
Dorothy Boswell	1600
Richd. Cretendon	280
Elizb. Anniers	250
Elizb. Snelling	250
Joseph Boswell	230
John Bullard	100
Anthony Elliot	100
Wm. Armistead	100
Peter Kemp	650
Majr. Peter Beverley	800
Ditto per Tillids Lands	150
Dudley Jolley	100
Robt. Couch	100
	31603

Glocester Rent Roll

A Rent Roll of Abbington Parish

Mr. Guy Smith	30
James Cary	50
Wm. Sawyer	150
Edwd. Cary	100
Robt. Barlow	62
Tho. Cleaver Sworne	200
Edwd. Stevens	80
Henry Stevens	60
Chillion White	100
Jerimah Holt	350
of Ditto for the Widdo Babb	150
Robt. Yarbborrow	100
Robt. Starkey	100
Henry Seaton	170

Hugh Howard	200
Capt. Booker	1000
Jno. Stoakes	300
Jno. Dobson	400
Wm. Dobson	950
Edmd. Dobson	350
Hugh Allen	1250
George Jackson	117
Jno. Teagle	30
Widdo Jones	45
Mary Thomas	100
Thomas Seawell	200
Benj. Lane	50
Valentine Lane	80
Jeffry Garves	33
Thomas Coleman	250
Johanna Austin	40
Majr. Burwell	3300
Jno. Satterwight	50
Jerimiah Holt Junr.	150
Charles Stevens	75
Richd. Roberts for wife	300
Jno. Sadler	125
James Steavens	100
Susannah Stubbs	300
Richd. Foster	150
Henry Mitchell	50
Nathanll. Russell	550
Elizb. Richardson	500
Wm. Camp	175
James Row	300
John Butler	100
John Smith Esqr.	2000
Ditto for Robt. Byron	400
Capt. Blackbourne	550
Peter Richeson	250
Benja Clements	500
Thomas Graves	70
Robt. Page	75
Joseph More	150
Richard Dixon	200
Elizb. Turner	150
Owen Grathmee	250
Richd. Woodfolk	125
Jno. Waters	50
Wm. Hilliard	80
Richd. Heywood	100
Mary Hemingway	150
Wm. Kemp	75
Robt. Francis	104
Joshua Broadbent	200
Joseph Coleman	200
Grustam Clent	100
Philip Grady	150
Jno. Hall	125
Tho. Walker	300
Jno. Mixon	400
Tho. Sanders	450
Wm. Smith for Kittson	50
John Banister	2750
Madm. Mary Page	3000
Jno. Lewis Esq.	2000
	28426
Richd. Cordell	
Ware	31603
Petso	41123
Kingston	46537
	147698

A Perfect Role of the Land in Middlesex County Anno Dom. 1704

Richard Atwood	100
Richard Allin	150
Tho. Blewford	100
Mrs. Blaiss	300
John Bristow	140
Robt. Blackley	100
Coll Corbin	2260
Coll Carter	1150
John Cheedle	50
Wm. Carter	170
Widdo Chaney	800
Nath. Cranke	50
Tho. Dyatt	200
John Davie	75
Wm. Daniell	150
Robt. Daniell	225
Henry Freeman	200
John Goodrich	50
Geo. Goodloe	50
Geo Guest	50
Richd Gabriell	30
Wm. Finley	50
Wm. Gardner	100
Robt. George	180
David George	150
Widdo. Hazellwodd	200
John Hoare	100
Richd. Reynolds	50

Jno. Southerne	100
Richd. Shurly	200
Tho. Hapleton	200
Wm. Southworth	50
Wm. Jones	300
Evan Jones	50
Esqr. Wormley Estate	5200
Wm Churchhill	1950
Jacob Briston	100
Jno. Pace	200
John Logie	300
John Price	519
Henry Perrott	1100
Richd Kemp	1100
Tho Kidd	250
Francis Weeks	225
Widdo Weeks	225
Henry Webb	100
Tho Wood	70
Robt. Williamson	200
Tho Lee	100
Edmd. Mickleburrough	200
Valentine Mayo	100
Wm. Mountague	500
Garrett Minor	225
Marvill Mosseley	225
Joseph Mitcham	75
Minie Minor	225
Humphrey Jones	150
Jno. North	200
Henry Tugill	200
Henry Thacker	1875
Thomas Tozeley	500
Charles Moderas	100
Wm. Mullins	150
John Smith	700
James Smith	400
Harry Beverley	1000
George Wortham	400
Capt. Grimes	900
Sarah Mickleborough	1000
Christo. Robinson	4000
John Vibson	100
James Daniell	150
James Curtis	300
Tho. Cranke	54
Phil. Calvert	200
John Hipkins	100

Richd. Daniell	210
Geo. Blake	100
Edwd Williams	100
Pat Mammon	100
Alexander Murray	250
Poplar Smith	550
Olixer Seager	380
Edwd Gobbee	90
Henry Barnes	200
John Davis	100
Paul Thilman	300
Hugh Watts	80
Edwd Clark	300
Charles Williams	100
Edwin Thacker Estate	2500
Thomas Dudly	200
Thomas Mackhan	200
Richd. Paffitt	200
Tho. Hiff	100
Peter Bromell	100
Tho Blakey	100
John Robinson	1350
Roger Jones	100
John Nicholls	200
George Berwick	100
Widdo Hurford	50
Widdo Hackney	300
Wm. Kilbee	600
Ezikiah Rhodes	300
John Handiford	100
John Miller	200
Wm. Scarborow	200
Wm. Herne	75
Robt. Dudley	300
Widdo Mason	100
Peter Chilton	100
Francis Dobson	150
James Dudley	200
Capt. Berkley	750
Wm. Sutton	150
Sr. Wm. Skipwith	350
Coll Kemp	900
Wm. Barbee	150
Wm. Wallis	300
Adam Curtin	200
Capt. Wm Armistead	2325
	49008

A True & Perfect Rent Roll of all the Lands held in Essex County this present year 1704

Abbott Wm.	150
Andrews Geo	200
Adcock Edwd	230
Adcock Henry	250
Acres James	100
Arving Wm.	100
Allin Erasmus	100
Allin Wm.	100
Ayres Wm.	200
Acres Wm.	200
	1630
Baulwar James	800
Bendall John	135
Butler John	125
Bowers Arthur	600
Baulwar James	200
Beesley Wm.	100
Barron Andrew	50
Bartlett Tho.	100
Brown Buskinghan	400
Beeswell Robt.	100
Beeswell Robt. Junr.	150
Brown Wm.	420
Brown Charles	1000
Buckner Richd.	1200
Buckner Tho.	1000
Brice Henry	400
Bourn Jno.	100
Beverly Harry	1000
Battail John	1100
Baulwar John	50
Booth Widdo	800
Butler Jno.	100
Butcher Jno.	150
Bendrey Widdo	700
Bird Widdo	100
Beckham Symon	100
Brutnall Richd	100
Brook Robt.	400
Ball Jno.	150
Brooks James	100
Billington Mary	200
Brooks Peter	275
Bowman Peter	400
Brooks Robt.	150
Brasur Jno.	300
Brush Richd.	250
Baker Henry	350

Bradburn Richd.	100
Brown Francis	150
Brown Danll. Junr.	150
Bryom Henry	100
Burnett Tho. Junr.	1000
Baughan James Senr.	600
Baughan James	150
Baughan Henry	100
Brown Danll. Senr.	450
Brown Tho.	50
Blackiston Argail	200
Burnett John	365
Burnett Tho. Junr.	130
Bailer Jno.	800
Brakins Qrtr.	250
Bell Thomas	100
	19980
Condute Nathll.	20
Cary Hugh	50
Connoly Edwd.	200
Cogwell Fredirick	250
Copland Nicho.	300
Cattlett Jno.	1800
Covengton Richd.	1000
Cook John	112
Chew Larkin	300
Crow Tho.	300
Covington Wm.	400
Cheney John	200
Cole Wm.	200
Cheney Wm.	700
Corbin Tho. Qr	440
Cockin Tho.	120
Coates Samll	300
Cooper Richd.	100
Cooper Tho.	100
Copland Jno.	175
Crow Jno.	440
Chew Larkin	550
Cooper Wm.	50
Compton Wm.	50
Cox Wm.	500
Callaway Jos.	87
Coleman Robt.	450
Cobnall Symon	100
Chamberlain Leond.	350
	9764

Daniell James	100
Devillard Jacob	80
David Tho.	150
Dudding Andrew	230
Davis Evans	150
Dobbins Danll.	550
Dressall Timo.	175
Daughty John	200
Dyer Wm.	100
Daingerfield Jno.	270
Daingerfield Wm.	270
Dunn Wm.	220
Dyer Jeffrey	100
Day Richd.	100
Dicks Thomas	500
	12959
Evans Rice	200
Edmondson James	500
Elliott Alice	75
Evitt Tho.	100
Emondson Tho.	700
Flowers Isaac	250
Faulkner Nicho.	100
Farrell Charles	50
Franklin Nicho.	130
Foster Robt.	200
Foster Jno.	200
Fisher Jonathan	250
Fisher Benja.	150
Frank Tho.	175
Fullerton James	400
Fossett Wm.	100
Ferguson Jno.	150
Faulkner Edwd.	530
	17219
Green George	300
Gray Abner	350
Goulding Wm.	200
Gannock Wm.	2100
Gaines Barnerd	450
Griffin Tho.	200
Gibson Jonathan	700
Grigson Tho.	300
Gouldman Francis	300
Goulding John	200
Goulding Edwd.	380
Good Richd.	200
Garnett John	150
Glover John	100
Hawkins John	1066
Hinshaw Samll.	200
Hutson Tho.	100
Harrison James	400
Harrison Andrew	300
Hilliard Thomas	100
Harper Wm.	240
Harmon Henry	75
Hoult Richd.	100
Humphrie Joe	100
Hail Jno.	900
Harper John	748
Harper Tho.	350
Hould David	100
Hudson Wm.	100
Hinds Thomas	100
Howerton Thomas	175
Hodges Arth	100
Hows Qrtr	300
Harwood Peter	125
Harway Tho.	1000
Hudson Tho.	50
Hudson Wm.	300
Hill Leond.	300
Harwar Samll.	300
Jamison David	250
Jones Wm.	165
Jenkins David	50
Jewell Tho.	100
Johnson Widdo.	300
Jones Walter	100
Johnson Richd.	50
Johnson Wm.	650
Jones John	300
Jones Richd.	350
Jenkins John	93
Jones Wm.	300
Journey Wm.	243
Johnson Thomas	500
Jones Rice	500
Key Robt.	209
Kerby Henry	60
Landrum John	300
Landrum James	100
Long Richd.	300
Lomax John	2000
Loyd George	800
Lawson Claudy	100
Little Abraham	60
Lacy John	100
Law John	300
Lattaine Lewis	250
Leveritt Robt.	100
Micou Paul	150

Martin John	400
Morgain John	100
Miller John	150
Medor Tho.	300
Moseley Benja.	1100
Mottley John	100
Morris John	200
Moss Robt.	180
Merritt Tho.	124
Merritt John	100
Munday Tho.	500
Magcon David	400
Mice Hno.	200
Mosseley Robt.	100
Mayfield Robt.	100
Matthews Richd.	250
Moseley Edwd.	550
Merriweather Francis	3200
Mefflin Zach	400
Michaell Jno.	200
Merriweather Tho.	2100
Mefflin Lath	400
Medor John	100
Morse John	400
Matthews Benja.	200
Mountegue Wm.	850
Newbury Nathll.	200
Nixson Henry	500
North Wm	900
Newton Nicho.	100
Nightingall John	100
Osman James	300
Presser John	450
Poe Samll.	800
Pley Widdo.	800
Parker Jno.	250
Pitts Jon.	200
Piskell Jno.	300
Pain Jno.	135
Price Wm.	100
Peteras Tho.	200
Powell Honor	72
Powell Wm.	72
Powell Place	72
Powell Tho.	72
Payne Widdow	1000
Perkin Henry	300
Prichett Roger	167
Paggett Edmd.	700
Price John	1100
Pickett John	800
Perry Samll.	225
Price Wm.	100
Quarter Xtpher Robinson	2200
Quartr Tho. Corbin	4000
Qrtr Robt. Thomas	200
Quartr John Hay	1000
Quartr. Wm. Smith	3000
Quartr Gawen Corbin	2000
Quartr Peter Ransom	300
Quartr David Gwin	950
Quartr Wm. Upshaw	1000
Quartr Leversons	600
Quartr Tho Todd	550
Ridgdall John	300
Ramsey Tho.	550
Rowze Ralph	610
Rucker Peter	500
Rowze Edwd.	300
Royston John	1000
Roberts Edmd.	300
Rebs Henry	400
Reeves Joseph	200
Reeves James	200
Roberts John	50
Richardson Robt.	200
Reynolds James Senr.	500
Reynolds James	500
Ransom Peter	1200
Strange Jno.	100
Stepp Abra.	390
Samll. Antho.	300
Sail Cornelius	73
Salmon John	60
Spiers Jno.	160
Smith Wm.	150
Stokes Richd.	500
Smith Charles	3000
Sullenger Peter	400
Sales Widdo	1150
Shipley Jno.	200
Spearman Job	300
Smith Francis	500
Stallard Samll.	100
Ship Jos	350
Short Tho.	150
Scott Wm.	1100
Stogell Jno.	100
Stephens Jno.	100
Slaughter Phebe	352
Smith Jno.	75
Smith Jonas	100
Sanders John	300
Stanton Jno.	95
Shepherd Jeremiah	300
Smith Tho.	50

Shackelford Francis	300
Sthrashley Tho	200
Staners Tho	500
Snead Tho	950
Shackelford Henry	50
Thorp Widdo	400
Tinsley Tho.	111
Thacker Samll.	110
Tomlin Widdo	400
Taliaferro Francis	1300
Thornton Fran.	700
Tomlin Wm.	1600
Thomas John	100
Taliaferro Charles	300
Thomas Wm.	200
Taliaferro John	2000
Turner George	200
Tomlin Wm.	950
Trible Peter	100
Taylor Richd.	650
Tilley Matthew	200
Vanters Bartho	400
Virget Job	50
Vincent Vaus	450
Wakeland Wm.	100
Wood Tho.	50
Winslow Tho.	150
Winslow Henry	100
Williams John	450
Williams Wm.	100
Wilson David	50
Wilton Richd.	150
Wheeden Edwd.	50
Ward Widdo.	200
Whitehorn Widdo.	260
Wms. Emanuell	100
Watkins Thomas	400
Waters John	150
Webb James	200
Webb John	200
Wead Wm.	200
Wood Tho	300
Williamson Tho	100
Williamson Wm.	100
Williamson John	100
Webb Robert	375
Webb Isaac	200
Woodnatt Henry	300
Waginer John	400
Ward Geo.	350
Wheeler Tho	250
Young Wm.	1000
Young Giles	100
Muscoe Salvator	100
Moody John	150
Maguffe John	100
Brookins Quartr.	250
Smith Jno. Quartr	1000
Newton Henry	100
Newton Henry	175
Nowell Dall	400
Nowell Widdo	300
Garrett Tho	1000
Gould Price	200
Green Samll.	97
Gouldman Fran.	300
Gawdin Wm.	100
Grimmall Wm.	100
Gaitwood John	400
Games John	475
Samll. Thompson	1000
	140580

Lands held in the above said County the Rents not paid and held by the severall Gentlemen as followth vizt.

John Smith Esqr. of Glocester County	800
Wm. Buckner of Glocester by information	1500
Jno. Lightfoot Esqr. New Kent County	900
Jno. Bridgate in Engld.	700
Richd. Wyatt & Jno. Pettus of King & Queen Cty.	800
Wm. Berry of Richmond County	400

Richard Covington

Accomack Rent Roll

A

Alexander Richards	150
Arthur Upshot	2020
Antho. West	700
Ann Simkins	1000
Arthur Donas	100
Arnoll Harrison	630
Alex. Harrison	400

Alex. Bagwell	413
Anne Chase	200
Arthur Frame	500
Alexdr West	550
Abraham Lambedson	100
Alex Benstone	270
Anne Blake Widdo	120
Anne Bruxe	180
Ar. Arcade Welburn	1854
	9187

B

Burnell Niblett	100
Majr. Bennit Scarbrough	521
	621

C

Corneline Hermon	321
Christo Stokly	200
Charles Scarbrough	1000
Charles Leatherbeny	1100
Charles Bally	959½
Charles Pywell	150
Churchhil Darby	125
Charles Evill	550
Charles Champison	270
Christo Hodey	500
Cornelius Lofton	166
Charles Stockley	170
Charles Taylor	580
Catherine Gland	217
	6312½

D

Dorman Derby	225
Daniell Derby Senr.	300
Dorothy Littlehouse	250
David Watson	200
Delight Shield	300
Daniel Derby Junr	125
Daniel Harwood	100
Dennis Mores	200
Daniel Gore	3976
	5676

E

Coll Edmd Scarbrough	2000
Edwd Hitchins	170
Edwd Turner	750
Edwd Killam	720
Edmd Allin	200
Edwd Bagwell for Coll Wm. Custis	200
Edmd. Jones	800
Elizb. Tinley	200
Edwd Taylor	300
Edmd Tatham	200
Edmd Bally	800
Edmd Ayres	1000
Edwd. Miles	413
Elizb. Mellchop	210
Edwd. Bell	101
Edwd. More	500
Edwd. Gunter	600
Edwd Brotherton	600
Elias Blake	430
Edwd Robins	782
Edwd Bally	300
Elias Taylor	1500
Elizb. Wharton	200
Mrs. Elizb Scarbrough	4205
	17181

F

Mr. Francis Mackenny	5109
Francis Robts.	200
Francis Wainhouse	700
Francis Crofton	200
Francis Young	100
Finley MackWm	100
Francis Ayres	300
Francis Jester	200
Francis Benstone	400
Francis Wharton	600
	7909

G

Geo. Anthony	100
Geo. Hastup	300
Coll Geo Nicho Halk	2700
Capt. Geo Parker	2609
Gervis Baggally	700
Garrat Hictlims	170
Geo Parker Sco. Side	1200
Griffin Savage	650
Geo Middleton Senr	588
Geo Trevit	400
Geo. Pounce	400
Geo Middleton Junr	150
Geo Johnson	200

Capt. Geo Hope	900
	11067

H

Henry Armtrading	175
Henry Chance	445
Henry Selman	180
Henry Ubankes	400
Henry Lurton	363
Henry Stokes	208
Henry Custis	774
Henry Bagwell	412
Henry Read	350
Henry Ayres	250
Hill Drummond	483
Henry Toules	300
Henry Hickman	135
Henry Gibbins	250
Henry Truett	240
	4965

J

John Tounson	200
Joseph Stokley	664
Jno. Read	200
Jno. Blake	310
Joseph Ames	375
Joseph Clark	200
Jno. Fisher	200
James Gray	900
Jno. Huffington	240
Jno. Legatt	300
James Lary	100
James Longoe	200
Jno. Merrey	350
Jno Milloy	500
Jno. Pratt	50
Jno. Revell	1450
Jno Road	110
Jno. Rowles	650
Jno. Savage Senr	350
Jno Charles	480
Jno Willis Senr	430
Jno Willis Junr	350
James Fairfax	900
Joseph Milby	830
John West Junr	500
Jno Jenkins	400
Jonathan James	150
John Rodgers	100
Jno Collins	100
Jno Sincocke	125
Jno Metcalfe, Isaac Metcalfe and Samll. Metcalfe	600
Joseph Touser	200
Jno Stanton	200
Jno Bally	1000
	13715

Jno Melson	180
Jno Bernes Senr	657
Jno Littletone	200
John Nock	300
Jno Killy	100
Jacob Morris	200
Jno Morris	640
Jona. Aylworth	200
James Davis	1000
Jno Parkes	200
Jno Evans	200
Jno Hull	100
Jno Blocksom	700
Jno Abbott	1170
Jno Arew	234
Jno Grey	116
Jno Baker	400
Jno Wharton	150
James Taylor	100
Jno Glading	207
Jno Loftland	167
James Smith	756
Majr Jno Robins	2700
Jno Collins for Asban	1666
James Walker	525
Jno Whelton	90
Jno Marshall	1666
Jona Owen	230
Jacob Wagaman	150
Capt John Broadhurst	1100
Jno Dyer	200
Mr. John Watts	2450
Jno Booth	300
John Bradford	364
Ingold Cobb	150
Jno Griffin	150
Jno Mitchell	400
John Parker	970
James Alexander	1250
Jno Burocke	200
James Sterferar	50
Jno Perry	217
Jno Drummond	1550
Jno Carter on Foxs Island	203

Jno Warington	100
Jno Bagwell	465
Jno Wise Senr	800
Jno Wise Junr	400
Jno Dix	500
Isaac Dix	500
Jno Hickman	454
Jno Onians	200
Coll Jno Custis Esqr	5950
John Coslin	50
	46692

M

Michaell Recetts	300
Mrs. Mattilda West	3600
Marke Evell	250
Mary Wright	200
	4350

N

Nicholas Mellchops	285
Nathaniel Williams	64
Nathaniell Rattcliff	300
	649

O

Owen Collonell	500
Overton Mackwilliams	200
Obedience Pettman	115
	815

P

Peter Major	113
Philip Parker	150
Peter Rogers	167
Perry Leatherbury	1750
Peter Turlington	79
Peter Ease	250
Philip Fisher	433
Peter Chawell	250
	3192

R

Robt. Bell	650
Richd Bally Senr.	2100
Richd Bally Junr	180
Richd Garrison	468
Roules Major	157
Rouland Savage Senr	950
Robt. Taylor	95
Richd. Rodgers	450
Richd Killam	1900
Robt. Wattson	425
Richd Jones	500
Robt. Hutchinson	934
Reynold Badger	150
Robt. West	400
Richd Cuttler	450
Robt. Cole	125
Richd Drummond	600
Robt. Stocomb	300
Robt Norton	1050
Richd Grindall	350
Roger Hickman	135
Robt Lewis	200
Roger Abbott	450
Richard Hill	350
Ralph Justice	1050
Richd Hinman	1800
Robt Davis	384
Ragnall Aryes	300
Roger Miles	200
Richd Bundike	773
Richd Kittson	1300
Robt. Bally	100
Richd Starlin	150
Richd Flowers	200
Richd Price	100
Robt. Pitts	2300
Robt Adkins	200
Rebeckha Benstone	270
Richd Hillayres	300
	22816

S

Samuell Benstone	300
Sarah Beach	300
Sillvanus Cole	250
Symon Sosque	325
South Littleton Widdo	2870
Stephen Woltham	244
Steph. Warrington	400
Symon Mitchell	300
Stephen Drummond	300
Selby Harrison	50
Sollomon Evell	125
Samll Young	50
Sarah Reyley	150
Sebastian Dellistations Senr	500

Sebastian Dellistations Junr	400
Skinner Wollope	2485
Samll. Sandford	3250
Sebastian Silverthorn	150
Symon Smith	200
Sarah Coe	900
Samll Taylor	1232
Sarah Evins	150
Sebastian Croper	600
Samuell Jester	200
	15731

T

Tho Burton	600
Tho Bud	500
Tho Boules	300
Tho Clark	100
Tho Middleton	350
Tho Stringer	600
Tho Haule	500
Tho Taylor	100
Tho Fockes	300
Tho Bagwell	465
Madm Tabitha Hill	3600
Tho Rose	7
Tho Webb	50
Tho Savage	450
Tho Jones	100
Tho Scott	100
Tho Reyley	225
Tho Ternall	150
Tho Simpson	520
Tho Coper	711
Tho Miles	202
Thomas Bonwell	300
Tho Bell Senr.	100
The Bell Junr	100
Tho Touson Kiquotan	800
Tho Stockley	363
Tho Jester	100
Tho Smith	300
Thomas Crippin	648
Tho Wilkinson	50
Tho Jenkinson	374
Tho Moore	166
Tho Allen	700
Tho Smith Savannah	200
Tho Perry	232
Tho Tonnson	400
Tho Smith Gingateague ...	693
Lieut Coll Robinson	600
	15956

W

Wm. Robins	200
Wm Patterson	200
Wm Bevens	400
Wm Matthews	400
Wm Shepherd	200
Wm Whett	400
Winfred Woodland	333
Wm Andrews	300
Wm Custis	1500
Wm Darby	83
Wm Fletcher	200
Wm Killam	450
Wm Lingoe	300
Wm Major	130
Wm Meeres	150
Wm Mack Sear	800
Wm Savage	150
Wm Waite	110
Wm Sill	200
Wm Waite Junr	600
Wm Bradford	3500
Wm Rogers	200
Wm Wise	400
Wm Finey	800
Wm Consalvins	100
Wm Phillips	200
Wm Parker	362
Wm Cole	375
Wm Merill	150
Wm Johnson	150
Wm Lewis	150
Walter Hayes	130
Wm Chance	450
Wm Milby	250
Wm Nicholson	600
Wm Burton	500
Wm Willett	842
Wm Hudson	270
Wm Lewis	300
Wm Young	144
Wm Liechfield	154
Wm Bunting	150
Wm Nock Junr	400
Wm Lucas	300
Mary Mellechop	498
Wm Daniell	200
Wm Silverthorn	160
Wm Garman	475
Wm White	600
Wm Broadwater	500
Wm Taylor	100
Wm Williamson	600
Wm Brittingham	538

Wm. Benstone Jun.	270
Wm Dickson for Mr. Littleton	1050
Wm Waite Senr	225
Wm Taylor	1400
	24599
	196899½

Added to this Rent Roll the following Lands of which the Quit Rents may possibly be recovered tho the Owners live out of the Country Viz.

Jonas Jackson	500
Robt. Andrews	500
Joseph Morris	200
Robt. Meros	200
Hillory Stringer	950
Tho Fisher	133
Jno Fisher	133
Timo Coe	4100
David Hagard	130
	6846

An Account of what Land in Accomack County the owners whereof are not dwellers.

Tho Preson of Northampton	200
Geo Corbin Ditto	150
Joshua Fichett Ditto	200
Alexdr Merey Maryld	200
Tho Dent	500
Mr. Wm Kendalls orphans of Northampton County.	2850
Mr Hancock Lee dividing Creeks	4050
Richd Watters in Maryland	1057
Francis Lailor Northamp..	100
Obedience Johnson Qtrs...	300
Henry Smith at the Southerd	1000
Grattiance Michell North..	200
Matt. Tyson Southerd	300
Teagle Woltham Maryld..	200
Peter Waltham New Engld	200
Jno Waltham Maryld	200
	11707

Jno Wise Sheriff

The Rent Roll of Northampton County for the Year of our Lord God 1704

A

Andrews Robt.	300
Andrews Andrew	100
Addison John	350
Abdell Tho	125
Abdell Jno	200
Abdell Wm	125
Alligood John	300
Angell James	100
Alligood Henry	100

B

Bullock Geo	100
Boner Geo	150
Brown Tho	1862
Benthall Joseph Senr	793
Benthall Joseph Junr	150
Branson Francis	100
Bateson	200
Billot Jno	400
Bell Geo	400
Billott Wm	100
Brewer Jno	50
Blackson Jno	100
Brooks Jeane	100
Beadwine Jno	200
Berthall Danll	258
Baker John	400
Brickhouse Geo	2100

C

Cob Samll	130
Coape Wm	200
Custis Jno Coll	3400
Collier Bartho.	150
Carpenter Charles	240
Cox Jno	500
Church Samll	143
Cleg Jno. Senr	204
Clog Henry	204
Carvy Richd	100
Cowdry Josiah	167
Cormeck Mich	100
Clerk Jno	100

Corban Geo 250
Clerk Geo 833
Caple Nath 100
Callinett Jno 100
Crew John 300
Costin Francis 275
Custis Majr John 3250
Custis Hancock 50
Chick Tho. 100

Downing Jno. 70
Dewy Geo 300
Dewy Jacob 100
Delby Margery 450
Dowty Rowland 150
Dunton John 170
Dunton Tho 400
Dowman John 100
Dullock John 100
Denton Tho 400
Dunton Tho Junr 120
Dunton Wm 420
Dunton Benj 220
Duparks Tho 90
Davis Jno 850
Dunton Joseph 120
Dixon Michaell 460

E

Eshon Jno 600
Evans John 200
Edmunds David 500
Evans Tho 300
Esdoll Geo 100
Eyres Tho 1133
Eyres Nich 325
Eyres Capt Jno 774
Eyres Anne Wido. 733
Esdoll Edwd. 100

F

Fisher John 637½
Francisco Dan 150
Fisher Tho 637½
Foster Robt. 150
Fabin Paul 60
Frost Tho 100
Frank Jno 500
Floyd Charles 378
Freshwater Geo 200
Frizell Geo 140
Freshwater Wm 200
Fitchett Joshua 100
Floyd Berry & Matthew .. 555

G

Gogni David 150
Gill Robt. 200
Gascoyne Robt. 125
Gascoyne Wm 525
Greene Jno Senr 2200
Giddens Tho 227
Grice Peter 200
Godwin Devorix 600
Goffogan Tho 100
Guelding Charles 200
Griffith Jerimiah 345
Griffith Benja 200

H

Hill Francis 100
Henderson John 250
Haggaman Isaac 750
Harmonson Jno 1600
Harmonson Henry 1250
Hanby Charles 25
Hanby Richd 75
Hanby Danll 50
Hanby John 150
Harmonson Capt Wm 308
Harmonson Geo 1586
Harmonson Tho 400
Hawkins Jno Senr 66
Hawkins Jno Junr 66
Hawkins Gideon 66
Hunto Groton 485
Hunt John 440
Hunt Tho 290
Hall Francis Widdo 340

J

Johnson John Senr 250
Johnson John Junr 100
Johnson Jacob 350
Isaacs John Jnr 100
Joynes Major 150
James Joan Widdo 250
Johnson Obedience Capt ... 400
Johnson Tho Junr 75
Johnson Thomas Senr ... 400
Jackson Jonah & John 625
Joynes Edmd 200
Joynes Edwd 200
Johnson Jeptha Senr 50

Jacob Phillip Senr	350
Johnson Jepha Junr	200
Johnson Obedience & Jepha Sen	250
Johnson Edmd	400
Jacob Richd	200
Jacob Abraham	50

K

Kendall Wm	2410
Knight John	100

L

Lawrence John	120
Lailler Luke	100
Lucas Tho	100
Lewis Robt	100
Littleton Susannah Wido.	4050
Luke John	400

M

Marshall Geo	250
Farshall Jno	250
Maddox Tho	1500
Michaell Yeardly	400
Matthews John	275
Major John	390
Map John	50
Moore Matthew	175
Mackmellion Tho	300
More Gilbert	225
Morraine John	119½
More Jno	545
More Eliner	175

N

Nicholson Wm	600
Nottingham Wm	150
Nottingham Joseph	150
Nottingham Richd	350
Nottingham Benja	300
Nelson John	100

O

Only Clement	200
Odear John	100

P

Parramore Tho	400
Preson Tho	610
Powell Frances Widdo	1225
Palmer Samll	1562
Pyke Henry	150
Powell John	636⅓
Pittett Tho	300
Pittet Justian	200
Pittett John	275
Powell Samll	200
Paine Daniell	150
Piggott Ralph	1368

R

Read Thomas	150
Rascow Arthur	100
Ronan Wm	150
Roberts Jno	200
Richards Lettis	150
Robins Jno Majr	1180
Robins Littleton	1000
Rabishaw Wm	55
Roberts Obedience	260
Robinson Benjamin	250

S

Shepherd Jno	200
Smith Joseph	250
Smith Samll	150
Smith Jno	200
Savage Tho	450
Smith Tho	400
Smith Abrah	300
Seady Antho	120
Sott Widdo	750
Smith Richd minor	300
Scot Geo	100
Smith Richd	99
Scot Jno	100
Scott Henry	800
Scot David	300
Smith Peter	450
Sanders Richd	100
Smaro John	800
Shepherd Tho	140
Sanders Eustick	100
Sanderson John	636
Savidge John	410
Stringer Hillary	1250
Savidge Capt Tho	1600
Savidge Elkington	750
Scot Wm Senr	153
Straton Benja	745
Smith Geo	133
Stockley Jno Senr	370
Shepheard Widdo	830
Seamore John	200

T

Tilney John	350
Tryfort Barth	147
Teague Simeon	100
Turner Richd	50
Teague Tho	200
Tankard Wm	450
Tanner Paul	148

W

Webb Henry	100
Wills Thorn	300
White John	400
Wilson Tho	250
Westerhouse Adryan Senr.	200
Walker John	300
Ward Tho	120
Walter John	400
Waterfield Wm	200
Warren John	525
Warren Argoll	350
Widgeon Robt	100
Wilkins Jno	150
Webb Edwd	200
Wilcock Jno	200
Warren James	50
Waterson Wm	855
Warren Robt.	190
Water Lieut-Coll Wm	700
Webb Charles	133¼
Willett Wms	2650
Waterson Richd	150
Wilkins Argoll	150
Walter Elizb Widdo	100
Warren Joseph	50
	99671

Lands not paid for vizt

Gleab formerly Capt Foxcrofts	1500
John Majr at Occahannock	200
Hogbin not being in Virginia	100
Tho Smith	300
Tho Marshall orphan	75
Jno Rews not in Virginia	100
	2275

The total on the other side is	99671 acres	
Added to it ye Glebe land	1500	
	101171 acres	

The preceding Sheets are true copys of the Rentrolls for the year 1704 given in and accounted for by the several Sherifs in April 1705 and sworne to before his Excellcy according to which they made up their accounts of the Quitrents with

Will Robertson Clerk.

INDEX

INDEX

VIRGINIA UNDER THE STUARTS

VIRGINIA UNDER THE STUARTS

1607-1688

BY

THOMAS J. WERTENBAKER, Ph.D.

VIRGINIA UNDER THE STUARTS

Dedicated

to my mother

PREFACE

It was in May, 1910, that the author came to Princeton for an interview with President Woodrow Wilson concerning an appointment as Instructor in the Department of History, Politics, and Economics. He was elated when President Wilson engaged him, though not happy over the $1,000 salary. Yet with this sum to fall back on he borrowed $200, and took a trip to England.

In London he went treasure hunting, the treasure of old documents relating to the history of colonial Virginia. He sought out the British Public Record Office, off Chauncery Lane, and was soon immersed in the mass of letters, official reports, journal of the Assembly, and other papers.

The author was prepared to find valuable historical materials in London, for he had spent the summer of 1908 studying the William Noel Sainsbury and the McDonald abstracts and transcripts of the documents in the Record Office deposited in the Virginia State Library. But he was staggered at the extent of the manuscript collection on Virginia history alone. Among the scores of volumes are thirty-two devoted to the correspondence of the Board of Trade, seventeen to the correspondence of the Secretary of State, twenty-two to entry books, letters, commissions, warrants, etc.

When the summer waned he left for America taking with him many pages of closely written notes. But what he had learned served to whet his appetite for more, so that in 1912 and again in 1914 he was back, going over volume after volume, searching eagerly for fear some important point would escape him. The mass of abstracts and notes which he accumulated formed the basis of this volume .

In fact, any political history of Virginia in the colonial period must be based on the documents in the Public Record

Office, since most of the copies left in Virginia have been lost or destroyed. Today, however, colonial historians no longer have to visit London to consult them, since transcripts have been made and deposited in the Library of Congress.

In recent years the American Council of Learned Societies has made available other collections of manuscripts which have thrown new light on early Virginia history. The most important of these are the Coventry Papers at Longleat, the residence of the Marquess of Bath. Many of the letters deal with Bacon's Rebellion, and include the correspondence between Berkeley and Bacon, accounts of the Indian war, complaints of the misgovernment of Berkeley, the account of the evacuation of Jamestown written by Berkeley, accounts of Bacon's death and the collapse of the rebellion.

This new material adds new weight to the conclusions reached in this book—that the causes of Bacon's Rebellion were deep-seated, that it grew out of the discontent caused by the Navigation Acts, the heavy taxes, the corrupting of the Assembly by Berkeley, and the misuse of the courts. It in no way shakes the conviction expressed by Thomas Mathews, who himself was involved in the rebellion, that the Indian war was the excuse for it rather than the cause.

Yet certain recent historians have contended that this violent uprising was not a protest against injustice and misgovernment. One has gone so far as to call it merely a quarrel between a rash young man and an old fool. We could with equal justice call the American Revolution just a quarrel between George Washington and George III. Mathews tells us that it was the general opinion in Virginia at the time that it was not Bacon who was chiefly responsible for the uprising, but Thomas Lawrence. Bacon "was too young, too much a stranger there, and of a disposition too precipitate to manage things to that length they were carried," he pointed out, "had not thoughtful Mr. Lawrence been at the bottom."

But neither Lawrence's hatred of Berkeley, nor Bacon's rashness, nor Berkeley's folly, nor the Indian war suffice to explain the rebellion. When the news of the uprising reached Charles II, he thought it past belief that "so considerable body of men, without the least grievance or oppression, should rise up in arms and overthrow the government". He was quite right. Had there been no grievances and oppression there would have been no uprising.

That Bacon's Rebellion is explained in part by poverty and suffering is clear. Philip Ludwell said that the rebel army was composed of men "whose condition . . . was such that a change could not make worse." The men who fought so valiantly against the Indians and Berkeley's forces, braved the King's anger, faced death on the gallows were called in contempt "the bases of the people," "the rabble," the "scum of the people," "idle and poor people," "rag, tag, and bobtail." The Council reported that there were "hardly two amongst them" who owned estates, or were persons of reputation. Berkeley complained that his was a miserable task to govern a people "where six parts of seven at least are poor, indebted, discontented, and armed."

So when Bacon sent out his agents to every part of Virginia to denounce the governor for not permitting an election for a new Assembly, accusing him of misgovernment, and complaining of the heavy and unequal taxes, they "infested the whole country." Berkeley stated that the contaigion spread "like a train of powder." Never before was there "so great a madness as this base people are generally seized with." When, in panic, he dissolved the Long Assembly and called for a new election, all except eight of those chosen were pro-Bacon men.

One cannot but ask why. Surely the voters would not have sided with this young man who had been in Virginia but a few months had he not taken the lead in protesting against the many wrongs to which they had been subjected. And had those who rushed to arms, risking their property, if not their necks, done so merely because of a quarrel between Bacon and Berkeley, they would have been more than base, they would have been fools.

What these wrongs were Bacon and his followers tell us in what they called the Declaration of the People. Berkeley and his favorites they denounced "for having upon specious pretences of public works raised great unjust taxes upon the commonalty for the advancement of private favorites and other sinister ends . . . ; for having abused and rendered contemptible the magistrates of justice, by advancing to places of judicature scandalous and ignorant favorites . . . ."

In a burning manifesto, denouncing the injustice and corruption of the ruling group, Bacon said: "We appeal to the country itself what and of what nature their oppressions have been, and by what cabal and mystery the design of many of those whom we call great men have been transacted and carried on . . . . See what sponges have sucked up the public wealth and whether it hath not been privately contrived away by unworthy favorites, by vile juggling parasites, whose tottering fortunes have been repaired and supported by the charge." The constant breach of laws, unjust prosecutions, excuses, and evasions, proved that the men in power were conducting public affairs "as if it were but to play a booty, game, or divide a spoil."

In view of these statements recent attempts to prove that Bacon was no true patriot and not interested in righting the people's wrongs seem strange indeed. It is hardly credible that he was merely pretending when he wrote these fiery words, that he posed as the champion of the people to further his personal ambitions, that he trumped up charges against Berkeley because of the disagreement over the Indian war.

But, it has been said, Bacon showed no interest in the passage of the reform laws enacted by the Assembly of June 1676, refused to have them read before his army, and complained that the Burgesses had not lived up to his expectations. Had he been really interested in reform, would he not have gloried in these laws and have praised the Assembly for passing them?

Any such conclusion falls flat when we consider the conditions under which this session was held. The Burgesses had hardly taken their seats when Bacon, who had been elected as one of the members to represent Henrico County, was captured. Though Berkeley pardoned him and restored him to his seat in the Council, he was a virtual prisoner during the first few days of the session. So he looked on with growing resentment as the governor overawed the Burgesses and reform measures were set aside.

Then, suddenly, the entire situation changed. Bacon got permission to return to Henrico because his wife was ill. Once there he placed himself at the head of his army of enraged frontiersmen and marched rapidly on Jamestown. When this news reached the little capital, the governor, his Council, and the Burgesses were panic stricken. Since resistance was useless, every thought was of appeasement. A series of reform laws, which struck at the very roots of Berkeley's system of rule through placemen, was introduced in the Assembly, rushed through, and signed by the governor.

Not knowing what had happened during his absence, on his arrival Bacon mounted the steps to the Long Room of the State House where the Assembly met, to urge them to right the people's wrongs. Thomas Mathews, who was present, says that "he pressed hard, nigh an hour's harangue on preserving our lives from the Indians, inspecting the revenues, the exorbitant taxes, and redressing the grievances and calamities of that deplorable country." It was only when he had finished that someone spoke up to tell him that "they had already redressed their grievances." To contend that Bacon was not interested in laws which he himself had so passionately urged and which had obviously been passed to conciliate him and his followers is merely to attempt to disprove the obvious.

Philip A. Bruce, in a statement published in 1893, in the *Virginia Magazine of History and Biography,* points out that Bacon's Rebellion "preceded the American Revolution by a century, an event which it resembled in its spirit, if not in its causes and results. Bacon is known in history as the Rebel, but the fuller information which we have now as to the motives of his conduct shows that he can with more justice be described as Bacon the Patriot. He headed a powerful popular movement in which the sovereignty of the people was for the first time relied upon on American soil by a great leader as the justification of his acts. The spirit breathing through the Declaration of the People is the spirit of the Declaration of Independence." Nothing which has been brought out in the sixty-four years since Dr. Bruce wrote these words has shaken or can shake their truth. Bacon was the torchbearer of the Revolution.

Attempts to defend Sir John Harvey are as unconvincing as those to belittle Bacon. Certainly the Sackville Papers, recently made available to historians, contain nothing to warrant any change in the conclusion, long accepted by Virginia historians, that Harvey's expulsion was richly deserved.

Charles Campbell, in his *History of the Colony and Ancient Dominion of Virginia,* thus describes Harvey's administration: "He was extortionate, proud, unjust, and arbitrary; he issued proclamations in derogation of the legislative powers of the Assembly; assessed, levied, held, and disbursed the colonial revenue without check or responsibility; transplanted into Virginia exotic English statutes; multiplied penalties and exactions and appropriated fines to his own use; he added the decrees of the court of high commission of England to the ecclesiastical constitutions of Virginia." Could we have a more perfect description of a despot?

It remains to point out a few errors which crept into the original manuscript. On page 21 "the falls of the Appomattox" should be "the first bend of the Appomattox; on page 75 "John Pott" should be "Francis Pott"; on page 82 "Matthew Kemp" should be "Richard Kemp".

Princeton, New Jersey THOMAS J. WERTENBAKER
August, 1957

CONTENTS

ABBREVIATIONS USED IN NOTES

Arb. Smith, *Works of Captain John Smith,* Edward Arber.

Scobell, *Scobell's Collection of Acts and Ordinances of General Use.*

F. R., *The First Republic in America,* Alexander Brown.

Gen., *The Genesis of the United States,* Alexander Brown.

Force, *Tracts and Other Papers Relating to the Colonies in North America,* Peter Force.

Nar. of Va., *Narratives of Early Virginia,* Lyon G. Tyler.

Va. Car., *Virginia Carolorum,* E. D. Neill.

Hen., *The Statutes at Large,* W. W. Hening.

Proceedings of Va. Co., *Proceedings of the Virginia Company of London.*

Cradle of Rep., *The Cradle of the Republic,* Lyon G. Tyler.

Bruce, Inst. Hist., *Institutional History of Virginia in the Seventeenth Century,* P. A. Bruce.

Bruce, Ec. Hist., *Economic History of Virginia in the Seventeenth Century,* P. A. Bruce.

Miller, *The Legislature of the Province of Virginia,* E. I. Miller.

P. R. O., British Public Record Office.

Stith, *History of Virginia,* William Stith.

Osg., *American Colonies in the Seventeenth Century,* H. L. Osgood.

Neill, Va. Co., *History of the Virginia Company of London,* E. D. Neill.

Fiske, Old Va., *Old Virginia and her Neighbors,* John Fiske.

Burk, *History of Virginia,* John Burk.

Va. Hist. Reg., *Virginia Historical Register.*

Beverley, *History of Virginia,* Robert Beverley.

Va. Mag., *Virginia Magazine of History and Biography.*

Wise, *The Early History of the Eastern Shore of Virginia,* J. C. Wise.

Southern Lit. Mess., *Southern Literary Messenger.*

Campbell, *History of Virginia,* Charles Campbell.

McD., *McDonald Papers,* Virginia State Library.

Jour. H. of B., *Journals of the House of Burgesses.* Manuscript copies in the Virginia State Library.

Justice in Virginia, *Justice in Colonial Virginia,* O. P. Chitwood.

Sains., *Sainsbury Papers,* Virginia State Library.

Mass. S. IV., *Massachusetts Historical Collections, Series IV.*

T. M., *The Beginning, Progress and Conclusion of Bacon's Rebellion.*

W. & M. Q., *William and Mary Quarterly.*

Inds' Pros., *Indians' Proceedings.*

Bac's Pros., *Bacon's Proceedings.*

Ing's Pros., *Ingram's Proceedings.*

Cotton, *Our Late Troubles in Virginia,* Mrs. A. Cotton.

Va. Vet., *Virginia Vetusta,* E. D. Neill.

CHAPTER I

The Founding of Virginia

In December, 1606, three little vessels—the *Sarah Constant,* the *Discovery* and the *Goodspeed*—set sail from England under Captain Christopher Newport, for the distant shores of Virginia.[1] After a long and dangerous voyage across the Atlantic the fleet, on the sixth of May, 1607, entered the Chesapeake Bay.[2] The adventurers spent several days exploring this great body of water, landing parties to investigate the nature of the shores, and to visit the Indian tribes that inhabited them. They were delighted with the "faire meddowes, . . . full of flowers of divers kinds and colours", and with the "goodly tall trees" of the forests with "Fresh-waters running" between, but they had instructions not to settle near the coast, lest they should fall victims to the Spaniards.[3] So they entered the broad mouth of a river which they called the James, and made their way cautiously up into the country. On the twenty-third of May they found a peninsula in the river, which afforded a convenient landing place and was easy to defend, both from the Indians and the Spaniards. This place they called Jamestown. Landing their men, they set immediately to work building houses and erecting fortifications. Thus did the English begin their first permanent settlement in the New World.

The bold band of adventurers that came thus hopefully into this beautiful and smiling country little realized that before them lay only dangers and misfortunes. Could they have foreseen the terrible obstacles to founding a colony in this land, they would have hesitated before entering upon the enterprise.

Four things conspired to bring misfortune and disaster upon

[1] F. R., pp. 21, 22. [2] F. R., p. 23.
[3] Arb. Smith, lxi-lxii.

Virginia. The form of government prescribed by the King and the Company was unsuited to the infant settlement, and its defects kept the colonists for many months in turmoil and disorder. The Indians proved a constant source of danger, for they were tireless in cutting off stragglers, ambushing small parties and in destroying the crops of the white men. Famines came at frequent intervals to weaken the colonists and add to their misfortunes. But by far the most terrible scourge was the "sicknesse" that swept over Virginia year after year, leaving in its wake horrible suffering and devastation.

The charter that James I granted to the London Company served as a constitution for Virginia, for it prescribed the form of government and made regulations that none could disregard. It provided for a Council, resident in England, to which was assigned the management of the colony and the supervision of its government.[4] This body was appointed by the King and was strictly answerable to him through the Privy Council for its every act.[5] The immediate government of the colony was entrusted to a local Council, selected by the Council in England, and responsible to it. The Virginia Council exercised extraordinary powers, assuming all administrative, legislative and judicial functions, and being in no way restrained by the wishes or demands of their fellow colonists.[6] Although they were restricted by the charter and by the instructions of the Council in England, the isolation of the settlement and the turbulent spirit of the adventurers made them reckless in enforcing their own will upon the colonists. More than once they were guilty of unpardonable harshness and cruelty.

The charter did not provide for the appointment of a Governor. The nominal leadership of the colony was entrusted to a President, chosen by the local Council from among its members. This officer had no duty distinct from that of the Councillors, other than to preside at their meetings and to cast a double or deciding vote in case of deadlock.[7] He

[4] Gen., p. 55.

[5] Gen., p. 56

[6] Gen., pp. 55, 70, 73.

[7] Gen., p. 77.

was to serve but one year and if at any time his administration proved unsatisfactory to his colleagues, they could, by a majority vote, depose him. In like manner, any Councillor that had become obnoxious could be expelled without specific charges and without trial.[8] These unwise provisions led naturally to disorder and strife, and added much to the misfortunes of the infant colony.[9]

The selections for the Council were made some days before the fleet sailed, but the Company, fearing a conflict of authority during the voyage, thought it best that they should be kept secret until the colonists had reached Virginia. The names of the appointees were embodied in "several instruments" which were entrusted to the commanders of the vessels, with instructions that they should be opened within twenty-four hours after they had arrived off the coast of America.[10] Upon entering the Chesapeake Bay the adventurers read the papers, and found that Christopher Newport, the commander of the fleet, Edward Wingfield, Bartholomew Gosnold, George Kendall, John Ratcliffe, John Martin and John Smith were those that had been chosen.[11]

After the landing the Council met, were sworn to office, and then elected Wingfield President.[12] Captain John Smith, who had been accused of mutiny during the voyage, was not allowed to take his seat, and was kept under restraint until the twentieth of June.[13]

Hardly had the founding of Jamestown been effected when the weakness of the constitution became apparent. The meetings of the Council were discordant and stormy. The mem-

[8] Gen., p. 67.

[9] Gen., pp. 342, 411.

[10] Gen., p. 77.

[11] Arb. Smith, p. 91.

[12] Arb. Smith, p. 91.

[13] Arb. Smith, p. 91; F. R., pp. 27, 32. Smith denied the justice of these charges. "Now Captaine Smith, who all this time from their departure from the Canaries, was restrained as a prisoner, upon the scandalous suggestions of some of the chiefe (envying his repute); who fained he intended to ursurpe the government, murder the Councell, and make himself king; that his confederats were dispearsed in all the three ships, and that divers of his confederats that revealed it, would affirme it: for this he was committed." Arb. Smith, p. 92.

bers were utterly unable to act with vigor and determination, or to agree upon any settled course of action in establishing the little colony. The President, because of the limitation of his powers, could do nothing to restore harmony or to enforce his own wishes and policies. Confusion and mismanagement resulted. In less than a month after the first landing the inefficiency of the government had created such discontent that the colonists petitioned the Council for redress.[14] It was only the tact and moderation of Captain Newport that appeased the anger of the settlers and persuaded them to submit to the decrees of the governing body.[15]

On the second of July, Newport, with his little fleet, sailed for England, leaving the ill-fated colonists to their own resources.[16] No sooner had he gone than the spirit of discord reappeared. The quarrels within the Council became more violent than ever, and soon resulted in the complete disruption of that body. Captain Kendall, who seems to have been active in fomenting ill feeling among his colleagues, was the first to be expelled. Upon the charge of exciting discord he was deprived of his seat and committed to prison.[17]

As Captain John Smith had, before the departure of Newport, been allowed to take his place in the Council, there were now five members of that body. The number was soon reduced to four by the death of Captain Gosnold, who fell a victim to the sickness.[18] One would imagine that the Council, thus depleted, would have succeeded in governing the colony in peace, but the settlers were given no respite from their wrangling and disputes. In September, Ratcliffe, Smith and Martin entered into an agreement to depose President Wingfield and to oust him from the Council. Before they proceeded against him, however, they pledged each other that the expulsions should then stop, and that no one of the three should be attacked by the other two.

The Councillors then appeared before Wingfield's tent with a warrant, "subscribed under their handes, to depose the

[14] Arb. Smith, liii.

[15] Arb. Smith, liv.

[16] F. R., p. 39.

[17] Arb. Smith, lxxvii.

[18] Arb. Smith, lxxvi.

President; sayeing they thought him very unworthy to be eyther President or of the Councell, and therefore discharged him of both".[19] They accused him of misappropriating funds, of improper division of the public stores, of being an atheist, of plotting to desert Virginia in the pinnace left at Jamestown by Captain Newport, of combining with the Spaniards for the destruction of the colony. Wingfield, when he returned to England, made a vigorous defense of his conduct, but it is now impossible to determine whether or not he was justly accused. After his expulsion from office, he was summoned before the court by the remnant of the Council to answer these numerous charges. It might have gone hard with him, had he not demanded a hearing before the King. As his enemies feared to deny him this privilege, they closed the court, and committed him to prison on board the pinnace, where he was kept until means were at hand to send him to England.[20]

The removal of the President did not bring peace to the colony. If we may believe the testimony of Wingfield, the triumvirate that now held sway ruled the settlers with a harsh and odious tyranny. "Wear," he says, "this whipping, lawing, beating, and hanging, in Virginia, known in England, I fear it would drive many well affected myndes from this honourable action."[21] One day Ratcliffe, who had been chosen to succeed Wingfield, became embroiled with James Read, the smith. Read forgot the respect due his superior, and struck the new President. So heinous a crime was this affront to the dignity of the chief officer of the infant colony, that the smith was brought to trial, convicted and sentenced to be hanged. But he saved his life, upon the very eve of his execution, by revealing to Ratcliffe a plot against the government, headed, he declared, by Captain Kendall.[22] Immediately Kendall, who had long been an object of suspicion, was tried for mutiny, found guilty and executed.[23]

In December, 1607, when the colony was suffering severely for the want of food, Captain Smith led an expedition into the

[19] Arb. Smith, lxxix.

[20] Arb. Smith, lxxxi.

[21] Arb. Smith, lxxxiv.

[22] Arb. Smith, lxxxiv.

[23] Arb. Smith, lxxxv.

territory of the Chickahominies in quest of corn.[24] During his absence the President, despite the protests of Martin, admitted Captain Gabriel Archer to the Council.[25] Archer, who seems to have been a bitter enemy of Smith, had no sooner attained this place of power, than he set to work to ruin the adventurous captain. "Being settled in his authority", he "sought to call Master Smythes lief in question, and . . . indicted him upon a Chapter in Leviticus for the death" of two men under his charge, that had been murdered by the Indians. He was to have had his trial upon the very day of his return from his thrilling adventures with the savages. His conviction and immediate execution would doubtless have resulted, had not the proceedings against him been interrupted by the arrival of the First Supply from England.[26] Captain Newport, whose influence seems always to have been exerted in favor of moderation and harmony, persuaded the Council to drop the charges against Smith, to release him from restraint, and to restore him to his seat in the Council.

Of extraordinary interest is the assertion of Wingfield that the arrival of the fleet "prevented a Parliament, which ye newe Counsailour (Archer) intended thear to summon".[27] It is not surprising that the settlers, disgusted as they were with the violence and harshness of their rulers, should have wished to share in the government. But we cannot but wonder at their boldness in attempting to set aside the constitution given them by the King and the Company. Had they succeeded in establishing direct government by the people, it could not be supposed that James would have permitted it to continue. But the attempt is very significant, as indicating that they were desirous, even at this early date, of having a voice in the management of affairs.

Archer and the unfortunate Wingfield sailed with the fleet when Captain Newport returned to England, and a few months later Martin followed them.[28] Since, with the First

[24] Arb. Smith, lxxxv.
[25] F. R., p. 54.
[26] Arb. Smith, lxxxvi.
[27] Arb. Smith, lxxxvi.
[28] F. R., p. 58.

Supply had come a new Councillor, Matthew Scrivener, the governing body once more numbered three.

During the summer of 1608 Smith was frequently away, chasing the phantom of the passage to the South Sea, but this did not prevent the usual quarrels. If we may believe the account in Smith's history, Ratcliffe was deposed from the Presidency because of "pride and unreasonable needlesse cruelty" and for wasting the public stores.[29] It is probable that for some weeks Scrivener conducted the government, while Ratcliffe was kept a prisoner.[30] In September, Captain Smith, returning from a voyage in the Chesapeake Bay, "received the letters patents, and took upon him the place of president".[31]

Smith was now supreme in the government, for the Council was reduced to two, and his casting vote made his will superior to that of Scrivener. But he was not long to enjoy this power. In October, 1608, Captain Newport, arriving with the Second Supply, brought with him two "antient souldiers and valient gentlemen"—Richard Waldo and Peter Wynne—both bearing commissions as Councillors.[32] Soon afterward Ratcliffe was restored to his seat. The Council, thus recruited, resumed its control over the colony, "so that although Smith was President yet the Council had the authority, and ruled it as they listed".[33]

Two months later, when Newport sailed again, Ratcliffe returned to England. Smith wrote the English Council, "Captaine Ratcliffe is . . . a poore counterfeited Imposture. I have sent you him home, least the company should cut his throat."[34] The next spring Waldo and Scrivener, with nine others, were caught in a small boat upon the James by a violent gale, and were drowned.[35] As Captain Wynne soon succumbed to the sickness, Smith became the sole surviving Councillor.[36] During the summer of 1609 the colony was governed, not, as the King and Company had designed, by a Council, but by the will of this one man.

[29] Arb. Smith, pp. 114, 115.

[30] Arb. Smith, p. 119.

[31] Arb. Smith, p. 121; F. R., p. 61.

[32] F. R., p. 68; Arb. Smith, p. 122.

[33] Arb. Smith, p. 122.

[34] Arb. Smith., p. 444.

[35] F. R., 70.

[36] F. R., 71.

In the meanwhile the London Company was becoming aware that a mistake had been made in entrusting the government of the colony to a body of Councillors. The reports of Wingfield, Archer, Newport and Ratcliffe made it evident that the lack of harmony in the Council had been a serious hindrance to the success of the enterprise.[37] Feeling, therefore, that this "error in the equality of the governors . . . had a little shaken so tender a body", the managers held an especial meeting to effect a change.[38] A new charter was drawn up by Sir Edwin Sandys, approved by the Company and assented to by the King.

In this document James relinquished into the hands of the Company not only the direct management of the colony, but the power of drawing up a new and more satisfactory system of government. Acting under this authority, Sandys and his associates abolished the Council and entrusted the entire control of the colony to an all-powerful Governor. The disorder that had so impeded the success of the enterprise was to be crushed under the iron hand of a despot. Doubtless Sandys would have attempted to establish representative government at once in Virginia, had conditions favored so radical a change. But the colony was too young and feeble, and James could hardly be expected to give his consent. Yet the many liberal members of the Company were deeply interested in Virginia and were determined, should a favorable opportunity occur, to establish there an Assembly similar in character to the English Parliament.

The granting of the new charter aroused extraordinary interest in the fortunes of the colony throughout England and stimulated the Company to renewed efforts.[39] Thousands of pounds were contributed to defray the expenses of another expedition, and hundreds of persons responded to the appeals for settlers. The first Governor was a man of ability and distinction—Thomas Lord De la Warr. Sir Thomas Gates was made Lieutenant-Governor, George Summers, Admiral, and Captain Newport, Vice-Admiral.[40] De la Warr found it

[37] F. R., p. 73.
[38] F. R., p. 73.
[39] F. R., p. 80.
[40] F. R., p. 84.

impossible to leave at once to assume control of his government, but the other officers, with nine vessels and no less than five hundred colonists, sailed in June, 1609.[41] Unfortunately, in crossing the Gulf of Bahama, the fleet encountered a terrific storm, which scattered the vessels in all directions. When the tempest abated, several of the ships reunited and continued on their way to Jamestown, but the *Sea Adventure,* which carried Gates, Summers and Newport, was wrecked upon an island in the Bermudas.[42] As a result of this misfortune none of the leaders of the expedition reached Virginia until May, 1610, ten months later.

The other vessels, with most of the settlers, arrived at Jamestown in August, 1609. The newcomers told Captain Smith of the Company's new plan of government, and requested him to relinquish the old commission. This the President refused to do. All the official papers relating to the change had been aboard the *Sea Adventure,* and he would not resign until he had seen them.[43] A long and heated controversy followed, but in the end Smith gained his point.[44] It was agreed that until the arrival of the *Sea Adventure* the colony should remain under the old charter, and that Smith should continue to act as President until the twentieth of September, when he was to relinquish the government to Captain Francis West.[45]

This arrangement did not restore harmony. West felt aggrieved that Captain Smith should insist upon continuing the old order of affairs despite the known wishes of the Company, and took occasion to ignore and slight his authority. This so angered the President that he is said to have plotted with the Indians to surprise and cut off a party of men that his rival was leading up the James. Before this could be accomplished, however, Smith met with a serious accident, which led to his immediate overthrow. "Sleeping in his Boate . . . accidentallie, one fired his powder-bag, which tore the flesh . . . in a most pittifull manner; but to quench the

[41] F. R., p. 84.

[42] Gen., pp. 1329, 1330, 346, 400; Force, III; Arb. Smith, p. 635.

[43] F. R., p. 93.

[44] Gen., pp. 331, 347.

[45] Gen., pp. 331, 332; F. R., p. 98.

tormenting fire . . . he leaped over-board into the deepe river, where ever they could recover him he was neere drowned."[46] Three former Councillors—Ratcliffe, Archer and Martin—who had come over with the new fleet, availed themselves of the helplessness of their old foe to rid the colony of his presence. Claiming, with some justice, that if Smith could retain his office under the old charter, they were by the same power still members of the Council, they held a meeting, deposed him from the Presidency and sent him back to England.[47] Having thus disposed of the troublesome Captain, they looked about them for some man suitable to head the colony until the arrival of Gates. Neglecting the claims of West, whom they probably considered too inexperienced for the place, they selected Captain George Percy.[48]

In the meanwhile, the crew and passengers of the *Sea Adventure* were stranded in the Bermudas, upon what was called Devil's Island. Some of their number were daring enough to venture out into the ocean in the longboat, in an attempt to reach the colony, but they must have perished, for they were never heard from again.[49] The rest of the company, seeing no other way of escape, built two pinnaces and, in May, 1610, sailed away in them for Jamestown. A few days later, upon their arrival in Virginia, Gates received the old patent and the seal from the President and the period of the first royal government in Virginia came to an end.[50]

But the "faction breeding" government by the Council was by no means the only cause of trouble. Far more disastrous was the "sicknesse". When the first expedition sailed for Virginia, the Council in England, solicitous for the welfare of the emigrants, commanded them to avoid, in the choice of a site for their town, all "low and moist places".[51] Well would it have been for the colonists had they obeyed these

[46] Arb. Smith, p. 484.

[47] Ratcliffe wrote the Earl of Salisbury, "This man is sent home to answere some misdemenors, whereof I perswade me he can scarcely clear himselfe from great imputation of blame." Gen., p. 334.

[48] F. R., p. 108.

[49] F. R., p. 115.

[50] F. R., p. 117.

[51] Gen., p. 84.

instructions. Captain Smith says there was in fact opposition on the part of some of the leaders to the selection of the Jamestown peninsula, and it was amply justified by the event. The place was low and marshy and extremely unhealthful.[52] In the summer months great swarms of mosquitoes arose from the stagnant pools of water to attack the immigrants with a sting more deadly than that of the Indian arrow or the Spanish musket ball.

Scarcely three months had elapsed from the first landing when sickness and death made their appearance. The settlers, ignorant of the use of Peruvian bark and other remedies, were powerless to resist the progress of the epidemic. Captain George Percy describes in vivid colors the sufferings of the first terrible summer. "There were never Englishmen," he says, "left in a forreign country in such miserie as wee were in this new discouvered Virginia. Wee watched every three nights, lying on the bare-ground, what weather soever came; . . . which brought our men to bee most feeble wretches. . . . If there were any conscience in men, it would make their harts to bleed to heare the pitifull murmurings and outcries of our sick men without reliefe, every night and day for the space of sixe weekes; in the morning their bodies being trailed out of their cabines like Dogges, to be buried."[53] So deadly was the epidemic that when Captain Newport brought relief in January, 1608, he found but thirty-eight of the colonists alive.[54]

Nor did the men that followed in the wake of the *Sarah Constant,* the *Discovery* and the *Goodspeed* fare better. In the summer of 1608, the sickness reappeared and once more wrought havoc among the unhappy settlers. Captain Smith, who probably saved his own life by his frequent exploring expeditions, on his return to Jamestown in July, "found the Last Supply al sicke".[55] In 1609, when the fleet of Summers and Newport reached Virginia, the newcomers, many of whom were already in ill health, fell easy victims to malaria and dysentery. Smith declared that before the end of 1610 "not

[52] Arb. Smith, p. 5.

[53] Arb. Smith, lxxii.

[54] F. R., p. 55.

[55] Nar. of Va., p. 146.

past sixtie men, women and children" were left of several hundred that but a few months before had sailed away from Plymouth.[56] During the short stay of Governor De la Warr one hundred and fifty, or more than half the settlers lost their lives.[57]

Various visitors to Virginia during the early years of the seventeenth century bear testimony to the ravages of this scourge. A Spaniard named Molina, writing in 1613, declared that one hundred and fifty out of every three hundred colonists died before being in Virginia twelve months.[58] DeVries, a Dutch trader to the colony, wrote, "During the months of June, July and August it is very unhealthy, then people that have lately arrived from England, die, during these months, like cats and dogs, whence they call it the sickly season."[59] This testimony is corroborated by Governor William Berkeley, who reported in 1671, "There is not now oft seasoned hands (as we term them) that die now, whereas heretofore not one of five escaped the first year."[60]

In 1623 a certain Nathaniel Butler, in an attack upon the London Company, called "The Unmasked Face of our Colony in Virginia", drew a vivid, though perhaps an exaggerated picture of the unhealthfulness of the climate. "I found the plantations," he said, "generally seated upon meer salt marshes, full of infectious bogs and muddy creeks and lakes, and thereby subjected to all those inconveniences and diseases which are so commonly found in the most unsound and most unhealthy parts of England, whereof every country and climate hath some." It was by no means uncommon, he declared, to see immigrants from England "Dying under hedges and in the woods", and unless something were done at once to arrest the frightful mortality Virginia would shortly get the name of a slaughter house.[61]

The climate of eastern Virginia, unhealthful as it undoubtedly was in the places where the first settlements were made,

[56] Many of these, however, died of starvation or were killed by the Indians. Nar. of Va., p. 200.

[57] Nar. of Va., p. 212.

[58] Nar. of Va., p. 220; Gen., p. 648.

[59] Va. Car.

[60] Hen., Vol. I; Gen., p. 499.

[61] Proceedings of Va. Co., p. 171.

cannot be blamed for all the epidemics that swept the colony. Much of the ill health of the immigrants was due to unwholesome conditions on board the ships which brought them from England. The vessels were usually crowded far beyond their real capacity with wretched men, women and children, and were foul beyond description.[62] Not infrequently great numbers died at sea. One vessel is reported to have lost a hundred and thirty persons out of a hundred and eighty-five. On the ships that left England in June, 1609, both yellow fever and the London plague appeared, doing fearful havoc, and making it necessary to throw overboard from two of the vessels alone thirty-two unfortunate wretches.[63] The diseases thus started, often spread after the settlers had reached their new homes, and under favoring conditions, developed into terrible epidemics.[64]

Less deadly than the "sicknesse", but still greatly to be dreaded, was the hostility of the Indians.[65] The natives, resentful at the attempt of the white men to establish themselves in their midst, proved a constant menace to the colony. Their superstitious awe of the strange newcomers, and their lack of effective weapons alone prevented untiring and open war. Jamestown was but a few days old when it was subjected to a violent assault by the savages. On the twentieth day of May, 1607, the colonists, while at work without their arms in the fields, were attacked by several hundred Indians. In wild dismay they rushed into the fort, while the savages followed at their heels. "They came up allmost into the ffort, shot through the tents, appeared in this Skirmishe (which lasted hott about an hower) a very valient people." The guns of the ships came to the aid of the English and their thunders struck dismay into the hearts of the savages. Yet they retired without panic, taking with them their dead and wounded. Four of the Council, standing in the front ranks, were wounded by the natives, and President Wingfield, while fighting valiently, had an arrow shot through his beard, "yet scaped hurte".[66]

[62] Gen., p. 489.

[63] Gen., p. 329.

[64] F. R., p. 98.

[65] Gen., p. 503.

[66] Arb. Smith, lii.

A few days after this event a gentleman named Clovell came running into the fort with six arrows sticking in him, crying, "Arm, arm". He had wandered too far from the town, and the Indians, who were still prowling near, shot him from ambush. Eight days later he died.[67] Thus at the very outset, the English learned the nature of the conflict which they must wage against the Indians. In open fight the savages, with their primitive weapons, were no match for them, but woe to any of their number that strayed far from the fort, or ventured into the long grass of the mainland. So frequently were small parties cut off, that it became unsafe for the English to leave their settlements except in bodies large enough to repel any attack.[68]

The epidemics and the wars with the Indians conspired to bring upon the colony still another horrible scourge. The constant dread of attack in the fields and the almost universal sickness made it impossible for the settlers to raise crops sufficient for their needs. During the summer of 1607 there were at one time scarce five able men at Jamestown, and these found it beyond their power even to nurse the sick and bury the dead. And in later years, when corn was planted in abundance, the stealthy savages often succeeded in cutting it down before it could be harvested. There can be no surprise then that famines came at frequent intervals to add to the misery of the ill-fated colonists. The most terrible of these visited Virginia in the winter of 1609-10. Smith's Historie gives a graphic account of the suffering during those fearful months. Those that escaped starvation were preserved, it says, "for the most part, by roots, herbes, acornes, walnuts, berries, now and then a fish: they that had starch in these extremities, made no small use of it; yea, even the very skinnes of our horses. Nay, so great was our famine, that a Salvage we slew and buried, the poorer sort took him up againe and eat him; and so did divers one another boyled and stewed with roots and herbs: And one amongst the rest did kill his wife, powdered her, and had eaten part of her before it was knowne; for which hee was

[67] Arb. Smith, liii.

[68] Force, Vol. III, Tract I, p. 17; Gen., p. 405, 419, 456.

executed, as hee well deserved. . . . This was the time, which to this day we call the starving time; it were too vile to say, and scarce to be believed, what we endured."[69]

The misery of the wretched settlers in time of famine is vividly described in a letter written in 1623 by a servant to his parents. The people, he said, cried out day and night, "Oh that they were in England without their limbs . . . though they begged from door to door". He declared that he had eaten more at home in a day than was now allowed him in a week, and that his parents had often given more than his present day's allowance to a beggar at the door. Unless the ship *Sea Flower* came soon, with supplies, his master's men would have but half a penny loaf each a day for food, and might be turned away to eat bark off the trees, or moulds off the ground. "Oh," he said, "that you did see my daily and hourly sighs, groans, tears and thumps that I afford mine own breast, and rue and curse the time of my birth and with holy Job I thought no head had been able to hold so much water as hath and doth daily flow from mine eyes."[70]

Thus was the immigrant to Virginia beset on all sides with deadly perils. If he escaped the plague, the yellow fever and the scurvy during his voyage across the Atlantic, he was more than apt to fall a victim to malaria or dysentery after he reached his new home. Even if he survived all these dangers, he might perish miserably of hunger, or be butchered by the savage Indians. No wonder he cursed the country, calling it "a miserie, a ruine, a death, a hell".[71]

It is remarkable that the enterprise, in the face of these stupendous difficulties, should ever have succeeded. The explanation lies in the great enthusiasm of all England for this attempt to extend the British domains to the shores of the New World, and in the devotion of a few brave spirits of the London Company, who would not be daunted by repeated failures. It mattered not to them that thousands of pounds were lost in the undertaking, that many hundreds of men

[69] Force, Vol. III, Tract I, p. 17; Nar. of Va., p. 295; Gen., pp. 330, 392, 401, 404, 456.

[70] Va. Vet.

[71] Nar. of Va., p. 117.

perished, the English flag and the English religion must gain a foothold upon the American continent.

Sir Thomas Gates found the colony in a pitiable condition. The tomahawk of the Indians, famine and pestilence had wrought terrible havoc with the settlers. A mere handful of poor wretched men were left to welcome the newcomers and to beg eagerly to be taken away from the ill-fated country. The town "appeared rather as the ruins of some auntient fortification, then that any people living might now in habit it: the pallisadœs he found tourne downe, the portes open, the gates from the hinges, the church ruined and unfrequented. . . . Only the block house . . . was the safetie of the remainder that lived: which yet could not have preserved them now many days longer from the watching, subtile, and offended Indians."[72]

Nor was it in the power of Gates to remedy these conditions, for he had brought with him from Devil's Island but a limited supply of provisions. So, with great reluctance, the Lieutenant-Governor decided to abandon Virginia rather than sacrifice his people. As the colonists climbed aboard the vessels which were to take them from the scene of their sufferings, they would have set fire to the town had not Gates prevented with his soldiers. He, himself, "was the last of them, when, about noon, giving a farewell with a peale of small shott, he set sayle, and that night, with the tide, fell down . . . the river."[73]

But it was not destined that this enterprise, which was of such importance to the English nation, should be thus abandoned. In April, 1610, De la Warr, the Lord Governor, had sailed for Virginia with three vessels, about a hundred and fifty immigrants and supplies for the relief of the colony.[74] Reaching Cape Comfort June the sixteenth, he learned from a small party there of the intended desertion of Jamestown. Immediately he sent a pinnace up the river to meet Gates, advise him of his arrival and to order his return to the aban-

[72] Gen., p. 405.

[73] Gen., p. 406; Force, Vol. III, Tract I, p. 18.

[74] F. R., p. 127.

doned town. Upon receiving these welcome tidings, Gates bore "up the helm" for Jamestown, and the same night landed all his men.[75] Soon after, the Governor reached the town and took formal possession of the government.

De la Warr began his administration by listening to a sermon from the good pastor, Mr. Buck. He then made an address to the people, "laying some blames on them for many vanities and their idleness", and promising, if occasion required, to draw the sword of justice.[76]

The Governor was not unrestrained in his authority over the colonists, for he was to "rule, punish, pardone and governe according to such directions" as were given him by the London Company. In case of rebellion or mutiny he might put into execution martial law. In matters not covered by his instructions he was to "rule and governe by his owne discretion or by such lawes" as he should think fit to establish.[77] The Council, which had formerly been all-powerful, was now but an advisory body, appointed by the Governor and removable at his discretion. De la Warr chose for his Council Sir Thomas Gates, Sir George Somers, Captain George Percy, Sir Ferdinando Weinman, Captain Christopher Newport and William Strachey, Esquire.[78]

Forgetting their former quarrels and factions, the people united in a zealous effort to serve their noble Governor. "You might shortly behold the idle and restie diseases of a divided multitude, by the unity and authority of the government to be substantially cured. Those that knew not the way to goodnes before, but cherished singularity and faction, can now chalke out the path of all respective dutie and service."[79]

For a while peace and prosperity seemed to have come at last to the little colony. All set to work with a good will to build comfortable houses and to repair the fort. The chapel was restored. The Governor furnished it with a communion table of black walnut and with pews and pulpit of cedar. The font was "hewn hollow like a canoa". "The church was so

[75] F. R., p. 128; Force, Vol. III, Tract I, p. 19; Gen., p. 407.

[76] Gen., p. 407.

[77] Gen., p. 379.

[78] F. R., p. 131.

[79] Force, Vol. III, Tract I, p. 20.

cast, as to be very light within and the Governor caused it to be kept passing sweet and trimmed up with divers flowers." In the evening, at the ringing of the bell, and at four in the afternoon, each man addressed himself to prayer.[80] "Every Sunday, when the Lord Governor went to Church he was accompanied with all the Councillors, Captains, other officers, and all the gentlemen, and with a guard of fifty Halberdiers in his Lordships Livery, fair red cloaks, on each side and behind him. The Lord Governor sat in the choir, in a green velvet chair, with a velvet cushion before him on which he knelt, and the Council, captains, and officers, on each side of him."[81]

But the misfortunes of the colony were far from being at an end. The principal causes of disaster had not yet been removed. Before many weeks had passed the "sickly season" came on, bringing the usual accompaniment of suffering and death. "Not less than 150 of them died of pestilent diseases, of callentures and feavors, within a few months after" Lord De la Warr's arrival.[82] So universal was the sickness among the newcomers that all the work had to be done by the old settlers, "who by use weare growen practique in a hard way of livinge".[83]

The war with the Indians continued without abatement, causing constant alarm to the settlers and keeping them closely confined to their forts. At one time fourteen were treacherously massacred by the Queen of Appomattox. The English revenged themselves by attacking the savages, burning their villages and destroying their crops, but they could not force them into friendly relations.[84]

Lord De la Warr, himself, was assailed by a series of maladies, that came near costing him his life. "Presently after my arrival in James Town," he wrote, "I was welcomed by a hot and violent Ague, which held mee a time. . . . That disease had not long left mee, till . . . I began to be distempered with other greevous sickness, which successively & sev-

[80] F. R., pp. 129, 130.
[81] F. R., p. 130.
[82] F. R., p. 134.
[83] F. R., p. 134.
[84] F. R., pp. 135, 136.

erally assailed me: for besides a relapse into the former disease; . . . the Flux surprised me, and kept me many daies: then the cramp assaulted my weak body, with strong paines; & afterward the Gout afflicted me in such sort, that making my body through weaknesse unable to stirre, . . . drew upon me the disease called Scurvy . . . till I was upon the point to leave the world."[85] Realizing that it would be fatal for him to remain longer in Virginia, the Lord Governor set sail with Captain Argoll for the West Indies, where, he hoped, he would recover his health.[86] As Gates had left the colony some months before, the government fell into the experienced hands of Captain George Percy.[87]

In the meanwhile the London Company, undismayed by their former failures, were preparing a new expedition, which they hoped would establish the colony upon a firm footing. Three hundred immigrants, carefully selected from the better class of working men, were assembled under the command of Sir Thomas Dale, and, on March the twenty-seventh, 1611, embarked for Virginia. Upon the arrival of the fleet at Jamestown, Dale received the letters patent from Captain Percy, and assumed command of the colony as Deputy for Lord De la Warr.[88]

The new Governor seems to have perceived at once that the chief source of disaster had been the location of the settlement upon the Jamestown peninsula. The small area which this place afforded for the planting of corn, and the unhealthfulness of the climate rendered it most undesirable as the site for a colony. Former Governors had refused to desert the peninsula because of the ease with which it could be defended against the Indians. But Dale at once began a search for a spot which would afford all the security of Jamestown, but be free from its many disadvantages. This he succeeded in finding up the river, some fifty miles from Jamestown.[89] "I have surveyed," he wrote, "a convenient strong, healthie and sweet seate to plant the new towne in, from whence might be no

[85] Gen., p. 479.
[86] Gen., p. 480.
[87] F. R., p. 137.
[88] F. R., p. 137.
[89] Gen., p. 492; Arb. Smith, p. 507; F. R., p. 150.

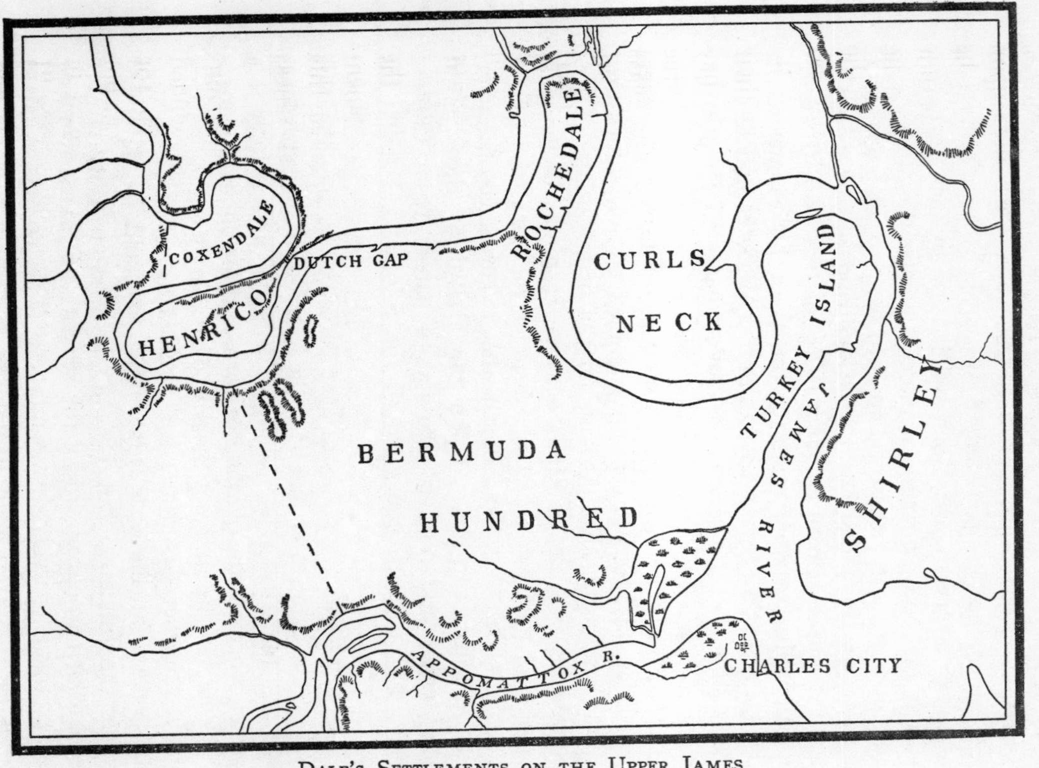

Dale's Settlements on the Upper James

more remove of the principall Seate." This place, which he named Henrico, was located not far from the point of juncture of the James and the Appomattox, at what is now called Farrar's Island. Here the river makes a sweeping curve, forming a peninsula about one square mile in extent.

In August, 1611, Sir Thomas Gates, returning to assume the command of the colony, pushed vigorously the work upon the new settlement.[90] Dale was sent up the river with no less than three hundred men, with directions to construct houses and fortifications. The settlers, working with new life and vigor in the more wholesome air of the upper James, soon rendered the place almost impregnable to attack from the Indians. They cut a ditch across the narrow neck of the peninsula, and fortified it with high palisades. To prevent a sudden raid by the savages in canoes from the other shore, five strong block houses were built at intervals along the river bank. Behind these defenses were erected a number of substantial houses, with foundations of brick and frame superstructures. Soon a town of three streets had been completed, more commodious and far more healthful than Jamestown.[91]

When this work had been completed, Dale led a force of men across to the south bank of the river and took possession of the entire peninsula lying between the Appomattox and the James. An Indian settlement just below Turkey Island bend was attacked and destroyed, and the savages driven away. The English built a palisade over two miles long and reinforced at intervals with forts and block houses, from the James at Henrico to the falls of the Appomattox. These fortifications secured from the attacks of the savages "many miles of champion and woodland", and made it possible for the English to lay out in safety several new plantations or hundreds. Dale named the place Bermuda, "by reason of the strength of the situation".

Here, for the first time, something like prosperity came to the colony. Although the "sicknesse" was not entirely eliminated even at Henrico, the percentage of mortality was greatly

[90] Gen., p. 474.

[91] Arb. Smith, pp. 509, 510; F. R., p. 157; Cradle of Rep., p. 136.

reduced. Soon there were in Virginia several hundred persons that had lived through the fatal months of June, July and August and were thoroughly "seasoned" or immune to the native disorders. Not until 1618, when the settlers, in their greed for land suitable for the cultivation of tobacco, deserted their homes on the upper James for the marshy ground of the lower country, and new, unacclimated persons began arriving in great numbers, did the pestilence again assume its former proportions.

Thus protected from the ravages of disease and from the assaults of the savages, Dale's men were able to turn their attention to the cultivation of the soil. Soon they were producing an annual crop of corn sufficient to supply their more pressing needs. And it was well for them that they could become, to some extent, independent of England, for the London Company, at last discouraged by continued misfortune, was often remiss in sending supplies. Clothing became exceedingly scarce. Not only were the gaudy uniforms of De la Warr's time lacking, but many persons were forced to imitate the savages by covering themselves with skins and furs.[92] The Company, however, succeeded in obtaining for them from the King many suits of old armor that were of great value in their wars with the savages. Coats of mail and steel that had become useless on the battlefields of Europe and had for years been rusting in the Tower of London, were polished up and sent to Virginia. Thus, behind the palisades of Henrico or in the fort at Jamestown one might have seen at this time soldiers encased in armor that had done service in the days of Richard III and Henry VII.[93]

The London Company, when they sent Sir Thomas Gates to Virginia with the letters patent of 1609, gave directions that the utmost severity should be used in putting an end to lawlessness and confusion. Gates, who had fought against the Spaniards in the Netherlands and had the soldier's dislike of insubordination, was well suited to carry their wishes into effect. No sooner had he arrived from Devil's Island in 1610 than he posted in the church at Jamestown certain laws, orders

[92] F. R., p. 226. [93] F. R., p. 172.

and instructions which he warned the people they must obey strictly.[94] These laws were exceedingly severe. It was, for instance, ordered that "every man and woman daly twice a day upon the first towling of the Bell shall upon the working daies repaire into the Church, to hear divine Service upon pain of losing his or her dayes allowance for the first omission, for the second to be whipt, and for the third to be condemned to the Gallies for six Months". Again, it was decreed that "no man shall give any disgracefull words, or commit any act to the disgrace of any person . . . upon paine of being tied head and feete together, upon the guard everie night for the space of one moneth. . . . No man shall dare to kill, or destroy any Bull, Cow, Calfe, Mare, Horse, Colt, Goate, Swine, Cocke, Henne, Chicken, Dogge, Turkie, or any tame Cattel, or Poultry, of what condition soever, . . . without leave from the Generall, upon paine of death. . . . There shall no man or woman . . . dare to wash any unclean linnen . . . within the Pallizadoes, . . . nor rench, and make clean, any kettle, pot or pan . . . within twenty foote of the olde well . . . upon pain of whipping."[95]

During the administration of Gates and De la Warr these laws seem not to have been enforce vigorously, but were utilized chiefly *in terrorem.*[96] Under Dale and Argoll, however, not only were they put into merciless operation, but were reinforced with a series of martial laws, drawn from the code in use among the armies of the Netherlands.

The Divine, Moral and Martial Laws, as they were called, undoubtedly brought about good order in the colony, and aided in the establishment of prosperity, but they were ill suited for the government of free-born Englishmen. They were in open violation of the rights guaranteed to the settlers in their charters, and caused bitter discontent and resentment.

At times they were enforced with odious harshness and injustice. Molina declared that the Governors were most cruel in their treatment of the people, often using them like

[94] F. R., p. 126; Gen., pp. 342, 345, 528, 529; Force, Vol. III, Tract II, pp. 9-19.

[95] Force, Vol. III, Tract II, pp. 9-10 [96] Bruce, Inst. Hist., Vol. I, p. 474

slaves.[97] The Virginia Assembly of 1624 gives a vivid, though perhaps an exaggerated, picture of the severity of the government. "The Colony . . . remained in great want and misery under most severe and Cruell lawes sent over in printe," they said, "and contrary to the express Letter of the Kinge in his most gracious Charter, and as mercylessly executed, often times without tryall or Judgment." Many of the people fled "for reliefe to the Savage Enemy, who being taken againe were putt to sundry deathes as by hanginge, shooting and breaking uppon the wheele and others were forced by famine to filch for their bellies, of whom one for steelinge of 2 or 3 pints of oatmeale had a bodkin thrust through his tounge and was tyed with a chain to a tree untill he starved, if a man through his sicknes had not been able to worke, he had noe allowance at all, and soe consequently perished. Many through these extremities, being weary of life, digged holes in the earth and there hidd themselves till they famished."[98] In 1612, several men attempted to steal "a barge and a shallop and therein to adventure their lives for their native country, being discovered and prevented, were shot to death, hanged and broken upon the wheel".[99] There was some criticism in England of the harshness of the laws, but Sir Thomas Smith, then the guiding spirit of the London Company, declared that they were beneficial and necessary, "in some cases *ad terrorum,* and in others to be truly executed".[100]

As time passed and the population of the colony increased, it became necessary to extend beyond the confines of Jamestown and Henrico. The cultivation of tobacco, which was rapidly becoming the leading pursuit of the people, required more ground than was comprised within the fortified districts. Even the expansion of the settlement upon the upper James to other peninsulas along the "Curls of the River" could not satisfy the demand for arable land. At one time the very streets of Jamestown were planted with tobacco.[101] Soon the people, despite their dread of the savages, were deserting their palisades, and spreading out in search of fertile soil.

[97] Gen., p. 648.
[98] Nar. of Va., pp. 422, 423.
[99] F. R., pp. 148, 172.
[100] Gen., pp. 529, 530.
[101] Bruce, Ec. Hist., Vol. I, p. 222.

This recklessness brought upon the colony a renewal of the disastrous epidemics of the earlier period, and exposed the planters to imminent danger from the savages. Fortunately, however, at this very time the long sought peace with the Indians was brought about by the romantic marriage of Pocahontas, the daughter of the powerful chief Powhatan, with Captain John Rolfe.

In the spring of 1613 Sir Samuel Argoll, while cruising in the Rappahannock in quest of corn, learned from the natives that the princess was visiting Japazaws, a neighboring king, at his village upon the Potomac. Argoll at once resolved to capture the daughter of the greatest enemy of the white men, and to hold her until all the tools and weapons stolen by the Indians had been returned.[102] Hastening into the country of the Potomacs, he demanded the maid of Japazaws. The king, fearing the hostility of the English more than the anger of Powhatan, consented, although with great reluctance, and she was placed aboard Argoll's ship.

The news of the capture of his favorite child filled Powhatan with rage and grief. Imploring Argoll to do Pocahontas no harm, he promised to yield to all his demands and to become the lasting friend of the white men.[103] He liberated seven captives and sent with them "three pieces, one broad Axe, and a long whip-saw, and one canow of Corne".[104] Knowing that these did not constitute all the tools in the hands of the king, the English refused to relinquish Pocahontas, but kept her a prisoner at Jamestown.[105]

The young princess was treated with consideration and kindness by Governor Dale. Her gentle nature, her intelligence and her beauty won the respect and love of the sternest of her captors. Dale himself undertook to direct her education. "I was moved," he exclaimed, "by her desire to be taught and instructed in the knowledge of God, her capableness of understanding, her aptness and willingness to receive any good impression. . . . I caused her to be carefully instructed in the Christian religion, who, after she had made

[102] Gen., p. 642.
[103] Gen., p. 643.
[104] Gen., pp. 643, 644.
[105] Nar. of Va., p. 308.

some good progress therein, renounced publicly her Country's idolatry; openly confessed her Christian faith; and was, as she desired, baptized."[106]

Before many months had passed the charm of this daughter of the American forest had inspired a deep love in the breast of Captain John Rolfe. This worthy gentleman, after struggling long against a passion so strange and unusual, wrote Dale asking permission to wed the princess. I am not ignorant, he said "of the inconvenience which may . . . arise . . . to be in love with one whose education hath bin rude, her manners barbarous, her generation accursed".[107] But I am led to take this step, "for the good of the plantation, for the honour of our countrie, for the glory of God, for my owne salvation, and for the converting to the true knowledge of God and Jesus Christ, an unbeleeving creature, like Pokahuntas. To whom my heartie and best thoughts are, and have a long time bin so intangled, and inthralled in so intricate a laborinth, that I was awearied to unwinde myselfe thereout."[108]

Dale, overjoyed at this opportunity to secure the friendship of the Indians, consented readily to the marriage. Powhatan, too, when he learned of his daughter's affection for Captain Rolfe, expressed his approval of the union, and sent Apachisco, an uncle of the bride, and two of her brothers to represent him at the ceremony.

Both English and Indians regarded this wedding as a bond of friendship between the two races. Apachisco, acting as deputy for Powhatan, concluded with Governor Dale a peace which lasted eight years and was fairly well kept by both parties.[109] "Besides this," wrote Captain Ralph Hamor, "we became in league with our next neighbors, the Chicahamanias, a lustie and daring people, free of themselves. These people, as soone as they heard of our peace with Powhatan, sent two messengers with presents to Sir Thomas Dale and offered . . . their service."[110] Thus was one of the greatest menaces to

[106] Arb. Smith, p. 512.
[107] Nar. of Va., p. 241.
[108] Nar. of Va., pp. 240, 241.
[109] F. R., p. 205; Arb. Smith, p. 514.
[110] Arb. Smith, p. 515.

the prosperity of the colony removed. Now the settlers could cultivate the soil, or hunt and fish without fear of the treacherous savage, and leave their cattle to range in comparative safety. John Rolfe himself wrote, "The great blessings of God have followed this peace, and it, next to him, hath bredd our plentie—everie man sitting under his fig tree in safety, gathering and reaping the fruits of their labors with much joy and comfort."[111]

In 1616 Sir Thomas Dale, who had been in command of the colony since the departure of Gates in 1614, returned to England, leaving the government in the hands of Captain George Yeardley. Despite the harshness and cruelty of Dale and Gates, they must be credited with obtaining the final success of the colony. These two stern soldiers of the Dutch wars had found the settlers dispirited, reduced in numbers, fighting a losing battle against pestilence, starvation and the savages. By their rigid discipline and able leadership they had brought unity and prosperity, had taught the people how to resist the sickness, and had secured a long peace with the Indians.[112] Dale left about three hundred and fifty persons in Virginia, most of them thoroughly acclimated and busily engaged in building up prosperity for the colony.

Tobacco was already becoming the staple product of Virginia. As early as 1612 Captain Rolfe had been experimenting with the native leaf, in an effort to make it suitable for the English market.[113] In 1613 he sent a part of his crop to London, where it was tested by experts and pronounced to be of excellent quality.[114] The colonists were greatly encouraged at the success of the venture, for the price of tobacco was high, and its culture afforded opportunities for a rich return. Soon every person that could secure a little patch of ground was devoting himself eagerly to the cultivation of the plant. It even became necessary for Dale to issue an order that each man should "set two acres of ground with corn", lest the new craze should lead to the neglect of the food supply.[115] In

[111] F. R., p. 226.

[112] F. R., pp. 230, 236.

[113] Bruce, Ec. Hist., Vol. I, p. 211.

[114] F. R., p. 197; Bruce, Ec. Hist., Vol. I, p. 217.

[115] F. R., p. 228; Gen., p. 782.

1617 *The George* sailed for England laden with 20,000 pounds of tobacco, which found a ready market at five shillings and three pence a pound. John Rolfe's discovery was opening for Virginia a veritable gold mine.

Fortunately the King, in 1612, had granted the Company an exemption for seven years from custom duties upon goods brought from the colony. So, for a while, at least, the Crown could not appropriate to its own use the profits from the Virginia tobacco. Since, however, the exemption had only a few years more to run, the Company hastened to secure what immediate returns were available. They took from the planters the entire crop, giving them for it three pence per pound, while they themselves were able to obtain a much larger price from the English dealers.

The profits thus secured were at once utilized in new measures for increasing and strengthening the colony. Encouraged by the discovery in Virginia of so profitable a commodity, the Company became convinced that now at last success was at hand. "Broadsides" were sent out to the British people, depicting in glowing terms the advantages of the country, and asking for immigrants and for financial support. Once more a wave of enthusiasm for the enterprise swept over England. Money was contributed liberally. The clergy, interested in the spread of the Anglican Church, and in the conversion of the savages, worked ardently for the success of the colony. Soon vessel after vessel was being fitted out for the voyage across the Atlantic, and hundreds of artisans and laborers were preparing to risk their all in the New World.[116]

[116] F. R., p. 209.

CHAPTER II

THE ESTABLISHMENT OF REPRESENTATIVE GOVERNMENT

King James I, from the beginning of his reign, was deeply desirous of planting the English nation upon the shores of the New World. It was with envy and alarm that he witnessed the extension of the power of Spain and of the Roman Catholic church across the Atlantic, while his own subjects were excluded from a share in the splendid prize. He must have perceived clearly that if the English wished to maintain their position as a great naval and mercantile people, the establishing of colonies in America was imperative. Peru, Mexico and the West Indies added greatly to the wealth and power of the Spanish King; why should England not attempt to gain a foothold near these countries, before it became too late?

But James had no desire to arouse the hostility of Philip III. Despite religious differences, despite the hatred of the English for the Spaniards, he had reversed the policy of Elizabeth by cultivating the friendship of these hereditary enemies. And so wedded was he to this design, that later, when his son-in-law, Frederick of the Palatinate, was being overwhelmed by a coalition of Catholic nations, he refused to affront Spain by coming to his rescue. Yet he knew that Philip considered America his own, and would resent any attempt of the English to establish colonies on its shores. So the crafty James resolved to disguise the founding of a royal colony under the guise of a private venture.[1] If the Spaniards complained of the occupation of their territory, he could free himself from blame by placing the responsibility upon the London Company. "If it take not success," his advisors told the King, "it is done by their owne heddes. It is but the attempt of private gentlemen, the State suffers noe losse, noe disreputa-

[1] F. R., p. 6.

tion. If it takes success, they are your subjects, they doe it for your service, they will lay all at your Majesty's feet and interess your Majesty therein."[2]

James was quite liberal in granting charters to those that had undertaken the settlement, and he encouraged them as much as was consistent with his friendship for Spain. It was truly written of him after his death, "Amongst the . . . workes of the late Kinge, there was none more eminent, than his gracious inclination . . . to advance and sett forward a New Plantation in the New World."[3] That he was deeply interested in the undertaking is shown most strikingly by his consent to the establishment of the Puritans in America. James hated the tenets of Calvin from the depths of his soul, and could have no desire to see them infect the English settlements in America, yet his solicitude for the welfare of the colony induced him to yield to the request of the Pilgrims for permission to settle there. How much greater was his foresight than that of Louis XIV, who, by refusing to allow the persecuted Huguenots to settle in any part of his domains, deprived the French colonies of what might have been their most numerous and valuable recruits! When some of the leading men of the London Company pleaded with James for the Puritans, the King lent a ready ear. He was asked to allow them "liberty of conscience under his . . . protection in America; where they would endeavour the advancement of his Majesty's dominions, and the enlargement of the interests of the Gospel". James replied that it was "a good and honest motion". He refused to tolerate them by public authority and would not confirm under the broad seal their petition for leave to worship as they chose, but he let it be understood that they were not to be molested in their new homes in any way.[4] And in this promise they finally decided to put their trust, feeling that "if afterwards there should be a purpose or desire to wrong them, though they had a seale as broad as ye house flore, it would not serve ye turn; for ther would be means a new found to recall or reverse it".[5]

[2] F. R., p. 76.
[3] Gen., p. 1027.
[4] F. R., p. 265.
[5] F. R., p. 271.

But the chief glory of the establishment of the English in America must be given to the patriotic and persevering men of the Virginia Company. It is erroneous and unjust to accuse them of mean and mercenary motives in founding and maintaining the colony at Jamestown. Some of them, perhaps, were dazzled with visions of a rich harvest of gold and silver, but most must have realized that there was small chance of remuneration. Many were merchants and business men of great foresight and ability, and it is quite evident that they were fully aware of the risks of the undertaking in which they ventured their money. What they did hope to gain from the colony was the propagation of the English Church, the extension of the English nation and its institutions, and the increase of British trade.

Over and over again it was asserted that the first object of the enterprise was to spread the Christian religion. In 1610 the London Company declared it their especial purpose "to preach and baptize . . . and by propagation of the Gospell, to recover out of the armes of the Divell, a number of poore and miserable soules, wrapt up unto death, in almost invincible ignorance".[6] The first draft of the Virginia charter of 1606 declared that the leading motive of this "noble work", was "the planting of Christianity amongst heathens".[7] The charter of 1609 asserted that the "principle effect, which we can desire or expect of this action, is the conversion and reduction of the people in those parts unto the true worship of God".[8]

That they were also actuated by a desire to extend the British possessions and trade is attested by numerous documents and letters. The Company declared it their purpose to promote the "honor and safety of the Kingdome, the strength of our Navy, the visible hope of a great and rich trade".[9] One of the leading shareholders wrote that the colony should be upheld for "ye Honor and profitt to our Nation, to make provinciall to us a land ready to supply us with all

[6] Gen., p. 339. [7] F. R., p. 6.

[8] Gen. p. 236. Compare F. R., pp. 262, 263, 264, 31, 248, 80; Gen., pp. 49, 146.

[9] F. R., p. 80.

necessary commodytyes wanting to us: In which alone we suffer ye Spanish reputation and power to swell over us."[10] The colonists themselves declared that one of the objects of the settlement of America was the extension of British territory and the enriching of the kingdom, "for which respects many noble and well minded persons were induced to adventure great sums of money to the advancement of so pious and noble a worke".[11]

The Company, in fact, did no more than take the lead in the work. It was really the English nation that had decided to second their King in gaining a foothold in America, and it was they that insisted that this foothold should not be relinquished. Again and again the London Company appealed to the people for support, and never without success, for all classes of Englishmen felt that they were interested in this new venture. The spirit of the nation is reflected in the statement of the Council for Virginia in 1610, that the Company "are so farre from yielding or giving way to any hindrance or impeachment . . . that many . . . have given their hands and subscribed to contribute againe and againe to new supplies if need require".[12]

But although James I and his people were agreed as to the necessity of extending the English nation to America, they were not in accord in regard to the form of government which should be established there. The King, who was always restive under the restraint placed upon him by the English Parliament, had no desire to see the liberal institutions of the mother country transplanted to Virginia. He wished, beyond doubt, to build a colonial empire which should be dependent upon himself for its government and which should add to the royal revenues. In this way he would augment the power of the Crown and render it less subject to the restraint of Parliament. But to found colonies that would set up little assemblies of their own to resist and thwart him, was not at all his intention.

On the other hand, many of the leading spirits of the Lon-

[10] F. R., p. 49.

[11] Gen., p. 50.

[12] Gen., p. 355.

don Company hoped "to establish a more free government in Virginia".[13] Some, perhaps, feared that the liberties of the English people might be suppressed by the King, and they looked hopefully to this new land as a haven for the oppressed. "Many worthy Patriots, Lords, Knights, gentlemen, Merchants and others . . . laid hold on . . . Virginia as a providence cast before them."[14] In the meetings of the Company were gathered so many that were "most distasted with the proceedings of the Court, and stood best affected to Religion and Liberty", that James began to look upon the body as a "Seminary for a seditious Parliament".[15]

The leader of these liberals was Sir Edwin Sandys. This man, who was widely known as an uncompromising enemy of despotism, was heartily detested by the King.[16] In his youth he had gone to Geneva to study the reformed religion and while there had become most favorably impressed with the republican institutions of the little Swiss state. He was afterwards heard to say that "he thought that if God from heaven did constitute and direct a forme of government on Earth it was that of Geneva".[17] Returning to England, he had entered Parliament, where he had become known as an eminent advocate of liberal principles. He had contended for the abolition of commercial monopolies; had demanded that all accused persons be given the assistance of counsel; had denounced many of the unjust impositions of the Crown; had raised "his voice for the toleration of those with whom he did not wholly agree"; and had aided in drawing up the remonstrance against the conduct of James towards his first Parliament.[18]

But Sandys and his friends were not without opposition in the London Company. Many of the "adventurers", as the stockholders were called, were by no means willing to permit the liberal party to utilize the Company as an instrument for propagating their political tenets. The great struggle between the forces of progress and reaction that was convulsing

[13] F. R., p. 558.
[14] F. R., p. 85.
[15] F. R., p. 237.
[16] F. R., vi.
[17] F. R., p. 251.
[18] F. R., p. 75.

Parliament and the nation, was fought over again in the Quarter Courts. At times the meetings resounded with the quarrels of the contending factions. Eventually, however, Sandys was victorious, and representative government in America was assured.

Sandys seems to have planned to secure from the King successive charters each more liberal than its predecessor, and each entrusting more fully the control of the colony to the Company. This could be done without arousing the suspicions of James under the pretext that they were necessary for the success of the enterprise. When at length sufficient power had been delegated, Sandys designed to establish in Virginia a representative assembly, modelled upon the British Parliament.

Under the provisions of the charter of 1606 Virginia had been, in all but form, a royal colony. The King had drawn up the constitution, had appointed the Council in England, and had controlled their policies. This charter had granted no semblance of self-government to the settlers. But it was declared "They shall have and enjoy all the liberties, franchises, and immunities . . . to all intents and purposes, as if they had been abiding and born, within . . . this realm of England".[19] This promise was not kept by the Kings of England. Several of the provisions of the charter itself were not consistent with it. In later years it was disregarded again and again by the royal commissions and instructions. Yet it was of the utmost importance, for it set a goal which the colonists were determined to attain. Throughout the entire colonial period they contended for all the rights of native Englishmen, and it was the denial of their claim that caused them to revolt from the mother country and make good their independence. Provision had also been made for trial by jury. James had decreed that in all cases the Council should sit as a court, but in matters of "tumults, rebellion, conspiracies, mutiny, and seditions . . . murther, manslaughter", and other crimes punishable with death, guilt or innocence was to be determined by a jury of twelve. To what extent the Council made use of the jury

[19] Gen., pp. 60, 61.

system it is impossible to say, but Wingfield states that on one occasion he was tried before a jury for slander, and fined £300.[20]

The second charter had been granted in 1609. This document is of great importance because through it the King resigned the actual control of the colony into the hands of the Virginia Company. And although this did not result immediately in the establishment of representative government, it strengthened the hands of Sandys and made it possible for him to carry out his designs at a future date. Under this charter the Company might have set up liberal institutions at once in Virginia, but conditions were not ripe, either in England or in America, for so radical a change.

In 1612 the third charter had been granted. This had still further strengthened the Company and made them more independent of the King. It gave them the important privilege of holding great quarterly meetings or assemblies, where all matters relating to the government of the colony could be openly discussed. Still Virginia remained under the autocratic rule of Dale and Gates.

In 1617 or 1618, however, when the liberals were in full control of the Company, it was decided to grant the colonists the privilege of a parliament.[21] In April, 1618, Lord De la Warr sailed for Virginia to reassume active control of affairs there, bringing with him instructions to establish a new form of government. What this government was to have been is not known, but it was designed by Sir Edwin Sandys, and beyond doubt, was liberal in form.[22] Possibly it was a duplicate of that established the next year by Governor Yeardley. Most unfortunately, Lord De la Warr, whose health had been shattered by his first visit to Virginia, died during the voyage across the Atlantic, and it became necessary to continue the old constitution until the Company could appoint a successor.[23]

In November, 1618, George Yeardley was chosen Governor-General of Virginia, and was intrusted with several documents by whose authority he was to establish representative govern-

[20] Arb. Smith, lxxxiii.

[21] F. R., p. 266.

[22] F. R., p. 266.

[23] F. R., pp. 281, 282.

ment in the colony.[24] These papers, which became known as the Virginia Magna Charta, were the very corner-stone of liberty in the colony and in all America. Their importance can hardly be exaggerated, for they instituted the first representative assembly of the New World, and established a government which proved a bulwark against royal prerogative for a century and a half.

Governor Yeardley sailed from England January, 1619, and reached Virginia on the 29th of April. After some weeks of preparation, he issued a general proclamation setting in operation the Company's orders. It was decreed, "that all those who were resident here before the departure of Sir Thomas Dale should be freed and acquitted from such publique services and labors which formerly they suffered, and that those cruel laws by which we had so long been governed were now abrogated, and that now we were to be governed by those free laws which his Majesty's subjects live under in Englande. . . . And that they might have a hand in the governing of themselves, it was granted that a General Assembly should be held yearly once, whereat were to be present the Governor and Counsell, with two Burgesses from each plantation freely to be elected by the inhabitants thereof; this Assembly to have power to make and ordaine whatsoever lawes and orders should by them be thought good and proffittable for our subsistence."[25]

The exact date of the election for Burgesses is not known.[26] The statement that the representatives were to be "chosen by the inhabitants" seems to indicate that the franchise was at once given to all male adults, or at least to all freemen. "All principall officers in Virginia were to be chosen by ye balloting box." From the very first there were parties, and it is possible that the factions of the London Company were reflected at the polls in the early elections. The Magna Charta made provision for the establishment of boroughs, which were to serve both as units for local government and as electoral districts. No attempt was made to secure absolute uniformity of population in the boroughs, but there were no glaring inequali-

[24] F. R., p. 293.

[25] F. R., p. 312.

[26] F. R., p. 315.

ties. With the regard for the practical which has always been characteristic of Englishmen, the Company seized upon the existing units, such as towns, plantations and hundreds, as the basis of their boroughs. In some cases several of these units were merged to form one borough, in others, a plantation or a town or a hundred as it stood constituted a borough. As there were eleven of these districts and as each district chose two Burgesses, the first General Assembly was to contain twenty-two representatives.[27]

The Assembly convened at Jamestown, August 9th, 1619. "The most convenient place we could finde to sitt in," says the minutes, "was the Quire of the Churche Where Sir George Yeardley, the Governor, being sett down in his accustomed place, those of the Counsel of Estate sate nexte him on both hands excepte onely the Secretary then appointed Speaker, who sate right before him, John Twine, the clerk of the General Assembly, being placed nexte the Speaker, and Thomas Pierse, the Sergeant, standing at the barre, to be ready for any service the Assembly shoulde comand him. But forasmuche as men's affaires doe little prosper where God's service is neglected, all the Burgesses tooke their places in the Quire till a prayer was said by Mr. Bucke, the Minister. . . . Prayer being ended, . . . all the Burgesses were intreatted to retyre themselves into the body of the Churche, which being done, before they were fully admitted, they were called in order and by name, and so every man tooke the oathe of Supremacy and entered the Assembly."[28]

The body at once claimed and made good its right to exclude Burgesses who they thought were not entitled to seats. The Speaker himself raised an objection to admitting the representatives of Warde's plantation, because that settlement had been made without a commission from the London Company. But Captain Warde promised to secure a patent as soon as possible, and the objection was waived. The Assembly refused absolutely, however, to seat the Burgesses from Martin's Hundred. Captain Martin had been one of the first Council for Virginia, and as a reward for his long services had been

[27] Nar. of Va., pp. 249, 250.

[28] Nar. of Va., p. 251.

granted privileges that rendered him almost independent of the government at Jamestown. He was summoned before the Assembly and requested to relinquish these extraordinary rights, but he refused to do so. "I hold my patent," he said, "for my service don, which noe newe or late comer can meritt or challenge."[29] So the Assembly, feeling that it would be mockery to permit the Burgesses from Martin's Hundred to assist in the making of laws which their own constituents, because of their especial charter, might with impunity disobey, refused to admit them.[30]

The legislative powers granted the Virginia Assembly in the Magna Charta, and continued with slight alterations after the revocation of the charter of the London Company, were very extensive. The Assembly could pass laws dealing with a vast variety of matters appertaining to the safety and welfare of the colony. Statutes were enacted in the session of 1619 touching upon Indian affairs, the Church, land patents, the relations of servants and landlords, the planting of crops, general morality in Virginia, the price of tobacco, foreign trade, etc. The collected laws of the entire colonial period fill many volumes, and cover a vast variety of subjects. But there were three things which limited strictly the Assembly's field of action. They must pass no statutes contravening first, the laws of England; secondly, the charters; thirdly, the instructions sent them by the London Company. When the colony passed into the hands of the King, all statutes were forbidden that conflicted with the charters, or with the instructions of the Crown. These restrictions lasted during the entire colonial period, but they were not always carefully regarded. The Company, and later the King, retained two ways of nullifying legislation which was unauthorized, or was distasteful to them. First, there was the veto of the Governor. As the guardian of the interests of England and his monarch, this officer could block all legislation. Secondly, the Company, and later the King, could veto laws even though the Governor had consented to them.

[29] F. R., p. 317.

[30] Nar. of Va., pp. 252, 253, 254, 255, 260, 261.

But the most important power exercised by the Assembly was its control over taxation in Virginia. In the very first session it made use of this privilege by ordering, "That every man and manservant of above 16 years of age shall pay into the handes and Custody of the Burgesses of every Incorporation and plantation one pound of the best Tobacco".[31] The funds thus raised were utilized for the payment of the officers of the Assembly.

The levy by the poll, here used, was continued for many years, and became the chief support of the government. As the colony grew, however, and the need for greater revenues was felt, customs duties and other forms of taxation were resorted to. Large sums were raised by an export duty upon tobacco. At times tariffs were placed upon the importation of liquors, slaves and other articles. But these duties had to be used with great care, for the carrying of the colony was done chiefly by English merchants, and Parliament would permit nothing detrimental to their interests.

The Assembly claimed the exclusive right to levy general taxes. The Governor and Council time and again tried to wrest this privilege from them, but never with success.[32] The Burgesses, realizing that their hold upon the exchequer was the chief source of their power, were most careful never to relinquish it. From time to time the Governors sought to evade this restraint by levying taxes under the guise of fees. But this expedient invariably excited intense irritation, and yielded a revenue so small that most Governors thought it best to avoid it entirely. Of more importance were the quit-rents, a tax on land, paid to the King by all freeholders. But this was frequently avoided, and, except at rare intervals, the funds raised by it were left in Virginia to be expended for local purposes. The greatest blow to the power of the Burgesses was struck by the King in 1680, when he forced through the Assembly a law granting to the government a perpetual income

[31] Nar. of Va., p. 276.

[32] In 1662 the Assembly granted power to the Governor and Council for three years to levy a small tax by the poll. The county taxes for defraying local expenses, were assessed and collected by the justices of the peace. The vestries controlled the raising of the parish dues.

from the export duty on tobacco. This revenue, although not large, was usually sufficient to pay the Governor's salary, and thus to render him less dependent upon the Assembly. Finally, it must not be forgotten that the English government, although it refrained from taxing the colony directly, imposed an enormous indirect tax by means of a tariff upon tobacco brought into England. These duties were collected in England, but there can be no doubt that the incidence of the tax rested partly upon the Virginia planters. Despite these various duties, all levied without its consent, the Assembly exercised a very real control over taxation in Virginia, and used it as an effective weapon against the encroachments of the Governors.

From the very first the General Assembly showed itself an energetic and determined champion of the rights of the people. Time and again it braved the anger of the Governor and of the King himself, rather than yield the slightest part of its privileges. During the decade preceding the English Revolution only the heroic resistance of this body saved the liberal institutions of the colony from destruction at the hands of Charles II and James II.

The General Assembly was not only a legislative body, it was also a court of justice, and for many years served as the highest tribunal of the colony. The judicial function was entrusted to a joint committee from the two houses, whose recommendations were usually accepted without question. Since this committee invariably contained more Burgesses than Councillors, the supreme court was practically controlled by the representatives of the people. During the reign of Charles II, however, the Assembly was deprived of this function by royal proclamation, and the judiciary fell almost entirely into the hands of the Governor and Council.

The General Assembly consisted of two chambers—the House of Burgesses and the Council. In the early sessions the houses sat together and probably voted as one body.[33] Later, however, they were divided and voted separately. The Burgesses, as time went on, gradually increased in numbers until they became a large body, but the Council was always small.

[33] Miller, p. 41.

The Councillors were royal appointees. But since the King could not always know personally the prominent men of the colony, he habitually confirmed without question the nominations of the Governor. The members of the Council were usually persons of wealth, influence and ability. As they were subject to removal by the King and invariably held one or more lucrative governmental offices, it was customary for them to display great servility to the wishes of his Majesty or of the Governor. It was very unusual for them to oppose in the Assembly any measure recommended by the King, or in accord with his expressed wishes. Although the Councillors were, with rare exceptions, natives of Virginia, they were in no sense representative of the people of the colony.

As the upper house of the Assembly, the Council exercised a powerful influence upon legislation. After the separation of the chambers their consent became necessary for the passage of all bills, even money bills. Their legislative influence declined during the eighteenth century, however, because of the growing spirit of liberalism in Virginia, and the increasing size of the House of Burgesses.

The executive powers entrusted to the Council were also of very great importance. The Governor was compelled by his instructions to secure its assistance and consent in the most important matters. And since the chief executive was always a native of England, and often entirely ignorant of conditions in the colony, he was constantly forced to rely upon the advice of his Council. This tendency was made more pronounced by the frequent changes of Governors that marked the last quarter of the seventeenth century. So habitually did the Council exercise certain functions, not legally within their jurisdiction, that they began to claim them as theirs by right. And the Governor was compelled to respect these claims as scrupulously as the King of England respects the conventions that hedge in and limit his authority.

Before the end of the seventeenth century the Council had acquired extraordinary influence in the government. With the right to initiate and to block legislation, with almost complete control over the judiciary, with great influence in administrative matters, it threatened to become an oligarchy of almost unlimited power.

But it must not be supposed that the influence of the Council rendered impotent the King's Governor. Great powers were lodged in the hands of this officer by his various instructions and commissions. He was commander of the militia, was the head of the colonial church, he appointed most of the officers, attended to foreign affairs, and put the laws into execution. His influence, however, resulted chiefly from the fact that he was the representative of the King. In the days of Charles I, in the Restoration Period and under James II, when the Stuarts were combating liberal institutions, both in England and in the colonies, the Governor exercised a powerful and dangerous control over affairs in Virginia. But after the English Revolution his power declined. As the people of England no longer dreaded a monarch whose authority now rested solely upon acts of Parliament, so the Virginians ceased to fear his viceroy.

The powers officially vested in the Governor were by no means solely executive. He frequently made recommendations to the Assembly, either in his own name or the name of the King, and these recommendations at times assumed the nature of commands. If the Burgesses were reluctant to obey, he had numerous weapons at hand with which to intimidate them and whip them into line. Unscrupulous use of the patronage and threats of the King's dire displeasure were frequently resorted to. The Governor presided over the upper house, and voted there as any other member. Moreover, he could veto all bills, even those upon which he had voted in the affirmative in the Council. Thus he had a large influence in shaping the laws of the colony, and an absolute power to block all legislation.

Such, in outline, was the government originated for Virginia by the liberal leaders of the London Company, and put into operation by Sir George Yeardley. It lasted, with the short intermission of the Commonwealth Period, for more than one hundred and fifty years, and under it Virginia became the most populous and wealthy of the English colonies in America.

The successful cultivation of tobacco in Virginia, as we have seen, put new life into the discouraged London Company. The shareholders, feeling that now at last the colony would grow and prosper, exerted themselves to the utmost to secure desirable settlers and to equip them properly. Soon fleets of considerable size were leaving the English ports for America, their decks and cabins crowded with emigrants and their holds laden with clothing, arms and farming implements.[34] During the months from March 1620 to March 1621 ten ships sailed, carrying no less than 1051 persons.[35] In the year ending March, 1622, seventeen ships reached Virginia, bringing over fifteen hundred new settlers.[36] And this stream continued without abatement until 1624, when disasters in Virginia, quarrels among the shareholders and the hostility of the King brought discouragement to the Company. In all, there reached the colony from November, 1619, to February, 1625, nearly five thousand men, women and children.[37]

Although tobacco culture was the only enterprise of the colony which had yielded a profit, it was not the design of Sandys and his friends that that plant should monopolize the energies of the settlers. They hoped to make Virginia an industrial community, capable of furnishing the mother country with various manufactured articles, then imported from foreign countries. Especially anxious were they to render England independent in their supply of pig iron. Ore having been discovered a few miles above Henrico on the James, a furnace was erected there and more than a hundred skilled workmen brought over from England to put it into operation. Before the works could be completed, however, they were utterly demolished by the savages, the machinery thrown into the river, all the workmen slaughtered,[38] and the only return the Company obtained for an outlay of thousands of pounds was a shovel, a pair of tongs and one bar of iron.[39] Efforts were made later to repair the havoc wrought by the Indians and to reëstablish the works, but they came to nothing. Not

[34] F. R., p. 376.
[35] F. R., p. 415.
[36] F. R., p. 464.
[37] F. R., p. 612.
[38] Bruce, Ec. Hist., Vol. II, pp. 448, 449.
[39] *Ibid.*

until the time of Governor Spotswood were iron furnaces operated in Virginia, and even then the industry met with a scant measure of success.

The Company also made an earnest effort to promote the manufacture of glass in Virginia. This industry was threatened with extinction in England as a result of the great inroads that had been made upon the timber available for fuel, and it was thought that Virginia, with its inexhaustible forests, offered an excellent opportunity for its rehabilitation. But here too they were disappointed. The sand of Virginia proved unsuitable for the manufacture of glass. The skilled Italian artisans sent over to put the works into operation were intractable and mutinous. After trying in various ways to discourage the enterprise, so that they could return to Europe, these men brought matters to a close by cracking the furnace with a crowbar. George Sandys, in anger, declared "that a more damned crew hell never vomited".[40]

In order to show that they were sincere in their professions of interest in the spiritual welfare of the Indians, the Company determined to erect a college at Henrico "for the training up of the children of those Infidels in true Religion, moral virtue and civility".[41] The clergy of England were enthusiastic in their support of this good design, and their efforts resulted in liberal contributions from various parts of the kingdom.[42] Unfortunately, however, the money thus secured was expended in sending to the college lands a number of "tenants" the income from whose labor was to be utilized in establishing and supporting the institution.[43] As some of these settlers fell victims to disease and many others were destroyed in the massacre of 1622, the undertaking had to be abandoned, and of course all thought of converting and civilizing the savages was given up during the long and relentless war that ensued.

Even more discouraging than these failures was the hostility of the King to the cultivation of tobacco in Virginia, and his restrictions upon its importation into England. Appeals were

[40] Bruce, Ec. Hist., Vol. II, pp. 442, 443.

[41] F. R., p. 322.

[42] F. R., p. 335.

[43] F. R., p. 336.

made to him to prohibit the sale of Spanish tobacco, in order that the Virginia planters might dispose of their product at a greater profit. This, it was argued, would be the most effective way of rendering the colony prosperous and self sustaining. But James, who was still bent upon maintaining his Spanish policy, would not offend Philip by excluding his tobacco from England. Moreover, in 1621, he issued a proclamation restricting the importation of the leaf from Virginia and the Somers Isles to fifty-five thousand pounds annually.[44] This measure created consternation in Virginia and in the London Company. The great damage it would cause to the colony and the diminution in the royal revenue that would result were pointed out to James, but for the time he was obdurate.[45] Indeed, he caused additional distress by granting the customs upon tobacco to a small association of farmers of the revenue, who greatly damaged the interests of the colony. In 1622, James, realizing that his policy in regard to tobacco was injuring the exchequer, made a compromise with the Company. The King agreed to restrict the importation of Spanish tobacco to 60,000 pounds a year, and after two years to exclude it entirely. All the Virginia leaf was to be admitted, but the Crown was to receive one third of the crop, while the other two thirds was subjected to a duty of six pence a pound.[46] This agreement proved most injurious to the Company, and it was soon abandoned, but the heavy exactions of the King continued. Undoubtedly this unwise policy was most detrimental to Virginia. Not only did it diminish the returns of the Company and make it impossible for Sandys to perfect all his wise plans for the colony, but it put a decided check upon immigration. Many that would have gone to Virginia to share in the profits of the planters, remained at home when they saw that these profits were being confiscated by the King.[47]

Yet the strenuous efforts of the London Company would surely have brought something like prosperity to the colony had not an old enemy returned to cause the destruction of hundreds of the settlers. This was the sickness. For some years

[44] Bruce, Ec. Hist., Vol. I, p. 264.
[45] Bruce, Ec. Hist., Vol. I, p. 265.
[46] Bruce, Ec. Hist., Vol. I, p. 269.
[47] P. R. O., CO1-3.

the mortality had been very low, because the old planters were acclimated, and few new immigrants were coming to Virginia. But with the stream of laborers and artisans that the Sandys régime now sent over, the scourge appeared again with redoubled fury. As early as January, 1620, Governor Yeardley wrote "of the great mortallitie which hath been in Virginia, about 300 of ye inhabitants having dyed this year".[48] The sickness was most deadly in the newly settled parts of the colony, "to the consumption of divers Hundreds, and almost the utter destruction of some particular Plantations".[49] The London Company, distressed at the loss of so many men, saw in their misfortunes the hand of God, and wrote urging "the more carefull observations of his holy laws to work a reconciliation".[50] They also sent directions for the construction, in different parts of the colony, of four guest houses, or hospitals, for the lodging and entertaining of fifty persons each, upon their first arrival.[51] But all efforts to check the scourge proved fruitless. In the year ending March, 1621 over a thousand persons died upon the immigrant vessels and in Virginia.[52] Despite the fact that hundreds of settlers came to the colony during this year, the population actually declined. In 1621 the percentage of mortality was not so large, but the actual number of deaths increased. During the months from March, 1621, to March, 1622, nearly twelve hundred persons perished. It was like condemning a man to death to send him to the colony. Seventy-five or eighty per cent. of the laborers that left England in search of new homes across the Atlantic died before the expiration of their first year. The exact number of deaths in 1622 is not known, but there is reason to believe that it approximated thirteen hundred.[53] Mr. George Sandys, brother of the Secretary of the London Company, wrote, "Such a pestilent fever rageth this winter amongst us: never knowne before in Virginia, by the infected people that came over in ye *Abigall,* who were poisoned with . . . beer and all falling sick & many dying, every where dispersed the contagion, and

[48] F. R., p. 372.
[49] F. R., p. 377.
[50] F. R., p. 377.
[51] F. R., p. 377.
[52] F. R., p. 415.
[53] F. R., p. 506.

the forerunning Summer hath been also deadly upon us."[54] Not until 1624 did the mortality decline. Then it was that the Governor wrote, "This summer, God be thanked, the Colony hath very well stood to health".[55] The dread sickness had spent itself for lack of new victims, for the immigration had declined and the old planters had become "seasoned".

History does not record an epidemic more deadly than that which swept over Virginia during these years. It is estimated that the number of those that lost their lives from the diseases native to the colony and to those brought in from the infected ships amounts to no less than four thousand.[56] When the tide of immigration was started by Sir Edwin Sandys in 1619, there were living in Virginia about nine hundred persons; when it slackened in 1624 the population was but eleven hundred. The sending of nearly five thousand settlers to Virginia had resulted in a gain of but two hundred. It is true that the tomahawk and starvation accounts for a part of this mortality, but by far the larger number of deaths was due to disease.

Yet hardly less horrible than the sickness was the Indian massacre of 1622. This disaster, which cost the lives of several hundred persons, struck terror into the hearts of every Englishman in Virginia. The colonists had not the least intimation that the savages meditated harm to them, for peace had existed between the races ever since the marriage of Rolfe and Pocahontas. Considering the protection of their palisades no longer necessary after that event, they had spread out over the colony in search of the most fertile lands. Their plantations extended at intervals for many miles along both banks of the James, and in the case of a sudden attack by the Indians it would obviously be difficult for the settlers to defend themselves or to offer assistance to their neighbors.

The apparent friendship of the Indians had created such great intimacy between the two races, that the savages were received into the homes of the white men and at times were fed at their tables.[57] At the command of the London Company

[54] F. R., p. 506.
[55] F. R., p. 608.
[56] P. R. O., CO1-36-37.
[57] Stith, p. 210.

itself some of the Indian youths had been adopted by the settlers and were being educated in the Christian faith. So unsuspecting were the people that they loaned the savages their boats, as they passed backward and forward, to formulate their plans for the massacre.[58]

The plot seems to have originated in the cunning brain of Opechancanough. This chief, always hostile to the white men, must have viewed with apprehension their encroachment upon the lands of his people. He could but realize that some day the swarms of foreigners that were arriving each year would exclude the Indians from the country of their forefathers. Perceiving his opportunity in the foolish security of the English and in their exposed situation, he determined to annihilate them in one general butchery.

His plans were laid with great cunning. Although thousands of natives knew of the design, no warning reached the white men until the very eve of the massacre. While Opechancanough was preparing this tremendous blow, he protested in the strongest terms his perpetual good will and love, declaring that the sky would fall before he would bring an end to the peace.[59] In order to lull the suspicions of the planters, "even but two daies before the massacre", he guided some of them "with much kindnesse through the woods, and one Browne that lived among them to learne the language", he sent home to his master. The evening before the attack the Indians came as usual to the plantations with deer, turkeys, fish, fruits and other provisions to sell.[60]

That night, however, a warning was received, which although too late to save the most remote settlements, preserved many hundreds from the tomahawk. Chanco, an Indian boy who had been adopted by an Englishman named Race, revealed the entire plot to his master. The man secured his house, and rowed away before dawn in desperate haste to Jamestown, to give warning to the Governor. "Whereby they were prevented, and at such other plantations as possibly intelligence could be given."[61]

[58] Stith, p. 210.
[59] Arb. Smith, p. 573.
[60] Arb. Smith, p. 573.
[61] Arb. Smith, p. 578.

The assault of the savages was swift and deadly. In all parts of the colony they fell upon the settlers, and those that had received no warning were, in most cases, butchered before they could suspect that harm was intended. Sometimes the Indians sat down to breakfast with their victims, "whom immediately with their owne tooles they slew most barbarously, not sparing either age or sex, man woman or childe".[62] Many were slain while working in the fields; others were trapped in their houses and butchered before they could seize their weapons. The savages, "not being content with their lives, . . . fell againe upon the dead bodies, making as well as they could a fresh murder, defacing, dragging, and mangling their dead carkases into many peeces".[63]

That the plot was so successful was due to the completeness of the surprise, for where the English made the least resistance the savages were usually beaten off. A planter named Causie, when attacked and wounded and surrounded by the Indians, "with an axe did cleave one of their heads, whereby the rest fled and he escaped; for they hurt not any that did either fight or stand upon their guard. In one place where they had warning of it, (they) defended the house against sixty or more that assaulted it."[64]

At the plantation of a Mr. Harrison, where there were gathered seven men and eighteen or nineteen women and children, the savages set fire to a tobacco house and then came in to tell the men to quench it. Six of the English, not suspecting treachery, rushed out, and were shot full of arrows. Mr. Thomas Hamor, the seventh man, "having finished a letter he was writing, followed after to see what was the matter, but quickly they shot an arrow in his back, which caused him to returne and barricado up the dores, whereupon the Salvages set fire to the house. But a boy, seizing a gun which he found loaded, discharged it at random. At the bare report the enemy fled and Mr. Hamor with the women and children escaped."[65] In a nearby house, a party of English under Mr. Hamor's brother, were caught by the Indians without arms, but they

[62] Arb. Smith, p. 573.
[63] Arb. Smith, p. 574.
[64] Arb. Smith, p. 575.
[65] Arb. Smith, p. 576.

defended themselves successfully with spades, axes and brickbats.[66]

One of the first to fall was Reverend George Thorpe, a member of the Virginia Council, and a man of prominence in England.[67] Leaving a life of honor and ease, he had come to Virginia to work for the conversion of the Indians. He had apparently won the favor of Opechancanough, with whom he often discoursed upon the Christian religion. At the moment of his murder, his servant, perceiving the deadly intent of the savages, gave him warning, but his gentle nature would not permit him to believe harm of those whom he had always befriended, and he was cut down without resistance.[68]

The barbarous king failed in his design to destroy the English race in Virginia, but the massacre was a deadly blow to the colony. No less than three hundred and fifty-seven persons were slaughtered, including six Councillors. The news of the disaster brought dismay to the London Company. For a while they attempted to keep the matter a secret, but in a few weeks it was known all over England. Although the massacre could not have been foreseen or prevented, it served as a pretext for numerous attacks upon Sandys and the party which supported him. It discouraged many shareholders and made it harder to secure settlers for the colony. Even worse was the effect in Virginia. The system of farming in unprotected plantations, which had prevailed for some years, had now to be abandoned and many settlements that were exposed to the Indians were deserted. "We have not," wrote the Assembly, "the safe range of the Country for the increase of Cattle, Swyne, etc; nor for the game and fowle which the country affords in great plentye; besides our duties to watch and warde to secure ourselves and labor are as hard and chargeable as if the enemy were at all times present."[69]

The massacre was followed by a venomous war with the Indians, which lasted many years. The English, feeling that their families and their homes would never be safe so long as the savages shared the country with them, deliberately planned

[66] Arb. Smith, p. 576.

[67] Stith, p. 211.

[68] Stith, pp. 211, 212.

[69] F. R., pp. 576, 577.

the extermination of all hostile tribes in Virginia. Their conversion was given no further consideration. "The terms betwixt us and them," they declared, "are irreconcilable."[70] Governor Wyatt wrote, "All trade with them must be forbidden, and without doubt either we must cleere them or they us out of the Country."[71]

But it soon became apparent that neither people would be able to win an immediate or decisive victory. The Indians could not hope to destroy the English, now that their deeply laid plot had failed. In open battle their light arrows made no impression upon the coats of plate and of mail in which the white men were incased, while their own bodies were without protection against the superior weapons of their foes. On the other hand, it was very difficult for the colonists to strike the savages, because of the "advantages of the wood and the nimbleness of their heels".[72] Even though they "chased them to and fro", following them to their villages and burning their huts, they found it very difficult to do them serious harm.

Finally the English hit upon the plan of bringing distress upon the savages by destroying their corn. Although the Virginia tribes subsisted partly upon game, their chief support was from their fields of maize, and the entire failure of their crop would have reduced hundreds of them to the verge of starvation.[73] Each year the white men, in small companies, in various parts of the country, brought ruin to the corn fields. Sometimes the savages, in despair at the prospect of famine, made valiant efforts to defend their fields, but were invariably beaten off until the work of destruction was done.

The natives retaliated with many sudden raids upon the more exposed parts of the colony, where they burned, pillaged and murdered. The planter at work in his fields might expect to find them lurking in the high grass, while their ambushes in the woods made communication from plantation to plantation very dangerous. "The harmes that they do us," wrote the Assembly, "is by ambushes and sudden incursions, where they

[70] F. R., p. 576.
[71] F. R., p. 508.
[72] F. R., p. 576.
[73] Bruce, Ec. Hist., Vol. I, pp. 155 to 159.

see their advantages."[74] In 1625 Captain John Harvey declared that the two races were "ingaged in a mortall warre and fleshed in each others bloud, of which the Causes have been the late massacre on the Salvages parte. . . . I conceive that by the dispersion of the Plantations the Salvages hath the advantage in this warre, and that by their suddaine assaults they do us more harme than we do them by our set voyages".[75]

When the English had recovered from the first shock of the massacre, they planned four expeditions against the tribes living on the river above Jamestown. Mr. George Sandys attacked the Tappahatomaks, Sir George Yeardley the Wyanokes, Captain William Powell the Chickahominies and the Appomatocks, and Captain John West the Tanx-Powhatans. The savages, without attempting to make a stand, deserted their villages and their crops and fled at the approach of the English. Few were killed, for they were "so light and swift" that the white men, laden with their heavy armor, could not overtake them.[76] In the fall Sir George Yeardley led three hundred men down the river against the Nansemonds and against Opechancanough. The natives "set fire to their own houses, and spoiled what they could, and then fled with what they could carry; so that the English did make no slaughter amongst them for revenge. Their Corne fields being newly gathered, they surprised all they found, burnt the houses (that) remained unburnt, and so departed."[77]

It is remarkable that the colonists could continue this war while the sickness was raging among them. At the very time that Yeardley was fighting Opechancanough, hundreds of his comrades were dying "like cats and dogs". "With our small and sicklie forces," wrote Mr. George Sandys, "we have discomforted the Indians round about us, burnt their houses, gathered their corn and slain not a few; though they are as swift as Roebucks, like the violent lightening they are gone as soon as perceived, and not to be destroyed but by surprise or famine."[78]

[74] F. R., p. 576.

[75] F. R., p. 611.

[76] Arb. Smith, p. 594.

[77] Arb. Smith, p. 559; F. R., pp. 475, 495.

[78] F. R., p. 510.

How bitter was the war is shown by an act of treachery by the English that would have shamed the savages themselves. In 1623, the Indians, discouraged by the destruction of their crops, sent messengers to Jamestown, asking for peace. The colonists determined to take advantage of this overture to recover their prisoners and at the same time to strike a sudden blow at their enemy. Early in June, Captain William Tucker with twelve well armed men was sent "in a shalope under colour to make peace with them". On the arrival of this party at the chief town of Opechancanough, the savages thronged down to the riverside to parley with them, but the English refused to consider any terms until all prisoners had been restored. Assenting to this, the savages brought forth seven whites and they were placed aboard the vessel. Having thus accomplished their purpose, the soldiers, at a given signal, let fly a volley into the midst of the crowd, killing "some 40 Indians including 3 of the chiefest".[79]

In 1624 the English won a great victory over the most troublesome of the Indian tribes, the Pamunkeys. Governor Wyatt, in leading an expedition against this people had evidently expected little resistance, for he brought with him but sixty fighting men. The Pamunkeys, however, had planted that year a very large crop of corn, which they needed for the support of themselves and their confederates, and they determined to protect it at all hazards. So Wyatt and his little band were surprised, on approaching their village to find before them more than eight hundred warriors prepared for battle. The English did not falter in the face of this army, and a fierce contest ensued. "Fightinge not only for safeguards of their houses and such a huge quantity of corn", but for their reputation with the other nations, the Pamunkeys displayed unusual bravery. For two days the battle went on. Whenever the young warriors wavered before the volleys of musketry, they were driven back into the fight by the older men. Twenty-four of the English were detached from the firing line and were employed in destroying the maize. In this they were so successful that enough corn was cut down "as by Estimation

[79] F. R., pp. 514, 515.

of men of good judgment was sufficient to have sustained fower thousand men for a twelvemonth". At last the savages in despair gave up the fight and stood nearby "rufully lookinge on whilst their Corne was cutt down". "In this Expedition," wrote the colonists, "sixteene of the English were hurte our first and seconde day, whereby nyne of the best shott were made unserviceable for that tyme, yett never a man slayne, nor none miscarried of those hurtes, Since when they have not greatly troubled us, nor interrupted our labours."[80]

The series of misfortunes which befel the London Company during the administration of Sir Edwin Sandys culminated in the loss of their charter. For some time King James had been growing more and more hostile to the party that had assumed control of the colony. It is highly probable that he had had no intimation, when the charter of 1612 was granted, that popular institutions would be established in Virginia, and the extension of the English parliamentary system to America must have been distasteful to him. The enemies of Sandys had been whispering to the King that he "aymed at nothing more than to make a free popular state there, and himselfe and his assured friends to be the leaders of them".[81] James knew that Sandys was not friendly to the prerogative of the Crown. It had been stated "that there was not any man in the world that carried a more malitious heart to the Government of a Monarchie".[82]

In 1621 the controlling party in the London Company was preparing a new charter for Virginia. The contents of this document are not known, but it is exceedingly probable that it was intended as the preface to the establishment of a government in the colony far more liberal than that of England itself. It was proposed to have the charter confirmed by act of Parliament, and to this James had consented, provided it proved satisfactory to the Privy Council.[83] But it is evident that when the Councillors had examined it, they advised the King not to assent to it or to allow it to appear in Parliament. Indeed the document must have stirred James' anger, for not

[80] P. R. O., COI-3.
[81] F. R., p. 530.
[82] F. R., p. 529.
[83] F R., p. 393.

only did he end all hopes of its passage, but he "struck some terrour into most undertakers for Virginia", by imprisoning Sir Edwin Sandys.[84]

Even more distasteful to the King than the establishment of popular institutions in the little colony was the spreading of liberal doctrines throughout England by the Sandys faction of the Company. James could no longer tolerate their meetings, if once he began to look upon them as the nursery of discontent and sedition. The party that was so determined in its purpose to plant a republican government in Virginia might stop at nothing to accomplish the same end in England. James knew that national politics were often discussed in the assemblies of the Company and that the parties there were sometimes as "animated one against the other" as had been the "Guelfs and Gebillines" of Italy.[85] He decided that the best way to end these controversies and frustrate the designs of his enemies was to annul the charter of the Company and make Virginia a royal colony.

The first unmistakable sign of his hostility came in June 1622, when he interfered with the election of their treasurer. It was not, he told them, his intention "to infringe their liberty of free election", but he sent a list of names that would be acceptable to him, and asked them to put one of these in nomination. To this the Company assented readily enough, even nominating two from the list, but when the election was held, the King's candidates were overwhelmingly defeated.[86] When James heard this, he "flung himself away in a furious passion", being "not well satisfied that out of so large a number by him recommended they had not made any choice".[87] The incident meant that James had given the Company an unmistakable intimation that it would be well for them to place the management of affairs in the hands of men more in harmony with himself, and that they had scornfully refused.

The Company was now doomed, for the King decided that the charter must be revoked. He could not, of course, annul a grant that had passed under the Great Seal, without some pre-

[84] F. R., pp. 436, 437.

[85] F. R., p. 542.

[86] F. R., p. 477.

[87] F. R., p. 478.

tence of legal proceedings, but when once he had determined on the ruin of the Company, means to accomplish his end were not lacking. John Ferrar wrote, "The King, notwithstanding his royal word and honor pledged to the contrary . . . was now determined with all his force to make the last assault, and give the death blow to this . . . Company."[88]

James began by hunting evidence of mismanagement and incapacity by the Sandys party. He gave orders to Captain Nathaniel Butler, who had spent some months in Virginia, to write a pamphlet describing the condition of the colony. *The Unmasking of Virginia,* as Butler's work is called was nothing less than a bitter assault upon the conduct of affairs since the beginning of the Sandys administration. Unfortunately, it was not necessary for the author to exaggerate much in his description of the frightful conditions in the colony; but it was unfair to place the blame upon the Company. The misfortunes of the settlers were due to disease and the Indians and did not result from incapacity or negligence on the part of Sandys. The Company drew up "A True answer to a writing of Information presented to his Majesty by Captain Nathaniel Butler", denying most of the charges and explaining others, but they could not efface the bad impression caused by the *Unmasking.*[89]

In April, 1623, James appointed a commission to make enquiry into the "true estate of . . . Virginia".[90] This body was directed to investigate "all abuses and grievances . . . all wrongs and injuryes done to any adventurers or planters and the grounds and causes thereof, and to propound after what sort the same may be better managed".[91] It seems quite clear that the commissioners understood that they were expected to give the King "some true ground to work upon", in his attack on the Company's charter.[92] In a few weeks they were busy receiving testimony from both sides, examining records and searching for evidence. They commanded the Company to deliver to them all "Charters, Books, Letters, Petitions,

[88] F. R., pp. 531, 532.

[89] F R., p, 524.

[90] F. R., p. 520.

[91] F. R., p. 520.

[92] F. R., p. 521.

Lists of names, of Provisions, Invoyces of Goods, and all other writing whatsoever" They examined the clerk of the Company, the messenger and the keeper of the house in which they held their meetings.[93] They intercepted private letters from Virginia, telling of the horrible suffering there, and made the King aware of their contents.[94]

In July the commission made its report. It found that "the people sent to inhabit there . . . were most of them by God's visitation, sicknes of body, famine, and by massacres . . . dead and deceased, and those that were living of them lived in miserable and lamentable necessity and want. . . . That this neglect they conceived, must fall on the Governors and Company here, who had power to direct the Plantations there. . . . That if his Majesty's first Grant of April 10 1606, and his Majesty's most prudent and princely Instructions given in the beginning . . . had been pursued, much better effects had been produced, than had been by the alteration thereof, into so popular a course."[95] James was much pleased with the report, and it confirmed his determination to "resume the government, and to reduce that popular form so as to make it agree with the monarchial form".[96]

Before taking the matter to the courts, the King resolved to offer the Company a compromise. If they would give up the old charter, he said, a new one would be granted them, preserving all private interests, but restoring the active control of the colony to the Crown. The government was to be modelled upon the old plan of 1606, which had already given so much trouble. "His Majesty," the Company was told, "hath . . . resolved by a new Charter to appoint a Governor and twelve assistants, resident here in England, unto whom shall be committed the government. . . . And his Majesty is pleased that there shall be resident in Virginia a Governor and twelve assistants, to be nominated by the Governor and assistants here . . . whereby all matters of importance may be directed by his Majesty."[97] The Company was commanded

[93] F. R., p. 541.
[94] F. R., p. 535.
[95] F. R., pp. 519, 520.
[96] F. R., p. 542.
[97] F. R., p. 551.

to send its reply immediately, "his Majesty being determined, in default of such submission, to proceed for the recalling of the said former charters".[98]

A special meeting of the stockholders was called, October 30th, 1623, to consider the King's proposal. Every man present must have known that the rejection of the compromise would mean the loss of all the money he had invested in the colony, and that if the King's wishes were acceded to his interests would be preserved. But the Company was fighting for something higher than personal gain—for the maintenance of liberal institutions in America, for the defence of the rights of English citizens. After a "hot debate" they put the question to the vote, and the offer was rejected, there being "only nine hands for the delivering up of the Charters, and all the rest (being about three score more) were of a contrary opinion".[99]

As a last hope the Company resolved to seek the assistance of Parliament. A petition was drawn up to be presented to the Commons, and the shareholders that were members of that body were requested to give it their strenuous support when it came up for consideration. The petition referred to Virginia as a "child of the Kingdom, exposed as in the wilderness to extreme danger and as it were fainting and labouring for life", and it prayed the House to hear "the grievances of the Colony and Company, and grant them redress".[100] The matter was brought before the Commons in May, 1624, but before it could be considered, a message was received from the King warning them "not to trouble themselves with this petition as their doing so could produce nothing but a further increase Schisme and factions in the Company". "Ourself," he announced, "will make it our own work to settle the quiet, and wellfare of the plantations."[101] This was received with some "soft mutterings" by the Commons, but they thought it best to comply, and the Company was left to its fate.[102]

In the meanwhile the King had placed his case in the hands

[98] F. R., p. 542.

[99] F. R., p. 554.

[100] F. R., pp. 595, 596.

[101] F. R., pp. 597, 598.

[102] F. R., p. 598.

of Attorney-General Coventry, who had prepared a *quo warranto* against the Company.[103] Although all hope of retaining the charter was gone, the Sandys party were determined to fight to the end. They voted to employ attorneys and to plead their case before the King's Bench. The *quo warranto* came up June 26th, 1624, and "the Virginia Patent was overthrown", on a mistake in pleading.[104] With this judgment the London Company practically ceased to exist, and Virginia became a royal province.

[103] F. R., p. 587.

[104] F. R., pp. 601, 602.

CHAPTER III

THE EXPULSION OF SIR JOHN HARVEY

The people of Virginia sympathized deeply with the London Company in its efforts to prevent the revocation of the charter. The Governor, the Council and the Burgesses gave active assistance to Sandys and his friends by testifying to the wisdom of the management and contradicting the calumnies of their enemies. In the midst of the controversy the Privy Council had appointed a commission which they sent to Virginia to investigate conditions there and to gather evidence against the Company. This board consisted of John Harvey, John Pory, Abraham Piersey and Samuel Matthews, men destined to play prominent rôles in Virginia history, but then described as "certayne obscure persons".[1] When the commissioners reached the colony they made known to the Assembly the King's desire to revoke the charter and to take upon himself the direction of the government. They then asked the members to subscribe to a statement expressing their gratitude for the care of the King, and willingness to consent to the contemplated change. The Assembly returned the paper unsigned. "When our consent," they said, "to the surrender of the Pattents, shalbe required, will be the most proper time to make reply: in the mean time wee conceive his Majesties intention of changing the government hath proceeded from much misinformation."[2]

After this they ignored the commissioners, and addressed themselves in direct letters and petitions to the King and the Privy Council.[3] They apprehended, they wrote, no danger from the present government, which had converted into freedom the slavery they had endured in former times.[4] They prayed that their liberal institutions might not be destroyed

[1] F. R., p. 556; Osg., Vol. III, p. 47. [2] F. R., p. 574.
[3] F. R., p. 572. [4] Osg., Vol. III, p. 50.

or the old Smith faction of the Company placed over them again.[5] These papers they sent to England by one of their number, John Pountis, even refusing to let the commissioners see them. But Pory succeeded in securing copies from the acting secretary, Edward Sharpless.[6] The Council, upon learning of this betrayal, were so incensed against the secretary that they sentenced him to "stand in the Pillory and there to have his Ears nailed to it, and cut off".[7] His punishment was modified, however, so that when he was "sett in the Pillorie", he "lost but a part of one of his eares".[8] The King, upon learning of this incident, which was represented to him "as a bloody and barbarous act", became highly incensed against the Council.[9]

In the meanwhile James had appointed a large commission, with Viscount Mandeville at its head, "to confer, consult, resolve and expedite all affaires . . . of Virginia, and to take care and give order for the directing and government thereof".[10] This body met weekly at the house of Sir Thomas Smith, and immediately assumed control of the colony.[11] Their first act was to decide upon a form of government to replace the Virginia Magna Charta. In conformance with the wishes of the King they resolved to return to the plan of 1606. In their recommendations no mention was made of an Assembly. It seemed for a while that the work of Sandys was to be undone, and the seeds of liberty in Virginia destroyed almost before they had taken root. Fortunately, however, this was not to be. The commission, perhaps wishing to allay the fears of the colonists, reappointed Sir Francis Wyatt Governor, and retained most of the old Council. This made it certain that for a while at least the government was to be in the hands of men of lofty character and liberal views.[12] More fortunate still for Virginia was the death of James I. This event removed the most determined enemy of their Assembly, and placed upon the throne a man less hostile to the Sandys faction, less determined to suppress the liberal institutions of the colony.

[5] Osg., Vol. III, p. 50.
[6] F. R., p. 584.
[7] F. R., p. 584.
[8] P. R. O., CO1-3.
[9] F. R., p. 584.
[10] F. R., p. 634 .
[11] Osg., Vol. III, p. 74.
[12] F. R., p. 639 .

Soon after his accession Charles I abolished the Mandeville commission and appointed in its place a committee of the Privy Council.[13] For a while he seemed inclined to restore the Company, for he consulted with Sandys and requested him to give his opinion "touching the best form of Government".[14] But he finally rejected his proposals, declaring that he had come to the same determination that his father had held. He was resolved, he said, that the government should be immediately dependent upon himself and not be committed to any company or corporation.[15] But, like his father, he was "pleased to authorise Sir Francis Wyatt knight to be governor there, and such as are now employed for his Majesties Councell there to have authoritie to continue the same employment". No provision was made for a representative body, the power of issuing decrees, ordinances and public orders being assigned to the Council.

But the Assembly was saved by the unselfish conduct of Wyatt and Yeardley and their Councils.[16] Had these men sought their own gain at the expense of the liberty of their fellow colonists, they would have welcomed a change that relieved them from the restraint of the representatives of the people. The elimination of the Burgesses would have left them as absolute as had been Wingfield and the first Council. But they were most anxious to preserve for Virginia the right of representative government, and wrote to England again and again pleading for the reëstablishment of the Assembly.[17] "Above all," they said, "we humbly intreat your Lordships that we may retaine the Libertie of our Generall Assemblie, than which nothing can more conduce to our satisfaction or the publique utilitie."[18] In 1625 Yeardley himself crossed the ocean to present a new petition. He pleaded with Charles "to avoid the oppression of Governors there, that their liberty of Generall Assemblyes may be continued and confirmed, and that they may have a voice in the election of officers, as in other Corporations".[19] After the overthrow of the Company char-

[13] F. R., p. 640.
[14] F. R., p. 641.
[15] F. R., pp. 641, 642.
[16] F. R., p. 647.
[17] F. R., p. 648.
[18] F. R., p. 573.
[19] P. R. O., CO1-3-7.

ter, there could be no legal election of Burgesses and no legislation save by proclamation of the Governor and Council. Yet Wyatt, in order to preserve as far as possible some form of representative government, held conventions or informal meetings of leading citizens, to confer with the Council on important matters. They issued papers under the title of "Governor, Councell and Collony of Virginia assembled together",[20] and it is possible that the people elected their delegates just as they had formerly chosen Burgesses. Since, however, acts passed by these assemblages could not be enforced in the courts, all legislation for the time being took the form of proclamations.[21]

Finally Charles yielded to the wishes of the people, and, in the fall of 1627, sent written instructions to the officials in Virginia to hold an election of Burgesses and to summon a General Assembly.[22] The King's immediate motive for this important step was his desire to gain the planters' acceptance through their representatives of an offer which he made to buy all their tobacco. In the spring of 1628 the Council wrote, "In obedience to his Majesties Commands wee have given order that all the Burgesses of Particular Plantations should shortly be assembled at James Citty that by the general and unanimous voice of the whole Colony his Majesty may receave a full answere."[23] Although the Assembly must have realized that its very existence might depend upon its compliance with the King's wishes, it refused to accept his proposition. The planters were willing to sell their tobacco to his Majesty, but only upon more liberal terms than those offered them. Charles rejected the counter-proposals of the Virginians, with some show of anger, but he did not abolish the Assembly, and in ensuing years sessions were held with great regularity.[24]

The apprehensions of the colonists during this trying period were made more acute by the resignation of Sir Francis Wyatt. In the winter of 1625-26 the Council wrote the Virginia commissioners, "The Governor hath long expected a

[20] P. R. O., CO1-3-5.
[21] Hen., Vol. I, pp. 129, 130.
[22] F. R., p. 648; P. R. O., CO1-4.
[23] P. R. O., CO1-20.
[24] Bruce, Ec. Hist., Vol. I, p. 287.

Successor, and the necessity of his private estate compelling him not to put off any longer his return for England, wee hope it is already provided for."[25] Great must have been the relief in the colony when it was learned that Sir George Yeardley had been chosen to succeed Governor Wyatt. Yeardley had been the bearer of the Virginia Magna Charta, under which the first Assembly had been established, and his services had not been forgotten by the people. But he was not destined to see the restoration of the Burgesses, for he died in November, 1627.[26] We have lost, wrote the Council in great grief, "a main pillar of this our building & thereby a support to the whole body".[27]

By virtue of previous appointment, Captain Francis West, brother of the Lord De la Warr who had lost his life in the service of Virginia, at once assumed the reins of government. Captain West continued in office until March 5th, 1629, when he resigned in order to return to England.[28] John Harvey, a member of the Virginia commission of 1624, was the King's next choice for Governor, but pending his arrival, the office fell to one of the Council—Dr. John Pott. This man had long been a resident of Virginia, and had acted as Physician-General during the years when the sickness was at the worst. He is described as "a Master of Arts . . . well practiced in chirurgery and physic, and expert also in the distilling of waters, (besides) many other ingenious devices".[29] He had made use of these accomplishments to poison large numbers of Indians after the massacre of 1622.[30] This exploit caused the temporary loss of his place in the Council, for when James I settled the government after the fall of the Company, Pott was left out at the request of the Earl of Warwick, because "he was the poysoner of the salvages thear".[31] In 1626 his seat was restored to him. He seems to have been both democratic and convival, and is described as fond of the company of his inferiors, "who hung upon him while his good liquor lasted".[31]

[25] P. R. O., CO1-4.
[26] F. R., p. 647.
[27] P. R. O., CO1-4-18.
[28] Gen., p. 1047.
[29] Neill, Va. Co., p. 221.
[30] F. R., p. 568.
[31] F. R., p. 639.
[32] Fiske, Old Va., Vol. I, p. 252.

In the spring of 1630 Sir John Harvey arrived in Virginia.[33] This man proved to be one of the worst of the many bad colonial governors. Concerned only for his own dignity and for the prerogative of the King, he trampled without scruple upon the liberties of the people, and his administration was marked throughout by injustice and oppression.

His first efforts as Governor were to attempt to win the friendship and support of one of the Council and to bring humiliation and ruin upon another. He had been in Virginia but a few weeks when he wrote the King asking especial favors for Captain Samuel Matthews. "This gentleman," he said, "I found most readie to set forward all services propounded for his Majesties honor, . . . and without his faithful assistance perhaps I should not soe soon have brought the busines of this Country to so good effect." It would be a just reward for these services, he thought, to allow him for a year or two to ship the tobacco of his plantation into England free of customs.[34] At the same time Harvey seemed bent upon the utter undoing of Dr. Pott. Claiming that the pleasure loving physician while Governor had been guilty of "pardoninge wilfull Murther, markinge other mens Cattell for his owne, and killing up their hoggs", Harvey suspended him from the Council and, pending the day of his trial, confined him to his plantation.[35]

It seems quite certain that this treatment of the two Councillors was designed to impress upon the people a just appreciation of the Governor's power. Harvey felt keenly the restriction of the Council. It had been the intention of James and after his death Charles to restore the government of the colony to its original form, in which all matters were determined by the Council. "His Majesties . . . pleasure," wrote the Privy Council in 1625, "is that all judgements, decrees, and all important actions be given, determined and undertaken by the advice and voices of the greater part."[36] If these instructions were adhered to, the Governor would become no more than the presiding officer of the Council. To this posi-

[33] Bruce, Ec. Hist., Vol. I, p. 130.
[34] P. R. O., CO1-5-29.
[35] P. R. O., CO1-5.
[36] F. R., p. 644.

tion Harvey was determined never to be reduced. He would, at the very outset, show that he was master in Virginia, able to reward his friends, or to punish those that incurred his displeasure.

Dr. Pott could not believe that the proceedings against him were intended seriously, and, in defiance of the Governor's commands, left his plantation to come to Elizabeth City. "Upon which contempt," wrote Harvey, "I committed him close prisoner, attended with a guard." At the earnest request of several gentlemen, the Governor finally consented that he might return to his plantation, but only under bond. Pott, however, refused to avail himself of the kindness of his friends, and so was kept in confinement.[37] On the 9th of July he was brought to trial, found guilty upon two indictments, and his entire estate confiscated.[38]

That Pott was convicted by a jury of thirteen men, three of them Councillors, is by no means conclusive evidence of his guilt. The close connection between the executive and the courts at this time made it quite possible for the Governor to obtain from a jury whatever verdict he desired. In fact it became the custom for a new administration, as soon as it was installed in power, to take revenge upon its enemies by means of the courts.

Pott's guilt is made still more doubtful by the fact that execution of the sentence was suspended "untill his Majesties pleasure might be signified concerning him", while the Council united in giving their security for his safe keeping.[39] Harvey himself wrote asking the King's clemency. "For as much," he said, "as he is the only Physician in the Colonie, and skilled in the Epidemicall diseases of the planters, . . . I am bound to entreat" your Majesty to pardon him.[40] It would seem quite inexplicable that Harvey should go to so much trouble to convict Dr. Pott, and then write immediately to England for a pardon, did not he himself give the clue to his conduct. "It

[37] P. R. O., CO1-5-31.

[38] P. R. O., CO1-5-32; Hen., Vol. I., p. 145.

[39] P. R. O., CO1-5; Hen., Vol. I, p. 146.

[40] P. R. O., CO1-5.

will be," he said, "a means to bring the people to . . . hold a better respect to the Governor than hitherto they have done."[41] Having shown the colonists that he could humble the strongest of them, he now sought to teach them that his intercession with the King could restore even the criminal to his former position.

When Dr. Pott was at Elizabeth City his wife was reported to be ill, but this did not deter her from making the long and dangerous voyage to England to appeal to the King "touching the wrong" done her husband.[42] Charles referred the matter to the Virginia commissioners, who gave her a hearing in the presence of Harvey's agent. Finding no justification for the proceedings against him, they wrote Harvey that for aught they could tell Pott had demeaned himself well and that there seemed to have been "some hard usage against him".[43] The sentence of confiscation seems never to have been carried out, but Pott was not restored to his seat in the Council.[44]

This arbitrary conduct did not succeed in intimidating the other Councillors. These men must have felt that the attack upon Dr. Pott was aimed partly at the dignity and power of the Council itself. If Harvey could thus ruin those that incurred his displeasure, the Councillors would lose all independence in their relations with him. Soon they were in open hostility to the Governor. Claiming that Harvey could do nothing without their consent, and that all important matters had to be determined "by the greater number of voyces at the Councell Table", they entered upon a policy of obstruction. It was in vain that the Governor declared that he was the King's substitute, that they were but his assistants, and that they were impeding his Majesty's business; they would yield to him only the position of first among equals. Early in 1631 Harvey was filling his letters to England with complaints of the "waywardness and oppositions of those of the Councell". "For instead of giving me assistance," he declared, "they stand Contesting and disputing my authoritie, avering that I can doe nothinge but what they shall advise me, and that my power extendeth

[41] P. R. O., CO1-5-32.
[42] P. R. O., CO1-5-33.
[43] P. R. O., CO1-5-33.
[44] P. R. O., CO1-6.

noe further than a bare casting voice."[45] He had received, he claimed, a letter from the King, strengthening his commission and empowering him to "doe justice to all men, not sparinge those of the Councell", which he had often shown them, but this they would not heed. "I hope," he wrote, "you never held me to be ambitious or vainglorious, as that I should desire to live here as Governor to predominate, or prefer mine owne particular before the generall good." My position in Virginia is most miserable, "chiefly through the aversions of those from whom I expected assistance". He had often tried to bring peace and amity between them, but all to no purpose, for he was scorned for his efforts. He would be humbly thankful if his Majesty would be pleased to strengthen his commission, "that the place of Governor and the duty of Councellors may be knowne and distinguished".[46]

It is probable that the Councillors also wrote to England, to place before the King their grievances against Harvey, for before the end of the year letters came from the Privy Council, warning both sides to end the dispute and to proceed peacefully with the government of the colony. In compliance with these commands they drew up and signed a document promising "to swallow up & bury all forepart Complainte and accusations in a generall Reconciliation". They thanked their Lordships for advice that had persuaded their "alienated & distempered" minds to thoughts of love and peace and to the execution of public justice. The Council promised to give the Governor "all the service, honor & due Respect which belongs unto him as his Majesties Substitute".[47] It is quite evident, however, that this reconciliation, inspired by fear of the anger of the Privy Council, could not be permanent. Soon the Council, under the leadership of Captain Matthews, who had long since forfeited Harvey's favor, was as refractory as ever.

A new cause for complaint against the Governor arose with the founding of Maryland. In 1623 George Calvert, the first Lord Baltimore, had received a grant of the great southeastern promontory in Newfoundland, and had planted there a

[45] P. R. O., CO1-6-34.

[46] P. R. O., CO1-6-35, 57.

[47] P. R. O., CO1-6-37.

colony as an asylum for English Catholics. Baltimore himself had been detained in England for some years, but in 1627 came with his wife and children to take personal control of his little settlement. His experience with the severe Newfoundland winter persuaded him that it would be wise to transfer his colony to a more congenial clime. "From the middle of October," he wrote Charles I, "to the middle of May there is a sad face of winter upon all the land; both sea and land so frozen for the greater part of the time as they are not penetrable . . . besides the air so intolerable cold as it is hardly to be endured. . . . I am determined to commit this place to fishermen that are able to encounter stormes and hard weather, and to remove myself with some forty persons to your Majesties dominion of Virginia; where, if your Majesty will please to grant me a precinct of land, with such privileges as the King your father . . . was pleased to grant me here, I shall endeavour to the utmost of my power, to deserve it."[48]

In 1629 he sailed for Virginia, with his wife and children, and arrived at Jamestown the first day of October. His reception by Governor Pott and the Council was by no means cordial. The Virginians were loath either to receive a band of Catholics into their midst, or to concede to them a portion of the land that they held under the royal charters. Desiring to be rid of Baltimore as speedily as possible, they tendered him the oath of supremacy. This, of course, as a good Catholic he could not take, for it recognized the English sovereign as the supreme authority in all ecclesiastical matters. Baltimore proposed an alternative oath of allegiance, but the Governor and Council refused to accept it, and requested him to leave at once. Knowing that it was his intention to apply for a tract of land within their borders, the Virginians sent William Claiborne after him to London, to watch him and to thwart his designs.

Despite Claiborne's efforts a patent was granted Baltimore, making him lord proprietor of a province north of the Potomac river, which received the name of Maryland. Baltimore, with his own hand, drew up the charter, but in April, 1632, before it had passed under the Great Seal, he died. A few weeks

[48] Fiske, Old Va., Vol. I, pp. 262, 263.

later the patent was issued to his eldest son, Cecilius Calvert. The Virginians protested against this grant "within the Limits of the Colony", claiming that it would interfere with their Indian trade in the Chesapeake, and that the establishment of the Catholics so near their settlements would "give a generall disheartening of the Planters".[49] But their complaints availed nothing. Not only did Charles refuse to revoke the charter, but he wrote the Governor and Council commanding them to give Lord Baltimore every possible assistance in making his settlement. You must, he said, "suffer his servants and Planters to buy and transport such cattle and comodities to their Colonie, as you may conveniently spare . . . and give them . . . such lawful assistance as may conduce to both your safetyes".[50]

The second Lord Baltimore appointed his brother, Leonard Calvert, Governor of Maryland, and sent him with two vessels and over three hundred men to plant the new colony. In February, 1634, the expedition reached Point Comfort, where it stopped to secure from the Virginians the assistance that the King had promised should be given them.

They met with scant courtesy. The planters thought it a hard matter that they should be ordered to aid in the establishment of this new colony. They resented the encroachment upon their territories, they hated the newcomers because most of them were Catholics, they feared the loss of a part of their Indian trade, and they foresaw the growth of a dangerous rival in the culture of tobacco. Despite the King's letter they refused to help Calvert and his men. "Many are so averse," wrote Harvey, "that they crye and make it their familiar talke that they would rather knock their Cattell on the heades than sell them to Maryland."[51] The Governor, however, not daring to disobey his sovereign's commands, gave the visitors all the assistance in his power. "For their present accomodation," he said, "I sent unto them some Cowes of myne owne, and will do my best to procure more, or any thinge else they stand in need of."[52] This action secured for Harvey the praise of the

[49] P. R. O., CO1-6-39.

[50] P. R. O., CO1-6-39.

[51] P. R. O., CO1-6-46.

[52] P. R. O., CO1-6-46.

Privy Council, but it made him more unpopular with his Council and the people of Virginia.

After a stay of several weeks at Point Comfort, Calvert sailed up the Chesapeake into the Potomac, and founded the town of Saint Mary's. This, however, was not the first settlement in Maryland. In 1631, William Claiborne, returning from England after his unsuccessful attempt to block the issuing of Baltimore's charter, had established a settlement upon Kent Island in the Chesapeake Bay. Here he had built dwellings and mills and store houses, and had laid out orchards and gardens. In thus founding a colony within Baltimore's territory he was sustained by the Council. When Calvert arrived in 1634 he sent word to Claiborne that he would not molest his settlement, but since Kent Island was a part of Maryland, he must hold it as a tenant of Lord Baltimore. Upon receipt of this message Claiborne laid the matter before his colleagues of the Virginia Council, and asked their commands. The answer of the Councillors shows that they considered the new patent an infringement upon their prior rights and therefore of no effect. They could see no reason, they told Claiborne, why they should render up the Isle of Kent any more than the other lands held under their patents. As it was their duty to maintain the rights and privileges of the colony, his settlement must continue under the government and laws of Virginia.

Despite the defiant attitude of the Virginians, it is probable that Calvert would have permitted the Kent Islanders to remain unmolested, had not a report spread abroad that Claiborne was endeavoring to persuade the Indians to attack Saint Mary's. A joint commission of Virginians and Marylanders declared the charge false, but suspicion and ill will had been aroused, and a conflict could not be avoided. In April, 1635, Governor Calvert, alleging that Claiborne was indulging in illicit trade, fell upon and captured one of his merchantmen. In great indignation the islanders fitted out a vessel, the *Cockatrice,* to scour the Chesapeake and make reprisals. She was attacked, however, by two pinnaces from Saint Mary's and, after a severe conflict in which several men were killed, was forced to surrender. A few weeks later Claiborne gained revenge by defeating the Marylanders in a fight at the mouth of the Potomac.

In these encounters the Kent Islanders had the sympathy of the Virginia planters. Excitement ran high in the colony, and there was danger that an expedition might be sent to Saint Mary's to overpower the intruders and banish them from the country. Resentment against Harvey, who still gave aid and encouragement to Maryland, became more bitter than ever. His espousal of the cause of the enemies of Virginia made the planters regard him as a traitor. In 1635 Samuel Matthews wrote to Sir John Wolstenholme, "The Inhabitants also understood with indignation that the Marylanders had taken Capt. Claibournes Pinnaces and men . . . which action of theirs Sir John Harvey upheld contrary to his Majesties express commands."[53] The Councillors held many "meetings and consultations" to devise plans for the overthrow of the new colony, and an active correspondence was carried on with Baltimore's enemies in England in the vain hope that the charter might yet be revoked.[54]

Matters were now moving rapidly to a crisis. Harvey's administration became more and more unpopular. Sir John Wolstenholme, who kept in close touch with the colony, declared that the Governor's misconduct in his government was notorious at Court and in the city of London.[55] When, in the spring of 1635, he was rudely thrust out of his office, the complaints against him were so numerous that it became necessary to convene the Assembly to consider them.[56]

To what extent Harvey usurped the powers of the General Assembly is not clear, but it seems very probable that he frequently made use of proclamations to enforce his will upon the people.[57] It was quite proper and necessary for the Governor, when the houses were not in session, to issue ordinances of a temporary character, but this was a power susceptible of great abuse. And for the Governor to repeal statutes by proclamation would be fatal to the liberties of the people. That Harvey was guilty of this usurpation seems probable from the fact that a law was enacted declaring it the duty of the people

[53] P. R. O., CO1-6-52.
[54] P. R. O., CO1-6-46.
[55] P. R. O., CO1-8-60.
[56] Hen., Vol. I, p. 223.
[57] Bruce, Inst. Hist., Vol. II, p. 324.

to disregard all proclamations that conflicted with any act of Assembly.[58]

Also there is reason to believe that Harvey found ways of imposing illegal taxes upon the people. John Burk, in his *History of Virginia,* declares unreservedly that it was Harvey's purpose "to feed his avarice and rapacity, by assessing, levying, and holding the public revenue, without check or responsibility".[59]

In 1634 an event occurred which aroused the anger of the people, widened the breach between the Governor and the Council, and made it evident to all that Harvey would not hesitate upon occasion to disregard property rights and to break the laws of the colony. A certain Captain Young came to Virginia upon a commission for the King. Wishing to build two shallops while in the colony and having need of a ship's carpenter, Young, with the consent of Harvey, seized a skilled servant of one of the planters. This arbitrary procedure was in direct defiance of a statute of Assembly of March, 1624, that declared that "the Governor shall not withdraw the inhabitants from their private labors to any service of his own upon any colour whatsoever".[60]

Upon hearing of the incident Captain Samuel Matthews and other members of the Council came to Harvey to demand an explanation. The Governor replied that the man had been taken because Young had need of him "to prosecute with speed the King's service", and "that his Majesty had given him authority to make use of any persons he found there".[61] This answer did not satisfy the Councillors. Matthews declared "that if things were done on this fashion it would breed ill bloude in Virginia", and in anger "turning his back, with his truncheon lashed off the heads of certain high weeds that were growing there".[62] Harvey, wishing to appease the Councillors, said, "Come gentlemen, let us goe to supper & for the night leave this discourse", but their resentment was too great to be smoothed over, and with one accord rejecting his invitation,

[58] Hen., Vol. I, p. 264.

[59] Burk, Vol. II, pp. 28, 29.

[60] Hen., Vol. I, p. 124.

[61] P. R. O., CO1-8.

[62] P. R. O., CO1-8.

"they departed from the Governour in a very irreverent manner".[63]

Harvey, in his letters to the English government tried to convey the impression that he was uniformly patient with the Council, and courteous in all the disputes that were constantly arising. That he was not always so self restrained is shown by the fact that on one occasion, he became embroiled with one of the Councillors, Captain Stevens, and knocked out some of his teeth with a cudgel.[64] Samuel Matthews wrote that he had heard the Governor "in open court revile all the Councell and tell them they were to give their attendance as assistants only to advise with him". The Governor attempted, he declared, to usurp the whole power of the courts, without regard to the rights of the Councillors, "whereby justice was now done but soe farr as suited with his will, to the great losse of many mens estates and a generall feare in all".[65]

In 1634 the King once more made a proposal to the colonists for the purchase of their tobacco, and demanded their assent through the General Assembly. The Burgesses, who dreaded all contracts, drew up an answer which was "in effect a deniall of his Majesties proposition", and, in order to give the paper the character of a petition, they all signed it. This answer the Governor detained, fearing, he said, that the King "would not take well the matter thereof, and that they should make it a popular business, by subscribing a multitude of hands thereto. as thinking thereby to give it countenance".[66] The Governor's arbitrary action aroused great anger throughout the colony. Matthews wrote Sir John Wolstenholme, "The Consideration of the wrong done by the Governor to the whole Colony in detayning the foresaid letters to his Majesty did exceedingly perplex them whereby they were made sensible of the condition of the present Government."[67]

The crisis had now come. During the winter of 1634-35 the Councillors and other leading citizens were holding secret meetings to discuss the conduct of the Governor. Soon Dr.

[63] P. R. O., CO1-8.
[64] P. R. O., CO1-8-63.
[65] P. R. O., CO1-8.
[66] P. R. O., CO1-8.
[67] P. R. O., CO1-8.

John Pott, whose private wrongs made him a leader in the popular discontent, was going from plantation to plantation, denouncing the Governor's conduct and inciting the people to resistance. Everywhere the angry planters gathered around him, and willingly subscribed to a petition for a redress of grievances. In April, 1635, Pott was holding one of these meetings in York, at the house of one William Warrens, when several friends of the Governor presented themselves for admission. "A servant meeting them told them they must not goe in . . . whereupon they desisted and bended themselves to hearken to the discourse among them." In the confusion of sounds that came out of the house they could distinguish many angry speeches against Harvey and cries against his unjust and arbitrary government. When Pott read his petition, and told the assemblage that it had the support of some of the Councillors, they all rushed forward to sign their names.

When Harvey heard of these proceedings he was greatly enraged. Summoning the Council to meet without delay, he issued warrants for Dr. Pott and several others that had aided in circulating the petition. "After a few days Potts was brought up prisoner, having before his apprehending bin in the lower parts of the Country there also mustering his names at a meeting called for that purpose."[68] He does not seem to have feared the angry threats of the Governor, for when put in irons and brought before the Council, he readily consented to surrender the offending petition. At the same time he asserted "that if he had offended he did appeal to the King, for he was sure of noe justice from Sir John Harvey". When some of the other prisoners, in their hearing before the Council, asked the cause of their arrest, the Governor told them they should be informed at the gallows.

Shortly after this the Council was summoned to deliberate on the fate of the accused. The Governor, fearing that he might not secure conviction from a jury, "declared it necessary that Marshall law should be executed upon" them. When the Councillors refused to consent to any other than a legal trial, Harvey flew into a furious passion. For a while he paced

[68] P. R. O., CO1-8-48.

back and forth in the room hardly able to contain himself. At length he sat down in his chair, and with a dark countenance commanded his colleagues to be seated. A long pause ensued, and then he announced that he had a question that they must answer each in his turn, without deliberation or consultation. "What," he enquired, "doe you think they deserve that have gone about to persuade the people from their obedience to his Majesties substitute?" "And I begin with you," he said, turning to Mr. Minifie. "I am but a young lawyer," Minifie replied, "and dare not uppon the suddain deliver my opinion." At this point Mr. Farrar began to complain of these strange proceedings, but Harvey commanded him to be silent. Captain Matthews also protested, and the other Councillors soon joined him in refusing to answer the Governor's question. "Then followed many bitter Languages from him till the sitting ended."

At the next meeting Harvey asked what the Council thought were the reasons that the petition had been circulated against him, and demanded to know whether they had any knowledge of the matter. Mr. Minifie replied that the chief grievance of the people was the detaining of the letter of the Assembly to the King. This answer seems to have aroused the Governor's fury, for, arising from his seat, and striking Mr. Minifie a resounding blow upon the shoulder, he cried, "Doe you say soe? I arrest you upon suspicion of treason to his Majesty." But Harvey found that he could not deal thus arbitrarily with the Councillors. Utie and Matthews rushed up and seizing him cried, "And we you upon suspicion of treason to his Majestie". Dr. Pott, who was present and had probably been waiting for this crisis, held up his hand as a signal to confederates without, "when straight about 40 musketiers . . . which before that time lay hid, came . . . running with their peeces presented" towards the house. "Stay here," commanded Pott, "until there be use of you."

In the meanwhile the Councillors crowded around Harvey. "Sir," said Matthews, "there is no harm intended you save only to acquaint you with the grievances of the Inhabitants and to that end I desire you to sit downe in your Chayre."

And there, with the enraged Governor seated before him, he poured out the recital of the people's wrongs. When he had finished there came an ominous pause. Finally Matthews spoke again. "Sir," he said, "the peoples fury is up against you and to appease it, is beyond our power, unlesse you please to goe for England, there to answer their complaints." But this Harvey refused to do. He had been made Governor of Virginia by the King, he said, and without his command he would not leave his charge.

But before many days the Governor changed his mind. He found himself deserted by all and entirely in the power of the Councillors. As sentinals were placed "in all wayes & passages so that noe man could travell or come from place to place", he could make no effort to raise troops. Dr. Pott and the other prisoners were set at liberty. A guard was placed around Harvey, ostensibly to protect him, but really with the purpose of restraining him. A letter came from Captain Purifee, a Councillor then in the "lower parts" of the colony, which spoke of designs of the people to bring Harvey to account for his many wrongs. In alarm the Governor consented to take the first ship for England. He endeavored, however, to name his successor, to induce Matthews, Pierce, and Minifie to go with him to England, and to secure a promise from the Council not to molest Maryland. But they would consent to none of these things.

In the meantime an Assembly had been called to consider the innumerable grievances against the Governor. When they met at Jamestown, Harvey sent them a letter, declaring the session illegal and ordering them to disperse to their homes. "Notwithstanding his threats . . . the assembly proceeded according to their former intentions." Harvey then dispatched a letter to the Council, ordering them to send him his royal commission and instructions, but these documents had been intrusted to the keeping of Mr. Minifie with directions not to surrender them. The Council then turned themselves to the task of selecting a successor to Harvey. Their unanimous vote was given to Captain Francis West, the senior member of the board and formerly Governor. Feeling that since the expulsion of Harvey had been primarily a movement to protect the rights of the people, the Burgesses should have some voice in the election of the new Governor, they appealed to the Assembly for the ratification of their choice. West was popular in the colony, and "the people's suffrages" were cast for him as willingly as had been those of the Council. The Assembly then drew up resolutions setting forth the misconduct of Harvey and justifying their course in sending him back to England. These documents were entrusted to one Thomas Harwood, who was to deliver them to the King. Of what happened after Harvey's departure we have little record, but it is probable that the colonists revenged themselves upon the deposed Governor by confiscating all his ill gotten possessions.

It was decided that Dr. Pott should go to England to stand trial as his appeal to the King had taken the case beyond the jurisdiction of the Virginia courts. He and Harwood sailed upon the same vessel with Sir John. It is not hard to imagine with what dark looks or angry words Pott and Harvey greeted each other during their long voyage across the Atlantic. Doubtless Harwood and Pott held many a consultation upon what steps should be taken when they reached England to secure a favorable hearing for the colony, and to frustrate Harvey's plans for revenge. It was Harwood's intention to hasten to London, in order to forestall the Governor and "to make friends and the case good against him, before he could come".[69] But Sir John was too quick for him. Hardly had the ship touched the dock at Plymouth, than he was off to see the mayor of the city. This officer, upon hearing of the "late mutiny and rebellion" in Virginia, put Pott under arrest, "as a principal author and agent thereof", and seized all the papers and letters that had been entrusted to Harwood. Having thus gotten his hands upon the important documents, Harvey proceeded to London to complain of the indignities shown him and to ask for the punishment of his enemies.

When Charles I learned that the Virginians had deposed his Governor and sent him back to England, he was surprised

[69] P. R. O., CO1-8-61.

and angered. It was, he said, an assumption of regal power to oust thus unceremoniously one of his officers, and he was resolved to send Harvey back, if for one day only. And should the Governor acquit himself of the charges against him, he was to be inflicted upon the colony even longer than had at first been intended. The case came before the Privy Council in December 1635.[70] In the charges that were made against Harvey nothing was said of the illegal and arbitrary measures that had caused the people to depose him. All reference was omitted to the detaining of the Assembly's letter, to the support given Maryland, to the abuse of the courts, to illegal taxes and proclamations. Possibly the agents of the Virginians felt that such accusations as these would have no weight with the ministers of a monarch so little in sympathy with liberal government, so they trumped up other charges to sustain their cause. Despite the assertion of Harwood that Harvey "had so carryed himself in Virginia, that if ever hee retourned back thither hee would be pistolled or Shott", he was acquitted and restored to his office. West, Utie, Mathews, Minifie and Pierce, whom Harvey designated as the "chief actors in the munity", were ordered to come to England, there to answer before the Star Chamber the charge of treason.[71]

As the time approached for him to return to Virginia, Harvey began to show symptoms of nervousness. Feeling possibly that the threats of "pistolling" were not to be taken lightly, he requested the King to furnish him a royal vessel in which to make the journey. The appearance of one of the King's own ships in the James, he thought, would "much abate the bouldness of the offenders". This request was granted, and, after some months of delay, Harvey set forth proudly in the *Black George*. But Charles had not cared to send a really serviceable vessel to Virginia, and for a while it seemed that the *Black George* would relieve the colonists of their troubles by taking Sir John to the bottom. The vessel, it would appear, sprank a leak before it had been many hours at sea, and was forced to return to port. The Governor then decided that

[70] P. R. O., CO1-8-62.

[71] P. R. O., CO1-8-61.

a merchant vessel would suffice for his purposes, and set sail again, upon a ship of the Isle of Wight.

He reached Point Comfort in January, 1637. Not wishing to wait until his ship reached Jamestown before asserting his authority, he landed at once and established a temporary capital at Elizabeth City. He had received instructions to remove from the Council all the members that had taken part in the "thrusting out", and he brought with him commissions for several new members. Orders were issued immediately for this reconstructed Council to convene in the church at Elizabeth City. There, after the oath had been administered, he published a proclamation of pardon to all persons implicated in the "mutiny", from which, however, West, Matthews, and the other leaders were excluded. The Governor then proceeded to displace all officials whom he considered hostile to his administration. "Before I removed from Elizabeth City," he wrote, "I appointed Commissioners and sheriffs for the lower counties, and for the plantation of Accomack, on the other side of the Bay."

The "thrusting out" did not cause Harvey to become more prudent in the administration of the government. His restoration, which Charles had meant as a vindication of the royal authority, the Governor seems to have interpreted as a license for greater tyranny. If the accusations of his enemies may be credited, he went to the greatest extremes in oppressing the people and in defying their laws. With the Council now completely under his control, he was master of the courts, and inflicted many great wrongs by means of "arbitrary and illegal proceedings in judgment". Confiscations and other "most cruel oppressions", it was declared, were used to punish all that showed themselves hostile to his government. He and his officers did not scruple to impose many unjust fines, which they converted "to their own private use", nor to strike terror into the people with whippings and "cutting of ears".[72]

Nor did Sir John neglect to take revenge upon those old enemies that had so defied and humiliated him. West, Utie, Matthews and Pierce were sent at once to England, and their

[72] Report of Com. on Hist. Mans. 3.

goods, cattle and servants seized. Beyond doubt it was against Samuel Matthews that Harvey bore the most bitter animosity, and it was his estate that suffered most. The Governor had been heard to say that if one "stood, tother should fall, and if hee swomme, the other should sinke". Matthews was one of the wealthiest men of the colony, his property consisting largely of cattle, but Sir John now swore that he would not leave him "worth a cow taile". At the next session of the Quarter Court, suit was entered against Matthews by one John Woodall, for the recovery of certain cattle. The learned judges, upon investigation, found that in the year 1622 Matthews held two cows rightfully belonging to Woodall. It was their opinion that the increase of these cows "unto the year 1628 . . . might amount unto the number of fifteen". "Computing the increase of the said fifteen head from the year 1628 to the time of their inquiry, they did return the number of fiftye head to the said Woodall."[73]

When Matthews heard that his estate had been seized and "havoc made thereof", he entered complaint with the Privy Council and secured an order requiring Harvey to restore all to his agents in Virginia. But the Governor was most reluctant to give up his revenge upon his old enemy. For seven months he put off the agents and at last told them that he had received new orders from the Privy Council, expressing satisfaction with what had been done and bidding him proceed.[74] Thereupon Secretary Kemp and other friends of the Governor entered Matthews' house, broke open the doors of several chambers, ransacked all his trunks and chests, examined his papers, and carried away a part of his goods and eight of his servants.[75] Soon after, however, Harvey received positive commands from the Privy Council to make an immediate restoration of all that had been taken. In January, 1639, he wrote that he had obeyed their Lordships exactly, by calling a court and turning over to Matthews' agents many of his belongings.[76] But Harvey denied that he had ever appropriated the estate to his own use, and claimed that he had been

[73] P. R. O., CO1-10-14.
[74] P. R. O., CO1-9-121.
[75] P. R. O., CO1-9-121.
[76] P. R. O., CO1-10-6.

misrepresented by "the Cunning texture of Captain Mathews, his complaint".[77]

Among those that felt most keenly the Governor's resentment was a certain clergyman, Anthony Panton. This man had quarrelled with Harvey's best friend and chief advisor in the stormy days of the expulsion, Secretary Matthew Kemp. Panton had incurred Kemp's undying resentment by calling him a "jackanapes", "unfit for the place of secretary", and declaring that "his hair-lock was tied up with ribbon as old as St. Paul's".[78] The belligerent parson was now brought to trial, charged with "mutinous speeches and disobedience to Sir John Harvey", and with disrespect to the Archbishop of Canterbury. His judges pronounced him guilty and inflicted a sentence of extreme rigor. A fine of £500 was imposed, he was forced to make public submission in all the parishes of the colony, and was banished "with paynes of death if he returned, and authority to any man whatsoever to execute him."[79]

In the meanwhile the Governor's enemies in England had not been idle. Matthews, Utie, West and Pierce, upon landing in 1637, had secured their liberty under bail, and had joined with Dr. Pott in an attempt to undermine Harvey's influence at Court. Had Sir John sent witnesses to England at once to press the charges against them before the Star Chamber, while the matter was still fresh in the memory of the King, he might have brought about their conviction and checked their plots. But he neglected the case, and Charles probably forgot about it, so the whole matter was referred to the Lord Keeper and the Attorney-General where it seems to have rested.[80] The exiles had no difficulty in finding prominent men willing to join in an attack upon Harvey. Before many months had passed they had gained the active support of the "sub-committee" of the Privy Council to which Virginia affairs were usually referred.[81] Harvey afterwards complained that members of this committee were interested in a

[77] P. R. O., CO1-10-6.
[78] Fiske, Old Va., Vol. I, p. 295.
[79] P. R. O., CO1-10-32.
[80] P. R. O., CO1-10-73.
[81] P. R. O., CO1-10-10.

plan to establish a new Virginia Company and for that reason were anxious to bring discredit upon his government.[82] It was not difficult to find cause enough for removing Sir John. Reports of his misconduct were brought to England by every vessel from the colony. Numerous persons, if we may believe the Governor, were "imployed in all parts of London to be spyes", and to "invite the meanest of the planters newly come for England into Taverns", where they made them talkative with wine and invited them to state their grievances.[83]

The English merchants trading to Virginia also entered complaint before the Privy Council against Harvey's administration. They sought relief from a duty of two pence per hogshead on all tobacco exported from the colony, from a fee of six pence a head on immigrants, and a requisition of powder and shot laid upon vessels entering the James.[84] The Privy Council, always careful of the welfare of British trade, wrote the Governor and the Council, demanding an explanation of these duties and requiring an account of the powder and shot. Harvey replied at great length, justifying the duties and begging their Lordships not to credit "the malitious untruths of such who by all means do goe about and studie to traduce us".

But the Privy Council, not waiting to receive all of Harvey's defense, decided to remove him and to appoint in his place Sir Francis Wyatt.[85] The new Governor was directed to retain the old Council and to confirm Kemp as Secretary.[86] But he was authorized to restore to Matthews any part of his estate yet withheld from him, and to reopen in the Virginia courts the case against Anthony Panton.[87] The day of reckoning had now arrived. When Wyatt reached Virginia, he lost no time in bringing Harvey to account for his misdeeds. He was arraigned before the courts, where he was forced to answer countless complaints of injustice and oppression, and to restore to their owners his ill gotten gains. Kemp wrote, in March, 1640, that Sir John was being persecuted with great rigor, that most of his estate had been confiscated, and at the

[82] P. R. O., CO1-10-10.
[83] P. R. O., CO1-10-15.
[84] P. R. O., CO1-10-5.
[85] P. R. O., CO1-10-3.
[86] P. R. O., CO1-10-43.
[87] P. R. O., CO1-10-26, 32.

next court would assuredly be swept away.[88] A few weeks later Harvey wrote to Secretary Windebank, to relate his misfortunes. "I am so narrowly watched," he complained, "that I have scarce time of priviledge for these few lines, which doe humbly crave of you to acquaint his Majesty how much I groan under the oppressions of my prevayling enemies, by whom the King's honor hath soe much suffered and who are now advanced to be my judges, and have soe farr already proceeded against me as to teare from me my estate by an unusuall way of inviting my creditors to clamour." He wished to return to England, there to repair his fortunes and seek revenge upon his enemies, but for some time he was detained in Virginia. The new Governor thought best to keep him in the colony where it would be difficult for him to plot against the administration. Harvey wrote, "I am denyed my passage for England notwithstanding my many infirmities and weaknesses of body doe crave advice and help beyond the skill and judgment which this place can give."[89]

"Sir John being . . . layed flatt," the Governor next turned his attention to Kemp.[90] Sir Francis, who had strong reasons for hating the Secretary, summoned him into court to explain his offenses against Anthony Panton. Realizing that he had little hope of clearing himself, Kemp sought to leave for England, but his enemies restrained him. "I am extremely injured," he wrote in April, 1640, "and shall suffer without guilt, unless my friends now assist me, . . . the Governor and Council here . . . aim at my ruin."[91]

But Wyatt feared to retain Harvey and Kemp permanently in Virginia. Both had powerful friends who might take the matter before the King or the Privy Council. So, in the end, both made their way to England, taking with them the charter and many important letters and records.[92] It was now their turn to plot and intrigue to overthrow the party in power.[93] And so quickly did their efforts meet success that before Wyatt had been in office two years he was recalled and Sir William Berkeley made Governor in his place.

[88] P. R. O., CO1-10-61.
[89] P. R. O., CO1-10-67.
[90] P. R. O., CO1-10-64. I.
[91] P. R. O., CO1-10-64.
[92] Report of Com. on Hist. Man., 3.
[93] Report of Com. on Hist. Man., 3.

CHAPTER IV

Governor Berkeley and the Commonwealth

Sir William Berkeley, who succeeded Governor Wyatt in 1642, is one of the striking figures of American colonial history. Impulsive, brave, dogmatic, unrelenting, his every action is full of interest. He early displayed a passionate devotion to the house of Stuart, which remained unshaken amid the overthrow of the monarchy and the triumph of its enemies. When the British Commons had brought the unhappy King to the block, Berkeley denounced them as lawless tyrants and pledged his allegiance to Charles II. And when the Commonwealth sent ships and men to subdue the stubborn Governor, they found him ready, with his raw colonial militia, to fight for the prince that England had repudiated. Throughout his life his chief wish was to win the approbation of the King, his greatest dread to incur his censure.

Berkeley did not know fear. When, in 1644, the savages came murdering through the colony, it was he that led the planters into the forests to seek revenge. In 1666, when a Dutch fleet sailed into the James and captured a number of English vessels, the Governor wished to sally out in person with a few merchantmen to punish their temerity.

He possessed many of the graces of the courtier, and seems to have charmed, when he so desired, those with whom he came in contact. His friends are most extravagant in his praises, and their letters refer to him as the model soldier, statesman and gentleman.

The overthrow of Sir Francis Wyatt was a severe blow to the enemies of the old Harvey faction. Anthony Panton entered a protest against the change of administration, claiming that it had been brought about by surreptitious means and that no just complaint could be made against Governor Wyatt.[1] At

[1] Report of Commission on Hist. Manuscripts. 3.

his petition Berkeley was ordered to postpone his departure for Virginia until the matter could be investigated further. Upon signing an agreement, however, to protect the interests of Wyatt and his friends, he was allowed to sail and reached the colony in 1642.

The new Governor soon showed that he had no intention of persecuting Harvey's enemies, or of continuing the bitter quarrels of the preceding administrations. In his first Council we find Samuel Matthews, William Pierce and George Minifie, all of whom had been implicated in the "thrusting out".[2] Whether proceeding under directions from the English government, or actuated by a desire to rule legally and justly, he conferred a priceless blessing upon the colony by refusing to use the judiciary for political persecution. So far as we can tell there was no case, during his first administration, in which the courts were prostituted to personal or party ends. Thomas Ludwell afterwards declared that it was a convincing evidence of Berkeley's prudence and justice that after the surrender to the Commonwealth, when his enemies might easily have hounded him to his ruin, "there was not one man that either publickly or privately charged him with injustice".[3] In March, 1643, he affixed his signature to a law allowing appeals from the Quarter Courts to the Assembly. This right, which seems not to have been acknowledged by Sir John Harvey, was of the very highest importance. It gave to the middle class a share in the administration of justice and afforded an effectual check upon the abuse of the courts by the Governor and Council.

Berkeley greatly endeared himself to the poor planters by securing the abolition of a poll tax that contributed to the payment of his own salary.[4] "This," the Assembly declared, "is a benefit descending unto us and our posterity which we acknowledge contributed to us by our present Governor."[5] Berkeley also made an earnest effort to relieve the burden of the poor by substituting for the levy upon tithables "assessments proportioning in some measure payments according

[2] Hen., Vol. I, p. 235.

[3] P. R. O., CO1-20.

[4] Hen., Vol. I, pp. 236, 237.

[5] Hen., Vol. I, pp. 236, 237.

to mens abilities and estates" But the colonial legislators soon found a just distribution of the taxes a matter of great difficulty, and we are told that the new measures, "through the strangeness thereof could not but require much time of controverting and debating".[6] In 1648 the experiment was abandoned and the old oppressive tax upon tithables revived.[7]

During the first administration of Berkeley numerous other measures were adopted tending to augment the liberty and prosperity of the people. In 1643 a law was passed prohibiting the Governor and Council from imposing taxes without the consent of the Assembly.[8] At the same session Berkeley assented to a statute exempting the Burgesses from arrest during sessions of Assembly and for ten days after dissolution.[9] The fees of the Secretary of State were limited and fixed in order to prevent excessive and unjust charges by that officer.[10]

That the colonists were not insensible of the Governor's liberal conduct is shown by their generosity to him on more than one occasion. In 1642 they presented him with an "orchard with two houses belonging to the collony . . . as a free and voluntary gift in consideration of many worthy favours manifested towards the collony".[11] In 1643, when the war in England caused the suspension of Berkeley's pensions and allowances from the King, the Assembly voted a tax of two shillings per poll on all tithable persons as a temporary relief.[12]

When Sir William assumed the government in 1642 he was conscious that an effort was being made in England to restore the old London Company of Virginia, and it became his first care to thwart this design. In 1639 George Sandys had been sent to England as the agent of the Assembly and had presented a petition in the name of the Virginia planters, to the House of Commons, for the restoration of the old corporation.[13] The Assembly of April, 1642, called together by Berkeley, repudiated entirely the action of their agent, declaring

[6] Hen., Vol. I, p. 237.
[7] Hen., Vol. I, p. 356.
[8] Hen., Vol. I, p. 244.
[9] Hen., Vol. I, p. 263.
[10] Hen., Vol. I, p. 265.
[11] Hen., Vol. I, p. 267.
[12] Hen., Vol. I, pp. 280, 281.
[13] Hen., Vol. I, p. 230.

that he had misunderstood his instructions. The renewal of the Company, they said, was never "desired, sought after or endeavoured to be sought for either directly or indirectly by the consent of any Grand Assembly or the common consent of the people". They drew up a petition to the King, expressing their desire to remain under his immediate care and protection, citing the many blessings of the present order of government, and drawing the most melancholy picture of their sufferings before the revocation of the charter. "The present happiness," they said, "is exemplified to us by the freedom of yearly assemblies warranted unto us by his majesties gratious instructions, and the legal trial per juries in all criminal and civil causes where it shall be demanded."[14]

This declaration of loyalty and contentment, reaching Charles at a time when so many of his subjects were rising in rebellion against his authority, was most pleasing to the unfortunate monarch. "Your acknowledgement," he replied to the Governor and the Assembly, "of our grace, bounty, and favour, towards you, and your so earnest desire to continue under our immediate protection, is very acceptable to us." "And," he continued, "as we had not before the least intention to consent to the introduction of any company over that our Colony, we are by it much confirmed in our resolution, as thinking it unfit to change a form of government wherein our subjects there . . . receive much contentment and satisfaction.[15]

In the early years of Berkeley's administration the colony experienced another horrible Indian massacre. As in 1622 the blow came without warning. The cruel and barbarous war that followed the first massacre had long since come to an end and for many years there had been peace between the two races. It is true that the friendly relations that resulted from the marriage of Rolfe and Pocahontas had not been restored, that the Indians were not allowed to frequent the English settlements, that no weapons were sold them, but the peace was fairly well observed and there was no reason to suspect the savages of treachery.

[14] Hen., Vol. I, p. 231.

[15] Va. Hist. Reg., Vol. I, p. 160.

The plot originated in the brain of Opechancanough. This remarkable savage was long supposed to have been the brother of Powhatan, but newly discovered evidence tends to show that this was not the case. It is known that he belonged to a foreign tribe that came from the far southwest. Having, it is supposed, been defeated in a battle with the Spaniards, he had led his people to Virginia and united them with the tribes under the command of Powhatan. This tremendous march must have consumed many months, and have been beset with countless dangers, but Opechancanough overcame them, and "conquered all along from Mexico" to Virginia.[16] He was now an extremely aged man. Being unable to walk he was carried from place to place upon a litter. His eyelids were so heavy that he could not of his own volition move them, and attendants stood always ready to raise them whenever it became necessary for him to see.[17] But his mind was clear, his force of will unshaken, and the Indians paid him the reverent obedience that his able leadership demanded.

Opechancanough planned the massacre for April 18th, 1644, and it was carried out upon that date with the utmost ferocity.[18] The slaughter was even greater than in 1622, and no less than five hundred Christians are said to have been destroyed.[19] But this calamity fell almost entirely upon the frontier counties at the heads of the great rivers, and upon the plantations on the south side of the James. The savages could not penetrate to the older and more populous communities of the lower peninsula. For this reason the disaster, horrible as it was, did not overwhelm the entire colony and threaten its destruction as had the massacre of 1622.

Another deadly war with the savages ensued immediately. Sir William Berkeley several times placed himself at the head

[16] P. R. O., CO5-1371-6 to 16. [17] Beverley.

[18] The Assembly, in 1645, ordered that the 18th of April be celebrated ever afterwards for the deliverance of the colony from the savages. Hen., Vol. I, p. 290. The year is fairly well determined by the fact that mention of an Indian war occurs for the first time, during this period, in the statutes of the session of Assembly of October, 1644. Hen., Vol. I, p. 285.

[19] Beverley.

of large expeditions and carried fire and destruction to many Indian villages.[20] As in the former war, the naked and poorly armed natives could not withstand the English, and, deserting their homes, they usually fled into the woods at their approach. And again the white men brought famine upon them by going out each year in the months of July and August to cut down their growing maize.[21] In order to protect the isolated frontier plantations the Governor ordered the people to draw together in fortified camps, strong enough to resist the assaults of a large body of the savages.[22] "He strengthened the weak Families," it was said, "by joining two or three . . . together and Palizaded the houses about."[23]

Despite these wise measures the savages would probably have continued the war many years had not Opechancanough fallen into the hands of the English. The old king was surprised by Sir William Berkeley, and, because of his decrepitude, was easily captured.[24] He was taken in triumph to Jamestown, where the Governor intended to keep him until he could be sent to England and brought before Charles I. But a few days after the capture, a common soldier, in revenge for the harm done the colony by Opechancanough, shot the aged and helpless prisoner in the back.[25]

Soon after this event the Indians sued for peace. Discouraged and starving, they promised to become the friends and allies of the whites forever, if they would cease their hostility and grant them their protection. A treaty was drawn up and ratified by the Assembly and by the new Indian king Necotowance.[26] It provided that the savages should acknowledge the King of England as their sovereign and overlord; that Necotowance and his successors should pay as tribute "the number of twenty beaver skins at the goeing of the Geese yearly"; that all the land between the York and the James from the falls of both rivers to Kecoughtan should be ceded to the English; that all white prisoners and escaped negroes should be returned. In compensation the English agreed to protect

[20] P. R. O., CO1-30-71; CO1-41-111.
[21] P. R. O., CO5-1371-6 to 16.
[22] CO5-1371-6 to 16.
[23] CO5-1371-6 to 16.
[24] P. R. O., CO1-41-111.
[25] Beverley.
[26] Hen., Vol. I, p. 323.

the savages from the attacks of their enemies and to resign to them as their hunting ground the territory north of the York River.[27] This peace, which was most beneficial to the colony, was not broken until 1676, when the incursions of the wild Susquehannocks involved the native Virginia tribes in a new conflict with the white men.[28]

During the civil war that was at this time convulsing England most of the influential Virginia planters adhered to the party of the King. They were, with rare exceptions, members of the established church, and could have little sympathy with a movement that was identified with dissenters. If the triumph of Parliament was to bring about the disestablishment of the Church, or even the toleration of Presbyterians and Independents, they could not give them their support. Moreover, loyalty to the House of Stuart was strong in Virginia. The very remoteness of the planters from the King increased their reverence and love. They could not be present at court to see the monarch in all his human weakness, so there was nothing to check their loyal imaginations from depicting him as the embodiment of princely perfection. Nor had the wealthy families of the colony aught to anticipate of economic or political gain in the triumph of Parliament. Possessed of large estates, monopolizing the chief governmental offices, wielding a great influence over the Assembly and the courts, and looking forward to a future of prosperity and power, they could not risk their all upon the uncertain waters of revolution. Some, no doubt, sympathized with the efforts that were being made in England to limit the King's power of taxing the people, for the colony had always contained its quota of liberals, but the dictates of self-interest must have lulled them into quiescence. And the Governor, in this hour of need, proved a veritable rock of loyalty for the King. None that showed leanings towards the cause of Parliament could expect favors of any kind from Sir William Berkeley. Moreover, if they spoke too loudly of the rights of the people and of the tyranny of monarchs, they might find themselves under arrest and charged with treason.

[27]Hen., Vol. I, p. 323.

[28] P. R. O., CO1-30-71.

But there was another faction in Virginia, composed largely of small planters and freedmen, which sympathized with the aims of their fellow commons of the mother country. Prominent among these must have been a small number of Virginia Puritans, who had for some years been subjected to mild persecution. The overwhelming sentiment of the colony had long been for strict uniformity in the Church "as neere as may be to the canons in England", and several statutes had been passed by the Assembly to suppress the Quakers and Puritans.[29] In 1642, Richard Bennett and others of strong Calvinistic leanings, sent letters to Boston requesting that Puritan ministers be sent to Virginia, to minister to their non-conformist congregations.[30] The New Englanders responded readily, despatching to their southern friends three ministers of distinction—William Thompson, John Knowles and Thomas James. Despite the laws against non-conformity these men anticipated little interference with their work and even brought letters of introduction from Governor Winthrop to Sir William Berkeley.[31] Little did they know the temper of the new Virginia Governor. So far from welcoming this Puritan invasion Berkeley determined to meet it with measures of stern repression. A bill was put through the Assembly requiring all ministers within the colony to conform to the "orders and constitutions of the church of England", both in public and in private worship, and directing the Governor and Council to expel all dissenters from the country.[32] Disheartened at this unfriendly reception, James and Knowles soon returned to New England, leaving Thompson to carry on the work. This minister, in defiance of the law, lingered long in Virginia, preaching often and making many converts.

Among those that embraced the Calvinistic tenets at this time was Thomas Harrison, formerly Berkeley's chaplain. Harrison seems to have regarded the massacre of 1644 as a judgment of God upon the colonists for their persecution of the Puritans. His desertion of the established Church aroused both the anger and the alarm of the Governor and in 1648 he

[29] Hen., Vol. I, p. 123, 149, 277.

[30] Bruce, Inst. Hist., Vol. I, p. 254.

[31] Bruce, Inst. Hist., Vol. I, p. 254.

[32] Hen., Vol. I, p. 277.

was expelled from his parish for refusing to use the Book of Common Prayer. Later he left the colony for New England.

This persecution, although not severe enough to stamp out dissent in Virginia, could but arouse among the Puritans a profound dissatisfaction with the existing government, and a desire to coöperate with their brethren of England in the great contest with the King. Although not strong enough to raise the Parliamentary standard in the colony and to seek religious freedom at the sword's point, the Puritans formed a strong nucleus for a party of opposition to the King and his Governor.

Moreover, in addition to the comparatively small class of Puritans, there must have been in the colony hundreds of men, loyal to the established church, who yet desired a more liberal government both in England and in Virginia. A strong middle class was developing which must have looked with sympathy upon the cause of the English Commons and with jealousy upon the power of the Virginia Governor and his Council. There is positive evidence that many poor men had been coming to Virginia from very early times, paying their own passage and establishing themselves as peasant proprietors. Wills still preserved show the existence at this period of many little farms of five or six hundred acres, scattered among the great plantations of the wealthy. They were tilled, not by servants or by slaves, but by the freemen that owned them. Depending for food upon their own cattle, hogs, corn, fruit and vegetables, and for the other necessities of life upon their little tobacco crops, the poor farmers of Virginia were developing into intelligent and useful citizens. They constituted the backbone of a distinct and powerful middle class, which even at this early period, had to be reckoned with by aristocracy and Governor and King.

This section of the population was constantly being recruited from the ranks of the indentured servants. The plantations of the rich were tilled chiefly by bonded laborers, brought from the mother country. So long as land was plentiful in Virginia the chief need of the wealthy was for labor. Wage earners could not supply this need, for the poor man would not till the fields of others when he could have land of his own almost for the asking. So the planters surmounted this difficulty by bringing workmen to the colony under indenture, to work upon their farms for a certain number of years. Many a poor Englishman, finding the struggle for existence too severe at home, thus surrendered for a while his liberty, that in the end he might acquire a share in the good things of the New World. After serving his master five or six years the servant usually was given his liberty and with it fifty acres of land and a few farm implements. Thus equipped, he could, with industry and frugality, acquire property and render himself a useful citizen in his adopted country. There can be no doubt that many hundreds of former servants, become prosperous, did unite with the free immigrants of humble means to form a vigorous middle class.

Nothing could be more natural than that the small farmers should regard Parliament as the champion of the poor Englishman at home and in the colony. They knew full well that if Charles should triumph over the Commons, his victory would mean greater power for their Governor, greater privilege for the wealthy planters. On the other hand, the King's defeat might bring increased influence to the middle class and to the Burgesses.

It is not possible to determine how numerous was the Parliamentary party in Virginia, but the faction was powerful enough to cause serious apprehension to the loyalists. So bitter was the feeling that fears of assassination were entertained for Sir William Berkeley, and a guard of ten men was granted him. We are "sensible", declared the Assembly, in 1648, "of the many disaffections to the government from a schismaticall party, of whose intentions our native country of England hath had and yet hath too sad experience".[33]

But the commons of Virginia were not prepared to raise the standard of revolt. They must have lacked organization and leaders. Most of the aristocracy and wealth of Virginia was arrayed against them, while the government was in the hands of a man noted for his passionate attachment to the Throne.

[33] Hen., Vol. I, p. 355.

The Parliamentary party must have felt it best to await the event of the struggle in England, pinning their hopes upon the success of their comrades there. But even after Parliament had won the victory, after the King had been executed, they were not strong enough to overthrow Berkeley's government and force Virginia into obedience to the Commonwealth.

The news of the death of Charles I filled the royalists of Virginia with grief and anger. It seemed to them that the cause of law and order and religion in the unhappy kingdom had fallen with their monarch. Moreover, they could but expect the victorious party, after settling all at home, to extend their arms to the little colony and force upon them a reluctant obedience to the new government. But the intrepid Berkeley was determined never to submit until compelled to do so by force of arms. Charles II was proclaimed King. The Assembly was called together and a law enacted declaring it high treason to question, even by insinuation, the "undoubted & inherent right of his Majesty . . . to the Collony of Virginia, and all other his majesties dominions".[34] The Assembly referred to Charles I in terms of reverence and affection, as their late blessed and sainted King, and, unmindful of consequences, denounced his executioners as lawless tyrants. For any person to cast dishonor or censure upon the fallen monarch, or to uphold in any way the proceedings against him, or to assert the legality of his dethronement, was declared by the Assembly high treason. "And it is also enacted," they continued, "that what person soever, by false reports and malicious rumors shall spread abroad, among the people, any thing tending to change of government, . . . such persons, not only the authors of . . . but the reporters and divulgers thereof, shall be adjudged guilty."[35]

Even before the news of these events reached England, Sir William had aroused the anger of Parliament by his persecution of the Puritans. Some of the people of Nansemond county had written, complaining of the banishment of Mr. Harrison, whom they described as an able minister and a man of splendid character. The English Council wrote Berkeley

[34] Hen., Vol. I, p. 360. [35] Hen., Vol. I, p. 361.

commanding him to restore Mr. Harrison to his parish. "Wee know," they said, "you cannot be ignorant that the use of the common prayer book is prohibited by the parliament of England."[36] And when they learned that the colony had refused to acknowledge the Commonwealth, and still adhered to the House of Stuart, they were determined to punish the Virginians for their temerity. Since it would be exceedingly inconvenient at this time of uncertainty and change to send an expedition across the Atlantic, it was decided to bring the colonists to their senses by cutting off their foreign trade. An act was passed by Parliament in October, 1650, declaring that since the colony had been settled by the English at great cost to the nation, it should rightly be under the authority of the present government; that divers persons in Virginia had committed open treason, "traytorously by force and Subtilty" usurping the government and defying the Commonwealth; and in order to repress speedily the rebellious colonists and to inflict upon them a merited punishment, they were to be forbidden all "Commerce or Traffique with any people Whatsoever". The full force of the English navy was to be used in carrying out this act, and all commanders were directed to seize and bring in foreign vessels found trading with the colony. No English ships were to sail for Virginia without special license from the Council of State.[37]

This was a dire threat indeed. To cut off all commerce with England and foreign countries would bring utter ruin upon the planters, for their tobacco crop would then be without a market. Even now, however, the Governor did not falter in his loyalty. He felt, no doubt, that Parliament would have difficulty in enforcing this act, and he looked to the Dutch merchantmen to take off the tobacco.

Before an Assembly called together in March, 1651, Berkeley delivered an address ringing with defiance of Parliament. "Gentlemen," he said, "you perceave by the Declaration that the men of Westminster have set out, . . . how they meane to deale with you hereafter. . . . Indeed me thinks they might have proposed something to us which might have strengthened

[36] Sp. Dom. Inter., 1-94. [37] Scobell, Vol. II, p. 132.

us to beare those heavy chaines they are making ready for us, though it were but an assurance that we shall eat the bread for which our owne Oxen plow, and with our owne sweat we reape; but this assurance (it seems) were a franchise beyond the Condition they have resolv'd on the Question we ought to be in: For the reason why they talk so Magisterially to us is this, we are forsooth their worships slaves, bought with their money and by consequence ought not to buy, or sell but with those they shall Authorize with a few trifles to Coszen us of all for which we toile and labour. . . . The strength of their argument runs onely thus: we have laid violent hands on your Land-lord, possessed his Manner house where you used to pay your rents, therefore now tender your respects to the same house you once reverenced. . . . They talke indeed of money laid out in this country in its infancy. I will not say how little, nor how Centuply repaid, but will onely aske, was it theirs? They who in the beginning of this warr were so poore, & indigent, that the wealth and rapines of three Kingdomes & their Churches too cannot yet make rich."

The Governor then began an impassioned appeal to the Assembly to remain firm in their loyalty to the Crown. "Surely Gentlemen," he cried, "we are more slaves by nature, than their power can make us if we suffer ourselves to be shaken with these paper bulletts, & those on my life are the heaviest they either can or will send us. . . . You have heard under what heavy burthens the afflicted English Nation now groans, and calls to heaven for relief: how new and formerly unheard of impositions make the wifes pray for barrenness and their husbands deafnes to exclude the cryes of their succourles, starving children. . . . Consider your selves how happy you are and have been, how the Gates of wealth and Honour are shut to no man, and that there is not here an Arbitrary hand that dares to touch the substance of either poore or rich: But that which I woud have you chiefly consider with thankfullnes is: That God hath separated you from the guilt of the crying bloud of our Pious Souveraigne of ever blessed memory: But mistake not Gentlemen part of it will yet stain your garments if you willingly submit to those murtherers hands that shed it; I tremble to thinke how the oathes they will impose will make those guilty of it, that have long abhor'd the traiterousnesse of the act. . . . Gentlemen by the Grace of God we will not so tamely part with our King, and all these blessings we enjoy under him; and if they oppose us, do but follow me, I will either lead you to victory, or lose a life which I cannot more gloriously sacrifice then for my loyalty, and your security."[38]

When the Governor had completed his appeal the obnoxious act of Parliament was read aloud. The Assembly then passed a series of resolutions, reiterating their loyalty to the Crown, denouncing the Commons as usurpers and regicides, and defending themselves against the charge of treachery and rebellion. They had, they declared, adhered always to the "Lawes of England", which enjoined upon them the oaths of allegiance and supremacy, and they refused now, at the bidding of Parliament, to break their word by renouncing their King. They could not be expected to give passive obedience to every party that possessed themselves of Westminster Hall, where the heads of divers factions had followed each other in quick succession. They had been accused of usurping the government of the colony, but their records would show that they had never swerved from their allegiance. And it ill became the Parliament that had overthrown the English constitution to bring such accusations. Finally, they declared, "we are resolv'd to Continue our Allegeance to our most Gratious King, yea as long as his gratious favour permits us, we will peaceably trade with the Londoners, and all other nations in amity with our Soveraigne: Protect all forraigne Merchants with our utmost force in our Capes: Allwaies pray for the happy restoration of our King, and repentance in them, who to the hazard of their soules have opposed him."[39]

As Berkeley had foreseen, the English found it impossible to enforce a strict blockade. The government could not spare war vessels enough to close the Virginia capes, and foreign merchantmen continued to sail unmolested into the James and the York, bringing goods to the planters and taking off their tobacco. Indeed the Dutch took advantage of this quarrel

[38] Va. Mag., Vol. I., p. 77.

[39] Va. Mag., Vol. I, pp. 75 to 81.

between colony and mother country to extend their American trade at the expense of the English merchants. The Council of State was soon made to realize by the complaints that poured in from the London shippers, that the "Blockade Act" was injuring England more than the refractory colony.

At this moment, several leaders of the Virginia Parliamentary party came to the Council at Westminster and represented to it the necessity of fitting out an expedition to overthrow the Berkeley government. They could plead that the blockade had proved ineffective, that the honor of the Commonwealth demanded the prompt subjection of the impudent Governor, that the coöperation of the Virginia commons would make the task easy. Nor could they omit to remind the Councillors that it was their duty to bring relief to their fellow Puritans of Virginia.

At all events the Council, seeing the necessity of prompt action, sent forth a well armed expedition under the command of Captain Robert Denis to subdue both the Barbadoes and Virginia. But wishing to avoid, if possible, open hostilities, at the same time they sent commissioners to treat with the colonists and persuade them to submit peaceably to the Commonwealth. The Council of State evidently expected active assistance from the Parliamentary party in the colony in these efforts to establish the new political order, for they gave directions to the commissioners to raise troops in the plantations, to appoint captains and other officers, and to guarantee freedom to all servants that volunteered to fight with the Commonwealth forces. They were given power to grant pardon to all that submitted, making such exceptions as they thought proper, and were directed to establish a new government in accord with the present constitution of England.

When, in the spring of 1652, the British fleet sailed up the James river, Captain Denis found the intrepid Berkeley prepared for a strenuous resistance. With the guns of the warships approaching his capital, with English soldiers ready for a landing, with a strong party in the colony in sympathy with the invaders, he might well have despaired. Resistance would certainly entail enormous misfortunes upon the colony—

bloodshed, devastation, civil strife—and success could be but temporary. Should he beat off the present expedition, others too powerful to be resisted would undoubtedly follow, and the punishment of the colony would be but the more severe.

Yet the Governor did not falter. He called around him the full strength of the colonial militia, posted them to good advantage, and himself took active command. Several Dutch vessels that had been trading in the James were pressed into service, filled with men and moored in close to Jamestown, with their guns trained upon the approaching enemy. Behind them were several land batteries. The whole made an imposing appearance, and might well have given apprehension to the invaders.

Fortunately, however, the threatened conflict was averted by the persuasion of the Parliamentary commissioners. These men, anxious to avoid civil war, availed themselves of the authority given them by the Council of State, to offer very lenient terms of surrender. Some of them seem to have preceded the fleet to Virginia, to consult with their friends and to formulate plans to render the Governor's resistance ineffectual. It is not improbable that these efforts were seconded by some of the most prominent men of the colony. Two members of the Council itself, it is said, who possessed goods of great value upon vessels in the fleet, received warning that their property would be at once confiscated, if they gave their support to the Governor. They therefore were constrained to advocate submission. With division in the ranks of the colonists and with the invaders ready for action, even Berkeley was at last forced to give way and consent to a capitulation.

The terms of surrender were drawn up at Jamestown and agreed to by the commissioners on the one hand, and by the Governor, Council and Burgesses on the other. It was agreed first, that Virginia should acknowledge its due allegiance to the Commonwealth of England, and "to the lawes there established". This submission, it was declared, was "a voluntary act, not forced nor constrained by a conquest upon the country".[40] It was also stipulated "that the people of Virginia have

[40] Hen., Vol. I, p. 363.

free trade as the people of England do enjoy to all places and with all nations according to the lawes of that commonwealth". Even more interesting was the agreement "that Virginia shall be free from all taxes, customs and impositions whatsoever, and none to be imposed on them without consent of the Grand Assembly, and soe that neither fforts nor castles bee erected or garrisons maintained without their consent". When these terms of surrender were reported to the English government, Parliament thought that the commissioners had been too liberal in their concessions, and some of the articles were not ratified.

The commissioners granted full pardon and indemnity for all "acts, words or writeings done or spoken against the parliament" and any persons refusing to take the oath of allegiance to the new government were given "a yeares time . . . to remove themselves and their estates out of Virginia". The use of the Book of Common Prayer was permitted for one year in the parishes that so desired, and no ministers were deprived of their charges or their livings.[41]

Separate articles were drawn up between the commissioners and the Governor and Council. Neither Berkeley nor the Councillors were to be compelled, during the ensuing twelve months, to take the oath of allegiance. They were not to be censured for speaking well in private of the King. They were given leave to sell all their property and to quit the country without molestation. They were permitted to send a message to Charles II, giving an account of the surrender.[42]

The commissioners were now confronted with the all-important task of establishing a new government. They had been given power by the Council of State to hold an election of Burgesses granting the franchise to all who had taken the oath of allegiance. Feeling, doubtless, a reluctance to assume the entire responsibility of moulding a new constitution, they resolved to wait until the Burgesses assembled and to consult with them in all their measures. The election was held without delay, and the members were sworn in on April 26th, 1652.

The Burgesses and the commissioners then entered upon a long and serious debate concerning "the settling and govern-

[41] Hen., Vol. I, pp. 363-365. [42] Hen., Vol. I, pp. 365-367.

ing of Virginia".[43] The English Council had not, it would seem, given specific directions in regard to this work, so the members of the little constitutional convention were practically at liberty to do what they chose. Realizing, however, that all might be changed if it proved unsatisfactory to Parliament, they proceeded cautiously. Their chief concern was to establish a tentative government that would prevent present confusion and could later be perfected by the Council of State. It so happened, however, that the English, amid the confusion of the times, neglected to attend to this matter, and the work of the convention remained essentially unaltered throughout the Commonwealth period.

The House of Burgesses, since it had been officially recognized by the Council of State, was made the chief governing body of the colony. Except for the veto of the English government its power was to be unlimited. It was to elect the Governor and to specify his duties. If his administration proved unsatisfactory it might remove him from office. The Burgesses were also to elect the Council, to prescribe its functions and limit its power. This proud body, which had formerly been so powerful, was now to exist only on the suffrage of the House. It was even debated whether Councillors should be admitted to membership in the General Assembly. The appointment of all officials was also to "appertain to the Burgesses, the representatives of the people", but it was agreed that for the present most of the first nominations should be left to the Governor and the commissioners.[44]

Thus did Virginia become in all but name a republic. In England, the long cherished hope of the patriots for liberty was to be disappointed by the usurpation of Oliver Cromwell, and the victory of Parliament over the stubborn Charles was to result only in the substitution of one despot for another. But the commons of Virginia, although they had played an insignificant rôle in the great drama of the times, were to reap the reward which was denied their cousins of England. Their government for the next eight years was to be truly representative of the people. Nor did the English government often

[43] Hen., Vol. I, p. 371.

[44] Hen., Vol. I, pp. 371, 373.

interfere with their affairs. Busy with his numerous wars and with the cares of administration, the Protector never found time to acquaint himself thoroughly with what was happening in Virginia. In 1653, and again in 1658, Cromwell promised to make some definite regulations for the government of the colony, but he was interrupted on each occasion before he could put his resolutions into effect. That it was his intention, however, to keep the appointment of the Governor in his own hands seems certain. In 1654 the Assembly received word that his Highness had decided then to continue Colonel Bennett, of whose good character he had heard, in the execution of his office, until he could further signify his pleasure. In 1657, the Council of State requested Cromwell to appoint some person to go to Virginia as its Governor, but this he failed to do.[45] With the exception of such spasmodic interruptions as these, and the partial enforcement of the Navigation Acts, the colony was left almost to its own devices throughout the Commonwealth period.

By the unanimous vote of the commissioners and the Burgesses Mr. Richard Bennett was made Governor. This choice must have been satisfactory both to the English government and the Parliamentary party in the colony. Mr. Bennett had been one of the few prominent Virginia Puritans and had left the colony during the persecution of dissenters by Sir William Berkeley. As a member of the commission he had been instrumental in bringing about the surrender and saving the colony from civil war. It was agreed that he should serve for one year, "or untill the next meeting of the Assembly", but as his administration proved most satisfactory he was continued in office by Cromwell until March 31st, 1655.[46]

The new government, however, was not to be established entirely without disorder and strife. In the interval between the surrender and the assembling of the Burgesses affairs on the Eastern Shore assumed a threatening aspect. The people of Northampton, many of whom seem formerly to have been favorable to the Commonwealth, became ill affected to the new

[45] Sp. Dom. Int., 1-75; Hen., Vol. I, p. 510; Bruce, Inst. Hist., Vol. II, p. 302.

[46] Hen., Vol. I, pp. 371, 408.

régime, even before it was well begun. A number of things conspired to bring about this change. Among the inhabitants of Northampton were a number of Dutch who had settled there during the preceding decade. When war broke out between Holland and England in 1652 it was rumored that these people were conspiring with the Indians to bring about another massacre in Virginia. Groundless as these suspicions were, they infuriated the English and caused grave fears for the safety of the Dutch planters. When the justices of the peace took precautions to protect the unfortunate foreigners their action caused discontent and bitterness against the new government. Moreover, the Navigation Acts, recently passed by Parliament, restricting foreign trade would, if enforced, prove especially damaging to the people of the Eastern Shore. Finally, Northampton had not been represented in the Assembly since 1647, except for one Burgess in 1651, and the belief had sprung up that the county was to become independent of the government at Jamestown. For various reasons, therefore, Northampton was hostile to the government. And when the Parliamentary commissioners imposed upon them a tax of forty-six pounds of tobacco per poll, the people of the county voiced their anger in no uncertain terms, and selected a committee of six to draw up a statement of their grievances and present it to the new Assembly.

"Wee," they protested, "the Inhabitants of Northampton Countie doe complanye that from tyme to tyme wee have been submitted & bine obedient unto the paymt of publeq taxacons. Butt after ye yeare 1647, since yt tyme wee Conceive & have found that ye taxes were very weightie. But in a more espetiall manner . . . the taxacon of fforty sixe pounds of tobacco p. poll (this present yeare). And desire yt ye same bee taken off ye charge of ye Countie; furthermore wee alledge that after 1647, wee did understand & suppose or Countie or Northampton to be disioynted & sequestered from ye rest of Virginia. Therefore that Llawe wch requireth & inioyneth Taxacons from us to bee Arbitrarye & illegall; fforasmuch as wee had neither summons for Ellecon of Burgesses nor voyce in their Assemblye (during the time aforesd) but only the Singular Burgess in September, Ano., 1651. Wee conceive that wee may Lawfullie ptest agt the pceedings in the Act of Assemblie for publiq Taxacons wch have relacon to Northmton Countie since ye year 1647."[47]

Thus early in the history of the colony was enunciated the principle that taxation without representation is unjust and illegal. The men of Northampton do not speak of the doctrine as something new, but as a thing understood and recognized. Certain it is that the people of Virginia, in all periods of their colonial history, realized the vast importance of confining the power of taxation to their own Assembly.

But the leaders of the new government did not receive the petition with favor. They were willing to give Northampton her due quota of Burgesses, but they were angered at the suggestion of separation. Moreover, the disorders on the Eastern Shore became more pronounced and the justices were compelled to seek aid from the Council in protecting the Dutch. In June, 1653, the turbulent people met and, amid scenes of disorder, denounced the action of the authorities. When a voice from the crowd cried out that the justices were a "company of asses and villyanes", the people roared out their approval. The Assembly, at its meeting in June, 1653, was forced to take active steps to suppress the agitation and to restore order upon the peninsula. Mr. Bennett with several members of the Assembly, was sent to Northampton, "for the settlement of the peace of that countie, and punishinge delinquents". In this he seems to have been entirely successful, for we hear no more of disorders upon the Eastern Shore during this period.[48]

When the commissioners and the Burgesses, in 1652, established anew the gubernatorial office, they were somewhat vague in defining the duties belonging to it. They first declared that Mr. Bennett was to exercise "all the just powers and authorities that may belong to that place lawfully".[49] But that it was not their intention to give the new officer the prerogatives enjoyed by the royal Governor is shown by their further statement that he was to have such power only as should

[47] Wise, p. 139.

[48] Wise, pp. 114, 115; Hen., Vol. I, p. 380.

[49] Hen., Vol. I, p. 371.

be granted him from time to time by the Assembly.[50] This lack of clearness led, quite naturally, to several clashes between the legislative and executive branches of the government.

At the session of Assembly of July, 1653, the Burgesses showed that they would brook no interference from the Governor with their affairs. On the eve of the election of the Speaker, they received a message from Mr. Bennett and the Council advising them not to choose a certain Lieutenant-Colonel Chiles. Although it was clearly shown that this gentleman could not serve with propriety, the Burgesses gave him the election, merely, it would seem, as a rebuke to the presumption of the Governor.[51]

Edward Digges, who succeeded Mr. Bennett, seems to have had no clash with the Assembly, but during the next administration, when Samuel Matthews was Governor, the executive made a determined effort to break the power of the Burgesses. At the session of 1658, the Governor and the Council sent a message to the Assembly declaring that body dissolved.[52] This move startled the Burgesses. The royal Governors had always possessed the right of dissolving the House, but no such authority had been delegated to the new executive. Moreover, it was inconsistent with the theory, upon which everyone had acted since the surrender in 1652, that all power resided in the representatives of the people. "The said disolution," replied the House, "as the case standeth is not presidentall neither legall according to the lawes, now in force, Therefore wee humbly desire a revocation of the said declaration."[53]

Although the Burgesses replied thus courteously they were deeply angered. Rightly judging this to be a challenge to their power, they resolved to show once more that they were supreme in the government. They voted, therefore, to ignore the dissolution. And it was ordered that if any member left his seat he was to be censured "as a person betraying the trust reposed in him by his country".[54] An oath of secrecy was administered to all present, while the Speaker was directed to

[50] Hen., Vol. I, p. 372.
[51] Hen., Vol. I, pp. 377, 378.
[52] Hen., Vol. I, p. 499.
[53] Hen., Vol. I, p. 499.
[54] Hen., Vol. I, p. 500.

"sign nothing without the consent of the major part of the house".

Staggered by the determined attitude of the Burgesses, the Governor and Council at once showed signs of weakening. They were willing, they said, to allow the Assembly to continue its deliberations, provided the work were brought to a speedy conclusion. The "dispute of the power of disolving and the legality thereof" they wished to refer to the Lord Protector. But the House resolved unanimously that this answer was unsatisfactory. The withdrawal of the dissolution was not enough, the Governor and Council must acknowledge that their act was illegal and therefore had never taken effect. "The House, unsatisfied with these answers, appointed a committee to draw up a report for the manifestation and vindication of the Assembly's power which after presentation to the House to be sent to the Governour and Councell."[55] This committee recommended the immediate dismissal of the Council, and proposed resolutions declaring the "power of government to reside in such persons as shall be impowered by the Burgesses (the representatives of the people) who are not dissolvable by any power now extant in Virginia, but the House of Burgesses". Upon receiving this report the House proceeded to annul "all former election of Governour and Councill". Since the executive had presumed to abuse its authority by defying the body that had appointed it to office, it must be removed to evince to all the supremacy of the House. The Burgesses seem not to have laid the blame for this crisis upon the Governor, but upon some of the Councillors, who were endeavoring to make their own power supreme in the government. Colonel Matthews was, therefore, reëlected, and invested with "all just rights and privileges belonging to the Governour and Captain Generall of Virginia".[56]

Fearing that the Council might offer resistance to their decrees, the Burgesses commanded the serjeant-at-arms of the Assembly and the sheriffs of James City county not to execute any warrant, precept or command" from any other person than the Speaker of the House. The Secretary of State,

[55] Hen., Vol. I, p. 501. [56] Hen., Vol. I, pp. 502, 503.

Colonel William Claiborne, was directed to deliver up the public records. But the Governor and Council seem not to have thought of resistance, and submitted to the recall and to a new election by the Assembly. Although they had just resolved that "for the future none bee admitted a councellor but such who shall be nominated, appointed and confirmed by the house", the Burgesses now allowed the Governor to propose to them a list of names for the new Council. It would seem that Nathaniel Bacon and Francis Willis were regarded as the instigators of the dissolution, for they were the only members of the Council which had signed the offensive order who were not now reëlected.[57]

When the Assembly met again, in March, 1659, it found that its supremacy was once more threatened. A letter had been received from Henry Lawrence, President of the Council of State in the home government, which seemed to imply that the Governor and his Council and not the Burgesses, were to hold the chief power in Virginia. Lawrence declared that the "looseness" of affairs in the colony had induced Cromwell to take active steps for the settlement of its constitution, but that these measures had been brought to a sudden halt by the Lord Protector's death. The matter was, however, still before the Council of State, and the colony might soon expect some definite orders from its deliberations. In the meanwhile, he wrote, "their Lordships do will and require you the present Governour and Councill there to apply yourselves . . . to the peaceable and orderly management of the affairs of that collony, according to such good lawes and customes as have been heretofore used and exercised among you".[58]

The Burgesses were deeply agitated by this letter. They at once passed resolutions promising to obey the commands of the Council of State, but they determined to write the new Lord Protector, Richard Cromwell, asking that the privileges of the Burgesses be confirmed. In this crisis the Governor gave striking evidence of his liberal inclinations by coming before the House to promise them his support. "He acknowledged the supream power of electing officers to be by the

[57] Hen., Vol. I, pp. 499, 505. [58] Hen., Vol. I, p. 510.

present lawes resident in the Grand Assembly", and offered to "joyne his best assistance with the countrey in makeing an addresse to his Highnesse for confirmation of their present priviledges".[59]

In the meanwhile an act was prepared making some important changes in the constitution, but confirming the power of the Burgesses. It was proposed, first, that Colonel Matthews "bee the Governour and Captain Gennerall of Virginia for two yeares ensueing, and then the Grand Assembly to elect a Governour as they think fitt, the person elect being then one of the Councell". The personnel of the Council was to remain unchanged and for the future its members were to serve for life, "except in case of high misdemanors". Lastly the Governor was to have the privilege of nominating the Councillors, but the Burgesses could confirm or reject at their discretion.[60] The Council at first assented to these proposals, "till the pleasure of his Highness be further signified", but later, it seems, they "expressly declined the said act", and declared the Assembly dissolved.[61] Whether or not the Burgesses submitted to this dissolution and left the Governor and Council to govern the colony as they chose, does not appear. It is quite probable that the executive, in the interval between the sessions of Assembly of March 1659 and March 1660, based its right to rule, not upon the commission of the Burgesses, but upon the authority given it in Lawrence's letter.

In May, 1659, Richard Cromwell resigned the reigns of government, and England was left a prey to confusion and uncertainty. The Virginians did not know to what government to give their allegiance. None could tell whether military despotism would be established in England, or another Cromwell would arise, or the House of Stuart be restored. To add to their troubles, in January, 1660, Colonel Matthews died, leaving them without a Governor. March 13th, the Assembly convened.

The Burgesses at once took steps to reëstablish their questioned prerogatives. An act was passed declaring that

[59] Hen., Vol. I, p. 512.
[60] Hen., Vol. I, p. 517.
[61] Hen., Vol. I, p. 537.

"whereas by reason of the late frequent distractions there being in England noe resident absolute and gen'll confessed power; Be it enacted and confirmed, That the supreame power of the government of this country should be resident in the Assembly, And that all writts issue in the name of the Grand Assembly of Virginia, until such a comand and comission come out of England as shall be by the Assembly adjudged lawfull".[62]

Their next care was to elect a new Governor. Strangely enough their choice fell upon that staunch advocate of royalty, Sir William Berkeley. When the surrender had been made to the parliamentary commissioners in 1652, the Governor had secured for himself the right to quit the colony any time within the ensuing year. But circumstances had prevented his sailing during this period, and later he resolved to remain in Virginia. During the eight years of the Commonwealth period he had lived in retirement, obedient to the new government, but longing for the restoration of the Stuarts. Why he was now called forth by the Assembly to take once more the most important office in Virginia, cannot be certainly determined. It seems strange that the Burgesses in one act should assert their own sovereignty in the most emphatic terms, and in the next elect as their Governor this ardent servant of the Crown. If it had been their only aim to choose a leader of executive ability, they did not lack men of power and experience whose love of popular government was unquestioned. Berkeley had in his first administration ruled justly and well, but there is no reason to think that Virginia had been more prosperous and happy under him than under the Commonwealth Governors. It seems then most probable that the Assembly was actuated in its choice by an apprehension that the monarchy might be restored. If the English should invite Charles to reclaim his lost inheritance, it would be of much advantage to the colony to have at its head the former royal Governor. It would make the restoration in Virginia easy and peaceful, for the staunchest republican would not dare resist, with Charles II on his throne and Sir William Berkeley ruling at Jamestown. Moreover, it could but please

[62] Hen., Vol. I, p. 530.

the King and recommend the colony to his favor. On the other hand, the Assembly was careful to reserve all real authority to itself. Sir William was to be its servant, not its master. If, out of the confusion in England, should emerge a real republic, they could force the Governor either to acknowledge the new power or to resign his commission. In fact the office was at first proffered him only upon condition that he would submit to any power, whatever it might be, that succeeded in fixing itself over the English people.[63]

But to this requirement Berkeley would by no means consent. He was willing, during the present interregnum, to hold office from the people of Virginia, but never from any English power save that of the Crown. In an address to the Assembly, outlining his conduct during the troubles of the past eleven years, he made it quite clear that his sympathies had undergone no change. "When I came first into this Countrie," he said, "I had the Commicon and Commands of my most gracious master King Charles of ever blessed memory. . . . When God's wrath lay heavie upon us for the sins of our nation, my ever honoured Master was put to a violent death, and immeadiately after his Royall Sonne . . . sent me a Commicon to governe here under him. . . . But the Parliament, after the defeat at Worcester, (by the instigation of some other intent) sent a small power to force my submission to them, which finding me defenceless, was quietly (God pardon me) effected. But this parliament continued not long after this, but another supream power outed them, whoe remained not long neither, nor his sonne after him. . . . And now my intelligence is not enough to tell me what incorporate, mixt, or individuall power there is. . . . Under all these mutable governments of divers natures and constitutions, I have lived most resigningly submissive: But, Mr. Speaker, it is one duty to live obedient to a government, and another of a very different nature to Command under it. . . . You have, Mr. Speaker, with great wisdome and providence taken care of my obedient prostrating to the Supreame power the authoritie you would entrust me with,

[63] Southern Lit. Mess., Jan. 1845.

for which I give you my humble thanks; for this wisdome of yours hath animated my caution of assumeing this burden, which is so volatile, slippery and heavy, that I may justly feare it will breake my Limbs." It might be thought by some, he said, that the emergency would excuse his accepting this authority, but the King would judge him, and if his information were prejudiced, his punishment might be severe. He did not fear death, he was too old for that, but an imprudent, criminal death he abhorred. In conclusion he declared that these and other considerations must dissuade him from accepting the proffered office.

But the Assembly persisted in its determination to make him Governor. If he scrupled to promise to serve under the enemies of the Crown, that promise would not be required of him. Let him be Governor of Virginia, by their authority only, and only so long as the confusion in England continued. If a new Protector, or a new Commonwealth gained the ascendency, and demanded Virginia's submission, he might resign. If England returned to its obedience to the Throne, he could petition the King for a new commission. To this Berkeley assented. "Wee have all," he said, in another short address, "had great and pressing feares of offending a Supreame power which neither by present possession is soe, nor has a publiquely confessed politique capacity to be a Supream power. I alsoe, Mr. Speaker, have my pressing feares too, and I am seriously afraid to offend him, who by all Englishmen is confessed to be in a naturall politique capacity of being a Supreame power." He therefore, he said, made this declaration in the presence of God, that if any government became fixed in London, he would immediately lay down his commission. When this was recorded and they were still of the same mind, he was ready most thankfully to serve them.[64]

Thus did Sir William Berkeley a second time become Governor of Virginia. It must have been with trepidation that this man, who had so often denied the right of any officer to serve save by the King's commands, accepted now this commission from the hands of the people. The stern hater of

[64] Southern Lit. Mess., Jan. 1845.

republicanism was becoming the head of an independent little republic. For such Virginia was and must continue to be until there should appear in England some fixed government to which it could submit. "I am," Berkeley wrote Governor Stuyvesant of New Amsterdam, "but a servant of the assembly's; neither do they arrogate any power to themselves, further than the miserable distractions of England force them to. For when God shall be pleased in his mercy to take away and dissipate the unnatural diversions of their native country, they will immediately return to their own professed obedience."[65]

The restoration of the monarchy took place May 29th, 1660. When the news reached Virginia some weeks later, the people accepted the change without opposition, and probably with relief, for they were weary of uncertainty and confusion. Berkeley's unaffected joy was mingled with a deep apprehension that the King might be angered at his accepting office without his consent. But Charles was not so unmindful of his staunch support at a time when the fortunes of the monarchy were at their lowest ebb as to reproach him for this act, which might, and probably did, redound to his advantage. He soon relieved the Governor's fears by sending a new commission. In a passion of joy and gratitude Berkeley wrote his thanks. "I . . . doe most humbly throwe myselfe at your Ma'ties feet," he said, "in a dutifull thankfullness to your Majestie, that you yett think me worthy of your Royall Commands. It is true, . . . I did something, which if misrepresented to your Majestie, may cause your Majestie to think me guilty of a weakness I should ever abhor myself for. But it was noe more . . . than to leape over the fold to save your Majesties flock, when your Majesties enemies of that fold had barred up the lawfull entrance into it, and enclosed the Wolves of Scisme and rebellion ready to devour all within it. Nor did I adventure on this, without the advice and impulsion of your Majesties best Subjects in these parts. . . . I always in all conditions had more fear of your Majesties ffrownes than the Swords or Tortures of your Enemies."[66]

[65] Campbell, p. 74.

[66] Southern Lit. Mess., Jan., 1845.

And so the Commonwealth period in Virginia came to an end. The colony had benefited greatly by the eight years of semi-independence and self-government. The population had increased rapidly. In 1649, there had been about 15,000 people in Virginia, while six years after the Restoration, the Governor estimated their number at 40,000. This great gain was due chiefly to accelerated immigration from England. The overthrow and execution of the King had sent many of his followers to seek shelter with Sir William Berkeley, others had come to escape the confusion and horrors of civil war, while the numerous prisoners taken in battle had furnished abundant material for the never-ending stream of indentured servants. Gentleman and tradesman and laborer alike were welcome, for land was abundant and the colony's only need was men. Nor was prosperity yet strangled by the strict enforcement of the Navigation Acts. Dutch vessels continued to sail through the capes in defiance of England and to carry off the planters' tobacco. Not until the closing years of the Commonwealth period did the increasing freight rates and the decreasing price of tobacco indicate that the "Hollanders" were being more strictly excluded.[67]

Equally important was the training received by the people in self-government. For eight years they had been their own masters, enacting such laws as they chose, and free from the restraining hand of the King. There had been no royal Governor to veto their bills, or threaten the Burgesses, or intimidate the voters, or overawe the Council, or sway the courts of justice. And the experience was priceless. It schooled them in governmental affairs and taught them self-reliance, patience and stubbornness to oppose oppression. Having tasted the sweets of freedom, they were ill prepared ever again to tolerate injustice and misgovernment. If there had been no Commonwealth period in Virginia, possibly there had never been a Bacon's Rebellion.

[67] Bruce, Ec. Hist., Vol. I, pp. 357-360.

CHAPTER V

The Causes of Bacon's Rebellion

There were many who hailed the restoration of the monarchy as the dawn of an era of prosperity and happiness for Virginia. The colony, despite the efforts of some of its people, had remained loyal to the Crown until overpowered by force of arms. It might well expect especial favor and care from its prince, now that he was firmly established upon his throne.[1] Of the ability and justice of the Governor Virginia had had ample experience during the ten years of his first administration.

Never was a people doomed to more bitter disappointment. The years which followed the Restoration were crowded with misfortunes greater than any that had befallen the colony since the ghastly days of the Great Sickness. Charles II, far from showing gratitude to his Old Dominion, overwhelmed it with injustice and oppression. The Virginians were crushed with tremendous duties on their tobacco and with ruinous restrictions upon their trade. The titles to their plantations were threatened by a grant of the entire colony to two unworthy favorites of the King. Governor Berkeley, embittered by the humiliation of the Commonwealth period, and growing avaricious and crabbed with advancing years, soon forfeited that respect and love which his former good conduct had gained him. His second administration was marred by partiality, oppression and inefficiency. The people were deprived of their right of suffrage by continued prorogation of the Assembly. Local government fell into the hands of small aristocratic cliques, while the poor were ground down with unequal and excessive taxes. Two wars with Holland added to the misfortunes of the colonists. Even the Heavens seemed to join with their enemies, for the country was visited

[1] P. R. O., CO1-34-95.

by a terrific hurricane which swept over the plantations, destroying crops and wrecking houses. These accumulated misfortunes brought such deep suffering upon the colony that hundreds of families were reduced to poverty and many were forced into debt and ruin. No wonder that the commons, finally driven to desperation, should have risen in insurrection against the Governor and the King.

First among the causes of distress during this unhappy period must be placed the Navigation Acts. England, in the middle of the 17th century, was engaged in an unsuccessful contest with Holland for the carrying trade of the world. The merchantmen of Amsterdam and Flushing found their way even to Maryland and Virginia, where their low freight rates and the liberal prices they gave for tobacco, assured them a hearty welcome. The exports of the colonies to England itself were not infrequently carried in Dutch bottoms. This was a source of much anxiety and annoyance to the British government. It seemed unjust that the American colonies, which had been founded at such tremendous cost, should now prove as great a source of wealth to Holland as to the mother country. And it could not but anger the English shippers to find themselves elbowed by these foreigners in the ports of the Bermudas or the rivers of Virginia.

In 1651, the British Parliament, thinking it necessary to give their merchants some protection from this lively competition, passed the first of the Navigation Acts. Under its provisions no goods of the growth or manufacture of Asia, America or Africa should be introduced into England in any but English ships, of which the owner, master and three-fourths of the sailors were English subjects; and all foreign commodities imported to England should be conveyed directly thither from the place of growth or manufacture.[2] This law injured the Virginians by excluding the Dutch carriers from the tobacco trade with England and thus causing a sharp rise in freight rates. During the early years of the Commonwealth period it was frequently avoided, but before 1660 the English government began to enforce it more strictly.

[2] Scobell, Vol. II, p. 132.

Nor did the people get relief with the restoration of the monarchy. Charles II proved more solicitous that Parliament for the welfare of the English merchants; even more indifferent to the complaints of the colonists. A new Navigation Act was passed in 1660 which struck a deadly blow at the prosperity of Virginia. Under its provisions all goods sent to the colonies, even though of foreign growth or manufacture, were to be exported from England, and all tobacco, sugar, wool, etc., produced in the colonies, must be shipped only to England or to her dominions.[3]

Thus were the colonies sacrificed upon the altar of greed. The new act injured the Virginia planters in several ways. Since all their tobacco must now be brought to English ports, they could no longer seek the most advantageous markets. Had the demand for the commodity in England been more elastic, the consequences of this provision might not have been disastrous. Declining prices would have so stimulated the demand that the English could have consumed the entire crop. But the King's customs kept up the price to the consumer, and made it impossible for the merchants to dispose of the vast quantities of the leaf that had formerly gone to Holland and other countries.[4] Moreover, the varieties sold to the Dutch were not popular in England, and could not be disposed of at any price. Soon the market became so glutted that the merchants refused to take more than half the crop, leaving the remainder to rot upon the hands of the planters.

There followed in Virginia a sharp decline in prices. The Dutch had given the colonists three pence a pound for their tobacco.[5] A few years after the Restoration the planters considered themselves fortunate if they could dispose of their crops at a half penny a pound. Much was sold at a farthing.[6] Now since tobacco was the staple product of Virginia and the main support of the people, this rapid decline in its value was disastrous. Frequent complaints were sent to England that

[3] Bruce, Ec. Hist., Vol. I, p. 357.

[4] Governor Berkeley wrote in 1666 that the King's customs from the Virginia and Maryland tobacco would amount "unto about £100,000".

[5] Bruce, Ec. Hist., Vol. I, p. 354. [6] P. R. O., CO1-21.

the colonists could not maintain themselves and their families upon the meagre returns from their tobacco. "Twelve hundred pounds is the medium of men's yearly crops," wrote Secretary Ludwell in 1667, "and a half penny per pound is certainly the full medium of the price given for it." This made an average income for each planter of but fifty shillings. When the poor man had paid his taxes for the necessary support of the government, very little remained to him to clothe his wife and children. "So much too little," he adds, "that I can attribute it to nothing but the mercy of God, that he has not fallen into mutiny and confusion."[7] In 1673 the Governor and the Council declared that the colony was full of indigent persons, who could barely support themselves with their utmost exertions.[8]

Not only did the act of 1660 depress the price of tobacco, but it increased the already excessive freight rates. Since the bulk of the colonial exports had now to be brought directly to England, in English ships, the masters of Plymouth or London could double or triple their charges. Simultaneously there occurred a pronounced rise in the cost of manufactured goods. The far-famed skill of the Dutch workmen had made it possible for them to produce many articles more cheaply than the English, and to underbid them in their own colonies. But now that all foreign goods were excluded, the planters were forced to purchase the more expensive product of the English workshops.

Thus were the Virginians cut with a two-edged sword. At the very time that their incomes were being diminished, they were confronted by an increase in the cost of living. Nor could they, as Lord Baltimore declared they might, alleviate these evils by industry and thrift. For the more strenuous were their efforts to increase the tobacco crop, the greater would be the glut in the English market and the more disastrous the drop in prices.

The poor colonists found an able, but an unsuccessful ad-

[7] P. R. O., CO1-21.

[8] P. R. O., CO1-30-51. Compare Petition of Governor Berkeley, Aug. 22, 1662, CO1-16.

vocate, in a London merchant named John Bland. "If the Hollanders," he wrote in a paper addressed to the King, "must not trade to Virginia how shall the Planters dispose of their Tobacco? The English will not buy it, for what the Hollander carried thence was a sort of Tobacco, not desired by any other people, . . . the Tobacco will not vend in England, the Hollanders will not fetch it from England; what must become thereof?" But Charles II, who knew little of economic matters, and cared nothing for the welfare of the colonists, ignored Bland's convincing appeal. No alleviation was given Virginia, and she was allowed to drift on through poverty and desperation to rebellion.

In a vain attempt to make the colony independent of the English manufacturers and to turn the people from the excessive planting of tobacco, the Assembly passed a series of acts designed to encourage local industrial establishments. It was especially desired that Virginia should make her own cloth, for the cost of the English fabrics was excessive.[9] To stimulate the art of spinning and weaving the Assembly offered rewards for the best pieces of linen and woollen goods produced in the country. A bounty was placed on the manufacture of silk.[10] In 1666, the establishment of cloth works in each county was made compulsory by act of Assembly.[11] "Whereas," it was declared, "the present obstruction of trade and the nakedness of the country doe suffitiently evidence the necessity of provideing supply of our wants by improveing all meanes of raysing and promoteing manufactures amonge ourselves, . . . Be it enacted . . . that within two yeares at furthest . . . the commissioners of each county court shall provide and sett up a loome and weaver in each of the respective counties."[12] Nor were other industries neglected. Tanhouses were erected in various places "to tanne, curry and make the hides of the country into leather and shoes".[13] Bounties were offered for the construction of vessels, in the

[9] Hen., Vol. II, pp. 120, 121.

[10] P. R. O., CO1-19; Hen., Vol. II, p. 272.

[11] Hen., Vol. II, p. 238.

[12] Ibid.

[13] Hen., Vol. II, p. 123.

hope that Virginia might rival the prosperous ship-builders of New England.[14]

These experiments added a heavy burden to the poor tax-payer, while they accomplished little for the relief of the colony. Virginia, with its scattered plantations and its lack of skilled artisans, could not hope to compete with the work-shops of England. The commissioners, whether from corruption or from lack of ability, proved poor business managers, and their ill success occasioned loud and bitter complaints.

In May, 1661, Governor Berkeley sailed for England to combat a new design to revive the Virginia Company. It is quite probable that he took occasion during his stay at court to protest against the Navigation Acts.[15] But he found it impossible to turn the King and Parliament from what had become their settled colonial policy. Ten years later, when the Lords of Trade and Plantations asked him what impediments there were to the improvement of trade in the colony, the Governor blurted out the truth with his accustomed vigor. "Mighty and destructive by that severe act of Parliament which excludes us from haveing any Commerce with any Nacon in Europe but our owne, Soe that wee cannot add to our plantacon any Comodity that growes out of itt . . . ffor it is not lawfull for us to carry a pipe-staff or a Bushel of Corne to any place in Europe out of the King's dominions. If this were for his Majesty's Service or the good of his Subjects wee should not repine what ever our Sufferings are for it. But on my Soule it is the Contrary for both."[16]

In seeking relief from the evil consequences of the Navigation Acts the Virginians turned to their cousins of New England.[17] And the hardy sailors of Massachusetts and Connecticut, tempted by the high prices of manufactured goods in the southern colonies, brought their wares into the James, the York and the Potomac, where they entered into lively competition with the English merchants. Nor did they hesitate,

[14] P. R. O., CO1-19; Hen., Vol. II, p. 178.
[15] P. R. O., CO1-16; Hen., Vol. II, p. 17.
[16] P. R. O., CO1-26-77; Hen., Vol. II, p. 315.
[17] P. R. O., CO1-24.

when occasion offered, to defy the law by transporting the Virginia tobacco to foreign markets.[18] But England was unwilling to leave the colonists even this small loophole. Parliament decided, in 1672, to place a duty of one penny a pound upon tobacco shipped from one colony to another, and the payment of this duty did not give liberty to the owners to transport it to a foreign country. This act completely crippled the intercolonial trade. A few years later, after Bacon's Rebellion, when the Virginia counties were presenting their grievances to the King's commissioners, the people of Lower Norfolk requested that the act of 1672 might be repealed. The only notice taken of their petition was the contemptuous comment of the commissioners that it was wholly mutinous for them "to desire a thing contrary to his Majesty's Royall pleasure & benefitt and also against an Act of Parliament".[19]

It had been suggested, when the price of tobacco began to fall, that the evil might be remedied by governmental restraint upon the annual crop. The diminution of the demand for the leaf, brought about by the loss of the foreign market, was to be met by a corresponding limitation upon the supply. Prices would thus be restored and the planter would receive a greater return for a much smaller output. But for this remedy to be effective, it would be necessary to secure the coöperation of Maryland and perhaps North Carolina, as a cessation in Virginia would accomplish little, if no restraint were put upon the planters of the other colonies. Moreover, since the proposed step might diminish the revenue from the customs, it would be necessary to obtain the consent of the King.

In 1662 many of the planters and merchants petitioned Charles II to forbid the planting of tobacco in Maryland and Virginia for one year.[20] At first this appeal was rejected and the colonists were commanded to refrain from presenting similar petitions in the future. Later, however, the Privy Council secured a reversal of this decision and an order was issued authorizing the Assembly to appoint commissioners to

[18] P. R. O., CO1-30; Bruce, Ec. Hist., Vol. I, p. 357.
[19] P. R. O., CO5-1371-328; Va. Mag., Vol. III, p. 38.
[20] Bruce, Ec. Hist., Vol. I, p. 389.

confer with the Marylanders upon the best means of lessening the excessive crops.[21] Accordingly a meeting was held at Wiccocomico, May 12, 1664, which recommended that the planting of tobacco after the twentieth of June each year should be prohibited. The report met with the approval of the Virginians and was promptly ratified by the Assembly, but the Marylanders believed that a partial cessation would be detrimental to their interests and their legislature refused to give its consent.

But as prices sank lower and lower, and poverty became more general, the Virginians once more appealed to Maryland, this time for a total cessation for one year. Numerous letters were exchanged upon the subject, but at first nothing was accomplished. After many months had been consumed in useless negotiations Governor Berkeley, in the dead of winter, himself journeyed to Maryland and at last succeeded in convincing the leading men of that colony of the necessity of the measure. As a result, the Maryland Assembly passed an act prohibiting all tobacco planting in their province from February 1666 to February 1667, provided Virginia and North Carolina should do likewise.[22] The Assembly at Jamestown promptly passed a similar law, but the North Carolinians, owing to Indian troubles, delayed their action so long that the Marylanders repudiated the entire agreement.

Somewhat discouraged the colonists again sent commissioners, this time to Saint Mary's, to resume the broken thread of negotiations. Here at last success seemed to crown their efforts, for all differences were adjusted, and the cessation was agreed upon by the three colonies.[23] But the joy of Virginia at this happy outcome was soon turned to grief and indignation, for the Marylanders received a letter from Lord Baltimore, "in absolute and princely terms prohibiting the execution of the . . . articles of cessation".

"This overtook us," wrote Governor Berkeley, "like a storm and enforced us like distressed marriners to throw our dear bought commodities into the sea, when we were in sight of our

[21] Bruce, Ec. Hist., Vol. I, p. 390. [22] P. R. O., CO1-20.
[23] P. R. O., CO1-20. Ludwell to Arlington.

harbour, & with them so drown'd not only our present reliefs but all future hopes of being able to do ourselves good, whilst we are thus divided and enforced to steere by anothers compasse, whose needle is too often touched with particular interest. This unlimited and independent power . . . of the Lord Baltimore doth like an impetuous wind blow from us all those seasonable showers of your Majesty's Royall cares and favours, and leaves us, and his own province withering and decaying in distress and poverty. . . . This unreasonable and unfortunate prohibition . . . hath not only increased the discontent of many of the inhabitants of his province, but hath raised the grief and anger of allmost all your . . . subjects of this colony to such a height as required great care to prevent those disturbances which were like to arise from their eluded hopes and vain expences."[24]

Can there be any doubt that the Navigation Acts and the futility of all attempts to escape their baleful effects, were largely instrumental in bringing on Bacon's Rebellion? As prosperity and contentment are the greatest safeguards of the public peace, so poverty, nakedness and distress are breeders of sedition. Philip Ludwell spoke of Bacon's army as "a Rabble of the basest sort of People; whose Condicion was such as by a chaunge could not admitt of worse".[25] Had England been less selfish in her treatment of Virginia, there would not have been so many indigent men in the colony eager to join in this wild uprising against the government. Berkeley himself admitted, in 1673, that at least one third of the freemen had been rendered so desperate by poverty and debt that in times of foreign war their loyalty to England could not be relied upon.[26]

But Charles II was indifferent to the welfare of these distant subjects and blind to their growing dissatisfaction. Just when the situation was most critical, he aroused their anger and grief to the highest pitch, by making a gift of the entire colony to Lord Culpeper and the Earl of Arlington. Previously he had granted that portion of Virginia which

[24] P. R. O., CO1-21. Governor and Council to the King.

[25] P. R. O., CO1-37-16. [26] P. R. O., CO1-80-51.

lies between the Potomac and the Rappahannock rivers, known as the Northern Neck, to Lord Hopton and several other noblemen. These patentees were to receive fees, remainders, reversions and escheats, and were given power to grant patents for all land that had not been taken up. This had caused the people of Virginia, and especially those residing in the Northern Neck, great uneasiness, and had proved a serious hindrance to the settling of that region. The Assembly, dreading the clash of jurisdiction which this grant made almost inevitable, had sent agents to England to persuade the King to annul the patent, or permit the purchase of the tract by the colony. While they were working to this end, there came the unexpected news that Arlington and Culpeper had received a grant of the entire colony. Without consulting in the least the desires of the people, Charles had given them over to two unscrupulous favorites, with the indifference he might have shown in presenting a necklace to his mistress. The colonists, "to their unspeakable griefe and Astonishment", felt now that they were "reduced to a far worse condition than that wherein they had adventured their lives and fortunes for the planting that Country under the Company".[27]

The privileges and powers granted in this patent, had they ever been exercised by Arlington and Culpeper, would have rendered the government at Jamestown almost a nullity. The two lords were to receive all escheats, quit-rents, duties and reservations belonging to the Crown; they were given power to divide the territory into counties, hundreds and parishes; to erect churches and present ministers to them; to make manors, fairs, and markets; to appoint sheriffs, surveyors, and other important officers; to issue patents for land; to appropriate to their own use all arrears of "rents and other profits", accruing since the year 1669.

In great alarm the Virginia Assembly directed the agents in England to use their utmost endeavors to have this grant recalled. At the same time they drew up a statement of their objections to the patent, showing how unjust and ruinous

[27] P. R. O., CO1-34-101.

were its provisions. It was in direct conflict with numerous royal concessions and patents, given them from time to time under the Great Seal. There was good reason to fear that the lords, by their deputies, might impose upon them new rents and services. They might demand new surveys and new patents for land which had long been occupied. They might, in fact, completely devastate the government of all its "just powers and authorities".

The agents, upon receiving these instructions, went to the Lords Patentees to request them to resign the most obnoxious of their new powers.[28] In case they refused, the agents threatened to appeal at once to the King. Arlington and Culpeper received them courteously, and, after numerous delays, consented to relinquish the patent, provided Virginia would offer no objection to the passing of a new grant, assuring them the quit-rents and escheated property. The agents were well satisfied with this settlement, for it would relieve the colony of its fear of proprietary government, while the grant of the rents and escheats would impose little additional burden.[29]

In order, however, to prevent the giving away of such disturbing powers in the future, they petitioned the King to grant "Letters Pattents for the incorporacon" of the colony.[30] In this new charter they desired first that permission be given Virginia to purchase the Northern Neck. They next requested the King to promise that Virginia should have no other dependence than upon the Crown of England, "nor in the future be cantonized into parcells by grants made to particular persons". "And for the prevention of surreptitious grants" they desired his Majesty to promise in the charter that nothing should again pass concerning Virginia until a hearing had been given to some person impowered by the colony to represent their interests. Of even greater importance was their desire, "That there shall bee no Taxe or Imposition layd on the people of Virginia, but by their owne

[28] P. R. O., CO1-28-20; Burk, Vol. II, Appendix XXXVI.
[29] Hen., Vol. II, pp. 518-543; Burk, Vol. II, Appendix XXXIII-LXII.
[30] P. R. O., CO1-34-95.

Consente, and that Express'd by the Representatives in Assembly."[31]

The whole matter came before the King in Council, June 23, 1675, and was referred to the judgment of Attorney-General William Jones and Solicitor-General Francis Winnington.[32] In October these officers reported that in their opinion the patent of incorporation would be beneficial both to the colony and the King's service, and ought to be granted. Charles thereupon gave directions that the papers be drawn up for his signature. But here, for some unknown reason, the matter came to a halt. Several months passed and the patent had not been issued.[33] At last, April 19, 1676, at the urgent request of the agents, his Majesty directed that the Lord Chancellor cause the papers to pass the Great Seal at once. But before this could be done, news came to England of Bacon's Rebellion, and the King immediately reversed his order. Later, other Letters Patent were granted, but they were very different from those sought by the agents, and contained little more than a bare declaration of the colony's direct dependence upon the Crown of England.[34]

This unsatisfactory business caused great irritation among the colonists. The heavy expense of carrying on the negotiations in England "made them desperately uneasie, especially when, after a whole Year's Patience . . . they had no Encouragement from their Agents".[35] A tax of fifty pounds of tobacco per poll, imposed for the purchase of the Northern Neck, aroused widespread dissatisfaction. In April, 1676, Governor Berkeley, fully conscious of the mutterings of revolution, was awaiting with anxiety the arrival of favorable news from the agents. "There are divers," he wrote, "that would fain persuade the people that al their high taxes will bring them no benefit, so that if the most advantageous terms had been proposed to us it would have been impossible to have

[31] P. R. O., CO1-34-96; CO1-34-100; CO1-33-108; CO1-34-95; Hen., Vol. II, p. 529.

[32] P. R. O., CO1-34-100.

[33] P. R. O., CO1-36-48; Hen. Vol. II, p. 534.

[34] P. R. O., CO389.6-133 to 137; Burk, Vol. II, Appendix LXI.

[35] Beverley.

persuaded the people to have parted with more tobacco til a more certain demonstration had been given them of what is already done. I appeased two mutinies this last year raysed by some secret villaines that whispered amongst the people that there was nothing intended by the fifty pounds levy but the enriching of some few people."[36] In 1677, after Bacon's Rebellion, the King's commissioners heard from all sides that the imposition of this tax was one of the main causes of discontent.[37]

The wars of 1664 and 1672 with Holland added much to the distress in Virginia. The bold Dutch mariners, angered at the injury done them by the Navigation Acts, preyed upon the English merchantmen in every sea. Woe to the tobacco ship that encountered a hostile privateer, in its journey across the Atlantic! The English vessels were not safe even in the Virginia rivers, under the guns of their forts. Twice the daring Dutch came through the capes and into the James River itself, where they wrought great damage to the shipping.

It was the custom, during these times of danger, for the merchant vessels of Virginia and Maryland to cross the Atlantic in large fleets, under the protection of English men-of-war. In May 1667, some twenty vessels were anchored in the mouth of James River, near Newport News, awaiting the remainder of their fleet before sailing. Three leagues above them lay the *Elizabeth,* a frigate of forty-six guns, sent by the King for the protection of the colony. She was undergoing repairs, however, having become "soe disabled in her Maste and Leaky in her Hull as that she could not keep at sea", and for the moment afforded little proctection to the merchantmen riding below.[38]

At this juncture, a fleet of five Dutch warships, under the command of Abraham Crimson, appeared off the coast, bent on mischief to the English shipping. The Hollanders, learning of the exposed position of the tobacco fleet from the crew of a shallop which fell into their hands, determined upon a bold attack. On their way to the capes they encountered a

[36] P. R. O., CO1-36-37.
[37] P. R O., CO5-1371-292, 331.
[38] P R. O., CO1-21-61.

ship of London bound from Tangier to Virginia. The English master, Captain Conway, "fought them very well for two hours, but at last being wounded himself and over powered with men, was taken by them".[39]

The Dutchmen came into Chesapeake Bay June 4, and anchored there over night. The next morning, taking advantage of a fair easterly breeze, they sailed boldly into the mouth of the James. In order to take their prey entirely by surprise they flew the English colors, and as they passed the merchantmen, hailed them in English and sang out their soundings in English. Proceeding directly up to the unsuspecting frigate, they threw aside their disguise with the roar of three volleys. The captain of the *Elizabeth* had gone ashore, to attend a wedding it was said, and had left but thirty men on board.[40] Without officers, and surprised by superior numbers, the sailors could make no effective resistance. Several rushed to their guns, but they fired only one piece of ordnance before they were forced to surrender. While some of the Dutchmen were securing the *Elizabeth*, the others turned upon the helpless merchantmen and succeeded in capturing the entire fleet. Several of the ships might have saved themselves by running into the Elizabeth River, where the enemy would not have dared to follow them, but they seemed paralyzed with surprise and fell an unresisting prey.[41]

Great was the grief and rage of Sir William Berkeley when news of this disaster reached him. How could he answer to the King for the loss of the royal frigate and twenty English merchantmen? With great promptness and resolution he decided to fit out all available vessels in the colony for a sally upon the enemy. In the upper James were three merchantmen and in the York nine. If these could be supplied quickly with guns and men, there might yet be time to defeat the Dutch and rescue the captured ships. The Governor, who was ever reckless in exposing his person, resolved to direct the attack himself in the good ship *Admirall*. But

[39] P. R. O., CO1-21-61.
[40] P. R. O., CO1-21-63.
[41] P. R. O., CO1-21-61, 62.

some of the masters by no means relished the thought of risking their vessels and their cargoes in a battle with the Dutch. When the Governor impressed them into the King's service by putting the broad arrow upon their masts, they pretended obedience, but used such delays that the fleet could not be prepared in time. Captain Lightfoot, of the *Elizabeth*, grieved by the loss of his ship, "very passionately resolved to hazard himself in the *Admirall*", while several members of the Council and forty other gentlemen volunteered their services. Upon the shore were assembled four regiments of militia, ready to embark should they be needed. Yet the masters continued their procrastination day after day until the Dutch escaped.

Nor had Admiral Crimson shown any haste to be off. Soon after the battle he had burned five or six of the merchantmen, "for want of men to man them". It had also been necessary for him to destroy the frigate, which was still out of repair and far from seaworthy. He had sent parties ashore several times to secure water, which he greatly needed, but they had been driven back with ease. After a stay of five or six days in James River, he sailed away with his prizes, leaving the Governor to dismiss his militia and write home his accusations against the masters.[42]

Warned by this experience, the English government, upon the outbreak of the war of 1672, sent two men-of-war to Virginia. These vessels, in July 1673, were stationed at the mouth of the James guarding a large fleet of merchantmen, when news came that nine Dutch warships were approaching the capes. Instantly preparations were made to fight them. Several of the tobacco ships were forced into service and fitted with guns. Sailors were taken from the smaller vessels to help man the larger. But before all could be put in readiness the enemy came through the capes and anchored at Lynhaven Bay.[43]

The English had as yet little apprehension for the safety of their merchantmen, for they could at any time run under the guns of a fort at Nansemond, or could retreat up the

[42] P. R. O., CO1-21-61, 62, 63. [43] P. R. O., CO1-30-51, 53, 71.

James while their men-of-war held back the enemy. At this moment, however, there appeared across the waters of the Chesapeake eight sail of the Maryland fleet, unconscious of their danger and bearing down upon the Dutch. The English commanders realized that only instant action could save them. Taking with them six of the tobacco ships they sailed out to give battle.

"But before they came within reach of gun shot 4 of the merchant ships came on ground." One turned back to the James. But the other three ships went on, and unaided fought six of the largest Dutchmen. For three hours the battle continued with great fury. At last Captain Gardner, one of the English commanders, "judging that the enemy (if he checkt them not) would be in with (the) merchant ships riding in James river . . . tacked alone upon them with Extra ordinary courage, and for at least one houre fought them all. . . . But, having all his greate maste and his fore topmast desperately wounded, and most of his rigging shot", he was at last forced to retire. "With as much courage as conduct (and beyond the hopes or expectation of those who saw that brave action) (he) disengaged himselfe . . . and brought off all the Marylanders but one." The Virginia fleet, "which were neere 40 sail", secured "almost a tides way before the enemy, which undoubtedly saved many which otherwise would have bin lost". Some of the merchantmen took refuge at Fort Nansemond, where the enemy dared not attack them, others retreated up the river towards Jamestown. Unfortunately five of them, in the confusion of the flight, ran aground and were afterwards captured. The four ships which had grounded before the battle also fell into the hands of the Dutch. Thus, despite the gallant conduct of the English, the enemy succeeded in capturing a large part of the tobacco fleet.[44]

Great as was the distress caused by the depredations of the Dutch, the planters suffered even more during these wars by the stagnation of trade. The great risk incurred in crossing the ocean necessarily brought an increase both in freight

[44] P. R. O., CO1-30-51, 53.

rates and in the cost of manufactured goods. In 1667 the Governor and Council declared that the planters were "inforced to pay 12 pounds to £17 per ton freight" on their tobacco, "which usually was but at seven pounds".[45] Conditions were even worse during the second war. In 1673 Berkeley complained that the number of vessels that dared come to Virginia was so small, that they had "not brought goods and tools enough for one part of five of the people to go on with their necessary labor". "And those few goods that are brought," he added "have Soe few (and these hard Dealing) Sellers and Soe many Indigent and necessitous buyors that the Poore Planter gets not the fourth part . . . for his tobacco which he usually has had in other times."[46]

In this period, so full of suffering and misfortune, the year 1667 was especially noteworthy for its long series of disasters. In November Secretary Thomas Ludwell wrote Lord Berkeley, "This poore Country . . . is now reduced to a very miserable Condicon by a continuall course of misfortune. In Aprill . . . we had a most prodigeous Storme of haile, many of them as bigg as Turkey Eggs, which destroyed most of our younge Mast and Cattell. On the fifth of June following came the Dutch upon us, and did soe much mischiefe that we shall never recover our reputations. . . . They were not gone before it fell to raineing and continued for 40 dayes together, which Spoiled much of what the haile had left of our English Graine. But on the 27th of August followed the most Dreadful Hurry Cane that ever the colony groaned under. It lasted 24 hours, began at North East and went round northerly till it came to west and soe on till it came to South East where it ceased. It was accompanied with a most violent raine, but no Thunder. The night of it was the most Dismall tyme that ever I knew or heard off, for the wind and rain raised soe Confused a noise, mixt with the continuall Cracks of falling houses. . . . The waves (were) impetuously beaten against the Shoares and by that violence forced and as it were crowded up into all Creeks, Rivers and bayes to that prodigeous height that it hazarded the drownd-

[45] P. R. O., CO1-21-61. [46] P. R. O., CO1-30-17.

ing many people who lived not in sight of the Rivers, yet were then forced to climbe to the topp of their houses to keep them selves above water. (The waves) carryed all the foundation of the fort at point Comfort into the River and most of our Timber which was very chargably brought thither to perfect it. Had it been finished and a garison in it, they had been Stormed by such an enemy as noe power but Gods can restraine. . . . Had the Lightning accompanied it we could have beleeved nothing else from such a confusion but that all the elements were at Strife, which of them should doe most towards the reduction of the creation into a Second Chaos. It was wonderful to consider the contrary effects of that Storme, for it blew some shipps from their Anchors and carryed them safe over shelves of Sand where a wherry could Difficultly passe, and yet knockt out the bottome of a ship . . . in eight foot water more than she drew. But when the morning came and the Sun risen it would have comforted us after such a night, had it not lighted us to ye Ruines of our plantations, of which I thinke not one escaped. The nearest computation is at least 10,000 houses blowne downe, all the Indian Graine laid flatt upon the ground, all the Tobacco in the fields torne to pieces and most of that which was in the houses perished with them. The fences about the Corne fields (were) either blown down or beaten to the ground by trees which fell upon them & before the owners could repaire them the hoggs & Cattell gott in and in most places devoured much of what the Storme had left."[47]

In the midst of the second Dutch war came another scourge no less distressing than the great hurricane. Throughout the 17th century cattle raising was one of the most important industries of the small Virginia proprietors. No planter, however insignificant his holdings, was without his cow and his calf.[48] They constituted a most important portion of his wealth, and an indispensable source of support. In the winter of 1672-3 occurred an epidemic which destroyed more

[47] P. R. O., CO1-21.

[48] This is shown by the wills of this period, many of which have been published in the Virginia Magazine of History and Biography.

than half the cattle of Virginia. The mortality was increased by the cold, which was unusually severe. Many men, in an effort to preserve the poor beasts, gave them all their corn and thus brought hunger upon themselves. Before relief came with the spring, fifty thousand cattle had perished.[49]

Perhaps the people of Virginia might have borne patiently all these misfortunes, had their Governor ruled them with wisdom and justice. Certain it is they would never have turned in wild anger to strike down his government, had that government not done much to make their condition intolerable. Sir William Berkeley was accused of destroying the representative character of the Assembly, of initiating a notorious spoils system, of intimidating Burgesses, of winking at embezzlement of public funds. And, although most of these charges were brought by the Governor's bitter enemies, some of them were undoubtedly true.

In Virginia, during this period, the commons could guard their interests only by means of the House of Burgesses. All other organs of government were controlled by Berkeley and his friends. The people had no voice in the selection of vestrymen, or sheriffs, or justices of the peace, and no control over their actions. The Council was entirely submissive to the Governor's will. Its members not only held their seats at Sir William's pleasure, but were the recipients of numerous other favors that bound them closely to his interest. Thus in the executive, in all branches of the judiciary, and in the upper house of Assembly the Governor was all-powerful.

If then he could control the Burgesses and make them subservient to his desires, he would remove the only obstacle to almost complete despotism. Nor was it a matter of very great difficulty for him to gain a mastery of the House. In every county he could nominate government candidates, and exert tremendous pressure to secure their election. If necessary, they might be seated by fraud at the polls or false returns by the sheriff.[50] "It is true," Bacon declared, "that the people's hopes of redemption did ly in the Assembly, as their Trusts, and Sanctuary to fly to, but I would have all men consider

[49] P. R. O., CO1-30-17; CO1-30-51. [50] Hen., II, p. 356.

first how poore people are debarred of their fair election, the great men in many places haveing the Country in their debte and consequently in their aw. Secondly how meanly we are provided of men of Learning, ability and courage, nay indeed of honesty, to stand up in the people's behalf and oppose the oppressing party."[51]

And if ever, despite these difficulties, the candidates of the people were elected, the Governor might still win their support in the House, by a judicious use of the patronage. He controlled enough offices of honor and profit to reward richly his friends in the Assembly. If the Burgess was careful never to thwart the wishes of the Governor, or to vote against his measures, he might reasonably expect a collectorship, a sheriff's place, a commission in the militia, or possibly a seat in the Council. A large percentage of the members of the House were office-holders.[52]

If half the charges brought against Berkeley are to be believed, he was guilty of instituting a system of political corruption as effective as that maintained in France by Guizot during the reign of Louis Philippe. He has assumed to himself, it was declared, "the sole nominating, appointing and commissionating of all . . . officers both civil and military amongst us . . . (they) being . . . (the better to increase . . . his party) multiplied to a greate number. . . . All which offices he bestowed on such persons (how unfitt or unskillfull soever) as he conceived would be most for his designs. And that the more firmely to binde and oblige them thereunto and allure others to his party, he . . . permitted or connived at the persons soe commissionated by him . . . unwarrantably . . . to lay and impose what levies and imposicons upon us they should or did please, which they would often extort from us by force and violence, and which for the most part they converted to their owne private lucre and gaine. And . . . Sir William Berkeley, haveing by these wayes and meanes, and by takeing upon him contrary to law the granting collectors places, sherifs, and other offices of profitt to whome he best pleased, he soe gained uppon and obliged all

[51] P. R. O., CO5-1371-241, 246.

[52] Bruce, Inst. Hist., Vol. I, p. 489.

the greatest number of the men of parts and estates in the whole country (out of which it was necessary our representatives and Burgesses should be elected) hath there by soe fortifyed his power over us, as of himselfe without respect to our laws, to doe what soever he best pleased, and from time to time . . . to gaine and procure great quantities of Tobacco and mony from us to his proper use over and besides the Thousand pounds yearly salary . . . and over and besides the fees, profitts and per quisites to the place of Governour belonging."[53]

Bacon himself declared, in justification of his rebellion, that oppression and injustice were rife in the colony, and that it was useless to appeal to the Assembly for redress. "The poverty of the Country is such," he said, "that all the power and sway is got into the hands of the rich, who by extortious advantages, having the common people in their debt, have always curbed and oppressed them in all manner of wayes." The poor, he declared, were kept in such perpetual bondage that it was not possible for labor or industry to extricate them. The great men of the colony had brought misery and ruin upon the common people by perverting all equity and right. The perpetual breach of laws, remiss prosecutions, excuses and evasions, but too plainly attested that things were carried by the men at the helm, "as if it were but to play a booty, game or divide a spoile". "Now consider," he adds, "what hope there is of redress in appealing to the very persons our complaints do accuse."[54]

And when once the Governor had obtained a House that was subservient to his will, he might, by his power of prorogation, continue it indefinitely. During the years from the Restoration to Bacon's Rebellion, there were not more than two general elections, and probably only one—that of 1661.[55]

[53] Va. Mag., Vol. III, pp. 135, 136. [54] P. R. O., CO5-1371-241.

[55] P. R. O., CO5-1371-316, 319. The Assembly which met in March, 1661, was continued by successive prorogations until October, 1665. This fact is placed beyond question by the copies of the Acts of Assembly now preserved in the British Public Record Office. But there is no statement in these copies that the session of June 5, 1666, had been prorogued from an earlier date. Nor is there any indication given in Hening's

Under these circumstances the Assembly could no longer be said to represent the voters of the colony. The Burgesses might defy or betray the people as they chose, they could not be made to answer at the polls for their misconduct. And their is ample proof that this Long Assembly attended more to the commands of the Governor than to the wishes of electors that could no longer elect. Even Sir William's best friends admitted that his authority in Virginia was almost despotic. Secretary Thomas Ludwell, writing in 1666, declared that the Governor was "the sole author of the most substantial part" of the government, "either for Lawes or other inferior institutions".[56] "Our representatives," complained the Charles City commons eleven years later "(of which for this county in nine yeares time last past there hath been a verry doubtful election as we conceive) have been overswayed by the power and prevalency of . . . Sir Wm. Berkeley and his councell, divers instances of which wee conceive might be given, and have neglected our grievances made knowne to them."[57]

That this overthrow of representative government in the

Statutes that this was not a new Assembly. (Hen., Vol. II, p. 224.) These two omissions, then, might lead us to infer that there was a general election in 1666. But there is other evidence tending to show that the Assembly of 1661 was not dissolved until 1676. Thus William Sherwood wrote during Bacon's Rebellion that the rabble had risen against the Assembly and seemed weary of it, "in that itt was of 14 years continuance". (P. R. O., CO1-37-17; Va. Mag., Vol. I, p. 170.) The account of the Rebellion given in the Collections of the Massachusetts Historical Society also declares that the session had "continued fowerteene yeares". (Mass. S. IV, Vol. IX, p. 169.) The Isle of Wight grievances state that the people of that county had not had an election of Burgesses for twelve years. (Va. Mag., Vol. II, p. 380.) Lists of the members at the sessions of September, 1663, and of October, 1666, have been preserved by Hening. Nineteen Burgesses of the Assembly of 1663 appear also in 1666; eleven have lost their seats and in their places are fifteen new members. But this settles nothing, for it is quite possible that if an election was held in 1666, the Governor's influence might have secured the return of many old Burgesses. There was no election from June 1666 to June 1676. It must remain, then, undetermined whether the Long Assembly continued for ten or for fifteen years.

[56] P. R. O., CO1-20.

[57] Va. Mag., Vol. III, pp. 141, 142.

colony and the substitution of the Governor's despotic sway contributed greatly to the anger and desperation of the people, there can be no doubt. The evidence comes not only from the rebels and from the county grievances, but from disinterested persons, and even Berkeley's friends. "Whatever palliations," wrote Governor Thomas Notley, of Maryland, in 1677, "the grate men of Virginia may use at the Councell board in England, . . . yett you may be sure . . . much . . . if not every tittle" of the accusations against them are true. "If the ould Course be taken and Coll: Jeoffreys build his proceedings upon the ould ffoundation, its neither him nor all his Majesties Souldiers in Virginia, will either satisfye or Rule those people. They have been strangely dealt with by their former Magistracy."[58] William Sherwood, if we may believe his own statement, forfeited Sir William's favor by reporting in England that "the general cry of the country was against ye Governour". And "it is most true", he added, "that the great oppressions & abuse of ye people by ye Governours arbitrary will hath been ye cause of the late troubles here".[59]

The illegitimate influence of Berkeley over the Assembly was the more galling to the people inasmuch as they had no voice in local government. The justices of the peace, who exercised the most important powers in the counties, received their commissions, not by popular election, but by executive appointment. And the Governor, although often influenced in his selections by the advice of the Council, gave little heed to the wishes of the commons. His appointees were invariably men of means and influence, and could be relied upon to uphold the interests of the aristocracy and the Governor.

The justices were members of the county courts, and as such exercised judicial, executive and legislative functions in local affairs. The courts met every second month, and were empowered to settle cases involving not more than ten pounds sterling.[60] Individual justices could "try and determine any cause to the value of twenty shillings or two hundred pounds of tobacco".[61] Far more important was the power of the

[58] P. R. O., CO1-40-88.
[59] P. R. O., CO1-40-43.
[60] Bruce, Inst. Hist., Vol. I, p. 542.
[61] P. R. O., CO1-20.

courts to impose direct taxes. The county levy was usually very heavy. In fact, during the Restoration period, it often exceeded the public levy voted by the Assembly. In Lower Norfolk county, during the years from 1666 to 1683, the local assessment amounted to 188,809 pounds of tobacco.[62] This sum seems to us now almost insignificant, but it proved a very real burden to the indigent freemen of that unhappy period. Yet perhaps the people would not have complained had the assessments been voted by a body elected by themselves or representative of their interests. They were bitterly angered, however, that they should be taxed without their own consent and against their wishes, by appointees of the Governor; and the sense of wrong was aggravated by the fact that the taxes were often voted by the courts in secret session, not without grave suspicions of abuses and fraud.[63] "It has been the custome," it was declared in the Surry grievances, "of the County Courts att the laying of the levy to withdraw into a private Roome by which the poor people not knowing for what they paid their levy did allways admire how their taxes could be so high."[64] "Wee desire," declared the people of the Isle of Wight, "to know for what wee doe pay our Leavies everie year and that it may noe more be layd in private."[65] From Charles City came the most startling charges of fraud and oppression. "The Commisoners or Justices of peace of this county," it was declared, "heretofore have illegally and unwarrantably taken upon them without our consent from time to time to impose, rayse, assess and levy what taxes, levies and imposicons upon us they have at any time thought good or best liked, great part of which they have converted to theire own use, as in bearing their expense at the ordinary, allowing themselves wages for severall businesses which ex officio they ought to do, and other wayes, as by account of the same on the booke for levies may appeare."[66]

The people were even deprived, during Berkeley's second administration, of the right of electing the vestries. These

[62] Bruce, Inst. Hist., Vol. II, 566.
[63] Hen., Vol. II, 357.
[64] Va. Mag., Vol. II, p. 172.
[65] Va. Mag., Vol. II, p. 389.
[66] Va. Mag., Vol. III, p. 142.

bodies had always been composed of the foremost men in each parish. At this period they succeeded in shaking off entirely the control of the commons by themselves filling all vacancies in their ranks.[67] Since they exercised the power of imposing a tax to pay the ministers' salaries and meet other obligations of the parishes, this attempt to make themselves self-perpetuating was a matter of no little importance.[68] The people expressed their disapproval in the most emphatic terms, and after Bacon's Rebellion requests came from many counties that the vestrymen might be chosen, as formerly, by the whole body of parishioners.[69]

The unjust poll-tax, which was then used in the public, county and parish levies, was an unending source of discontent. There can be no doubt that it bore with too great weight upon the poor people. "They complain," wrote Gyles Bland, on the eve of the Rebellion, "that great Taxes are imposed upon them every yeare, by wayes very unequall, Laying them very heavily, by the Poll, whereby the Poorer sort are in the hardest Condition."[70] It must be remembered, however, that many of the servants and slaves were listed as tithables, or persons subject to the poll tax. This of course tended to increase the share of the wealthy. Yet the inequality was very real and the burden upon the poor very heavy. The number of tithables assessed of a man was by no means an accurate gage of his wealth. Later in the century, with the great influx of negro slaves, the burden upon the rich planters increased and became more nearly proportionate to their ability to pay.

Bland suggested that all inequality might be eliminated by adopting a land-tax. "Which," he said, "seems to be the most equal imposition and will generally take off the complaint of the people, although perhaps some of the richest sort will not like it, who hold greater proportions of land than they actually plant."[71] The King's commissioners also thought the land tax just, but considered it "impracticable there".

[67] Bruce, Inst. Hist., Vol. I, p. 67.

[68] Bruce, Inst. Hist., Vol. I, p. 77; Hen. Vol. II, p. 356.

[69] Va. Mag., Vol. II, pp. 172, 289, 388.

[70] P. R. O., CO1-36-54. [71] P. R. O., CO1-36-54.

When the people of Warwick county asked, "That all persons may be rated and taxed according to their Estates", the commissioners reported that this was "a thing to be wish'd but never to be granted them". If the King should command it, they knew not how it would be relished by the landed men, since the common usage had been always taxing by poll.[72]

The universal discontent was still further increased by the wasteful and lax use of public funds. The money which was wrung from the poor people by these unequal taxes, was seldom wisely or economically expended. Much was squandered upon foolish projects, costly in the extreme, and impossible of accomplishment. Such was the attempt to build a city at Jamestown. For many years it had been a matter of regret to the English government that Virginia should remain so entirely a rural country. Not realizing that this was but the result of exceptional economic conditions and not a sign of weakness or decay, they sought more than once to force the building of towns by legislative enactments. Thus, in 1662, in accordance with the King's wishes, the Assembly passed an act providing for the erection of thirty-two brick houses at Jamestown.[73] Each county was required to build one of these houses, a levy of thirty pounds of tobacco per poll being laid for that purpose. This attempt was foredoomed to failure, for if economic conditions could not develop cities in the colony, the mere erection of houses upon the unhealthful Jamestown peninsula could accomplish nothing. We learn from Bacon's Proceedings that the town at the time of the Rebellion consisted of "som 16 or 18 howses, . . . and in them about a dozen families (for all the howses are not inhabited) getting their liveings by keeping ordnaries, at extraordnary rates". That there was corruption or inefficiency in carrying out the orders of the Assembly seems certain. The people of Isle of Wight county complained of "the great Quantities of Tobacco levyed for Building Houses of publick use and reception at Jamestown, which were not habitable, but fell downe before the Finishing of them".[74]

[72] P. R. O., CO5-1371-315. [73] Hen., Vol. II, p. 172.
[74] P. R. O., CO5-1371-316-19, 304-5.

There were also accusations of laxness and fraud in the erecting and management of the public industrial plants. Very grievous taxes have been laid on the poor people, it was claimed, "for building work houses and stoare houses and other houses for the propogating & encouragem't of handicraft and manufactury, which were by our Burgesses to our great charge and burthen by their long and frequent sitting invented and proposed. Yet for want of due care the said houses were never finished or made useful, and the propagating & manufactury wholy in a short time neglected, and noe good ever effected . . . save the particular profitt of the Undertakers, who (as is usually in such cases) were largely rewarded for thus defrauding us."[75]

Even more frequent and bitter complaints originated with the construction of forts upon the various rivers to protect the colony and the merchant ships from foreign foes. At the outbreak of the war of 1664 it was resolved to build a fortress at Jamestown. The ships' masters were not satisfied with the selection of this site, for obviously it afforded no protection to vessels trading upon the Potomac, York or Rappahannock, and very little to those upon the lower James. After one hundred pounds sterling had been expended at Jamestown, the structure partly completed and fourteen guns brought up, the merchants procured orders from the English government that the fort be transferred to Old Point. The Governor and Council were most reluctant to make this change, but the commands were so positive they dared not disobey. So the guns were conveyed back down the river and the work begun again. But many serious difficulties were encountered. "We have been at 70,000lb tobacco charge," wrote Thomas Ludwell in 1667, "and have lost several men in the worke and many of the materials by storms breaking our rafts whereon we float the timber to that place. . . . After all (we) were forced to quit the work as of impossible manage, for great were the difficulties, and so insupportable would the charge have been."[76] A few months after, when the Dutch

[75] Va. Mag., Vol. III, p. 142; P. R. O., CO1-37-41.
[76] P. R. O., CO1-21.

captured the tobacco fleet in the mouth of the James, this fort seems to have been deserted. It was utterly destroyed by the great hurricane of the following August.

Thereupon it was decided to build five new forts, two on the James and one upon each of the other great rivers. The charges for these structures were to be borne entirely by the counties upon the rivers they were to defend. Whether from mismanagement or dishonesty large sums of money were expended in this undertaking with but little good effect. Berkeley wrote that the colony lacked the skill either to construct or maintain the forts. "We are at continuall charge," he declared, "to repaire unskilfull & inartificall buildings." The King's commissioners in 1677, testified that the forts were made of "mudd and dirt", and could be of little service against the enemy.[77] At the beginning of the Dutch war of 1672 the Assembly found them in poor condition and incapable of offering resistance to the enemy. "For as much," it was declared, "as the materials . . . were not substantial or lasting, some have suffered an utter demolition, some very ruinous and some capable of repair." It was thereupon ordered that the forts be at once restored and authority was given for new taxes to cover the cost.[78]

One at least of the reconstructed forts proved of service in the hour of need, for it was under the guns of Nansemond that many of the merchantmen ran in July 1673, from the pursuing Dutch men-of-war. But the people could see in them only a pretext for increasing their taxes. And it was quite impossible to make them believe that such sums could be expended to so little purpose save by fraud or embezzlement. The Charles City commons declared that great quantities of tobacco had been raised for building forts "which were never finished but suffered to goe to ruine, the artillery buried in sand and spoyled with rust for want of care".[79] From James City county came the complaint that although heavy taxes had been paid for fortifications, there was in 1677 "noe Place of defence in ye Country sufficient to secure his Majestys Sub-

[77] P. R. O., CO5-1371-292, 7.
[78] P. R. O., CO1-29-31.
[79] Va. Mag., Vol. III, p. 142.

jects against any Forreign Invasion". The King's commissioners substantiated this statement. "We are well assured," they said, "of the Truth of this Complaint, and doe know that the Forts erected could be of noe use, Endurance or defence. . . . Yet were they of great Expence to the People who paid Excessively for Building them."[80]

The Assembly had from time to time sought to make the merchants trading to Virginia aid in the defense of the colony, by imposing upon them Castle Duties, in the form of a toll of powder and shot. The masters had more than once complained of this duty, but as it was not very burdensome it was allowed to remain. Had all the ammunition thus received been used as intended by law, the people would have been saved great expense, and the forts made more serviceable. But the contributions, if we may believe the complaints of the people, were often stolen by the collectors. "Notwithstanding," said the Isle of Wight commons, "the great quantities of ammunition payd by ships for fort duties for the countries service . . . wee are forced to provide powder and shott at our proper charges."[81] The Nansemond grievances were more explicit in their accusations of fraud. "They Complayne that the Castle duties, accustomed to be paid by the Masters of Shipps in Powder & Shott for the service and security of the Country, is now converted into Shoes and stockings &c as best liketh the Collectors of it and disposed to their own private advantage."[82]

It would not be just to give credence to all the accusations made against Berkeley. The King's commissioners who conducted the investigation into his conduct, were his enemies; while many of the charges were brought by those who had taken part in the Rebellion. Thus the testimony against him is in most cases distinctly partisan. Moreover those that were closely associated with Sir William often expressed extravagant admiration for his ability and energy, and love for his character.[83] "He hath," wrote the Council in 1673, "for

[80] P. R. O., CO5-1371-292, 7; CO1-21.
[81] Va. Mag., Vol. II, p. 387.
[82] P. R. O., CO5-1371-330, 331.
[83] P. R. O., CO1-20, 21.

neare 30 years governed this colony with that prudence and justice which hath gained him both love and reverence from all the Inhabitants here."[84]

Singularly enough Berkeley seems to have prided himself upon his ability as a ruler. He never forgot the compliment paid him by the people in 1660, when they insisted, even against his will, upon making him their Governor. And long after he had forfeited their confidence and esteem he imagined himself as popular as in his first administration. It was a bitter blow to his pride when the commons rose against his government in 1676. His proclamations bear testimony to his pain that the youthful Bacon should have usurped his place in the affections of the people.[85] His letter to the King asking to be recalled from his government was undoubtedly dictated by wounded pride. Upon the eve of his final departure for England he did not scruple to write Colonel Jeffreys, "I will confesse to you that I beleeve that the Inhabitants of this Colony wil quickly find a difference betweene your management and mine."[86]

It would be difficult to reconcile this attitude of mind with Berkeley's oppressive administration, did we not know his views upon governmental matters. He had never been in sympathy with republican institutions. It was the height of folly, he thought, to allow the people to participate either in administrative or legislative affairs. The King alone should rule; the people's duty was to obey. It was but five years before the Rebellion that he wrote to the Lords of Trade and Plantations, "I thanke God there is noe ffree schooles nor printing (in Virginia)[87] and I hope wee shall not have these hundred yeares, for learning has brought disobedience & heresaye and sects into the world and printing has divulged them, and libells against the best Government: God keepe us from both."[88] A man that could utter such sentiments as these

[84] P. R. O., CO1-30-71. [85] P. R. O., CO1-37-1.

[86] P. R. O., CO1-40-54.

[87] Mr. P. A. Bruce, in his Institutional History of Virginia in the Seventeenth Century, has shown that this statement is incorrect.

[88] P. R. O., CO1-26-77.

would not scruple to throttle, if he could, all representative institutions in his government. If he intimidated voters and corrupted the Burgesses, it was perhaps because he thought himself justified in any measures that would render the Governor, the King's substitute, supreme in the government.

But whatever is the verdict of posterity upon the conduct and motives of Sir William Berkeley, the causes of the Rebellion stand out with great clearness:—England's selfish commercial policy, the Culpeper-Arlington grant, the Dutch wars, storms and pestilence, inefficient if not corrupt government, excessive taxes. The only wonder is that the insurrection did not occur earlier. In fact two mutinies did break out in 1674, when the excessively heavy taxes of that year were announced, but the rebels lacked leaders and were suppressed without great difficulty.[89] As early as 1673 the defection of the planters was so great that it was feared many might attempt to deliver the colony into the hands of the Dutch. Berkeley wrote that a large part of the people were so desperately poor that they might reasonably be expected upon any small advantage of the enemy to "revolt to them in hopes of bettering their Condition by Shareing the Plunder of the Country with them".[90] A certain John Knight reported "that the planters there doe generally desire a trade with the Dutch and all other nations and would not be singly bound to the trade of England, and speake openly there that they are in the nature of slaves, soe that the hearts of the greatest part of them are taken away from his Majesty".[91] Thus the downtrodden planters, alienated from England, angered at the Governor, even distrusting their own Assembly, waited but an occasion and a leader to rise in open rebellion. A new Indian war offered the occasion, and they found their leader in young Nathaniel Bacon.

[89] P. R. O., CO1-36-37; CO1-36-54. [90] P. R. O., CO1-30-51.
[91] P. R. O., CO1-30-78.

CHAPTER VI

BACON'S REBELLION

For many years Virginia had been at peace with the neighboring Indians.[1] The long series of wars which had filled most of the first half of the seventeenth century had broken the spirit and power of the Pamunkeys, the Nansemonds and the Nottoways.[2] The remnants of these nations had become dependent upon the English, paying them tribute and looking to them for protection from their enemies.[3] In 1675, however, these friendly relations were disturbed by a southward movement of some of the northern Indians. Large bodies of the warlike Senecas, pressing upon the Susquehannocks at the head of the Chesapeake Bay, were driving them down into Maryland and Virginia. Here their indigence and their restlessness became a menace to the whites and an element of disturbance to their relations with the other tribes.[4]

In the summer of 1675 a party of savages rowed across the Potomac river, committed several murders and made good their escape into Maryland.[5] In anger and alarm the planters of Stafford county seized their arms to protect their homes and to avenge their neighbors. A band of thirty or more, led by Colonel Mason and Captain Brent, pursued the savages up the Potomac into the Maryland woods.[6] Coming in the early dawn upon two diverging trails, "each leader with his party took a separate path". "In less than a furlong either found a cabin", one crowded with Doeg Indians, the other with Susquehannocks. The king of the Doegs, when he saw his hut surrounded by Brent's men, "came trembling forth,

[1] Mass. S. IV, Vol. IX, p. 165; P. R. O., CO1-30-71.
[2] Hen., Vol. I, pp. 323, 380. [3] Hen., Vol. II, p. 141.
[4] T. M., p. 9; Mass. S. IV, Vol. IX, pp. 165, 167.
[5] T. M., p. 9; P. R. O., CO5-1371-370; CO1-36-36; CO1-36-37.
[6] T. M., p. 8; Mass. S. IV, Vol. IX, p. 165.

and wou'd have fled". But Captain Brent, "catching hold of his twisted lock, which was all the hair he wore", commanded him to deliver up the men guilty of the recent murders. "The king pleaded ignorance and slipt loos", whereupon Brent shot him dead. At this the savages in the cabin opened fire, and the Virginians answered with a deadly volley. "Th' Indians throng'd out at the door and fled." "The English shot as many as they cou'd, so that they killed ten . . . and brought away the kings son." "The noise of this shooting awaken'd th' Indians in the cabin which Coll. Mason had encompassed, who likewise rush'd out and fled, of whom his company shot ffourteen."[7]

This unfortunate affair was the beginning of a deadly war between the English and the Indians, which brought untold suffering upon the people of Maryland and Virginia. The Susquehannocks, enraged at the slaughter of their warriors, became the most implacable enemies of the white men. Joining with the other tribes in a league against the English, they began a series of outrages and murders which continued many months, and cost the lives of hundreds of men, women and children. During the year 1676 alone, more people were butchered in Virginia by the savages than fell in the massacre of 1644.[8] This fearful mortality was due to the fact that the Indians were now supplied with firearms. Governor Berkeley and his friends, in their greed to secure the valuable beaver and otter skins, had not hesitated to purchase them with powder, shot and guns.[9] The savages had now almost entirely discarded the bow and arrow, and were so skilful with their new weapons that the English often hired them "to kill Deare".[10] So that when the war cry was once more heard upon the frontier, the savages, although less numerous than in the days of Powhatan or Opechancanough, were far more to be feared.

It was Maryland that first felt the resentment of the savages.

[7] T. M., pp. 8-9; P. R. O., CO5-1371-370; Mass. S. IV, Vol. IX, p. 165.
[8] P. R. O., CO1-39-10; CO1-36-78; W. & M. Q., Vol. IX, p. 10.
[9] W. & M. Q., Vol. IX, p. 6; T. M., p. 11.
[10] W. & M. Q., Vol. IX, p. 6.

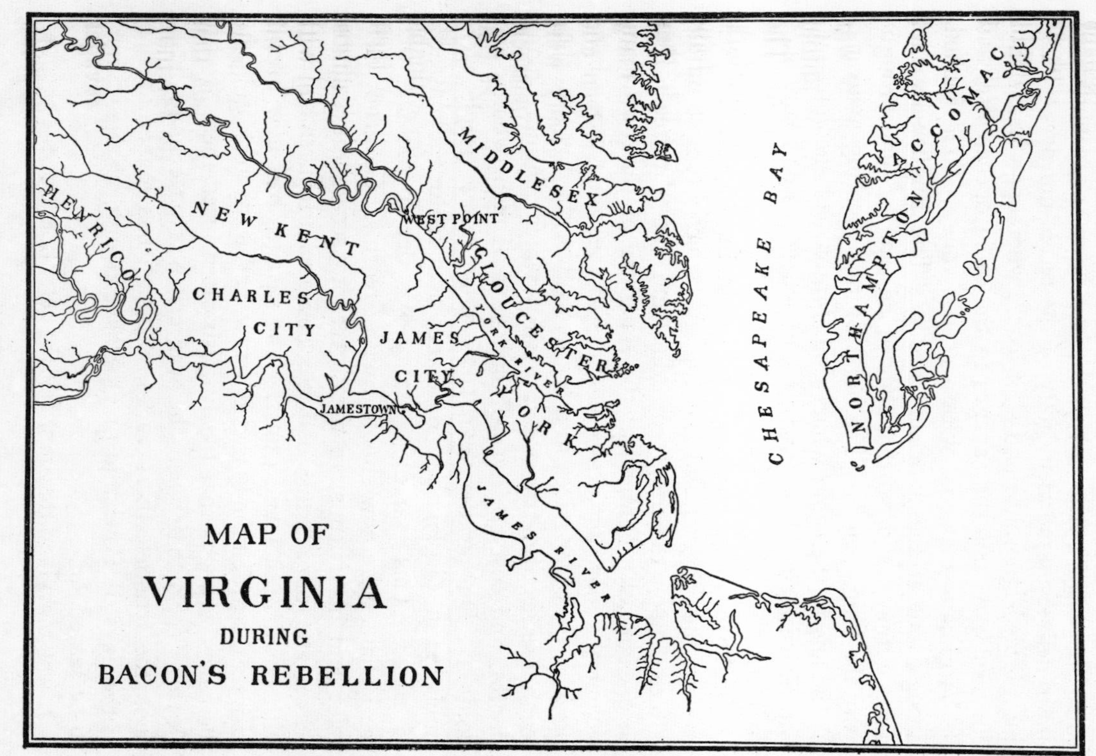

MAP OF
VIRGINIA
DURING
BACON'S REBELLION
HENRICO
NEW KENT
CHARLES
CITY
JAMES
CITY
JAMESTOWN
WEST POINT
MIDDLESEX
GLOUCESTER
YORK RIVER
JAMES RIVER
CHESAPEAKE BAY
NORTHAMPTON
ACCOMAC

The people of this province had taken no part in the attack of Mason and Brent, but the Susquehannocks were not in the humor to make nice distinctions. In seeking revenge for the murder of their braves they held all whites equally guilty, and fell immediately upon the nearest plantations. Thus were the Marylanders made to suffer for the rashness of the Virginia frontiersmen.

Feeling that it was his duty to aid the neighboring province in this war brought on by the hasty action of two of his own officers, and fearing that depredations upon the Virginia frontiers could not long be prevented, Sir William Berkeley decided to join Governor Calvert in a vigorous attack upon the savages. Colonel John Washington, great-grandfather of George Washington, at the head of several hundred men, was despatched across the Potomac to effect a junction with the Maryland troops.[11] The combined forces of the two colonies are said to have numbered "neer a thousand men".[12]

Unable to withstand this army in the open field, the Indians fell back upon a fort which they had erected upon the north bank of the Potomac, and here awaited the approach of the English. Their fortress had been constructed with such care and skill that the white men were unable to carry it by storm. The outer works consisted of lines of tree trunks, from five to eight inches in diameter, "watled 6 inches apart to shoot through", their tops firmly twisted together. Behind this was a ditch, and within all a square citadel, with high walls and "fflankers having many loop-holes". The fire of the red-skins from behind these works proved so deadly that hopes of a successful assault had to be abandoned. Nor could breaches be effected, for the allies were not provided with heavy guns. The moist and swampy ground surrounding the fort made it impossible to approach by means of trenches.[13]

So the English cast their camp before the fort hoping to starve out the enemy. Lines were drawn about the place, as closely as the nature of the ground would permit, while boats

[11] Mass. S. IV, Vol. IX, p. 165; P. R. O., CO1-36-78.
[12] P. R. O., CO5-1371-369; T. M., p. 9.
[13] T. M., p. 10.

patrolled the river to cut off escape to the Virginia shore. Fearing, no doubt, that lack of provisions would soon make it necessary for them to come to terms with the besiegers, the Indians sent out several of their leaders to treat for peace. But so deep was the animosity aroused by the recent murders, that the white men violated the flag of truce by detaining these envoys, and finally beating out their brains.[14] This flagrant act aroused the Indians to a desperate defense. In numerous sallies they inflicted severe loss upon the besiegers, and captured enough horses to supply themselves with food. At last, after six or seven weeks of fighting, they resolved to effect their escape. On a dark night, when the English were least expecting it, they sallied forth, bringing with them their women and children. Awakening the white men with their savage yells, they burst in among them, killing and wounding many, and before resistance could be made, were through the lines and gone.[15]

And now the Virginians were made to pay dearly for their part in this ill-managed affair. Early in January, 1676, the Susquehannocks crossed the Potomac and came plundering and murdering through the frontier counties.[16] Separating into small bands, the Indians fell upon the more isolated plantations, and in a few days had killed no less than thirty-six persons. Those whose wretched fate it was to be captured, were put to death with all the tortures that devilish ingenuity could devise. Some were roasted, others flayed alive. The sufferings of the victims were long and protracted, while the savages knocked out their teeth or tore off their nails or stuck feathers and lighted wood into their flesh.[17]

In terror the people of the frontier began to desert their homes, seeking shelter in the more populous settlements.[18]

[14] T. M., p. 9; P. R. O., CO392.1-173, 178; Cotton, p. 3; Inds' Pros. p. 5; P. R. O., CO5-1371-370.

[15] P. R. O., CO1-36-78; CO5-1371-369; T. M., pp. 9-10; Inds' Pros., pp. 7-8; Mass. S. IV, Vol. IX, p. 165.

[16] P. R. O., CO5-1371-370.

[17] Inds' Pros., p. 7; P. R. O., CO5-1371-370; CO1-36-66; Mass. S. IV, Vol. IX, p. 176.

[18] W. & M. Q., Vol. IX, p. 7.

In a few weeks one parish, upon the upper waters of the Rappahannock, was reduced from seventy-one plantations to eleven.[19] Those that remained were concentrated upon the largest farms, which they fortified with palisades and redoubts.[20]

When the news of these atrocities reached Sir William Berkeley, hasty preparations were made for an expedition against the invaders. Sir Henry Chicheley was put at the head of forces of horse and foot, with orders to give immediate pursuit to the savages. But just as all was in readiness and the command to march hourly expected, the Governor decided that the expedition should be abandoned. Chicheley's commission was annulled, his forces disbanded and the soldiers sent to their homes.[21]

What induced Berkeley to take this strange step none could tell. The murders of the savages were continuing. The frontier was defenseless. Messages were coming from the exposed plantations imploring aid. Why should he desert the people and expose them to the fury of the Indians? It is possible that he detected symptoms of mutiny among the troops and thought it better to abandon the expedition than to run the risk of a rebellion. He was well aware of the discontent of the people, and his letters to England show that he dreaded an insurrection.[22] The unhappy planters ascribed the Governor's strange conduct to avarice. He and his friends had a monopoly of the Indian trade, and it was hinted that he preferred to allow the atrocities to continue rather than destroy his source of revenue. He was determined, was the cry, "that no bullits would pierce beaver skins".[23] More probable seems the explanation that Berkeley hoped to prevent further depredations by the help of the Pamunkeys and other friendly tribes, and feared that an invasion of the Indian lands might defeat this purpose.[24]

But an Assembly was summoned in March and instructed

[19] P. R. O., CO5-1371-372; Va. Mag., Vol. III, p. 35.

[20] T. M., p. 10.

[21] P. R. O., CO5-1371-373, 411.

[22] P. R. O., CO1-30-51; CO1-36-37.

[23] T. M., p. 11; W. & M. Q., Vol. IX, p. 7; P. R. O., CO5-1371-375.

[24] P. R. O., CO1-36-36.

by the Governor to take immediate measures to secure the frontier.[25] Acting, no doubt, under Berkeley's influence, the Assembly resolved not to carry the conflict into the enemy's territory, but to wage a defensive war. Forts were to be erected upon the upper waters of the great rivers, and manned with regular troops as a protection to the outer plantations. To defray the cost, new and heavy taxes were put upon the people.[26]

This last act of the Long Assembly caused bitter dissatisfaction. The border counties had hoped that provision would be made for an expedition against the Indians. No headway could be made unless the whites took the offensive and hunted down the savages in their own villages. The erection of forts was useless.[27] The Indians would experience no difficulty in avoiding them in their murderous raids. They could approach the remote plantations, or even those far within the frontiers, without fear of detection by the soldiers, for the numerous swamps and dense woods afforded them ample covert. It was not intended that the forts should be used as bases for expeditions into the enemy's country; nor could the soldiers leave them to pursue and punish the plundering savages. What then, it was asked, could be the value of fortresses, if they were to defend only the ground upon which they stood?[28]

The event proved the people right. The forts, when built, were but slight obstacles to the invasions of the Indians. The murders became more frequent than before. The impotency of the defenses of the colony seems to have inspired them to more terrible and vigorous attacks. The cry against the forts became more bitter. "It was a design," the people thought, "of the grandees to engross all their tobacco into their own hands".[29] As the cries of their women and children grew more piteous and distressing, the men of the frontier spoke openly of disobedience. Rather than pay the taxes for the

[25] Mass. S. IV, Vol. IX, p 165; Hen., Vol. II, p. 326.
[26] P. R. O., CO5-1371-373; Hen., Vol. II, pp. 327-329.
[27] Inds' Pros., pp. 8, 9.
[28] P. R. O., CO5-1371-378.
[29] P. R. O., CO5-1371-374.

accursed forts they would plant no more tobacco. If the Governor would not send an expedition against the Indians, they themselves would march out to avenge their wrongs. The forts must be dismantled, the garrisons dismissed.[30]

From all parts of the colony came the insistent demand that the Assembly, which had so long been but a mockery of representative government, should be dissolved and the people given a free election.[31] But Berkeley was not the man to yield readily to this clamor. Never, in all the long years that he had ruled over Virginia, had he allowed the rabble to dictate his policies. He would not do so now. When petitions came from the frontiersmen, asking leave to go out against the Indians, he returned a brusk and angry refusal.[32] A delegation from Charles City county met with a typical reception from the irritable old man. As they stood humbly before him, presenting their request for a commission, they spoke of themselves as the Governor's subjects. Upon this Berkeley blurted out that they were all "fools and loggerheads". They were subjects of the King, and so was he. He would grant them no commission, and bade them be gone, and a pox take them.[33] Later he issued a proclamation forbidding under heavy penalties all such petitions.[34]

Unfortunately, at this juncture came news that large bodies of Indians were descending upon the upper waters of the James, and that another bloody assault might soon be expected.[35] In terror and anger the people of Charles City county seized their arms, determined to repel this threatened storm, with or without the Governor's permission. Parties went about from place to place beating up volunteers with the drum. The magistrates were either in sympathy with the movement, or were unable to prevent it.[36] Soon a considerable body of rough, determined men were assembled, awaiting only a leader to march out against the enemy.

This leader they found in one of the most interesting and

[30] P. R. O., CO5-1371-378; Inds' Pros., p. 8.
[31] P. R. O., CO5-1371-379; CO1-37-17.
[32] P. R. O., CO5-1371-375.
[33] P. R. O., CO1-40-106.
[34] P. R. O., CO5-1371-375.
[35] Ibid.
[36] Ibid.

picturesque characters in Virginia history. Nathaniel Bacon is depicted as twenty-nine years of age, black-haired, of medium height and slender, melancholy, pensive, and taciturn. In conversation he was logical and convincing; in oratory magnetic and masterful.[37] His successful expeditions against the Indians and the swift blows he directed against the loyal forces mark him as a military commander of no mean ability.[38]

Bacon was almost a stranger in Virginia, for he had left England less than two years before.[39] He was fortunate, however, in having a cousin, also named Nathaniel Bacon, high in the favor of Sir William Berkeley.[40] It was doubtless through the influence of this relative that the young man attained a position of great influence, and was appointed to the Council itself.[41] But submission to the will of the imperious Governor was the price paid by all that wished to remain long in favor in Virginia. Bacon did not approve of Berkeley's arbitrary government; he disliked the long continuation of the Assembly, the unjust discriminations, the unusual taxes, the incapacity of officials; and it was not in his fiery temper to conceal his opinions. Soon, it would seem, the frowns of the Governor began to fall upon him, and he grew weary of coming to Council.[42]

Bacon had made his home in Henrico, at that time one of the extreme frontier counties. His marked ability, his liberal education, his place in the Council soon gave him a position of great influence among his rough but hardy neighbors. None could be better suited to assume command over the desperate volunteers that had gathered in Charles City county.

But it was a very serious step to accept the leadership of this band which had taken arms in defiance of the Governor's commands. It would expose him to the charge not only of disobedience, but of open rebellion. Bacon, however, like all

[37] Bac's Pros., p. 9.
[38] P. R. O., CO5-1371-376.
[39] Cotton, p. 4; Mass. S. IV, Vol. IX, p. 180; P. R. O., CO1-37-1.
[40] Va. Mag., Vol. II, pp. 125-129.
[41] P. R. O., CO5-1371-375.
[42] Va. Mag., Vol. III, pp. 134-135.

that dwelt upon the frontiers, was angered at the inadequate protection given by the government. When news came to him that depredations had been committed upon one of his own plantations, and that his overseer had been killed, he was eager to take revenge.[43]

Now some of Bacon's friends, as anxious as he for an Indian expedition, and thinking him most proper to conduct it, suggested his name to the volunteers. The men were quite willing to accept so influential a commander, but it was not so easy to persuade Bacon to take the dangerous place. He consented, however, to row across the river, and visit the soldiers in their camp. Here the men gathered around him, and with joyous shouts of, "A Bacon! A Bacon!" proclaimed him their leader. His friends pressed him to accept. They would, they said, accompany him on his expedition. If the Governor ordered them to disband, they would defy him. "They drank damnation to their souls", if they should prove untrue to him. Touched by these proofs of confidence, and fired perhaps with ambition, the young man yielded, and Bacon's Rebellion had begun.[44]

From the very first the movement assumed the character of an insurrection.[45] Amid the hearty applause of his rough followers, Bacon spoke of the negligence, the incapacity and wickedness of the government. Their betrayal into the hands of the savages was but one of many grievances. The laws were unjust, the taxes oppressive. Something must be done to redress these wrongs and to end misgovernment.[46] And as the poor people flocked in to him, he listed their names in a huge round-robin and bound them to him by an oath of fidelity.[47]

A message was dispatched to the Governor to request a commission authorizing the expedition against the Indians.[48]

[43] P. R. O., CO5-1371-376; W. & M. Q., Vol. IX, pp. 4, 7.

[44] P. R. O., CO5-1371-376.

[45] P. R. O., CO1-36-54; CO1-36-37; CO1-37-1.

[46] P. R. O., CO5-1371-376, 7; CO1-36-54; CO1-37-1; Mass. S. IV, Vol. IX, p. 166.

[47] P. R. O., CO5-1371-376, 7.

[48] W. & M. Q., Vol. IX, p. 7; Mass. S. IV, Vol. IX, p. 166.

But Bacon promised his men that if Sir William withheld his assent, he would lead them forth without it; and in the meanwhile, without waiting for the Governor's reply, he crossed over into New Kent, "a county ripe for rebellion", where he expected to strengthen his position and perhaps attack the Pamunkeys.[49] This nation had for many years been friendly to the English, and had more than once given them invaluable assistance against other Indian tribes. Their present queen was the widow of Tottopottomoi, who had been killed while fighting as the ally of the white men against the Richahecrians.[50] They now occupied land allotted them by the Assembly, upon the frontier of New Kent, where, it was supposed, they would act as a protection to the colony against the raids of hostile tribes.[51] When the Susquehannocks began their depredations Governor Berkeley expected valuable assistance from these allies, whom he termed his "spyes and intelligence" to search out "the bloody enimies".[52] But the Pamunkeys not only failed to check the invasion of the Susquehannocks, but seem to have joined with them in the work of bloodshed and pillage. The people of the frontier believed that almost all the Indians were leagued together for their ruin. The Pamunkeys, they were sure, had taken part in the recent atrocities. And as they were their close neighbors, knowing all their customs and all their habitations, they were especially fitted for the work of destruction. The New Kent planters were now impatient to march out against them to take revenge for the recent horrible murders. But the Pamunkeys, upon hearing of Bacon's approach, deserted their reservation and took refuge in the wilderness.[53]

It is not hard to imagine the Governor's anger when he heard of these proceedings. Despite the testimony of the frontiersmen, he had refused to believe the Pamunkeys guilty, and he still relied upon them for assistance against the Susquehannocks. Bacon's proceedings, in frightening them

[49] P. R. O., CO5-1371-377; W. & M. Q., Vol. IX, p. 4.

[50] Hen., Vol. I, p 422; Burk, Vol. II, pp. 104-106; Force, Vol. I, Tract VIII, p. 14.

[51] Hen., Vol. I, p. 380.

[52] Mass. S. IV, Vol. IX, pp. 166, 180.

[53] Mass. S. IV, p. 166.

from their lands, upset all his plans of defense. Yet had the volunteers contented themselves with attacking the Indians, it is conceivable that Berkeley would have yielded. But when they took up arms without his permission, put themselves under the command of a discontented Councillor, and demanded redress of grievances from the government, it was necessary for him to resort to repression. The commission was refused and a proclamation issued denouncing Bacon's conduct as illegal and rebellious. He and his men were offered pardon, but only on condition that they lay down their arms, and return immediately to their obedience.[54]

But the mutineers would not obey. Are we, they complained, to return passively to our homes, there to be slaughtered by the savage foe? The Governor has given us no protection. The Indians are coming. Already the blood of our butchered relatives cries aloud to Heaven. We hope we have still enough English blood in our veins to think it more honorable to die in fair battle with the enemy, than to be sneakingly murdered in our beds. If we lie still, we are destroyed by the heathen; if we defend ourselves, we are accounted rebels and traitors. But we will fight. And if we must be hanged for killing those that will destroy us, let them hang us, we will venture that rather than lie at the mercy of our barbarous enemies. So, turning their backs upon the plantations, they struck out into the dense woods.[55]

When Berkeley heard that his authority was still defied, and his pardon rejected, he was resolved at all hazards to compel obedience. Gathering around him a party of three hundred gentlemen, "well armed and mounted", he set out, on the third of May, to intercept the rebels.[56] But learning, upon his arrival at the falls of the James, that Bacon had crossed the river and was already far away, he decided to encamp in the frontier counties and await his return.[57]

But he sent out a party under Colonel Claiborne to pursue the Pamunkeys, and induce them, if possible, to return to their

[54] P. R. O., CO5-1371-377; CO1-36-55; CO1-37-1.

[55] P. R. O., CO5-1371-377; CO1-36-66; CO1-37-14.

[56] Mass. S. IV, Vol. IX, p. 167. [57] P. R. O., CO5-1371-377.

reservation. The savages were found entrenched in a strong position, "encompassed with trees which they had fallen in the branch of an Impassable swamp".[58] Their queen refused to abandon this retreat, declaring that since the Governor had not been able to command the obedience of Bacon, he could not save her people from his violence. But she promised that the Pamunkeys should remain peaceable and should take no part in the raids of the Susquehannocks. "Of this the Governor was informed, who resolved not to be soe answered but to reduce her and the other Indians, soe soone as Bacon could be brought to submit."[59]

On May the tenth Berkeley issued a new proclamation. The taking of arms by Bacon, he said, against his wishes and commands, was an act of disloyalty and rebellion. If permitted to go unpunished, it would tend to the ruin and overthrow of all government in the colony. It was his duty to use all the forces at his command to suppress so dangerous a mutiny. Should the misguided people desert their leader, and return to their allegiance, he would grant a free and full pardon. And as Nathaniel Bacon had shown himself by his rash proceedings utterly unworthy of public trust, he suspended him from the Council and from all other offices held by him. It was amazing, he said, that after he had been Governor of Virginia so many years, and had done always equal justice to all men, the people should be seduced and carried away by so young and turbulent a person as Bacon.[60]

But although Berkeley was determined to suppress the rebels by force of arms, the attitude of the commons in other parts of the colony became so threatening that he was forced to make some concessions. To the great joy of the people he dissolved the unpopular Long Assembly, and ordered a new election. It was with sorrow, he declared, that he departed with the present Burgesses, who had given frequent proof of ability and wisdom. But the complaints of many inhabitants of the long continuance of the old Assembly had induced him to grant a free election. And if any man had grievances against

[58] Mass. S. IV, Vol. IX, p. 168. [59] Ibid.
[60] P. R. O., CO1-37-1.

his government, or could accuse him of injustice or bribery, he was to present his complaint by his Burgesses to the Assembly, where it would be examined.[61]

It was indeed time for the Governor to act, for the rebellion was spreading to the older and more populous counties.[62] The people there too were denouncing the forts, and demanding redress of grievances. Some began to arm, and it seemed not improbable that the entire colony might soon be ablaze. Hastening back to his residence at Green Spring, he sought to appease the people by dismantling the obnoxious forts and dismissing their garrisons.[63]

In the meanwhile Bacon was making his way through the woods southward from the falls of the James in pursuit of the Susquehannocks that had committed the recent murders upon the frontier.[64] These savages had not attempted to return to their homes north of the Potomac, but had retired to the country of the Occaneechees, where they had entrenched themselves in two forts.[65] The Occaneechees dwelt in the southernmost part of Virginia, near the site of Clarksville.[66] They are described as a stout people, and the most enterprising of traders. Their chief town, situated upon an island in the Roanoke River and defended by three strong forts, was "the Mart for all the Indians for att least 500 miles" around.[67] The beaver skins stored in this place at the time of Bacon's expedition are said to have valued no less than £1,000.[68] Persicles, their king, was reported to be an enlightened ruler, "a very brave man & ever true to ye English".[69]

It was toward this island that Bacon led his men. But a quest for Indian allies took him far out of his route. Every-

[61] P. R. O., CO1-36-64. Berkeley's proclamation, addressed to the sheriff of Rappahannock county, dissolving the Assembly, and the proclamation denouncing Bacon as a traitor were both issued in Henrico, on May 10, 1676.

[62] P. R. O., CO5-1371-379.

[63] P. R. O., CO5-1371-379, 411.

[64] W. & M. Q., Vol. IX, p. 1; Va. Mag., Vol. I, p. 180; P. R. O., CO1-36-77; CO1-37-16.

[65] Va. Mag., Vol. I, p. 180.

[66] W. & M. Q., Vol. XI, p. 121.

[67] Mass. S. IV, Vol. IX, p. 167.

[68] Ibid.

[69] P. R. O., CO1-37-16; Va. Mag., Vol. I, p. 182.

where he found the savages reluctant to aid him, even those nations that had formerly been most friendly to the English now holding aloof from them. This embarrassed him greatly for he had relied upon receiving aid from several tribes, and his food was not sufficient for a long march. As the little army went further and further into the wilderness, they began to face the possibility of starvation. When at last they approached the Occaneechee country and received promises of aid from Persicles, their provisions were nearly exhausted.[70]

Upon reaching the Roanoke the English crossed the north branch of the river and encamped upon the Occaneechee island.[71] To his deep satisfaction, Bacon found Persicles embroiled with the Susquehannocks, and already preparing for their destruction. When these wanderers from the north first came to him, Persicles had received them with kindness and had relieved their needs. But they, "being exercised in warr for many years with the Senecaes, and living on rapin, endeavoured to beat the Ockinagees of their own Island".[72] Persicles had defeated them, however, and forced them to take refuge in their two forts.[73]

Now the Susquehannocks, in their southward march, had subdued and brought with them some members of the Mannakin and Annelecton tribes.[74] These savages, although they lived with their conquerors, had no love for them, and were quite willing to join in any plan for their destruction. Persicles, it would seem, was plotting with them to surprise and cut off the Susquehannocks, when Bacon appeared with his men. Fearing, no doubt, that the participation of the English in the attack would render secrecy impossible, Persicles left them on the island, and went out alone against the enemy.[75] The Mannakins and Annelectons proved true to their allies and the Susquehannocks were easily defeated. Persicles returned in triumph, bringing with him several prisoners. These he

[70] P. R. O., CO1-36-77.

[71] Va. Mag., Vol. I, p. 181.

[72] Mass. S. IV, Vol. I, p. 167.

[73] Ibid.

[74] Va. Mag., Vol. I, p. 181; P. R. O., CO1-37-16; W. & M. Q., Vol. IX, p. 2.

[75] P. R. O., CO1-37-16.

wished the English to execute, but they "refused to take that office".[76] Thereupon he himself put them to death with all the usual Indian tortures, "running fyer brands up their bodys & the like".[77]

But now the friendship of Persicles and the English came abruptly to an end. The Berkeley party afterwards claimed that Bacon deliberately picked a quarrel with his allies, and attacked them without provocation.[78] It would be unjust, however, to place too much confidence in these charges. Bacon's men found themselves in a most critical situation. They were many miles from the plantations, surrounded by the savages, their provisions exhausted. Persicles, they asserted, had failed to keep his promise to supply them with food. He was assuming a threatening posture, manning his forts, and lining the river bank with his warriors. For Bacon to retreat from the island under these circumstances, would have exposed his company to destruction. To remain passive was to starve.[79]

As the English became more insistent in their demands for food, Persicles retired to one of his forts, and refused further conference. Many of the savages, seeing hostilities imminent, deserted their cabins and began to rush in through the entrances of their fortresses. But Bacon interposed his men, and succeeded in shutting out many of them.[80] Now from the Indians across the river came a shot, and one of the English fell dead.[81] Instantly Bacon ordered a general attack. The defenseless men, women and children left in the cabins were mercilessly butchered. At the same time fire was opened upon the forts. The soldiers rushed up to the portholes, and poured their volleys directly in upon the wretched savages.[82] A hideous din arose. The singing and howling of the warriors was mingled with the moans of the dying. Fire was set to one of the forts, in which were the king's wife and children. As the flames arose, three or four braves made a dash for

[76] P. R. O., CO1-36-77.

[77] Mass. S. IV, Vol. IX, p. 167; P. R. O., CO1-37-16; CO1-36-77.

[78] Mass. S. IV, Vol. IX, p. 167.

[79] P. R. O., CO1-36-77.

[80] Mass. S. IV, Vol. IX, p. 168.

[81] P. R. O., CO1-37-16.

[82] W. & M. Q., Vol. IX, p. 7.

safety through the line of the English. All others in this fort, including the king's family, perished amid the burning timbers.[83]

The next day the fight was continued from morn till night. Several times the savages sallied forth from their remaining forts, and placing themselves behind trees, opened fire upon the English. But Bacon's frontiersmen were accustomed to this method of warfare. So well were they posted and so cleverly concealed, that most of the enemy were picked off as they stood. At last Persicles himself led forth a party of about twenty men in a desperate attack upon his enemy. With great bravery they rushed around the English in a wide circle, howling and firing. But they too were unsuccessful. Persicles was killed. Several of his men were shot on the bank of the river, and fell into the water. Of all this party seven only were seen to escape.[84]

It now seemed hopeless for the Indians to fight further. With their king and many of their warriors dead, and with one of their forts in ruins, their ultimate destruction was certain if they remained upon the island. So, with their women and children, they deserted the remaining forts and escaped. How they managed to slip past the victorious white men and make their way across the river is not explained. Thinking it best not to follow, Bacon secured his plunder, and turned his face back towards the plantations.[85]

The news of the victory over the savages was received with enthusiasm in the frontier counties. Bacon had been popular with the people before; he now became their idol.[86] He and his men, upon their return, found the entire colony deeply interested in the election of a new House of Burgesses. In various places popular candidates, men in sympathy with Bacon, were being nominated.[87] In Henrico county the people showed their contempt for the Governor's proclamations by electing Bacon himself.[88]

[83] P. R. O., CO1-36-77. [84] W. & M. Q., Vol. IX, p. 7.

[85] P. R. O., CO1-36-77; CO1-36-16; T. M., p. 11.

[86] W. & M. Q., Vol. IX, p. 5. [87] P. R. O., CO5-1371-379.

[88] Bac's Pros., p. 11; T. M., p. 12.

But it would be a matter of no little risk for him to go to Jamestown to take his seat in the Assembly. While surrounded by his loyal frontiersmen in his own county he might well ignore the proclamations against him, but if he put himself in the Governor's power, that fiery old man might not hesitate to hang him as a rebel. His friends would not allow him to go unprotected, and insisted upon sending with him a guard of forty or fifty armed men.[89] Embarking with this company in a sloop, Bacon wended his way down the crooked James to the capital. He cast anchor a short distance above the town and sent to the Governor to know whether he would be allowed to take his seat in the Assembly without molestation.[90] For reply Sir William opened fire upon the sloop with the guns of the fort.[91] Whereupon Bacon sailed further up the river out of danger.[92] But that night he landed with twenty of his men, and unobserved by any, slipped silently into town.[93]

In the place resided Richard Lawrence and William Drummond, both deeply impressed with the need of reform in Virginia, and both in sympathy with Bacon's movement. Repairing to Lawrence's house, Bacon conferred with these two friends for several hours.[94] Upon reëmbarking he was discovered. Alarm was immediately given in the town and several boats filled with armed men pursued him up the river. At the same time Captain Gardner, commanding the ship *Adam and Eve,* was ordered to follow the fugitives, and capture or sink the sloop. For some hours Bacon eluded them all. Finally, however, about three the next afternoon, he was driven by the small boats under the guns of the *Adam and Eve,* and forced to surrender.[95] Coming on board he was entrusted to Captain Gardner and Captain Hubert Farrill, and by them conducted to the Governor.[96]

As the prisoner was led before him, the old man lifted his

[89] P. R. O., CO5-1371-369; CO1-37-16, 17; Bac's Pros., p. 11; Mass. S. IV, Vol. IX, p. 170.

[90] P. R. O., CO5-1371-379.

[91] Ibid.

[92] Ibid.

[93] Ibid.

[94] P. R. O., CO5-1371-380; CO1-37-16; Mass. S. IV, Vol. IX, p. 170.

[95] Ibid.

[96] Ibid.

eyes and arms to Heaven, exclaiming, "Now I behold the greatest Rebell that ever was in Virginia!"[97] After some moments he added, "Mr. Bacon, doe you continue to be a gentleman? And may I take your word? If so you are at liberty upon your parol."[98] Later, when the rebel expressed gratitude at this mild treatment and repentance for his disobedience, Berkeley promised to grant him a free pardon. And should he offer a humble submission, he was to be restored to his seat in the Council, and even receive the long desired commission.[99]

In this unexpected leniency the Governor was probably actuated not by magnanimity, but by policy, or perhaps necessity. When the rebel was out upon his Indian expedition, Sir William had not scrupled to tell Mrs. Bacon that he would most certainly hang her husband, if ever he got him in his power.[100] But now he dared not do so. Bacon was regarded by a large part of the people as their leader in a struggle for justice and liberty; to treat him too harshly might set the entire colony ablaze. In fact, many frontiersmen, when they heard of the capture of their hero, did hasten down to Jamestown with dreadful threats of revenge should a hair of his head be touched.[101] And throughout the colony the mutterings of impending insurrection were too loud to be mistaken or ignored.[102]

A few days after the capture, at a meeting of Council and Assembly, the Governor arose from his chair, saying, "If there be joy in the presence of the angels over one sinner that repenteth, there is joy now, for we have a penitent sinner come before us. Call Mr. Bacon." Whereupon the rebel entered, and dropping upon his knee, presented his submission. "God forgive you," said the Governor, "I forgive you." "And all that were with him?" asked one of the Council. "Yea," said Sir William, "all that were with him."[103] That very day Bacon was restored to his seat in the Council.[104] The soldiers

[97] CO5-1371-380.
[98] Ibid.
[99] Va. Mag., Vol. I, p. 171; Hen., Vol. II, p. 543.
[100] W. & M. Q., Vol. IX, p. 5.
[101] T. M., p. 15.
[102] W. & M. Q., Vol. IX, p. 8.
[103] T. M., pp. 12-13.
[104] P. R. O., CO1-37-16.

that had been captured with him were freed from their chains and permitted to return to their homes.[105] And, to the great joy of the people, it was publicly announced by one of the Burgesses, that Bacon had been granted a commission as general in the Indian war.[106] Feeling that all was now well, and that their presence in Jamestown was no longer necessary, the sturdy frontiersmen shouldered their fusils, and returned to their plantations.[107]

But the reconciliation could be but temporary. Bacon's repentance and submission had been forced from him while helpless in the Governor's power. He did not consider it morally binding. And so long as the people's grievances were not righted, and the Indian war was neglected, he could not be content to remain inactive and submissive. On the other hand, Sir William probably felt that his promise of a commission had been exacted by the unlawful threats of Bacon's friends, and might be broken without dishonor.[108]

After waiting several days for his papers, Bacon became suspicious of the Governor's intentions, and set out for his home in Henrico.[109] Berkeley consented to his departure, and he took "civill leave", but immediately afterwards he repented bitterly that he had let his enemy thus slip through his fingers. It is probable that information came to him just too late, that Bacon was again meditating resistance. Parties of men were sent out upon the roads and up the river to intercept his flight. The very beds of his lodging house were searched in desperate haste, in the hope that he had not yet left Jamestown. But all in vain. Bacon had ridden quietly out of town, without servants or friends, and was now far on his way towards the frontier.[110]

On his arrival at Henrico, his old comrades flocked around him, eager to be led out against the Indians, and confident in the belief that Bacon was authorized to command them. And when they learned that he had not secured a commission, and was once more a fugitive, they "sett their throats in one com-

[105] Mass. S. IV, Vol. IX, p. 170; P. R. O., CO1-37-16.

[106] W. & M. Q., Vol. IX, p. 8.

[107] Ibid.

[108] Ibid.

[109] W. & M. Q., Vol. IX, p. 9.

[110] Va. Mag., Vol. I, p. 171.

mon key of Oathes and curses, and cried out aloud, that they would either have a Commission . . . or else they would pull downe the Towne".[111] And as the news spread from place to place, rough, angry men came flocking in to Bacon, promising that if he would but lead them to the Governor, they would soon get him what he pleased. "Thus the raging tumult came downe to Towne."[112]

Vague rumors began to reach the Assembly that Bacon was marching on Jamestown at the head of five hundred men.[113] By June the twenty-second, it became definitely known that the rebels were approaching.[114] Berkeley sent out several messengers to demand their intentions, but could get no satisfactory reply. Hasty preparations were made to defend the town.[115] The neighboring militia was summoned. Four guns were dragged to Sandy Bay to command the narrow neck of land that connected the peninsula with the left bank of the river.[116] It was proposed to construct palisades across the isthmus. Early on the morning of the 23d, Berkeley went out himself to direct the mounting of the guns.[117] But it was too late. On all sides the people were crying, "To arms! To arms! Bacon is within two miles of the town." The rebels were threatening, it was reported, that if a gun was fired against them, they would kill and destroy all.[118] Seeing that resistance would be useless, and might be fatal, the Governor ordered the guns to be dismounted, withdrew his soldiers, and retired to the state house.[119]

And so the rebels streamed unresisted into the town, a motley crew of many sorts and conditions: Rough, weather-beaten, determined frontiersmen, bent on having the commission for their leader; poor planters, sunk deep in debt, denouncing the government and demanding relief from their taxes; freedmen whose release from bondage had brought them little but hunger and nakedness. Moderation and reason were not to be expected of such a band, and it is not strange

[111] P. R. O., CO5-1371-381.
[112] P. R. O., CO5-1371-382.
[113] Mass. S. IV, Vol. IX, p. 171.
[114] P. R. O., CO1-37-17.
[115] P. R. O., CO1-37-16.
[116] P. R. O., CO1-37-17.
[117] Ibid.
[118] Ibid.
[119] Ibid.

that many of them talked openly of overthrowing the government and sharing the property of the rich among themselves. Sixteen years of oppression and injustice were bearing their natural fruit—rebellion.[120]

"Now tagg, ragg & bobtayle carry a high hand."[121] Bacon leaves a force to guard Sandy Bay, stations parties at the ferry and the fort, and draws up his little army before the state-house.[122] Two Councillors come out from Berkeley to demand what he wants. Bacon replies that he has come for a commission as general of volunteers enrolled against the Indians. And he protests that if the Assembly intends a levy for new forces, his men will refuse to pay it. The ragged troops shout their approval with cries of "Noe Levies! Noe Levies!"[123]

It is easy to imagine with what anger the Governor drew up and signed the commission. But he dared not refuse it. He was in the power of the rebels, who were already muttering threats of bloodshed and pillage. To defy them might bring instant ruin.[124] When the commission was brought out, and Bacon had read it to his soldiers, he refused to accept it, declaring the powers granted insufficient. Thereupon he drew up the heads of a new paper, in which his loyalty to the king and the legality of his past actions were attested, and an appointment given him as general of all the forces in Virginia used in the Indian war.[125]

These new demands throw the old Governor into an uncontrollable rage. He rushes out to Bacon, gesticulating wildly, and declaring that rather than sign such a paper he will have his hands cut off.[126] In his excitement he opens his bosom, crying out, "Here, shoot me, fore God fair mark."[127] Then he offers to measure swords with the rebel before all his men, shouting, "Let us settle this difference singly between ourselves."[128] But Bacon ignores these ravings. "Sir," he says, "I come not nor intend to hurt a haire of your Honors head.

[120] P. R. O., CO1-37-16.
[121] P. R. O., CO1-37-17.
[122] P. R. O., CO1-37-16, 17; T. M., p. 16.
[123] P. R. O., CO1-37-17.
[124] P. R. O., CO1-37-16.
[125] Ibid.
[126] P. R. O., CO1-37-16.
[127] P. R. O., CO5-1371-382.
[128] P. R. O., CO1-37-16.

And for your sword, your Honor may please to put it up, it will rust in the scabbard before ever I shall desire you to draw it. I come for a commission against the Heathen who daily inhumanly murder us and spill our bretherens blood."[129]

In the general distraction somebody takes the proposals to the Burgesses, now sitting in an upper chamber of the state house. Bacon struts impatiently below, muttering threats and "new coyned oathes".[130] At a window of the Assembly room are a number of faces, looking out on the exciting scenes below. Bacon calls up to them, "You Burgesses, I expect your speedy result." His soldiers shout, "We will have it, we will have it." At a command from Bacon the rebels cock their fusils, and take aim at the crowded window. "For God's sake hold your hands," cry the Burgesses, "forbear a little and you shall have what you please."[131] And now there is wild excitement, confusion and hurrying to and fro. From all sides the Governor is pressed to grant the commission in Bacon's own terms. At last he yields, and the paper is signed.

But new humiliation awaited him. The next morning Bacon entered the House of Burgesses with an armed guard, demanding that certain persons active in obeying the Governor's orders should be deprived of all offices, and that recent letters to the King denouncing him as a rebel should be publicly contradicted. When Berkeley heard of these demands, he swore he would rather suffer death than submit to them. But the Burgesses, who thought it not unlikely that they might soon have their throats cut, advised him to grant whatever was demanded.[132] So a letter was written to the King, and signed by the Governor, the Council and the Burgesses, expressing confidence in Bacon's loyalty and justifying his past actions.[133] Several of Berkeley's friends were committed to

[129] P. R. O., CO5-1371-382. [130] P. R. O., CO1-37-16.

[131] P. R. O., CO5-1371-382. In the various accounts left us of these scenes there is usually agreement upon the essential points. But in details and the sequence of events there is much discrepancy. The author has endeavored to present the facts in accordance with the greatest weight of evidence.

[132] P. R. O., CO1-37-16, 17.

[133] P. R. O., CO5-1371-383; CO1-37-15.1.

prison. Blank commissions for officers to command under Bacon in the Indian war were presented for signature. The Governor granted all, "as long as they concerned not life and limb", being "willing to be ridd of him". The Assembly finished its session, and thinking to appease the rebels, sent their laws out to be read before them. But they rose up like a swarm of bees, and swore they would have no laws.[134] Yet the legislation of this session was exceedingly liberal. The elections had been held at a time when the people were bitterly angry with the Governor and disgusted with the old régime. In several counties popular candidates, men bent upon reform, had been elected over Berkeley's friends.[135] These men, aided by the menacing attitude of the people, had initiated a series of bills designed to restrict the Governor's power and to restore to the commons their rightful share in local government. But it was probably the presence of Bacon with his ragged troops at Jamestown that brought about the final passage of the bills. The Governor and the Council would hardly have given their consent, had they not been forced to do so at the sword's point.

Indeed these laws aimed a telling blow at the aristocratic cliques that had so long controlled all local government. It was to be illegal in the future, for any man to serve as sheriff for two consecutive terms.[136] Surveyors, escheators, clerks of the court and sheriffs should hold only one office at a time.[137] The self-perpetuating vestries which had long controlled the parishes and levied church taxes, were to give place to bodies elected tri-annually by the freemen.[138] An act was passed restricting the power of the county courts. For the future the people were to elect representatives, equal in number with the justices, to sit with them, and have a voice "in laying the countie assessments, and of making wholesome lawes".[139] Councillors were no longer to be exempt from taxation. The act of 1670, restricting the right to vote for Burgesses to freeholders was abolished, and the franchise

[134] P. R. O., CO1-37-16.
[135] P. R. O., CO5-1371-379.
[136] Hen., Vol. II, p. 353.
[137] Hen., Vol. II, p. 354.
[138] Hen., Vol. II, p. 359.
[139] Hen., Vol. II, p. 357.

extended to all freemen.[140] And since "the frequent false returns" of elections had "caused great disturbances", it was enacted that any sheriff found guilty of this crime should be fined twenty thousand pounds of tobacco.[141]

Hardly had the Assembly closed its session when the news was received that the Indians were again on the war-path, having killed eight persons in the upper counties. This caused great alarm in the rebel army, and Bacon found it necessary the next day to lead them back to the frontier that they might guard their homes and families.[142]

Here active preparations were made for a new expedition against the savages. Now that Bacon had a commission signed by the Governor and confirmed with the public seal, men were quite eager to follow him. On all sides volunteers flocked in to offer their services against the brutal enemy. Even Councillors and Burgesses encouraged their neighbors to enlist, declaring that no exception could be taken to the legality of the commission.[143] Thus hundreds swallowed "down so fair a Bait, not seeing Rebellion at the end of it".[144]

In the meanwhile, the Governor, angered at the great indignities put upon him, was planning to regain his lost authority. A petition was drawn up in Gloucester county by Sir William's friends, denouncing Bacon, and asking that forces be raised to suppress him.[145] Although most of the Gloucestermen, it would seem, had no part in this request, Berkeley crossed over the York River to their county and began to enlist volunteers.[146] But he met with little success. Even in this part of the colony Bacon was the popular hero, and men refused to serve against him. It seemed outrageous to many that while he was out to fight the common enemy, the Governor should attack him in the rear. All his desperate efforts were in vain. Sick at heart and exhausted from exertions too great for his age, he is said to have fainted away in the saddle.[147]

The news that Berkeley was raising forces reached Bacon

[140] Hen., Vol. II, p. 356.
[141] Ibid.
[142] P. R. O., CO1-37-16.
[143] CO5-1371-384, 385.
[144] P. R. O., CO5-1371-383.
[145] Mass. S. IV, Vol. IX, p. 181.
[146] P. R. O., CO5-1371-385.
[147] P. R. O., CO5-1371-387; T. M., p. 20.

at the falls of James River, just as he was going to strike out into the woods. "Immediately he causes the Drums to Beat and Trumpets to sound for calling his men to-gether."[148]. "Gentlemen and Fellow Soldiers," he says, when they are assembled, "the news just now brought me, may not a little startle you as well as myselfe. But seeing it is not altogether unexpected, wee may the better beare it and provide our remedies. The Governour is now in Gloster County endeavouring to raise forces against us, having declared us Rebells and Traytors. . . . It is Revenge that hurries them on without regard to the Peoples safety. (They) had rather wee should be Murder'd and our Ghosts sent to our slaughter'd Country-men by their actings, then wee live to hinder them of their Interest with the Heathen. . . . Now then wee must be forced to turne our Swords to our own Defence, or expose ourselves to their Mercyes. . . . Let us descend to know the reasons why such a proceedings are used against us . . . (why) those whome they have raised for their Defence, to preserve them against the Fury of the Heathen, they should thus seek to Destroy. (Was there) ever such a Theachery . . . heard of, such Wickednesse and inhumanity? But they are damned Cowards, and you shall see they will not dare to meet us in the field to try the Justnesse of our Cause."[149]

Whereupon the soldiers all cried, "Amen. Amen." They were ready to follow him. They would rather die fighting than be hanged like rogues. It would be better to attack the Governor at once than have him come upon their rear while they were engaged in the woods with the savages.[150] And so, with universal acclaim, they gathered up their arms, and set out to give battle to the Governor.

But Berkeley had fled. Upon finding that the militia of Gloucester and Middlesex would not support him, he had taken ship for the Eastern Shore. Here, for the time being, he was safe from the angry rebels. It would be difficult for Bacon to secure vessels enough to transport his men over to Accomac; to march them hundreds of miles around the head of Chesapeake Bay was out of the question.

[148] P. R. O., CO5-1371-385.
[149] P. R. O., CO5-1371-385.
[150] P. R. O., CO5-1371-386.

The flight of the Governor left Bacon undisputed master of all the mainland of Virginia. Everywhere he was hailed by the people as their hero and deliverer. Those that still remained loyal to Sir William either fled with him or rendered their submission to the rebel. For a while, at least, he could prosecute the Indian war and redress the public grievances without fear of interruption.[151]

But now Bacon was confronted with the question of what attitude he should assume to the English government. Berkeley had written home denouncing him as a rebel and traitor. The King assuredly would not tolerate his conduct. No doubt preparations were already being made to send British troops to the colony. Should he defy the King and resist his soldiers in the field of battle?

Bacon made up his mind to fight. The dense woods, the many swamps and creeks, the vast distances of the colony would all be favorable to him. He would resort to the Indian method of fighting. His men were as brave as the British; were better marksmen. Five hundred Virginians, he was sure, would be a match for two thousand red coats. If England sought to bring him to his knees, by blockading the coast and cutting off all foreign trade, he would appeal to the Dutch or even to the French for assistance. Assuredly these nations would not neglect so favorable an opportunity of injuring their old rival and enemy. He even cherished a wild dream of leading his rebels back into the woods, to establish a colony upon an island in the Roanoke river.[152]

But Bacon knew that the people would hesitate to follow him into open resistance to England. Ties of blood, of religion, of interest were too strong. All the injustice done them by the King, all the oppression of the Navigation Acts, could not make them forget that they were Englishmen. So he found it necessary to deceive them with a pretence of loyalty. He himself took the oath of allegiance and supremacy, and he imposed it upon all his followers. His commands were issued in the King's name. He even went to the absurd extremity of

[151] P. R. O., CO5-1371-387.

[152] P. R. O., CO5-1371-232-240; CO1-39-38.

declaring it for the service of the Crown to disobey the King's commands, to arrest the King's Governor, to fight the King's troops.[153]

Realizing that resistance to his plans would come almost entirely from the upper classes, Bacon made especial efforts to seduce the wealthy planters. On August the third, a number of influential gentlemen assembled upon his summons at Middle Plantation, to discuss the means of protecting the people from the Indians, and preventing civil war. After delivering a long harangue, justifying his own actions and denouncing the Governor, Bacon requested the entire company to take three oaths which he had prepared. First, they were to promise to assist him in prosecuting the Indian war. Secondly, they must combat all attempts of the Governor and his friends to raise troops against him. Thirdly, they were asked to declare it consistent with their allegiance to the King to resist the royal troops until his Majesty could be informed by letter from Bacon of the justice of his cause.[154] This last article caused prolonged and bitter controversy. But Bacon locked the doors, it is said, and by persuasion and threats induced them all to sign. The three oaths were taken by no less than sixty-nine prominent men, among them Thomas Swann, Thomas Milner, Philip Lightfoot and Thomas Ballard.[155]

Bacon now felt himself strong enough to take active control of the administration of the government. He did not assume, however, the title of Governor, but styled himself "General by the consent of the people".[156] Nor did he venture to proceed in the alteration of laws or the redress of grievances without the advice and support of the representatives of the people. In conjunction with four members of the Council, he issued orders for an immediate election of a new Assembly, to meet on the fourth of September, at Jamestown.[157]

Having settled these matters, Bacon turned his attention to two military expeditions—one against the Indians, the other

[153] P. R. O., CO1-37-41.

[154] P. R. O., CO1-37-42.

[155] Ibid.

[156] P. R. O., CO1-37-41.

[157] P. R. O., CO1-37-43.

against the Governor. The continued activity of the savages and the exposed condition of the frontier demanded his personal attention, but he was resolved not to leave the lower counties exposed during his absence to attack from the Eastern Shore. Seizing an English ship, commanded by a Captain Larrimore, which was lying in James River, he impressed her, with all her crew, into his service against the Governor. In this vessel, with a sloop and a bark of four guns, he embarked a force of two hundred or more men.[158] The expedition was placed under the command of Captain William Carver, "a valiant, stout Seaman", and Gyles Bland, both devoted to Bacon's cause and high in his favor. They were ordered to patrol the coast to prevent raids upon the Western Shore, and, if possible, to attack and capture the Governor.

Bacon himself hastens to Henrico, "where he bestirs himself lustily in order to a Speedy March against the Indians". It was his intention to renew his attack upon the Occaneechees and the Susquehannocks, but for some reason he gave up this design to turn against the Pamunkeys. Hastening across from the James to the York, Bacon met Colonel Gyles Brent, who brought with him reinforcements from the plantations upon the upper waters of the Rappahannock and Potomac. Their united forces marched to the extreme frontier and plunged into the wilderness. Discovering a narrow path running through the forest, the English followed it to a small Pamunkey village situated upon a neck of land between two swamps. As Bacon's Indian scouts advanced upon the place they were fired upon by the enemy. Whereupon the English came running up to assault the village. But the Pamunkeys deserted their cabins and fled into the adjacent swamps, where the white men found it impossible to pursue them. All made good their escape except one woman and one little child.[159]

Continuing his march, Bacon stumbled upon an old squaw, the nurse of the Pamunkey queen, whom he ordered to act as his guide. But the woman, unwilling to betray her people, led him far astray, many miles from the Indian settlements. The

[158] P. R. O., CO5-1371-388; Burk, Vol. II, p. 271.
[159] P. R. O., CO5-1371-390.

English followed her "the remainder of that day & almost another day" before they discovered that they were being deceived. When sure of her treachery, "Bacon gave command to his soldiers to knock her on the head, which they did, and left her dead on the way".[160] The army now wandered around at random in the woods, following first one path and then another, but could not discover the enemy. The appointed time for the new Assembly was approaching, and it was imperative for Bacon to be at Jamestown to open the session. He was resolved, however, not to return to the colony until he had struck a decisive blow at the Indians. Sending a message to the people "that he would be with them with all possible speed", he resumed his discouraging quest.[161]

But the Indians still eluded him. It seemed a hopeless task to discover their villages amid the dense woods and treacherous swamps. His men became discouraged. "Tyred, murmuring, impatient, hunger-starv'd", many begged him to lead them back to the plantations. But Bacon would not abandon the expedition. He would rather die in the woods, he said, than disappoint the confidence reposed in him by the people. Those that felt it necessary to return home, he would permit to depart unmolested. But for himself, he was resolved to continue the march even though it became necessary to exist upon chincapins and horse flesh.[162] Whereupon the army was divided, one part setting out for the colony, the other resuming the search for the savages.

That very day Bacon runs upon the main camp of the Pamunkeys and immediately attacks them. The savages are encamped upon a "piece of Champion land", protected on three sides by swamps, and covered with a dense growth of "small oke, saplings, Chinkapin-Bushes and grape vines". As the English charge in among them they offer little resistance, but desert their habitations and flee. Some are shot down, many are captured. Bacon takes possession of all their goods—"Indian matts, Basketts, Match cotes, parcells of Wampameag and Roanoke, Baggs, Skins, ffurs", etc.

[160] P. R. O., CO5-1371-391.
[161] P. R. O., CO5-1371-392.
[162] P. R. O., CO5-1371-392.

The poor queen fled for her life with one little boy, and wandered fourteen days in the woods, separated from her people. "She was once coming back with designe to throw herself upon the mercy of the English", but "happened to meet with a deade Indian woman lying in the way, . . . which struck such terror in the Queen that fearing their cruelty by that ghastly example, shee went on . . . into the wild woodes". Here she was preserved from starvation by eating part of a terrapin, found by the little boy.[163] After this victory, Bacon secured his plunder and his captives, and hastened back to the plantations.

In the meanwhile the expedition against Accomac had ended in disastrous failure.[164] Carver and Bland had been given instructions to capture the Governor, and Bacon proposed, if ever he got him in his power, to send him to England, there to stand trial for his misgovernment and his betrayal of the people to the barbarous Indians.[165] Even though it was quite probable that the King would send him back, the colony would for a time be rid of his troublesome presence.

Upon the arrival of the little fleet off the coast of Accomac, it was decided to send Carver ashore under a flag of truce, to treat with the Governor.[166] Leaving Bland to guard the fleet with a force not superior in number to the English sailors, Carver set out in the sloop "with the most trusty of his men".[167] In the meanwhile Captain Larrimore and his sailors, who resented their enforced service with the rebels, were plotting to betray them to the enemy. In some way Larrimore contrived to get a message to Berkeley, requesting him to send out a party of loyal gentlemen in boats, and promising to deliver his ship into their hands.[168] The Governor at first was loath to venture upon such a hazardous undertaking.[169] The whole thing might be a snare to entrap his men. Yet his situation was desperate; he must take desperate chances.

[163] P. R. O., CO5-1371-393.
[164] P. R. O., CO5-1371-393.
[165] P. R. O., CO5-1371-394.
[166] Ibid.
[167] T. M., p. 22.
[168] P. R. O., CO5-1371-394; Burk, Vol. II, p. 271.
[169] Burk, Vol. II, p. 271.

Placing a party of twenty-six men in two small boats, he sent them out under the command of Colonel Philip Ludwell, to surprise the ship.[170] Fearing that Carver might return before the capture could be effected, Berkeley "caressed him with wine", and detained him with prolonged negotiations. Upon reaching the ship, Ludwell and his men rowed up close under her side, and clambered in at "the gun room ports". "One courageous gentleman ran up to the deck, and clapt a pistoll to Bland's breast, saying you are my prisoner."[171] The rest of the company followed upon his heels, brandishing their pistols and swords. Captain Larrimore and his crew caught up spikes, which they had ready at hand, and rushed to Ludwell's assistance. The rebels, taken utterly by surprise, many no doubt without arms, "were amazed and yielded".[172]

A short while after, Carver was seen returning in the sloop from his interview with the Governor. "They permit the boat to come soe neere as they might ffire directly downe upon her, and soe they alsoe commanded Carver on Board & secured him. When hee saw this surprize he stormed, tore his haire off, and curst, and exclaimed at the Cowardize of Bland that had betrayed and lost all their designe."[173] Not long after he was tried for treason by court martial, condemned, and hanged.[174]

Elated by this unexpected success, the Governor determined to make one more effort to regain his lost authority. The rebels were now without a navy; they could not oppose him upon the water, or prevent his landing upon the Western Shore. With the gentlemen that had remained loyal to him, the troops of Accomac, many runaway servants and English sailors he was able to raise a force of several hundred men.[175] Embarking them in Captain Larrimore's ship, in the *Adam and Eve,* and sixteen or seventeen sloops, he set sail for Jamestown.[176]

[170] Ibid.

[171] T. M., p. 22.

[172] T. M., p. 22.

[173] P. R. O., CO5-1371-394.

[174] T. M., p. 23; P. R. O., CO5-1371-52, 54.

[175] The account of the King's commissioners places the number at six hundred; in Bacon's Proceedings it is given as one thousand.

[176] P. R. O., CO5-1371-394; Bac's Pros., p. 21.

In the meanwhile the appointed date for the convening of the Assembly had come. It is probable that the members were arriving to take their seats when the news of the Governor's approach reached the town.[177] Bacon was still absent upon the Pamunkey expedition. There seems to have been no one present capable of inspiring the rebels with confidence, or of leading them in a vigorous defense. When the sails of the Governor's fleet were seen, on the seventh of September, wending their way up the river, the place was thrown into the wildest confusion. Sir William sent a message ashore, offering a pardon to all, with the exception of Lawrence and Drummond, that would lay down their arms and return to their allegiance.[178] But few seem to have trusted him, "feareing to meet with some afterclaps of revenge".[179] That night, before the place could be fully invested, the rebels fled, "every one shifting for himselfe with no ordnary feare".[180] "Collonell Larence . . . forsooke his owne howse with all his wealth and a faire cupbord of plate entire standing, which fell into the Governour's hands the next morning."[181]

This was the unwelcome news which greeted Bacon upon his return from the Indian expedition. So many of his soldiers had left for their homes before the final defeat of the Pamunkeys, that he now had with him less than one hundred and fifty men.[182] Yet he resolved to march at once upon Jamestown to attack the Governor. His little band gave him enthusiastic assurance of loyal support. He knew that he had the well wishes and prayers of the people, while his opponents were "loaded with their curses". Berkeley's men, although so much more numerous than his own, he believed to be cowards that would not dare appear against him in the field. Victory would be easy and decisive.[183]

So, after delaying a short while to gather reinforcements from New Kent and Henrico, he marched with extraordinary swiftness down upon the enemy.[184] Everywhere along the

[177] Bac's Pros., p. 22.
[178] Bac's Pros., p. 22.
[179] Bac's Pros., p. 22.
[180] Bac's Pros., p. 22.
[181] Bac's Pros., p. 22.
[182] P. R. O., CO5-1371-394.
[183] P. R. O., CO5-1371-395.
[184] P. R. O., CO5-1371-395.

route he was hailed by the people as their deliverer. The sight of the sullen Indian captives that he led along with him "as in a Shew of Triumph", caused enthusiastic rejoicing. Many brought forth fruit and other food to refresh his weary soldiers. The women swore that if he had not men enough to defeat the Governor, they themselves would take arms and follow him. All prayed for his success and happiness, and exclaimed against the injustice of his enemies.[185]

Before Berkeley had been in possession of Jamestown one week, Bacon was upon him. On the evening of September the thirteenth, the little rebel band arrived at Sandy Bay, driving before them a party of the Governor's horse.[186] With singular bravado, Bacon himself rode up to the enemy, fired his carbine at them, and commanded his trumpets to sound their defiance.[187] Few thought, however, he would attempt to capture the town, for the Governor's position was very strong. The narrow isthmus, by which alone the place could be approached, was defended by three heavy guns planted behind strong palisades.[188] Upon the left, "almost close aborde the shore, lay the ships, with their broadesides to thunder" upon any that dared to assault the works. The loyal forces had recently been augmented to a thousand men, and now outnumbered the rebels three to one. Yet Bacon seems to have meditated from the first an attack upon the place, and was confident of success.[189]

Although his men had marched many miles that day he set them immediately to work within gun-shot of the enemy, building an entrenched camp.[190] All night long, by the light of the moon, the soldiers toiled, cutting bushes, felling trees and throwing up earthworks. But it soon became apparent that their utmost efforts would not suffice to complete the trenches before dawn, when the enemy's guns would be sure to open upon them. In this dilemma, Bacon hit upon a most unmanly expedient to protect his men at their work. Sending out several small parties of horse, he captured a number of ladies, the

[185] P. R. O., CO5-1371-395.
[186] P. R. O., CO5-1371-396.
[187] P. R. O., CO5-1371-397, 400.
[188] Bac's Pros., p. 24.
[189] Bac's Pros., p. 24.
[190] P. R. O., CO5-1371-396.

wives of some of Berkeley's most prominent supporters. "Which the next morning he presents to the view of there husbands and ffriends in towne, upon the top of the smalle worke hee had cast up in the night, where he caused them to tarey till hee had finished his defence."[191] The husbands were enraged that the rebels should thus hide behind the "white aprons" of their innocent wives, but they dared not make an assault.

When, however, the ladies were removed, "upon a Signall given from ye Towne the Shipps fire their Great Guns and at the same tyme they let fly their small-Shott from the Palaisadoes. But that small Sconse that Bacon had caused to be made in the night, of Trees, Bruch, and Earth soe defended them that the Shott did them noe damage at all, and was returned back as fast from the little Fortresse."[192]

Fearing that this cannonade will be followed by an assault upon his works, Bacon places a lookout on the top of a near-by brick chimney, which commands a view of the peninsula. On the sixteenth, the watchman announces that the enemy are preparing for an assault, and the rebels make ready to give them a warm reception. The Governor's forces, six or seven hundred strong, dash across the Sandy Bay, in an attempt to storm Bacon's redoubts.[193] Horse and foot "come up with a narrow front, pressing very close upon one another's shoulders". But many of them fight only from compulsion, and have no heart for their task. At the first volleys of shot that pour in upon them from the rebel army, they throw down their arms and flee. They marched out, as one chronicler says, "like scholars going to school . . . with heavy hearts, but returned hom with light heels".[194] Their officers were powerless to stem the rout, until they were safe under the protection of the palisades.[195]

[191] Cotton, p. 8; Bac's Pros., p. 24. The report of the commissioners places this incident some days later, after the assault of the 15th. The author has followed the account given in Bacon's Proceedings, which seems to him probably more correct. Bacon could have no object in exposing the ladies after his trenches were completed, his heavy guns mounted and the enemy defeated.

[192] P. R. O., CO5-1371-397.

[193] Bac's Pros., p. 25.

[194] Bac's Pros., p. 25.

[195] P. R. O., CO5-1371-398, 400.

The Governor's losses in dead and wounded were very small, but the moral effect of his defeat was great. The rebels were so elated at their easy victory, and so scornful of their cowardly opponents, "that Bacon could scarce keep them from immediately falling to storm and enter the Towne".[196] On the other hand, the loyal troops were utterly discouraged. Many of them, that had been "compelled or hired into the Service", and "were intent only on plunder", clamored for the desertion of the place, fearing that the victorious rebels would soon burst in upon them.[197]

"The next day Bacon orders 3 grate guns to be brought into the camp, two whereof he plants upon his trench. The one he sets to worke against the Ships, the other against the entrance into the towne, for to open a pasage to his intended storm."[198] Had the rebels delayed no longer to make an assault it seems certain they could have carried the palisades with ease, taken many of the enemy, and perhaps captured the Governor himself. The loyal soldiers were thinking only of flight. "Soe great was the Cowardize and Basenesse of the generality of Sir William Berkeley's party that of all at last there were only some 20 Gentlemen willing to stand by him." So that the Governor, "who undoubtedly would rather have dyed on the Place than thus deserted it, what with (the) importunate and resistless solicitations of all was at last over persuaded, nay hurried away against his will".[199] "Takeing along with him all the towne people, and their goods, leaveing all the grate guns naled up, and the howses emty", he left the place a prey to the rebels.[200] "So fearful of discovery they are, that for Secrecy they imbarque and weigh anchor in the Night and silently fall down the river."[201]

Early the next morning Bacon marched across the Sandy Bay and took possession of the deserted town.[202] Here he learned that the Governor had not continued his flight, but had cast anchor twenty miles below, where he was awaiting

[196] P. R. O., CO5-1371-400.
[197] Ibid.
[198] Bac's Pros., p. 25.
[199] P. R. O., CO5-1371-400.
[200] Bac's Pros., p. 26.
[201] P. R. O., CO5-1371-400.
[202] P. R. O., CO5-1371-401; Bac's Pros., p. 26.

a favorable opportunity to recapture the place.[203] At the same time, news came from the north that Colonel Brent, Bacon's former ally, was collecting troops in the counties bordering upon the Potomac River, and would soon be on the march to the Governor's assistance, with no less than a thousand men.[204] Should this new army, by acting in concert with the fleet, succeed in blocking Bacon up at Jamestown, the rebels would be caught in a fatal trap. The peninsula could hardly be defended successfully against superior forces by land and water, and they would be crushed between the upper and nether millstones. On the other hand, should they desert the town, in order to go out against Brent, Berkeley would undoubtedly return to take possession of it, and all the fruits of their victory would be lost.

After long consultation with his chief advisors, Bacon decided to destroy the town.[205] That very night he set fire to the place, which in a few hours was reduced to ashes. Not even the state-house, or the old church were spared. Drummond and Lawrence, it is said, showed their unselfish zeal for the cause by applying the torch to their homes with their own hands.[206] As the Governor, from his ships, saw in the distance the glare of the burning buildings, he cursed the cowardice of his soldiers that had forced him to yield the place to the rebels. But as it could now serve him no longer as a base, he weighed anchor, and set sail for Accomac.[207]

Deserting the ruined town, Bacon led his men north to Green Spring, and thence across York River into Gloucester county. Here there came to him a messenger riding "post haste from Rapahanock, with news that Coll: Brent was advancing fast upon him".[208] At once he summons his soldiers around him, tells them the alarming news, and asks if they are ready to fight. The soldiers answer "with showtes and acclamations while the drums thunder a march to meet the promised conflict".[209]

[203] Bac's Pros., p. 26.
[204] Bac's Pros., p. 26.
[205] P. R. O., CO5-1371-401.
[206] P. R. O., CO5-1371-405.
[207] P. R. O., CO5-1371-401; CO1-39-22; Bac's Pros., p. 26.
[208] Bac's Pros., p. 26.
[209] Bac's Pros., p. 26.

Bacon had advanced not "above 2 or 3 days jurney, but he meets newes . . . that Brents men were all run away, and left him to shift for himselfe".[210] Like the troops that had so signally failed of their duty in the battle of Sandy Bay, these northern forces had no desire to meet Bacon. Many of them were undoubtedly pressed into service; many were in sympathy with the rebellion. At all events they deserted their leaders before the hostile army came in sight, and fled back to their homes.

Thus Bacon once more found himself master of all the mainland of Virginia. But his situation was more critical than it had been in July and August. Many of the prominent gentlemen that had then given him their support, and had taken his three oaths, were now fighting on the side of the Governor. It was quite certain that royal forces were being equipped for an expedition to Virginia, and might make their appearance within the capes before many more weeks. Moreover, the disastrous failure of Carver and Bland had left him without a navy and exposed all the Western Shore to attack from the loyal forces in Accomac.

Realizing his danger, Bacon felt it necessary to bind the people to him more closely. Summoning the militia of Gloucester to meet him at their county court-house, he delivered a long harangue before them and tendered them an oath of fidelity. They were asked to swear that if the King's troops attempted to land by force, they would "fly to-gether as in a common calamity, and jointly with the present Army . . . stand or fall in the defense of . . . the Country". And "in Case of utmost Extremity rather then submitt to so miserable a Slavery (when none can longer defend ourselves, our Lives and Liberty's) to acquit the Colony.[211]

The Gloucestermen were most reluctant to take this oath. A Mr. Cole, speaking for them all, told Bacon that it was their desire to remain neutral in this unhappy civil war. But the rebel replied that if they would not be his friends, they must be his enemies. They should not be idle and reap the benefit of liberty earned by the blood of others. A minister, named

[210] Bac's Pros., p. 26.

[211] P. R. O., CO5-1371-402.

Wading, who was active in persuading the men to refuse the oath, was committed to prison by Bacon, with the warning that the church was the proper place for him to preach, not the camp. Later, it seems, fearing the consequences of further refusal, the Gloucester troops yielded and took the binding engagement.[212]

Bacon now turned his thoughts, it is said, to an expedition against Accomac. But his preparations were never completed. For some time he had been ill of dysentery and now was "not able to hould out any longer".[213] He was cared for at the house of a Mr. Pate, in Gloucester county, but his condition soon became worse.[214] His mind, probably wandering in delirium, dwelt upon the perils of his situation. Often he would enquire if the guard around the house was strong, or whether the King's troops had arrived. Death came before the end of October.[215] Bacon's place of burial has never been discovered. It is supposed that Lawrence, to save the body of his friend from mutilation by the vindictive old Governor, weighted the coffin with stones and sunk it in the deep waters of the York.[216]

The death of Bacon proved an irreparable loss to the rebels. It was impossible for them to find another leader of his undaunted resolution, his executive ability, his power of command. No one could replace him in the affections of the common people. It would not be correct to attribute the failure of the rebellion entirely to the death of this one man, yet it undoubtedly hastened the end. Had he continued at the head of his faithful army, he might have kept the Governor indefinitely in exile upon the Eastern Shore, or even have driven him to take refuge upon the water. In the end Bacon would have been conquered, for he could not have held out against the English fleet and the English troops. But he would have made a desperate and heroic resistance.

The chief command fell to Lieutenant-General Ingram.

[212] P. R. O., CO5-1371-401; Bac's Pros., p. 27.

[213] Bac's Pros., p. 28.

[214] P. R. O., CO5-1371-404.

[215] Bacon's Proceedings places the death of Bacon on Oct. 18; the Commissioners give the date as Oct. 26.

[216] T. M., p. 24.

The selection seems to have been popular with the soldiers, for when it was announced, they "threw up their caps, crying out as loud as they could bellow, God save our new Generall".[217] Ingram is depicted by some of the chroniclers as a man of low birth, a dandy and a fool, but there is reason to believe their impeachment too harsh. Although he lacked Bacon's force of character and had no executive ability, as a general he showed considerable talent, and more than held his own against the Governor.

The mastery of the water was an advantage to Berkeley of the very greatest importance. The numerous deep rivers running far up into the country made it easy for him to deliver swift, telling blows at any point in the enemy's position. In order to guard the James, the York and the Rappahannock it became necessary for the rebels to divide their forces into several small bands. On the other hand, the entire strength of the loyalists could be concentrated at any time for an unexpected attack.

Ingram made his chief base at West Point, where the Mattapony and the Pamunkey unite to form the broad and stately York.[218] Here he could watch both banks of the river, and could concentrate his men quickly either upon the Peninsula, or in Gloucester or Middlesex. At this place were gathered several hundred rebels under Ingram himself. But it was deemed wise to leave other detachments at various places lower down in the country, to prevent the enemy from landing, and to suppress any rising of the people in favor of the Governor. At the house of Colonel Bacon, in York county, a force of thirty or forty men were posted under the command of Major Whaly.[219] "The next Parcell, considerable, was at Green Spring, the Governours howse, into which was put about 100 men and boys." Their leader, a Colonel Drew, fortified the place strongly, barricading all approaches, and planting three large guns "to beate of the Assailants". Another small detachment, under Colonel Hansford, was posted "at the Howse where Coll: Reade did once live", the site of famous old Yorktown.[220]

[217] Ing's Pros., p. 32.

[218] Ing's Pros., p. 39.

[219] Ing's Pros., p. 40.

[220] Ing's Pros., p. 39.

This last post, situated near the mouth of the river, was especially exposed to attack from the Eastern Shore. A few days after the death of Bacon, Major Robert Beverley, with a small force, sailed across the bay to effect its capture.[221] The rebels "kep a negligent Gard", and were caught completely by surprise. Hansford was taken prisoner, with twenty of his men, and brought in triumph to Accomac.

Here he was at once charged with treason, tried by court martial, and condemned to die. He pleaded passionately to "be shot like a soldier and not to be hanged like a Dog. But it was tould him . . . that he was not condemned as he was merely a soldier, but as a Rebell, taken in Arms."[222] To the last he refused to admit that he was guilty of treason. To the crowd that gathered around the scaffold to witness his execution he protested "that he dyed a loyal subject and a lover of his country".

"This business being so well accomplish'd by those who had taken Hansford, . . . they had no sooner deliver'd there Fraight at Accomack, but they hoyse up there sayles, and back againe to Yorke River, where with a Marvellous celerity they surprise one Major Cheise-Man, and som others, amongst whom one Capt. Wilford, who (it is saide) in the bickering lost one of his eyes, which he seemed little concern'd at, as knowing that when he came to Accomack, that though he had bin starke blinde, yet the Governour would take care for to afford him a guide, that should show him the way to the Gallows."[223]

The Governor was resolved to make the rebel leaders pay dearly for the indignities they had put upon him. Those that were so luckless as to fall into his hands, were hastened away to their execution with but the mockery of a trial. Doubtless Berkeley felt himself justified in this severity. To him rebellion against the King was not merely a crime, it was a hideous sacrilege. Those guilty of such an enormity should receive no mercy. But this cannot explain or excuse the coarse

[221] The news of Hansford's capture reached Captain Morris near Nansemond Nov. 12th.

[222] Ing's Pros., p. 33.

[223] Ing's Pros., p. 35.

brutality and savage joy with which he sent his victims to the scaffold. It is impossible not to feel that many of these executions were dictated, not by motives of policy or loyalty, but by vindictiveness.

Nothing can make this more evident that the pathetic story of Madam Cheesman. "When . . . the Major was brought in to the Governor's presence, and by him demanded, what made him to ingage in Bacon's designes? Before that the Major could frame an Answer . . . his Wife steps in and tould his honr: that it was her provocations that made her Husband joyne in the Cause that Bacon contended for; ading, that if he had not bin influenced by her instigations, he had never don that which he had don. Therefore (upon her bended knees) she desires of his honr . . . that shee might be hang'd, and he pardon'd. Though the Governour did know, that that what she had saide, was neare to the truth," he refused her request and spurned her with a vile insult. It is with a sense of relief that we learn that her husband died in prison and was thus saved the ignominy of the gallows.[224]

Encouraged by his successes, Berkeley now planned a more formidable invasion of the Western Shore. Public sentiment, he hoped, was beginning to turn in his favor. The death of Bacon had deprived the rebellion of all coherency and definiteness of purpose. The country was getting weary of the struggle, and was anxious for the reëstablishment of law and order. In Gloucester and Middlesex especially there were many prominent planters that awaited an opportunity to take up arms against the rebels. And although the common people were indifferent to the Governor's cause, they would be forced to enlist under him could he but get a firm foothold in those counties.[225]

So he sailed into York River with a fleet of four ships and several sloops, and a force of one hundred soldiers.[226] Landing a party, under command of Major Robert Beverley, upon the north bank, he surprised and captured a number of the enemy at the residence of a Mr. Howard.[227] He then set up

[224] Ing's Pros., p. 36.

[225] Ing's Pros., p. 38.

[226] Ing's Pros., p. 38.

[227] Ing's Pros., p. 38.

his standard at the very house in which Bacon had died, and sent out summons to all loyal citizens to come to his support. Here there soon "appeared men enough to have beaten all the Rebells in the countrey, onely with their Axes and Hoes".[228] They were quickly organized into an army and placed under the command of Major Lawrence Smith.[229] Almost simultaneously the people of Middlesex began to take up arms in support of the Governor, and for a while it seemed that the rebels would be overwhelmed and driven back upon the frontiers.

But Ingram acted with vigor and promptness. He dispatched a body of horse, under Lientenant-General Walkelett, to attack and disperse the Middlesex troops before their numbers become formidable. With the main body of the rebels he himself remained at West Point, to watch the movements of the enemy in Gloucester. When Major Smith heard of Walkelett's advance, he at once hastened north to intercept him, leaving a garrison at Mr. Pate's house, to guard that post and maintain intact his communication with the fleet in York River. But he was not quick enough. Before he could complete his march, news came to him that Walkelett had dispersed the Middlesex troops and was preparing to give battle to him.[230]

In the meanwhile, Ingram, hearing that Smith had marched north, "by the advice of his officers strikes in betweene him and his new made Garrisson at M. Pates. He very nimbly invests the Howse", and forces its defenders to surrender. Hardly had he accomplished this task, "but M. L. Smith, having retracted his march out of Middlesex . . . was upon the back of Ingram before he was aware". This new move placed the rebels in no little peril, for the Gloucester forces were between them and their base at West Point. Defeat at this juncture would have meant utter destruction for Ingram's army.

As the two bands faced each other, "one Major Bristow (on Smith's side) made a Motion to try the equity, and justness of the quarrill, by single combett . . . proffering him-

[228] Ing's Pros., p. 40.
[229] Ing's Pros., p. 40.
[230] Ing's Pros., p. 40.

selfe against any one (being a Gent.) on the other side. . . . This motion was as redely accepted by Ingram, as proffered by Bristow; Ingram swaring, the newest oath in fashion, that he would be the Man; and so advanceth on foot, with sword and Pistell, against Bristow; but was fetched back by his owne men", who had no desire to risk their leader in this duel.[231]

But the Gloucester troops were not inspired to deeds of courage by the intrepidity of their champion. They had no desire to encounter the veterans that had defeated the Governor before Jamestown and twice hunted the savages out of their hidden lairs. Despite all the efforts of their officers they opened negotiations with Ingram and agreed to lay down their arms. No less than six hundred men, it is said, thus tamely surrendered to the rebels. Major Smith and some of his officers, when they found themselves betrayed by their men, fled and made good their escape. Other "chiefe men" fell into the enemy's hands and were held as prisoners of war. Ingram "dismist the rest to their own abodes".[232]

It was a part of the Governor's plan to secure a foothold also upon the right bank of the river and to drive the rebels out of York county. With this in view, he sent out one hundred and twenty men, under Captain Hubert Farrill, to surprise and capture the rebels commanded by Major Whaly, at Colonel Bacon's house. To advise and assist Farrill, Colonel Ludwell and Colonel Bacon himself accompanied the expedition. They decided to steal silently up to the place in the early hours of the morning before dawn, drive in the sentries and "enter pell mell with them into the howse". But their plans miscarried woefully. "The Centrey had no sooner made the challenge . . . who comes there? . . . but the other answer with their Musquits (which seldom speakes the language of friends) and that in so loud a maner, that it alarmed those in the howse to a defence, and then to a posture to salley out." The attacking party took refuge "behinde som out buildings, . . . giving the Bullits leave to grope their owne way in the dark". Here they stood their ground for a short while and then fled back to their boats. Several were

[231] Ing's Pros., p. 42.

[232] Ing's Pros., p. 42.

taken prisoners, but none were killed save Farrill himself, "whose commission was found droping-wett with blood, in his pockett".[233]

The failure of these operations in the York were partly offset by successes in the southern counties. Late in December a loyal force, consisting in part of English sailors, landed on the right bank of the James and defeated a party of the rebels, killing their leader and taking thirteen prisoners. Four days later, they captured one of the enemy's forts. Soon large parts of Isle of Wight and Surry had been overrun and the people reduced to their allegiance. During the first week of January several hundred rebels gathered upon the upper James to retrieve their waning cause, but they seem to have melted away without accomplishing anything, and at once all the south bank of the river submitted.[234]

Almost simultaneously in all other parts of the colony the rebellion collapsed. The defeats of the Governor in Gloucester, Middlesex and York had not long postponed the end. The failure of the movement was due, not to military successes by Berkeley, but to hopeless internal weakness. Since the death of Bacon the insurgent leaders had been unable to maintain law and order in the colony. Ingram, although he showed some ability as a general, proved utterly unfitted to assume control of civil affairs. Bacon, when Sir William fled to Accomac, had grasped firmly the reins of government, calling a part of the Council to his assistance, summoning a new Assembly, and retaining sheriffs and justices in their offices. Like Cromwell, he had shown himself not only a soldier, but a civil ruler of force and ability. But Ingram could not command the respect and obedience of the people. Under him the machinery of government seems to have broken down. The unhappy colony was given over to disorder and anarchy. We are inclined to wonder why Drummond or Lawrence did not assume the chief command in the government after Bacon's death. Both were men of intelligence and ability, both esteemed by the people, and both devoted heart and soul to the

[233] Ing's Pros., p. 43.
[234] P. R. O., CO5-1371-416; CO1-37-52; CO1-39-10.

rebellion. For some reason, neither could take the leadership, and affairs fell into hopeless confusion.

Without a government to supply their needs, or to direct their movements, the rebel bands found it necessary to maintain themselves by plundering the estates of the Governor's friends. Many wealthy planters paid for their loyalty with the loss of their cattle, their sheep, their corn and wheat, and often the very furniture of their houses. At times the rebel officers could not restrain their rough soldiers from wanton waste and destruction. Crops were ruined, fences thrown down, houses burned.[235] Disgusted with this anarchy, and seeing that Ingram could not preserve order, many of the people began to long for the end of the rebellion. Even the misgovernment of Berkeley was better than lawlessness and confusion.

Ingram himself seems to have perceived that the end was at hand. Intelligence came to him that some of his own party, dissatisfied with his conduct, were awaiting an opportunity to deprive him of the chief command. The long expected arrival of the English troops would bring swift and complete ruin, for under the present conditions, he could not hope for success against them. So he soon became quite willing "to dismount from the back of that horse which he wanted skill, and strength to Manidge". Could he but secure a pardon from the Governor, he would gladly desert the failing cause of the people, and return to his allegiance.[236]

Nor was Sir William less anxious to come to terms with Ingram. It had been a bitter humiliation to him to be thrust headlong out of his government by the rebellious people. It would add to his shame to be restored by English troops. Could he but reduce the colony before the arrival of the red coats, his position would appear in a much better light, both in Virginia and in England. So he sent a Captain Grantham to negotiate with Ingram and to offer him immunity and pardon in return for prompt submission. The rebel leader willingly accepted these terms and returned to his allegiance.[237]

[235] P. R. O., CO1-40-45.

[236] Ing's Pros., p. 45.

[237] Ing's Pros., p. 45; P. R. O., CO5-1371-416.

More delicate was the task of inducing the troops at West Point to follow the example of their general. It was a question whether Ingram, "or any in the countrye could command them to lay down their arms". An attempt to betray them, or to wring the sword out their hands by violence would probably end in failure. It was thought more prudent to subdue "these mad fellows" with "smoothe words", rather than by "rough deeds". So Grantham presented himself to them, told of Ingram's submission and offered them very liberal terms of surrender. They were to be paid for the full time of their service since the granting of Bacon's commission; those that so desired were to be retained in arms to fight the Indians; all servants among them were to secure immediate release from their indentures. Deserted by their leader and tempted by these fair promises, the men were at last persuaded to yield. Grantham embarked them on the fleet and took them down to Tindall's Point, there to make their submission and "kiss the Governour's hand".[238]

Almost at the same time overtures were made by the Governor to General Walkelett. Could this man be induced to surrender himself and his troops, the last great obstacle to peace would be removed. So anxious was Sir William to seduce him from the cause of the rebels, that he offered him not only his pardon, but part of the plunder taken by Bacon from the Indians.[239] Walkelett assented, and agreed to lead his troops to Tindall's Point, and "declare for ye King's Majesty, the Governour & Country". He was to find there "a considerable Company of resolved men", to assist him in case his own party offered resistance.[240] This arrangement seems to have been carried out successfully and Walkelett's entire command was taken.[241]

The collapse of the rebellion sounded the death knell of those "chiefe Incendiaries" Drummond and Lawrence. These men had long protested against Berkeley's arbitrary government, and had been largely instrumental in bringing on the insurrection. Bacon had considered them his chief advisors

[238] Ing's Pros., p. 46; P. R. O., CO5-1371-416.

[239] P. R. O., CO1-39-13.

[240] P. R. O., CO5-1371-501.

[241] P. R. O., CO5-1371-416.

and friends. So deep was the Governor's hatred of them that in his recent proclamations he had excepted them from the general pardon.[242]

When Ingram and Walkelett surrendered, these "arch rebels" were stationed on the south side of the York River, at a place called Brick House. When they heard of Ingram's intended desertion, they made desperate but futile efforts to prevent his designs. Failing in this, they determined to gather around them the remnants of the rebel forces and march towards the frontier, in hopes of kindling anew the waning spirit of resistance. "They sent downe to Coll: Bacons to fetch of the Gard there, under . . . Whaly, to reinforce their own strength." Whaly, whose position was more exposed than their own, promptly obeyed, and succeeded in bringing off his force with "the last remains of Coll: Bacon's Estate". The rebel leaders now mustered about three hundred men, and with these they retreated through New Kent, "thinking (like the snow ball) to increase by their rouleing". "But finding that in stead of increasing there number decreast; and that the Moone of there fortune was now past the full, they broke up howse-keeping, every one shifting for him selfe."[243]

And now the chief rebels were hunted down like wild beasts by the Governor's troops. Thomas Hall, formerly clerk of the New Kent county court, Thomas Young, Major Henry Page, and a man named Harris were captured and led before Sir William. They were all tried by court martial, on shipboard off Tindall's Point, convicted of treason, and at once sent to their execution.[244]

A few days later Drummond was found, exhausted and half starved, hiding in Chickahominy swamp.[245] When he was brought before the Governor, that resentful old man could not restrain his joy. He is said to have "complimented him with the ironicall sarcasm of a low bend", declaring that he was more welcome than any other man in Virginia, or even his own brother.[246] The next day Berkeley went to Colonel Bray's house and here Drummond was conducted on foot to

[242] P. R. O., CO1-39-10; Ing's Pros., p. 47.

[243] Ing's Pros., p. 48.

[244] Ing's Pros., p. 49.

[245] Drummond was captured Jan. 14, 1677.

[246] T. M., p. 23; Ing's Pros., p. 49.

stand his trial. "In his way thither he complained very much that his Irons hurt him, and . . . expressed abundance of thankes for being permitted to rest himselfe upon the Roade, while he tooke a pipe of Tobacco."[247] But he refused the offer of a horse, saying he would come soon enough to his death on foot.

At his trial he was treated with brutal harshness, his clothes stripped from his back and his ring torn from his finger. Although the rebellion was now over, he was denied jury trial, and was condemned by court martial after a hearing of but half an hour. Some months later, when this matter came to the attention of the English Privy Council, the Lord Chancellor exclaimed that "he knew not whether it were lawful to wish a person alive, otherwise he could wish Sir William Berkeley so, to see what could be answered to such barbarity".[248]

Thus ended the rebellion. Apparently it had accomplished nothing for the cause of liberty or the relief of the oppressed commons. Few of the abuses that had caused the people to take arms had been rectified. The taxes were heavier than ever, the Governor was more severe and arbitrary. English troops were on their way to the colony to enforce submission and obedience. Charles II, irritated at the independent spirit of the Virginians, was meditating the curtailment of their privileges and the suppression of their representative institutions. Yet this attack of an outraged people upon an arbitrary and corrupt government, was not without its benefits. It gave to future Governors a wholesome dread of the commons, and made them careful not to drive the people again into the fury of rebellion. It created a feeling of fellowship among the poor planters, a consciousness of like interests that tended to mould them into a compact class, ready for concerted action in defense of their rights. It gave birth in the breasts of many brave men to the desire to resist by all means possible the oppression of the Stuart kings. It stirred the people to win, in their legislative halls, victories for the cause of liberty, as real as those which Bacon and his followers had failed to secure on the field of battle.

[247] Ing's Pros., p. 50.

[248] Burk, Vol. II, p. 266; P. R. O., CO1-41-74, 75; CO389.6. Lawrence and Whaly made good their escape into the forest. They probably perished, however, from exposure, or at the hands of the Indians.

CHAPTER VII

The Period of Confusion

When the news reached England that the common people of Virginia were in open revolt against their Governor, and had driven him from his capital, the King was not a little surprised and alarmed. The recollection of the civil war in England was still fresh enough in his memory to make him tremble at the mutterings of rebellion, even though they came from across the Atlantic. Moreover, since the customs from the Virginia tobacco yielded many thousand pounds annually, he could but be concerned for the royal revenue. If the tumults in the colony resulted in an appreciable diminution in the tobacco crop, the Exchequer would be the chief loser. Nor did the King relish the expense of fitting out an army and a fleet for the reduction of the insurgents.

His anxiety was increased by lack of intelligence from the colonial government. Several letters telling of Bacon's coercion of the June Assembly had reached him, but after that months passed without word from the Governor or the Council. From private sources, however, came reports of "uproars so stupendous" that they could hardly find belief.[1] It was rumored in England that Sir William had been defeated, driven out of the colony, and "forced to lie at sea".[2]

Charles seems to have perceived at once that Berkeley must have been responsible for the Rebellion. He probably cared very little whether the old Governor oppressed the people or not, so long as he kept them quiet, but it was an inexcusable blunder for him to drive them into insurrection. Charles himself, it is said, had resolved long before, never to resume his travels; he now wondered why Sir William had brough upon himself this forced journey to Accomac. He decided to institute an investigation to find out what the Governor ha

[1] P. R. O., CO 389.6-177. [2] Ibid.

been doing so to infuriate the people. A commission, consisting of Colonel Herbert Jeffreys, Sir John Berry and Colonel Francis Moryson, was appointed to go to Virginia to enquire into and report all grievances and pressures.[3]

Early in June, 1676, Berkeley had written the King, complaining that his age and infirmities were such that he could no longer perform properly his office in Virginia, and requesting that he be allowed to retire from active service.[4] The Council had protested against this resignation, but Charles thought it best to take Sir William at his word and to recall him from the government he had not been able to preserve in peace and quiet. In honor of his long service, and his well known loyalty, he was, however, to retain "the title and dignity of Governor".[5] He was ordered to return to England "with all possible speed", to report upon his administration and to give an account of the extraordinary tumults in the colony.[6] During his absence the duties of his office were to be entrusted to Colonel Herbert Jeffreys, who was to bear the title of Lieutenant-Governor.[7] He was not, however, to be the deputy or assistant of Sir William, and "to all intents and purposes" was made Governor-in-chief. Berkeley was to be "no wayes accountable" for his actions good or bad.[8]

The King instructed Colonel Jeffreys, before attempting to subdue the rebels by force of arms, to exhaust all peaceable means of securing their submission. In order to make this task more easy, he drew up and had printed a proclamation of pardon, which he directed him to publish throughout the colony. All, it declared, with the sole exception of Bacon, that should surrender themselves, and take the oath of allegiance and supremacy, were to receive free and full forgiveness. Charles felt that most of the colonists were at heart still loyal, and would, if their grievances were redressed, be glad to accept his royal offer of grace.

[3] The commission had consisted at first of Sir John Berry, Colonel Francis Moryson and Thomas Fairfax. P. R. O., CO1-37-53.
[4] P. R. O., CO389.6-113, 174.
[5] P. R. O., CO389.6-113.
[6] P. R. O., CO389.6-121, 174, 175.
[7] P. R. O., CO389.6-113.
[8] P. R. O., CO389.6-137, 139, 140, 144; CO1-38-7.

But he did not rely entirely upon gentle measures, for, after all, the stubborn Virginians might distrust his promises and reject the pardon. So he resolved to send to the colony a strong body of troops to bring them to their senses, if necessary, at the point of the bayonet. A thousand men, thoroughly equipped for active service, were put under the command of Colonel Jeffreys and embarked for the colony.[9]

In the meanwhile, Governor Berkeley, having regained his authority, was busily engaged in reimbursing himself and his friends for their losses in the Rebellion. There can be no doubt that many of the loyalists had suffered severely by the depredations of the insurgents.[10] Those that followed the Governor into exile upon the Eastern Shore, had been compelled to leave their estates to the mercy of the enemy. And the desperate rebels, especially after death had removed the strong arm of Bacon, had subjected many plantations to thorough and ruthless pillage. Crops had been destroyed, cattle driven off, farm houses burned, servants liberated. Almost every member of the Council had suffered, while Berkeley himself claimed to have lost no less than £10,000.[11]

Thus, it was with a spirit of bitterness and hatred that the loyalists, in January and February, returned to their ruined homes. Quite naturally, they set up a clamor for compensation from the estates of those that had plundered them. Now that the King's authority had been restored, and the cause they had contended for had triumphed, they demanded that the vanquished should be made to disgorge their plunder and pay for their wanton destruction. Surely the Governor's followers could not be expected to accept readily all these great losses as a reward for their loyalty.

But restoration upon a large scale would almost certainly entail injustice, and would fan again the flames of bitterness and hatred. It might be possible to restore many articles yet remaining in the hands of the rebels, but most of the plundered goods had long since been consumed. It was often impossible to determine what persons had been guilty of specific acts of

[9] P. R. O., CO389.6-116. [10] P. R. O., CO5-1371-149, 154.
[11] P. R. O., CO1-40-110; CO5-1371-27, 33, 62, 63, 64.

pillage, while many of the most active rebels were very poor men, from whom no adequate compensation could be obtained.

There ensued an undignified and pernicious scramble by the loyalists to seize for their own use the property of the few well-to-do insurgents. On all sides confiscation, unauthorized seizures, and violence marked the collapse of the Rebellion. In these proceedings Sir William took the lead. His servants went out, under pretence of searching for his stolen property, to take for his use the sheep, the cattle, and other goods of the neighboring rebels.[12] He showed, it was declared, "a greedy determination thoroughly to heale himselfe before hee car'd to staunch the bleeding gashes of the woefully lacerated country. . . . Making and treating men as delinquents, before any due conviction or attainder, by seizing their estates, cattle, servants and carrying off their tobacco, marking hogsheads and calling this securing it to the King's service."[13]

Even more unjustifiable was the conduct of Sir William in resorting to arbitrary compositions with his prisoners to fill his exhausted purse.[14] Men were arrested, thrown into jail, terrified with threats of hanging, and released only upon resigning to the Governor most or all of their estates.[15] One James Barrow was locked up at Green Spring and refused permission to plead his case before the Governor. He was told that his release could be secured only upon the payment of a ruinous composition. "By reason," he said, "of the extremity of Cold, hunger, lothsomnesse of Vermin, and other sad occasions, I was forct to comply."[16] Edward Loyd was held for twenty-one days, while his plantation was invaded, and his wife so frightened that she fell into labor and died.

It was proposed by the loyalists to share among themselves the estates of all that had been executed for treason, had died in arms against the King, or had fled from the colony to escape the Governor's vengeance.[17] It did not matter to them that the wretched widows and orphans of these men would be

[12] P. R. O., CO1-39-11, 17; CO5-1371-68, 69, 62, 63, 64, 78, 79, 81, 82, 132.

[13] P. R. O., CO5-1371-152.

[14] P. R. O., CO5-1371-132.

[15] CO1-40-1 to 37; CO1-40-43; CO5-1371-81, 82.

[16] P. R. O., CO1-40-23.

[17] P. R. O., CO5-1371-27, 33.

left destitute. Nor did they stop to consider that these estates, if forfeited at all, could not be seized legally for private use, but should revert to the Crown. They thought only of repairing their own ruined fortunes.[18]

In the midst of this confusion and lawlessness Berry and Moryson, with a part of the fleet and seventy of the English soldiers, arrived in the James River.[19] They had left Portsmouth November the nineteenth, but it was January the twenty-ninth before they reached Virginia.[20] Without waiting for Jeffreys and the main body of the fleet, they notified the Governor of their arrival and requested an immediate conference. Berkeley came aboard their flag-ship, the *Bristol,* February the first, where he was notified of their mission and intrusted with official letters.[21] He poured into the ears of the commissioners the recital of the exciting events of the past months—the destruction of Jamestown, Bacon's death, the surrender of Ingram and Walkelett, the execution of the leading rebels, the return of "the poore Scattered Loyal party to their ruined homes".[22] Although peace had been restored not three weeks before, he pretended astonishment that the King had thought it necessary to send soldiers to his aid.

Nor could he conceal his irritation at the mission of Berry and Moryson. That Charles should think it necessary to make an investigation of affairs in Virginia betokened a lack of confidence in the Governor. Berkeley's friends claimed, no doubt truly, that he was the author of every measure of importance adopted by the government of Virginia. An inquiry into conditions in the colony could but be an inquiry into his conduct. And the Governor, perhaps, knew himself to be guilty of much that he did not wish to have exposed before his royal master.

Moreover, Berkeley was not in the humor to brook interference at this juncture. He was inexorably resolved that the chief rebels should be brought to the gallows and that his own followers should be rewarded for their faithfulness. If

[18] P. R. O., CO1-39-38.

[19] P. R. O., CO5-1371-17, 20.

[20] Ibid.

[21] P. R. O., CO5-1371-27, 33.

[22] Ibid.

the commissioners intended to block these measures, or protest against his actions when in violation of law, they might expect his bitter hostility.

Before the commissioners had been in Virginia two weeks their relations with the Governor became strained. The disposing of the "delinquents Estates", they announced, must be referred to the King. Loyal sufferers should not secure restitution except by due process of law. Seizures of tobacco and other goods must stop. Soon the meetings in the cabin of the *Bristol* became so stormy that the commissioners decided to hold all future communication with Sir William in writing. This they thought necessary because his "defect of hearing" not only made privacy impossible, but looked "angrily, by loud and fierce speaking".[23]

A few days later Colonel Jeffreys arrived with the remainder of the fleet. He and his fellow commissioners found the whole country so ruined and desolate that they experienced considerable difficulty in securing a place of residence.[24] As the Governor disobeyed flatly the King's commands to entertain them at Green Spring,[25] they were compelled to accept the hospitality of Colonel Thomas Swann and make their home at his seat on the James River.[26] On the twelfth of February, Jeffreys, Berry and Moryson went to Green Spring, where they held a long conference with Berkeley and the Council.[27] Jeffreys produced his commission, and read the clauses which instructed Berkeley to return immediately to England, and to resign the government into his hands.[28]

It is easy to imagine with what anger Berkeley and his Council received this command. If Sir William must embark for England and give up his government to this stranger, they would be foiled in their revenge in the very moment of triumph. Jeffreys would probably put an end to the wholesale plundering of the rebels: the illegal distribution of confiscated estates, the seizure of goods, the unjust compositions. It was true that Sir William had written the King in June asking

[23] P. R. O., CO5-1371-55, 60.
[24] P. R. O., CO5-1371-90, 94.
[25] P. R. O., CO391.2-173, 178.
[26] P. R. O., CO5-1371-90, 94.
[27] P. R. O., CO5-1371-83, 85, 90, 94.
[28] P. R. O., CO289.6-121.

his recall, but many things had happened in Virginia since he penned that letter. He was passionately opposed to leaving his government at this juncture.

And the old man's quick wit found an excuse for remaining in Virginia. The word "conveniency" in his orders gave him a loophole.[29] It was evident to all that the King wished him to return without delay, but Berkeley pretended to believe that this word had been inserted in order to permit him to use his own convenience in selecting the date of departure. The question was put to the Council and this body gave a ready and joyous support to the Governor's interpretation. Jeffreys and the commissioners begged them to consider that the word referred not to Sir William's "conveniency", but to that of the King's service, yet they would not heed them.[30] So Jeffreys went back to Swann's Point in discomfiture and the old Governor remained in Virginia for three months more to carry to completion his plans of restitution and revenge.[31] That he should have dared thus to trifle with his royal master's commands, which all his life he had considered sacred, reveals to us vividly his furious temper at this juncture. The humiliation and indignities he had experienced during the Rebellion had deprived him of all prudence.

Had Colonel Jeffreys been a man of force he would not have submitted to this juggling with the King's commands. With a thousand British troops at his back, he could easily have arrested Sir William and forced him to take ship for England. Although this would have been harsh treatment for one that had so long served the King, it was fully justified by the Governor's flagrant disobedience. And it would have relieved the colony of the presence of a man whose inhuman cruelty had rendered him odious to the people. But Jeffreys knew that the Governor's brother, Lord John Berkeley, was high in the King's favor, and might take revenge should he resort to violent measures. So he contented himself with writing home his complaints, and sat quietly by, while Berkeley carried to completion his principal designs.

[29] P. R. O., CO5-1371-50, 83. [30] P. R. O., CO5-1371-93, 94.
[31] P. R. O., CO1-40-88.

The Governor was deeply displeased with the King's proclamation of pardon. Should he publish it at once, as he was ordered to do, it would greatly hinder him in his work of revenge and render more difficult his illegal seizures and confiscations. Since the pardon excepted only Bacon, under its terms such notorious rebels as Robert Jones, or Whaly, or even Lawrence, might come in out of the wilderness and demand immunity. This Berkeley was determined should not be. He thought at first of suppressing the pardon entirely, and of setting out one of his own based upon it, excepting the most notorious rebels.[32] The commissioners urged him to publish the papers unchanged, as the King would undoubtedly resent any attempt to frustrate his intentions.[33] And they insisted that there should be no delay. "Observing the generality of the people to look very amazedly one upon another", at the arrival of the English soldiers, as though dreading a terrible revenge by the King, they thought it highly desirable to "put them out of their paine".[34] It was, they declared, by no means unlikely that a new rebellion would break out, for the people were still deeply dissatisfied and "murmured extremely".

After several days of hesitation, Berkeley decided to issue the King's proclamation unchanged. Accordingly, on the tenth of February, to the great relief of "the trembling people", the printed copies brought over by the commissioners were made public.[35] But with them the Governor published a proclamation of his own, which limited and modified that of his Majesty.[36] Gyles Bland, Thomas Goodrich, Anthony Arnold, and all other rebels then in prison were to be denied the benefit of the pardon. The King's mercy was not to extend to Lawrence and Whaly; or to John Sturdivant, Thomas Blayton, Robert Jones, John Jennings, Robert Holden, John Phelps, Thomas Mathews,[37] Robert Spring, Stephen Earleton and Peter Adams; or "to John West and John Turner, who being legally condemned for rebellion made their escapes by

[32] P. R. O., CO1-39-24.

[33] P. R. O., CO5-1371-32.

[34] P. R. O., CO5-1371-55, 60.

[35] P. R. O., CO5-1371-32, 38.

[36] P. R. O., CO5-1371-276, 286.

[37] This Thomas Mathews was probably the author of the T. M. account of Bacon's Rebellion.

breaking prison"; or to Sara Grindon, "who by her lying and scandalous Reports was the first great encourager and Setter on of the ignorant" people; or even to Colonel Thomas Swann, Colonel Thomas Beale or Thomas Bowler, former members of the Council.[38] The commissioners thought it highly presumptuous in Berkeley thus to frustrate the King's wishes, and they were careful to let his Majesty know the Governor's disobedience, but the Council of Virginia endorsed all his actions and the people dared not disobey.

And so the trials and executions of the wretched rebels continued. As a result, no doubt, of the protests of the commissioners, the proceedings of the court martial were closed, and the accused were now examined before the court of oyer and terminer.[39] Gyles Bland, who for some months had been a prisoner aboard the *Adam and Eve,* was now made to answer for his participation in the Rebellion.[40] He possessed many powerful friends in England, but their influence could not save him. It was rumored that the Duke of York had blocked all efforts in his behalf, vowing "by God Bacon and Bland shoud dye".[41] Accordingly, on the eighth of March, he was condemned, and seven days later was executed.[42] Other trials followed. In quick succession Robert Stoakes, John Isles, Richard Pomfoy, John Whitson and William Scarburgh were sent to the scaffold.[43] Some of the Governor's friends expressed fear that the rabble might attempt to rescue these men, and "Counsell'd the not sending them to dye without a strong Guard", but the people dared not rise in their behalf.[44]

Robert Jones was condemned, but was saved from the gallows by the intercession of Colonel Moryson. Jones had fought with Charles I in the English civil wars, and now exhibited the wounds received in the service of the father as a plea for pardon for his rebellion against the son. Moryson was moved

[38] P. R. O., CO2-39-31; CO5-1371-276, 286.
[39] P. R. O., CO5-1371-125, 127. [40] P. R. O., CO1-39-38; CO1-41-79.
[41] T. M., p. 24.
[42] P. R. O., CO1-39-35; Hen., Vol. II, p. 550.
[43] P. R. O., CO1-39-35; Hen., Vol. II, p. 553.
[44] P. R. O., CO5-1371-152.

to pity at the plight of the old veteran and wrote to Madam Berkeley requesting her to intercede for him with the Governor.[45] "If I am at all acquainted with my heart," wrote the Lady in reply, "I should with more easinesse of mind have worne the Canvas Lynnen the Rebells said they would make me be glad off, than have had this fatal occasion of interceding for mercy."[46] None the less Berkeley consented to reprieve Jones, and many months later the King pardoned him.[47]

Anthony Arnold, who had been one of the most active of the rebel leaders, boldly defended the right of peoples to resist the oppressions of their rulers. He declared that kings "had no rights but what they gott by Conquest and the Sword, and he that could by force of the Sword deprive them thereof, had as good and just a Title to it as the King himselfe. . . . If the King should deny to doe him right he would make noe more to sheathe his sword in his heart or Bowells then of his own mortall Enemyes."[48] For these and other treasonable words this "horrible resolved Rebell and Traytor" was condemned to be "hang'd in Chaines in his own County, to bee a more remarkable Example than the rest".[49]

The Governor, even now, showed no inclination to put an end to the trials and executions. No sooner would the courts empty the jails of prisoners than he would fill them up again. The unhappy rebels, finding that the King's pardon gave them little protection, and that Berkeley excepted from it whom he wished, could not know where next the axe would fall.[50] None can say how far Sir William would have carried his revenge had not the Assembly requested him "to hold his hand from all other Sanguinary punishment".[51] This brought him to his senses and he consented, though with extreme reluctance, to dismiss his witnesses and juries, and put an end to the executions. And even then "he found out a new way" to punish his victims, "ffyning some of their Treasons and Rebellions and condemning others to banishment to England".[52]

[45] P. R. O., CO5-1371-178, 179. [46] P. R. O., CO5-1371-180, 181.
[47] P. R. O., CO1-45-3. [48] P. R. O., CO5-1371-152.
[49] P. R. O., CO5-1371-152; Hen., Vol. II, p. 550.
[50] P. R. O., CO5-1371-32, 152. [51] P. R. O., CO5-1371-152.
[52] P. R. O., CO5-1371-152.

The Governor's extreme severity and the insatiable greed of the loyal party brought the colony to the verge of another rebellion. The people were deeply angered. Had there appeared any person to lead them, "bould and courageous . . . that durst venture his neck", the commons were ready "to Emmire themselves as deepe in Rebellion as ever they did in Bacon's time".[53] For many months it was feared that Lawrence, "that Stubborn desperate and resolved Rebell", would emerge from seclusion to put himself at the head of a new swarm of mutineers.[54] Were he to appear at this juncture, not even the presence of the English troops could prevent Bacon's veterans from flocking to his standard. "Soe sullen and obstinate" were the people that it was feared they would "abandon their Plantacons, putt off their Servants & dispose of their Stock and away to other parts". Had England at this juncture become involved in a foreign war, the Virginians would undoubtedly have sought aid from the enemies of the mother country.[55]

Nor could the people expect relief or justice from the General Assembly which met at Green Spring, February the twentieth, 1677.[56] The elections had been held soon after the final collapse of the Rebellion, amid the general terror inspired by the numerous executions, and had resulted in an overwhelming victory for the loyalists. In many counties, staunch friends of the Governor had been put in nomination, and the commons given an opportunity of showing the sincerity of their repentance by electing them to the Assembly. William Sherwood declared that most of the Burgesses were Berkeley's "owne Creatures & choase by his appointments before the arrivall of the Commissioners".[57] In several places fraud as well as intimidation seems to have been used to secure the election of loyalists. The commons of Charles City complained that there had been illegal voting in their county and seventy of them signed a petition, demanding a new election, which they posted upon the court house door.[58] That the

[53] P. R. O., CO1-40-88.
[54] P. R. O., CO5-1371-132.
[55] P. R. O., CO5-1371-32.
[56] P. R. O., CO1-39-35.
[57] P. R. O., CO1-40-43.
[58] P. R. O., CO1-40-73, 106.

Assembly was in no sense representative of the people seems to have been recognized even in England, for some of the King's ministers declared that it had been "called when ye Country was yet remaining under great distractions, and uncapable of making their Elections after ye usual manner".[59]

Certain it is, that the House of Burgesses as well as the Council, was filled with ardent loyalists and friends of the Governor. They passed several acts confirming all Berkeley's recent measures, and inflicting further punishment upon the luckless rebels.[60] Some that had escaped the gallows were forced to pay heavy fines, others were banished.[61] Many were compelled to make humble submission, with ropes around their necks, upon their knees before the Governor or the county magistrates. Large sums of money were voted to reward the most active of Berkeley's supporters. All that had held command among the rebels, even Ingram and Walkelett, were made forever "incapable of any office civil or military in Virginia". To speak ill of the Governor and Council or of the justices of the peace, was declared a high crime, punishable by whipping. If the people, to the number of six, assembled in arms, they were to be considered mutineers and rebels. And the Burgesses showed great reluctance to reduce their own salaries, which the people considered so excessive. The Governor feared to insist upon it, "least perhaps he might thereby disoblige and thwart his own ends and interest in the Assembly", and only the positive commands of the King, delivered to them by the commissioners, could induce them to make any reduction at all.[62]

They passed resolutions praising the wisdom, the bravery, the justice and integrity of the Governor, and exonerating him for all blame for the outbreak of the Rebellion.[63] "The distempered humor predominant in the Common people", which had occasioned the insurrection, they declared the result of false rumors "inspired by ill affected persons, provoking an itching desire in them to pry into the secrets of the grand

[59] P. R. O., CO1-40-114.
[60] P. R. O., CO1-39-35.
[61] P. R. O., CO1-39-35.
[62] P. R. O., CO5-1371-168 to 175; CO1-39-35.
[63] P. R. O., CO1-39-38.

assembly".[64] They snubbed the King's commissioners, replying to their request for assistance in discovering the common grievances that the Assembly alone was the proper body to correct the people's wrongs.[65] Yet when the commons did come to the Burgesses with their complaints they were repulsed with harsh reproofs and even severe punishment. Certain grievances from Isle of Wight county were denounced as "libellous, Scandalous and rebellious" and "the chiefe persons in the Subscriptions" were to be punished "to the merits of their Crymes".[66] A petition from Gloucester county was declared to savor so strongly of the "old leaven of rebellion" that it must be expunged from the records. When the people of Nansemond appealed for a more just method of taxation, they were answered briefly, "It is conceived the pole is the equallest way."[67]

One is inclined to wonder why the people, thus finding the Assembly but an instrument of oppression in the Governor's hands, did not turn eagerly for support and relief to the King's commissioners. These men had invited them to bring in all their pressures, without restraint or fear of punishment. His Majesty, they announced, was anxious to know what had caused them to rise against his authority. All just complaints would be carefully considered and all grievances redressed.[68] But dread of Sir William's anger held the people back. Their chief grievance was the old Governor himself, but there were few that dared say so, even with the promise of the King's protection. The commissioners wrote Secretary Coventry that until "the awe of his stay" was removed, they could "never thoroughly search and penetrate into the bottome of the Businesse".[69] Berkeley, they said, continually impeded their investigations and prevented the people from testifying. It might be necessary for Colonel Jeffreys to send him home, before the mists he cast before them could be dispelled.[70] When he was gone, a short time would show boldly those things that as yet only cautiously peeped forth.[71]

[64] P. R. O., CO1-39-38.
[65] P. R. O., CO1-39-39.
[66] P. R. O., CO1-39-38.
[67] P. R. O., CO1-39-38.
[68] P. R. O., CO5-1371-39 to 44.
[69] P. R. O., CO5-1371-132.
[70] P. R. O., CO5-1371-182, 187.
[71] P. R. O., CO5-1371-193 to 198.

The violent opposition which the commissioners encountered from the Governor and the loyalists soon forced them to become the leaders of the defeated party. The poor people looked forward with hope to the day when Sir William would leave and Colonel Jeffreys assume control of the executive. Then, they were sure, the persecutions would end and justice be done them.

The hatred and contempt of the Governor's friends for Colonel Jeffreys and his colleagues is shown by an interesting and unique incident. Having heard that Sir William was at last preparing to sail for England, they went to Green Spring, on the twenty-second of April, to bid him farewell.[72] This they thought due his dignity and rank, even though their relations with him had been far from cordial.[73] As they left the house, after paying their respects to the Governor and his lady, they found Sir William's coach waiting at the door to convey them to their landing.[74] But before they rode away a strange man came forward, boldly putting aside the "Postillion that used to Ryde" and got up himself in his place. The Governor, several Councillors, and others saw what occurred, but did not offer to interfere. Lady Berkeley went "into her Chamber, and peep'd through a broken quarrell of the Glass, to observe how the Show look'd".[75] After reaching their boat, the commissioners found to their horror that the strange postilion was none other than the "Common Hangman that . . . put the Halters about the Prisoner's Necks in Court when they were to make their submission". This seemed to them so gross an insult, not only to the "Great Seal", but to their "persons as Gentlemen", that they were resolved to make his Majesty himself acquainted with it.[76] "The whole country rings of . . . the public Odium and disgrace cast upon us," they said, "as the Exchange itselfe shortly may."[77]

It is probable that Lady Berkeley alone was responsible for this incident, which, as the commissioners themselves said, looked "more like a woman's than a man's malice".[78] The

[72] P. R. O., CO5-1371-208 to 211

[73] P. R. O., CO5-1371-212, 213.

[74] P. R. O., CO5-1371-220, 231.

[75] P. R. O., CO5-1371-220, 231.

[76] P. R. O., CO5-1371-212, 213.

[77] P. R. O., CO5-1371-220, 231.

[78] P. R. O., CO5-1371-220, 231.

Governor denied with passionate vehemence that he was in any way guilty. "I have sent the Negro[79] to be Rebuked, Tortur'd or whipt, till he confesse how this dire misfortune happen'd," he wrote the commissioners, "but I am soe distracted that I scarce know what I doe."[80]

Even before Berkeley left the colony Colonel Jeffreys issued a proclamation, formally taking possession of the government.[81] For some time it had been apparent that the Lieutenant-Governor's long delay in entering upon his duties was greatly weakening him in the estimation of the people. Since he had been forced to sit idly by for several months while Sir William carried to completion matters of the utmost importance, and had not dared to take his office so long as it pleased the old man to linger in the colony, many thought, quite naturally, that he could not have been entrusted with full authority to act as Governor. And this opinion had been industriously furthered by the loyal party. The departure of Sir William, they declared, did not mean a permanent change of administration. Jeffreys was to act only as his deputy during his absence and would retire upon his return.[82] Feeling that these views, if universally accepted, would undermine his influence and authority, Jeffreys entered a vigorous denial in his proclamation. He had been appointed, he declared, to exercise the power of Governor, as fully as Berkeley or any of his predecessors had done. No man should dare to belittle his office or authority. Berkeley was going home at his own request because his great age and infirmities rendered him unfit to sustain further the burdens of his position. The new executive had refrained from assuming his duties earlier, "because an Assembly being . . . ready to convene, the issueing forth a new Summons . . . must needs have greatly retarded the publique Weale".[83] Nor did he scruple to claim the full title of "Governour and Captain Generall of Virginia".

This proclamation aroused Berkeley's deepest ire. "Your ejecting me," he wrote Jeffreys, "from having any share in

[79] Probably the real postilion. [80] P. R. O., CO5-1371-214 to 217.
[81] This proclamation was issued April 27, 1677. P. R. O., CO1-40-53.
[82] P. R. O., CO1-41-121; CO1-42-23. [83] P. R. O., CO1-40-53.

the Government whilst yet I am in the Countrey . . . I beleeve can neither be justified by your Comision nor mine." "You say that his Majesty out of the knowledge of my inability to govern did surrogate so able a man as Coll: Jeffreys to supply my defects. I wish from my heart Coll: Jeffreys were as well known to the King and Counsel as Sir William Berkeley is, for then the difference would be quickly decided." The letter was addressed to the "Right honorable Coll: Herbert Jeffreys, his Majesty's Lieutenant Governor of Virginia", and was signed "William Berkeley, Governor of Virginia till his most Sacred Majesty shall please to determine otherwise".[84]

In the meanwhile the letters of the commissioners, reporting Berkeley's disobedience to the King's commands, had arrived in England. Charles was angered, not only at his delay in surrendering the government, but also at his presumption in disregarding the royal proclamation of pardon. "You may well think," he wrote Berkeley, "we are not a little surprised to understand that you make difficulty to yield obedience to our commands, being so clear and plain that we thought no man could have raised any dispute about them. Therefore . . . we do . . . command you forthwith . . . without further delay or excuse (to) repair unto our Presence as We formerly required you."[85]

Secretary Coventry wrote even more severely. We understand, he said, that to the King's clear and positive orders for you to resign the government to Colonel Jeffreys, "upon certain pretences which are no wayes understood here, you have delayed at least if not refused obedience. . . . His Majesty . . . seemeth not a little surprised as well as troubled to find a person that had for so many years served his Royal Father and himself through ye worst of times with so unshaken a loyalty, and so absolute obedience and resignation, should now at one time fall into two such great errors as to affront his Proclamation by putting out one of his owne at ye same time with his, and in that to exempt several persons from pardon, which were by the King's owne Proclamation made capable

[84] P. R. O., CO1-40-54.
[85] This letter was written May 13, 1677.

of Pardon; then after positive orders given for your immediate return . . . you yet stay there . . . and continually dispute with his Majesty's commissioners. I will assure you, Sir, his Majesty is very sensible of these miscarriages, and hath very little hopes that ye people of Virginia shall be brought to a right sense of their duty to obey their Governours when the Governours themselves will not obey the King. I pray you, Sir, . . . take not councell from your owne nor any other body's passion or resentment, to take upon you to judge either conveniency or not conveniency of the King's orders, but obey them, and come over; and whatever you have to say . . . you will be heard at large."[86]

Even before these letters were written Sir William had left the colony. He had embarked for England, May the fifth, in Captain Larrimore's sturdy ship which had stood him in such good stead in the hour of need.[87] But the old man, worn out by his violent passions and unusual exertions, was physically unfit for the long voyage across the Atlantic. He became very ill on shipboard, and reached England a dying man. "He came here alive," wrote Secretary Coventry, "but so unlike to live that it had been very inhumane to have troubled him with any interrogacons."[88] The news of the King's displeasure at his conduct added much to his suffering. He pleaded for an opportunity "to clear his Innocency" even though the "tedious passage & griefe of mind" had reduced him "to extreame weaknesse".[89] That Charles did not refuse him this privilege is attested by a letter written to Berkeley by Secretary Coventry. "I am commanded by his Majesty," he said, "to let you know that his Majesty would speake with you as soone as you can, because there are some ships now going to Virginia, and his Majesty would see what further Instructions may be necessary to be sent by them."[90] But Berkeley could not attend the King, either to give information or to plead his own cause. His condition rapidly became critical, and a few days later he died.[91]

[86] P. R. O., CO389.6-195 to 198.
[87] P. R. O., CO1-40-88.
[88] P. R. O., CO389.6.
[89] P. R. O., CO1-40-110.
[90] P. R. O., CO389.6-207.
[91] P. R. O., CO389.6-210.

Hardly had Sir William breathed his last than Thomas Lord Culpeper "kissed the King's hand as Governour".[92] This nobleman had received a commission, July 8, 1675, which was to take effect immediately upon the death, surrender or forfeiture of the office by Berkeley.[93] It had never been Charles' intention that Colonel Jeffreys should remain permanently at the head of the government of Virginia, and he now notified him to prepare to surrender his office to the new Governor.[94] The King, who felt that the unsettled condition of Virginia required Culpeper's immediate presence, ordered him to depart "with all speed", and told the colonists they might expect him by Christmas "without fayle".[95] But this pampered lord, accustomed to the luxury of the court, had no desire to be exiled in the wilderness of the New World. By various excuses he succeeded in postponing his departure for over two years, and it was not until the spring of 1680 that he landed in Virginia.[96] Thus, for a while, Colonel Jeffreys was left as the chief executive of the colony.

In the meanwhile the commissioners, freed from the baleful presence of the old Governor, were continuing their investigation into the causes of the Rebellion. Berkeley had advised them, when they first announced their mission, to carry out their work through the county courts.[97] But they had refused to accept this plan. The justices were almost all henchmen of Sir William, many were hated by the people and some were the objects of their chief accusations. Had the investigation been intrusted to their hands, they would most certainly have suppressed the principal complaints.[98] The commissioners, therefore, appointed especial officers in the counties to hear the people's grievances, draw them up in writing and bring them in for presentation to the King.[99] Even

[92] P. R. O., CO389.6-212.

[93] P. R. O., CO5-1355-299; CO389.6-271 to 273.

[94] P. R. O., CO389.6-210, 215.

[95] P. R. O., CO389.6-210.

[96] P. R. O., CO5-1355-377.

[97] P. R. O., CO5-1371-45.

[98] Nothing can show this more clearly than the reception in the Assembly, which was largely composed of justices of the peace, of the county grievances.

[99] P. R. O., CO391.2-180.

then the loyal party attempted, by intimidation, to prevent the commons from explaining without reserve what had caused them to take up arms against the government. Sir William, they were careful to report, would most certainly return, and any that dared charge him or his friends with corruption might expect the severest punishment.[100] But the announcement by the commissioners that his Majesty himself had promised his protection to all informants relieved the fears of the people and many came forward with the story of their wrongs.[101] These seem to have been faithfully drawn up by the officers and in time presented to the King.

The loyal party complained loudly that the commissioners used in this matter none but the enemies of the Governor.[102] Lord John Berkeley declared that they had sought information from such only as were known "to be notorious actors in the rebellion".[103] But the commissioners were undoubtedly right in insisting that all grievances should come from those that had been aggrieved. They themselves, they declared, were not responsible for the truth of the charges; their function was only to receive and report them. The King had sent them to Virginia to make the royal ear accessible to the humblest citizen. This could be done only by brushing aside the usual channels of information and going directly to the commons themselves. That some of the accusations were exaggerated or even entirely false seems not improbable; many were undoubtedly true. Posterity must accept them, not as the relation of established truth, but as the charges of a defeated and exasperated party.

In their work of investigation the commissioners found that they had need of the records of the House of Burgesses. In April, 1677, after the adjournment of the session at Green Spring, they came to Major Robert Beverley, the clerk of the Assembly, and demanded "all the Originall Journals, Orders, Acts", etc., then in his custody.[104] Beverley required them to show their authority, and this they did, by giving him a sight

[100] P. R. O., CO5-1371-132. [101] P. R. O., CO5-1371-132.

[102] P. R. O., CO391.2-180; Burk, Vol. II, pp. 259, 260.

[103] P. R. O., CO391.2-173 to 178; Burk, Vol. II, p. 260.

[104] P. R. O., CO1-41-87.

of that part of their commission which concerned his delivery of the records.[105] He then offered to allow them to examine any of the papers necessary to the investigation, but he refused absolutely to relinquish their custody.[106] The commissioners, who distrusted Beverley and perhaps feared that he might conceal the records, "took them from him by violence".[107]

When the Assembly met in October, 1677, the House of Burgesses sent a vigorous protest to Colonel Jeffreys against these proceedings of the commissioners. Their action, they declared, "we take to be a great violation of our privileges". The power to command the records which the commissioners claim to have received from the King, "this House humbly suppose His Majesty would not grant or Comand, for that they find not the same to have been practiced by any of the Kings of England in the likewise. . . . The House do humbly pray your Honour . . . will please to give the House such satisfaction, that they may be assured no such violation of their privileges shall be offered for the future."[108]

When Charles II heard of this bold protest he was surprised and angered. It seemed to him a "great presumption of ye said Assembly . . . to call in Question" his authority.[109] Referring their representation to the Lords of Trade and Plantations, he directed them "to examine ye same, & to Report" what they thought "fitt to be done in Vindication of . . . (the) Royall Authority, & for bringing the said Assembly to a due sence & acknowledgement of their Duty & Submission".[110] The Lords gave it as their opinion that the declaration was so "Seditious, even tending to Rebellion", that the new Governor should be directed to rebuke the Assembly and punish the "authors and abettors of this presumption".[111] The King commanded Lord Culpeper to carry these recommendations into effect. On the third of July, 1680, Culpeper brought the matter before the Virginia Council, preparatory to delivering the rebuke. But the Councillors made a vigorous defense of the action of the Assembly, and unanimously ad-

[105] P. R. O., CO1-42-138.
[106] P. R. O., CO5-1376-273.
[107] P. R. O., CO5-1376-273.
[108] P. R. O., CO1-41-87.
[109] P. R. O., CO1-42-141.
[110] P. R. O., CO1-42-141.
[111] P. R. O., CO391.2-300, 301.

vised the Governor to suspend the execution of the King's command.[112] After some hesitation, Culpeper yielded, and the matter was referred back to the Privy Council. Charles was finally induced to rescind the order, but he insisted that all reference to the declaration "be taken off the file and razed out of the books of Virginia".[113]

The work of the commission being completed, Berry and Moryson, in July, 1677, sailed with the royal squadron for England.[114] Their report, which was so damaging to the Virginia loyalists, was not allowed to go unchallenged. Sir William Berkeley, upon his death bed, had told his brother, Lord John Berkeley, of the hostility of the commissioners, and charged him to defend his conduct and character. And Lord Berkeley, who was a member of the Privy Council and a man of great influence, did his best to refute their evidence and to discredit them before the King.[115] Their entire report, he declared, was "a scandalous lible and invective of Sir William . . . and the royal party in Virginia".[116] His brother's conduct had been always prudent and just, and it was noticeable that not one private grievance had ever been brought against him before this rebellion.[117] The meetings of Lord Berkeley with the commissioners in the Council chamber were sometimes stormy. On one occasion he told Berry, "with an angry voice and a Berklean look, . . . that he and Morryson had murdered his brother". "Sir John as sharply returned again" that they had done nothing but what they "durst justify".[118]

As the other members of the Privy Council protected the commissioners, and upheld their report, the attacks of the angry nobleman availed nothing. Secretary Coventry averred that Berry and Moryson had been most faithful in carrying out the King's directions, and he showed his confidence in their honesty and their judgment by consulting them upon all important matters relating to the colony.[119] And for a while, their

[112] P. R. O., CO5-1355-354.
[113] Sains., Vol. XVIII, p. 129.
[114] P. R. O., CO1-41-17.
[115] Burk, Vol. II, p. 263.
[116] Burk, Vol. II, p. 259; P. R. O., CO391.2-180.
[117] Burk, Vol. II, p. 264.
[118] Burk, Vol. II, p. 266.
[119] P. R. O., CO391.2-180.

influence in shaping the policy of the Privy Council in regard to Virginia was almost unlimited.

Nor did they scruple to use this great power to avenge themselves upon those men that had so antagonized them and hindered their investigation. Robert Beverley they represented to the Privy Council as a man of low education and mean parts, bred a vulgar seaman and utterly unfit for high office.[120] Colonel Edward Hill was the most hated man in Charles City county.[121] Ballard, Bray and some of the other Councillors were rash and fiery, active in opposing the King's orders and unjust to the poor people.[122] The Privy Council was so greatly influenced by these representations that they determined to reconstruct the Virginia Council, upon lines suggested by Berry and Moryson. Colonel Philip Ludwell, Colonel Ballard and Colonel Bray were expressly excluded from the Council, while Colonel Hill and Major Beverley as "men of evil fame and behavior" were deprived of all governmental employment whatsoever, and "declared unfit to serve His Majesty".[123] On the other hand, Colonel Thomas Swann, who had been excluded from the Council by Governor Berkeley, was now, for his kindness to the commissioners, restored to his seat.[124]

The departure of Sir William Berkeley by no means ended the opposition to Colonel Jeffreys. A part of the Council, realizing that continued hostility could result only in harm to themselves, made their peace with the new administration, and were received into favor, but the more violent of the loyal party remained defiant and abusive. Philip Ludwell, Beverley, Hill, Ballard and others openly denounced Jeffreys as a weakling, entirely unsuited for the important office he now occupied, and did their best to render him unpopular with the people.[125] The Lieutenant-Governor retaliated with considerable spirit, depriving some of their lucrative offices, and suspending others

[120] P. R. O., CO1-41-121. Major Beverley was of good family. His military leadership in Bacon's Rebellion, and his services as clerk of the Assembly, testify to his ability. Va. Mag., Vol. II, p. 405.

[121] P. R. O., CO1-41-121.

[122] P. R. O., CO391.2-173 to 178.

[123] P. R. O., CO391.2-305.

[124] P. R. O., CO391.2-173 to 178.

[125] P. R. O., CO1-41-138; CO1-42-117.

from the Council. Ludwell, whose conduct had been especially obnoxious, was ousted from the collectorship of York River.[126] Ballard was expelled from a similar office.[127] And many months before the changes in the Council ordered by the English government became known in Virginia, no less than six of the most active loyalists had been suspended by the Lieutenant-Governor.[128]

But events soon took a more favorable turn for the Berkeley party. The departure of Berry and Moryson deprived Jeffreys of his staunchest friends and advisors. And, before the end of the summer, he was prostrated by the Virginia sickness, which was still deadly to those unaccustomed to the climate of the colony. For several months he was too ill to attend properly to his duties or to resist the machinations of his enemies, and the government fell into the hands of the Council.[129] And since this body, despite its pretended support of the Lieutenant-Governor, was at heart in full sympathy with Beverley and Ludwell and the other loyalists, the policy of the administration was once more changed. The work of extortion was actively resumed and the courts again busied themselves with suits against the former rebels.[130]

But consternation seized the Green Spring faction, as the loyalists were now called, upon the arrival of the King's order, annulling Berkeley's proclamation of February 10, 1677, and reaffirming the general pardon.[131] If this command were put into effect, most of the confiscations secured since the Rebellion, would become illegal, and restitution would have to be made. So desperately opposed to this were the loyalists that they resolved to suppress the King's letter. They believed that it had been obtained by the influence of the commissioners, and this, they hoped, would soon be rendered nugatory by the presence at court of Sir William Berkeley. If they could keep the order secret for a few weeks, new instructions, dictated by the Governor, might arrive to render

[126] Va. Mag., Vol. XVIII, p. 18; P. R. O., CO1-42-55.
[127] Sains., Vol. XVII, p. 19.
[128] P. R. O., CO1-41-121.
[129] P. R. O., CO1-42-17.1, 23.
[130] P. R. O., CO1-42-23.
[131] P. R. O., CO1-42-17.1, 23.

its execution unnecessary. Colonel Jeffreys protested against their disobedience, but he was too weak to oppose the will of the Council.[132] So, for six weeks, his Majesty's grace "was unknown to ye poore Inhabitants", while the innumerable suits and prosecutions were pushed vigorously. Not until October the twenty-sixth, when all hope of its revocation had been dispelled by fresh information from England, did the Council consent to the publication of the letter.[133]

In September, 1677, writs were issued for an election of Burgesses.[134] Had Jeffreys not been ill, he would perhaps have refused to allow a new session of the Assembly. The contest at the polls could but result in a victory for the Green Spring faction, as the electoral machinery was in their hands. The Lieutenant-Governor, although he had removed some of the higher colonial officials, had made few changes in the personnel of the county courts.[135] The sheriffs, by resorting to the old methods, made sure of the election of most of the nominees of the loyal party. Complaints came from James City county, New Kent county and other places that intimidation and fraud had been used to deprive the people of a fair election.[136] If we may believe the testimony of William Sherwood, the Berkeley faction carried things with a high hand. "The Inhabitants of James City County," he wrote, "did unanimously elect me a Burgess . . . but several of my professed enemies . . . procured another writt for a new election, with a positive command not to choose me. The people then being under amazement consented to whome soever the Sheriffe would returne, & so my enemies to make their party the stronger in ye house . . . causd three Burgesses to serve for James City County."[137]

"By this means," wrote Colonel Daniel Parke, "and by persuading the burgesses that Sir William Berkeley was coming in Governour again, (the loyal party) got all confirmed that was done at the Assembly before held at Greene Spring."[138] In order to compensate themselves for their great losses and to fulfil the promises made by Berkeley to his followers during

[132] P. R. O., CO1-42-17.1, 23.

[133] P. R. O., CO1-42-17.1.

[134] P. R. O., CO1-42-23.

[135] P. R. O., CO1-42-23.

[136] P. R. O., CO1-42-17.1.

[137] P. R. O., CO1-42-23.

[138] P. R. O., CO1-42-17.1.

the Rebellion, they levied a tax upon the people of one hundred and ten pounds of tobacco per poll. "This with the county tax and parish tax," said Parke, "is in some counties 250lbs, in some 300, and in some 400lbs, which falls very heavie upon the poorer people." The county grievances were again rejected by the Burgesses as false and scandalous, and the persons presenting them were severely punished.[139] But the Assembly expressed an earnest desire to bring about a reconciliation between the hostile factions in the colony, and prescribed a heavy penalty for the use of such opprobrious epithets as "traytor, Rebell Rougue, Rebell", etc.[140]

The news of Berkeley's death was a severe blow to the Green Spring party. All the hope they had entertained that he would accomplish the overthrow of the work of the commissioners, at once fell to the ground. But thev were somewhat consoled by the appointment of Lord Culpeper. This nobleman was related to Lady Berkeley, and they had good reason to believe he would reverse the policy of the present administration and ally himself with the loyalists.[141]

In the meanwhile the Lieutenant-Governor was regaining his health and spirits, and was taking a more active part in public affairs. He had been deeply angered with Colonel Philip Ludwell for his many insults, and he now determined to prosecute him "for scandalizing the Governor, and abusing the Authority of his Majesty".[142] Ludwell's unpardonable crime, it would seem, consisted in calling Jeffreys "a pitiful little Fellow with a perriwig".[143] He had also been heard to say that the Lieutenant-Governor was "a worse Rebel than Bacon", that he had broken the laws of Virginia, that he had perjured himself, that he "was not worth a Groat in England". Nor was it considered a sufficient excuse that Ludwell had made those remarks immediately after consuming "part of a Flaggon of Syder".[144] The jury found him guilty of "scandalizing the Governor", but acquitted him of any intention of abusing his Majesty's authority. The General Court, upon the

[139] P. R. O., CO5-1376. [140] P. R. O., CO5-1376.
[141] P. R. O., CO1-42-55; Va. Mag., Vol. II, p. 408.
[142] Va. Mag., Vol. XVIII, p. 20. [143] Va. Mag., Vol. XVIII, p. 12.
[144] Va. Mag., Vol. XVIII, p. 11.

motion of Colonel Jeffreys, referred the case to the King and Privy Council, that they might "advise a punishment proportionable to the offence".[145] Against this decision the defendant, as he had an undoubted right to do, appealed to the General Assembly. Ludwell felt, no doubt, that should the appeal be allowed, his great influence in the House of Burgesses would secure him a light sentence. But the court declared the case so unprecedented that the whole matter, including the question of appeal, must be decided by the King.

With the return of hot weather, Colonel Jeffreys, not yet being acclimated, or "seasoned", as the Virginians expressed it, again became seriously ill.[146] The Council elected a president to act in his place and once more assumed control of the administration.[147] The Green Spring faction, whom only the Lieutenant-Governor could restrain, again lifted its head and endeavored "to continue their old exactions & abuses".[148] Feeling, perhaps, a sense of security in their remoteness from the King, which made it impossible for him to watch their actions closely, or to mete out to them prompt punishment, they still disregarded his pardon and his reiterated commands.[149] "The colony would be as peaceful as could be wished," wrote William Sherwood in August, 1678, "except for the malice of some discontented persons of the late Governor's party, who endeavour by all ye cunning contrivances that by their artifice can be brought about, to bring a Contempt of Colonel Jeffreys, our present good Governor. . . . Those persons who are the troublers of the peace . . . are . . . Lady Berkeley, Colonel Philip Ludwell, Colonel Thomas Ballard, Colonel Edward Hill, Major Robert Beverley, all of which are cherished by Mr. Secretary Ludwell (who acts severely.) It is to be feared, unless these fiery Spiritts are allayed or removed home, there will not be that settled, happy peace and unity which otherwise might be, for they are entered into a faction, which is upheld by the expectation of my Lord Culpeper's doing mighty things for them & their interest."[150]

[145] Va. Mag., Vol. XVIII, p. 23.
[146] P. R. O., CO1-42-103.
[147] Va. Mag., Vol. IX, p. 307.
[148] P. R. O., CO1-42-103.
[149] P. R. O., CO1-42-107.
[150] P. R. O., CO1-42-117.

Colonel Jeffreys died in November, 1678.[151] It was the fortune of this Governor to come to the colony in one of the greatest crises of its history. Had he been a man of ability and firmness he could have rendered the people services of great value. He might have put an end to the reign of terror inaugurated by Berkeley, prevented the unending law suits, confiscations and compositions, reorganized the county courts and assured to the people a fair election of Burgesses. He seems to have wished to rule justly and well, but he was too weak to quell the strife between the rival factions and bring quiet to the distracted colony.

So bitter was the loyal party against Colonel Jeffreys, that after his death they sought to revenge themselves upon his widow. The Lieutenant-Governor had received no part of his salary from March, 1678, to the day of his death, and had, as a result, incurred considerable debt. As Mrs. Jeffreys was unable to meet all her husband's obligations, she was detained in Virginia, and, according to one account, thrown into prison.[152] "T'is plain," she wrote Secretary Coventry, "they seek my Life in malice to my husband, though none of them can tax him with any injustice. . . . I cannot hope to outlive this persecution, but I most humbly beseech you to intercede for me to his Majesty, that my child may not be ruined."[153] Mrs. Jeffreys later received the arrears due her husband, and was thus enabled to free herself from the power of her enemies.[154]

Upon the death of Colonel Jeffreys, Sir Henry Chicheley, by virtue of a commission granted in 1674, assumed control of the government.[155] The new Governor had long served with distinction in the Council, and seems to have been a "most loyal, worthy person and deservedly beloved by the whole country".[156] But he was now too "old, sickly and crazy" to govern the colony with the vigor and firmness that were so greatly needed.[157] During the eighteen months of his administration the people were "not reconciled to one another", and "ill blood" only too often was manifested by both factions.[158]

[151] Va. Mag., Vol. IX, p. 307.
[152] P. R. O., CO5-1355-304, 305, 309.
[153] P. R. O., CO5-1355-305.
[154] P. R. O., CO5-1355-370.
[155] Va. Mag., Vol. IX, p. 307.
[156] P. R. O., CO1-41-121.
[157] Sains., Vol. XVII, p. 230.
[158] Sains., Vol. XVII, p. 230.

Sir Henry had himself been a severe sufferer by the Rebellion. He had fallen into Bacon's hands and had even, it would seem, been threatened with death, in retaliation for Berkeley's execution of Captain Carver. Yet he attempted to rule impartially and well. Writs were issued in the spring of 1679 for an election of Burgesses, and the people were protected from intimidation at the polls. The Assembly, as a result, showed itself more sane, more sensitive to the wishes of the commons, than had been either of the sessions of 1677.[159] Several laws were enacted redressing some of the most flagrant evils of the old governmental system of Berkeley. The voters of each parish were empowered to elect two men "to sitt in the severall county courts and have their equall votes with the severall justices for the makeing of by lawes".[160] An act was passed putting a limit upon the excessive fees charged by the collectors of the customs.[161] And the clamor of the loyalists for the payment of their claims upon the treasury were unheeded, and all public debts were referred for settlement to the next session.[162]

Chicheley's administration came temporarily to an end with the arrival of Lord Culpeper. The period from the close of the Rebellion to May, 1680, when the new Governor-General took the oath of office, seems, at first sight, characterized only by confusion and disaster. The violent animosities, the uncertainty of property rights, the lack of a firm and settled government kept the people in constant uneasiness and discontent. The numerous banishments and executions had deprived the colony of some of its most intelligent and useful citizens, while the plundering of both parties during the Rebellion, and the numberless forfeitures that followed the establishment of peace, had reduced many men to poverty. Nor had the most pressing of the grievances that had caused the people to rise against the government been redressed. The Navigation Acts were still in force, the commons were yet excluded from their rightful share in the government, the taxes were more oppressive than ever.

[159] Hen., Vol. II, p. 433.
[160] Hen., Vol. II, p. 441.
[161] Hen., Vol. II, p. 443.
[162] Hen., Vol. II, p. 456.

Yet amid the melancholy confusion of the times, important changes for the better were taking place. Never again was an English Governor to exercise the despotic power that had been Sir William Berkeley's. This was not due to the greater leniency of the British government, or to lack of ambition in the later Governors. But the Rebellion and the events following it, had weakened the loyalty of the people and shown them the possibility of resisting the King's commands. The commons, angered at the severity of the punishment inflicted upon the rebel leaders, and disappointed in the royal promise that their grievances should be redressed, regarded the government with sullen hostility. The wealthy planters resented what they considered Charles' ingratitude for their loyal support in the hour of need, and complained bitterly of his interference with their attempts to restore their ruined fortunes. Throughout Berkeley's administration their interests had seemed to be identical with those of the Governor, and they had ever worked in harmony with him. With the advent of Colonel Jeffreys, however, they had been thrown into violent opposition to the executive. Their success in thwarting the policies of the Lieutenant-Governor, and in evading and disobeying the King's commands gave them a keen appreciation of their own influence and power. They were to become more and more impatient of the control of the Governors, more and more prone to defy the commands of the English government.

The awakened spirit of resistance bore rich fruit for the cause of liberty. The chief difficulty heretofore experienced by the commons in defending their rights was the lack of intelligent and forceful leaders. These they now secured through the frequent quarrels of the wealthy planters with the Governors. More than once Councillors, suspended from their seats for disobedience, came forward as leaders in the struggle to preserve the rights of the people. In this capacity they rendered services of the highest importance. Strangely enough some of the leading spirits of the old Berkeley party became, by their continued opposition to the executive, champions of representative government in the colony. Had it not been for the active leadership of Robert Beverley and Philip Ludwell the cause of liberty might well have perished under the assaults of Charles II and James II.

The House of Burgesses was gradually becoming more representative of the people. The intimidation of voters practiced by the loyal party immediately after the Rebellion could not be continued indefinitely. As the terror inspired by Berkeley's revenge upon the rebels began to wane, the commons insisted more upon following their own inclinations at the polls. Moreover, the incessant quarrels of the Governors with the members of the aristocracy made it impossible for any clique to control again the electoral machinery. As the sheriffs and justices were no longer so closely allied with the executive as they had been in the Restoration period, false returns of Burgesses and other electoral frauds were apt to be of less frequent occurrence.

Thus, during the years immediately following the Rebellion, forces were shaping themselves which were to make it possible for the colony to resist those encroachments of the Crown upon its liberties that marked the last decade of the rule of the Stuart kings, and to pass safely through what may well be called the Critical Period of Virginia history.

CHAPTER VIII

The Critical Period

For some years after the Restoration the administration of English colonial affairs had been very lax. The Council of Plantations, which had served as a Colonial Office during the period from 1660 to 1672, had done little to control the Governors or to supervise and direct their policies. With the exception of one list of questions sent to Virginia in 1670, they had left Sir William Berkeley almost entirely to his own devices. September 27, 1672, the Council of Plantations was united with the Board of Domestic Trade to form the Council of Trade and Plantations. This new arrangement seems not to have been productive of good results, for in December, 1674, after the fall of the Cabal ministry, it was discontinued and the direction of colonial affairs entrusted to the King's Privy Council. This important body, finding its new duties very onerous, created a committee of twenty-one members, to whom the supervision of trade and plantations was assigned. In this way the King's most trusted ministers were brought into close touch with colonial affairs. We find now such prominent statesmen as Secretary Coventry, Secretary Williamson and Sir Lionel Jenkins carrying on extensive correspondence with the Governors, becoming interested in all their problems and needs, and demanding copies of all journals of Assembly and other state papers.[1]

This closer intimacy with the colonial governments led inevitably to a feeling of intolerance for local autonomy and for representative institutions, and to a determination to force upon the colonists a conformity with the policies and desires of the English government. Charles II and James II, instituted, in the decade preceding the English Revolution, a series of measures designed to curb the independence of the

[1] Osg., Vol. III, pp. 280, 281.

colonists. Some of the Assembly's long-established and most important rights were attacked. Many of its statutes were annulled by proclamation; its judicial powers were forever abolished; its control over taxation and expenditure was threatened; the privilege of selecting the Assembly clerk was taken from it; while even the right to initiate legislation was assailed.

The intolerant mood of the King and Privy Council is reflected in the instructions given Lord Culpeper upon his departure for Virginia. They included orders depriving him of the power, exercised freely by all former Governors, of calling sessions of the Assembly. "It is Our Will and pleasure," Charles declared, "that for the future noe General Assembly be called without Our special directions, but that, upon occasion, you doe acquaint us by letter, with the necessity of calling such an Assembly, and pray Our consent, and directions for their meeting."[2]

Even more dangerous to the liberties of the people was the attempt to deprive the Assembly of the right to initiate legislation. "You shall transmit unto us," Culpeper was commanded, "with the advice and consent of the Council, a draught of such Acts, as you shall think fit and necessary to bee passed, that wee may take the same into Our consideration, and return them in the forme wee shall think fit they bee enacted in. And, upon receipt of Our commands, you shall then summon an Assembly, and propose the said Laws for their consent."[3]

Most fortunately neither of these instructions could be enforced. The great distance of England from Virginia, and the time required to communicate with the King, made the summoning of the Assembly and the initiation of legislation without the royal assent a matter of absolute necessity. Lord Culpeper, with his Majesty's especial permission, disregarded these orders during his first visit to the colony, and later, to his great satisfaction, the Committee of Trade and Plantations "altered their measures therein".[4]

Culpeper was directed to secure in the colony a permanent

[2] P. R. O., CO5-1355-334; McD., Vol. V, p. 302.
[3] P. R. O., CO5-1355-313, 334.
[4] P. R. O., CO5-1355-334; McD., Vol. V, p. 302.

revenue for the King. It was rightly judged that the representatives of royal authority could never be entirely masters of the government while they were dependent for their salaries upon the votes of the Assembly. Sir William Berkeley, it is true, had rendered his position secure by obliging all "the men of parts and estates", but similar methods might be impossible for other Governors. The King and Privy Council did not, however, attempt to raise the desired revenue by imposing a tax upon the people without their own consent. An act levying a duty of two shillings a hogshead upon all tobacco exported from Virginia was drawn up by the Attorney-General for ratification by the Assembly.[5] The consent of the King in Council was duly received and the bill, with an act concerning naturalization and another for a general pardon, were sent to Virginia by Lord Culpeper. "These bills," the King told him, "we have caused to be under the Greate Seale of England. and our will is that the same . . . you shall cause to be considered and treated upon in our Assembly of Virginia."[6]

The revenue bill was quite similar to an act of Assembly still in force, which had imposed a duty upon exported tobacco, but an all-important difference lay in the disposal of the funds thus raised. The former statute had given the proceeds of this tax to the Assembly, "for the defraying the publique necessary charges",[7] but the new act was to grant the money "to the King's most excellent Majesty his heires and Successors for ever to and for the better support of the Government".[8]

In order to carry out these new designs for the government of the colony, the King ordered Lord Culpeper to prepare to sail at once. The Governor, however, was most reluctant to leave the pleasures of the court for a life in the American wilderness. His departure had already been long delayed, more than two years having elapsed since Charles had told the colonists to expect his speedy arrival. Yet he still delayed and procrastinated. On the third of December, 1679,

[5] P. R. O., CO5-1356; CO391.2-276, 325, 283 to 285.
[6] P. R. O., CO1-43-165. [7] Hen., II, p. 133.
[8] P. R. O., CO5-1376; Hen., Vol. II, p. 466.

an order was issued giving his Lordship "liberty to stay in Towne about his affaires until Monday next, and noe longer, and then to proceed forthwith" to the Downs, where "the Oxford frigat" was waiting to convey him to Virginia.[9] But as he still lingered in London, the Captain of the frigate was ordered to sail up the Thames to take him on board.[10] No sooner had he left his moorings, however, than Culpeper, probably in order to gain time, hastened away to the Downs. This so aroused the King's anger that he was pleased to direct one of his principal secretaries to signify by letter to Lord Culpeper his high displeasure at his delay and neglect of duty, and that his intentions were to appoint another Governor of Virginia unless he embarked as soon as the frigate returned to the Downs.[11] But now adverse winds set in, and Culpeper, with the tobacco fleet which had waited for him, was unable to sail until February 13, 1680.[12]

He arrived off the capes May the second, and eight days later took formal possession of his government. Immediately the Councillors and other leading planters flocked around him, eager to secure his support against the old rebellious party. Nor was their presentation of their cause ineffectual in winning the Governor's sympathy. "All things," he wrote Secretary Coventry, "are . . . far otherwise than I supposed in England, and I beleeve ye Council, at least I have seen through a mist."[13] It was to be expected then, that in settling the dispute that had so long troubled the colony he would favor the Berkeley faction. And this, so far as the King's commands would permit, he seems to have done. The wealthy planters expressed their satisfaction with his measures, and the commons, if they disapproved, feared to reveal their resentment. "His Excellency," wrote Colonel Spencer, "has with soe great prudence settled all the Affairs of the Country that our late different Interests are perfectly united to the general satisfaction of all his Majesty's Subjects in this colony."[14]

The Berkeley party was deeply displeased at the King's

[9] P. R. O., CO5-1355-372.

[10] P. R. O., CO5-1355-375.

[11] P. R. O., CO5-1355-375, 376.

[12] P. R. O., CO5-1355-378.

[13] P. R. O., CO5-1355-385.

[14] P. R. O., CO5-1355-384.

command to exclude Colonel Philip Ludwell from the Council. Recognizing in the order the influence of Colonel Jeffreys and the other commissioners, they assured the Governor that it had been secured by false representations. The Councillors declared "that they were very sencible of ye want of that Assistance they for many Years" had had from Colonel Ludwell, "whose good abilities, Knowne Integrity and approved Loyalty" rendered him most necessary to his Majesty's service. They therefore earnestly requested "his Excellency to Readmitt & Receive him to be one of ye Councill".[15] Culpeper yielded readily, and Ludwell was restored to his seat.

The Burgesses were chagrined at the order to oust Major Robert Beverley from all public employment. He was again the clerk of Assembly, for which office he was "their Unanimous Choyce", and his disgrace was regarded as a rebuke to the House.[16] Upon their earnest petition Culpeper consented that he should retain that important post in which he was soon to render signal service to the people and to incur again the anger of the King and his ministers.[17]

When the Assembly convened the Governor at once laid before it the Act of General Pardon, the Act of Naturalization and the Act for a Public Revenue. To the first and the second he obtained a prompt assent, but the third was strenuously resisted. The House of Burgesses was filled with gentlemen of the best families, men closely allied with the Council in position and interest, yet they were unwilling to permit any part of the public revenue to pass out of the control of the people.[18] "The House," they declared, "doe most humbly desire to be Excused if they doe not give their approbacon of his Majesties bill."[19] And so determined were they, that when the matter was again brought before them by the Governor they refused even to resume the debate.[20]

[15] P. R. O., CO5-1376-265. [16] Jour. H. of B., 1680, p. 1.

[17] Jour. H. of B., 1680, p. 7.

[18] Among the Burgesses were Captain William Byrd, Major Swann, Benjamin Harrison, Colonel Ballard, Colonel Mason, Colonel John Page, Colonel Matthew Kemp, William Fitzhugh, Isaac Allerton, John Carter and Captain Fox. P. R. O., CO5-1376-321.

[19] Jour. H. of B., 1680, pp. 13, 14. [20] Jour. H. of B., 1680, p. 27.

But Culpeper, fearful of the King's displeasure, and uneasy for the payment of his own salary, made strenuous efforts to secure the passage of the bill. He did not scruple to resort to bribery and intimidation to force obedience from the stubborn Burgesses. We have the testimony of the Governor himself to one notorious case of the misuse of the patronage. Among the leaders of the House of Burgesses was Isaac Allerton, a man of wealth and education, and an excellent speaker.[21] "He did assure me," Culpeper reported to the Privy Council, "of his utmost services in whatsoever the King should command him by his Governor, particularly as to a further Bill of Revenue for the support of ye Government, And I did engage to move his Majesty that hee should bee of the Council . . . though not to be declared till after the Session of next Assembly, when I am sure he can bee as serviceable if not more than any other person whatsoever."[22] This bargain was faithfully kept and in time Allerton, for thus betraying his trust, received his seat in the Council.[23]

Nor did Lord Culpeper hesitate to intimidate the Burgesses by threatening to demand the payment of all arrears of quit-rents. This tax, although belonging to the King from the first settlement of the colony, had not, for many years, been duly collected. It was now rumored, however, that the Privy Council intended, not only to enforce for the future a strict payment, but to demand a settlement for the accumulated arrears. In 1679 Sir Henry Chicheley had forwarded to his Majesty a petition from the Assembly asking relief from this great burden. If this be not granted, he wrote, the payments which have been so long due and amount to so vast a sum, will fall heavily upon all, but especially upon the poor.[24] Culpeper, knowing well the anxiety of the Burgesses upon this point, told them that if they expected the King to grant their petition, they must yield to his desire for a royal revenue in the colony.

Calling the Assembly before him, he urged them to resume their debate. "It looks," he said, "as if you could give noe reasons or as if you were affraid to be convinced. . . . I desire

[21] P. R. O., CO5-1356-125.
[22] P. R. O., CO5-1356-125, 126.
[23] P. R. O., CO5-1356-265.
[24] P. R. O., CO5-1355-361.

you to lay aside that irregular proceeding . . . and resume the debate." The Council, he added, had given their unanimous consent to the bill. "Consider the affaires of the Quitt Rents, Consider the King's favour in every thing you may aske even to a cessacon . . . and reflect if it be tante for you not to concurr in a thing that, I am assured, ye King . . . judges his owne and will soe use it and the more fully then if this Act pass."[25]

Thus threatened, the Burgesses finally yielded, and the bill became law. But they insisted upon adding to it two provisos: that the former export duty upon tobacco be repealed, and that the exemption of Virginia ship owners from the payment of the tax, which had been a provision of the former law, should be continued.[26] When some months later the matter came before the Committee of Trade and Plantations, their Lordships expressed much dissatisfaction at these amendments, declaring that the bill should have passed "in Terminis". Since, however, the first proviso in no way changed the sense of the act, and had been added only to prevent a double imposition, they recommended that it should be continued. But the second was declared null and void by order of the King, as "irregular and unfit to be allowed of".[27]

Lord Culpeper, immediately after the dismissal of the Assembly made ready to return to England. August 3, 1680, he read to the Council an order from the King granting him permission to leave the colony, and a few days later he set sail in *The James*.[28] The government was again left in the hands of the infirm Chicheley.[29]

Culpeper, upon his arrival in England, told the King that all was well in the colony, that the old contentions had been forgotten, and the people were happy and prosperous. But this favorable report, which was made by the Governor to palliate his desertion of his post, was far from being true. There was, as he well knew, a deep-seated cause of discontent in Virginia, that threatened constantly to drive the people again into mutiny

[25] Jour. H. of B., 1680, p. 32. [26] Jour. H. of B., 1680, p. 36.

[27] P. R. O., CO5-1355-388 to 394.

[28] P. R. O., CO5-1355-380; CO5-1376-286.

[29] P. R. O., CO5-1355-396.

and disorder. This was the continued low price of tobacco. In the years which had elapsed since Bacon's Rebellion, the people, despite their bitter quarrels, had produced several large crops, and the English market was again glutted. "What doth quite overwhelm both us and Maryland," complained the colonists, "is the extreme low price of our only commodity . . . and consequently our vast poverty and infinite necessity."[30] The Burgesses, in 1682, spoke of the worthlessness of tobacco as an "ineffable Calamity". "Wee are," they said, "noe wayes able to force a miserable subsistance from the same. . . . If force of penne, witt, or words Could truely represent (our condition) as it is, the sad resentments would force blood from any Christian Loyall Subjects heart."[31] Some months later the Council wrote, "The people of Virginia are generally, some few excepted, extremely poor, . . . not being able to provide against the pressing necessities of their families."[32] That the Privy Council was aware, as early as October, 1681, that these conditions might lead to another insurrection, is attested by a letter of the Committee of Trade and Plantations to Lord Culpeper. "We are informed," they wrote, "that Virginia is in great danger of disturbance . . . by reason of the extreme poverty of the People, occasioned by the low price of tobacco which, tis feared may induce the servants to plunder the Stores of the Planters and the Ships arriving there and to commit other outrages and disorders as in the late Rebellion."[33]

This universal distress created a strong sentiment throughout the colony in favor of governmental restriction upon the planting of tobacco. Unless something were done to limit the annual crop, prices would continue to decline. Many merchants, who had bought up large quantities of tobacco in England with the expectation that its value would eventually rise, "fell to insinuate with the easiest sort People how advantageous it would bee . . . if an Act of Assembly could be procured to cease planting tobacco for one whole year".[34]

[30] P. R. O., CO5-1355-408.
[31] Jour. H. of B., April 1682, p. 4.
[32] P. R. O., CO5-1356-179.
[33] P. R. O., CO5-1356-1, 2.
[34] P. R. O., CO5-1356-177.

When, in the spring of 1682, it became apparent that another large crop must be expected, an almost universal demand arose for the immediate convening of the Assembly for the passage of a law of cessation.

The Councillors, although themselves in favor of some restraint upon the huge output, advised the aged Deputy-Governor not to consent to a session at this juncture.[35] But Chicheley, persuaded, it was claimed, by the insistent arguments of Major Beverley, yielded to the desires of the people, and upon his own responsibility, issued writs summoning the Burgesses to convene at Jamestown, April 18, 1682.[36] Five days before the date of meeting, however, a letter arrived from the King, expressly forbidding an Assembly until November the tenth, when, it was hoped, Lord Culpeper would have returned to his government.[37] The letter also informed the Deputy-Governor that two companies of troops that had remained in Virginia ever since the Rebellion, could no longer be maintained at the expense of the royal Exchequer. Since many of the Burgesses were already on their way to Jamestown, Sir Henry decided to hold a brief session, in order to permit them, if they so desired, to continue the companies at the charge of the colony.[38] But he expressed his determination, in obedience to the King's commands, to forbid the consideration of any other matter whatsoever.

The Burgesses met "big with expectation to enact a Cessation".[39] The appeals of their constituents and the smart of their own purses made them desperately resolute to give the country relief from the present depressing conditions. When they learned that after all their session was to be in vain, and that they were to be allowed to vote only on the matter of continuing the companies, they were deeply concerned and angered. Addressing the Deputy Governor, they declared themselves overwhelmed with grief at the expectation of adjournment. They had, from all parts of the drooping country, passionately wended their way to Jamestown, to attend this Assembly, upon

[35] P. R. O., CO5-1356-73.

[36] P. R. O., CO5-1356-73, 156; Jour, H. of B., April 1682.

[37] P. R. O., CO5-1356-11, 12, 68, 72.

[38] P. R. O., CO5-1356-8.

[39] P. R. O., CO5-1356-68.

which the "last expiring hopes" of the "miserably indigent poor Country" were reposed. Should they be compelled to return to their homes, having accomplished nothing, the people would be struck with amazement, "like an unexpected death wound".[40]

The Deputy Governor, not daring to disobey the King, ignored their appeal, and bade them decide without delay whether or not they would continue the two companies. But the Burgesses would give no definite answer upon this matter, hoping by a policy of delay to win, in the end, Chicheley's consent to the cessation. After seven days of fruitless bickering Sir Henry, in anger at their obstinacy, prorogued the Assembly to November the tenth.[41] Before their dismissal, however, the Burgesses, in order to show that they had not been remiss in endeavoring to secure relief for the people, voted that the journal of their proceedings should be read publicly in every county.

Nor had they misjudged the desperate humor of the people. When it became known throughout the colony that the Assembly had done nothing to restrict the planting of tobacco, the anger of the poor planters could not be restrained. Some bold spirits proposed that the people should assemble in various parts of the country, and, in defiance of law and order, cut to pieces the tobacco then in the fields. If the King would not permit a cessation by law, they would bring about a cessation by force. A few days after the close of the Assembly, parties of men in Gloucester began the work of destruction. It required but little exertion to ruin the tender plants, and the rioters, passing from plantation to plantation, in an incredibly short time accomplished enormous havoc. Many men, filled with the contagion, cut up their own tobacco, and then joined the mob in the destruction of the crops of their neighbors.[42]

As soon as the news of this strange insurrection reached Jamestown, Chicheley dispatched Colonel Kemp to Gloucester with directions to muster the militia and to restore order by

[40] Jour. H. of B., April 1682, pp. 4, 5.

[41] Jour. H. of B., April 1682; P. R. O., CO5-1356-68.

[42] P. R. O., CO5-1356-65, 66, 67.

force of arms. This officer, with a troop of horse, fell upon one party of plant-cutters, and captured twenty-two of their number. "Two of the principal and incorrigible rogues" he held for trial, but "the rest submitting and giving assurances of their quiet and peacable behavior were remitted".[43] Other parties, intimidated by these vigorous measures, dispersed, and soon peace was restored throughout all Gloucester. But now news reached the Deputy-Governor "that the next adjacent county, being new Kent, was lately broke forth, committing the like spoyles on plants". And no sooner had the troops suppressed the rioters here than the disorders spread to Middlesex and other counties. It became necessary to issue orders to the commanders of the militia in each county to keep parties of horse in continual motion, to prevent the designs of the plant-cutters and arrest their leaders.[44] And then the rioters, who had at first carried on their work in the open day, "went in great companys by night, destroying and pulling up whole fields of tobacco after it was well grown".[45] Not until August were the disorders finally suppressed.

These troubles, coming so soon after Bacon's Rebellion, caused great apprehension, both to the colonial government and to the Privy Council. "I know," wrote Secretary Spencer, "the necessities of the inhabitants to be such . . . their low estate makes them desperate. . . . If they goe forward the only destroying Tobacco plants will not satiate their rebellious appatites who, if they increase and find the strength of their own arms, will not bound themselves."[46] And, although the actual rioters were "inconsiderable people", yet it was thought they had been instigated by men of position and wealth.[47]

Grave suspicion rested upon Major Robert Beverley.[48] It had been the importunities of "the over-active Clerk" that had persuaded Chicheley, against the advice of the Council, to convene the Assembly. It was he that had been the most industrious advocate of a cessation, that had fomented the disputes in the Assembly, that had most strenuously opposed

[43] P. R. O., CO5-1356-70.
[44] P. R. O., CO5-1356-71.
[45] P. R. O., CO5-1356-178.
[46] P. R. O., CO5-1356-71.
[47] P. R. O., CO5-1356-178.
[48] P. R. O., CO5-1356-74.

adjournment. And it was he, the Council believed, that had "instilled into the multitude . . . the right of making a Cessation by cutting up Plants".[49] Moreover, they thought it not improbable that he would lead the people into a new insurrection. The rabble regarded him with veneration and love. His activity in suppressing the Rebellion and his opposition to the county grievances of 1677 had been forgotten, and they saw in him now only the defender of the poor and helpless. Were he to assume the rôle of a Bacon and place himself at the head of the commons, he might easily make himself master of the colony. Although there was no evidence against him, "but only rudeness and sauciness", it was thought advisable to render him powerless to accomplish harm, by placing him under arrest.[50] He was taken without resistance by Major-General Smith, "though to his own great loss of 2 or 300 pounds, by the Rabbles cutting up his Tobacco plants within two days after out of Spight".[51]

Beverley was kept in strict confinement on board an English ship, the *Duke of York,* where for the time, he was safe from rescue by the people. But so fearful was the Council that he might plot for a general insurrection, that they issued orders forbidding him to send or to receive letters, and permitting him to speak only in the presence of the captain of the ship.[52] Even these harsh measures did not reassure them, and it was decided to send him to the Eastern Shore, where the people were most loyal to the government, and where rescue would be impossible.[53] As preparations were being made to effect his transfer, he escaped from the custody of the sheriff, and returned to his home in Middlesex. But he was soon recaptured, and conveyed to Northampton. Here, despite all the efforts of his friends and his own violent protests, he was kept in confinement for months. In the fall he applied for a writ of habeas corpus, but this was denied him under the pretext that the whole matter had been referred to the King, and was no longer within the jurisdiction of the Deputy-Governor

[49] P. R. O., CO5-1356-74.

[50] Hen., Vol. III, p. 543.

[51] P. R. O., CO5-1356-156.

[52] Hen., Vol. III, p. 544.

[53] Hen., Vol. III, p. 546.

and Council.[54] Since, however, all fear of a rebellion was now passed, he was permitted, upon giving bail to the sum of £2,000, to return to his home. But he was still restricted to the counties of Middlesex and Gloucester, was declared ineligible to public office and was forbidden to plead as an attorney in any colonial court.[55]

When the Privy Council learned of the plant-cutting in Virginia, they ordered Lord Culpeper "to repair to the Government with all possible speed, in order to find out, by the strictest enquiry, the abbetors and instruments of this commotion". And since they too were fearful of a new insurrection, they gave directions "that some person who shall be found most faulty may be forthwith punished".[56] "After which," the Privy Council advised, "and not before the Governor may be directed to consider of and propose, with the advice of the Council and the Assembly, . . . some temperament in relation to the Planting of Tobacco and raising the price of that commodity."[57]

Culpeper left England in October, 1682, upon "the Mermaid frigat", and, after a tedious and dangerous voyage of eleven weeks, arrived safely in Virginia. He was resolved that the persons responsible for the plant-cutting should be brought immediately to trial, and punished with the utmost rigor of the law. The strictest inquiry was made into the conduct of Major Beverley, and had there been evidence sufficient to convict him, the unfortunate Clerk would undoubtedly have suffered death upon the gallows. But since only the most trivial offenses could be adduced against him, Culpeper was forced to turn elsewhere for the victims demanded by the English government.

So the prosecution was now directed against some of the actual plant-cutters. In this, however, Culpeper found himself greatly embarrassed by Chicheley's previous treatment of the matter. The Deputy-Governor had, some months before, issued pardons to many of the chief offenders, and had permitted the others to give bail, thus treating their crime as "Ryot and noe more", and making the affair seem "as slight

[54] Hen., Vol. III, pp. 546, 547.
[55] Hen., Vol. III, p. 547.
[56] P. R. O., CO5-1356-76.
[57] P. R. O., CO5-1356-76, 77.

as possible to the people".[58] But Culpeper, despite this action of Sir Henry, ordered the arrest of four of the most notorious plant-cutters and charged them with high treason. Their trial created great excitement throughout the colony, but "despite the high words and threats" of the rabble, three of them were convicted. Two were executed—Somerset Davies at Jamestown, and Black Austin "before the Court-house in Glocester county, where the Insurrection first broke out".[59] The third was pardoned by the Governor. "Hee was extremely young," Culpeper wrote, "not past 19, meerely drawn in and very penitent, and therefore . . . I thought fit to mingle mercy with Justice and Repreeved him . . . to the end the whole country might be convinced that there was no other motive in the thing but purely to maintain Government."[60]

But although Culpeper was thus vigorous in punishing the disorders of the poor people, he did nothing to remove the cause of their turbulence—the low price of tobacco. By an order in Council of June 17, 1682, he had been directed to grant a cessation, should it seem expedient, and had been given a letter from Secretary Jenkins to Lord Baltimore, requiring the cooperation of Maryland.[61] But, upon finding the colony in peace and quiet, and the Assembly busy with other concerns, he "took advantage thereof", and kept secret this unexpected concession. Culpeper pretended to believe that the desired cessation would be of no real benefit to the planters, but it is clear that he was consciously betraying the colony to the greed of the royal Exchequer.[62] "I soe encouraged the planting of tobacco," he reported to the Privy Council ,"that if the season continue to be favorable . . . there will bee a greater cropp by far than ever grew since its first seating. And I am confident that Customs next year from thence will be £50,000 more than ever heretofore in any one year."[63] Immediately after, he declared that he well knew "that the great Cropp then in hand would most certainly bring that place into the utmost exigen-

[58] P. R. O., CO5-1356-157.
[59] P. R. O., CO5-1356-158.
[60] P. R. O., CO5-1356-159.
[61] P. R. O., CO5-1356-76, 77, 163.
[62] P. R. O., CO5-1356-164.
[63] P. R. O., CO5-1356-164.

cies again", and he promised to be prepared to quell the disturbances that would result.[64]

Before Lord Culpeper left England an order had been delivered to him "commanding that noe Governour of his Majesty's Plantations, doe come into England from his Government", without first obtaining leave from the King.[65] But so loath was he to remain long in Virginia, that as soon as he had dispatched the business of the April court, he once more set sail for England. "I judged it a proper time," he said, "to make a step home this easy quiet year, not out of any fondness to bee in England, . . . but for the King's service only."[66]

But Charles and the Privy Council were weary of Culpeper's neglect of duty. They decided to rid themselves of so untrustworthy an officer and to appoint in his place a man that would remain in the colony and carry out their wishes and policies. An inquisition was held upon his conduct, and his letters patent as Governor-General were declared void[67] On the 28th of September, 1683, a commission as Lieutenant- and Governor-General of Virginia was granted to Lord Howard of Effingham.[68]

Few British colonial Governors are less deserving of respect than Thomas Lord Culpeper. He was insensible of any obligation to guard the welfare of the people of Virginia, and was negligent in executing the commands of the King. He seems to have regarded his office only as an easy means of securing a large income, and he was untiring in his efforts to extort money from the exhausted and impoverished colony. Sir William Berkeley's salary as Governor had been £1,000, but Culpeper demanded and received no less than £2,000.[69] In addition, he was allowed £150 a year in lieu of a residence, received pay as captain of infantry and claimed large sums under the provisions of the Arlington-Culpeper grant.

Nor did he scruple to resort to open fraud in satisfying his greed. There were, in 1680, two companies remaining in

[64] P. R. O., CO5-1356-164, 169. [65] P. R. O., CO5-1356-87.
[66] P. R. O., CO5-1356-168, 169.
[67] P. R. O., CO5-1356-188, 239, 244, 114.
[68] P. R. O., CO5-1356-188.
[69] P. R. O., CO5-1356-56, 145, 146.

Virginia of the troops sent over to suppress Bacon's Rebellion. Having received no pay for many months, the soldiers were discontented and mutinous.[70] The Privy Council entrusted to Culpeper, upon his first departure for the colony, money to satisfy them, and to compensate the householders with whom they had been quartered.[71] At this period, as always in the seventeenth century, there was a great scarcity of specie in Virginia. But there circulated, usually by weight, various foreign coins, the most common of which was the Spanish piece of eight, about equal in value to five shillings in English money. My Lord, upon his arrival, industriously bought up all the worn coins he could secure, arbitrarily proclaimed them legal tender at the ratio of six shillings to one piece of eight, and then paid the soldiers and the landlords. This ingenious trick probably netted him over £1,000. Later he restored the ratio to five to one, so that he would lose nothing when his own salary became due. Of such stuff were some of the Virginia colonial governors.[72]

But Culpeper's many defects were not wholly unfortunate for the colony, for they rendered him unfit to carry out the designs of the King. His frequent absences from his government made it impossible for him to become thoroughly acquainted with conditions in the colony, or to bind the wealthy to him by a judicious use of the patronage. He was too weak, too careless to pursue a long continued attack upon the established privileges of the people.

It boded ill, therefore, for Virginia, when he was removed, and a commission granted to Lord Howard. The new Governor was well fitted for the task of oppression and coersion. Unscrupulous, deceitful, overbearing, resentful, persistent, he proved a dangerous foe to the representative institutions of the colony, and an able defender of royal prerogative. Had he not encountered throughout his entire administration, the united and determined resistance of the Burgesses, he might have overthrown all constitutional government. Well it was for Virginia that at this moment of imminent danger, the Bur-

[70] P. R. O., CO5-1376-287.

[71] P. R. O., CO1-42-152; CO391.2-276.

[72] Beverley.

gesses should have been so conscious of their duty and so resolute in executing it. They were still, as in most periods of colonial history, men of high social position, but they represented, not their own class, but the entire colony. And they were ever watchful to guard the interests of the commons.

Effingham took the oath of office in England, October 24, 1683,[73] and a few months later sailed for the colony.[74] No sooner had he set foot in Virginia than the struggle with the Burgesses began. The session of Assembly of April, 1684, was filled with their bitter disputes.

Consternation reigned in the House when Lord Howard produced an instruction from the King forbidding appeals from the inferior courts to the Assembly.[75] As early as October, 1678, Colonel Francis Moryson had advised the Privy Council to abolish the judicial powers of the Assembly, claiming that they were the source of the great influence and "arrogancy" of that body.[76] Their Lordships did not awaken at once to the importance of this matter, but before long they became convinced that Moryson was right. Accordingly Lord Culpeper, in his commission of 1682, was directed to procure the immediate repeal of all laws "allowing appeals to the Assembly".[77] But Culpeper, interested only in securing money from the Burgesses, failed to put this instruction into operation. "As to what concerns Appeals," he declared, "I have never once permitted any one to come to the Assembly, soe that the thing is in effect done. But having some thoughts of getting a Revenue Bill to pass, I was unwilling actually to repeal ye Laws relating thereunto till the next session of Assembly should be over, well knowing how infinitely it would trouble them."[78]

But Effingham had no such scruples, and told the Burgesses plainly the commands he bore from the King.[79] The House, in great dismay, requested the Governor and the Council to join them in an address to his Majesty, imploring him to restore a privilege which had so long been enjoyed "according to ye

[73] P. R. O., CO5-1356-244, 245.
[74] P. R. O., CO5-1356-248.
[75] Jour. H. of B., 1684, pp. 23, 24.
[76] P. R. O., CO1-42-138, 139.
[77] P. R. O., CO5-1356-53.
[78] P. R. O., CO5-1356-142.
[79] P. R. O., CO5-1356-22

Laws and antient Practice of the Country".[80] But Lord Howard replied coldly, "It is what I can in noe parte admitt of, his Majesty haveing been pleased by his Royal instruccons to direct & command that noe appeales be open to the General Assembly."[81]

Nor did the Assembly ever regain this important power. As late as 1691 we find the agent of the Burgesses in England asking in vain for the restoration of the right of appeals.[82] The change threw into the hands of the Governor and Council extraordinary power over the judiciary of the colony. The county justices, who sat in the lower courts, were the appointees of the Governor, and could not effectually resist his will. Moreover, as appeals lay from them to the General Court, they were powerless before the decisions of the superior tribunal. Thus the judiciary of the colony lost its only democratic feature.

The Burgesses, undismayed by their defeat in this matter, at this same session entered a vigorous protest against the King's right to annul acts of Assembly. During Berkeley's administration his Majesty had seldom exercised this power, but of late many acts had been repealed by proclamation without the consent or knowledge of the Assembly. This, the Burgesses claimed, was an unwarranted infringement upon the privileges granted them "by sundry Comissions, Letters and Instructions", that was most destructive of their cherished liberties and rights. And they demanded that henceforth their statutes should have the force of law until they had been "Repealed by the same Authority of Generall Assembly".[83] But they received no encouragement from the Governor. What you ask, he told them, "is soe great an entrenchment upon ye Royall authority that I cannot but wonder you would offer at it".[84]

Thereupon the House determined to appeal directly to the King, petitioning him not only to give up the right of repealing laws by proclamation, but to permit the continuation of appeals to the Assembly. Since the Governor refused to

[80] Jour. H. of B., 1684, p. 37.
[81] Jour, H. of B., 1684, p. 42.
[82] Justice in Va., p. 25.
[83] Jour. H. of B., 1684, p. 114.
[84] Jour. H. of B., 1684, p. 159.

transmit their address to his Majesty, they forwarded copies to Secretary Jenkins by two of their own members—Thomas Milner and William Sherwood.[85]

This address received scant consideration from the King and the Privy Council. "Whereas," James II wrote Effingham in October, 1685, "it hath been represented unto us by our Committee for Trade and Plantations, that they have received from some unknown persons a paper entitled an address and supplication of the General Assembly of Virginia . . . which you had refused to recommend as being unfit to be presented. . . . Wee cannot but approve of your proceedings. . . . And wee doe further direct you to discountenance such undue practices for the future as alsoe the Contrivers and Promoters thereof."[86] For their activity in this matter Sherwood and Milner "in ye following year were both turned out of all imployments to their great damage and disgrace".[87]

In the spring of 1685 Effingham received notification from the Privy Council of the death of Charles II and the accession of the Duke of York as James II.[88] He replied a few days later, "I have, with the greatest solemnity this place is capable of proclaimed his Majesty King James II in all the considerable places of this colony, where the great Acclamations and Prayers of the People gave a universal Testimony of their Obedience."[89] Despite these outward manifestations of joy, the people were by no means pleased to have a Roman Catholic monarch upon the English throne. When news reached Virginia that the Duke of Monmouth was in open rebellion, and had gained important successes over his Majesty's forces, there was grave danger that the commons of the colony might espouse his cause.[90] Many were so emboldened, wrote Effingham, "that their tongues ran at large and demonstrated the wickedness of their hearts, till I secured some and deterred others from spreading such false reports by my Proclama-

[85] P. R. O., CO5-1356-299, 301.
[86] P. R. O., CO5-1357-58.
[87] McD., Vol. VII, p. 88.
[88] P. R. O., CO5-1356-316.
[89] P. R. O., CO5-1356-328.
[90] P. R. O., CO5-1357-79, 80, 95, 96; Jour. H. of B., 1685, p. 49.

tion".[91] The defeat and execution of the Duke of Monmouth for a time ended all thought of resistance to the King.

But Effingham found the people sullen and discontented and the Burgesses more stubborn than ever. The session of Assembly of 1685 was, perhaps, the most stormy ever held in Virginia. The House made a strenuous and successful resistance to a vigorous attempt to deprive it of its control over taxation. In 1662, when the Assembly was dominated by Sir William Berkeley, an act had been passed empowering the Governor and Council to levy annually for three years a tax of not more than twenty pounds of tobacco per poll.[92] In 1680 the Council had requested Lord Culpeper to represent to the King the disadvantages of leaving taxation entirely in the hands of the Assembly, hoping that his Majesty would by proclamation revive the law of 1662.[93] The greatest item of expense to the government, they argued, arose from the Assembly itself, "ye charge of which hath been too often found to be twice as much as would have satisfied all publiq dues".[94] The matter was presented to the consideration of the Burgesses in 1680, but was lost in the committee room.[95]

The King and Privy Council, although they approved of the levy by the Governor and the Council, did not venture to grant them that power by royal proclamation. They instructed Lord Howard, however, in his commission of 1683, to propose for passage in the Assembly a law similar to that of 1662.[96] Accordingly, in 1684, Effingham placed the matter before the Burgesses and told them that it was the King's desire that they give their consent. But they ignored his message, and the Governor could not press the matter at that time. In the next session, however, he became more insistent. "I must remind you," he told the Burgesses, "of what was omitted in ye last Assembly . . . that a Law may passe whereby His Majesty's Governor with ye advice of ye Council may be empowered to lay a levy."[97] But the Burgesses

[91] P. R. O., CO5-1357-80.

[92] Hen., Vol. II, p. 24; P R. O., CO5-1376-281.

[93] P. R. O., CO5-1376-281.

[94] P. R. O., CO5-1376-281; CO5-1356-101.

[95] P. R. O., CO5-1376-362.

[96] P. R. O., CO5-1356-267.

[97] Jour. H. of B., 1685.

would not yield. "The House," they replied, ". . . do humbly signifye to your Excellency, that they can noe waies concede to or comply with that proposition, without apparent and signal violation of ye great trust with them reposed."[98] And when Effingham urged them to reconsider their action, they passed a resolution unanimously refusing to relinquish this their greatest privilege.

After the prorogation of the Assembly, Lord Howard wrote home his complaints against the stubborn Burgesses. "Your Lordships," he said, "will . . . find their total denyal that the Governor and Council should have any power to lay the least Levy to ease the necessity of soe frequent Assemblys. . . . This was propounded by mee to them before his Majesty's Instructions came to my hand that I should, . . . but nothing would prevail nor I beleeve will, unless his Majesty's special command therein."[99]

A long and acrimonious quarrel occurred over the quit-rents. Because of the lack of specie in the colony, it had always been necessary to collect this tax, when it was collected at all, in tobacco. In March, 1662, the Assembly had passed a law fixing the rate of payment at two pence a pound, which was then not far from the current price. But the decline in value of the commodity which had occurred since 1662, had resulted in a great diminution in the tax.

In July, 1684, the King wrote Effingham that he had taken over all the rights of Arlington and Culpeper to the quit-rents, and announced it his intention to use them for the support of the Virginia government. He directed the Governor to secure the repeal of the law of 1662 and to forbid all payments in tobacco. "You must . . . impower," he wrote, "the Officers of our Revenue to collect (them) . . . according to ye reservation of 2s per every hundred acres . . . to be paid in specie, that is in Mony."[100]

As tobacco sold, in 1684, at a half penny a pound, this order, had it been put into operation, would have quadrupled the value of the quit-rents, and increased materially the burdens

[98] Jour. H. of B., 1685.
[99] P. R. O., CO5-1357-85.
[100] P. R. O., CO5-1356-282.

of the planters. The Burgesses, in alarm, petitioned the Governor to allow the old arrangement to continue, declaring that the lack of specie made it impossible to comply with the King's order. And they refused to repeal the law of March, 1662.

Displeased at their obstinacy, the King, in August, 1686, nullified the law by proclamation. "Being now informed," he declared, "that several persons goe about to impede our Service . . . by imposing bad tobacco upon our collectors at the rate of 2d per llb, under pretence of an Act of Assembly of March 30, 1662, . . . Wee have thought fit to Repeal the said Act."[101]

Even then the Burgesses resisted. At the session of 1686 they petitioned on behalf of all the freeholders of the colony that the quit-rents should be paid as formerly. To make payment in specie, they declared, would not only be ruinous, but utterly impossible.[102] So angered were they and so determined not to obey, that Effingham found it expedient to consent to a compromise. It was agreed that the tax should be collected in tobacco as before, but at the rate of one penny per pound, which, as Effingham said, was not ad valorum. Thus the only result of this long quarrel was to double the value of the quit-rents, and to add greatly to the burdens of the impoverished and discontented people.[103]

Even more bitter was the contest over the so-called Bill of Ports. This measure was designed to remedy the scattered mode of living in Virginia, by appointing certain places as ports of landing and shipment, and confining to them all foreign trade. Throughout the seventeenth century almost all shipping was done from private wharves. The country was so interspersed with rivers, inlets and creeks, deep enough to float the largest vessels, that ports were entirely unnecessary. Each planter dealt directly with the merchants, receiving English manufactured goods almost at his front door, and lading the ships with tobacco from his own warehouse. This system, so natural and advantageous, seemed to the English Kings, and even to the colonists, a sign of unhealthful con-

[101] P. R. O., CO5-1357-113.
[102] Jour. H. of B., 1686, p. 17.
[103] Jour. H. of B., 1686, p. 37.

ditions. More than once attempts had been made to force the people to build towns and to discontinue the desultory plantation trade.

In 1679, Culpeper was ordered to propose a law in the Assembly requiring the erection of towns on each great river, to which all foreign trade should be confined. Accordingly, in 1680, a Bill of Ports was passed. "Wee are now grown sensible," wrote Secretary Spencer, "that our present necessities, and too much to be doubted future miseries, are much heightened by our wild and rambling way of living, therefore are desirous of cohabitation, in order whereunto in ye late Assembly an Act was made appointing a town in every County, where all Goods imported are to be landed, and all Goods exported to be shipt off. And if this takes effect, as its hoped it may, Virginia will then go forward which of late years hath made a retrograde motion."[104]

But this attempt ended in dismal failure. In 1681, when the shipmasters came to the appointed ports, they found that no shelter had been constructed for their goods. Thinking the law nullified, or not yet in operation, they traded as usual from private wharves. For this breach of the law, some of them were prosecuted in the colonial courts, to their own great loss and to the inconvenience of many of the planters.[105] Loud wrangling and bitter animosities resulted throughout the colony, and at length the King was compelled to suspend the law.[106]

In the Assembly of 1685 it was proposed to enact another Bill of Ports. Accordingly an act was drafted in the House of Burgesses and, in due time, sent up for the approval of the Council. The upper house, after making several alterations, consented to the bill and returned it to the Burgesses. The latter agreed to most of the changes, but struck out a clause restricting the towns to two upon each river, and added an amendment permitting one port to a county.[107] The Council in turn yielded, but inserted a new clause, "That there should bee ffees ascertained on Goods exported and imported for the

[104] P. R. O., CO5-1355-383.
[105] P. R. O., CO5-1356-177.
[106] P. R. O., CO5-1356-4.
[107] P. R. O., CO5-1407-310, 282.

support of those Officers which should bee obliged to reside in those Ports".[108] As "there was noe room in ye margint to write ye alteration . . . it was wrote in a piece of paper and affixt to ye Act".[109] When the bill came back to the House, Major Robert Beverley, who was again the clerk of the Assembly, acting it would seem upon his own initiative, tore off the paper containing this amendment. The bill then came before the House apparently assented to without change and was returned by them for the signature of the Governor and the Councillors. Neither Effingham nor any of the Council noticed the omission, and thinking their amendment had been accepted, signed the bill.[110] Thereupon it was engrossed, and sent up for the final signature of the Governor. But Effingham in reading the engrossed copy, discovered the omission, and refused to affix his name to the bill, claiming that it "was not engrost as assented to" by him and the Council.[111] "To which," wrote the Governor, "they sent mee word that the Bill could admit of noe alteration or amendment after it was attested by the Clerk of the General Assembly as assented to, and that it had by that the force of a Law. . . . I sent them word again that though any bill was assented to by mee and the Council, yet if I should afterwards perseive it would prove prejudicial . . . I had power to refuse the signing of it by vertue of His Majesty's negative voice. . . . But all would not persuade them out of their obstinacy, nay tho' I offered to lay that Bill aside till His Majesty's pleasure should bee known therein; And to sign all the others. . . . But nothing would please them but Invading, if not destroying, His Majesty's Prerogative." The Burgesses declared that they did not contest the Governor's right to the veto, but contended that when once he signed a bill, "it could not faile of having ye force of a Law".[112] Effingham, they complained, was claiming a "double negative Voice". So angry did they become that they refused to apportion the levy for defraying the public charges, and after many days of bitter contention the Governor was forced to prorogue them.

[108] P. R. O., CO5-1357-89.
[109] P. R. O., CO5-1407-310.
[110] P. R. O., CO5-1357-89.
[111] P. R. O., CO5-1357-89.
[112] Jour. H. of B., 1685.

"I did not disolve them," he wrote the Privy Council, "for these reasons. Because if his Majesty shall think fitt to have them dissolved, it will bee soe great a rebuke to them, when done by his Majesty's special command, that I hope it will deter them for the future to bee soe obstinate and peevish."[113] Accordingly, in August, 1686, the King wrote the Governor, "Whereas, we have been informed of ye irregular and tumultuous proceedings of the House of Burgesses of Virginia, at their late meeting, the members thereof having . . . presumed so far as to raise contests touching ye power of ye Negative Voice . . . which wee cannot attribute to any other Cause then the disaffected & unquiet Dispositions of those Members. . . . Wee have thought fitt hereby as a mark of our displeasure . . . to Charge . . . you forthwith to Dissolve the present Assembly."[114]

When this order reached Virginia the Assembly was again in session. "After I had passed the Acts," wrote Effingham, "I ordered His Majesty's Letter to bee publickly read to them, and then Dissolved them . . . and told them they were the first Assembly which had been soe dissolved and I hoped they would bee the last that should deserve it. I ordered copies of his Majesty's Letter to bee sent to the several County-Courts, that all the Inhabitants might know how displeasing such proceedings were to his Majesty."[115] "And now," he added, "the public debts being paid, . . . I shall not for the future have soe frequent Assemblys."[116]

More damaging to the Burgesses than this rebuke was the loss of the right to elect their own clerk. "I was severely angry with their Clerk," declared Effingham, "that he durst omit ye least clause, especially soe material an one . . . I sent to the Assembly to make him an example for it, But they rather maintained him."[117] Some months later the King sent orders that Beverley be tried for defacing the records and that he be once more deprived of all offices. Probably because of his great popularity, Beverley was never brought to trial, but

[113] P. R. O., CO5-1357-93.
[114] P. R. O., CO5-1357-119.
[115] P. R. O., CO5-1357-127.
[116] P. R. O., CO5-1357-133.
[117] P. R. O., CO5-1357-92; McD., Vol. VII, p. 222.

he was forced to relinquish his lucrative governmental posts.[118] In May, 1686, Nicholas Spencer wrote the Committee of Trade and Plantations, advocating the appointment of the clerk by the Governor. "I . . . beg leave to present," he said, "how necessary it is . . . that the clerk of the House . . . bee commissionated by his Majesty's Governour . . . and that his salary be appointed unto him out of his Majesty's revenue. This will take off his dependency on his great masters the House of Burgesses, and leave noe room for designed omissions."[119] Nothing loath, the King, in August, 1686, wrote Lord Howard, "Wee . . . require you . . . upon the Convening of the Assembly to appoint a fit person to execute the Office of Clerk of the House of Burgesses, & not to permit upon any pretense whatsoever any other person to execute ye said Office but such as shall bee soe chosen by you."[120]

Accordingly, at the session of April, 1688, the Governor, with the approbation of the Council, appointed Captain Francis Page as clerk of the House.[121] The Burgesses could but yield, but they told Effingham that the clerk was still their servant and ought to take the usual oath of secrecy. "I do declare," replied the Governor, "it was never my intention nor my desire that the Clerk should be as a spy upon your Actions and to declare to me your private Debates." It was therefore agreed that he should take the following oath: "You shall keep secret all private Debates of the said House of Burgesses."[122] Despite this, it was quite evident that the House was no longer to be master of its own clerk, and that he was to be in the future, to some extent at least, an emissary of the enemy seated in their midst.

The resolute and vigilant defense of the constitutional rights of Virginia made by the House in this the critical period of her history is deserving of the highest praise, because it was made in the face of vigorous personal attacks by Effingham upon the most active of the members. Every Burgess that voted against the measures proposed by the King or advocated by his Gov-

[118] Sains., Vol. XV, p. 30.
[119] McD., Vol. VII, p. 229.
[120] P. R. O., CO5-1357-119.
[121] Jour. H. of B., 1688, p. 1.
[122] Jour. H. of B., 1688, p. 17.

ernor, exposed himself not only to removal from office, but to active persecution. As we have seen, Mr. William Sherwood and Colonel Thomas Milner, for forwarding to the Privy Council the address of the Burgesses in 1684, had been dismissed from office.[123] "In ye year 1686 Mr. Arthur Allen & Mr. John Smith, who were Burgesses in ye year 1685, were turned out of all imployment Civill & Military to Mr. Allen's great damage, he being a surveyor of land at that tyme."[124] I have displaced Allen, wrote Effingham, because he was "a great promoter of those differences between mee and the Assembly concerning the King's negative Voice . . . as not thinking it fitt that those who are peevishly opposite to his Majesty's interest should have any advantage by his favor".[125] "In the year 1688 Mr. William Anderson, a member of ye Assembly in that year was soon after the Assembly by the Governor's order and Command put in ye Common goale and there detained 7 months, without Tryal, though often prayed for, and several courts past in ye time of his imprisonment. Nor could he obtain ye benefit of habeas corpus upon his humble petition. . . . Mr. Charles Scarburgh, a member of that Assembly, alsoe was, soon after ye Assembly, turned out of all imployment and as a mark of his Lordship's displeasure, a command was sent to ye clerk of ye county to raze his name out of ye records as a Justice of Peace."[126] "From whence," it was declared, "the people conclude these severities are inflicted rather as a terrour to others than for any personall crimes of their owne, and is of such ruinous consequence that either the public or particular interests must fall, for if none oppose, the country must languish under the severity of the government, or fly into a mutiny to save themselves from starving. If any do appear more zealous in prosecuting the countries complaints they know what to expect. It being observable that

[123] Sains., Vol. IV, p. 254.

[124] McD., Vol. VII, p. 26.

[125] McD., Vol. VII, p. 257. Some years later Effingham contradicted this statement. "They were not dismissed," he said, "from their imployments upon account of their proceedings in ye Assembly, but being Justices of Peace they oppenly opposed the King's authority in naming sheriffs by his Governour alledging that office ought to go by succession."

[126] McD., Vol. VII, pp. 437-441.

none has been thus punisht but those who were forward in the assembly to oppose the encroachments on the people, and promote the complaint to England, being out of hope of relief on the place."[127]

One is inclined to ask, when considering the incessant quarrels of the Governor and the Burgesses, why Lord Howard was less successful than Governor Berkeley had been in gaining an ascendency over the Assembly. During the Restoration Period the Burgesses had worked in entire harmony with Sir William, even when he advocated the oppressive measures that were so instrumental in bringing on Bacon's Rebellion. Effingham, on the other hand, found himself continually embroiled with the Assemblymen, and unable to force them into submission even with rebukes and persecution.

The explanation must be sought partly in the different characters of the two Governors. Berkeley was an abler man than Lord Howard, more tactful, more capable of utilizing the weapons at hand. His method of overwhelming the legislators with favors was more effective in winning their support than intimidation and threats. Moreover, Sir William, himself a Virginian by his long residence in the colony, carried out only his own policies, and by methods that did not openly assail the charter rights of the people. Effingham, on the other hand, was the instrument of the English King and his Councillors in an assault upon representative government in the colony. It was but natural that all classes, even the wealthy planters, should resist him with stubborn resolution. Nor was it possible for Effingham to control, as Sir William had done, the elections of Burgesses. The opposition of many sheriffs, whose duty it was to preside at the polls, to the administration, the greater vigilance of the House, and the independent spirit of the commons conspired to render the returns more accurate and the House more responsive to the will of the people. Finally, the poor planters found now, what they had lacked during the Restoration Period, cultured and able men to represent them in the Assembly. Without the aggressive leadership of Major Robert Beverley, Thomas Milner, Colonel Ballard, and other

[127] McD., Vol. VII, pp. 437-441.

prominent planters, the cause of the people might have been lost.

Even in the Council the commons had one staunch friend—Colonel Philip Ludwell. This restless man, who was unable to work in harmony with any Governor save Sir William Berkeley, sympathized with his old friends of the Green Spring faction in their resistance to Effingham. As early as 1684 he had aroused the Governor's suspicion by arguing in Council "for the undutiful Address which was sent to his Majesty",[128] and during the sessions of 1685 and 1686 it was thought that he was "an Instrument in Abbetting and formenting those Disputes & Exceptions the Assembly soe insisted on".[129]

Soon after, the Governor's distrust was heightened by two acts of favor shown by Ludwell to leaders of the opposition in the House of Burgesses. When ordered to oust Major Allen from his surveyor's place, he gave it to "Major Swan, one altogether as troublesom as the other & that only for the use of Allen". Upon receiving information that the King had declared Major Beverley "uncapable of any public imployment . . . hee presently gives his Surveyor's place, the best in the Country to his Son".[130] In the spring of 1686 the Governor made one last attempt to win Ludwell over from the people's cause. "I did," he wrote, "on the death of Colonel Bridger . . . give him a collector's place, in hopes to have gained him by it."[131] But Ludwell, unaffected by this attempted bribery, continued his active opposition to the arbitrary and illegal conduct of the Governor. At last, during the session of Assembly of 1686, there occurred an open breach. "His Lordship flew into a great rage and told . . . Ludwell he had formerly made remarks upon him, and that if he did not look the better to himself he should shortly suspend him from the Council."[132] Early in 1687 this threat was put into effect,[133] and the troublesome Councillor was for the second time deprived of his seat. But this persecution, which the people believed to be directed against Ludwell for his support

[128] P. R. O., CO5-1357-130. [129] CO5-1357-127.
[130] P. R. O., CO5-1357-129. [131] P. R. O., CO5-1357-130.
[132] McD., Vol. VII, pp. 437-441.
[133] Sains., Vol. IV, p. 226; P. R. O., CO5-1357-127.

of their cause, brought him into great popularity throughout the colony and made him the acknowledged leader of the opposition to the administration. In the elections for the Assembly of 1688 he was chosen by the freeholders of James City county to represent them in the House of Burgesses.[134] Effingham, however, would not allow him to take his seat, producing a clause from his commission which forbade suspended Councillors to become members of the Assembly.[135] Despite this exclusion, Ludwell could and did, by conferences with individual members, influence the actions of the House and lead them in their fight against the Governor.

The most important task that confronted the Burgesses when they assembled in 1688 was to call the Governor to account for many burdensome fees which he had imposed upon the people by executive order. First in importance was "a fee of 200 pounds of tobacco for the Seal affixed to Patents & other public instruments".[136] This the Burgesses considered a tax imposed without the authority or consent of the Assembly, and consequently destructive of the most cherished rights of the people. Moreover, it had, they claimed, deterred many from using the seal and had greatly impeded the taking up of land. They also protested against a fee demanded by the "Master of the Escheat Office of £5 or 1000lbs tobacco", and to one of thirty pounds of tobacco required by the Secretary for recording surveys of land.[137] "This House," they declared, "upon Examination of the many grievous Complaints . . . (have) been fully convinced and made sensible that many unlawful and unwarrantable fees and other dutyes have been, under colour of his Majesty's Royal authority, unjustly imposed . . . & that divers new unlawful, unpresidented & very burthensom and grievous wayes & devises have been of late made use of to the great impoverishing Vexing and utter undoeing of many of his Majesties Subjects of this his Dominion."[138]

The Burgesses were also deeply concerned at an instance of the unwarrantable use of the royal prerogative. In 1680 an

[134] McD., Vol. VII, pp. 437-441; Jour. H. of B., 1688, p. 13.
[135] P. R. O., CO5-1355-313; Jour. H. of B., 1688, p. 29.
[136] P. R. O., CO5-1357-218.
[137] Jour. H. of B., 1688, pp. 82, 83.
[138] Jour. H. of B., 1688, pp. 82, 83.

act had been passed concerning attorneys. Two years later, before the act had received the royal assent, it had been repealed by the Assembly. Later the King, by proclamation, had made void the act of 1682, and the Governor had insisted that this revived the law of 1680. Against this, the Burgesses in 1688 entered a vigorous protest. "A Law," they declared, "may as well Receive its beginning by proclamation as such revivall. . . . Some Governor may be sent to Govern us who under the pretense of the liberty he hath to construe prerogative and stretch it as far as he pleaseth may by proclamation Revive all the Lawes that for their great Inconveniences to the Country have been Repeal'd through forty years since."[139]

The Burgesses drew up a long paper, setting forth their many grievances, with the intention of presenting it to the Governor. They first, however, requested the Council to join them in their demand for redress. This the Council with some sharpness, refused to do. We are apprehensive, they replied, that the grievances "proceed from petulent tempers of private persons and that which inclines us the rather so to take them is from the bitterness of the Expressions".[140] Judging the Governor's temper from this reply of the Councillors, the Burgesses relinquished hope of redress from the executive and determined to petition the King himself. An humble address was drawn up, entrusted to Colonel Philip Ludwell and delivered by him at Windsor, in September, 1688, into the hands of James II. Before it could be considered, however, William of Orange had landed in England and King James had been overthrown.[141]

In the meanwhile a crisis in Virginia had been approaching rapidly. The people felt that their religion, as well as their liberties, was menaced by the rule of James II. In 1685, the King had directed Effingham "to permit a Liberty of Conscience to all persons", that would "bee contented with a quiet and peaceable enjoyment of it, not giving offence or scandal".[142] The people of Virginia understood well enough that this order was dictated, not by considerations of liberality, but

[139] Jour, H. of B., 1688, p. 50.
[140] Jour. H. of B., 1688, p. 116.
[141] P. R. O., CO5-1357-248.
[142] P. R. O., CO5-1357-38, 39.

by James' determination to favor the Catholic church. The feeling of uneasiness was increased when, in 1688, Effingham, declaring it no longer necessary for the Burgesses to take the oaths of allegiance and supremacy, admitted a Catholic to the Assembly.[143]

In October, 1688, James sent word to the Governor of the impending invasion of the Prince of Orange and commanded him to place Virginia in a posture of defense.[144] Immediately the colony was thrown into the wildest excitement, and, for a time, it seemed probable that the people would attempt the expulsion of Effingham. "Unruly and unorderly spiritts," the Governor afterwards testified, "laying hold of the motion of affairs, and that under the pretext of religion, . . . betook themselves to arms."[145] Wild rumors spread through the colony that the Papists of Maryland were conspiring with the Senecas to fall upon Virginia and cut off all Protestants in a new Saint Bartholomew's Eve.[146] The frontiersmen along the upper courses of the Rappahannock and the Potomac "drawing themselves into parties upon their defense", were "ready to fly in the face of ye government. Soe that matters were . . . tending to a Rebellion." However, the news of William's easy victory and the flight of James restored quiet to the colony. On February the nineteenth, 1689, the Privy Council wrote the Governor that William and Mary had ascended the throne of England,[147] and a few weeks later their Majesties were proclaimed at Jamestown with solemnity and thanksgiving.[148]

The Glorious Revolution was a victory for liberty even more important to Virginia than to England. It brought to an end those attacks of the English government upon the representative institutions of the colony that had marked the past ten years. It confirmed to the people the rights that had been guaranteed them, through a long series of patents dating back as far as 1606, and rendered impossible for all time the illegal oppressions of such men as Harvey, Berkeley, Cul-

[143] Jour. H. of B., 1688, p. 8; McD., Vol. VII, pp. 437-441.

[144] P. R. O., CO5-1357-229.

[145] McD., Vol. VII, p. 316.

[146] McD., Vol. VII, p. 316.

[147] P. R. O., CO5-1357-236.

[148] Sains., Vol. IV, p. 215.

peper and Effingham. Other Governors of despotic disposition were yet to rule Virginia—Nicholson, Andros, Dunmore—but it was impossible for them to resort to the tyrannical methods of some of their predecessors. The English Revolution had weakened permanently the control of the British government over the colony, and consequently the power of the Governor.

The advance of liberalism which was so greatly accelerated both in England and in America by the events of 1688 was halted in the mother country in the middle of the eighteenth century. But Virginia and the other colonies were not greatly affected by the reaction upon the other side of the Atlantic. Here the power of the people grew apace, encountering no serious check, until it came into conflict with the sullen Toryism of George III. Then it was that England sought to stifle the liberalism of the colonies, and revolution and independence resulted.

The changed attitude of the Privy Council towards Virginia was made immediately apparent by the careful consideration given the petition of the Burgesses. Had James remained upon the throne it is probable that it, like the address of 1684, would have been treated with neglect and scorn. But William received Ludwell graciously, listened to his plea "on behalf of the Commons of Virginia", and directed the Committee of Trade and Plantations to investigate the matter and to see justice done.[149]

Effingham, who had been called to England upon private business, appeared before the Committee to defend his administration and to refute Ludwell's charges. Despite his efforts, several articles of the petition were decided against him, and the most pressing grievances of the people redressed. The "Complaint touching the fee of 200lbs of tobacco and cask", it was reported, "imposed by my Lord Howard for affixing the Great Seal to Patents . . . in regard it was not regularly imposed . . . the committee agree to move his Majesty the same be discontinued".[150] Similarly their Lordships declared in favor of abolishing the fee of thirty pounds of tobacco

[149] P. R. O., CO5-1357-247, 248. [150] Sains., Vol. IV, pp. 233, 234.

required for registering surveys. The article touching the revival of repealed laws by proclamation was referred to the consideration of the Attorney-General and the Solicitor-General. These officers gave it as their opinion that his Majesty did have the right, by repealing acts of repeal, to revive laws, but the committee agreed to move the King that the Act of Attorneys should be made void by proclamation.[151]

This was a signal victory for the Burgesses, but Ludwell, who had personal scores to settle with the Governor, did not let matters drop here. After the lapse of several months he appeared once more before the Committee with charges against Effingham of misgovernment and oppression.[152] Referring to the quarrel over the Bill of Ports, in 1685, he accused him of exercising "two negative voices". He complained bitterly of his attacks upon those Burgesses that had opposed him in the Assembly, and of his abuse of the power of suspending Councillors. The money arising from fort duties, he said, which had formerly been accounted for to the Assembly, had, during Effingham's administration, "been diverted to other uses". The Governor had established new courts of judicature contrary to the wishes of the people.

These persistent attacks of Ludwell resulted in another victory, for the Committee decided that Effingham should no longer rule the colony. He was not displaced as Governor-General, but he was commanded to remain in England, and to leave the control of the administration to a Lieutenant-Governor. This, doubtless, was not unsatisfactory to Lord Howard, for he retained a part of his salary and was relieved of all the work and responsibility of his office. The Lieutenant-Governorship was given to Captain Francis Nicholson.[153]

Thus the colony emerged triumphant from the Critical Period. It is true the House of Burgesses had lost many privileges—the right to elect its own clerk, the right to receive judicial appeals, the right to control all revenues,—but they had retained within their grasp that all-important power—the levying of general taxes. And they had gained greatly in

[151] Sains., Vol. IV, p. 243. [152] Sains., Vol. IV, p. 246.
[153] Sains., Vol. IV, p. 254.

political experience. Long years of watchfulness, of resistance to encroachments upon their rights, had moulded them into a body that the most cunning executive could neither cajole nor intimidate. Unmindful of the anger of Governors, the rebukes of Kings, of personal loss, even of imprisonment, they had upheld the people's rights. And their descendants were to reap the reward of their faithfulness. The traditions of ability, probity and heroism established by the men of the Critical Period made possible that long and honorable career of the House of Burgesses and the important rôle it was to play in winning independence for America.

INDEX